Wars That
Changed History

Wars That Changed History

50 of the World's Greatest Conflicts

Spencer C. Tucker

An Imprint of ABC-CLIO, LLC
Santa Barbara, California • Denver, Colorado

Library of Congress Cataloging-in-Publication Data

Tucker, Spencer, 1937–
    Wars that changed history : 50 of the world's greatest conflicts / Spencer C. Tucker.
        pages   cm
    Includes bibliographical references and index.
    ISBN 978-1-61069-785-9 (alk. paper) — ISBN 978-1-61069-786-6 (ebook)   1. Military history.   2. War—History.   I. Title.
    D25.T83   2015
    355.0209—dc23   2015005734

ISBN: 978-1-61069-785-9
EISBN: 978-1-61069-786-6

19 18 17 16 15   1 2 3 4 5

This book is also available on the World Wide Web as an eBook.
Visit www.abc-clio.com for details.

ABC-CLIO, LLC
130 Cremona Drive, P.O. Box 1911
Santa Barbara, California 93116-1911

This book is printed on acid-free paper ∞
Manufactured in the United States of America

For Jack and Dana McCallum,
who were with us from the beginning.

Contents

Chronological Entry List

Alphabetical Entry List

Preface

Wars both fascinate and repel us; they are the ultimate test for humankind and bring in their wake death and destruction, sometimes on a vast scale, and sometimes advantage. This volume treats what I consider to be the 50 most significant wars in human history. The criterion in their selection was that they must have had major impact on subsequent historical development rather than being significant for costs, destruction, or new weapons. Selecting the 50 wars from among the thousands in history has been no easy task. I developed an initial list of some 70 wars and then asked colleagues to review it. Each individual subtracted some but also added others, making my final selections even more difficult! I am most grateful for the insight offered by Timothy Dowling, Jinwung Kim, Jerry Morelock, Eric Osborne, George Pesely, Paul Pierpaoli, and Harold Tanner. A number of them also read one or more of the completed entries. Professors Pesely and Kim were especially helpful in that regard.

For each conflict I discuss the causes, course, and significance as well as books for further reading. There are also fact boxes summing up each conflict. I have deliberately minimized attention to technological developments in order to deal with the course of the conflicts and keep the whole within the total number of words allowed me. In presenting the wars, where space permits I have included more detailed treatment of some pivotal battles.

Regarding dates and places, I have endeavored to use throughout modern dating (as opposed to the lunar calendar) and in most cases present place-names with older and alternate names in parentheses.

Some conflicts, most notably World War I and World War II, receive greater coverage than others. For both of these wars I have included significantly more detail on the causes in the belief that this will be of more interest to the reader and will also provide insight into the roots of current events.

Spencer C. Tucker

Thutmose III's Campaigns (ca. 1479–1459 BCE)

Dates	1479–1459 BCE
Location	The Middle East from the Euphrates River to northern Sudan
Combatants	Egypt vs. Caanan, Kadesh, Phoenicia, Mitanni, others
Principal Commanders	Egypt: Thutmose III Others: King of Kadesh
Principal Battles	Megiddo
Outcome	Considerable expansion of Egyptian territory

Causes

Pharaoh Thutmose III greatly expanded Egyptian territory. Born near Thebes sometime around 1504 BCE (although his life is well documented, virtually every source has different years for his life and events of his reign), Thutmose was crowned pharaoh at age 7 with his stepmother and future mother-in-law, Hatshepsut, and was the junior coregent for 22 years. During this time Hatshepsut followed a pacific foreign policy, and Egypt's hold on the Levant and Nubia weakened. Following the death of Hatshepsut and with Egyptian power in decline, the king of Kadesh led a revolt against Egyptian rule of some 300 cities of Palestine and Syria.

Thutmose III was anxious to assert his power and restore Egyptian authority in the Levant. After ordering the removal of Hatshepsut's name from all public buildings, Thutmose rebuilt the Egyptian Army, which had been largely dormant for decades. Much is known of his military campaigns, thanks to the royal scribe and army commander Thanuny who wrote about Thutmose's campaigns. Indeed, Thutmose's Battle of Megiddo is said to have been the first in history of which there is record by an eyewitness.

Course

In his second year as ruler, Thutmose marched the army into Palestine. Estimates of the size of his force range from 10,000 to 30,000 men. It is believed to have consisted largely of infantry, with some chariots. The infantrymen were armed with swords and axes and carried shields. The nobility fought from the chariots, probably as archers. Thutmose's adversaries were similarly armed.

The king of Kadesh had assembled a large force at the fortified city of Megiddo (Armageddon in Hebrew), north of Mount Carmel. Disregarding the advice of his generals, who feared an ambush, Thutmose chose the most direct route north to Megiddo, through a narrow pass. Apparently the king of Kadesh believed that the Egyptians would consider this route too risky, for he had deployed the bulk of his forces along another road to the east. Leading in person in a chariot, Thutmose pushed through Megiddo Pass, scattering its few defenders, then consolidated his forces while the king of Kadesh withdrew his covering troops back on Megiddo.

Preparing for what would probably be the largest battle of his many campaigns, Thutmose drew up his army in a concave formation of three main groups southwest of Megiddo and athwart the small Kina

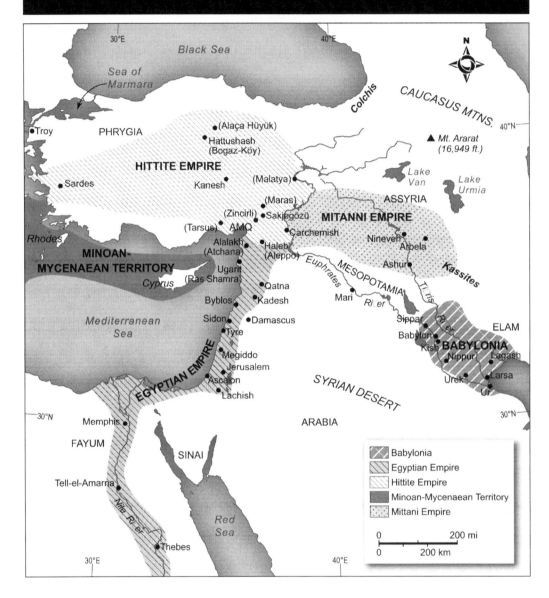

ANCIENT NEAR EAST, CA. 1400 BCE

River. Both flanks were on high ground, with the left flank extending to the northwest of Megiddo to cut off any enemy escape along a road from the city. The rebel force was drawn up on high ground near Megiddo.

While the southern wing of his army held his adversary in place, Thutmose personally led the northern wing in an attack that sliced between the rebel left flank and Megiddo itself, enveloping the enemy and winning the battle. (Although the month and day are set as a lunar date, May 21, the years vary, with 1457, 1469, and 1479 often given.) The surviving enemy soldiers fled, saved by the fact that the Egyptian soldiers halted their pursuit to loot the enemy camp, something that greatly displeased Thutmose.

Thutmose then subjected Megiddo to a siege, lasting as long as eight months. On its surrender, Thutmose took most of the rebel kings prisoner, although the king of Kadesh escaped. Thutmose did capture the king's son and took him back to Egypt as a hostage, along with the sons of other captured kings. Among the spoils of war were more than 900 chariots and 2,200 horses as well as 200 suits of armor. Reportedly, in the campaign Thutmose acquired 426 pounds of gold and silver. The Assyrian, Babylonian, and Hittite kings all sent him gifts, which the Egyptians interpreted as tribute.

During the next two decades, Thutmose mounted as many as 16 additional campaigns. His 2nd and 3rd campaigns appear to have been little more than tours of Canaan and Syria to exact tribute. There is no record of his 4th campaign. The 5th, 6th, and 7th campaigns were all against Phoenician cities in Syria and Kadesh on the Orontes (Asi) River. The 8th campaign was against the state of Mitanni on the other side of the Euphrates, which Thutmose and his men crossed in boats, taking the Mitannians by surprise. His 9th campaign was a new invasion of Syria, probably more a raid than anything else.

The 10th campaign, against the king of Mitanni, involved considerably more fighting. The two sides came together near Aleppo, with Thutmose again victorious. Details regarding Thutmose's 11th and 12th campaigns are unknown but probably involved Qatna and Nukhashshe. He returned to the latter for his 13th campaign, while his 14th was against the Shasu, possibly in present-day Lebanon or across the Jordan River. His 15th

campaign is obscure, but his 16th was sparked by a revolt led by Mitanni and involving major cities of Syria with significant fighting. Although Thutmose defeated the opposing armies, he failed to take Kadesh. His last campaign occurred late in his life and apparently in his 50th regnal year and was up the Nile southward into Nubia, but only as far as the Fourth Cataract.

Thutmose fully understood the value of sea power, and one of his accomplishments was the creation of a fleet that controlled the eastern Mediterranean. Thutmose apparently was never defeated in battle and established an empire that extended to the Euphrates River and included the subjugation of Palestine and Syria as well as part of the Hittite Empire in Asia Minor (modern-day Turkey).

Thutmose ensured the peace of his empire by taking to Egypt the children of the conquered kings as hostages. They were educated to respect the pharaoh and then installed as governors in their fathers' cities. Thutmose proved to be a capable and effective administrator. He used the tribute and captives of his wars to rebuild the cities and temples of Egypt. According to the scribes, his reign lasted 54 years. He probably died in 1450 BCE near Thebes.

Significance

Thutmose III is widely regarded as one of the greatest, if not the greatest, of Egyptian pharaohs. His campaigns brought the Egyptian Empire to its greatest extent, into present-day southern Turkey, central Syria, and up the Nile into Nubia. He created a new vision for Egyptians of their place and role in the world, and the imperial system he created lasted well into the Twentieth Dynasty (1189–1077 BCE).

Further Reading

Benson, Douglas. *Ancient Egypt's Warfare.* Ashland, OH: Book Masters, 1995.

Cline, Eric H., and David O'Connor, eds. *Thutmose III: A New Biography.* Ann Arbor: University of Michigan Press, 2006.

Cline, Eric H., and Jill Rubalcaba. *The Ancient Egyptian World.* New York: Oxford University Press, 2005.

Collins, Paul. *From Egypt to Babylon: The International Age, 1550–500 BC.* Boston: Harvard University Press, 2008.

Darnell, John Coleman, and Colleen Manassa. *Tutankhamun's Armies: Battle and Conquest during Ancient Egypt's Late Eighteenth Dynasty.* New York: Wiley, 2007.

Gabriel, Richard, and Donald Boose. *The Great Battles of Antiquity.* Westport, CT: Greenwood, 1994.

Gardiner, Alan. *Egypt of the Pharaohs.* Oxford: Oxford University Press, 1964.

Montet, Pierre. *Lives of the Pharaohs.* Cleveland, OH: World Publishing, 1968.

Nelson, Harold Hayden. *The Battle of Megiddo.* Chicago: University of Chicago Press, 1913.

Redford, Donald B. *The Wars in Syria and Lebanon of Thutmose III.* Leiden, the Netherlands: Brill Academic Publishers, 2003.

Spalinger, A. J. *War in Ancient Egypt: The New Kingdom.* New York: Wiley, 2005.

Steindorff, George, and Keith C. Seele. *When Egypt Ruled the East.* Chicago: University of Chicago Press, 1963.

Greco-Persian Wars (499–479 BCE)

Dates	499–479 BCE
Location	Eastern Mediterranean
Combatants	Greek city-states vs. Persian Empire
Principal Commanders	Greece: Miltiades, Leonidas, Themistocles, Pausanias Persia: Darius I, Xerxes, Mardonius
Principal Battles	Marathon, Thermopylae, Salamis, Plataea
Outcome	Greek victory. Greece is able to continue its experiment in democracy free of Persian control, and Greek culture spreads throughout the Mediterranean.

Causes

Often simply called the Persian Wars, the Greco-Persian Wars of 499–479 BCE are one of the most important conflicts in all recorded history. They were fought between the Achaemenid Empire of Persia and the Greek city-states and were the result of the expansion of Persian power. Then the world's mightiest empire, Persia was expanding westward and came into contact with the Greeks. The stage was set when in 547 BCE Persian king Cyrus II (Cyrus the Great, r. 559–530 BCE) conquered the Greek city-states that had been established in Ionia (the central coast of Anatolia in present-day Turkey). Cyrus then set up tyrants (rulers) over these.

In 499 Aristagoras, the tyrant of the Ionian city-state of Miletus, with Persian support, mounted an expedition to conquer the Greek island of Naxos, the largest island in the Cyclades island group in the Aegean Sea. This military effort was rebuffed. Fearing that this failure would bring his dismissal, Aristagoras then initiated a revolt of all Hellenic Asia Minor against Persian rule.

During the ensuing Ionian Revolt (499–493), Aristagoras appealed to the city-states of mainland Greece for support. King Darius I (Darius the Great, r. 522–486) demanded earth and water, symbols of submission from the Greeks. While some Greek city-states including Aegina submitted, others refused, and the Greco-Persian Wars began.

Course

Both Athens and Eretria sent military assistance to their fellow Greeks in Ionia. They also assisted the Ionian Greeks in capturing the Persian regional capital of Sardis in western Anatolia in 498. The Greeks wanted to sack Sardis, but a great fire destroyed the city. The Ionian Revolt continued for some time, with both sides essentially deadlocked throughout 497–495. In 496 the island of Cyprus revolted against Persia, as did Caria on the coast of Asia Minor. Persian forces transported there by the Phoenicians retook Cyprus, while a Phoenician fleet suppressed Caria. In 494 the Persians sent a large force against Miletus, the center of the Ionian Revolt. The Persians crushed an Ionian fleet of 333 triremes in a great sea battle off Lade in the gulf opposite Miletus, then captured and sacked Miletus itself. They destroyed much of the city, killed most of its men, and enslaved the women and children. The Persians then took all Ionian cities on the eastern shore of the Hellespont (Dardanelles) as well as Byzantium on the European side of the Bosporus and Chalcedon on the Asian side. In addition, they secured and sacked the islands of Chios, Lesbos, and Tenedos, in effect bringing large-scale fighting to a close. The last Greek resistance ended the next year, in 493.

Seeking to secure the western frontier of his empire from further revolts and from the interference of the mainland Greeks and also vowing to have revenge on Athens and Eretria, Darius now embarked on an effort to conquer all Greece. In 492 he dispatched his son-in-law Mardonius across the Hellespont at the head of a large fleet and army. The Persians subdued Thrace but suffered a check on the Macedonian border from a Thracian tribe. Meanwhile, the Persian fleet encountered a storm while rounding Mount Athos, and many of its ships were driven ashore and wrecked. Mardonius wisely returned to Persia, where Darius relieved him of command.

The next year, 491, as his shipyards turned out new vessels, Darius tested the morale of the Greek city-states by sending to them envoys demanding earth and water as symbols of vassalage. A number of the mainland cities, including most of those in northern Greece, submitted to the Persians, but not Athens or Sparta.

Darius launched his second invasion of Greece in 490. This time he gave command of the Persian forces to his nephew, Artaphernes, and a Median noble, Datis. At Tarsus on the Cilician coast, the invasion fleet of some 200 triremes and 400 transports took on board perhaps as many as 25,000 infantry and 1,000 cavalry. The ships then proceeded to Ionia and west through the Cyclades islands.

The Persians captured and sacked Naxos, which had resisted capture a decade earlier. Then the fleet proceeded westward across the Aegean Sea from island to island, picking up conscripts and taking children as hostages. By the time the Persians had landed on Euboea, they had gathered a force of perhaps 80,000 men, including rowers and conscripts.

When Eretria on Euboea refused to surrender, the Persians destroyed the

GREECE DURING THE PERSIAN WARS

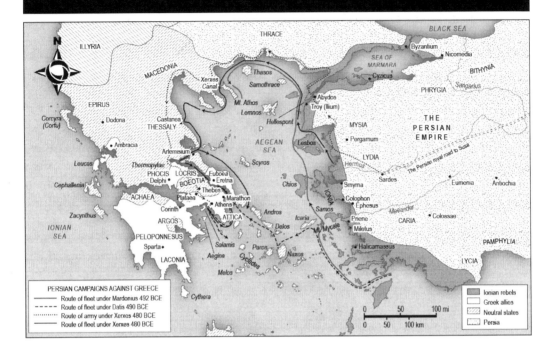

countryside and laid siege to the city. Eretria held out for a week until the defenders were betrayed from within the walls. In reprisal for Sardis, the Persian burned all the city's temples. The fleet then sailed west from Eretrea and made landfall on the Greek mainland in the Bay of Marathon, some 26 miles northeast of Athens. The Persians selected this site because Hippias, who had been deposed as the tyrant of Athens in 510 and had fled to Persia, told the Persians that the plain there would allow them to employ their cavalry, in which they were overwhelmingly superior to the Greeks. Hippias was with the Persian force and, following their anticipated victory, was to work with the pro-Persian faction in Athens and be installed as Persian governor of all Greece.

The Persians hoped that by landing at Marathon they might draw the Athenian army away from the city and destroy it or else hold the smaller Athenian force there while sending part of their army south to Athens by ship. Athens sent an appeal to Sparta, probably carried by the famed runner Pheidippides (Philippides); reportedly he once covered 140 miles in two days. The Spartan leaders agreed to assist, but they refused to suspend a religious festival that would delay their army's march north until the next full moon, on the night of August 11–12. It was then August 5.

News of the fall of Eretria brought fierce debate in Athens. Some wanted simply to prepare for a siege, but others, including Miltiades, urged that the army be sent out to fight. Reportedly, Miltiades pointed out that allowing the Persians to mount a siege would cut Athens off from Spartan aid (the Long Walls were not yet built) and increase the chances of treachery. Miltiades won the day. He argued that the city's only hope once the Persians landed at Marathon with their cavalry was to destroy them on the beachhead.

Some accounts have Athens freeing slaves. They and other freedmen and citizens traversed the mountains to Marathon. The Athenian force numbered some 10,000 hoplites (infantrymen). The little city-state of Platea sent unexpected aid—of as many as 1,000 hoplites. Callimachus commanded as war archon (*polemarchos*). Each of the 10 tribes of Athens had its own general, and Miltiades was only one of these.

The Athenians positioned themselves on high ground west of the plain, there to block a Persian advance overland toward Athens, and set about felling trees to inhibit the Persian cavalry. Not only did the Persians vastly outnumber the Greeks, but they had cavalry and archers where the Greeks had none. For several days (August 7–11), the two armies simply sat in place, some two miles apart. Both sides were waiting: the Athenians for the Spartans to arrive, the Persians for conspirators in touch with Hippias to seize power in Athens.

The Persians must have known that Spartan reinforcements would soon arrive, and with no word that pro-Persian conspirators in Athens had been successful, they evidently decided to send the bulk of their fleet to Phaleron Bay on the night of August 11–12 carrying a substantial land force, including the cavalry. They left behind a land force numbering perhaps 15,000 men.

If the Persians had hoped to win by treachery, it was the Greeks who actually did so. Ionian deserters got word to the Greeks before dawn on August 12, including information that the cavalry had departed. Miltiades realized that the

one hope the Athenians had was to attack swiftly, defeat the Persian land force, and then march to the relief of Athens before the other Persian force could disembark, perhaps in late afternoon.

Miltiades formed the Greeks into a line about a mile long so that its flanks rested on two small streams flowing to the sea. Beyond these were marshes north and south. The disposition of the Greek force thinned the center of the line, which contained the best troops, to perhaps only three to four men deep, but Miltiades kept the flanks, which had his least reliable troops, at full phalanx depth (normally about eight or more men deep). Thus, the Greeks had a weak center with powerful striking forces on either side. The Greeks were better armed, with long spears against javelins and short swords against daggers or scimitars. They were also better protected with bronze body armor, and they were more highly motivated, as they were fighting for their homeland.

Battle was joined that morning (August 12). The Greeks advanced slowly toward the Persian camp and the beach until they were 150–200 yards away and within bow range of the Persian archers, who were in front. The Greeks then charged the center of the Persian line to minimize the time they would be under arrow attack and easily broke through the ranks of lightly armed Persian bowmen, who had time only to get off a few arrows each before seeking safety behind the main Persian formation. The Persian infantry easily threw back the Greek center, but Greek discipline held as their line became concave. The heavy Greek flanks folded on the lightly armed Persian flanks, compressing the Persians in a double envelopment. It is not clear whether this was by design or simply accidental.

The Persian flanks and center now gave way as the troops fled for the beach and their transports, being cut down by the Greeks as they tried to get away. Some sort of Persian rear guard was organized to cover their embarkation, though, and most of the force escaped. It was then about 9:00 in the morning. The Greek historian Herodotus, who was writing well after the fact, proudly claimed that the Greeks only lost 192 men killed, while 6,400 Persians fell. The Greeks also destroyed seven Persian ships.

Miltiades sent word of the Greek victory to Athens by a runner, reportedly Pheidippides, on the first Marathon run. The Athenians could not pause to celebrate, for the two Persian naval forces were now making for Phaleron Bay. Leaving a detachment to guard the Persian prisoners and booty, the remainder of the Athenian army marched to Athens. They arrived in late afternoon, just as the Persian fleet was approaching shore for a landing. Realizing they were too late, the Persians withdrew. The Spartans did not arrive at Athens until several days later. They praised the victors and returned home. Had the Persians won and forced Athens to submit, they would have installed Hippias again as tyrant.

The Greeks had won one of the important battles of history. The victory was not conclusive, but it did hold the Persians at bay for a decade. Marathon, at least, allowed the Greeks to imagine that they might triumph a second time.

The next year, 489, Athens sent Miltiades and 70 ships against islands that had assisted the Persians. Miltiades attacked Pardos in the Cyclades islands but, following a monthlong siege, was forced to withdraw. This failure brought his political ruin and imprisonment and the ascendancy of Themistocles, which would have

wide repercussions for the second Persian invasion.

Following the defeat of his forces in Greece, during 486–485 Persian king Darius I immediately began raising a new and far larger force. To pay for it he raised taxes, which brought a revolt in Persian-controlled Egypt in the winter of 486–485 that disrupted grain deliveries and diverted Persian military resources to restore order in that important province. Darius died in late 486. His son and successor, Xerxes, was temporarily distracted by the Egyptian revolt, but once it had been crushed, he returned to the plans to invade Greece. Well aware of the Persian preparations, Athenian leader Themistocles took steps to meet the invasion, securing approval to increase the size of the Athenian Navy from 50 to 200 triremes.

When at last he set out on his planned expedition to Greece in 481, Xerxes commanded one of the largest invasion forces in history. Its exact size has been the subject of considerable debate. Modern reckoning puts it at perhaps 600 ships and three Persian Army corps of 60,000 men each. This was thus a Persian advantage of at least three to one on land and two to one at sea.

In the spring of 480 BCE, the Persian host reached the Hellespont. There Egyptian and Phoenician engineers had constructed a bridge that was among the most admired mechanical achievements of antiquity. The Greek historian Herodotus wrote that they distributed 674 ships in two rows athwart the strait, each vessel facing the current and moored with a heavy anchor. The engineers then stretched flaxen cables across the ships from bank to bank. These cables were bound to every ship and were made taut by the use of capstans on shore. Wooden planks were then laid across and fastened to the cables and to one another. The planks were covered with brushwood, which was covered with earth, and the whole was tamped down to resemble a road. A bulwark was erected on each side of this causeway to keep animals from being frightened of the sea.

According to Herodotus, during the course of seven days and nights the Persian forces passed over the bridge from Asia to enter Europe. The Persian invaders soon occupied Thrace and Macedonia. The northern Greek states were completely intimidated. Surrendering to fear or bribery, they allowed their own troops to be added to those of Xerxes. Only Plataea and Thespiae in the north prepared to fight.

For once, Athens and Sparta worked together. Athens provided the principal naval force, while Sparta furnished the main contingent of land forces sent north against the Persians. The land force was commanded by Leonidas, one of the kings of Sparta. The Greek plan was for the land forces to hold the Persians just long enough for the Greek fleet to be victorious and force a Persian withdrawal.

Themistocles now led the Athenian fleet northward. Joined by other Greek vessels, it numbered 271 frontline ships. The Persian fleet was more than 650 ships. A severe storm reduced the Persian numbers to around 500 serviceable warships, but this was still a comfortable advantage over the Greeks. In August the Greeks met the Persians in a naval battle off the northern coast of Euboea at Artemisium (ca. August 30). The battle was inconclusive, although the Greeks did manage to capture some 30 Persian vessels.

While the Greek fleet was sailing northward to Artemisium, the allied Greek land force of about 4,000 men under Leonidas had also marched northward and taken up position at the Pass of Thermopylae. Some 135 miles north of Athens, this site was selected because there a small force would be able to hold off a much larger one. Three hundred Spartan men-at-arms formed the nucleus of Leonidas's force, accompanied by perhaps 900 helots. Leonidas had chosen only fathers with sons so that no Spartan family line would be extinguished.

The same day that the ships from the two sides clashed at Artemisium, Xerxes launched his first attack against the Greek defenders, who were driven back. Xerxes then committed his elite Guards Division, the Ten Thousand Immortals, but they too were forced to withdraw in disorder. The pass was reportedly piled high with corpses. Xerxes tried again the next day, but the defenders also repelled this assault.

Leonidas and his men were overwhelmed not so much by the bravery of the Persians as by the treachery of the Greeks. On the second day of battle a Greek, Ephialtes of Malis, betrayed to Xerxes, apparently for reward, the secret of an indirect route over the mountains and then led a Persian force by that approach, routing a lightly held Phocian outpost and turning the Greek position. Meanwhile, Themistocles and the Greek fleet had been carrying out hit-and-run attacks against the Persian ships.

On the night of the second day of battle, learning from Ionian Greek deserters from Xerxes' army that the defenders at Thermopylae were going to be cut off, Leonidas permitted the allied Greeks to withdraw. Seven hundred Thespians and 300 Thebans refused and remained with the Spartans. All of the defenders were wiped out. Only 2 Spartans are said to have survived; 1 fell at the Battle of Plataea a year later, and the other is said to have hung himself in shame. Over the tomb of the Spartans is placed the most famous of Greek epitaphs: "Go, stranger, and tell the Lacedamonians [Spartans] we lie here in obedience to their laws."

The Battle of Thermopylae, which is also said to have claimed two younger brothers of Xerxes, had far more psychological than military importance. While some Greeks saw it as an excuse to ally with the Persians, others admired the Spartan example and redoubled their efforts to resist the invaders.

With news of the Greek defeat at Thermopylae, Themistocles sailed southward with the remaining Greek triremes to Salamis in order to provide security for the city of Athens. With no land barrier now remaining between Athens and the Persian land force, proclamation was made for every Athenian to save his family as best he could. Some fled to Salamis or the Peloponnese, and some of the men joined the crews of the returning triremes. When Persian king Xerxes and his army arrived at Athens, the city was devoid of civilians, although some troops remained to stage a largely symbolic defense of the Acropolis. The Persians soon secured it, however, and destroyed it by fire.

Xerxes now had to contend with the remaining Greek ships. He would either have to destroy them or leave behind a sufficiently large force to contain the Greek ships before he could invade the Peloponnese and bring an end to the Greek campaign. Everything suggested the former, for if he left the Greek force behind, his own ships would remain vulnerable to a Greek flanking attack. At the end of August the Persian fleet of something less than 500 ships appeared off Phaleron, east of the Salamis Channel. Themistocles now added to his fleet the reserve ships from Salamis and triremes from other states, altogether about 100 additional ships. The combined Greek fleet that assembled at

Salamis totaled about 310 ships, a force larger than that which took part in the Battle of Artemisium.

Xerxes and his admirals did not want to engage the Greek fleet in the narrow waters of the Salamis Channel. Accounts differ, but some have the Persians attempting, for about two weeks in early September, to construct causeways across the channel at its narrowest point so that they might take the island without having to engage the Greek ships. As Salamis now contained most of the remaining Athenian population and government officials, the Persians reasoned logically that their capture would bring the fleet's surrender. Massed Greek archers, however, gave those attempting to build the causeways so much trouble that the Persians abandoned this plan.

The causeway effort having failed, Xerxes met with his generals and chief advisers. With all except Queen Artemisia of Halicarnassus favoring engaging the Greek fleet in a pitched battle, Xerxes ordered advance elements of his fleet from Phaleron off Salamis. He hoped that putting part of his vast army in motion toward the Peloponnese would cause the ships provided by the Greeks of that region to return home, enabling him to destroy them later at his leisure. Failing that, Xerxes sought to do battle with the Greek ships in the open waters of the Saronic Gulf, where his superior numbers would be at advantage. If he had waited, Xerxes might simply have starved Salamis into submission.

With the Greek captains then in an uproar and with every possibility that the Peloponnesian ships would leave the coalition, Themistocles resorted to what will be heralded as one of the most famous stratagems in all military history. He sent a trusted slave to the Persians with a letter for Xerxes, informing him that

Themistocles had decided to change sides. He gave no reason for this decision but informed the Persian king that he now would work for a Persian victory. The Greeks, Themistocles said, were bitterly divided and would offer little resistance; indeed, there would be pro-Persian factions fighting the remainder. Furthermore, elements of the fleet were intending to use the cover of darkness to sail away the next night in order to link up with Greek land forces defending the Peloponnese. The Persians could prevent this only by not letting the Greeks escape.

This letter in fact contained much truth and was, after all, what Xerxes wanted to hear. It did not tell Xerxes what Themistocles wanted him to do, that is, to attack and engage the Greek ships in the narrows. Themistocles left this entirely to Xerxes, who took the bait. Actually, a blockade would have worked very much to the Persian advantage.

Xerxes, not wishing to lose the opportunity, acted swiftly. He ordered Persian squadrons patrolling off Salamis to block all possible Greek escape routes; the main fleet came into position that very night. The Persians held their stations all night waiting for the Greek breakout, which never occurred. Themistocles was counting on Xerxes' vanity and impatience, and as the Athenian leader expected, the Persian king chose not to break off the operation that he had begun. Compelled to give fight, the Greeks stood out to meet the Persians. Xerxes, seated on a throne at the foot of nearby Mount Aegaleus on the Attica shore across from Salamis, observed the battle.

Early in the morning (ca. September 20) the entire Persian fleet attacked, moving up the Salamis Channel in a crowded mile-wide front that precluded any possibility

of organized withdrawal should that prove necessary. The details of the actual battle are obscure, but the superior tactics and seamanship of the Greeks allowed them to take the Persians in the flank, and the confusion of minds, languages, and too many ships in narrow waters among the Persians all combined to decide the issue in favor of the Greeks.

In the Battle of Salamis the Persians, according to one account, lost some 200 ships, while the Greeks lost only 40. However, few of the Greeks, even from the lost ships, were killed. For the most part excellent swimmers, they were able to reach safety ashore when their ships floundered. The Greeks feared that the Persians might renew the attack, but when they awoke the next morning they found that the remaining Persian ships had departed. Xerxes had ordered them to the Hellespont to protect the bridge there.

The Battle of Salamis marked the end of the year's campaign. Xerxes left two-thirds of his forces in garrison in central and northern Greece and marched the remainder back to Sardis. A large number of Persians died of pestilence and dysentery on the way.

A year after the Battle of Salamis, the remaining Persian forces in northern Greece again invaded Attica. Commanded by Mardonius, brother-in-law of King Xerxes, they advanced from central Greece and again occupied the city of Athens. The Persians burned most of its buildings, and those that survived were razed. Sparta and some other Greek states, however, answered the Athenian appeal for assistance.

The Persian ground force numbered about 50,000 men, including 15,000 Greeks from northern and central Greece. The opposing Greek army, led by King Pausanias of Sparta, totaled about 40,000 men, including 10,000 Spartans and 8,000 Athenians. The Persians not only had the advantage in total numbers but also possessed more cavalry and archers.

When the Greeks threatened a flanking attack on the Persians, Mardonius withdrew northward behind the Asopus River. The Greeks followed and set up defensive positions on the other side of the river, which was about 25 miles northwest of Athens. Mardonius found it difficult to employ his cavalry and archers against the more heavily armed Greek hoplites, however. The two sides faced one another for several days. The Greeks were confident that they could defeat the Persians in a shock-action battle, but they were unable to entice the Persians into an attack. Meanwhile, the Persian cavalry harassed Greek foraging and water parties.

Finally, with the Greeks running out of supplies, Pausanias developed a plan to bring Mardonius to battle by a withdrawal closer to Plataea. Supposedly the Greek change of position was to be carried out entirely at night, but by dawn only about half the forces had departed. In the morning (ca. August 27), the Persians could view the much smaller Athenian and Spartan forces in march formation. Noting the Greek disorder, Mardonius immediately ordered an attack, hoping to prevail with his archers against the remaining hoplites. Although the outcome was in doubt for some time, the attackers approached the Greeks too closely, and the Greeks then mounted a countercharge. Greek reinforcements also came up, although Persian and allied cavalry proved effective against them.

This Battle of Plataea was fiercely fought, but the archers, who had only wicker armor and leather helmets, were unable to defend themselves at close quarters against the better-disciplined Greek

hoplites, with their bronze spears and metal breastplates and helmets. The Persians were overwhelmed. In the fighting the Greeks may have lost 1,360 men, while the Persians lost 10,000 or more, including some 1,000 allied Greeks. Mardonius and his personal guard were among those slain in the wild Persian retreat. The remaining 40,000 Persians were scattered in every direction. For all practical purposes, the Persian field army now ceased to exist.

In the simultaneous Battle of Mycale (which according to Greek tradition occurred the same day), the Greeks engaged the Persians near Samos. Unbeknownst to the Persian-backed ruler of Samos, a number of Samian envoys had appealed to King Leotychidas of Sparta, who led the combined Greek fleet of some 250 triremes from a base at Delos. The Samians informed Leotychidas that the Persians had detached their powerful Phoenician contingent and, with little more than 100 triremes remaining, were vulnerable to attack.

Departing Delos, Leotychidas sailed east to Samos. Afraid to risk a naval engagement with the Greeks, the Persians had drawn their ships up on land on the Mycale peninsula of Asia Minor, across the narrow channel from Samos. There they enjoyed land communications with Sardis and a line of retreat should that prove necessary. They also had the support of Persian general Tigranes and 6,000 Persian troops detached to keep watch over Ionia. The Persians had thrown up defensive works on land, including a wooden stockade, to protect their ships. In all, counting the troops under Tigranes, the Persians and their Ionian Greek allies numbered about 10,000 men.

In addition to these rowers and sailors, Leotychidas had at best 2,500 marines and 1,000 archers. But a number of the rowers may have been hoplites, drafted in the emergency. Despite the Persian numerical advantage, the Greeks decided to attack the Persians on land and attempt to destroy their ships.

With his small force and lacking heavy equipment, Leotychidas could not hope to take the Persian fortification by storm. He therefore decided to tempt Tigranes into attacking him. Leotychidas split his already small force into a group of Athenians and other Greek forces while he accompanied the majority of his men in secretly working overland in order to strike the Persians in the flank.

The Athenians attacked directly along the beach in full view of the Persians, and Tigranes took the bait. Seeing the small size of the Greek force, he ordered an attack from the defenses. In the resultant fighting, some of the Ionian Greeks abandoned the Persians and switched sides. With the battle in the balance, Leotychidas and the Spartans arrived just in time, and after hard fighting the Persians were routed. Perhaps 4,000 Persians perished, including Tigranes and his second-in-command. Greek losses were also heavy. The Greeks seized what booty they could, set fire to the Persian ships in the stockade, and sailed to Samos. The Persian threat to conquer Greece was ended.

Significance

The victory of little Greece in the Greco-Persian Wars was momentous for Western civilization, for it made Europe possible. It allowed the continuation of Greek independence and the dissemination and flowering of Greek literature and the arts. The Greeks were now able to continue their great experiment in liberty, and their control of the sea enabled them to export ideas of freedom and democracy as well as goods throughout the Mediterranean world. Greece entered upon its golden age. There were also those Greeks who believed that one day Greece might actually conquer the Persian Empire. Unfortunately for Greece in the long run, however, the Greeks were never able to unify themselves. The city-states were fiercely independent, which was the seed of their fall. Soon they were dominated by Macedonia, then the Romans, and after them the Turks. Greece did not win its independence from the Ottomans until the 1830s.

Further Reading

Boardman, John, N. H. L. Hammond, D. M. Lewis, and M. Ostwald, eds. *The Cambridge Ancient History,* Vol. 4, *Persia, Greece and the Western Mediterranean, c. 525 to 479 BC.* 2nd ed. Cambridge: Cambridge University Press, 1988.

Burn, A. R. *Persia and the Greeks: The Defense of the West, c. 546–478 BC.* Stanford, CA: Stanford University Press, 1984.

Creasy, Edward S. *Fifteen Decisive Battles of the World.* New York: Harper, 1951.

Farrokh, Keveh. *Shadows in the Desert: Ancient Persia at War.* London: Osprey, 2007.

Green, Peter. *The Greco-Persian Wars.* Berkeley: University of California Press, 1996.

Herodotus. *The History of Herodotus.* Edited by Manuel Komroff. Translated by George Rawlinson. New York: Tudor Publishing, 1956.

Hignett, G. *Xerxes' Invasion of Greece.* Oxford, UK: Clarendon, 1963.

Holland, Tom. *Persian Fire: The First World Empire and the Battle for the West.* Preston, Lancashire, UK: Abacus, 2006.

Kagan, Donald. *The Outbreak of the Peloponnesian War.* Ithaca, NY: Cornell University Press, 1989.

Lazenby, J. F. *The Defence of Greece.* Oxford, UK: Aris and Phillips, 1993.

Sealey, Raphael. *A History of the Greek City States, ca. 700–338 B.C.* Berkeley: University of California Press.

Peloponnesian Wars (460–404 BCE)

Dates	460–404 BCE
Location	Greece
Combatants	Greek city-states allied with Athens vs. Greek city-states allied with Sparta and Persia
Principal Commanders	Athens and its allies: Pericles, Alcibiades Sparta and its allies: Archidamus, Gylippus, Lysander
Principal Battles	Plataea, Syracuse, Athens
Outcome	The Greek city-states fail to unite, bringing a close to Greece's golden age and opening it to conquest.

Causes

The two Peloponnesian Wars (460–446 and 431–404 BCE) resulted from the great rivalry between the two major Greek states of Athens and Sparta and their respective allies. Greek historian and general Thucydides was an eyewitness to many of the important events. Sometimes referred to as the first scientific historian—for he endeavored to describe events as they actually occurred—Thucydides wrote the highly influential *History of the Peloponnesian War* that has had lasting influence on the discussion of strategy since. Thucydides described their cause in these words: "In my view the real reason, true but unacknowledged, which forced the war was the growth of Athenian power, and Spartan fear of it."

Indeed in the decades after the defeat of the second Persian invasion of Greece in 479 BCE, Athens substantially increased its power and influence, in effect becoming an empire. In 478 Athens took the lead in the creation of the Delian League. An organization of some 150–179 Greek city-states, it was established for the purpose of continuing warfare against Persia in the Aegean Sea and Ionia, where many of the league states were located. The league's name derived from Delos, the Aegean island where the meetings were held and where the league kept its treasury. Athens, however, increasingly overshadowed and bullied the other members of the Delian League until it had reduced them to tribute-paying states and members of what was in effect the Athenian Empire.

Tension between Athens and the powerful Peloponnesian state of Sparta had existed for some time. The Delian League only intensified this. Athenian strength was in the navy, and Athens grew increasingly wealthy through trade. Athens touted democracy and espoused literature and the arts. Sparta's strength was in its army, regarded as the finest in the Greek world. But it was also a strictly hierarchical society with no interest in the arts and even less in cultural refinements.

Sparta had protested the decision by Athens, taken after the defeat of the Persians, to rebuild its city walls that had been destroyed by the Persians in their occupation of Athens in 480. Without these, however, Athens would be vulnerable to attack by Sparta. Sparta took no action, but the Athenian decision clearly rankled.

In 465, the enmity between Athens and Sparta was revealed when a large-scale Helot revolt occurred in Sparta. Helots were slaves and worked in agriculture. Their considerable numbers made it possible for Spartan male citizens to concentrate on military training and become the most formidable land force of all Greece. Sparta appealed to other Greek city-states for assistance. Athens was among those responding. It dispatched a sizable force of 4,000 hoplites. Sparta retained the hoplites sent by the other states but dismissed those of Athens because, according to Thucydides, it feared that Athens might switch sides and take the part of the Helots. The Athenians were greatly offended by this treatment and terminated their alliance with Sparta as a result. When the rebellious Helots were subdued and a number left Sparta, Athens settled a number of them in the strategic city of Naupactus on the Gulf of Corinth.

Course of the First Peloponnesian War (460–446 BCE)

The First Peloponnesian War began in 460 BCE when Megara, a small Greek city-state strategically located on the Gulf of Corinth, withdrew from the Peloponnesian League. Led by Sparta, the Peloponnesian League was a military alliance formed in the 6th century BCE. Athens then welcomed Megara as an ally, which gave Athens a position on the strategically important Gulf of Corinth. Corinth—an ally of Sparta—then went to war against Athens, and the fighting then spread to other states belonging to the two leagues, including Sparta, and lasted until 446.

In 458 Athens commenced construction of the Long Walls, strengthening defenses that ran from the city to the port of Piraeus. A Spartan-led army defeated the Athenians in the Battle of Tanagra near Thebes, but in 457 thanks to its victory over the Boeotian city-state in the Battle of Oenophyta,

Athens acquired Boeotia. Fighting continued, but in 451 Athens and Sparta agreed to a five-year truce. Athens was considerably weakened militarily in 454 when it lost a fleet that was attempting to aid Egypt in its revolt against Persia. Fearing revolts by the other members of the Delian League, Athens moved the league treasury from Delos to Athens. Then in 449 Athens and Persia concluded the Peace of Callias, ending hostilities between them.

By 447, however, Athens faced a revolt in Boeotia. Athens sent troops there, who captured Chaeronea only to be defeated by the Boeotians at Coronea and forced to give up control of Boeotia. This Athenian defeat led to revolts against it on Euboea and in Megara and to further fighting with Sparta.

In 446 Euboea revolted, and Athens and Sparta agreed to the Thirty Years' Peace, which for all practical purposes ended the First Peloponnesian War. Athens was forced to give up all of its Peloponnesian possessions but retained Naupactus on the northern shore of the Gulf of Corinth. The peace also prevented armed conflict between Sparta and Athens if at least one of the two wanted arbitration. Neutral city-states could join either side. The peace settlement also recognized both the Delian League and the Peloponnesian League and thus recognition of the Athenian Empire in the Aegean.

Cause of the Second Peloponnesian War (431–404 BCE)

Following conclusion of the Thirty Years' Peace, Athens was free to expand to the north. In 440 Samos revolted against the Athenian Empire. This raised the prospects of a wider revolt against Athens, and indeed Sparta called a congress of the Peloponnesian League to decide whether to go to war with Athens at this time. Corinth,

GREECE DURING THE PELOPONNESIAN WAR

next to Sparta the most powerful member of the league, was opposed, and the congress decided against war. Meanwhile, Athens put down the revolt by Samos.

In 437 Athens secured Amphipolis, located on the northern Aegean Sea in present-day central Macedonia. Amphipolis was an important source of timber, which was of vital importance for its navy. This Athenian expansion, along with renewed aggression against Megara, reawakened concerns in Corinth. In 435 Corcyra, originally a colony of Corinth, went to war against and defeated Corinth. This led Corinth to greatly strengthen its navy. Alarmed at this, in 433 Corcyra allied with Athens, and a small Athenian contingent played a key role in the ensuing naval Battle of Sybota. Corinth

had tried to persuade Athens not to make an alliance with Corcyra, claiming that this would break the Thirty Years' Peace. Athens had made only a defensive alliance with Corcyra and had instructed its commanders not to fight unless the Corinthians threatened to invade Corcyra. The Athenians did get involved, however, and Corinth claimed that Athens had broken the treaty, which Athens denied.

After this the Athenians instructed the little city-state of Potidaea, which was a tributary ally of Athens but a colony of Corinth, that it must tear down its walls, send hostages to Athens, and dismiss its Corinthian magistrates. Angered by this Athenian action, the Corinthians encouraged Potidaea to revolt against Athens. In direct violation of the Thirty Years' Peace that called on both the Delian League and the Peloponnesian League to respect each others' affairs, Corinth also sent troop contingents into Potidaea to help defend it.

In another provocation, Athens imposed stringent trade restrictions on Megara, again an ally of Sparta, preventing it from trading with the Athenian Empire. Those historians who have placed major blame on Athens for the start of the war stress the devastating effect this would have had on the economy of Megara.

At the request of Corinth, a meeting of the Peloponnesian League was held at Sparta in 432. Although not invited, Athenians who happened to be there asked to speak and debated with the Corinthians. According to Thucydides, the Corinthians strongly criticized Sparta for its lack of action to this point and warned that continued inactivity would find Sparta bereft of allies. The Athenians used the forum to remind Sparta of the success Athens had enjoyed against Persia and the dangers to Sparta of war with Athens. They urged that Sparta seek arbitration under the terms of the Thirty Years' Peace. However, a majority of the assembly declared that Athens had in fact broken the peace. This was essentially a declaration of war.

Course

The two sides in the ensuing Second Peloponnesian War presented very different military strengths. Sparta and its allies, with the exception of Corinth, were essentially land powers, with the Spartans enjoying a near-mythic reputation as invincible. Athens was a true empire, with its dependencies spread out around the Aegean and its wealth coming through trade. The strength of Athens was thus understandably its navy.

The first phase of the war, from 431 to 421, is known to history as the Archidamian War, for Spartan king Archidamus II. It was centered on short land invasions of Attica. While the Spartans were able to devastate the surrounding countryside, the Long Walls held, protecting Athenian access to the port of Piraeus, which enabled it to secure foodstuffs and other needed supplies from its overseas empire. Thus, a Spartan siege would have been unsuccessful. Indeed, the longest Spartan presence in Attica was only some 40 days.

Athens had a brilliant *strategos* (general, from which word derives the term "strategy," the art of the general) in its great leader Pericles. He wisely avoided a confrontation with the superior Spartan Army in favor of naval actions. This strategy seemed vindicated by a victory by the Athenian fleet at Naupactus in 429.

In 430 BCE, however, a great plague had struck the densely populated city of Athens. It may have brought the deaths of more than 30,000 people or anywhere from one-third to two-thirds of the city population. The plague was certainly a major factor, and perhaps decisive, in the ultimate defeat of Athens. The situation was so dire in Attica that the Spartans even called off a further effort to invade Attica, so fearful were their soldiers of contracting the plague themselves.

The costliest casualty for Athens of the plague was Pericles himself, who succumbed in 429. Following his death, the Athenian leadership abandoned his wise, essentially defensive strategy centered on the navy, with unfortunate result for Athens. New Athenian leader Cleon and the Athenian general Demosthenes sought to pursue an aggressive strategy that would carry the war to Sparta.

In 428 Mytilene revolted against Athens. The Athenians crushed the revolt the next year. They then raided into Boeotia and Aetolia and proceeded to establish fortified positions in the Peloponnese.

The long war was marked by cruelties and breaches of honor on both sides, particularly for the small states caught between the major powers in the conflict. One such example was Plataea, which the Spartans decided to attack in 428. This Athenian ally and small Boeotian city-state was of no strategic value and had done nothing to invite attack. The invasion was in fact undertaken on the insistence of Sparta's ally Thebes, which wanted to acquire Plataea for itself.

Plataea had been the only other Greek state to aid Athens during the Battle of Marathon against Persia in 490 BCE, and following the Battle of Plataea in 479 that ended the Persian Wars, the Spartans had apparently administered an oath to all the Greeks who had taken part by which they restored the Plataeans to their land and city and upheld their independence. The oath also enjoined all to defend Plataea in upholding its independence. The Spartan attack on Plataea was thus a considerable embarrassment to and stain on Spartan honor. King Archidamus II gave the Plataeans the choice of abandoning their alliance with Athens and joining Sparta or at least pledging neutrality. The Plataeans requested a truce in order to request permission from Athens to surrender, hoping that Athens might allow them to strike some arrangement with the Spartans, since the city could not be rescued without an infantry battle that Athens could not then win. Athens refused, however, urging the Plataeans to remain true to their alliance and promising assistance. Plataea then rejected the Spartan demands, whereupon

Archidamus announced that the Spartans had not broken their oath and Plataea was responsible for what would ensue because it had rejected a reasonable offer.

A series of Spartan attempts to take Plataea by storm failed. Plataea had sent to Athens for safety much of its population, including all children and the elderly, leaving defense of the city to only 400 of its own men and 80 Athenians with 110 women to cook for them. Despite the small number of defenders, Plataea's walls were formidable and sufficient to hold off a large attacking force.

In September 428 BCE, the Spartans initiated a siege with a palisade entirely around the city. The Spartans spent more than two months utilizing a variety of materials to construct an embankment equal to the height of the city walls. At the same time, however, the Plataeans used wood to add to the height of their own walls. The defenders also built a second wall inside the first so that if the latter should be breached, the attackers would have to begin the process anew.

The Spartans sent their battering rams against the outer wall but were unsuccessful, with the defenders dropping large chained beams on the long metal-tipped rams. Archidamus then filled the short space between the embankment and the city wall with combustible materials and set these afire. The Plataeans thought that they were lost, but a fortuitous rain extinguished the flames.

With winter coming on, Archidamus ordered his men to build a more substantial double wall around the city and then sent half his force home for the winter. That winter on a stormy night, some of the Plataeans managed to get over the Spartan wall by means of ladders without being detected and then, after a brief skirmish, broke free; 212 made their way to Athens. The remaining defenders were simply starved into surrender in the summer of 427. The Spartans might easily have taken the city earlier by force but did not do so on the grounds that if peace was concluded with Athens, Sparta could continue to hold on to Plataea in the false claim that the defenders had left of their own free will.

To secure the Plataean surrender, the Spartans promised that each of the defenders would receive a fair trial by a panel of five Spartan judges. But the question put to each defender was whether he had rendered assistance to Sparta or its allies in the war. All were thus forced to answer no. At least 200 Plataeans and 25 Athenian men were subsequently put to death. All the women were sold into slavery.

Eventually the Spartans turned Plataea over to Thebes, which leveled the city entirely and divided up its land among its own citizens. Thereafter Thebes considered what had been Plataea to be part of its own territory. The Siege of Plataea offered ample embarrassment on all sides. The Athenians might easily have released their loyal ally to conclude reasonable terms with the Spartans or rendered the military assistance promised, but they did neither. The granting of Athenian citizenship to the surviving Plataeans was hardly adequate compensation.

One of the posts fortified by the Athenians in the Peloponnese was on the mainland just north of the small island of Sphacteria. The Spartans were determined to reduce it by military action, but Demosthenes outmaneuvered them, winning the 425 naval Battle of Pylos and trapping Spartans who had been stationed on previously uninhabited Sphacteria. Demosthenes then waited for them to surrender, but it fell to the militarily inexperienced

Cleon, who had boasted in the Athenian Assembly that he could defeat the Spartans to win the Battle of Sphacteria that same year. Thucydides says that there had been 420 hoplites there and that 292 were taken prisoner—a major bargaining chip in any peace negotiations. The Athenians could also prevent the annual Spartan invasions of Attica by threatening to kill the hostages.

Following these two Spartan defeats, in 424 the Spartan general Brasidas raised an army and marched it the length of Greece to Amphipolis in Thrace. An Athenian ally, Amphipolis controlled several nearby silver mines that provided substantial financial resources for the Athenian war effort. During the winter of 424–423, Brasidas laid siege to Amphipolis. In order to secure its surrender before an Athenian relief force under Thucydides could arrive, Brasidas offered its citizens generous terms, and they surrendered. The day of the surrender, Thucydides arrived. His tardy arrival earned him exile from Athens, which in turn led to many subsequent conversations with leaders from both sides in the war that found their way into his history.

The Athenians were defeated in their subsequent effort to retake Amphipolis. Both Cleon and Brasidas were among the dead. With the death of the two war leaders, the two sides agreed in 421 to the Peace of Nicias, also known as the Fifty-Year Peace. Among its provisions, both sides agreed to return all conquests in the war except for Nisaea, which would remain in Athenian hands, and Plataea, which had been taken by Thebes. Amphipolis was to be returned to Athens in return for Athens giving up the fort at Pylos. But the citizens of Amphipolis did not want to return to Athenian control and so could not honor that provision. Athens then kept

Pylos (eventually losing it in 409). Shortly thereafter, however, Athens and Sparta concluded an alliance, as a consequence of which Athens let the prisoners taken at Sphacteria go free.

Although Athens and Sparta were not directly involved, fighting continued in and around the Peloponnese. Athens lent support to Argos, a powerful democratic state in the Peloponnese that had managed to remain free of Spartan control. Argos then established a powerful coalition that included Mantinea and Elis. Supported by a small Athenian fleet, these city-states moved against the city of Tegea near Sparta itself. The Spartans then did battle to prevent this. At first the allies had the advantage, but they failed to capitalize on their early successes. On the brink of defeat, the Spartans rallied and won a complete victory in the 418 Battle of Mantinea in what was the largest land engagement within Greece itself during the long Peloponnesian Wars. As a result, Sparta reestablished its hegemony in the Peloponnese, and it and Argos agreed to a 50-year peace.

In 416 Athens attacked Melos and enslaved its inhabitants. The next year Athens received word that Segesta and Leontini, two allied Greek cities in Sicily, had been attacked by the neighboring city of Selinus and its protector, Syracuse. Athens had a long-standing interest westward, as in their colonization of Thurii in southern Italy in 444/443. Indeed, in 427 they had sent troops to Sicily on the occasion of war between Syracuse and Leontini. Concerned about the growing power of Syracuse, in 422 they sent out Phaeax to assess the situation. He had received some favorable responses from other city-states, but after a rebuff at Gela he had abandoned his diplomatic effort. The people of Syracuse

were of Dorian descent, as were the Spartans, while those of Egesta (Segesta) were reported to be of Trojan descent, and the inhabitants of Leontini were Ionian, as were the Athenians.

The Athenian decision to send a powerful expeditionary force to Sicily began the final phase of the Second Peloponnesian War. Alcibiades, a nephew of the great Athenian leader Pericles, convinced the Athenians that securing Sicily would provide them the resources with which to defeat their enemies. Grain from Sicily was then immensely important to the Peloponnese, and cutting it off could well win the war for Athens. The argument was correct, but actually securing Sicily was the problem.

The Athenians assembled a formidable force. Thucydides describes the force that set out in June 415 BCE as "by far the most costly and splendid Hellenic force that had ever been sent out by a single city up to that time." It numbered 134 triremes (100 of them from Athens and the remainder from Chios and other Athenian allies), 30 supply ships, and more than 100 other vessels. These carried, in addition to sailors, rowers, and marines, some 5,100 hoplites and 1,300 archers, javelin men, and slingers as well as 300 horses. In all, the expedition included perhaps 27,000 officers and men. Three generals—Alcibiades, Lamachus, and Nicias—commanded.

The original, sound plan was for a quick demonstration in force against Syracuse and then a return to Greece. But Alcibiades considered this a disgrace and urged that the expeditionary force stir up political opposition to Syracuse in Sicily. In a memorable council of war, Lamachus pressed for an immediate descent on Syracuse while the city was still unprepared and its citizens afraid, but Alcibiades prevailed.

The expedition's leaders then carried out a series of diplomatic approaches to leaders of the other Sicilian cities; all ended in failure, with no city of importance rallying to Athens. Meanwhile, Syracuse strengthened its defenses. Alcibiades was recalled to stand trial in Athens for impiety regarding the earlier defacing of religious statues by unknown persons, and Nicias and Lamachus launched an attack on Syracuse and won a battle there, but the arrival of winter prevented further progress, and they suspended offensive operations. What had been intended as a lightning campaign became a prolonged siege that sapped Athenian energies elsewhere.

Alcibiades meanwhile, fearing for his life, managed to escape from the ship taking him back to Athens and fled to Sparta. There he not only betrayed the Athenian plan of attack against Syracuse but also spoke to the Spartan assembly and strongly supported a Syracusan plea for aid. The Spartans responded by sending out to Sicily a force of their own commanded by Gylippus, one of their best generals.

In the spring of 414 BCE, the Athenians renewed offensive operations at Syracuse. Despite Syracusan work during the winter, the Athenians captured the town of Euryalus and drove the Syracusans behind their city's walls. The Athenians then constructed a fortification, known as the Circle, and other protective walls. They also destroyed several Syracusan counterwalls. Unfortunately for the Athenians, Lamachus was slain in the fighting, and leadership devolved to the ineffective Nicias.

Syracuse, now teetering on the brink of defeat, was in despair when a Corinthian ship made it into the harbor with news that help was on the way. Fortified by this development, the leaders of Syracuse vowed to fight on. Landing in northern Sicily, the Spartan expeditionary force under Gylippus then marched to Syracuse, Nicias failing to contest it en route. Gylippus's men then strengthened the defenses of Syracuse and in the spring of 413 won a stunning victory over the Athenian Navy, capturing its base.

Also, on the advice of Alcibiades, that same year Sparta had sent a land force to Attica and there established a permanent fortification at Decelea. This Spartan land presence not only prevented Athenians from farming the land of Attica year-round but also forced them to rely entirely on the sea for supplies at great expense. Sparta also secured control of the silver mines at Laurium in southeastern Attica, freeing some 20,000 Athenian slaves. With the loss of the mines Athens was forced to demand increased tribute from within its overseas empire, which heightened the possibility of revolts.

Rather than suffer a loss of prestige by abandoning the siege—the wise course under the circumstances—the Athenians decided to send out a second expedition. Led by Demosthenes, one of Athens's most distinguished generals, it numbered 73 triremes carrying 5,000 hoplites and 3,000 bowmen as well as slingers and javelin throwers, in all some 15,000 men. The expedition arrived at Syracuse in July 413.

Demosthenes attempted to destroy one of the Syracusan counterwalls, and when this proved unsuccessful he mounted a night attack. This caught the defenders by surprise, enabling the Athenians to capture Euryalus and much of the Epipolae plateau. But sufficient numbers of Gylippus's troops held fast, and the Syracusans carried out an immediate counterattack, which caught the Athenians disorganized and inflicted heavy casualties.

Cut off from supplies and prey to the defender's cavalry, the Athenians attempted a breakout from the harbor of Syracuse in September 413 with 110 ships, but they were contained by a great boom of block ships across the mouth of the great harbor as well as some 76 Corinthian and Syracusan ships. The naval battle ended in Athenian defeat, with Athens losing 50 ships to 26 of its enemies'.

The Athenians still had 60 triremes to only 50 for their enemies, and the generals wanted to try yet another breakout attempt. The crews refused, however, demanding an overland retreat. Instead of setting out at once in the midst of Syracusan victory celebrations, the Athenians ordered a pause of 36 hours because of a false report that the retreat route was blocked, a story spread to gain time until the victory celebrations had ended.

At length, the retreat occurred. One group of 6,000 men under Demosthenes was offered freedom if they deserted. They refused and fought on until the situation was hopeless. On receiving a guarantee that his men's lives would be spared, the Athenian commander surrendered. The other group of 1,000 men was also forced to surrender. Nicias and Demosthenes were killed, against the will of Gylippus. The 7,000 survivors from the 45,000–50,000 who took part in the expedition on the Athenian side were then sent off to the stone quarries of Syracuse. The expedition had also cost Athens some 200 triremes.

Had the advice of Lamachus been followed at the outset, there is little doubt that Syracuse would have fallen and that the main Sicilian cities would then have been forced to submit to Athens. As it was, the annihilation of the Athenian fleet and army in Sicily shook the Athenian Empire to its core. Thucydides expressed amazement that Athens was able to continue the fight for nearly another decade.

The islands of Euboea, Lesbos, and Chios now revolted against Athens. Sparta built 100 warships, and Persia set out to regain its lost Ionian dominions. Athens still had a number of triremes, set aside as an emergency reserve. These were now activated and formed the Athenian Navy for the remainder of the war. In Athens, oligarchs seized power. They sought peace, but the sailors of the fleet, now based at Samos, rejected this and vowed to fight on. They appointed Alcibiades as their leader, and in the Battle of Abydos in the Hellespont (Dardanelles) in 411 an Athenian fleet of 92 ships defeated a Spartan fleet of 97 ships commanded by Mindarus. The Spartans lost some of their own 30 triremes captured, along with 15 Athenian triremes that had been taken earlier. Pressure from Alcibiades and the fleet also led to the restoration of democratic government in Athens.

In the spring of 410, Alcibiades with 86 triremes then destroyed a Spartan fleet of 80 triremes under Mindarus in what was a combined sea-land battle at Cyzicus. Sparta offered to make peace, but the demagogue Cleophon, who had recently seized power in Athens, persuaded the Athenians to reject it, and the war continued.

Athens won a series of victories, and Alcibiades recaptured Byzantium, regaining Athenian control of the Bosporus, then returned to Athens in 408 or 407. At the same time Sparta and Persia resumed their cooperation in an effort to humble the resurgent Athens, and in 406 the Athenian victories came to an end when Spartan admiral Lysander defeated an Athenian fleet in the relatively minor Battle of Notium. Alcibiades was not reelected general, and he then exiled himself from Athens. Later that same year in the Battle of Arginusae, however, an Athenian fleet commanded by eight generals defeated a Spartan fleet under Callicratidas. The Athenians lost 25 ships, the Spartans 70. Bad weather, however, prevented the Athenians from rescuing their stranded crews or being able to completely defeat the Spartans. A subsequent controversial trial in Athens brought the execution of six of the Athenian top naval commanders. Not only had Athens lost a number of its top naval leaders, but this thoroughly demoralized the navy itself.

Spartan admiral Lysander was a capable naval commander. He also proved to be an astute diplomat and established close ties with Cyrus, the son of Persian king Darius II. This brought considerable Persian financial assistance to the Spartans. Lysander now sailed the Spartan fleet for the Hellespont, forcing the Athenian fleet to follow. In the 405 Battle of Aegospotami, Lysander outmaneuvered and totally defeated the Athenian fleet, reportedly destroying some 168 ships and capturing 3,000–4,000 Athenian sailors. Reportedly only 9 Athenian triremes escaped. It was not the battle itself but the subsequent Spartan blockade of the Hellespont that was decisive, however.

With Athens bereft of its navy, the siege was now complete, and the city surrendered in 404 BCE, its allies following suit, bringing the Second Peloponnesian War to a close. Athens lost what remained of its once proud navy (its navy being limited to 12 triremes), the Long Walls were torn down, and all of the city's overseas possessions were taken from it. Corinth and Thebes wanted the city destroyed and its inhabitants sold into slavery, but to its lasting credit, Sparta rejected this course of action, its leaders refusing to destroy a city that they said had done such fine service at a time of the greatest danger to Greece. Athens was taken into the Spartan system of states, to have "the same friends and enemies" as Sparta itself.

Significance

The Peloponnesian Wars marked the end of the golden age of Greece. Although Greek culture survived in its adoption and spread by Alexander the Great of Macedon and then Rome, Greece itself was largely devastated. The economies of the many Greek city-states were destroyed, and Greece lay open to conquest. Under the insistence of Sparta, Athens was for some 12–17 months under oligarchical rule. Democracy was restored in 403 BCE. Sparta was in turn humbled by Thebes, which defeated it in the Battle of Leuctra in 371 BCE. The adage that those unable to govern themselves are soon governed by others was borne out as far as Greece was concerned several decades later, when it was conquered by King Philip II of Macedon.

Further Reading

Bagnall, Nigel. *The Peloponnesian War: Athens, Sparta, and the Struggle for Greece.* New York: Thomas Dunne Books, 2006.

Cawkwell, George. *Thucydides and the Peloponnesian War.* London: Routledge, 1997.

Hanson, Victor Davis. *A War Like No Other: How the Athenians and Spartans Fought the Peloponnesian War.* New York: Random House, 2005.

Kagan, Donald. *The Outbreak of the Peloponnesian War.* Ithaca, NY: Cornell University Press, 1969.

Kagan, Donald. *The Peloponnesian War.* New York: Viking, 2003.

Kallet, Lisa. *Money and the Corrosion of Power in Thucydides: The Sicilian Expedition and Its Aftermath.* Berkeley: University of California Press, 2001.

Lazenby, J. F. *The Peloponnesian War: A Military Study.* New York: Routledge, 2004.

Strassler, Robert B., ed. *The Landmark Thucydides: A Comprehensive Guide to the Peloponnesian War.* New York: Free Press, 1998.

Thucydides. *The Peloponnesian War.* Translated by Richard Crawley. New York: E. P. Dutton, 1910.

Tritle, Larry. *A New History of the Peloponnesian War.* Malden, MA: Wiley-Blackwell, 2010.

Wars of Alexander the Great (335–323 BCE)

Dates	335–323 BCE
Location	Greece, Thrace, Asia Minor, Syria, Babylonia, Persia, India
Combatants	Macedon and allied Greek city-states vs. Persian Empire, Phoenicia, Egypt, Babylonia, Bactria, north Indians
Principal Commanders	Macedon: Alexander III, Parmenion, Antipater, Ptolemy, Hephaestion Persia: Darius III, Memnon, Bessus India: King Porus
Principal Battles	Granicus, Issus, Tyre, Gaza, Gaugamela, Hydaspes River
Outcome	Alexander conquers much of the known world and spreads Greek culture throughout (the fusion of Greek and Persian cultures being known as Hellenistic), with immense consequences for world history.

Causes

Following the successful defense of their homeland by the Greek city-states against invasions by forces of the vast Persian Empire in the Greco-Persian Wars (499–479), a number of Greeks harbored visions of turning the tables and conquering the Persian Empire, then the world's largest empire. Among these was Philip II, king of Macedon, who ruled that territory in the northeastern part of the Greek peninsula during 359–336. Inaugurating a new period in Greek history, Philip organized Macedonia for war and turned its army into a formidable military force, transforming it into arguably the finest military establishment the world had yet seen. Philip studied and understood the strengths, limitations, and utility of each type of military formation and melded these into a combined-arms team that included strong cavalry and artillery elements whereby the particular strength of each contributed to the success of the whole. Commanded by the king in person and, upon his death, by his son Alexander III (the Great), the army was not only well trained but efficiently organized and brilliantly administered, triumphing over all other forces it encountered.

Taking advantage of the sharp divisions and rivalries among the Greek city-states to the south, Philip expanded Macedonian territory in Illyria and toward the Danube and then in Thrace and Thessaly. He also greatly increased his influence in Greece.

Philip had long planned to invade Persia. He hoped to be able to do so at the head of an army that would include an allied Greek force, but the leading Greek city-states stole a march on him and concluded an alliance with King Artaxerxes of Persia. This forced Philip to move quickly against the Greeks before he could invade Persia.

In May 338 BCE Philip defeated the forces of Athens, Thebes, and their allies in the Battle of Chaeronea in Boeotia in central Greece. One of the most decisive battles in Greek history, it extinguished the independence of the city-states and saw Philip master of all Greece. Philip then established a federal system in the so-called League of Corinth that united most of the city-states and ended the struggles that had distracted them for so long. Sparta, however, refused to participate.

Philip then prepared to launch his invasion of the Persian Empire. This was ostensibly to free the Greek city-states of Asia Minor, but his grand design was to conquer Persia and secure the wealth of that vast empire. In 336 he sent his trusted general Parmenio to Asia Minor with an advance force. Philip was preparing to follow with the main invasion force when he was assassinated, possibly with the complicity of Olympias, his estranged wife. In any case, Philip was succeeded by his son Alexander, who prepared to implement his father's plan.

Course

The accession to the throne of Macedon of young Alexander (he was but 20 years old at the time) appeared to present an opportunity for the Greek city-states to reassert their independence, but Alexander quickly marched an army southward and, at Corinth, secured election as captain general of the Hellenic League, the same position held by his father. In 335 Alexander moved against areas under Macedonian control to the north, which also had become restive, crushing a revolt in southern Illyria. There he learned that Athens and Thebes had risen against him, probably under the influence of Darius III, the new king of Persia. Alexander immediately marched south into Greece with a sizable force. Moving quickly, he surprised and took Thebes, sacking and virtually destroying it. Athens surrendered and was treated generously, ending opposition in Greece to Alexander's rule.

His base of operations secure, in 334 BCE Alexander proceeded to invade the Persian Empire with a relatively small army of some 30,000 infantry and 5,000 cavalry. This included soldiers from the Greek states. Alexander left behind in Macedon his trusted general Antipater and 10,000 men to hold Macedonia and Greece in his absence. During the next decade Alexander not only conquered Persia but also campaigned in Egypt and as far as Uzbekistan, Afghanistan, and the Punjab. Everywhere victorious, his conquests created what became known as the Hellenistic world.

Alexander's army reached the Hellespont (present-day Dardanelles) in just three weeks and crossed without Persian opposition. His fleet numbered only about 160 ships supplied by the allied Greeks. The Persian fleet included perhaps 400 Phoenician triremes and its crews were far better trained, yet the Persian ships did not contest the crossing.

Alexander instructed his men that there was to be no looting in what was now, he said, their land. The invaders received the submission of a number of Greek towns in Asia Minor. Persian king Darius III was, however, gathering forces to oppose Alexander. Memnon, a Greek mercenary general in the king's employ, knew that Alexander was short of supplies and cash; he therefore favored a scorched-earth policy to eventually force Alexander to withdraw. At the same time, Darius would use his fleet to transport the army across the Aegean and invade Macedonia. Memnon advised that the Persians should avoid a pitched battle with Alexander at all costs. This, however, wounded Persian pride and influenced Darius to reject Memnon's wise advice.

The two armies met in May. The Persian force was approximately the same size as that of Alexander. The Persians took up position on the east bank of the swift Granicus River. The Persian force was strong in cavalry but weak in infantry, with perhaps as many as 6,000 Greek hoplite mercenaries. Memnon and the Greek mercenaries were in front, forming a solid spear wall supported by men with javelins. The Persian cavalry was on the flanks, to be employed as mounted infantry.

When Alexander's army arrived, Parmenio and the other Macedonian generals recognized the strength of the Persian position and counseled Alexander against attack. The Greek infantry would have to cross the Granicus in column and would be vulnerable while they were struggling to re-form. The generals urged that as it was already late afternoon, they should camp for the night. Although determined to attack, Alexander followed their advice.

That night, however, probably keeping his campfires burning to deceive the Persians, Alexander located a ford downstream and led his army across the river. The Persians only discovered the deception the next morning. The bulk of the Macedonian army was then already across the river and easily deflected a Persian assault. The rest of the army then crossed.

With Alexander having turned their position, the Persians and their Greek mercenaries were forced to fight in open country. Their left was on the river, their right anchored by foothills. The Persian cavalry was now in front, with the Greek mercenary infantry to the rear. Alexander placed the bulk of his Greek cavalry on the left flank, the heavy Macedonian infantry in the center, and the light Macedonian infantry, the Paeonian light cavalry, and his own heavy cavalry (known as the Companions) on the right. Conspicuous in magnificent armor and shield with an extraordinary helmet with two white plumes, Alexander took personal position on the right wing, and the Persians therefore assumed that the attack would come from that quarter.

Alexander initiated the Battle of the Granicus. Trumpets blared, and Alexander set off with the Companions in a great wedge formation aimed at the far left of the Persian line. This drew Persian cavalry off from the center, whereupon Alexander wheeled and led the Companions diagonally to his left, against the weakened Persian center. Although the Companions had to charge uphill, they pushed their way through an opening in the center of the Persian line. Alexander was in the thick of the fight as the Companions drove back the Persian cavalry, which finally broke.

Surrounded, the Greek mercenaries were mostly slaughtered. Alexander sent the 2,000 who surrendered to Macedonia in chains, probably to work in the mines. It would have made sense to have incorporated them into his own army, but he wanted to make an example of them for having fought against fellow Greeks.

Following the battle, Alexander proceeded to liberate the Greek coastal cities of Asia Minor. His only real opposition came at Miletus, which he captured

THE EMPIRE OF ALEXANDER THE GREAT

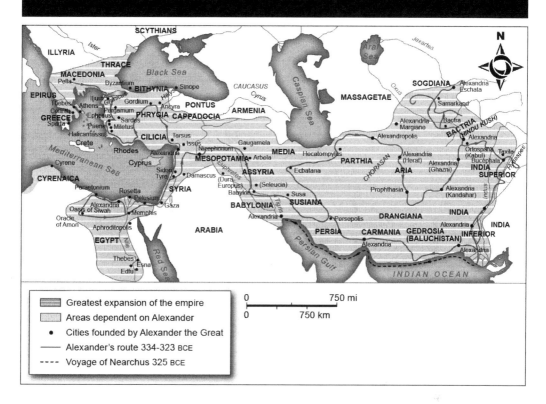

following a brief siege. Alexander then took the momentous decision of disbanding his fleet of some 160 triremes. He kept only the Athenian detachment, to serve as transports and provide hostages, and a squadron in the Hellespont. With the Persian fleet of more than 400 triremes dominating the eastern Mediterranean, he could not hope to win a sea battle, and maintaining the fleet was expensive. His commanders opposed this decision. The Persians might now easily cut off the army in Asia Minor and prevent both its resupply and its return to Macedonia and Greece. The Persians could also raid Greece and stir up revolts against Alexander there. Alexander, however, believed that his men would fight harder knowing that retreat was not possible. He also seems to have

profoundly distrusted his Greek allies, so much so that he was prepared to risk his entire campaign rather than entrust its safety to a Greek fleet. Alexander told his generals that he intended to move against the Persian fleet from the land instead, taking the Persian and Phoenician naval bases along the eastern Mediterranean coast. Indeed, during 334–333 he conquered much of the coast of Asia Minor.

Alexander's early military successes owed much to his reputation for mercy, justice, and toleration. It certainly helped his cause that his rule brought improved administration, lower taxes, and public works projects. The only difficult operation in this campaign occurred at Halicarnassus, where the defenders were led by Memnon. Alexander only took the city following a siege.

While Alexander secured the remaining coastal cities, Persian king Darius III now loosed Memnon, his only first-class general, against Alexander's lines of communication. Memnon soon took sick and died, however. Darius was busy gathering yet another army for another military test with the invader when he learned that Alexander had moved south into Syria. This news caused Darius to move before he was fully ready. Crossing the Amanus Mountains, Darius positioned his forces behind Alexander, cutting off his line of communications. With the potentially hostile cities of Phoenicia to the south, Alexander had no choice but to break off this campaign to turn and fight.

The two armies came together at Issus in southern Anatolia in early November 333 (possibly November 5). The size of the armies remains in dispute. Darius had more men—probably 75,000 and perhaps as many as 100,000 (Macedonian reports of 600,000 are sheer propaganda). Alexander had about 42,000 infantry and 5,000 cavalry. Darius positioned his army on the narrow coastal plain on the north side of the steep-banked Pinarus River, a front of about three miles. This meant that only part of his force could engage at any one time. Largely untrained troops held the Persian left and right, and Darius placed archers to their fronts to buttress them. In the center of the Persian line were the 2,000 Royal Bodyguards, the elite force in the army. Darius was with them in a great ornamental chariot. As many as 30,000 Greek mercenaries were on either side of the bodyguards, while Persian cavalry anchored the far right flank on the Gulf of Issus. If the Persians could but hold, Alexander's days would be numbered.

Alexander arrived before the Persian line in late afternoon. After completing his dispositions, he resumed the advance. His forces on a three-mile front, he halted just out of bowshot hoping the Persians would attack. As he occupied a strong, prepared defensive position, Darius understandably refused. Alexander then ordered his own men forward. Determining that the infantry on the Persian left was the weak part of the enemy line, Alexander placed his Macedonian heavy cavalry (the Companions) on the right of his line.

Battle was joined when the Persian archers let loose a volley of arrows, then withdrew back into the mass of infantry, as Alexander led the Companions in an assault against the light infantry on the Persian left, which almost immediately broke.

The Macedonian attack in the center did not go as well. The men had difficulty getting across the river, only to encounter its steep bank and stake palisades placed by the Persians. Desperate hand-to-hand fighting ensued, pitting the Macedonian infantrymen against equally tough Greek mercenaries. Alexander, meanwhile, rolled up the Persian left.

Alexander then shifted his cavalry to strike the rear of the Greek mercenaries and the Royal Bodyguards in an effort to kill or capture Darius. Alexander was wounded in the thigh during the fighting, some accounts say by Darius himself. But the horses on Darius's chariot were wounded and suddenly reared and bolted. Darius managed to control them but, in danger of capture, shifted to another smaller chariot and fled the field.

Things were not going well for Alexander elsewhere, and he was forced to break off his pursuit. He swung his right wing into the Persian army's Greek mercenaries from the flank and rolled them up. When the men of the Persian heavy cavalry saw this and learned of the flight of Darius, they too decamped. The retreat became a rout, but darkness forced Alexander to break off the pursuit.

Persian losses may have been as high as half of the force, or 50,000 men, while Alexander reported some 450 dead. Among the captives were Darius's wife, mother, and two daughters. The loot taken included some 3,000 talents in gold.

Issus was a glorious victory, but it was not decisive. More than 10,000 Greek mercenaries escaped and would form the nucleus of yet another army. Darius also still lived, and as long as this was the case, the fight would continue.

After Issus, Alexander returned to his strategy of capturing the Persian Mediterranean naval bases in order to secure his southern flank prior to resuming his eastward march to the extremities of the Persian Empire. Alexander's sieges of Tyre and Gaza in 332 are two of the great military operations in history.

Tyre was the most important of the Phoenician coastal city-states and ports. Ruled by King Azemilk and located in present-day Lebanon, Tyre was actually two cities. Old Tyre was located on an island about three miles in circumference, separated from the mainland city by a half mile of water more than 20 feet deep. The island citadel was protected by massive walls up to 150 feet high on the land side and reputedly was impregnable.

Alexander would have preferred to bypass Tyre, but he had to reduce it before he could move against Egypt lest Tyre be used as a base for Darius's fleet. Alexander predicted that once Tyre fell, the Phoenician ship crews, deprived of their bases,

would desert to the winning side. This observation was prescient.

Determined to hold out, the Tyrians rejected Alexander's overtures. They had full confidence in their defenses. Alexander himself had reservations, evidenced by his dispatching heralds to the Tyrians to urge a peaceful resolution. The Tyrian leaders, however, seeing this as a sign of weakness, slew the heralds and threw their bodies over the walls. This foolish act cemented Alexander's determination and won support for his plans from his generals.

Alexander secured mainland Tyre without difficulty, then in January 332 initiated siege operations against the island, ordering his chief engineer, Dyadis the Thessalian, to construct a great mole about 200 feet wide out from the land to bring up siege engines and reach the island. The Tyrians had some success in employing a fireship and archers against the mole, but Alexander secured ships and operated against the island himself. Meanwhile, work on the mole continued. Tyre finally fell at the end of July. Pent-up Macedonian frustration over the length and ferocity of the siege gave way to rage, with no quarter extended to the inhabitants. Reportedly, 8,000 Tyrians died during the siege, with the Macedonians killing another 7,000 afterward. Another 30,000 inhabitants, including women and children, were sold into slavery.

With Tyre destroyed, the Macedonian Army set out on foot in July or early August for Egypt. Some 160 miles from Tyre the army encountered the fortress city of Gaza, situated on a rocky hill. The city's governor, Batis, rejected calls for surrender. Macedonian siege operations here were quite difficult, as the siege engines sank in the sand. On occasion the defenders also sallied forth to destroy the

Macedonian siege equipment. On one such foray, Alexander was badly wounded in the shoulder by an arrow.

Alexander now again called on Dyadis, this time to build an earthen rampart around the city. In a considerable undertaking, completed in only two months, the Macedonians encircled Gaza with an earthen rampart topped by a wooden platform. The Macedonian troops finally breached the walls and entered the city. Another group gained access to Gaza by a tunnel.

Gaza fell after heavy fighting. Reportedly, the Macedonians slew 10,000 of the defenders, and the women and children were all sold as slaves. Batis was among those captured. Alexander ordered him lashed by his ankles behind a chariot and dragged around the city walls until dead. The sieges of both Tyre and Gaza demonstrated Alexander's thorough mastery of siege warfare and greatly added to his mystique of invincibility. Alexander was, however, fortunate that Darius III had not moved against the Macedonian lines of communication.

Darius offered Alexander 10,000 talents in gold, the territory of the empire west of the Euphrates River, and his daughter in marriage. Alexander rejected this overture, replying that he intended to conquer all Persia.

Having secured both Syria and Palestine, during 332–331 Alexander occupied Egypt. While there he founded Alexandria, only one of many cities to bear his name. While in Egypt, Alexander also traveled 200 miles into the desert to visit the Temple of Zeus Ammon and there received confirmation of his divinity as the son of Zeus.

Taking advantage of Alexander's absence and with funds supplied by Persia, during 331 King Agis III of Sparta led a revolt in Greece. Most of the southern Greek states joined it and laid siege to Megalopolis (present-day Megalopoli) in the southwestern Peloponnesus. Antipater marched south, however, and defeated the rebels outside Megalopolis. Antipater then sent Alexander reinforcements, who joined him in Egypt.

In April 331 Alexander departed Egypt with his army, marching north to Tyre and then east across the territory he had carved out of Asia Minor. This time, however, he moved directly against the distant cities of Persia, crossing the Euphrates on a bridge constructed by some of his men under his general and alleged lover Hephaestion.

Persian king Darius III had assembled a new army. Alexander had a maximum of 47,000 men: 31,000 heavy infantry (Phalangists) and 9,000 light infantry (Peltasts), along with 7,000 cavalry. Ancient sources credit Darius with a force of between 200,000 and 1 million men. This is almost certainly an exaggeration, for maintaining a force this large would have been almost impossible given the primitive logistics of the time. Probably he had no more than 100,000 men, of whom up to 40,000 were cavalry. But Alexander was certainly greatly outnumbered. His force was, however, well trained, well organized, and disciplined, while the Persian Army was a polyglot force drawn chiefly from the eastern provinces that included Persians, Medes, Babylonians, Syrians, Armenians, and Indois (the Greek term for inhabitants of India).

Darius III awaited Alexander on the plain at Gaugamela, some 60 miles from the city of Arbela (modern-day Erbil). Usually known as the Battle of Gaugamela, the clash here is sometimes erroneously known as the Battle of Arbela for the nearest settlement. Most probably it took place east of the city of Mosul in present-day northern Iraq.

Darius chose not to oppose Alexander's approach, trusting in superior numbers. Darius had selected the location to be able to utilize his superior numbers and employ his chariots, which had scythes mounted on their wheel hubs to cut down Alexander's forces like so much wheat. Some sources contend that Darius had the plain cleared of vegetation for ease of maneuver. He was confident that his preparations would bring him victory.

Alexander moved slowly to Gaugamela, hoping to wear down the defenders and exhaust their food stocks. When Alexander finally arrived, his chief of staff, Parmenio, urged a night attack to help offset the numerical disadvantage, but Alexander refused. Apart from the difficulty of maintaining control at night, Alexander opposed any effort to "steal victory like a thief." He would, he said, "defeat his enemies openly and honestly." As it turned out, Darius had feared a night assault and kept his troops awake all night. The next morning the men were exhausted, while those of Alexander were well rested.

Battle was joined on October 1, 331. Alexander, who fought with his Companion cavalry, commanded the right flank of his army, while Parmenio had charge of the left. Macedonian and Greek cavalry protected the two flanks. Alexander arranged the army in oblique formation, refusing his left and moving the army laterally to the right across the Persian front. His plan was to draw the Persians to the flanks, opening a weak point in the center of the Persian line. Everything depended on his flanks holding until Alexander could detect this weakness and strike a decisive blow.

Darius positioned himself in the center of the Persian line with his best infantry. Bessus commanded the cavalry on the Persian left wing with chariots in front, while Mazaeus commanded the right flank of other cavalry. With their vastly superior numbers of cavalry and much longer line, it appeared that the Persians must inevitably flank Alexander's army.

Darius ordered Bessus to release cavalry to ride around the Macedonian right wing and arrest Alexander's movement. Bessus committed some 11,000 cavalry to the effort, but they were halted by the numerically far inferior but better-trained Macedonian cavalry and the Greek mercenary infantry.

Darius then ordered the chariots positioned in front of his left wing to attack Alexander's elite force of Companion cavalry on the Macedonian right. Alexander's infantry screen of javelin throwers, archers, and light infantrymen somewhat blunted this chariot charge before it reached the Companions. The Companions then wheeled aside, allowing the remaining chariots to pass through unopposed, when they came up against the lances of the infantry. The gap then closed, and the Persian charioteers were annihilated in the Macedonian rear.

Darius then ordered a general advance. Mazaeus, who commanded the Persian right wing, moved against the Macedonian left led by Parmenion and sent cavalry in an attempt to get around the Macedonian line. At the same time, Bessus sought to push men around the Macedonian right to envelop it. These efforts elongated the Persian line as Alexander had hoped, weakening its center.

Having brought up reserves and detected a weak point in the Persian line, Alexander led his Companion cavalry and light infantry in a great wedge-shaped formation against it. Twice the Macedonians burst through gaps in the Persian line and drove close to Darius's own chariot.

Both Persian flanks were now threatened by the great gap torn in the center of the line. The possibility of encirclement led Bessus to retreat, his forces suffering heavy casualties from the pursuing Macedonians. Darius, now himself in danger of being cut off, panicked and fled. With the Persians in wild retreat, the Macedonians vigorously pressed their advance, scattering the vast Persian host.

Alexander's left wing, heavily engaged with Mazaeus's men, could not keep pace with the cavalry, and an attempt at encirclement failed. The victory was nonetheless sweeping. The Macedonians reported their casualties in the battle at some 500 killed and up to 3,000 wounded, while Persian losses were close to 50,000.

Alexander did not rest but after the battle advanced rapidly toward the Persian capital of Persepolis so as not to allow the Persian generals time to reorganize their forces. Bessus and other Persian generals, disgusted by Darius's conduct, murdered him in mid-330. Alexander caught such regicides as he could and executed them.

Alexander sent most of his men by the long route, while he led about a third of his force through the mountains on a shorter route through the Persian Gates (the strategic pass now known as Tang-e Meyran in modern-day Iran), held by a Persian army under Ariobarzan. The Persians halted the Macedonians at the narrow pass and reportedly inflicted heavy casualties. Either through a shepherd or prisoners, Alexander learned of a path

that flanked the Persian position and, in a highly dangerous move, led a number of his men by it at night and turned the Persian position. As a result, Alexander reached Persepolis before the guards of the treasury could hide its reputed 3,000 tons of gold and silver, the greatest known treasury in the world. He then destroyed the great palace, perhaps as a sign of the end of Persian power.

Alexander was now 25 years old. In 4 years he had broken the power of Persia forever and now ruled an empire of 1 million square miles. No one in the world could come close to him in wealth or power. The speed of what he accomplished stands unequaled before or since.

Alexander's tutor, Aristotle, had urged him to treat the Persians as slaves. Instead Alexander treated them as equals and employed them in administrative positions, something many of his troops could not understand. After organizing his new empire, in 329 Alexander campaigned in Parthia and Bactria. He then turned north across the Oxus River into Sogdiana. In 328 he subdued Sogdiana and then fought his way through the mountain passes north of the Kabul Valley and across the Indus River into India.

In May 326 Alexander triumphed over King Porus of the Punjab in the Battle of the Hydaspes River. In this engagement, Alexander deployed a force of only some 9,000 infantry and 5,000 cavalry, while Porus had perhaps 35,000 men and 100 war elephants. In the battle, Porus was wounded and taken prisoner. Alexander left him as a vassal king. Alexander then conquered the Punjab and sailed down the Indus River to the Indian Ocean.

Alexander planned to continue campaigning in north-central India and to proceed to the Ganges. He reached only the

Hyphasis (Beas) River when in July 326 his men mutinied and refused to go farther. Reluctantly Alexander agreed to halt, then led his army south down the Indus and was seriously wounded in battle. Recovering, he moved to the mouth of the Indus and there constructed a fleet. He sent part of his force under Nearchus across the Arabian Sea to the Persian Gulf. Another part of the army he sent back to Persepolis by way of the Bolan Pass and Kandahar. He accompanied the remainder through Baluchistan, his men suffering great hardship in the desert. Twice the army linked up with Nearchus's ships.

Returning to Persia and then to Mesopotamia in 324, Alexander concentrated on restoring order in his vast empire and attempting to combine the best of Greek and Persian cultures. He did not have the time necessary to make this work but died at age 32 of a fever, possibly malaria, after a drinking bout. As he was dying, he was asked to whom he left his vast empire. Reportedly he whispered "Kratisto" (meaning "to the strongest").

Significance

Following Alexander's death, first Perdiccas and then Antigonus the One-Eyed endeavored to maintain the unity of the empire. Soon, however, a dozen of Alexander's leading generals (the Diadochi, or successors) were fighting for control of the state. Although skillful generals, none had Alexander's vision or genius. By 309 BCE Alexander's direct family had been eliminated, and the contenders believed themselves strong enough to claim the title of king in their own areas of the Hellenistic world. Alexander's vision of a universal

commonwealth was thus lost. By 276 BCE the three major power centers of the Hellenistic empire were Macedon, Egypt, and the Seleucid Empire.

Despite the breakup of the empire, the cultural impact of Alexander's conquests was immense. The fusion of Greek and non-Greek culture, known as Hellenistic, impacted virtually all areas, including the arts but also education, government, and even city planning, and was still evident in the Byzantine Empire of the mid-15th century.

Further Reading

Burn, A. *Alexander the Great and the Hellenistic Empire.* 2nd ed. London: English Universities Press, 1951.

Engels, Donald W. *Alexander the Great and the Logistics of the Macedonian Army.* Berkeley: University of California Press, 1978.

Green, Peter. *Alexander of Macedon, 356–323 B.C.: A Historical Biography.* Berkeley: University of California Press, 1991.

Hammond, N. G. L. *Alexander the Great: King, Commander, and Statesman.* 3rd ed. London: Bristol Classical Press, 1996.

Hammond, N. G. L. *The Genius of Alexander the Great.* Chapel Hill: University of North Carolina Press, 1997.

Hammond, N. G. L. *The Macedonian State: Origins, Institutions, and History.* Oxford University Press, 1989.

Kern, Paul Bentley. *Ancient Siege Warfare.* Bloomington: Indiana University Press, 1999.

McCrindle, J. W. *The Invasion of India by Alexander the Great as Described by Arrian, Q Curtius, Diodorus, Plutarch, and Justin.* Westminster, UK: Archibald Constable, 1993.

Sekunda, Nick, and John Warry. *Alexander the Great: His Armies and Campaigns, 332–323 B.C.* London: Osprey, 1988.

Punic Wars (264–146 BCE)

Dates	264–146 BCE
Location	Western Mediterranean, Sicily, Spain, Italy, North Africa
Combatants	Rome vs. Carthage
Principal Commanders	Rome: Gnaeus Cornelius Scipio Asina, Publius Cornelius Scipio, Gaius Terentius Varro Carthage: Hamilcar Barca, Hannibal Gisco, Hannibal Barca, Hasdrubal Barca
Principal Battles	Tunes, Aegates Islands, Cannae, Metaurus River, Zama
Outcome	Rome obliterates Carthage and dominates the Mediterranean world.

Causes

The prolonged struggle for mastery of the Mediterranean world between Rome and Carthage was probably the largest series of wars in terms of numbers of men involved to that time in history, claiming the lives of hundreds of thousands of men on both sides. The term "Punic" comes from the Latin word *punicus* or *poenicus* and refers to the Phoenician ancestry of the Carthaginians, a seafaring people who built their wealth in trade and lived in present-day Tunisia. The 3,000-year-old city of Carthage is located on the Mediterranean on the Gulf of Tunis.

The three Punic Wars (264–241, 218–201, and 149–146 BCE) sprang out of the expansion of the Roman Republic into the western Mediterranean, which the Carthaginians considered their preserve. The First Carthaginian War was sparked by a struggle for control of the island of Sicily, specifically the city-state of Messana (present-day Messina). Around 271 BCE following the death of Agathocles, tyrant of Syracuse, a number of Italian mercenaries known as the Mamertines revolted against his successor, Hiero II. The Mamertines then established themselves at Messana, just across the straits of that name from Italy, setting up there what was for all intents and purposes a pirate state. Under threat by Hiero, one group of the Mamertines decided to call on Rome for assistance, while another faction appealed to Carthage. Carthage immediately responded, and Rome also decided to send troops, paving the way for war between the two.

Course of the First Punic War (264–241 BCE)

In 264 BCE the Carthaginians, who had allied with Hiero, reached Messana first and seized control of the city. They were, however, soon driven out by a Roman army under Appius Claudius Caudex, who then laid siege, without success, to Syracuse, also in Sicily. In 263, Roman military successes under Manius Valerius Maximus in eastern Sicily caused Hiero II to switch sides and ally with Rome against Carthage.

The next year the Romans besieged the Carthaginian possession of Agrigentum (Girgenti) in eastern Sicily, ably defended by Hannibal Gisco. The Romans defeated a Carthaginian relief force under Hanno, but Hannibal Gisco and his army escaped the city. The victory nonetheless gave Rome control over most of Sicily.

With the land successes in Sicily, the Romans embarked on a naval-building program so as to contest with Carthage control of the western Mediterranean. In only two months the Romans built and fitted out some 100 quinqueremes (warships with five superimposed banks of oars and as many as 300 oarsmen) and 20 triremes (three banks). In 260 in the Battle of the Lipari Islands, the first major naval contest between the two sides, the Carthaginians commanded by Boödes ambushed a Roman squadron under Consul Gnaeus Cornelius Scipio Asina in Lipara Harbor, Sicily. The inexperienced Roman crews panicked under the Carthaginian attack. The Carthaginians lost 4 ships sunk but captured all 17 Roman vessels and made prisoners of their crews. Scipio was among those taken.

The Romans, however, turned the tables later that same year in the Battle of Mylae, fought off the northern Sicilian coast. Consul Gaius Duilius won a decisive victory over the Carthaginians commanded by Hannibal Gisco. The Romans had some 130 ships and employed new tactics, meeting the Carthaginian ships bow-on and utilizing the corvus. With scant expertise at sea and their strength being their soldiers, the Romans devised a sort of gangplank, about 36 feet long with rails on either side and a spike on the underside at the end. Attached to a mast and lowered by pulley onto an enemy ship, where it was secured by the spike, the corvus provided a secure means for the legionnaires to cross to the enemy vessel. The Carthaginians also had 130 ships and lost 50 in the battle. Reportedly, 3,000 Carthaginians were killed and another 7,000 captured.

Having won control of the sea, the Romans then dispatched land forces to both

Corsica and Sardinia. In 256 they also sent an expeditionary force from Sicily to Africa. Commanded by M. Atilius Regulus and L. Manlius Volso, it numbered some 150,000 men in all and 330 galleys. To oppose it, the Carthaginians assembled some 350 ships, several of which were quinqueremes. Hamilcar (a common Carthaginian name) had command. In the ensuing Battle of Cape Ecnomus off the southern coast of Sicily, Roman tactics again prevailed. The Carthaginians lost more than 30 ships sunk and another 64 captured, while the Romans lost only 24.

The Roman land force then came ashore in North Africa, and Regulus won a decisive victory in the Battle of Adys. The Carthaginians sued for peace, but the Roman terms were so severe that the Carthaginians elected to continue the struggle. Toward that end, they acquired the services of Spartan soldier of fortune Xanthippus, who arrived in Carthage with a force of Greek mercenaries. Xanthippus reorganized and retrained the Carthaginian army and in 254 took to the field against the Roman army commanded by Regulus. Each side had about 20,000 men. In the Battle of Tunes (Tunis), also known as the Battle of Bagrades, Xanthippus made effective use of his cavalry, war elephants, and the phalanx formation of his infantry to inflict a decisive defeat on Regulus, capturing him and about half of his force. Only about 2,000 Romans escaped, rescued by the fleet.

The Roman fleet then sailed for home with what remained of the land force. During the return voyage, the Romans suffered one of the greatest maritime disasters in history. In a great storm off Camarina some 284 of 364 ships were lost, with perhaps 100,000 men drowned. This represented about 15 percent of all the available Roman adult manpower of fighting age. Some historians attribute the loss of the ships to their instability in stormy seas because of the heavy corvus at the bow. Roman resolve was demonstrated, however, when the Romans immediately set to work building new ships and putting together a new army. Within three months the Romans had constructed 220 new ships and raised another 80,000 men.

The Carthaginians sought peace terms and sent captured Roman general Regulus to Rome to arrange at least an exchange of prisoners. According to legend, Regulus advised Rome not to negotiate, then honored the terms of his parole by returning to Carthage, where he was tortured to death.

The Carthaginians reinforced their strongholds in Sicily and recaptured Agrigentum. The Romans, however, mounted a successful amphibious assault against Panormus in northwestern Sicily. Roman consul L. Caecilius Metellus commanded some 25,000 men of the reconstituted Roman army at Panormus in 251 and defeated about the same number of Carthaginians under Hasdrubal.

In 249 some 200 Roman galleys under Consul P. Claudius Pulcher engaged a Carthaginian fleet of similar size under Adherbal near Drepanum (Trapani), Sicily. The Romans attacked from seaward, while the Carthaginians sailed in line-ahead formation, close together. The Carthaginian maneuver caused the Roman ships to bunch up until they were almost too close to employ their oars and their sails masked each other. The Carthaginians then turned and engaged the Romans in a traditional side-by-side attack and were victorious. The Romans lost 93 ships and 8,000 men killed and another 20,000 taken prisoner. No Carthaginian ships were lost. Hamilcar Barca also repulsed both land and sea attacks by Rome at Eryx in western Sicily.

Shortly thereafter what was left of the Roman fleet was lost in a storm, and the Romans made no major efforts at sea for several years.

During 247–242 able Carthaginian general Hamilcar Barca campaigned in western Sicily. By dint of superior generalship, Hamilcar turned back all Roman efforts to take the Carthaginian possessions on the island. He also dispatched warships to harass the Roman coastal cities in Italy.

Reconstituting its sea power, in 242 BCE Rome sent Gaius Lutatius Catulus and an expeditionary force with about 200 galleys to western Sicily. In a series of land and sea operations, the Romans captured the Carthaginian strongholds of Lilybaeum and Drepanum. Following their defeats on land, the Carthaginians ordered a fleet of 200 galleys under Hanno to Sicily. In the ensuing Battle of the Aegates Islands in 241, Roman fleet commander Catulus, also with some 200 galleys, won a decisive victory, sinking 50 of the Carthaginian ships and capturing another 70.

Their defeat in the Battle of the Aegates Islands forced the Carthaginians to sue for peace that same year. In the peace treaty of 241, Carthage agreed to evacuate all Sicily and to pay Rome 3,200 talents over a 10-year period. Rome permitted Syracuse to keep eastern Sicily but organized the remainder of the island as its first overseas province.

Causes of the Second Punic War (218–201 BCE)

In 241 BCE unpaid Carthaginian mercenaries led by Matho revolted, and some 15,000 of them laid siege to Carthage in a bitter, drawn-out war that lasted until 238 or 237. Appointed to command the Carthaginian army, Hamilcar Barca defeated the rebels in the Battle of Utica and

PUNIC WARS, 264 – 146 BCE

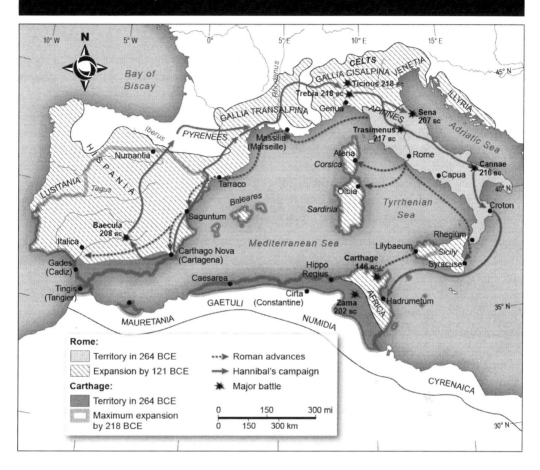

then ambushed and defeated another rebel army near Tunes. Hamilcar was then acknowledged as the leader of Carthage.

With the revolt of the mercenaries crushed and Carthage about to reassert its control over Sardinia, on the invitation of the mercenaries who had deserted to them from Sardinia, the Romans prepared to send an expedition there and declared war on Carthage. Carthage then had to cede Sardinia to Rome and pay an additional 1,200 talents to Rome beyond what they had agreed to pay in the peace treaty of 241. In 237 Rome occupied Corsica as well. That same year, Carthage sent

Hamilcar to Spain to expand Carthaginian holdings there in order to offset the loss to Rome of Sardinia and Sicily. Raising and financing the army almost entirely from his own resources, Hamilcar gradually expanded the initial Carthaginian outposts along the Spanish coasts. By the time of his death in 228, he had conquered most of the Iberian Peninsula to the Ebro and Tagus Rivers. On Hamilcar's death his son-in-law, Hasdrubal, took up the Carthaginian cause in Spain, consolidating the earlier conquests and concluding a treaty with Rome that recognized Carthaginian control of all Iberia south of the Ebro.

During 225–222, moreover, Rome had to deal with a large number of invading Gauls who had occupied much of northern Italy. In 222 at Clastidium in the Po Valley, Marcus Claudius Marcellus defeated the remnants of the Gallic force.

In 221 Hasdrubal was assassinated. Twenty-five-year-old Hannibal Barca, son of Hamilcar, succeeded him as commander of Carthaginian forces in Spain. During 221–218 Hannibal consolidated the Carthaginian position there, advancing Carthaginian control to the Durius (Douro, Deuro) River. Rome meanwhile allied with the city-state of Saguntum (Sagunto), south of the Ebro River.

In 219 Hannibal demanded the submission of Saguntum, the only area of Spain south of the Ebro River not under Carthaginian control. When Saguntum refused, Hannibal attacked the city and took it following an eight-months' siege. Rome meanwhile demanded that Carthage halt the siege and surrender Hannibal. When Carthage refused, Rome declared war.

Course of the Second Punic War

The Second Punic War, also known as the Hannibalic War, was essentially led by one man, Hannibal, against Rome. Because Rome now controlled the Mediterranean, Hannibal invaded Italy from land. Leaving in Spain about 20,000 men under his brother Hasdrubal to secure his base there, Hannibal planned to take the remainder of the army across southern Gaul and, by way of the Alps, into the Po Valley of northern Italy, there to recruit additional forces from among the Gauls, whose enmity toward Rome was long-standing, and force Rome into a two-front war by concluding an alliance with Philip V of Macedon.

The Romans, who had no idea of Hannibal's plans, hoped to take advantage of their command of the sea to send Consul Titus Sempronius with 30,000 men and 60 galleys to invade North Africa and take Carthage itself. Consul Publius Cornelius Scipio and his brother Gnaeus Cornelius Scipio were to invade Spain with another Roman army of some 26,000 men supported by 60 ships. Meanwhile, Praetor Lucius Manlius and a third Roman force of some 22,000 men would hold Cisalpine Gaul (the territory just south of the Alps) and prevent its population from joining Hannibal against Rome.

During March–June 218 Hannibal led 90,000 men into northern Iberia just south of the Pyrenees, bringing it under Carthaginian control. Leaving behind forces to garrison it, he then crossed the Pyrenees into southern Gaul, arriving there with some 50,000 infantry, 9,000 cavalry, and 80 war elephants. Learning of Hannibal's movements, Publius Cornelius Scipio landed his men at Massilia (Marseille) in the hopes of blocking Hannibal, who had already turned north up the Rhone Valley with the plan of crossing the Alps well inland. Scipio then proceeded to northern Italy with part of his force, sending his brother and most of the army to Spain.

In October despite an already considerable snowfall, Hannibal crossed the Alps into northern Italy, with many of his men and animals perishing from the cold or from combat with some tribes of the region. Hannibal now had only 20,000 infantry, 6,000 cavalry, and a few elephants.

Publius Cornelius Scipio took command of Manlius's army, which had been defeated by the Gauls, and moved rapidly to meet Hannibal at the Ticinus River. This battle in November 218, which was fought largely by cavalry alone, resulted in a Roman defeat and the wounding of Scipio. Learning of events, Sempronius moved his forces from Sicily by sea to Italy and marched to the Po Valley, where he joined Scipio to confront Hannibal, who now, thanks to the recruitment of Gauls, had 30,000 men. Hannibal provoked Sempronius, against the advice of Scipio, into attacking him at the Trebia River in December 218. Hannibal surprised Sempronius, sending his brother Mago and a Carthaginian force concealed in a ravine against the Roman flank and rear. Of 40,000 Romans in the battle, only 10,000 escaped; the remainder were slain. Hannibal's losses were probably on the order of 5,000 men. Also in 218, Gnaeus Cornelius Scipio Calvus landed north of the Ebro River in Spain and defeated the Carthaginians under Hanno (variously identified as Hannibal's nephew, a brother, or no relation) in the Battle of Cissa, securing for Rome the territory between the Ebro and the Pyrenees to the north.

Both sides were quiescent during the winter of 218–217, when they built up their forces. Hannibal learned of the appointment of new Roman consuls Gaius Flaminius and Gnaeus Servilius. Their two armies blocked the principal routes south toward Rome. Flaminius commanded 40,000 men at Arretium (Arezzo), while Servilius had 20,000 more at Ariminum (Rimini). In March 217 Hannibal carried out a brilliant movement with 40,000 men, crossing the Apennine mountain passes north of Genoa and moving south along the seacoast and through the supposedly impassable Arno marshes, outflanking the two consular armies. Reaching the Rome-Arretium road near Clusium (Chiusi), Hannibal placed his own forces between the two Roman armies and Rome itself.

Realizing that Hannibal had severed his line of communication with Rome, in April 217 Gaius Flaminius rushed his army south

without taking adequate security precautions. Hannibal set up an ambush position along a defile where the road passed Lake Trasimene. His heavy infantry halted the head of the Roman advance at the end of the defile, and the remaining Roman soldiers bunched up. Hannibal then closed off the Roman rear with his cavalry and sent his light infantry against the Roman left flank. About 30,000 Romans, including Flaminius, perished or were captured; only some 10,000 escaped. Hannibal then proceeded south, expecting to be joined by the cities nominally allied to Rome but actually under Roman control.

To meet this crisis, in May 217 the Roman Senate named as dictator Quintus Fabius Maximus. He adopted the wise strategy of avoiding direct battle with Hannibal in favor of harassing tactics to wear down his opponent. Try as he might, Hannibal was unable to draw Fabius into pitched battle. Such tactics were, however, anathema to many Romans, including Fabius's ambitious second-in-command, Marcus Minucius Rufus, and they earned Fabius the nickname of "Cunctator" (Delayer). Responding to public impatience, the Senate split command of the army between Fabius and Minucius, with each having two legions.

Aware of Minucius' impetuosity, Hannibal lured him into battle in October 217 by sending a small force to occupy a hill near Geronium but positioning his Nubian cavalry and infantry in ravines flanking the plain near the hill. Unaware that he was moving into a trap, Minucius ordered his men to take the hill, whereupon Hannibal struck. A rout in the Battle of Geronium appeared inevitable, but Fabius then appeared with his two legions. With his own forces somewhat scattered in the pursuit of Minucius's force and thus not ready to face Fabius, Hannibal retired. Acknowledging his error, Minucius thenceforth loyally supported Fabius.

During 217–211 BCE there was also fighting in Spain. Publius Scipio joined his brother Gnaeus there, and the two generals generally enjoyed success during the next years against Hannibal's brothers Hasdrubal and Mago (Magon). Encouraged by Rome, Numidian king Syphax revolted against Carthage in 213 BCE, but Hasdrubal returned to North Africa and joined Numidian prince Masinissa to defeat Syphax. The next year Hasdrubal returned to Spain with reinforcements, including Masinissa's cavalry. Meanwhile, the Scipios recaptured Saguntum.

Thanks to the time purchased by Fabius, Rome was able to assemble a large army. Two consuls, Aemilius Paullus and Terentius Varro, assumed command. Normally they would have had independent commands, but the Senate ordered them to combine their forces and to meet and defeat Hannibal once and for all. Together Paullus and Varro commanded eight enlarged legions (each of 5,000 infantry and 300 cavalry rather than 4,000 infantry and 200 cavalry).

The troops underwent a period of training, but by late summer they moved to near Hannibal's base at Cannae in northern Apulia on the Adriatic coast. Counting their allied forces, Varro and Paullus together commanded some 87,000 men, one of the largest land forces of antiquity. Hannibal had only some 50,000 Carthaginian and allied troops (40,000 infantry and 10,000 cavalry).

The two consuls alternated command daily, and on August 2, 216, Varro was in command and ordered both armies to engage the Carthaginians; Paullus reluctantly complied. The consuls led their forces onto an open plain on the right bank of the Aufidus River, with Paullus having detached some 10,000 of his men to guard his camp.

Varro positioned the Roman cavalry on both flanks and, since his forces were far superior in numbers, arranged the infantry in a much more compact center mass than was the custom. Varro's intention was to launch a power drive through the Carthaginian center, smashing a wide hole, then employ his superior numbers to annihilate first one Carthaginian wing and then the other.

Hannibal drew up his army in line-abreast formation, placing his cavalry, in which he was superior to the Romans, on the flanks. The Spanish and Gallic cavalry under Hasdrubal (Hannibal's brother of the same name was in Spain) were on the left, while the Numidian cavalry under his nephew Hanno was on the right. Hannibal placed his best-trained African heavy infantry on the flanks, with the center consisting of Spanish and Gallic infantry forming a convex position. Hannibal then personally supervised a slow planned withdrawal before the heavy Roman pressure.

Luring the Romans forward, Hannibal ordered his flanking cavalry to destroy their counterpart Roman cavalry. Meanwhile, the Roman center pinched out the forward bulge in the Carthaginian line and collapsed it inward. With the Romans apparently having broken through, Hannibal ordered his African infantry on each side to wheel in. At the same time, Hannibal's cavalry returned from its pursuit of the Roman cavalry and closed behind the rear of the close-packed Roman infantry, who were blinded by dust kicked up on the dry plain.

Hannibal's daring double envelopment on both flanks of a numerically superior enemy was one of the greatest tactical military masterpieces of history. During the course of the next several days the Carthaginians attacked both Roman camps and killed or captured many more Roman soldiers; only about 14,500 men escaped, Varro among them. The Carthaginian side suffered some 5,700 dead, of whom 4,000 were Celts, but probably two or three times this number were wounded. Cannae was a disaster for Rome, and it says much for the Roman state that it was able to recover from the defeat.

Hannibal was subsequently criticized for not having marched on the city of Rome after the victory, but Rome was a large fortified place, and Hannibal could not have besieged it effectively. Instead, he sought to induce revolts against Rome. Much of southern Italy, including Capua—the second-largest Roman city—did indeed revolt, as did Syracuse in Sicily. The Gauls also rose in the north and wiped out a Roman army sent to reconquer them. Yet most Roman subjects in central Italy remained loyal, and the Romans continued the fight. Never again, however, would their commanders allow a full Roman army to be drawn into open battle with Hannibal in Italy. Instead, those forces remaining in the field sought to harass Hannibal's supply lines and inhibit provisioning of his forces.

The Roman Senate appointed Marcus Junius Pera as dictator, with the principal field commander Proconsul Marcus Claudius Marcellus. He immediately marched south with two legions. Reassured by this action, the majority of its allies confirmed their loyalty to Rome. Although some Carthaginian reinforcements arrived at the end of the year, Roman naval superiority and the fact that the Carthaginian government was then dominated by one Hanno, a former political adversary of Hannibal's father, ensured that Carthage provided little support to its principal field commander.

For good reason the Second Punic War has been described as the contest of one man against a nation, for it was Hannibal alone, not Carthage, who conducted and animated it. Rome now had a total of some 150,000 men under arms in all theaters of the war (40,000 in defense of Rome itself), while Hannibal had only 40,000–50,000. Hannibal was thus forced to concentrate on securing a base of operations in southern Italy, where he enjoyed some success. The limitations of his resources were clearly revealed, and Rome was greatly strengthened vis-à-vis its allies, however, when Marcellus repulsed Hannibal's effort to take Nola in Campania, in the first battle for that city.

Two other significant battles also occurred in 216. In the Litana Forest in the Apennines in Cisalpine Gaul, a Roman army of some 25,000 men under Lucius Postumius Albinus was ambushed and slaughtered by the Boii tribe. And in Spain, the Scipio brothers Publius Cornelius and Gnaeus Scipio defeated Hasdrubal Barca and the Carthaginians near the Ebro River.

In Italy, utilizing Nola as a base of operations, Marcellus carried out raids against Hannibal's allies, who appealed to the Carthaginians for assistance. Marching on Nola, Hannibal failed to take that city when Marcellus mounted a counterattack. The battle ended with a heavy thunderstorm. The next day with much of Hannibal's army off foraging, Marcellus drew up his forces outside the city and attacked, but hearing the sound of battle Hannibal's foragers returned, and the bloody Second Battle of Nola ended in a draw. Hannibal went on to take Casilinum, and Carthaginian reinforcements arrived at Lochi.

In 214 Hannibal's nephew Hanno, with 18,000 men, was badly beaten at Beneventum (Benevento) by Roman general

Tiberius Gracchus with 20,000 men (most of them slaves who had been promised their freedom in return for victory). Fewer than 2,000 Carthaginians escaped. The Romans then retook Casilinum. Hannibal decided on a third attempt to take the Roman base of Nola. Marcellus resolved to meet him and sent his subordinate commander, Claudius Nero, with cavalry to attack the Carthaginian rear when he himself initiated the battle with Hannibal. The fighting lasted for several hours, but Nero failed to arrive in time, and the battle was inconclusive. Marcellus offered battle the next day, but Hannibal declined and withdrew into Apulia, hoping to take the port city of Tarentum.

Meanwhile, Syracuse rebelled against Rome and allied with Carthage. Sicily was in effect divided in two. Under Propraetor Appius Claudius Pulcher, Rome controlled the west and north. Staunchly pro-Roman Hiero, tyrant of Syracuse, had dominated the remainder of the island, but he died in late 216 or early 215. Hiero's young grandson Hieronymus succeeded him and that same year opened negotiations with Carthage. After little more than a year Hieronymus was murdered in a coup, and Syracuse became a democratic republic in which the Carthaginian faction prevailed over that favoring Rome.

Hippocrates and Epicydes, two brothers of Syracusan extraction but natives of Carthage, led the pro-Carthage group in Syracuse and hoped to make all Sicily a Carthaginian stronghold. The Syracusan government sent Hippocrates and 4,000 men, many of them Roman army deserters, to garrison the city of Leontini. From there, Hippocrates raided the Roman portion of the island.

Rome then dispatched Marcellus with an army to Sicily. He promptly retook Leontini and ordered that all Roman deserters taken prisoner were to be beaten with rods and then beheaded. Hippocrates and Epicydes, who had joined his brother at Leontini, escaped and subsequently spread the story that the Romans had massacred all inhabitants of the city, including women and children. Exploiting this lie, they brought the Syracusan soldiers over to their side and seized power in Syracuse. War with Rome was now inevitable.

Beginning probably in the spring of 213 BCE, Marcellus commenced military operations against Syracuse. He was supported by Appius Claudius Pulcher, who led Roman troops against the city from the land side, while Marcellus utilized 68 quinqueremes to blockade and attack Syracuse from the sea.

In the siege of 213–212, both sides employed a number of novel devices. Marcellus had four pairs of galleys specially prepared, ordering removal of the starboard oars from one side and the port oars from the other. The two ships were then lashed together, with scaling ladders mounted in their bows that could be raised by means of ropes attached to pulleys at the tops of masts in the center of the ships. The resulting craft was known as a *sambuca* because it somewhat resembled the harplike instrument of that name. The *sambuca* was designed to enable troops in the ships to reach the tops of the city walls.

On the land side the Romans employed *tolleni*, assault machines consisting of a boom in counterweight mounted on a mast with a large wicker or wooden basket attached to the far end of the boom. This basket, loaded with men, could be lifted up in the air by soldiers pulling down the other end of the boom by ropes wound around a capstan.

The Syracusans had a formidable asset in the celebrated geometrician Archimedes. Then in his 70s, he developed a number of innovative military devices. To attack the Roman ships, he arranged catapults and ballistae situated in batteries according to required range. He also developed a type of crane that extended over the walls and made use of a grapple, known as a claw, to hook onto a ship. A counterbalance enabled the crane to lift up the ship. Letting it go dashed the vessel to pieces. Another technique was to drop heavy stones on ships to crash through their hulls and sink them. A number of these boulders, one of which was said to weigh 10 talents (670 pounds), were dropped on the *sambucas,* destroying them. Archimedes also used smaller shorter-range catapults, known as scorpions, to hurl boulders and stones at the attackers. The most controversial story of the siege concerned Archimedes' supposed invention of so-called burning mirrors, whereby the sun's rays were reflected to set fire to the Roman ships.

All Roman attempts by land and sea proved failures, including a night attack from the sea against a section of the wall that seemed to offer maximum protection from the Syracusan war machines. With only heavy casualties to show for his efforts, Marcellus ended his effort to take the city by assault and settled in for a long-term siege and blockade. In the meantime, he sent some of his men to defeat the other rebel Sicilian cities, in one instance surprising a force under Hippocrates near Acila and inflicting some 8,000 casualties. Reportedly, only Hippocrates and 500 cavalry escaped.

Both sides reinforced. The Carthaginians dispatched an expeditionary force of 25,000 men, 3,000 cavalry, and 12 war elephants under the command of Himilco.

They also broke through the Roman blockade with 55 galleys. The Romans also built up their strength on the island, to three or four legions in addition to allied troops.

The siege continued through the winter, and early in 212 BCE Marcellus decided on a surprise attack. In negotiations regarding a prisoner exchange held outside Syracuse near a tower known as Galeagra, one of the Romans carefully calculated the height of the tower based on its even blocks of stone. Shortly thereafter Marcellus, taking advantage of the distraction of a major festival in Syracuse, sent 1,000 men with scaling ladders against the Galeagra tower at night. The ladders proved to be the correct height, and the assaulting troops took the defenders by surprise.

Before the night was over, the Romans had opened the Hexapylon Gate to other troops and captured much of the city. Other portions of Syracuse continued to hold out but suffered greatly from the ravages of disease, which seems to have hit the Romans less hard. Carthaginian ships continued to penetrate the blockade, but Marcellus was able to confront and turn back a massive Carthaginian convoy of 700 merchantmen protected by 150 warships.

With all hope gone, Epicydes fled Syracuse (Hippocrates had earlier died of disease), and in the summer of 212 Roman forces captured the remainder of the city, giving it over to pillage and fire. Although Marcellus had ordered that Archimedes be taken alive, he died within the city. Reportedly, he was working on a mathematical problem when Roman soldiers burst in on him. The soldiers were ignorant of the identity of the old man who demanded they not disturb his "circles" in the dirt, whereupon one of them dispatched him with a single sword thrust. The victory at

Syracuse solidified Rome's control over all Sicily.

In southern Italy in 213, meanwhile, Hannibal concentrated on besieging Tarentum while his nephew Hanno defeated Roman general Tiberius Gracchus at Bruttium. In 212 Hannibal captured Tarentum. Meanwhile, Consuls Quintus Fulvius Flaccus and Appius Claudius Pulcher initiated a siege of Capua, which was already short of food. Following an appeal for assistance, Hanno Barca collected food supplies at Beneventum (modern-day Benevento). While he was away on a foraging expedition, however, Flavius attacked the Carthaginian camp, taking it along with vast amounts of supplies destined for Capua and killing 6,000 Carthaginians and capturing another 7,000. Hanno escaped back to Bruttium, and the Roman siege of Capua continued. Hannibal then marched to Capua with 20,000 men, reaching the city despite a Roman force there of 80,000 men.

Although badly outnumbered, Hannibal skillfully defended Capua and defeated the Romans in a battle outside the city. To draw Hannibal away from Capua, the consuls marched their armies off in different directions, threatening Carthaginian strongholds. Hannibal pursued the Roman forces under Appius Claudius into Lucania but was unable to catch up with him. With 20,000 men, however, he destroyed a Roman army of 16,000 men under Marcus Centenius Penula near the Silarus River in southwestern Lucania. Only some 1,000 Romans escaped death or capture, with Centenius among the slain.

Shortly thereafter, Hannibal encountered and destroyed another Roman army of 18,000 men under Praetor Gnaeus Fulvius. Only 2,000 Romans escaped death or capture. The consuls resumed the Siege of Capua, but with the city now resupplied, Hannibal retired southward, where he tried but failed to capture Brundisium (Brundusium; present-day Brindisi).

In 211 Hasdrubal Barca, reinforced from Carthage, defeated Publius Cornelius Scipio and Gnaeus Scipio in two separate battles in the Upper Baetis Valley. Both brothers were slain. Hasdrubal's victories again gave Carthage control of all Spain south of the Ebro River.

That same year, 211, Roman forces completed the investment of Capua. New consuls Publius Sulpicius Galba and Gnaeus Fulvius Centumalus with 50,000 men guarded against an approach by Hannibal from the south, while Proconsuls Fulvius and Appius prosecuted the siege with 60,000 men. Following an appeal from Capua, Hannibal marched north with 30,000 men and reached the Roman lines. While he attacked from without, the Capuan forces sortied from the city. Fulvius repulsed Hannibal, however, and Appius halted the Capuans.

Hoping to draw the Romans away and raise the Siege of Capua, Hannibal marched on Rome. Indeed, the two consuls hurried after him, and Fulvius also took a small force from Capua, but Appius continued the siege. Hannibal, greatly outnumbered, did not try to test the defenses of Rome but merely demonstrated before the city before slowly retiring south again, harassed by the consular forces. Now on the verge of starvation, Capua was forced to surrender, the worst setback for Hannibal thus far in the war.

Sensing victory, in 210 the Romans went over on the offensive against Hannibal, hoping to destroy his bases in southern Italy. Hannibal, however, continued to win victories, defeating a Roman army under Proconsul Fulvius Centumalus in the Second Battle of Herdonia, in which

Centumalus was killed, then defeating Marcus Claudius Marcellus in the Battle of Numistro.

Following the death of Publius Scipio, Rome sent to command in Spain his 25-year-old son Publius Cornelius Scipio, who would become known as Scipio Africanus. With an army of nearly 28,000 men, in 210 Scipio established Roman control north of the Ebro River and then rapidly marched against the capital of New Carthage, the Carthaginian stronghold. Blockading New Carthage from the sea as well, Scipio took it by assault in 209.

Although Rome was now near bankruptcy and the population was close to starvation from the absence of men working the fields, it now had some 200,000 men against Hannibal with only 40,000, most of whom were Italians and few of them hardened veterans. Hannibal awaited reinforcements from his brother Hasdrubal in Spain, while Rome's immediate objective was to retake Hannibal's chief base of Tarentum.

In 209 in a hard-fought two-day battle, Hannibal was victorious over Marcellus, this time at Asculum, but the battle was not decisive strategically. Meanwhile, Fabius Cunctator (for the fifth time a consul) captured Tarentum, the result of treachery on the part of Hannibal's Italian allies. Despite this major loss, Hannibal continued military operations. Sensing his weakness, the Roman commanders were now more willing to engage him, although Marcus Claudius Marcellus was killed in an ambush.

In Spain in 208, Roman general Publius Cornelius Scipio defeated Hasdrubal in the Battle of Baecula near present-day Cordova. Hasdrubal's losses were not serious, however, and he now responded to Hannibal's appeal for assistance in Italy

even though it would no doubt mean the loss of Spain. Marching to Gaul, Hasdrubal wintered his army there, recruiting and training reinforcements. Early in 207 Hasdrubal crossed the Alps via the Cenis Pass and arrived in the Po Valley of northern Italy in April 207. The exact size of his force is unknown, but it may have been as many as 50,000 men, certainly too small to oppose the 15 Roman legions of perhaps 150,000 men then in position between him and Hannibal in the south.

Hasdrubal first initiated a siege of Placentia, probably to placate the Gauls in his army, but this proved unsuccessful. He then proceeded southward to Fanum Fortunae (Fano) on the Adriatic Sea, where he encountered Roman forces sent against him under Consul Livius Salinator. Having learned of his brother's siege of Placentia, Hannibal moved slowly north to join him, closely watched by four legions under Consul Gaius Claudius Nero. Unaware of the threat to his brother, Hannibal established camp at Canusium (Canosa), and Nero interposed his army between the two Carthaginian forces. Fortunately for the Romans, they captured two of Hasdrubal's couriers sent to Hannibal and learned of his intention to link up with Hannibal in Umbria. Leaving a force to keep watch on Hannibal, Nero proceeded northward with his best troops—some 6,000 infantry and 1,000 cavalry—to join Livius. Moving at a fast pace, Nero reached Fanum Fortunae after about a week's march and secretly joined Livius at night. Nero then convinced Livius that they should attack Hasdrubal before he could learn of the Roman reinforcements.

Both armies were drawn up for battle when Hasdrubal became aware of the increase in Roman numbers and decided to withdraw up the Via Flaminia at night.

Night movements are notoriously difficult to execute, and Hasdrubal's local guides may also have deserted, delaying him in gaining the road. In any case, the pursuing Nero caught up with the Carthaginians near the Metaurus River, and Hasdrubal hastily deployed for battle. His men were in three main bodies, somewhat separated from one another and thus not able to offer mutual support. The Romans probably had 40,000 men, the Carthaginians fewer. The battle began with an attack by the Spaniards on the Roman left, but in a bold move Nero, on the Roman right opposite the Gauls, discovering that his men were unable to get at the Gauls because of a ravine, left a small body of men to hold and moved with the rest southward behind the Roman lines, then marched north and got in behind the attacking Spaniards. Despite Hasdrubal's leadership, his men could not hold against this Roman pincer movement. Sensing defeat, Hasdrubal drove directly at the Romans to die fighting, which occurred. His army was largely destroyed. The battle probably claimed some 10,000 Carthaginian dead, while the Romans lost only 2,000.

Nero wasted no time but swiftly retraced his steps, taking only six days. News of the victory, the first time the Carthaginians had been defeated in Italy, was received with joy in Rome. Legend has it that Hannibal first heard of the battle when a Roman horseman approached the Carthaginian camp and hurled a sack at their lines. It was found to contain the head of Hasdrubal. However he learned of what had transpired, Hannibal broke camp on the news and marched his army south to the port of Bruttium.

The Roman victory in the Battle of the Metaurus River was strategically important because it meant that Hannibal now had little hope of actually defeating Rome.

Hannibal's remaining brother, Mago, landed near Genoa in 205 with 12,000 infantry and 2,000 cavalry but seems to have made no real effort to link up with Hannibal. Although Hannibal remained in Italy, undefeated, for six years after the Metaurus River battle, even his brilliant leadership could not compensate for his dwindling resources.

During 207–206, meanwhile, Scipio gained control of Spain despite fierce opposition from the remaining Carthaginian forces. In 206 in the Battle of Ilipa (Silpia), Scipio, with 48,000 men, outmaneuvered and double enveloped a force of 70,000 Carthaginians. This decisive victory gave Rome control of all Spain. Despite the tremendous odds against him, Hannibal managed to hold on in Bruttium. Fighting during 206–204 mostly consisted of low-intensity clashes.

Victorious in Spain, in 204 Scipio, now proconsul and having concluded an alliance with Masinissa, rival of Syphax for the throne of Numidia, arrived in North Africa with 30,000 well-trained and well-equipped legionnaires. The Romans landed near Utica, which Scipio invested. Scipio broke off the Siege of Utica, however, following the arrival of a large Carthaginian force under Hasdrubal Gisco and Syphax. Scipio withdrew to a fortified camp on the coast, and both sides then went into winter quarters.

Early in 203 Scipio mounted a surprise night attack on the Carthaginian and Numidian camps, destroying the two armies and burning their camps. He then renewed the Siege of Utica. Syphax and Hasdrubal Gisco raised a new army, but Scipio routed it in the Battle of Bagbrades near Utica, capturing Syphax.

Carthage sued for peace with Rome, but at the same time the Carthaginian leaders recalled Hannibal and Mago from Italy. Taking advantage of an ensuing armistice, Hannibal sailed from Italy with some 18,000 men, most of them Italians. Mago, who had been defeated by the Romans in Liguria, also sailed for North Africa with several thousand men but died at sea of his wounds.

With the return to North Africa of Hannibal, the scene was now set for the final struggle between Hannibal and Scipio, the two ablest generals of the war. More confident with Hannibal's return, Carthage broke the terms of the armistice by seizing Roman supply ships that had been scattered in a storm.

The final battle between the two sides took place probably in October 202. The exact location remains in dispute. Some historians place it on the plain of Zama, five days' march southwest of Carthage, while others say that the battle occurred at Naraggara (Sidi Youssef), west of Zama Regia (Seba Biar).

Hannibal moved west from Hadrumetum to near Zama and encamped less than four miles from the Roman camp. He then proposed a parley, to which Scipio agreed. The two men talked together with only an interpreter present. Hannibal apparently sought peace, but Scipio refused, replying that because of the recent Carthaginian treachery in attacking the Roman supply ships he would not agree to peace without a battle.

That battle occurred the next day. This time Scipio held the upper hand. Unknown to Hannibal, just before the battle Numidian king Masinissa joined the Romans with 4,000 cavalry and 6,000 infantry. Each side now had about 40,000 men, with Hannibal probably enjoying a slight overall numerical advantage, although Scipio had more cavalry.

Hannibal positioned more than 80 war elephants in front of his line. Behind these he placed his infantry in Roman fashion, in a series of three separate linear formations although not in maniples. The first body consisted of 12,000 seasoned mercenary troops: Liguria and Gaulish swordsmen, Balearic slingers, and Mauretanian archers. The second rank contained the less experienced Carthaginians and Libyan troops, while the third grouping was of Hannibal's best men, the seasoned veterans who had campaigned with him in Italy. Numidian cavalry protected Hannibal's left flank, and Carthaginian cavalry protected his right rank. Hannibal expected the first two bodies of infantry to absorb the initial Roman assault, whereupon he planned to attack the Romans with his veterans.

Scipio positioned his infantry facing the Carthaginian line of battle. His Italian cavalry were on the left flank, and his Numidian cavalry under Masinissa were on the right. Scipio's infantrymen were not in solid ranks but were subdivided into the smaller maniples, with spaces between the lines to help absorb the shock of the Carthaginian war elephants. Fearing these, Scipio placed the maniples one behind the other rather than in the gaps, thus abandoning the usual checkerboard Roman formation. At the beginning of the battle, these gaps were filled with *velites* (lightly armed troops).

The battle opened with Hannibal advancing his elephants toward the Roman lines. Undoubtedly the elephants were not well trained, for many of them soon became disoriented by Roman trumpets and bugles and bolted to their left, causing Hannibal's Numidian cavalry to stampede and greatly assisting in their rout by Masinissa's cavalry. Meanwhile, Scipio's Roman cavalry attacked and defeated the

Carthaginian cavalry on Hannibal's right, driving it from the field. The situation then resembled the Battle of Cannae but in reverse, with the Romans poised to envelop the Carthaginian flanks.

Although the first body of Hannibal's infantry fought well, the second failed to come up in time, leading the mercenaries in the first rank to believe that they had been deserted, whereupon they withdrew. Hannibal then brought up his seasoned veterans but earlier than planned. These ran into the retreating mercenaries. Scipio meanwhile re-formed his infantry before Hannibal could strike, and his cavalry fell on Hannibal's veterans from the flanks, cutting them to pieces. Scipio's horsemen then pursued, killing many of those attempting to flee.

The Romans won a decisive victory. Carthaginian losses were variously estimated at 20,000–25,000 killed and 8,500–20,000 captured. Only Hannibal and some of the cavalry escaped to Hadrumetum. Roman losses were on the order of only 1,500–2,500 killed, while Masinissa may have lost 2,500 men. The Battle of Zama was payback for Cannae. Well-trained Roman infantry, supported by superior cavalry, had annihilated a larger but poorly trained infantry force weak in cavalry.

Following the Battle of Zama, Hannibal urged the Carthaginians to sue for peace. According to the terms of the 201 BCE peace dictated by Scipio, Carthage was to retain its autonomy but was forced to give up all its elephants and all but 10 of its triremes. Carthage also ceded to Rome Spain and the Mediterranean islands it held and was obliged to pay a large indemnity of 10,000 talents over a 50-year span. Carthage was also obliged to agree not to wage war, even in Africa, without Roman approval.

A grateful Rome accorded Scipio the title "Africanus." Hannibal, however, took charge of the Carthaginian state and reformed its government, paying the heavy tribute demanded by Rome. In 195 Rome, fearing Hannibal, insisted that he be surrendered, forcing Hannibal to flee to Syria, where he was granted asylum. Learning that he was about to be turned over to Rome, Hannibal committed suicide there in 183. Meanwhile, Rome reestablished its control over Cisalpine Gaul during 202–191.

Cause of the Third Punic War (149–146 BCE)

Carthage observed the terms of its treaty with Rome and abstained from any provocation, but when Carthage again began to show signs of prosperity, Roman fears and hatred were aroused. No Roman could forget that it took 25 legions to win the Second Punic War. Roman leaders now intrigued with Masinissa, ruler of neighboring Numidia, encouraged him to encroach on what remained of Punic territory. Finally after many vain appeals to Rome, Carthage was goaded into an attempt at self-defense. In 150 BCE Carthage declared war, sending an army under Hasdrubal against Masinissa. This was technically a violation of the peace terms with Rome ending the Second Punic War whereby Carthage was only permitted to declare war with Roman consent.

Course of the Third Punic War

The Roman Senate agreed with its leader Cato that Carthage had to be destroyed and dispatched a sizable force to Utica in North Africa. That city had been Carthage's most important ally, but seeing the handwriting on the wall, it rallied to Rome just before the war. Utica's defection provided Rome with an important base less than 30 miles from Carthage. Two consuls commanded the Roman expeditionary force: Manius Manilius, who had charge of four legions totaling some 40,000–50,000 men, and Lucius Marcius Censorinus, who commanded the fleet with 50 quinqueremes.

The Third Punic War (149–146 BCE) was basically the Siege of Carthage. Given the disparity of resources, the Romans expected a short, profitable, and virtually bloodless campaign.

The Carthaginian leadership opened negotiations with the two consuls and was informed that they must surrender their fleet, arms, and missile weapons. The Roman position was that since Carthage would now be under Roman protection, it would have no need of weapons. The Carthaginians agreed to these terms. They surrendered their fleet, which was burned in the harbor, as well as a reported 200,000 sets of infantry weapons and 2,000 catapults. The consuls then announced that the inhabitants of Carthage would have to leave the city, as the Romans intended to destroy it. The Carthaginians would be permitted to rebuild at any other location as long as it was at least 10 miles (80 *stades*) from the sea.

Following initial shock and despair, the Carthaginian Council rejected this new Roman demand and declared war on Rome, shutting the gates of Carthage and commencing the manufacture of weapons. The Romans were surprised by this response, having assumed that with Carthage virtually disarmed its leaders would have no choice but to accept their demands.

The Romans mounted an assault on the city, led by Manilius from the land side and Censorinus from the sea. Carthage had excellent defenses, however, as the city was surrounded by three walls almost 50 feet high and sufficiently wide to contain troop quarters and stalls for elephants and horses. The Carthaginians easily repelled the first two assaults. When the Romans sent out troops to find timber to build additional catapults, they were surprised by Carthaginian forces under Hamilcon that had been harassing their base camps. In one such engagement, a cavalry force led by Himilco Phameas inflicted some 500 casualties on the Romans and seized a number of weapons.

Despite these setbacks, the Romans located the timber with which to build a number of new siege machines, including two very large ones with battering rams. The Romans made a breach in the wall, but the Carthaginians quickly repaired it and then mounted sorties from the city, setting fire to and destroying both siege engines. Scipio Aemilianus, tribune of the Fourth Legion, particularly distinguished himself in the fighting both in rescuing trapped legionnaires and in subsequent engagements against Hasdrubal.

In the spring of 148 BCE Carthaginian general Himilco defected, bringing with him to the Romans a reported 2,200 Carthaginian cavalry. Meanwhile, Consul L. Calpurnius Piso Caesoninus for the army and Legatus Lucius Hostilius Mancinus for the navy arrived at Carthage. They concentrated their resources against minor cities close to Carthage and destroyed most of these. Piso then retired for the winter to Utica.

In Rome, meanwhile, Scipio was elected at age 37 as consul of the people, and in 147 he set sail for Africa with additional forces. Landing at Utica, he proceeded to Carthage, rescuing Mancinus and a number of his men who had been cut off by the Carthaginians. Mancinus then returned to Italy, and Scipio began construction of extensive siege works at Carthage.

Meanwhile, the Carthaginians had secretly constructed 50 triremes, but instead of using the element of surprise to launch a sudden attack on the unprepared Roman fleet, the Punic admiral paraded his ships to give his crews practice and then returned to port. When he sallied out to do battle several days later the Romans were ready, and the Carthaginians, who had not fought well at sea for nearly half a century, were soundly defeated.

At the beginning of the spring of 146, Scipio launched a major offensive. Employing Carthaginian deserters as guides, the Romans managed to overcome the three lines of Carthaginian defenses and penetrate the city itself, with vicious fighting in the narrow streets and six-story buildings along them. The fighting was house to house and room to room, and the Romans laid plank bridges from houses already taken to the remainder, reaching the slopes of the Byrsa, the hill on which the citadel was situated. Once the buildings had been taken, Scipio ordered that the city be fired. The flames spread and raged for six days and nights. Many Carthaginians, young and old, were trapped and died. Roman engineers then leveled what remained.

The Carthaginian leadership at Byrsa then appealed to Scipio to spare the lives of those who wished to leave. He agreed, with the exception of Roman deserters. Reportedly, 50,000 people departed the Byrsa to be held under guard. This left only some 900 Roman deserters as well as Hasdrubal and his wife and their sons. Hasdrubal turned traitor, however, opening the gates to the Romans and begging Scipio for mercy. Hasdrubal's wife then appeared on the roof of the temple, which the defenders had set on fire. She denounced Hasdrubal

for his treachery, then leapt with her sons into the flames.

The Romans plundered what remained of Carthage (Scipio took nothing for himself) and utterly demolished it. The few towns that had supported Carthage were also destroyed. The 50,000 survivors of Carthage, all that remained of a presiege population of 500,000, were sold into slavery. The terrible destruction of the city gave rise to the term "Carthaginian Peace." Africa now became a Roman province.

Significance

With the end of the Punic Wars and the Macedonian Wars (which ran concurrently with the Punic Wars) and the defeat of Seleucid king Antiochus III the Great in the Roman-Syrian War (192–188), Rome became the preeminent Mediterranean power, a status it would retain until the fifth century CE. The Punic Wars also saw Rome acquire its first overseas provinces. One consequence of the Second Punic War was the creation of a standing Roman Army of four legions to hold the two new provinces in Spain. The men enlisted for long terms and were paid, but this standing professional army would have ominous consequences for the Roman political system. During the course of the wars, the Senate also greatly increased its power.

Further Reading
Bagnall, Nigel. *The Punic Wars: Rome, Carthage, and the Struggle for the Mediterranean.* New York: Thomas Dunne Books, 2005.

Caven, Brian. *The Punic Wars.* New York: Barnes and Noble, 1980.

De Beer, Gavin. *Hannibal: The Struggle for Power in the Mediterranean.* London: Thames and Hudson, 1969.

Eckstein, Arthur M. *Mediterranean Anarchy, Interstate War, and the Rise of Rome.* Berkeley: University of California Press, 2009.

Goldsworthy, Adrian. *The Fall of Carthage: The Punic Wars, 265–146 BC*. London: Cassell, 2001.

Healy, Mark. *Cannae, 216 B.C.: Hannibal Smashes Rome's Army*. London: Osprey Military, 1994.

Lazenby, J. F. *Hannibal's War: A Military History of the Second Punic War*. Norman: University of Oklahoma Press, 1998.

Livy. *Hannibal's War: Books 21–30*. Edited by J. C. Yardley and translated by Dexter Hoyos. New York: Oxford University Press, 2009.

Smith, R. Bosworth. *Carthage and the Carthaginians*. London: Longmans, Green, 1916.

Smith, R. Bosworth. *Rome and Carthage: The Punic Wars*. New York: Scribner, 1889.

Qin Wars of Unification (230–221 BCE)

Dates	230–221 BCE
Location	China
Combatants	Qin vs. Han, Zhao, Wei, Chu, Yan, Qi
Principal Commanders	Qin: King Ying Zheng (Emperor Qin Shi Huang), Wang Jian, Wang Ben, Li Xin Other States: King An, King Qian, Li Mu, King Fuchu, King Xi, King Jia, Xiang Yan, King Tian Jian
Principal Battles	Daliang
Outcome	The seven states of central China are formed into one state. The short-lived Qin dynasty gives its name to China and establishes the concept of a unified state.

Causes

The Qin Wars of Unification of 230–221 BCE were the direct result of the efforts of King Ying Zheng of Qin (later emperor as Qin Shi Huang) to control all northern China. Born Ying Zheng in Handan in 259 BCE, Qin Shi Huang (Ch'in Shih-hung) was nominally the son of the king of Qin but may have actually been the offspring of his father's powerful chancellor, Lü Buwei. Regardless of his patrimony, Ying Zheng succeeded to the throne at age 13 in 245 on the death of his father and assumed his personal rule at age 22 in 231 when he seized full power and dismissed Lü Buwei, who had been acting as regent.

As ruler, Ying Zheng put down a number of rebellions. He also built up the army, emphasizing the cavalry, and carried out a number of reforms, especially in agriculture. The king was determined to expand Qin territory. Most of the smaller states of northern and central China, such as the Ba, Shu, Zhongshan, Lu, and Song states, had already been absorbed by their more powerful neighbors, and by the time Ying Zheng had come to the throne there were seven major states in northern China: Qin, Han, Zhao, Wei, Chu, Yan, and Qi. Having consolidated his own kingdom, Ying Zheng now proceeded to conquer the other remaining feudal states of the Yellow River and lower and middle Yangtze River valleys in a series of campaigns from 230 to 221 BCE. His strategy was to attack and defeat one state at a time, described in one of the so-called Thirty-Six Stratagems as "befriend a distant state while attacking a neighbor." This meant first allying Qin with the Yan and Qi states and holding at bay the Wei and Chu states while conquering the Han and Zhao states.

Course

Han was the weakest of the seven states and had previously been attacked by Qin. In 230 led by Minister of Interior Teng, a Qin army moved south across the Huang He (Yellow River) and invaded Han. Cavalry played a major role in the campaign. That same year the Qin army captured the Han capital of Zheng (today Xinzheng in Zhengzhou in southern Henan Province). With the surrender of King An of Han, the whole of Han came under Qin control.

Zhao was the next state to fall. Qin had invaded Zhao before but had not been able to conquer it. Zhao, however, was struck by two natural disasters—an earthquake and a famine—and in 229 the Qin armies again invaded, this time in a converging attack by three armies on the Zhao capital of Handan. Capable Zhao general Li Mu avoided pitched battle, however, choosing to concentrate instead on the construction of strong defenses, which indeed prevented the Qin armies from advancing farther. Ying Zheng then bribed a Zhao minister to sow discord between Li Mu and Zhao King Qian, who as a result came to doubt his general's loyalty. Indeed, Li Mu was subsequently imprisoned and executed on King Qian's order. Learning of Li Mu's execution, in 228 the Qin armies again invaded Zhao. After several victories against the Zhao armies, Qin troops captured Handan and took King Qian. Ying Zheng then annexed Zhao.

That same year, 228, Qin general Wang Jian prepared for an invasion of Yan. Ju Wu, a Yan minister, suggested to Yan King Xi that he ally with Dai (present-day Yu, Zhangjiakou, in Heibei), then ruled by Prince Jia, the elder brother of the former king of Zhao, and also Qi and Chu. Crown Prince Dan opposed this course of action, however, believing it unlikely to succeed. Instead he sent an emissary, Jing Ke, to Qin with the head of a turncoat Qin general and orders to assassinate Ying Zheng. The assassination attempt failed, and Jing Ke was killed.

Using the attempted assassination as an excuse, Ying Zheng then sent an army against Yan. The Qin defeated the Yan Army, which had been strengthened with forces from Dai, in a battle along the eastern bank of the Yi River. Following their victory, the Qin army occupied the Yan capital of Yi (present-day Beijing). King Xi and his son Crown Prince Dan then withdrew with the remaining Yan forces into the Liaodong Peninsula. Qin general Li Xin pursued the Yan forces to the Ran River (present-day Hun River), where they destroyed most of the remaining Yan forces. To save his throne, King Xi ordered the execution of his son Crown Prince Dan, then sent his head to Qin in atonement for the assassination attempt on Ying Zheng, who accepted this "apology" and made no further military effort against Yan at this time.

In 222, however, Wang Ben led Qin forces in renewed warfare against Yan. The Qin army invaded the Liaodong Peninsula and captured King Xi. Yan was then annexed to the expanding Qin Empire.

In 225 Qin moved against Wei, first sending an army under Wang Ben that reportedly numbered 600,000 men to take more than 10 cities on the border with Chu in order to prevent that state from invading while the attack on Wei was proceeding. Wang Ben then moved against Daliang. It had natural defenses in that

GOVERNANCE IN THE QIN DYNASTY

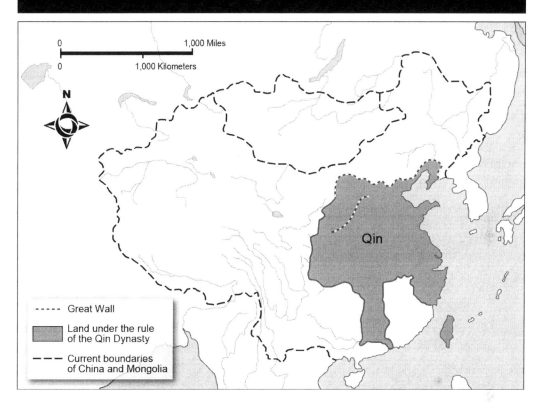

0   1,000 Miles

0   1,000 Kilometers

N

Qin

- - - - - Great Wall

Land under the rule of the Qin Dynasty

— — — Current boundaries of China and Mongolia

it was located at the confluence of the Sui and Ying Rivers. The city also had a very wide moat and four drawbridges that provided access to the city proper. Given the difficulties of taking Daliang, Wang Bei decided on an attempt to redirect the waters of the Yellow River and the Hong Canal in order to flood Daliang. It took his men more than three months to accomplish this considerable engineering feat while at the same time maintaining the Siege of Daliang. Wang Bei's plan worked. Reportedly, more than 100,000 people lost their lives in the flooding of the city. King Jia of Wei then surrendered, and Wei was added to Qin.

Chu was next. In 224 Ying Zheng called a conference to discuss the plans for the invasion. General Wang Jian said that no fewer than 600,000 men would be required, but General Li Xin claimed that 200,000 men would be sufficient to conquer Chu. Ying Zheng then appointed Li Xin and Meng Wu to lead 200,000 men in two armies against Chu, while Wang Jian retired from state service, supposedly the result of illness.

The Qin armies enjoyed initial success. Li Xin's men took Pingyu, while Meng Wu captured Qigiu. After then taking Yan (all three cities in present-day Henan), Li Xin led his army to rendezvous with Meng Wu. However, the Chu army, under Xiang Yan, had been avoiding a decisive encounter and was waiting for the opportunity to launch a counterattack. Xiang Yan's army now pursued Li Xin during a three-day period, catching up with him and carrying out a surprise attack, joined by forces under Lord Changjing, a relative of Ying Zheng, a descendant of the Chu royal family. The two Chu armies effectively destroyed Li Xin's army.

Informed of the crushing Chu victory over Li Xin, Ying Zheng then traveled to his retired general Wang Jian's residence and personally apologized for having doubted his advice. Wang Jian agreed to return to government service, this time in command of the force of 600,000 men he had initially recommended. Meng Wu became Wang Jian's deputy.

In 224 Wang Jian's army invaded Chu territory and made camp at Pingyu. Chu general Xiang Yan assembled the entire Chu army and attacked the Qin encampment but was repulsed. Wang Jian then held his position, refusing to attack the Chu force as Xiang Yan had wanted, and it subsequently withdrew. As the Chu army was doing so, Wang Jian launched a surprise attack and then pursued the Chu army into Qinan (northwest of present-day Qichun County, Huanggang, Hubei), where it was defeated and Chu commander Xiang Yan was killed in action.

In 223, Qin forces again invaded Chu and captured the capital city of Shouchun (present-day Shou in Lu'an, Anhui). King Fuchu of Chu was among those taken prisoner. Qin then annexed Chu. The next year, Wang Jian and Meng Wu attacked the Wuyu region (present-day Zhejiang and Jiangsu). It became part of the Qin territorial holdings.

In 221 BCE, Qi was the only state of north China not conquered by the Qin. Ying Zheng had early on bribed Qi chancellor Hou Sheng into advising King Tian Jian of Qi not to assist the other states, which were being conquered by Qin. Too late, King Tian Jian recognized the threat and sent his army to the border with Qin. Ying Zheng then used the excuse of Tian Jian's refusal to meet with the Qin king's envoy as justification for an invasion.

Avoiding the Qi forces massed on the border, commander of the Qin invasion force general Wang Ben moved his army into Qi from Yan territory. The army therefore met little resistance before arriving at the Qi capital of Linzi (north of present-day Zibo, Shandong). Taken by surprise, King Tian Jian surrendered without a battle. Qi was then absorbed by Qin.

Qin expansion had, however, eliminated the buffer zone between the Chinese states and the nomadic peoples of present-day Inner and Outer Mongolia, thus creating the need for the system of defensive fortifications known as the Qin Great Wall.

Upon absorbing Qi, Ying Zheng established the Qin dynasty, assuming the throne name of Qin Shi Huang (meaning "First Emperor of China"). As the first emperor of China, he had an enormous impact on the future of China and on the Chinese people. A reformer but also a strong-willed autocrat, he and his chief adviser Li Si pushed through a series of changes designed to solidify the unification. To diminish the threat of rebellion, the emperor required members of the former royal families to live in the capital of Xianyang, in Shaanxi Province.

Qin Shi Huang also abolished feudalism and divided his territory into 36 prefectures and then divided the prefectures into counties and townships, all of which were ruled directly by the emperor through his appointees. A uniform law code was established, and Qin Shi Huang decreed a standardized system of Chinese characters in writing. A new tax system was put in place that is said to have exacted a heavy financial toll on the Chinese people. Qin Shi Huang also established a uniform system of laws, weights and measures, and coinage. In an attempt to silence any criticism of his rule, in 213 Qin Shi Huang ordered the burning of all books in the empire and records of all other dynasties and the execution of those scholars who opposed him, along with their families. Stories that he ordered some 460 Confucian scholars buried alive in Xianyang are probably not true, however.

Qin Shi Huang and Li Si also undertook a series of mammoth construction projects, including setting hundreds of thousands of men to work building the great defensive wall that incorporated older walls. This wall served as a precedent when later regimes, most notably the Ming, also built systems of fortified walls as a means of defense against nomadic peoples to the north. The emperor also oversaw construction of a system of new roads designed to unify China economically and facilitate the passage of goods and troops radiating from the capital of Xianyang.

Qin Shi Huang is now also known for having ordered construction of his large mausoleum in Xian, guarded by life-sized terra-cotta warriors and horses. Discovered in 1974 and opened to the public in 1979, the 800 warriors and their horses guarding the tomb are regarded as one of the greatest archaeological finds of all time.

Around 212 BCE, Qin Shi Huang subsequently expanded Qin territory to the south (i.e., south of the Changjiang [Yangtze or Yangxi River]). His generals Meng Tian and Zhao Tuo conquered northern Korea (Goryeo, Koryo) as well as the areas later known as Fujian, Guangdong, Guangxi, and Tonkin (Tongking) in northern Vietnam.

Seeking to extend his life, Qin Shi Huang had been taking a medicine prescribed by his doctors that contained a small amount of mercury. He died, apparently of mercury poisoning, while on a tour of eastern China in Shaqiu Province in 210. In short order there was a strong reaction to his autocratic regime. His second son and successor, Hu Hai (Qin Er Shi), proved to be an inept ruler, and a great peasant rebellion, led by Chen Sheng and Wu Guang, soon began. This sparked a series of rebellions that, combined with infighting at court, brought the Qin dynasty to an end in 206 BCE.

Significance

The Qin Wars of Unification joined the seven states of central China into one state. Although the Qin dynasty itself was short-lived (221–206), it gave its name to China and produced the concept of a unified Chinese state.

Further Reading

Bodde, Derk. "The State and Empire of Qin." In *The Cambridge History of China*, Vol. 1, *The Ch'in and Han Empires, 221 B.C.–A.D. 220*, edited by Denis Twitchett and Michael Loewe, 21–102. Cambridge: Cambridge University Press, 1987.

Clements, Jonathan. *The First Emperor of China*. Stroud, Gloucestershire, UK: Sutton, 2006.

Tianchou, Fu, ed. *The Underground Terracotta Army of Emperor Qin Shi Huang*. Beijing: New World Press, 1988.

Wood, Francis. *The First Emperor of China*. London: Profile Books, 2007.

Zilin Wu. *Qin Shi Huang: The First Emperor of China*. Hong Kong: Man Hei Language Publications, 1989.

Gallic Wars (58–51 BCE)

Dates	58–51 BCE
Location	Gaul (modern France), western Germany, southern England
Combatants	Rome vs. the Gallic, German, and British tribes
Principal Commanders	Rome: Julius Caesar Gallic tribes: Vercingetorix German tribes: Ariovistus British tribes: Cassivellaunus
Principal Battles	Alesia
Outcome	Gaul's immense resources greatly increase Rome's strength, but Caesar is now a threat to the Roman state.

Causes

It should be noted at the outset that although there has been an immense amount of scholarly literature on Caesar and the Gallic Wars, these rely almost entirely on Caesar's own narrative of the war (of the eight books of the *Gallic Wars,* the first seven were written by Caesar himself, and the eighth was written after his death by Aulus Hirtius, who had served under him in Gaul). Although our source for the wars is thus exceptionally well informed, he also has a strong interest in presenting his own decisions and actions in a favorable light and suppressing those that put him in a bad light, especially as he was a political figure thinking of his political future.

In 58 BCE Roman leader Gaius Julius Caesar received appointment as governor of Gaul. Gaul then consisted of Cisalpine Gaul (in effect the Po Valley in northern Italy) and Transalpine Gaul (roughly the subsequent southern French provinces of Provence, Dauphiné, and Languedoc). Caesar had been a praetor in Rome in 62 and then spent 61 and the first part of 60 in Spain as a promagistrate. Returning to Rome, in 60 he joined with two others to oppose the ruling faction in the Roman Senate. This First Triumvirate (60–51) consisted of Caesar, popular general Gnaeus Pompeius Magnus (Pompey the Great), and wealthy businessman Marcus Licinius Crassus. The alliance was cemented by Pompey's marriage to Caesar's daughter Julia.

Under the division of spoils in the First Triumvirate, Caesar became one of two consuls in 59, followed by military command for 5 years (later increased to 10) in Illyricum (consisting of most of the former Yugoslavia and modern Albania, although Caesar's territory probably was largely limited to the coastal areas of present-day Croatia and Montenegro) and Gaul, first only in Cisalpine Gaul but when Roman governor of Transalpine Gaul Metellus Celer died, there as well. (In 55 when Pompey and Crassus were again consuls, they saw to it that Caesar's command was extended for another 5 years.)

Soon Caesar had initiated major warfare against several Gallic tribes. Although he portrayed this as a justifiable preemptive military action, most historians have concluded that the Gallic Wars were fought primarily to boost Caesar's political career and to pay off his massive debts. Still, Gaul was of considerable strategic importance to Rome, the territory of which had been invaded several times in the past by native tribes from the area and to northward. Conquering all Gaul would give Rome a natural frontier on the Rhine River. At the start of the fighting, Caesar had four legions at his disposal.

Course

When Caesar arrived in Gaul he learned that the 380,000 people of the Helvetian tribe, a quarter of whom were warriors, were on the move from the area of present-day Switzerland to Gaul with the intention of settling in the Rhône Valley. Caesar ordered the construction of fortifications to block the Helvetians from moving down the Rhône Valley, then gathered what scattered Roman forces he could along with contingents from other Gallic tribes fearful of being overrun by the Helvetians. With their southern advance blocked, the Helvetians continued west through the Jura north of the Rhône.

In June 58 BCE Caesar, with some 34,000 men, caught up with the Helvetians as they were crossing the Arar River (present-day Saône River), a tributary of the Rhône. Following a long night march, Caesar launched a surprise attack on those Helvetians remaining on the east bank. In the Battle of the Arar, Caesar virtually annihilated a force of some 30,000 warriors. The majority of the Helvetians, who had already crossed the Arar, continued westward to the larger Loire River, with Caesar in pursuit.

The next month, July, the Helvetians halted their movement, and some 70,000 of their warriors attacked Caesar, who then had about 30,000 legionnaires and 24,000 Gauls (4,000 of them cavalry). In the Battle of Bibracte (Mount Beuvray) Caesar's men held off the Helvetians and then drove on the enemy camp. In the ensuing wild fighting, some 130,000 Helvetians, including many women and children, perished. Roman losses were also heavy but are not known with any precision. The surviving Helvetians agreed to withdraw and return to their home east of the Jura Mountains.

Caesar did not rest on his laurels. During August–September 58 he agreed to aid the Aedui, Sequani, and Arverni tribes in east-central Gaul, who were being terrorized by a Germanic tribe led by Ariovistus. Caesar commanded about 50,000 men, Ariovistus perhaps 75,000. On September 10, 58, in the vicinity of modern-day Belfort, Caesar attacked Ariovistus and routed his army. Pursued by Caesar, what remained of the German force withdrew across the Rhine. Most of central Gaul now recognized Roman supremacy. Caesar then went into winter quarters.

Alarmed by Caesar's successes in southern and central Gaul, the Belgae peoples of northeastern Gaul formed an alliance against the Romans, planning to march south with a vast force of 300,000 men and destroy Caesar's army. Learning of the plan, Caesar struck first. In the spring of 57 he invaded Belgae territory with 40,000 Roman legionnaires and 20,000 Gallic auxiliaries. Galba, king of Suessiones (Soissons) and leader of the Belgae, managed to assemble on short notice 75,000–100,000 men and attempted without success to stop Caesar at the Axona River, probably in April 57. Caesar continued on, and a number of the tribes submitted to his authority. Others, led by the Nervii, prepared to resist.

Failing to take adequate reconnaissance precautions, a confident Caesar with 40,000 men was preparing to camp on the banks of the Sabis (Sambre) River in July when he was suddenly attacked by some 75,000 Nervii, led by Boduognatus. Desperate fighting ensued, with Caesar going from one legion to another, fighting in their front ranks in order to inspire his men. The well-disciplined legionnaires beat back the attackers and then took the offensive themselves. The Nervii reportedly suffered 60,000 dead, but Roman losses were also heavy.

Caesar continued his advance into Aduatuci territory, besieging and taking the surrender of their capital of Aduatuca (Tongres), but in September as the Romans marched into that place, the Aduatucis treacherously attacked them. The Romans beat back the attackers, and most of Belgica (present-day Belgium) submitted to Roman control. Caesar established winter quarters along the Loire River. He himself returned to Cisalpine Gaul as he did each winter to be certain of his political base.

During the winter of 57–56, the Veneti tribe of Armorica (Brittany) seized several of Caesar's ambassadors. In the spring, Caesar began a multipronged offensive against the Veneti, advancing into Armorica (that part of Gaul between the Seine and the Loire Rivers, including the Brittany peninsula) with three legions. Caesar's lieutenant, Decimus Brutus, commanding another legion and hastily constructed galleys, operated near the mouth of the Loire, while Publius Crassus (son of Caesar's triumvirate partner) invaded Aquitania in southwestern Gaul with more than a legion. In addition, two smaller forces under Titus Labienus and Qunitas Titurius Sabinus operated along the Rhine and in present-day Normandy, respectively.

The campaign was a slow one and consisted largely of a series of long but successful Roman sieges of fortified Veneti towns. The major engagement of the campaign in fact occurred at sea in the Battle of Morbihan Bay (Quiberon Bay), with Caesar observing from shore. Although the light Roman galleys experienced difficulty dealing with the larger Veneti sailing ships, the legionnaires were able to disable the Veneti ships by using sickles lashed to long poles to slash their opponents' sails. The Veneti were subdued, and Caesar dealt harshly with those responsible for mistreating his ambassadors. Although the other Roman operations encountered serious opposition, they too were successful.

In the fall of 56, Caesar marched against the remaining dissident tribes in Belgica. The Romans dispersed the Morinis and the Menapiis, but a number found refuge in the present-day Low Countries and the Ardennes. By the end of the campaign, however, Caesar had for all intents and purposes brought all Gaul under Roman rule, a considerable achievement.

During the winter of 56–55, the German Usipetes and Tenctheri (Tencteri) tribes crossed the Rhine into Gaul and settled in the lower Meuse River area. They numbered more than 400,000 people, a quarter of them warriors. Caesar marched to the Meuse River and, in May 55, entered into talks with the tribes with the goal of getting them to return to Germany. Learning that they planned to attack during the negotiations, Caesar decided to make an example of the two tribes and, in a treacherous maneuver of his own, mounted a preemptive strike during the negotiations.

In fighting in the area between the Meuse and the Rhine, Caesar's men killed all the

GAUL IN THE TIME OF JULIUS CAESAR

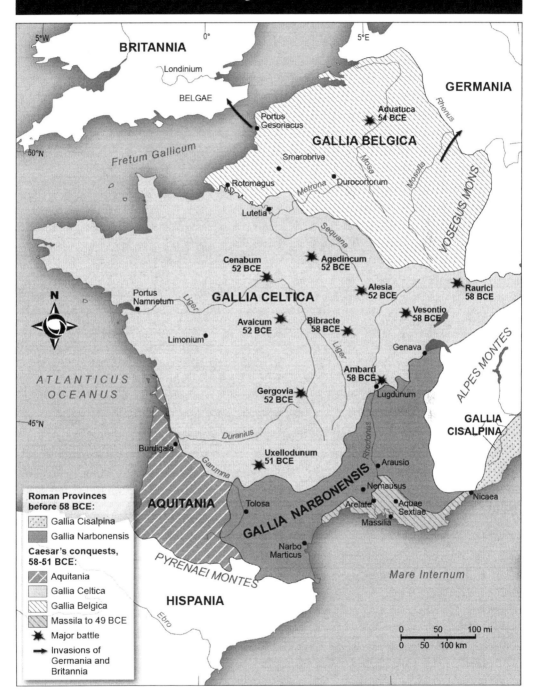

BRITANNIA

Londinium

BELGAE

GERMANIA

Portus
Gesoriacus

Aduatuca
54 BCE

GALLIA BELGICA

Fretum Gallicum

Smarobriva

Rotomagus

Durocortorum

Metrona

Lutetia

Sequana

Cenabum
52 BCE

Agedincum
52 BCE

Alesia
52 BCE

Raurici
58 BCE

Portus
Namnetum

GALLIA CELTICA

Vesontio
58 BCE

Avaicum
52 BCE

Bibracte
58 BCE

Limonium

Liger

Genava

Ambarri
58 BCE

ATLANTICUS
OCEANUS

Gergovia
52 BCE

Lugdunum

GALLIA
CISALPINA

45°N

Duranius

Burdigala

Garumna

Uxellodunum
51 BCE

Arausio

Nemausus

Nicaea

AQUITANIA

Tolosa

Arelate

Aquae
Sextiae

GALLIA NARBONENSIS

Massilia

**Roman Provinces
before 58 BCE:**

Gallia Cisalpina

Gallia Narbonensis

**Caesar's conquests,
58-51 BCE:**

Aquitania

Gallia Celtica

Gallia Belgica

Massila to 49 BCE

✶ Major battle

➜ Invasions of
Germania and
Britannia

Narbo
Marticus

PYRENAEI MONTES

Mare Internum

HISPANIA

Ebro

0   50   100 mi
0   50   100 km

VOSEGUS MONS

Rhenus

Mosa

Mosella

Liger

Rhodanus

ALPES MONTES

5°W   0°   5°E

50°N

warriors encountered. Caesar also ordered the massacre of all noncombatants, including women and children. His enemies in Rome used reports of events to condemn Caesar on a charge of bloodlust, but he insisted that this action was necessary to prevent further German invasions of Gaul.

During June 55 in one of great engineering feats of antiquity, Caesar ordered construction of a great bridge over the Rhine in the vicinity of present-day Bonn. In a clear act of intimidation, Caesar then marched his legions across the bridge into Germany, defeated several tribes, and then withdrew, destroying the bridge after him.

In August 55, Caesar invaded Britain with two legions. The landing near Dubra (Dover) was hotly contested, but covered by catapults on the Roman ships, the men got ashore. The Romans moved inland and remained in Britain for three weeks before returning to Gaul in what was little more than a raid.

Caesar again sailed to Britain in July 54, this time with some 800 small ships transporting five legions totaling some 22,000 men, including 2,000 cavalry. The Roman landing northeast of Dubra was unopposed. Following it, however, a severe storm destroyed many of the Roman ships and damaged others. As Caesar moved inland, crossing the Thames somewhere east of present-day London, a large force of Britons under the leadership of chieftain Cassivellaunus attempted to destroy the Roman entrenched base on the coast. When this failed, Cassivellaunus opened peace talks. Receiving the nominal submission of the Britons, Caesar returned to Gaul.

In the years 54–53 uprisings occurred in Gaul against Roman rule. Unrest was widespread, with the tribes involved probably numbering more than 1 million people. Now fully aware that they had been conquered by a Roman force of hardly more than 50,000 men, the dissident tribes staged an uprising. The revolt was centered on the Nervii, led by Ambiorix.

Taking advantage of the dispersion of Roman forces into eight separate camps across northern Gaul during the winter, in the year 53 Ambiorix attacked the camp of Quintus Titurius Sabinus, then offered him safe conduct. In violation of this pledge, Ambiorix then attacked the Romans while they were on the march, annihilating them. Ambiorix then moved against the Roman camp near modern-day Binche, where he attempted the same ruse with its commander, Quintus Cicero, who refused to oblige.

His fortified camp near Binche besieged by the Nervii, Cicero managed to get word of the situation to Caesar in north-central Gaul. Collecting some 7,000 men, the only ones immediately available, Caesar marched to the rescue. Leaving a strong force to contain Cicero, Ambiorix moved with 60,000 men to meet Caesar. After some maneuvering, the two sides came together near the Sabis River.

Caesar feigned indecision, causing Ambiorix to attack. The Romans were able to contain the attack, whereupon Caesar launched a counterattack and was victorious. Following the battle, Caesar relieved Cicero. Caesar was also joined by legionnaires under Labienus, who had managed to beat back his attackers. Consolidating his forces, Caesar then went into more secure winter quarters.

Caesar, his strength now raised to 10 legions, took the offensive in the early spring of 53 to crush the remaining centers of resistance in northern Gaul. In the ensuing campaign there was little actual fighting, but Caesar completely subdued the Belgae. As some German tribes assisted the rebels,

Caesar again ordered a bridge constructed over the Rhine, crossed some of his men over it, and carried out a military demonstration in Germany before withdrawing and dismantling the bridge after him. By the end of the summer, Caesar was again complete master of northern Gaul.

Caesar was, however, caught by surprise in late 53 by a widespread revolt in central Gaul. It was led by young Arverni chieftain Vercingetorix, certainly the most capable of the Gallic leaders Caesar ever faced. Vercingetorix raised a large army and trained it to a degree previously unknown for native Gallic forces. When the revolt began, most of Caesar's forces were in the recently pacified northern Gaul, while Caesar himself was in Italy.

Learning in January 52 of the revolt, Caesar hurried back to Gaul. Following a difficult winter march, he united his forces north of the Loire River. Leaving Labienus to hold northern Gaul, Caesar recaptured Cenabum (Orléans), where the rebellion had begun. Vercingetorix, however, rejected pitched battle with the Romans, waging a guerrilla war and destroying anything that might be useful to the Romans.

Although the Gauls mounted a spirited defense and Vercingetorix harassed the besiegers, who came close to running out of food, Caesar was able to capture Avaricum (Bourges) in March 52. He then moved south against the Arverni capital of Gergovia (near present-day Puy de Dôme), hoping to be able to capture it before it could be properly fortified. Vercingetorix was prepared. Taking advantage of Gregovia's natural siting on high ground, he had laid in ample supplies and denuded the countryside. Caesar again found himself short of supplies, and adding to his troubles, much of the rest of Gaul, including areas heretofore loyal to Rome, also rebelled. Caesar

sent for Labienus in northern Gaul to assist him before he could be overwhelmed. Unable to delay, Caesar attempted to take Gergovia by storm but failed and was forced to withdraw, moving northward to join Labienus, who was victorious at Lutetia (Paris). Caesar then reunited his own forces with those of Labienus south of the Seine.

Realizing that all Gaul was temporarily lost, Caesar withdrew to the southeast to reconstitute his forces in June 52. Vercingetorix, fielding the most effective Gallic military force assembled to that point in history of some 80,000 infantry and 15,000 cavalry, attempted to get in behind Caesar and prevent him from reaching the Saône Valley. Vercingetorix was able to place his army along the Vingeanne, a tributary of the Saône, blocking Caesar from moving south. Caesar attacked, and after an indecisive cavalry encounter, Vercingetorix retired and Caesar pursued.

Vercingetorix mistakenly retired to Alesia (Alise-Ste-Reine), situated on the top of Mount Auxois near the source of the Seine. Caesar surrounded Alesia with his army in July 52. Vercingetorix had more than 90,000 men, while Caesar had only 55,000. Of this number, only some 40,000 were legionnaires; the remainder were Gallic cavalry and auxiliaries.

Caesar ordered his legionnaires to construct two walls: one of contravallation and one of circumvallation, each roughly 10 miles in circumference. Each line incorporated a ditch 20 feet wide and deep, backed by two additional trenches 15 feet wide and deep. Behind these the Romans constructed ramparts with 12-foot-high palisades and towers every 130 yards. The Romans placed sharpened stakes facing outward in front of and in the ditches.

Caesar's foresight in having a defensive works facing outward was soon manifest.

Responding to appeals from Vercingetorix, a vast Gallic relief force of as many as 250,000 men and 8,000 cavalry gathered around Alesia and besieged the besiegers. Caesar had laid in considerable stocks of food and had an assured water supply, so he calmly continued his own siege operations. He repulsed two relief attempts mounted from without and one from within the siege lines, with heavy losses to the attackers.

In order to win additional time, Vercingetorix attempted to send out the women and children from Alesia, but Caesar refused to allow them through the lines. With the situation now hopeless and to save his people further disaster, Vercingetorix surrendered in October. Taken to Rome for Caesar's triumph there in 46, Vercingetorix was then executed.

The defeat of the Gauls at Alesia broke the back of their resistance to Rome. Their failure to unite cost the Gauls dearly. At least a third of their men of military age had been killed during the fighting, and another third were sold into slavery. The vast majority of Gauls now hastened to renew their fealty to Rome.

In the year 51 Caesar completed the Roman reconquest of Gaul. In mopping-up operations he traversed the entire province, impressing on the Gauls the futility of further resistance.

Significance

Their resistance at an end, the Gallic peoples prospered under Roman rule. The newly conquered territories, with a population of perhaps 5 million people, proved immensely important to Rome because of its vast resources of agriculture, stock breeding, mining, and metallurgy as well as its production of pottery and glass. Gaul would be an integral part of the Roman Empire for the next 500 years.

During the conquest of Gaul, however, Caesar's army had grown from 5 to 13 legions, making Caesar a threat to Rome itself. Chaotic conditions in Rome and his own growing jealousy of Julius Caesar's military reputation had led Pompey to agree in 52 BCE to his illegal election as sole consul and virtual dictator. This action further strained relations between the two men. The Gallic Wars thus paved the way for Caesar to contest with Pompey for control of the Roman Republic.

Further Reading

Caesar, Gaius Julius. *The Gallic War.* Edited and translated by Carolyn Hammond. New York: Oxford University Press, 1996.

Caesar, Julius. *War Commentaries of Caesar.* Translated by Rex Warner. New York: New American Library, 1960.

Fuller, J. F. C. *Julius Caesar: Man, Soldier, and Tyrant.* London: Eyre and Spottiswoode, 1965.

Gelzer, M. *Caesar: Politician and Statesman.* Translated by Peter Needham. Cambridge, MA: Harvard University Press, 1985.

Gilliver, Kate. *Caesar's Gallic Wars, 58–50 BC.* London: Osprey, 2002.

Goldsworthy, Adrian. *Caesar: Life of a Colossus.* New Haven, CT: Yale University Press, 2006.

Grant, Michael. *The Army of the Caesars.* New York: Scribner, 1974.

Grant Michael. *Julius Caesar.* New York: M. Evans, 1992.

Holland, Tom. *Rubicon: The Last Years of the Roman Republic.* New York: Doubleday, 2003.

Matyszak, Philip. *The Enemies of Rome: From Hannibal to Attila the Hun.* London: Thames and Hudson, 2004.

Walter, Gérard. *Caesar: A Biography.* Translated by Emma Craufurd. New York: Scribner, 1952.

Wyke, Maria. *Caesar: A Life in Western Culture.* Chicago: University of Chicago Press, 2008.

Caesarian-Pompeian Civil War (49–45 BCE)

Dates	49–45 BCE
Location	Spain, Italy, Greece, western Balkan Peninsula, Egypt, North Africa
Combatants	Julius Caesar and his supporters vs. Pompey the Great and most of the Roman Senate and supporters
Principal Commanders	Caesar: Julius Caesar, Mark Antony, Gaius Curio, Decimus Brutus Pompey: Gnaeus Pompeius Magnus (Pompey the Great), Ptolemy XII, Metellus Scipio
Principal Battles	Bagradas River, Dyrrhachium, Pharsalus, Alexandria, Nile, Zela, Thapsus, Munda
Outcome	The Great Roman Civil War ends the Roman Republic and establishes the Roman Empire.

Causes

Also known as Caesar's Civil War and the Great Roman Civil War, the Caesarian-Pompeian Civil War of 49–45 BCE was the last major politico-military conflict in Rome before the establishment of the Roman Empire, to which it directly contributed. It was essentially a confrontation between Roman military leaders Gaius Julius Caesar and Gnaeus Pompeius Magnus (Pompey the Great) over who would control Roman affairs. But this was also only the culmination of a long series of subversions of governmental institutions of the Roman Republic, beginning with Tiberius Gracchus in the second century BCE.

In the year 59, Caesar, Pompey, and wealthy nobleman Marcus Licinius Crassus had formed the First Triumvirate, in effect dividing power in the Roman Republic between them. The alliance was cemented by Pompey's marriage to Caesar's daughter Julia. Under the First Triumvirate, Caesar became one of two consuls in 59, followed by a military command for 5 years (later increased to 10) in Illyricum (constituting

most of the former Yugoslavia and modern Albania, although Caesar's territory was probably restricted to the coast of present-day Croatia and Montenegro) and Gaul on both sides of the Alps (France and northern Italy). Caesar's victory over the Gauls added a rich and populous territory, indeed one of the largest territorial additions in Roman history. During the conquest of Gaul his army had grown in strength from 4 legions, soon increased to 6, to 13 legions.

Pompey had received the governorship of Spain in 55 BCE but exercised it in absentia from the suburbs of Rome (as proconsul he had to stay outside the *pomerium*). In 53 Crassus was killed campaigning in Mesopotamia, and the First Triumvirate came to an end. In 52 amid increasing civil unrest in Rome, the Senate appointed Pompey sole consul. His wife, Caesar's daughter Julia, had died in 54, and Pompey was pressed by a conservative group of senators to break with Caesar, now a popular military hero in Rome and presumed champion of the people whose ambitions the senators greatly feared. The ensuing civil war was thus a test between Caesar and his legions and supporters (known as Populares) and Pompey, his legions, and the politically conservative and socially traditionalist leaders of the Roman Senate (known as the Optimates or Boni).

The Pompey-dominated Senate demanded that Caesar give up his military command. This action was in fact illegal, for Caesar was permitted to retain his command until his term expired. Caesar was then at Ravenna in Cisalpine Gaul with one legion only. He was willing to yield his command but wanted another consulship. If without office, he would be subject to prosecution by his enemies in the Pompey-controlled Senate for alleged irregularities during his consulship as well as supposed war crimes during his Gallic campaigns. According to the law, the earliest time Caesar could acquire a second consulship would be 48 BCE.

Caesar had the support of young tribune Gaius Curio, who vetoed Senate demands for the appointment of a successor for Caesar. Curio indeed presented a compromise whereby Caesar would resign, with Pompey simultaneously resigning his absentee governorship of Spain. A small group of senators brought its rejection. Near the end of that year following considerable political maneuvering, a majority of the Senate duly approved the plan, only to see a small faction again veto it. Deadlock was now complete. The day after its rejection, one of the consuls called on Pompey to assume command of all of the armed forces of the republic, which he promptly accepted, taking command of two Roman legions that were to have been sent to Syria.

In December 50 BCE the Senate ordered Caesar to give up his military command, disband his legions, and return to Rome (probably by March 1, 49, although there is considerable dispute among scholars over the exact date) or be declared a traitor. Tribune Marcus Antonius (Mark Antony), who had assumed Curio's role as Caesar's chief defender in Rome, left the city to join Caesar in northern Italy. The stage was set for civil war.

Course

Roman law specifically prohibited generals from bringing their legions into Italy proper without the express approval of the Senate. On the Adriatic coast, the border was marked by the Rubicon River south of Ravenna. Yet on January 10 or 11 (sources differ), 49 BCE, announcing that "the die is cast," Caesar defied the Senate and crossed the small Rubicon with his army into Italy proper. Although Caesar had only one legion immediately with him, he retained eight other battle-tested legions in Gaul. His total force thus numbered some 40,000 men, plus 20,000 auxiliaries. Ranged against Caesar, Pompey and his allies in the Senate could call on two legions in Italy (with eight more being raised there), seven in Spain, and substantial military resources in Greece, the East, and North Africa.

Caesar hoped to counter this formidable imbalance by the decisive approach that had brought him victory in Gaul. Moving swiftly south along the Adriatic, he collected additional forces and recruits. Pompey declared that Rome could not be defended, and he and most of the senators abandoned the city to Caesar in order to buy time to gather additional resources in southern Italy. The only setback for Caesar to this point was the news that Labienus, a former lieutenant of Pompey, had defected to him. All of Caesar's other key subordinates and legions remained loyal.

Because Pompey was slow both to react to the threat posed by Caesar and to mobilize his own legions, he and 25,000 men and most of the senators who had fled to the

ROMAN REPUBLIC AT THE DEATH OF CAESAR, 44 BCE

south withdrew to Brundisium (Brindisi). Pompey also rejected calls from Caesar that they end the fighting and restore their former alliance, Pompey claiming that he was Caesar's superior.

Pompey was confident of ultimate victory. He expected to raise substantial forces in the eastern Greek provinces and, with control of most of the Roman Navy, institute a blockade of the Italian coast. In March 49 BCE Pompey and a number of his senatorial allies sailed from Brundisium for Epirus.

Before Caesar could contemplate proceeding against Pompey in Greece, he had to eliminate the threat to his rear posed by Pompey's sizable army in Spain. Leaving Marcus Aemilius Lepidus as prefect in Rome and Mark Antony in charge of the rest of Italy, Caesar marched for Spain. Gaius

Antonius held Illyria for Caesar, while Cisalpine Gaul was under Licinius Crassus. Caesar sent Gaius Curio with other troops to secure Sicily and North Africa.

Pompey supporter Lucius Domitius Ahenobarbus landed by sea at Massilia (present-day Marseille) with a small number of men and persuaded its leaders to declare for Pompey. Caesar, having sent most of his army ahead to secure the passes over the Pyrenees that would give him access to Spain, invested Massilia in April with three legions. Caesar then hurried on to take charge of operations in Spain, leaving Gaius Trebonius to continue the siege operations by land and Decimus Brutus to raise a naval force and blockade Massilia from the sea. The siege continued during the entire time of Caesar's operations in Spain, although Brutus won a naval victory off Massilia against a joint Massilian-Pompeian force.

Taking advantage of Pompey's absence from the Italian mainland, Caesar moved quickly. In June 49, his legions secured the vital Pyrenees passes just in advance of a large force of 65,000 men loyal to Pompey and commanded by Lucius Afranius and Marcus Petreius. Frustrated by their inability to reach and secure the passes first, the two Pompeian generals awaited Caesar's arrival in Spain. Two additional Pompeian legions and about 45,000 auxiliaries under Vebellius Rufus and Marcus Terentius Varro held the remainder of Spain.

Both sides engaged in extended maneuvering in what is known as the Ilerda Campaign. Caesar was anxious to avoid pitched battle because of his considerable inferiority in numbers. His opponents were equally reluctant to engage because of Caesar's military reputation. Finally, through adroit maneuvering and rapid movement, Caesar cut off the withdrawal of the two legions and surrounded them, securing their surrender at Ilerda on August 2, 49. Following his victory, Caesar disbanded the two legions, gaining recruits in the process. He then marched to Gades (Cádiz) to overawe all Spain. Then, leaving a small force to complete the pacification of Iberia, Caesar returned to Massilia, which surrendered on September 6. Domitius escaped by sea.

After successfully establishing Caesar's authority in Sicily, his lieutenant Curio sailed for North Africa. Although initially triumphant near Utica against the forces of Pompeian general Attius Varus and his ally King Juba of Numidia, Curio was subsequently defeated by them in the Battle of the Bagradas River on August 24, 49; Curio committed suicide rather than surrender.

Caesar returned to Rome only to learn that his small fleet had been defeated in the Adriatic near Curicta (Krk). Pressuring the remnant of the Senate, in October 49 Caesar engineered his appointment as dictator. He held this position for only 11 days, sufficient to carry through several measures and to secure a second term as consul, with Publius Servilius Vatia Isauricus.

Caesar was not done with campaigning, for Pompey was still a great threat. In January 48 risking everything, for Pompey's ships controlled the Adriatic, Caesar crossed the Adriatic Sea from Brundisium with 12 understrength legions totaling perhaps 25,000 men. Successfully evading Pompey's fleet, Caesar landed on the coast of Epirus (present-day Albania), south of Pompey's base at Dyrrhachium (present-day Durrës, also known as Durazzo) in what is today western Albania. Caesar then ordered his ships to return to Brundisium to bring back an additional 20,000 men under Mark Antony, but Pompey's fleet blockaded Antony's ships at Brundisium.

Learning of Caesar's landing, Pompey marched there from Epirus, forestalling Caesar's attempt to seize Dyrrhachium. Surprisingly, Pompey, who commanded as many as 100,000 men, did not attempt to defeat Caesar, who possessed a quarter that number. Indeed, it was Caesar who took the initiative, mounting a number of bold moves south of Dyrrhachium.

In March 48 able to slip past Pompey's blockading fleet, Antony delivered Caesar's remaining legions north of Dyrrhachium. Informed of Antony's arrival, Pompey moved to defeat Caesar's forces in detail before they could unite, but Caesar was as usual quicker and managed to link up with Antony at Tirana and cut Pompey off from Dyrrhachium by land. Because his forces dominated at sea, however, Pompey was still able to communicate with his base of Dyrrhachium.

Realizing that the countryside was largely bereft of supplies and yet able to secure plentiful stocks for his own men from Dyrrhachium, Pompey decided to remain quiescent in the hopes of starving Caesar into submission. Caesar was able to secure sufficient food supplies, however. Always offensive minded, he initiated a bold siege of Pompey's beachhead with a force half the size of that of his adversary. Both sides constructed extensive fortifications.

On July 10, 48, battle was joined at Dyrrhachium. With his forces cut off from freshwater by Caesar's fortifications, Pompey initiated action at each end of Julius Caesar's contravallation line. With his own great numerical advantage and assisted by his fleet, Pompey easily broke through Caesar's fortifications. Facing disaster, Caesar withdrew his forces, suffering perhaps 1,000 killed in the fighting. Pompey's losses were far fewer. Caesar then withdrew southeast into Thessaly. Believing that Caesar had not been defeated and was attempting to draw him into a trap, Pompey failed to pursue aggressively. He also left behind a strong garrison at Dyrrhachium.

During July and early August, Caesar secured supplies and reconstituted his forces. His army and that of Pompey were camped next to the Epineus River a few miles from one another near Cynoscephalae in Thessaly on opposite sides of the Pharsalian Plain. Each day the two armies deployed, only to return to camp. Gradually, however, Caesar moved his own army closer to that of Pompey, hoping to entice him into an attack.

Caesar was still outnumbered, more than two to one. Pompey commanded some 45,000 infantry and 7,000 cavalry, while Caesar had only 22,000 infantry and 1,000 cavalry. Caesar's left flank rested on the steep banks of the Enipeus River. His right flank was the weak point. Here his cavalry were outnumbered seven to one. Caesar formed his infantry in three lines, but he held back six cohorts (about 2,000 men) in the so-called fourth line to cover his right rear. He extended the intervals between his cohorts to match the frontage of Pompey's line, which was drawn up in normal formation. Caesar's third line was, as usual, a reserve to the first two lines. Caesar took position with the fourth line.

Pompey, wary of his opponent, refused to allow his men to attack and held them stationary in a compact mass with the intent of breaking Caesar's charge. Pompey also believed that hurled javelins would be less effective if the men were stationary rather than running forward. Finally, Caesar ordered an attack on Pompey's stationary forces.

In the Battle of Pharsalus (August 9, 48 BCE), Caesar's men rushed forward, javelins leveled. But when they saw that Pompey's men were not running out to meet them, Caesar's veterans knew immediately to halt their charge so as not to wear themselves out. After a short interval they resumed the charge, hurling their javelins and then drawing their swords. Pompey's men threw their own javelins and then also resorted to their swords.

At the moment of the infantry impact, Pompey launched his cavalry on his left flank, supported by archers and slingers, against Caesar's horsemen. Although Caesar's cavalry fought well, they were no match for Pompey's vastly superior numbers. But at the decisive moment, Caesar wheeled out with his six reserve cohorts against Pompey's cavalry. They charged forward with such force that Pompey's cavalry were obliged to scatter. This left Pompey's archers and slingers unprotected.

They were overwhelmed and slain. Caesar then turned his fourth line against the left flank of Pompey's more numerous army and drove it in with a single envelopment from the rear.

At the same time Caesar ordered forward his third line, inactive to this point. This fresh force and the fourth line attacking from the rear caused Pompey's army to flee the field for its camp. Caesar would not allow his men to stop to plunder but instead pressed the pursuit. Pompey escaped with only a handful of followers, reaching the coast and sailing for Egypt.

Caesar's superior military leadership and bold innovation had carried the day against a capable yet unimaginative commander who had failed to divine his opponent's intentions. The Battle of Pharsalus cost Pompey 15,000 killed and 24,000 prisoners; Caesar's losses were some 1,200 killed and perhaps 2,000 wounded. Greece and Asia now declared for Caesar.

Caesar pursued Pompey to Egypt with only some 4,000 men and there learned that Pompey had been assassinated on September 29 on the orders of King Ptolemy XII by an Egyptian and two Roman centurions, one of whom had served under Pompey earlier. Caesar is said to have mourned the death of Pompey and subsequently put to death those who had murdered him. Pompey's lieutenants in Egypt meanwhile convinced Ptolemy XII, co-ruler of Egypt with his sister Cleopatra, to resist Caesar. With 20,000 men, Ptolemy besieged Caesar at Alexandria. Although Caesar controlled some of the eastern harbor of the city, he refused to flee. Sending an appeal for assistance, he ably defended the small part of the city and seafront he controlled. Land and naval reinforcements for Caesar then slowly arrived. Victorious in two desperate naval battles outside the harbor, Caesar lost a land battle on the harbor mole and a third naval battle nearby.

In January 47 Caesar's position again appeared desperate, but his luck held. Learning of the arrival of forces sent overland by his ally Mithridates of Pergamum, Caesar left only a small force to hold his existing positions in Alexandria and joined Mithridates outside the city for a battle with his opponents. Each side numbered about 20,000 men.

In the February 27 Battle of the Nile, Caesar and Mithridates utterly defeated the Egyptians. Ptolemy XII was among those slain. After relieving his forces in Alexandria, Caesar established firm control over Egypt, placing on the throne Cleopatra's younger brother, Ptolemy XIII. At the same time, Caesar became involved romantically with Cleopatra and with her fathered his only known biological son, Ptolemy XV Caesar, known as Caesarion. Caesar and Cleopatra never married, however, owing to Roman law prohibiting marriage with a non-Roman citizen.

Meanwhile, King Pharnaces of Bosporus Cimmerius, son of Mithridates the Great of Pontus, took advantage of the Roman civil war to re-create his father's Kingdom of Pontus. Pharnaces defeated Caesar's lieutenant Domitius Calvinus in the Battle of Nicopolis (Nikopol) in October 48 BCE. In April 47, Caesar sailed from Egypt with part of his army. Securing reinforcements in Syria, he then moved overland to meet Pharnaces and defeated him in the Battle of Zela in May 47. This victory was the subject of his famous message to Rome "Veni, vidi, vici" ("I came, I saw, I conquered"). Caesar then reorganized the eastern part of the empire, giving Mithridates of Pergamum nominal rule over Pharnaces' territory.

Returning to Rome from the East, Caesar was confronted with a mutiny among his troops who sought their back pay. Forced to appeal to them in person, he addressed the men as "citizens" rather than "soldiers," an implication that they were no longer in the army by reason of their insubordination. He asked what they wanted, and embarrassed to say that it was their back pay, they called out for their discharge. Caesar responded that they were discharged immediately and that their back pay would be forthcoming as soon as he had been victorious in Africa with other soldiers. The men, many of whom had served with him for more than a decade, were shocked at the news that he might not need them now, and they soon crowded around him demanding to accompany him to Africa.

After securing reinforcements in Sicily, Caesar sailed with some 25,000 men to engage Pompey's remaining lieutenants, who had concentrated there from Spain, Gaul, Greece, and other points in the empire. Metellus Scipio had command. He and his lieutenants, including Labienus, commanded some 50,000 men. Scipio had the support of King Juba's Numidian army of equal size and the Pompeian fleet.

Managing to avoid Scipio's fleet, Caesar landed at Ruspina (Monastir), which he made his base. Much of his fleet was scattered in a storm as it approached the coast, so initially Caesar had only a small portion of his men available. His opponents, however, failed to take advantage of the situation before Caesar could reassemble his scattered units. He recklessly allowed himself, with only 12,000 men, to be cut off from Ruspina by troops under Labienus but was able to cut his way out and regain Ruspina, where he was soon blockaded by the entire opposing force of 100,000 men.

Although reinforced, Caesar was still outnumbered two to one, but in typical fashion he took the offensive, marching inland with 40,000 men. Laying siege to Thapsus, he invited attack. Meanwhile, desertion and illness combined to reduce his opponents to about 60,000 men. Scipio and Juba attacked and were soundly defeated in the Battle of Thapsus in February 46. Caesar sustained fewer than 1,000 casualties; his opponents lost 10,000 dead and at least that number wounded or captured. The remaining Pompeians now fled to Spain, where Pompey's sons had begun a revolt. Caesar meanwhile returned to Rome.

After six months in Rome, Caesar sailed for Spain with a small force in December 46 BCE, joining there troops loyal to him for a combined total strength of perhaps 40,000 men. Learning that Gnaeus Pompeius (Pompey the Younger) and some 50,000–60,000 men were in the vicinity of Corduba (Cordova), Caesar moved his own force there and commenced his customary maneuvering and skirmishes to determine weaknesses and opportunities. Labienus, who was apparently in actual command of the Pompeian field army, withdrew southward to the coast in order to have naval support.

The two armies finally did battle on the plains of Munda near Osuna in southern Spain on March 17, 45 BCE. The Pompeian forces were in an excellent defensible position on a gentle hill less than a mile from the walls of Munda. Caesar commanded about 40,000 men in 8 legions (80 cohorts) and 8,000 cavalry, while Pompey and Labienus had as many as 70,000 men in 13 legions along with 6,000 light infantrymen and about 6,000 cavalry. Many on the Pompeian side had surrendered to Caesar in previous campaigns and had deserted his army to rejoin the Pompeians. They could thus be expected to fight with desperation, knowing they were likely to be executed if taken prisoner.

After an unsuccessful attempt to lure the Pompeians down the hill, Caesar reluctantly ordered a frontal assault. Pompey halted this and then ordered a counterattack that was almost successful. Indeed, Munda was among the most bitterly contested of Caesar's many battles. To bolster his men, Caesar went from legion to legion and personally fought in the front lines. Inspired by his example, Caesar's men ultimately broke through the enemy center, whereupon resistance collapsed and the battle became a massacre. All 13 Pompeian legion standards were taken, indicating the complete nature of Caesar's victory. The battle claimed some 30,000 dead on the Pompeian side. Caesar's losses were more than 1,000 dead and some 5,000 wounded. Labienus was killed in the fighting, while Pompey the Younger was subsequently taken prisoner and executed. His younger brother, Sextus Pompey, however, escaped to the seacoast and the safety of the Pompeian fleet. Gaius Didius, a naval commander loyal to Caesar, ultimately captured most of the Pompeian ships, although Sextus continued to carry out piratical operations along the coast.

Following the Battle of Munda, Caesar left Quintus Fabius Maximus to lay siege to Munda while he pacified the rest of the province. Corduba surrendered to him. Those men taken with arms were executed, and the city was forced to pay a heavy indemnity. After a protracted siege, Munda also surrendered.

In July 45 Caesar returned to Rome, where he was recognized as the undisputed ruler and in effect the uncrowned monarch. In 46 BCE he secured appointment by the Senate as dictator for 10 years. Although the formality of elections continued, Caesar held power. What Caesar intended is unclear. In 44 he caused his dictatorship to be extended for life and secured deification. He seems to have wanted the

kingship, but the Roman public apparently opposed this step, and he was not to have the time to convince them otherwise.

Always rational and logical, Caesar carried out extensive reforms. He began projects to restore Corinth and Carthage, the destruction of which had marked the end of Mediterranean trade, and projects he believed would bring employment for the Roman urban poor. He reformed local government by moving toward decentralization, and he reformed the calendar. (A month in the calendar was renamed July after him.) Caesar made many provincials citizens, including the entire province of Cisalpine Gaul.

Not all Romans approved of Caesar's reforms. Many traditionalists, powerful vested interests, and republicans were upset by his changes and cosmopolitan attitude. Shortly after he extended his dictatorship to life, a group of senators, some of whom had been his supporters and some of whom had been Pompeians whom he had spared, plotted against him. Caesar was assassinated on March 15, 44 BCE, stabbed to death in Rome. Believing they had killed a tyrant and were restoring liberty, the senators brought anarchy instead.

Significance

Caesar's victory in the Caesarian-Pompeian Civil War ensured the end of the Roman Republic and led to the establishment of the Roman Empire (27 BCE–476 CE). A struggle now ensued over control of the Roman state. Surprisingly, no action was taken initially against those responsible for Caesar's murder, but public anger forced them to flee. In alliance with other senators, the conspirators hoped to raise provincial armies there and return to Rome to restore the republic. In Rome, the two leading contenders for power were Caesar's principal lieutenant

Mark Antony and Marcus Aemilius Lepidus (Caesar's colleague as consul in 46 and his master of the horse at the time of Caesar's death). Caesar's 18-year-old nephew, adopted son in Caesar's will, and legal heir Gaius Octavius (Octavian) was not in Rome at the time of Caesar's death and only became a major contender later. Antony considered himself Caesar's heir and refused to acknowledge Octavian, now Gaius Julius Caesar Octavianus. Antony, Octavian, and the republicans then engaged in an inevitable struggle over control of the Roman state. Cicero led the effort to try to revive the republic, but in the end the issue was decided on the battlefield. A fair amount of fighting ensued, with the most important battles being Philippi in 42 and Actium in 31 BCE. Following his victory at Actium, Octavian became the first Roman emperor, ruling from 27 BCE until his death in 14 CE.

Further Reading

Appian. *The Civil Wars.* Translated with an introduction by John Carter. New York: Penguin Classics, 1996.

Canfora, Luciano. *Julius Caesar: The Life and Times of the People's Dictator.* Translated by Marian Hill and Kevin Windle. Berkeley: University of California Press, 2007.

Fields, Nic. *Julius Caesar.* New York: Osprey, 2010.

Fields, Nic. *Pompey.* New York: Osprey, 2012.

Gelzer, Matthias. *Caesar: Politician and Statesman.* Cambridge, MA: Harvard University Press, 1985.

Goldsworthy, Adrian. *Caesar: Life of a Colossus.* New Haven, CT: Yale University Press, 2006.

Goldsworthy, Adrian. *Caesar's Civil War, 49–44 BC.* New York: Osprey, 2002.

Grant, Michael. *The Army of the Caesars.* New York: Scribner, 1974.

Grant, Michael. *History of Rome.* New York: Scribner, 1978.

Grant, Michael. *Julius Caesar.* New York: M. Evans, 1992.

Jiménez, Raymond L. *Caesar against Rome: The Great Roman Civil War.* Westport, CT: Praeger, 2000.

Sheppard, Si, and Adam Hook. *Pharsalus 48 BC: Caesar and Pompey; Clash of the Titans.* New York: Osprey, 2006.

Barbarian Invasions of the Roman Empire (363–476)

Dates	363–476
Location	Balkan Peninsula, South-Central Europe, Asia Minor, France, Spain, Italy, North Africa
Combatants	Rome vs. Quadi, Huns, Visigoths, Alemanni, Franks, Ostrogoths, Vandals
Principal Commanders	Roman Empire: Valentinian, Valens, Flavius Gratianus (Gratian), Theodosius I, Promotus, Aetius Visigoths: Fritigern, Alaric Ostrogoths: Tribigild Huns: Attila
Principal Battles	ad Salices, Argentaria, Adrianople, Châlons
Outcome	The Barbarian invasions are the major factor behind the demise of the Roman Empire. Europe is divided into a number of small states but is nonetheless preserved from Asian control.

Causes

Throughout its existence, the Roman Empire was surrounded on almost all sides by hostile peoples. The Romans called them "barbarians" because they spoke neither Greek or Latin. The point needs to be made, however, that this was not necessarily a struggle between barbarism and civilization, for the Roman Empire was itself a brutal place where the chief amusements were to pit men against one another in a fight to the death, pit wild animals against defenseless people, and nail those who opposed the empire's policies to a cross to die.

With the exception of Persia, the barbarian peoples had never come under the sway of Greco-Roman culture. As with the Chinese, who in about 200 BCE built the Great Wall to hold their own "barbarians" at bay, the Romans established their own defensive lines beyond which the barbarians were not to pass. After several centuries of relative stability, however, the peoples beyond the Roman Empire's frontiers came under considerable pressure from other peoples moving out of Asia and pressed against and through Rome's barriers.

There were many such barbarian incursions—too many in fact for inclusion here. In the mid-fifth century the Angles and Saxons overran Britain, while the Franks invaded Gaul. The Vandals reached Roman Africa by 429. The Goths were also active. The movement of the Huns west from China drove other peoples before them. The Huns now forced the Ostrogoths (East Goths) west, and they in turn pushed against the Visigoths (West Goths), driving them into the Danube River Valley, which was the northern border of the Roman Empire. The Ostrogoths were in Asia Minor in 382 and in Italy in 402. The Visigoths (West Goths) moved on Constantinople (present-day Istanbul) about 380.

At its height, the Roman Empire counted more than 100 million people. Bounded by the Rhine and Danube to the north, Britain to the northwest, Spain to the west, North Africa to the south, and Asia Minor to the east, it was a vast area to govern from one administrative center, and in 285 Emperor Diocletian (r. 284–305) split the empire into two. From this point forward there were usually two emperors, one for the East and the other for the West. A few emperors, such as Constantine I the Great (r. 311–337), ruled both parts, but there were two bureaucracies and two capital cities (Constantinople in the East, Milan and then Ravenna in the West). Also, following the death of Emperor Constantine in 337, the empire experienced a seemingly never-ending series of succession struggles. The barbarian "invasions" of the Roman Empire are far too numerous and complex to treat here in any detail. What follows is largely a general outline, with concentration on key events.

Course

In 364 following the death of western emperor Jovian (r. 364–365), the army selected as his successor an able general, Valentinian. As Emperor Valentian I (r. 364–375) he quickly appointed his brother, Valens, to be coruler in the East, sending him to Constantinople to deal with the ongoing problem of the Persians, while he concentrated on shoring up the empire's Danubian defenses against barbarian incursions there.

Valens (r. 364–378) had a low opinion of the Goths, and in 367 he ordered the imprisonment of a number of Goth mercenaries. Goth king Ermanaric protested this

BATTLE OF ADRIANOPLE, AUGUST 9, 378

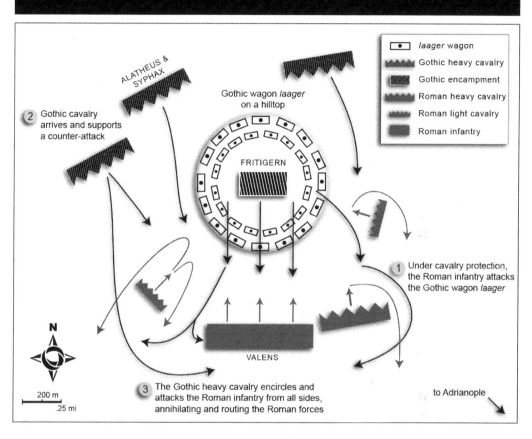

ALATHEUS & SYPHAX

2 Gothic cavalry arrives and supports a counter-attack

Gothic wagon *laager* on a hilltop

FRITIGERN

▭•▭	*laager* wagon
▰▰▰	Gothic heavy cavalry
▨	Gothic encampment
▰▰▰	Roman heavy cavalry
▰▰▰	Roman light cavalry
▬	Roman infantry

1 Under cavalry protection, the Roman infantry attacks the Gothic wagon *laager*

VALENS

N

200 m
.25 mi

3 The Gothic heavy cavalry encircles and attacks the Roman infantry from all sides, annihilating and routing the Roman forces

to Adrianople

and sent a Visigoth army under Athanaric south of the Danube River. During the ensuing fighting and negotiations, Valens released the imprisoned mercenaries. At the same time, however, he and Generals Victor and Arintheus crossed the Danube into Visigoth territory and in 369 forced a treaty on the Visigoths by which they recognized the Danube as the boundary between their territory and that of Rome. Had Valens been more accommodating toward the Visigoths, he might well have secured a large loyal population from which to draw soldiers.

Following the renewal of warfare with the Persians, in 373 Valens departed Constantinople for Antioch to campaign against them. While Valens had been occupied with the Persians, during 374–375 western emperor Valentinian had been fighting the Quadis and Sarmatians. Roman general Marcellinus had treacherously killed Gabinus, king of the Quadis, when the latter was trying to resolve a border dispute peacefully. The infuriated Quadis then attacked and laid waste to Pannonia and much of the upper and middle Danube region. Valentinian arrived from Gaul and forced the Quadis back across the Danube but died in 375 while in the midst of preparations for a punitive expedition across the Danube. Valentinian's 16-year-old son

Flavius Gratianus (Gratian) succeeded him as western emperor. Gratian (r. 375–383) was immediately confronted by pressure from the Goths to northward.

In the early 370s the Huns were on the move westward. Fearsome warriors and apparently descendants of the Xiongnu (Hsiung-nu) tribes driven from Mongolia by the Chinese two centuries earlier, they invaded and conquered the area between the Volga and Don Rivers. The Huns won a decisive victory over the Alans here in the Battle of the Tanais River (ca. 373) and within two years had completely conquered Alan territory. In 376 Goth forces fought but failed to halt a major Hun invasion west of the Dnieper River. Goth king Ermanaric was either killed or committed suicide fighting the Huns; his successor, Withimer, was also slain fighting them.

Hunish victories forced the Ostrogoths, led by Alatheus and Saphrax, to flee westward across the Dniester. Visigoth leader Athanaric wanted to fight the invaders, but some 700,000 to 1 million of his people, led by Fritigern and Alavius, fled in panic to the Danube. Athanaric and the remainder of the Visigoths sought refuge in the Carpathian and Transylvanian forests.

The Visigoths appealed to Valens for refuge and protection. He reluctantly agreed, insisting that the warriors give up their weapons and that all male children be surrendered to the Romans as hostages. Agreeing to these conditions, the Visigoths began crossing the Danube into Roman territory. Most of the boys were given up and scattered around the empire in Asia Minor, but many warriors kept their weapons, bribing local Roman officials with gold and other valuables as well as the favors of their wives and daughters. Meanwhile, the remnants of the Ostrogoth community reached the Danube and also appealed for sanctuary. Although this was refused, they crossed the river into Roman territory anyway, pillaging widely.

Eastern Roman officials, overwhelmed by the large influx of refugees, made little or no effort to accommodate the new arrivals. In fact, they mistreated and exploited them economically, often forcing them to sell their children into slavery to stay alive. Visigoth leaders Fritigern and Alavius at first sought to cooperate with the Romans; rebuffed, they negotiated with the Ostrogoths.

The Romans made matters worse by treacherously attacking Visigoth leaders during a parley in 377. The Romans killed Alavius, but Fritigern was able to escape. He immediately assembled an army and attacked and defeated the Romans under Lupicinus at Marianopolis (Shumla, in eastern Bulgaria). Fritigern then joined other forces under Alatheus and Saphrax in the area between the lower Danube and the Black Sea (known today as Dobruja, shared by Romania and Bulgaria). Thus began the Goth War of 377–382.

Valens responded to the Goth pressure by concluding a hasty peace with the Persians that in effect yielded all Armenia to them. Returning to Europe in 377, Valens sent strong troop reinforcements to Thrace. His generals Richomeres, Trajanus, and Profuturus drove the Goths north into a marshy area of the mouth of the Danube in present-day Bulgaria. The Goths employed their wagons to build makeshift forts, and in the Battle of ad Salices ("by the Willows") they fought a bloody but indecisive battle in which both sides suffered heavy casualties. (The battlefield was described for years afterward as "white with bones.")

While the Romans were preparing another attack, Fritigern and most of the remaining Goths managed to escape through the marshes. The Goths then split into several bands and went on a rampage through Thrace and Moesia aided by some Sarmatian, Alan, and Hun horsemen. One of the larger groups of barbarians headed for the town of Dibaltum, where they surprised a Roman force making camp there. The Roman general Barzimeres led his cavalry in a mad charge against the Goths, saving the rest of his force but at the cost of his own life.

By 378 the entire northern frontier of the Roman Empire was ablaze from the mouth of the Rhine to the lower Danube. Valens now sought reinforcements from his nephew Gratian in Italy. Gratian, gathering forces to assist his uncle, was instead obliged to march to Gaul. There he defeated major invasions by the Alemannis and Franks. In the May 378 Battle of Argentaria (near present-day Colmar) he nearly wiped out an Alemanni army of 40,000 men under their ruler Prianus, who was slain. Crossing the Rhine, Gratian then led a punitive expedition into Germany, pacifying the frontier with Gaul and allowing him to march in the Danube River Valley to join his uncle.

In the summer of 378, meanwhile, Valens's generals drove the Goths back in Thrace toward the city of Adrianople, west of Constantinople on the Maritza River. Valens's principal general, Sebastian, had trained a small reliable force, and he now conducted a series of successful hit-and-run attacks. Sebastian recommended a continuation of this strategy, believing that it would eventually force the Goths to depart. Valens, however, favored a large pitched battle, believing that his forces would have the advantage against what he considered to be poorly trained Goth levies.

Some eight miles from Adrianople (Hadrianopolis), Fritigern and the Visigoths set up camp in an excellent defensive position on high ground with a perimeter circle of wagons. The Visigoths were primarily an infantry force, while the Ostrogoths provided the bulk of the cavalry. The Goth cavalry then departed to forage for provisions to feed the camp population of perhaps 300,000 people (100,000 warriors and 200,000 women and children).

Jealous of Gratian's success and anxious to achieve a glorious victory of his own before his nephew could arrive with reinforcements, Valens foolishly decided to press the issue, departing Adrianople with his legions at dawn on August 9 after leaving behind under suitable guard his treasury and baggage. After a rapid advance in extreme heat over rough ground, at about 2:00 p.m. Valens and his legions came on Fritigern's camp. Valens commanded some 50,000 men; Fritigern had twice that number, the majority of them cavalry.

Fritigern sent negotiators to Valens to buy time for the Ostrogoth cavalry to return. Valens also stalled in order to rest and deploy his men, but he finally broke off negotiations. Before the Romans could complete their deployment of infantry in the center and cavalry on the wings, however, the Goth cavalry returned and fell on the Roman right-wing cavalry. Although the Roman cavalry fought well, it was badly outnumbered and broke. When this happened, the Ostrogoth cavalry under Alatheus and Saphrax drove against the still not completely deployed Roman infantry. Blinded by dust kicked up by the horses, the foot soldiers were driven back into a mass so tight that many could not even draw their swords, let alone use them.

The Ostrogoths then subjected the Roman infantry to attack by arrows. Seeing the situation, Fritigern attacked with his infantry, their long slashing swords and battle-axes exacting a terrible toll. Reportedly some 40,000 Romans perished, including both Valens and Sebastiani.

Called by one Roman historian the greatest defeat for Rome since the Battle of Cannae in 216 BCE, the Battle of Adrianople (Hadrianopolis, Edirne) did not immediately affect the Roman Empire, however. The Goths rampaged through the Balkans for a time, but Gratian appointed Theodosius, son of his father's great general of the same name and a successful military commander in his own right, as the new Roman emperor in the East. Establishing his headquarters at Thessalonika, Theodosius worked to build up the defenses of Greece and Thrace and to restore the morale and discipline of the shattered Roman military in the East.

By 381 Theodosius I, known to history as Theodosius the Great (r. 379–395 in the East and after 392 also in the West), had begun to send out units to confront and destroy smaller barbarian detachments in sharp, small actions, wearing down his enemy in the process. After restoring order in Thrace, Theodosius mounted two successful campaigns against the Goths during 382–383, defeating Fritigern in central Thrace. The Visigoth leader died at this time, possibly in battle with the Romans.

While Theodosius was active in Thrace, his general Promotus was operating against the Ostrogoths under Altheus and Saphrax south of the Danube. Demonstrating great ability, patience, and a conciliatory approach, Theodosius was finally able to pacify completely both Thrace and Moesia, in the process driving large numbers of Goths north of the Danube. In October 382

he concluded a peace settlement, permitting other Goths to settle down and become citizens of the empire in return for military service.

The Gothic War had far-reaching political significance. The Goths had defeated and killed a Roman emperor, destroyed a Roman army, and laid waste to much of the empire's Balkan holdings. The Roman Empire also for the first time had negotiated a peace settlement with barbarians inside the territory of the empire. This was not lost on other barbarian peoples. Within 100 years the western empire would collapse under the pressure of continued invasions as the empire was carved up into barbarian kingdoms.

Following the death of Theodosius in 396, rule over the Roman Empire passed to his two largely incapable sons, Arcadius in the East and Honorius in the West. Visigoth chieftain Alaric took advantage of the situation to ravage much of Thrace and Greece. He was briefly delayed by capable Roman general Stilicho, who had marched an army from Italy to Greece. Fearing Stilicho and his own brother more than the Goths, Arcadius insisted that Stilicho return to Italy, and Stilicho reluctantly obeyed, allowing Alaric to resume his plundering, now joined by two other Gothic leaders, the Ostrogoth Tribigild and a Visigoth general, Gainas, who was formerly in the Roman Army. Together they and their men laid waste to much of Asia Minor.

Only Stilicho's enterprise kept the empire together. During 395–400 he was in effect the uncrowned ruler of the empire. In 401 Alaric led an invasion of northern Italy but was driven out in 403 following a series of victories by Stilicho. Alaric and the Visigoths returned in 409 and moved against Rome. Rome surrendered on August 24, 410, following a brief siege. Alaric then turned Rome over to his troops, permitting a controlled six-day sack of the city in the first occasion that Rome had ever been occupied by foreign invaders. Alaric was preparing to invade Sicily when he died. The Visigoths then temporarily took up residence in Provence.

In 405 another Gothic chieftain, Radagaisus, led a large invasion of northern Italy, but the next year Stilicho defeated him at Florence. Radagaisus was executed, and his followers were enslaved. Stilicho, however, was murdered in 408 on the instigation of jealous western emperor Honorius.

In 406 another barbarian people, the Vandals, who had also been pushed eastward by the Huns, were joined by the other Germanic tribes of the Alan and Suebi peoples in an invasion of Gaul. Rebuffed by the Franks, they entered Iberia and conquered all of it by 428.

The Huns also continued their westward drive. They first tested the Eastern Roman Empire in 409. Crossing the Danube into Thrace, they were then expelled. Led by their great chieftain Attila, known to Christians as "the Scourge of God," they again crossed the Danube and, after destroying a Roman army near Constantinople in 440, extracted a considerable tribute from eastern emperor Theodosius II. Moving westward, in 451 they crossed the Rhine into Gaul.

In order to meet the threat posed by the Huns, Aetius, the de facto Roman ruler in the West, raised a large army consisting of his Gothic Roman legions and allied forces, including those of King Theodoric of Toulouse, who was convinced that the security of his kingdom rested on loyalty to the empire. Meanwhile, as half of

Attila's forces laid waste to much of northern Gaul, in early April 451 Attila and the remainder of his men arrived in the Loire Valley and laid siege to Aurelianum (present-day Orléans) on the Loire. Apparently King Sangiban of the Alans had sent word to Attila that he would surrender the city, but he went back on this with the arrival of Aetius and Theodoric.

On the arrival at Aurelianum of Aetius and Theodoric and their men, Attila sent for the remainder of his army and withdrew northward. Crossing the Seine, Attila left a Gepid force to cover his withdrawal, but Aetius destroyed Attila's rear guard in a night attack, reportedly inflicting 15,000 casualties. The Battle of Châlons (also known as the Battle of Campus Mauriacus) occurred the next day.

The exact date is in dispute. Possibilities range from late June to late September 451. The place is also in dispute, but most historians believe that it occurred on the Mauriac Plain (present-day Mery-sur-Seine), about 20 miles northwest of Troyes and 35 miles south of Châlons-sur-Marne.

Attila selected a defensive position somewhere between Troyes and Châlons that was most likely to favor his cavalry. Aetius arrived, his own forces joined by a number of Frankish deserters from Attila's forces. Still, Aetius was badly outnumbered.

The battle began late in the day, perhaps about 5:00 p.m., in a struggle for possession of an important ridgeline. The Visigoths reached the ridge first and then repelled the advancing Huns. The two opposing sides then closed in sanguinary combat. Elderly King Theodoric fell from his horse and was trampled to death by his own men. The Visigoths then turned and rolled up the Hun left flank. Reportedly, Attila narrowly escaped death or capture.

Aetius and his men broke through the Gepid line. Attila then ordered the Huns to stage a fighting retreat to their camp, which was encircled with wagons. As darkness fell, the Visigoths attempted to storm the camp but were repulsed.

Casualties in the battle were such that neither side sought a resumption of fighting the next day. Contemporary estimates of the dead in the battle range from 165,000 to 300,000, although even the smaller figure is believed to be a gross exaggeration. Nonetheless, the coalition victory at Châlons is correctly regarded as one of the most decisive in history. It probably saved Western Europe from falling under Asiatic control. The battle also established the Merovingian dynasty of the Franks (who give their name to France) under Meroveus, who fought in the battle against the Huns. While remaining allies of the Romans, Meroveus and his son Childeric nonetheless continued to expand Frankish control in Gaul.

After the battle Aetius and Thorismund considered trying to cut off and starve out the Hunnish camp. Perhaps Aetius feared that completely ending the Hunnish threat would too greatly strengthen the Visigoths in Gaul. In any case, Attila was permitted to depart and withdraw across the Rhine. Thorismund, the new king of the Visigoths, returned with his warriors to Toulouse and there consolidated his rule.

In 452 Attila and the Huns invaded Italy from across the Julian Alps, destroying Aquileia. To escape the invaders, the inhabitants of Venetia sought refuge on islands off the coast in what is traditionally regarded as the founding of the city of Venice. Attila next destroyed Padua. Aetius, aware of events, hurried from Gaul to Italy with a small force and took up position along the Po to block the principal river crossings. Attila then learned that one of his lieutenants had suffered defeat in northeastern Illyricum (today parts of Albania, Croatia, and Bosnia). Famine and pestilence were now rampant in Italy, greatly increasing pressure on Attila, who also was finding it difficult to secure food. At this point Pope Leo I arrived in Attila's camp to confer with him. Tradition holds that the pope's saintly demeanor so impressed Attila that he now decided to withdraw, but it is more likely that Leo offered Attila a bribe.

Attila died in 453 before he could mount yet another invasion of the Western Roman Empire, and his vast empire soon collapsed as his sons maneuvered among themselves for the throne and as the subject peoples of the empire revolted. The Huns soon disappeared from European history. In 454, meanwhile, jealous western emperor Valentinian II caused the death of Aetius. The successionist struggles, if anything, intensified.

Meanwhile, the Vandals, pressed by the Visigoths in Iberia during 415–419, invaded North Africa in 429. By 435 they had conquered all North Africa except eastern Numidia (present-day Tunisia). They then took Corsica, Sardinia, and Sicily. In 455 they also took and sacked Rome before withdrawing. The next year they invaded Spain and soon secured all Iberia, which they then held for the next two centuries. In 476 Odoacer deposed the last western Roman emperor, Romulus Augustus, and became the first king of Italy. The Eastern Roman Empire, or Byzantine Empire, continued until it too was conquered by the Muslims in their great Siege of Constantinople of 1453.

Significance

Although other factors were clearly at play in its demise, the barbarian invasions were a major factor in the destruction of the Roman Empire. Europe was now divided into a number of small states. Despite the considerable cost in depopulation wrought by the fighting, Europe itself had been preserved from Asiatic control. Militarily the Goth influence led to a sharp increase in the numbers of cavalry, and the army of the Eastern Roman Empire became predominantly a cavalry force. This would continue for the next 1,000 years until the 15th century, when cavalry was neutralized by the longbow and the crossbow.

Further Reading

Barford, Paul M. *The Early Slavs: Culture and Society in Early Medieval Eastern Europe.* Ithaca, NY: Cornell University Press, 2001.

Burns, Thomas S. *Barbarians within the Gates of Rome.* Bloomington: Indiana University Press, 1994.

Burns, Thomas S. *Rome and the Barbarians, 100 B.C.–A.D. 400.* Baltimore: Johns Hopkins University Press, 2003.

Curta, Florin. *The Making of the Slavs: History and Archaeology of the Lower Danube Region, c. 500–700.* New York: Cambridge University Press, 2001.

Ferrill, Arthur. *The Fall of the Roman Empire: The Military Explanation.* London: Thames and Hudson, 1986.

Gibbon, Edward. *Decline and Fall of the Roman Empire.* 6 vols. New York: Everyman's Library, 2010.

Grant, Michael. *The Army of the Caesars.* New York: Scribner, 1974.

Heather, Peter. *Empires and Barbarians: The Fall of Rome and the Birth of Europe.* New York: Oxford University Press, 2010.

Heather, Peter. *The Goths.* London: Blackwell, 1996.

Luttwak, Edward, ed. *The Grand Strategy of the Roman Empire.* Baltimore: Johns Hopkins University Press, 1976.

MacMullen, Ramsay. *Corruption and the Decline of Rome.* New Haven, CT: Yale University Press, 1990.

Whittaker, Charles. *Frontiers of the Roman Empire.* Baltimore: Johns Hopkins University Press, 1994.

Williams, Stephen, and Gerard Friell. *Theodosius: The Empire at Bay.* New Haven, CT: Yale University Press, 1995.

Muslim Wars of Expansion (623–732)

Dates	623–732
Location	Middle East, North Africa, Spain, Mediterranean, Central Asia
Combatants	Muslims vs. Byzantines, Persians, Libyans, Tunisians, Berbers, Indians, Ottoman Turks, Chinese, Iberians, Franks
Principal Commanders	Muslim: Muhammad, Khalid ibn al-Walid, Abu Bekr, Abu Jahl, Abd ul-Malik, Tarik ibn Ziyad, Suleiman the General, Maslama, Abd-ar-Rahmān Persians: Mihran, Rustam Byzantines: Mahan, Heraclius, Constans II, Justinian II, Leo III Franks: Charles Martel
Principal Battles	Badr, Trench, Mecca, Muta, Fihl, Bridge, Yarmouk, al-Qādisiyyah, Ram Hormuz, Nahavend, Lycia, Armorium, Cyzicus, Constantinople, Sebastopolis, Guadalete, Tours
Outcome	The Muslims create a vast empire stretching from the Indus River in the east to the Atlantic Ocean in the west.

Causes

The wars of Muslim territorial expansion are traced to the Prophet Muhammad and his desire and that of his followers to spread their new faith. Inspired by what he believed to have been a series of divine revelations beginning in 610, Muhammad began espousing a new monotheist and egalitarian religion known as Islam. In 622 he organized the tribes of Yathrib (now Medina) into a community under the will of God (Allah) as revealed in his teachings. As with Moses, however, Muhammad was both prophet and military commander, and he sought to expand the faith by force of arms.

Course

Muhammad's initial military campaign was against the prominent trading city of Mecca. Beginning in 623 Muhammad raided Meccan caravans, and in early 624 he ordered out a dozen men to attack a small caravan from Yemen to Mecca. Acting as pilgrims bound for Mecca, his followers located the caravan and joined it. They faced the problem of it being a holy month in Arabia during which warfare was forbidden. If they obeyed this stricture they would reach the holy city of Mecca, where fighting was also forbidden. In order to carry out their mission, the raiders decided to violate the first rule and fell on the guards, killing one and capturing two others.

Widely condemned for the raid, Muhammad replied that the merchants of Medina were guilty of greater sins than any violation by his men of the holy month. As a consequence of the raid, however, the leaders of Mecca were determined to destroy Muhammad. To accomplish this, they planned to send out as bait a rich caravan from Sinai to Mecca, tricking Muhammad

into a battle in which he would be badly outnumbered and destroyed.

Muhammad took the bait, and in early March 624 he led some 300 men from Medina to intercept the caravan. Most of his men were on foot. Reportedly, they had only 70 camels and 2 horses. The Meccans sent out almost 1,300 men. Led by Abu Jahl, they were far better armed and equipped. They had some 700 camels and 100 horses, and reportedly half the men were protected by chain mail armor.

Meccan caravan leader Abu Sufyan learned by careful reconnaissance the location of Muhammad's ambush force and diverted the convoy accordingly. It arrived safely in Mecca, and Abu Sufyan so informed Abu Jahl. Seeing no need for battle in these circumstances, however, some 400 Meccans deserted Abu Jahl. Determined to do battle with Muhammad, Abu Jahl informed the remainder that they would travel to the wells at Badr, some 25 miles southwest of Mecca, and there celebrate the safe passage of the caravan.

Muhammad's men were lying in wait at Badr. Learning from pickets of Abu Jahl's approach, Muhammad called a council on the evening of March 14. After representatives of both his Mecca and Medina followers pledged their support, Muhammad announced that he intended to give battle. On the advice of his second-in-command Abu Bakr, Muhammad ordered all the wells except one stopped up, then positioned his men around it.

On March 15 Abu Jahl's men arrived, nearly out of water. They approached the one serviceable well, situated on rising ground. Muhammad, seated under a tent, ordered his men to maintain their positions and attack only on his order. In the meantime, they met Abu Jahl's men with arrows. Reportedly, a sandstorm struck the

Meccans as they advanced, causing their attack to falter. Muhammad then ordered his own men forward. The Meccan force broke and ran, leaving behind 70 dead and an equal number as prisoners. Abu Jahl was wounded in the battle and was among those taken prisoner. He was beheaded after he refused to acknowledge Allah as the real victor.

Many people in Arabia chose to see the victory of Muhammad's badly outnumbered and poorly armed and equipped force in the Battle of Badr as a sign from God. The battle added immensely to Muhammad's reputation, especially as a military leader. Defeat at Badr would probably have brought his death.

Muhammad's forces were, however, defeated in the Battle of Ohod in 625. Two years later in the Battle of the Trench (also known as the Battle of the Confederates) during late April to early May 627, some 3,000 followers of Muhammad withstood a two-week siege of Medina by some 10,000 Meccan and allied forces. Following a period of truce, fighting resumed, and Muhammad and his followers captured Mecca by assault in 630. Mecca then converted to Islam.

Meanwhile, a long period of warfare between the Byzantine Empire and Persia during 602–628 had severely weakened both states and their ability to stand against a tide of Muslim conquest. In the initial Muslim raid into Byzantine Palestine in 629, however, the Byzantines turned back the Muslims in the Battle of Muta.

By the time of Muhammad's death from natural causes in June 632, he had established control over most of Arabia and created there a theocratic state. Abu Bekr became the first caliph, or successor to Muhammad. Initially there was some resistance to his rule, but in the so-called Ridda Wars (632–634), assisted by his great general Khalid ibn al-Walid, Abu Bekr put down revolts by several apostates, the last being Musaylima in the Battle of Akraba in 633. The Arab tribes were again united.

The new Arabian state now confronted the two great empires of Persia and Byzantium. With both these states now seriously weakened, Islamic forces took the offensive, first expanding beyond Arabia in 632. Taking advantage of chaos in the Persian Sasanian Empire following the death of King Kavadh II, Khalid ibn al-Walid led an invasion of Persian Mesopotamia. Concurrently, Amr ibn al-As invaded Byzantine territory in Palestine and Syria. Byzantine forces replied with a counteroffensive. Khalid ibn al-Walid marched to Amr's relief and in the Battle of Ajnadain, between Gaza and Jerusalem, defeated Byzantine forces under General Theodore in July 634. Khalid pursued the Byzantines and again defeated them in the Battle of Fihl (Pella or Gilead) near Baisan in January 635. Continuing north, Muslim commander Abu Ubaidah ibn al-Jarrah and Khalid once more defeated Byzantine forces, under Baanes, in the Battle of Marjal-Saffar near Damascus. The Muslims then took Emesa (Homs) and Damascus.

Upon the departure of Muslim general Khalid ibn al-Walid for Palestine, Persian general Mihran defeated the remaining Muslim forces in the Battle of the Bridge (on the Euphrates River) in 634. However, reinforcing Muslim forces halted the Persian pursuit the next year in the Battle of Buwayb, south of Kufa.

In mid-August 636, Arab forces of the Rashidun Caliphate, led by Abu Ubaidah ibn al-Jarrah and Khalid ibn al-Walid, came together with Byzantine Empire forces under Mahan in Palestine next to the Yarmouk (Yarmuk, Yarmūk) River, the

EXPANSION OF ISLAM, 814

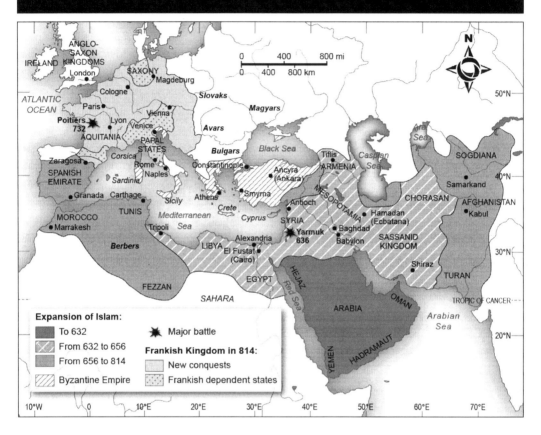

largest tributary of the Jordan. The battle was the culmination of Caliph Abu Bekr's order in 634 for Muslim forces to invade Syria that had seen the Arabs capture Damascus and most of Palestine. Faced with these developments, Byzantine emperor Heraclius assembled a large force at Antioch. Organized as five separate armies, it was a polyglot force that included native Byzantines as well as Slavs, Franks, Armenians, Georgians, and Christian Arabs.

Heraclius sought to take advantage of the fact that the Arab forces were separated into four main armies, at Palestine, in Jordan, at Caesarea, and at Emesa in Syria. The emperor planned to concentrate his own forces and defeat the Arabs in detail.

In June 636 he sent reinforcements under his son Constantine to Caesarea, hoping to tie down Arab forces there, while ordering his remaining four armies on converging axes toward Damascus and Emesa. With this Byzantine advance, the Arabs abandoned their conquests of both Emesa and Damascus.

Meanwhile, the Arabs learned the broad outlines of the Byzantine plan from prisoners, and in a council of war Abu Ubaidah ibn al-Jarrah accepted the advice of his subordinate, Khalid ibd al-Walid, to withdraw from northern and central Syria and concentrate on the plain of Yarmouk, which was more suitable for cavalry operations. Close to the Rashidun stronghold of Najd, this location also offered an escape route.

The Byzantines camped just north of the Wadi-ur-Raqqad. The two sides conducted protracted negotiations, but these soon collapsed. Muslim accounts place the Byzantine force at 200,000–250,000 men and their own army at only 24,000–40,000. Modern estimates are on the order of 50,000–100,000 for the Byzantines and only 7,500–25,000 for the Arabs. Whatever the figures, all accounts agree that the Arabs were heavily outnumbered.

Byzantine commander Mahan formed his four armies in a line of battle some 12 miles wide. On the Muslim side, Khalid offered to assume command of the army for the battle; Abu Ubaidah, who lacked the experience of his subordinate, accepted. Khalid's forces held a total front of about 10 miles, with the Muslim left anchored on the Yarmouk River.

The battle opened in mid-August 636 with the two armies less than a mile apart and lasted six days. The Byzantines began with an advance by all four armies in line. The initial assault was not a strong one, however, as Mahan was endeavoring to locate weak points in the Muslim line.

On the second day Mahan attacked at dawn, launching two armies against the Muslim center to fix the Muslim forces in place, but with the main thrusts coming on the flanks. The Byzantines made considerable headway in each of their flanking attacks and came close to achieving victory. Khalid's cavalry reserve was the difference; it shored up first the Muslim right, then the left. On the third day the Byzantines attacked again, this time trying to break through where the Muslim right flank joined the center. Again the Muslim mobile reserve averted disaster and pushed the Byzantines back.

On the fourth day the Byzantines again came close to victory. Believing that the previous day's assault had severely weakened the Muslim right wing, Mahan resumed the attack there. The Armenian portion of the Byzantine army broke completely through the Muslim line and drove on their camp. Khalid's cavalry reserve again averted disaster. Khalid split it into two main bodies to attack the Armenians on each flank. Facing Muslim forces on three sides, the Armenians were forced to withdraw, and the original line was restored.

Early on the fifth day, Mahan dispatched an emissary to the Muslims asking for a truce of several days to conduct negotiations. Abu Ubaidah was willing to accept the proposal, but Khalid was opposed, and the battle continued, although there was no major fighting that day.

To this point, the Muslims had remained on the defensive. On the sixth day, assuming correctly that Byzantine morale was flagging, Khalid ordered an attack. He planned to use his cavalry to defeat that of the Byzantines, leaving their infantry without cavalry support and open to attacks from the flanks and rear. He also planned a major simultaneous flanking attack on the Byzantine left that would roll up their line against the river ravine to the west. While Mahan was attempting to organize his own cavalry, the Muslim cavalry struck en masse, forcing the Byzantine horsemen to withdraw to the north and abandon the infantry. Khalid then directed his cavalry to attack the rear of the Armenian infantry on the Byzantine left. Under the pressure of a three-pronged attack of Muslim cavalry from the rear and infantry from the east and south, the Armenians broke, carrying the rest of the Byzantine army with them. Pinned against the steep ravines of the Yarmouk so closely that they were hardly able to use their weapons, the Byzantines were slaughtered in large numbers. Many others were killed or maimed by falling into the ravines.

The Battle of Yarmouk secured Syria and Palestine for the Muslims. Khalid then reoccupied both Damascus and Emesa. Emperor Heraclius returned to Constantinople to consolidate his forces against a Muslim drive in Egypt.

Caliph Umar (Omar) dispatched Sa'd ibn Abi Waqqas and a new Arab 30,000-man army against Persia. Sa'd defeated a Sassanid Persian force of 50,000 men under Rustam in the Battle of al-Qādisiyyah during November 16–19, 636. This strategically significant encounter led to the Muslim capture of the Persian capital of Ctesiphon several months later. Sa'd and the Arabs defeated the Persians again in the Battle of Jalula in December 637.

During 637–645 the Arabs completed the conquest of Syria and Palestine. Among prominent places taken were Jerusalem and Antioch (638), Aleppo (639), Caesarea and Gaza (640), and Tripoli (645). Most fell after lengthy sieges. At the same time, during 639–641 the Arab forces conquered all of remaining Byzantine Mesopotamia.

Egypt was the next Muslim target, beginning in 639. In July 640, General Amir ibn al-As was victorious over Byzantine forces in the Battle of Babylon, near Helliopolis. Following long sieges, he captured the fortified cities of Babylon in April 641 and Alexandria in September 642.

During 640–650 the Arab armies conquered what remained of Persian territory. Following decisive Muslim Arab victories in the Battle of Ram Hormuz in 640 and the Battle of Nahavend in 641, organized Persian resistance came to an end. During the next decade the Arabs solidified their control over what had been the Sassanid Persian

Empire, with the Oxus River the boundary between Arab and Turkish territory.

During 642–643 the Muslims expanded into North Africa from Egypt. Under Abdullah ibn Zubayr, they captured Cyrene and Tripoli, then raided farther west. In 645 Muslim forces under Amr turned back an ineffectual Byzantine effort to recapture Alexandria. A revolt within the city, however, forced Amr to retake Alexandria by storm.

At the same time, the Arabs were taking to the sea. The growing strength of their naval forces in the eastern Mediterranean was shown in their capture in 649 of Cyprus. The Arabs also raided Sicily in 652 and secured Rhodes in 654.

In 655 Byzantine emperor Constans II personally led a large fleet to attack the Arabs. Constans had perhaps 1,000 warships; the Arabs under Abdullah ibn Sa'd had far fewer. The Battle of Lycia, or Battle of the Masts (Dhat al-sawari), occurred at Phoinike (off the Lycian coast). The Byzantines had the best of the fighting on the first day of the two-day battle, but the two sides agreed to a truce for the night, and Abdullah used this respite to lash his ships together with chains and win the battle the next day. This was the first great Arab victory at sea, on the second day. Reportedly, some 500 Byzantine ships were destroyed. Emperor Constans was wounded but escaped.

During 657–661 a civil war occurred within the Rashidun Caliphate. The revolt of Talha and Zubayr, although suppressed in Basra with the Battle of the Camel in 657, sparked civil war and shelved Arab plans to attack Constantinople. The civil war brought the division of Islam into the Sunni and Shia factions. Because of this, new caliph Mur'awiya concluded peace with the Byzantine Empire in 659, agreeing to pay an annual tribute. Mur'awiya founded the Umayyad dynasty, the rule of which traditionally dates from 661 to 750.

During 661–663, Ziyad ibn Abihi carried out the first Muslim raids against India. These penetrated Sind and the lower Indus River Valley. In 664, repeated Muslim invasions of Afghanistan from 652 brought the temporary capture of Kabul.

In 668 warfare was renewed between the Byzantine Empire and the Umayyad Caliphate. Muslim forces invaded Anatolia and reached Chalcedon on the Asian side of the Bosporus. They crossed the Bosporus to attack Constantinople itself but were repulsed in 669. The Byzantines then virtually destroyed the Arab army at Armorium and retook the city. The Byzantines also repulsed the Arab naval attack on Constantinople.

In 672 the Byzantines virtually destroyed an Arab fleet in the Battle of Cyzicus in the Sea of Marmora. The Byzantine use of a combustible mixture known as Greek fire, perhaps the first time it was employed in warfare at sea, was a major factor in the victory. Undeterred by this setback, the Arabs soon dispatched other forces and maintained an intermittent land and sea blockade of Constantinople during 673–677. The Byzantines were hard-pressed because the Arabs also raided Anatolia, and concurrently the Slavs attacked Thessalonika. This war was effectively ended by the Byzantine naval victory in the Sea of Marmora off Syllaeum. Again, Greek fire played a key role. The withdrawing Arab ships were caught in a storm, and nearly all were lost. The Byzantines also defeated the Arabs on land. Caliph Mur'awiya then agreed to peace terms; the Arabs agreed to evacuate Cyprus and to pay an annual tribute to Constantinople and to maintain the peace for 30 years.

In 674, meanwhile, Arab forces invaded and conquered Transoxiana in Central Asia. The next year the Byzantines were forced to embark on a struggle in the Balkans. Taking advantage of war between the Byzantine Empire and the Umayyads, the Slavs invaded Thessalonika but were repulsed. Isperich, ruler of the Bulgars, led a large invasion force across the Danube and defeated Byzantine forces sent against him. In 680 he forced Emperor Constantine IV to cede the province of Moesia.

In 681 Arab forces reached Morocco. An Arab army led by Okba ibn Nafi gained the Atlantic before being driven back into Cyrene by the Berbers, who acted in alliance with the Byzantine forces at Carthage. Okba was killed during the withdrawal.

In 685 Justinian II become sole Byzantine emperor on his father's death. Only 16 years old, he took advantage of peace with the Arabs to recover the Balkans, which had come under the control of Slavic tribes. Defeating the Bulgars during 688–689, Justinian entered Thessalonika, the second most important Byzantine city in Europe. He then resettled the Bulgars in Anatolia and secured 30,000 of them for his army.

Emboldened by the additional manpower, Justinian renewed the war with the Arabs during 690–692 but was defeated by the Umayyads in the Battle of Sebastopolis (Sevastopol) on the western shore of the Black Sea in 692. The Byzantine loss resulted from the defection of upward of 20,000 Slavs because of harsh treatment under Justinian and Arab bribes. Reportedly, in the aftermath of the battle the emperor ordered the deaths of every Slavic family in Bithynia. The Arabs then took all Armenia.

During 690–691 there was civil war within the Umayyad Caliphate. Forces under Caliph Abd ul-Malik (r. 685–705) reconquered Iraq and Arabia, taking Medina in 691 and Mecca in 692. By 698 Abd ul-Malik was again the undisputed ruler of all Muslim territory.

Arab operations continued in North Africa, where during 693–698 their forces conquered Tunisia. Byzantine influence in North Africa came to an end with the capture of Carthage in 698. Meanwhile, Justinian II's harsh rule led to his overthrow as emperor.

In 699 Ibn al-Ash'ath led an Arab army in revolt against al-Hajjaj ibn Yusuf, overall governor of the eastern Muslim territories. Marching to Iraq, ibn al-Ash'ath occupied Basra and then moved against Kufa, winning the indecisive Battle of Dair al-Jamajim against al-Hajjaj and forcing him into Kufa. After receiving reinforcements, al-Hajjaj defeated ibn al-Ash'ath in the Battle of Maskin on the Dujail River in 701, ending the rebellion.

In 703 the Berbers defeated an Arab army under Hassan ibn No'man near Mount Aurasius (Aures Mountains) in present-day Algeria, but two years later they concluded an alliance with the Arabs that allowed the latter to conquer all North Africa.

Deposed Byzantine emperor Justinian II escaped imprisonment and worked out a secret arrangement with the Bulgars. Thanks to their military support, he returned to power in Constantinople in 705 and began a six-year reign of terror there before his forces were defeated by 711 in intermittent wars with both his former ally Terbelis, ruler of the Bulgars, and the Arabs.

During 705–715 Caliph al-Walid, the son of Caliph Abd ul-Malik, pushed the caliphate to the greatest territorial extent of any Muslim empire under one ruler. Additions included Bokhara, Samarkand, Khwarizm (Kiva), Ferghana, and Tashkent. Muslim forces also raided into Sinkiang, as far as Tashkent, in 713. Kabul was taken in 708, and the Sind was secured during 708–712. Multan was taken after a long siege, and Umayyad raids extended into the Punjab. The Gujaras repulsed subsequent Arab raids into Rajputana and Gujrat, however. During 708–711, Arab forces under Musa ibn Nusair conquered northwestern Africa.

In 710 having reached the Strait of Gibraltar, Musa ibn Nusair launched raids across it into Spain. Visigoth forces under Count Julian initially repelled these, but Julian soon concluded an alliance with Musa whereby the latter promised assistance against Julian's sovereign, Visigoth king of Spain Roderick. In July an Arab reconnaissance led by Abu Zora Tarif crossed the straits and landed in Spain in the vicinity of Algeciras.

The following year Musa sent 7,000 men under Tarik ibn Ziyad across the straits to Gibraltar, which was then named for him (Gebel-al-Tarik, or the Rock of Tarik). Tarik moved northwest and, between the Barbate and Guadalete Rivers, met a Visigoth army of some 90,000 men, led in person by King Roderick. Tarik had been reinforced but still commanded only some 12,000 men. Despite the great disparity in numbers, Tarik triumphed in the Battle of the Guadalete, near present-day Medina-Sidonia, on July 19, 711. This Muslim victory was made possible by widespread Visigothic dissension, outright treachery, and wholesale defections. Roderick was drowned attempting to flee.

Tarik then won another victory at Ecija. Consolidating his hold over southern Spain, he captured the Visigothic capital of Toledo without opposition. Musa then arrived and, except for a few small strongpoints in the

Asturias, completed the Muslim conquest of Spain in 712. That same year, Muslim forces raided north of the Pyrenees for the first time.

In 710 also, Muslim forces invaded Anatolia, conquering Cilicia in 711 and securing partial control of Galatia in 714. In 711 meanwhile Emperor Justinian II, who seemed more interested in punishing his own subjects than anything else, was defeated and killed in battle with an army led by his general Philippius in northwestern Armenia. Unfortunately for the empire, Philippius proved hopelessly inept as a ruler, with the result that the Bulgars reached Constantinople in 712 and the Arabs captured Ceicia and then invaded Pontus, taking Amasia (Amasya). The Byzantine Army then mutinied, replacing Philippius in 713 with Amastasius II, who restored internal order and began the reorganization and reform of the army. Certain elements in the army resisted this, and a new rebellion saw Amastasius replaced by Theodosius III in 715. He captured Constantinople following a six-month siege and sent his predecessor off to a monastery. In the meantime, however, a major Muslim force reached the ancient Greek city of Pergamum in Aeolis, some 16 miles from the Aegean. The failure of Theodosius to meet this threat brought to the throne one of his generals, Leo the Isaurian, who took the title of Leo III. In 716 Muslim forces under Yemenite general Yazid ibn Mohallin invaded and conquered the Transcaspian region.

The chief Muslim goal throughout the seventh and eighth centuries remained the acquisition of Constantinople. This great Byzantine capital city controlled the Bosporus and thus access between the Mediterranean and Black Seas. It also guarded the entrance to South-Central Europe. The

Arabs had tried before in 655 and in 669. Several attempts in the 670s were turned back when the Byzantines defeated the attackers at sea.

The greatest threat to the city and to Byzantium came in 717 under Caliph Suleiman (r. 715–717). Aware of Arab preparations, Leo III ordered granaries in Constantinople restocked and repairs made to the city walls. He also secured weapons and ordered siege engines installed.

Constantinople was secure as long as its sea communications remained open. The city was built on a promontory flanked on the north by the so-called Golden Horn, an inlet of the Bosporus forming a natural harbor, and on the south by the Sea of Marmora. The city was protected on its western, or landward, side by both inner and outer walls; the inner wall had been built under Emperor Constantine the Great. The outer wall was constructed under Emperor Theodosius II and was some four miles in length. Normally the city population numbered about half a million people, but in 717 it must have swelled from refugees.

Until the invention of gunpowder, the only practical way to take a strongly held city was by blockading and starving its population. This meant closing both the Bosporus and the Dardanelles—a difficult feat because Constantinople flanked the Bosporus from the south. Everything depended on the Byzantine fleet, which was markedly inferior in numbers to that of the attackers.

Maslama, brother of the caliph, commanded the operation against Constantinople. He took personal command of the land force of some 80,000 men and gave command of the 1,800-ship fleet transporting another 80,000 men to Suleiman the General. The attackers also had some 800 additional ships preparing in African and

Egyptian ports, while the caliph assembled a reserve army at Tarsus.

Maslama crossed over the Dardanelles to Europe, probably in July 717, and then moved overland to Constantinople, arriving there on August 15. He ordered his troops to entrench before the city, then attempted a land attack, which the Byzantines beat back. Maslama then ordered his men to surround his camp with a deep ditch and decided to reduce the city by blockade. He instructed Suleiman the General to divide his fleet into two squadrons, one to cut off supplies from reaching Constantinople via the Aegean and Dardanelles and the other to move through the Bosporus and sever communications with the city from the Black Sea.

In early September the second Muslim fleet got under way to sail north of the Golden Horn, where Leo III had his fleet. The entrance to the harbor was protected by a great chain, suspended between two towers, that could be raised or lowered. When the blockading squadron approached, the strong current in the Bosporus threw the leading ships into confusion. Leo immediately ordered the chain lowered, stood out with his galleys, and attacked the broken Muslim formation with Greek fire, destroying 20 ships and capturing others before retiring to the Golden Horn on the approach of Suleiman's main body.

Suleiman the General made no further attempt to force the strait, and Leo was thus able to bring in supplies and prevent Constantinople's surrender through starvation. To add to Maslama's difficulties, his brother, Caliph Suleiman, suddenly died, and his successor, Omar II, a religious bigot, was no soldier. Omar continued the siege by land, but then winter set in and was unusually severe with snow. Many

of the besiegers died in these conditions, among them Suleiman the General.

In the spring of 718, an Egyptian squadron of 400 ships arrived. Passing Constantinople at night, it closed the Bosporus. It was followed by a squadron from Africa of 360 ships and the reserve army to reinforce the land troops, who had reportedly been reduced to cannibalism. Although closure of the Bosporus would have in time forced Constantinople to surrender, a large number of the crewmen on the Egyptian ships were impressed Christians, and many were able to desert and provide accurate intelligence to Leo.

Choosing an opportune time when his enemy was unprepared, Leo again ordered the boom lowered and sortied from the Golden Horn to engage the Egyptian ships. The Christian crewmen deserted en masse; many Muslim vessels were destroyed by Greek fire, and others were captured. This gave Leo control of the Bosporus. He followed it up by ferrying over to the Asiatic side a sizable land force. It trapped and routed a number of Muslim troops.

Leo was also active diplomatically. He arranged an alliance with Terbelis, king of the Bulgars, who then marched against Maslama, defeating him, probably in July 718, somewhere south of Adrianople. Some 22,000 Muslim troops are said to have been killed. Leo made adroit use of disinformation as well, scattering reports that the Franks were preparing to send large forces.

The caliph finally recalled Maslama, who raised the siege on August 15. It had lasted exactly one year. The fleet embarked the army, landing them on the Asiatic shore of the Sea of Marmora. The ships then sailed for the Dardanelles, but en route they encountered a great storm. Reportedly only 5 galleys out of some

2,560 in the siege returned to Syria and Alexandria. Of the land forces, which some estimates place at more than 200,000 men, no more than 30,000 made it home.

Leo's victory at Constantinople was decisive. In 739 he also won a land victory that compelled the Muslims to withdraw from western Asia Minor. In the process he may have saved not only his empire but also West European civilization.

In 719 the Muslims in Spain took Narbonne in France, but two years later they met defeat at Toulouse. In 725 they occupied Carcassonne and Nîmes, and the next year they advanced up the Rhône River Valley and ravaged Burgundy. The Franks appeared in no position to oppose the Muslim advance. The ruling Merovingian dynasty was in decline, and effective power had passed into the hands of the mayor of the palace. In 714 Charles had assumed this title and was king in all but name.

In 732 Muslim governor of Spain Abd-ar-Rahmān launched a full-scale invasion of Aquitaine, then ruled by Duke Eudo. The Muslim invaders defeated Eudo at Bordeaux, then sacked and burned that city. From Bordeaux Abd-ar-Rahmān moved north, pillaging and destroying as he advanced. He took Poitiers and moved toward Tours because of reports of that city's wealth. Eudo meanwhile appealed for assistance to Charles, who had been fighting the Germanic tribes along the Danube. Charles agreed to assist if Eudo would submit Aquitaine to Frankish control, to which Eudo agreed. Putting together an army, Charles crossed the Loire, probably at Orléans. The Muslim army, now burdened down by plunder, fell back on Poitiers.

Little is known about the composition of Abd-ar-Rahmān's army or its size, which has been variously estimated at 20,000 to 80,000 men. The bulk were probably mounted Moors. A mule train followed the troops, probably carrying plunder rather than supplies, for the army lived off the land. Its tactics centered on wild, headlong charges.

The Frankish army was basically an infantry force and smaller than that of the invaders. Only the nobles had horses, and these were used only during the march. There was little discipline on either side.

The sudden appearance of Charles's force caused consternation among the Muslims, who were so heavily weighed down with loot that they were no longer mobile. Abd-ar-Rahmān considered abandoning the plunder but did not, possibly because his men would have refused such an order. The two armies faced one another for seven days, with Charles awaiting the arrival of reinforcements.

Few details exist concerning the actual battle. It most likely occurred at a site later called Moussais-la-Bataille on October 25, 732. Probably the armies first came into contact near Tours, and Abd-ar-Rahmān withdrew toward Poitiers; when he found that the army's booty had not gotten farther south, he decided to accept battle. As the Muslims were solely an offensive force, this meant an attack. Realizing this, Charles drew up his own forces in a solid phalanx formation.

The battle opened with a furious Muslim cavalry charge. Although repeated again and again, the Muslims were unable to break the Frankish phalanx. Toward dusk, Eudo and a force of Aquitanians turned one of the Muslim flanks and launched an attack on Abd-ar-Rahmān's camp, where the bulk of the loot was located. Abd-ar-Rahmān died in the battle, which was over by nightfall.

The next morning scouts reported to Charles that the foe had fled south, abandoning the bulk of their plunder. Frankish chroniclers provided fantastic figures of 360,000 Muslims killed against only 1,500 for Charles, but actual losses were more likely along the lines of 2,000 for the Muslims and 500 for the Franks.

There was no pursuit, for Charles on foot could not pursue a retiring mounted force, and the capture of the loot prohibited such an operation. Probably Charles also deemed it wise not to remove all Muslim pressure from Eudo in order to ensure his loyalty. Therefore, he collected the loot and recrossed the Loire. For his role in the victory, Charles became known to posterity as Charles Martel (Charles the Hammer).

The Battle of Tours saw the deepest Muslim penetration into Europe, east and west. It may not have saved Western Europe from Arab rule, but it certainly made Charles supreme in Gaul and enabled him to establish the Carolinigian dynasty, which reached its zenith under his grandson Charlemagne. In 735 Eudo died; Charles overran Aquitaine and compelled Eudo's two sons to pay homage to him. After this Charles undertook several campaigns against the Muslims in the Rhône Valley, sufficient that a few years later they withdrew south of the Pyrenees for good.

An Arab invasion of the Byzantine Empire in 739, at first successful, was halted by Emperor Leo III in the Battle of Akroïnon (Afyon Karahisar). In 741 new Byzantine emperor Constantine V (r. 741–775) invaded Syria in renewed war with the Arabs but was almost immediately forced to withdraw on news of a revolt led by his brother-in-law, Artavasdus, and supported by those favoring the veneration of religious images. Returning to Constantinople, Constantine V crushed the revolt, then again invaded Syria, taking

some border areas in 745. Constantine's fleet was also victorious at sea against the Arabs near Cyprus, and the Muslims were forced from that island in 746. Constantine then campaigned in Armenia, regaining part of it during 751–752. He was aided by considerable turmoil and outright fighting within the Umayyad Caliphate during 743–750, the result of dynastic struggles and religious strife.

Significance

In 750 Caliph Abu'l Abbas established the Abbasid Caliphate. The Abbasids moved the capital from Damascus to Baghdad. Recurring revolts in Syria and Mesopotamia in favor of the deposed Umayyad family allowed the Byzantines to raid deep into Arab territory. Although Umayyad leader Abd-ar-Rahmān established a separate state at Córdoba in Spain, sporadic warfare between Muslim and Christians there ultimately led to the Reconquista, or reconquest of the Iberian Peninsula by the Christian forces that spanned 700 years. Although warfare continued, the Arabs made no major new conquests. The age of the great Arab conquests was at an end.

Further Reading

Blankinship, K. *The End of the Jihad State.* Albany: State University of New York Press, 1994.

Butler, A. J. *The Arab Conquests of Egypt.* 2nd ed. Brooklyn, NY: A&B Publishing, 1998.

Collins, Roger. *The Arab Conquest of Spain, 710–797.* Oxford, UK: Blackwell, 1989.

Dixon, A. A. *The Umayyad Caliphate, 65–86/684–705.* London: Luzac, 1971.

Donner, Fred. *The Early Islamic Conquests.* Princeton, NJ: Princeton University Press, 1981.

Fregosi, Paul. *Jihad in the West: Muslim Conquests from the 7th to the 21st Centuries.* Amherst, NY: Prometheus Books, 1998.

Gibbon, Edward. *The History of the Decline and Fall of the Roman Empire,* Vol. 6. Edited by J. B. Bury. London: Methuen, 1912.

Graham, Mark, and Akbar Ahmed. *How Islam Created the Modern World.* Beltsville, MD: Amana Publications, 2006.

Haldon, J. J. *Byzantium in the Seventh Century.* Cambridge: Cambridge University Press, 1990.

Jandora, John. *The March from Medina.* Clifton, NJ: Kingston, 1990.

Kaegi, Walter. *Byzantium and the Early Islamic Conquests.* Cambridge: Cambridge University Press, 1992.

Karsh, Efraim. *Islamic Imperialism: A History.* New Haven, CT: Yale University Press, 2007.

Kennedy, Hugh. *The Great Arab Conquests: How the Spread of Islam Changed the World We Live In.* Cambridge, MA: Da Capo, 2007.

McGraw, Donner F. *The Early Islamic Conquests.* Princeton, NJ: Princeton University Press, 1981.

Nicolle, David. *Armies of the Muslim Conquest.* London: Osprey, 1993.

Pirenne, Henri. *Mohammed and Charlemagne.* Mineola, NY: Courier Dover Publications, 2001.

Runciman, Steven. *Byzantine Civilization.* New York: Barnes and Noble, 1994.

Shoufani, E. *Al-Riaddah and the Muslim Conquest of Arabia.* Toronto: University of Toronto Press, 1973.

Vasiliev, Alexander Alexandrovich. *History of the Byzantine Empire, 324–1453.* Madison: University of Wisconsin Press, 1990.

Ye'or, Bat. *The Decline of Eastern Christianity: From Jihad to Dhimmitude.* Madison, NJ: Fairleigh Dickinson University Press, 1996.

Charlemagne's Wars (772–814)

Dates	772–814
Location	Spain, Italy, Germany, Central Europe
Combatants	Franks and allies vs. Saxons, Basques, Lombards, Bavarians, Moors, Avars
Principal Commanders	Franks: Charlemagne Saxons: Widukind Bavarians: Tassilo III Lombards: Desiderius
Principal Battles	Pavia, Roncesvalles Pass, Detmold, Hase River, Barcelona
Outcome	Charlemagne greatly expands the Frankish Empire to the east and unites most of Europe from the Pyrenees to the Elbe. His reign also sees the center of European power shift from the Mediterranean to the Rhine.

Causes

In 732 Charles Martel (the Hammer), ruler of the Franks in all but name, had defeated Muslim forces invading northward from Spain in the Battle of Tours. Charles's son Pepin Le Bref (the Short, Pepin III) united the major tribes of Western Europe, ousted the last of the titular Merovingian kings, and became king of the Franks. On his death in 768 the throne passed to his two sons, Charles and Carloman II. At St. Denis outside Paris they were anointed joint kings by Pope Stephen III. Charles was eager to expand Frankish territorial holdings. Born on April 2, 741 (or 747 or 748, depending on sources), and physically impressive, charismatic, and highly intelligent (although not well educated), Charles, subsequently known as Charlemagne (Charles the Great, Karl der Grosse), turned out to be one of history's great military commanders. In 769 a revolt occurred against the brothers in Gascony and Aquitaine, the latter having been taken by Pepin only the year before after a decade-long war with Duke Waifer of Aquitaine.

Course

The revolt in Aquitaine, which extended as far north as Angoulême, was led by Hunald. Charles sought Carloman's support, but the latter refused to take part, and Charles led an army southward to Bordeaux, where he established a fort and forced Hunald to flee to the court of Duke Lupus II of Gascony. Lupus, however, turned Hunald over in exchange for peace. Charles thus firmly reestablished Frankish control over both Aquitaine and Gascony.

Assisted by their mother Bertrada, Charles and Carloman maintained a tenuous relationship. In 770 Charles concluded a treaty with Duke Tassilo III of Bavaria and married Lombard princess Desiderata, daughter of King Desiderius. Fearing a Frankish-Lombard alliance, Pope Stephen III at first opposed the match. Stephen need not have worried, for a year later Charles repudiated the marriage, possibly on grounds that Desiderata was incapable of bearing children. In any case, she returned to her father's court at Pavia. Certainly this event greatly strained relations between the Franks and the Lombards. Charlemagne then married a 13-year-old Swabian named Hildegard. Desiderius was prepared to ally with Carloman to defeat Charles, but before hostilities could occur, Carloman died on December 5, 771,

apparently from natural causes. Seeking protection for herself and her sons, Carloman's widow Gerberga then fled to Desiderius's court at Pavia.

In 772 in the first major attack by Christian forces against the Moors of Spain, Charles crossed the Pyrenees with an army and laid waste to much of the Ebro River Valley. In 777 he led a larger invasion of Spain that was repulsed at Saragossa (Zaragoza), then withdrew the next year. In 772 Charles invaded Saxon territory in retaliation for a raid by the Saxons. Although he defeated them in pitched battle, he was continually frustrated by Saxon uprisings as soon as the Frankish troops had departed.

Meanwhile, Pope Adrian I appealed to Charles for assistance against Desiderius, who was encroaching on papal territory. Charles readied his army while at the same time urging peaceful settlement of the dispute. In the summer of 773, however, having received confirmation that Desiderius had indeed invaded papal territory and refused a large monetary settlement from Adrian to evacuate the territories taken, Charles marched toward northern Italy.

The size of Charles's army is unknown, but he divided it for the passage through the Alps. His uncle Bernard led part of the army through the St. Bernard Pass, while Charles led the remainder through the Dora Susa via Mount Cenis. As they descended the Alps, Charles's force found its way blocked by Lombard fortifications. Charles's initial assault against these failed, but he found a way to take the Lombards in the flank. The defenders then fled to Pavia, perhaps prompted by news that Bernard was moving in from the east.

In September 773 Charles's combined force arrived before the walled city of Pavia. The Frankish siege of that place

CHARLEMAGNE'S WARS, 772 – 814

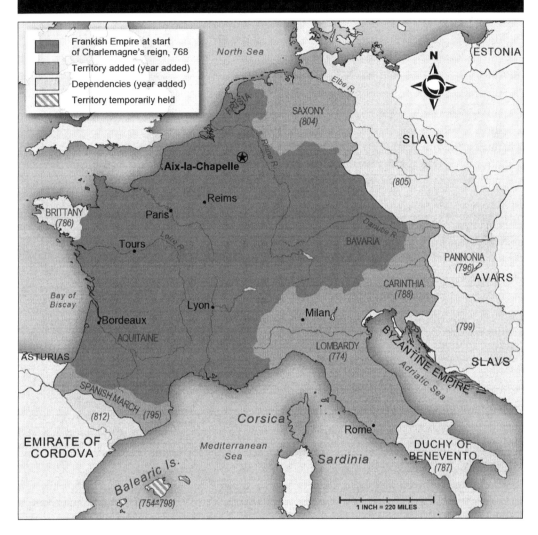

lasted 10 months. Although Charles did not possess siege engines, the defenders had not anticipated the need, and the city was poorly provisioned. King Desiderius was among those trapped at Pavia, although his son Adelchis had fled to the stronger walled city of Verona, there to watch over the wife and children of Charles's deceased brother Carloman. Charles's force must have been fairly large, for he had sufficient numbers to send a force to Verona, which

succumbed without a fight. Adelchis then fled to Constantinople, and Charlemagne secured Carloman's wife and children.

With famine now taking hold at Pavia and no other force coming to its aid, Desiderius surrendered the city in June 774. Charles sent Desiderius off to France to enter a monastery. Having captured Pavia and other Lombard cities, Charles then absorbed the Lombard kingdom into his rising Frankish empire, naming himself king of both the Franks and the Lombards. In effect, Charles's victory made him supreme in northern Italy. He also reached accommodation with Adrian. While recognizing Adrian's claim to much of Italy, Charles failed to oblige the pope in actually conquering it for him.

In 777 Charles invaded northern Spain. His first expedition against the emir of Cordova was successful. His second in 778 was a disaster when the Christian Basques of Pamplona made common cause with the Muslims to ambush in the Roncesvalles Pass his rear guard, commanded by his nephew Roland. The death of Roland in the fighting became the subject of the great epic poem *The Song of Roland.* Regarded as the most outstanding example of the chansons de geste, it was also the first major work of French literature.

In 780 Charles carried out a successful punitive expedition against the Duke of Benevento in southern Italy. Charles defeated the Saxons in two major battles of 783 in Detmold and the Hase River, then subdued them in a winter campaign of 785–786. Only weak sporadic resistance occurred thereafter. In 787 Charles carried out a second successful punitive expedition against the Duke of Benevento. That same year, Charles invaded Bavaria and defeated its ruler Duke Tassilo III, reestablishing Frankish control in 788.

During 791–796 Frankish armies under Charles and his son Pepin operated in the Danube River area, defeating the Avars, a people who had come out of Asia and settled in present-day Hungary in the late 780s. Charles and Pepin campaigned east of the Theiss River, taking territory as far as Lake Boloton. They also conquered portions of present-day Croatia and Slovenia and later (799 and 803) put down Avar revolts.

In 796 Charles invaded northern Spain. He then drove the Muslims south of the Ebro River and successfully besieged Barcelona during 800–801. Beginning in 800 the Norse began raids against the northern German coast that reached up the Elbe River, but Charles and his subordinates built up Frankish naval power at Boulogne and repelled these. Charles was now easily the most important ruler in Europe north of the Alps.

In 799, Pope Leo III had been forced to flee Rome. Traveling to Paderborn, he there met with Charles, who agreed to restore him to power in Rome. Charles arrived in the city in November 800 and held a council there on December 1. On December 23 Leo swore an oath of innocence, and at mass on Christmas Day, December 25, 800, as Charles knelt at the altar in Saint Peter's Basilica to pray, Leo crowned him "Imperator Romanorum" (Emperor of the Romans), thus arrogating to himself the right to appoint the emperor of the Romans and at the same time implying papal superiority over the emperor he had created. This, in effect, also nullified the claim of the Byzantine or Eastern Roman Empire rulers.

In achieving his conquests, Charlemagne clearly understood the importance of religion, and he was quick to cloak his own ambition in a staunch Christianity and use the conversion of the conquered to his faith as justification for the territorial conquests. Although he defeated the Lombards in battle, Charlemagne recognized the superiority of their cavalry and made effective use of a reorganized Lombard cavalry in his own army in the defeat of the Avars. Discipline was the key to his military success.

By the end of his reign Charlemagne had established a military system whereby he would call on a vassal lord to provide men for military service. This meant that the ruler would no longer have to worry about raising the men himself. As it evolved, the system provided for lords, vassals, and fiefs.

Unlike his Frankish predecessors, Charlemagne was able to maintain armies in the field over extended periods, at great distances, and in winter. This was made possible by the introduction of an efficient logistical system that relied both on foraging and convoyed supply trains. He increased the reach of his cavalry by providing it with mule pack trains and also established fortified posts along the frontier of conquered territory, connecting each by road. These well-stocked posts allowed Charlemagne to carry out cavalry operations at any time of year for purposes of both pacification and new offensive action.

Charlemagne reintroduced the bow as an important weapon in his arsenal, although for reasons that are not clear it largely disappeared as a military weapon after his death. He also had an efficient staff and training system as well as a highly effective intelligence service. Imperial ordinances specified the specific obligations of vassals in providing manpower, including the organization of the soldiers and the equipment necessary.

During 800–803 Charlemagne enjoyed general success in a campaign against the Byzantine Empire for control of Venetia and the Dalmatian coast. The fighting occurred on land in Dalmatia and at sea in the Adriatic, but he did not press the effort and eventually reached a negotiated agreement with Byzantine emperor Nicephorus I by which Charlemagne surrendered territory taken in Dalmatia in return for recognition of Frankish control over Istria and the title "Emperor of the West." At the same time, Frankish forces fought the Basques and took Barcelona (801).

Charlemagne chose to locate his imperial capital in Northern Europe at Aachen (Aix-la-Chapelle). Greatly interested in education and the arts, he established a palace school under the monk Alcuin in order to train individuals for state service. Among the accomplishments of the school was the creation of a more efficient way of writing known as Carolingian minuscule.

Following one of the longest reigns in European history, Charlemagne died at Aachen on January 28, 814. He was succeeded as emperor by his son, the ineffectual Louis I the Pious (r. 814–840). On Louis's death, full-scale civil war broke out almost immediately between his three sons. Louis II (Louis the German) allied with Charles the Bald against their elder brother and new emperor Lothair I (r. 840–855). In the Battle of Fontenay (Fontenat) in 841 Charles and Louis defeated Lothair and forced him to sue for peace, which led to the Treaty of Verdun in 843. Under its terms, Charlemagne's three grandsons divided the empire among themselves. Lothair I retained the hollow title of emperor and was king of Italy, Burgundy, and the so-called middle kingdom of Lotharingia. (Its territory extended north from the Jura Mountains to the North Sea through the Meuse and Rhine Valleys.) Louis secured the German lands to the east, while Charles held the future French lands to the west.

Significance

As a general Charlemagne was bold, resourceful, and imaginative. He believed passionately in God and in himself and his own strategic plan. He planned his campaigns carefully and had excellent mastery of logistics. As a ruler he was wise and just. A superb administrator, he held his various realms together effectively.

Today heralded as the father of both modern France and Germany (Charlemagne and Karl der Grosse, respectively), Charlemagne ultimately ruled over the area of present-day northern Spain, France, Belgium, Luxembourg, the Netherlands, Germany, Austria, Slovenia, Croatia, and northern Italy. He was the first to unite most of Europe from the Pyrenees to the Elbe.

The period of Charlemagne's rule saw a fundamental shift in the center of European power from the Mediterranean, which had been the center of Greek and Roman civilizations, to the Rhine. Although his military system was primitive next to that of the Macedonians, Romans, and Byzantines, it nonetheless functioned effectively and marked a significant departure from European warfare at the beginning of the Middle Ages. Charlemagne's military system also served as the basis for the feudal system that characterized the Middle Ages.

Further Reading

Barbero, Alessandro. *Charlemagne: Father of a Continent.* Berkeley: University of California Press, 2004.

Becher, Matthias. *Charlemagne.* New Haven, CT: Yale University Press, 2005.

Biel, Timothy. *Charlemagne.* San Diego: Lucent Books, 1997.

Chamberlin, Russell. *The Emperor Charlemagne.* New York: Franklin Watts, 1986.

Collins, Roger. *Charlemagne.* Toronto: University of Toronto Press, 1998.

Einhard the Frank. *The Life of Charlemagne.* Translated by A. J. Grant. Ann Arbor: University of Michigan Press, 1979.

Ganshof, F. L. *The Carolingians and the Frankish Monarchy: Studies in Carolingian History.* Translated by Janet Sondheimer. Ithaca, NY: Cornell University Press, 1971.

McKitterick, R. *Charlemagne: The Formation of a European Identity.* Cambridge: Cambridge University Press, 2008.

Riché, Pierre. *The Carolingians: A Family Who Forged Europe.* Philadelphia: University of Pennsylvania Press, 1993.

Russell, Charles Edward. *Charlemagne, First of the Moderns.* Boston: Houghton Mifflin, 1930.

Santosuosso, Antonio. *Barbarians, Marauders, and Infidels: The Ways of Medieval Warfare.* Boulder, CO: Westview, 2004.

Scholz, Bernhard Walter, and Barbara Rogers. *Carolingian Chronicles: Royal Frankish Annals and Nithard's Histories.* Ann Arbor: University of Michigan Press, 1970.

Sypeck, Jeff. *Becoming Charlemagne: Europe, Baghdad, and the Empires of A.D. 800.* New York: Ecco/HarperCollins, 2006.

Wilson, Derek. *Charlemagne.* New York: Doubleday, 2006.

Norman Conquest (1066)

Dates	1066
Location	England
Combatants	Normans vs. Anglo-Saxons
Principal Commanders	Normans: Duke William of Normandy Anglo-Saxons: King Harold I
Principal Battles	Hastings
Outcome	William becomes king and creates an efficient administrative system in England centered on the Crown. This is of great future advantage to England, especially in its contests with France, which are another consequence of William's rule.

Causes

The Norman invasion and conquest of England in 1066 resulted from the ambition of one man, Duke William of Normandy. Then probably the most powerful French noble and also potential master of France, William also laid claim to the throne of England. In 1064 Harold Godwinson, Earl of Wessex and chief adviser to English king Edward the Confessor (r. 1042–1066), had arrived by ship in Normandy either, as William claimed, as an emissary from Edward to confirm William as his successor or because, as Harold later claimed, his ship had been wrecked on the Norman coast. In any case, during Harold's time in Normandy, William extracted from him an oath in which Harold recognized him as Edward's successor and promised to aid William in securing the Crown.

On his return to England, Harold soon was forced to side against his brother Tostig, who led a popular uprising against Edward. Tostig was driven into exile and sought refuge with his wife's brother-in-law, Baldwin of Flanders, William's father-in-law and ally. In January 1066 Edward died, commending his family and kingdom to Harold. The principal English nobles then assembled and elected Harold king of England.

When this news reached William, he resolved to secure by whatever means necessary his claimed inheritance. He first sent emissaries to Harold demanding that he fulfill his oath. Harold's position was weak. England was disunited, and Harold was not of a royal line. Indeed, two important earls in northern England refused to acknowledge his rule. Harold won over one by marrying his sister, and in April Harold secured general recognition as king.

William's position was much stronger. Not only did William rule the rich duchy of Normandy, but his alliances with other prominent French nobles were strong, and he enjoyed the support of much of European opinion, which regarded Harold as a usurper. William isolated Harold diplomatically and even secured the support of Pope Alexander II. To weaken Harold further, William encouraged Harold's brother Tostig to lead Norse forces on raids against the English coast. Although Harold defeated Tostig's men and forced them back to their ships, the raids had an important ancillary effect, because they led Harold to believe that William's invasion was imminent.

Course

William's army was centered on mounted cavalry and had been well tested in various military campaigns. William would have to requisition ships to transport his men and horses to England. A more serious problem lay in the vagaries of the weather for a crossing of the English Channel.

Edward had disbanded the small English fleet, so Harold had to scrape together and transform into warships various fishing and commercial vessels to meet the Norman invasion. Harold could count only on a small force of professionals for his army. Only with difficulty would he be able to assemble a larger citizen force, the fyrd, for which there would be pay for two months. Although many of his professional soldiers were mounted, the major fighting was on foot. Archery was not yet important as an English weapon of war.

Harold mobilized both his land and sea forces and kept them on guard throughout the summer. At the end of September their terms of service and money and provisions for them had all expired. No sooner had the English forces disbanded than Harold received word that Norwegian king Harald

BATTLE OF HASTINGS, OCTOBER 14, 1066

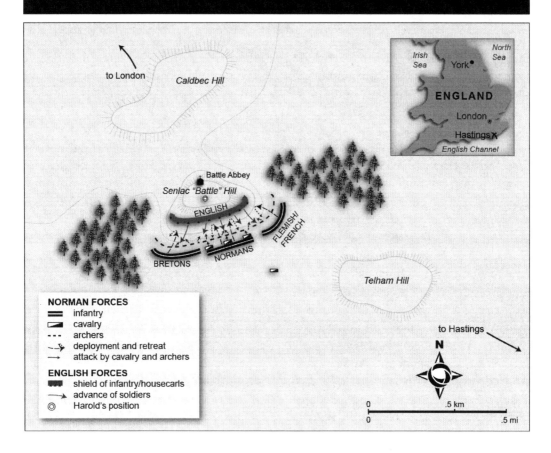

Hardrada, accompanied by Tostig, had invaded the north.

The Norwegian forces, sailing in some 300 ships, landed near York on September 18, 1066. Two days later at Gate Fulford, the invaders defeated English forces under Earls Edwin and Morcar. On learning of the invasion, Harold immediately marched north with such forces as had not already been disbanded; on September 25 at Stamford Bridge, he all but wiped out the Norwegians. Both Harald Hardrada and Tostig were among the dead. Harold allowed the survivors (reportedly not more than two dozen boatloads full) to return to Norway. However, Harold had also sustained heavy losses, and the battle thus had tremendous consequences for the upcoming struggle with William.

William's forces were ready in early August, but for some reason he did not then sail. He did attempt to depart in mid-September, but contrary winds prevented it. On September 27 the winds finally shifted to the south, and the fleet set out. Landing in England at Pevensey the next day, William marched his army to Hastings, the coastal terminus of the road to London. He then set about ravaging the countryside in an effort to draw Harold into battle.

Harold was at York on October 1 celebrating his victory at Stamford Bridge when he learned of William's arrival. Harold immediately hurried south, stopping only briefly in London to gather additional men. He also ordered out some 70 vessels to prevent William's ships from escaping. Harold erred in not remaining in London longer to gather more men, but he was by nature impulsive and offensively minded.

Harold departed London on October 11 to cover the 60 miles to Hastings, probably hoping to catch William by surprise with a night attack, but arrived too late on October 13 and decided to let his men rest. The two armies were about seven miles apart when Harold made camp. Learning of Harold's approach, William decided to strike first.

William advanced on the Saxon forces at dawn on October 14. Although William may have enjoyed a slight numerical advantage, each side probably had about 6,000 men. The fight was also even in terms of training and equipment. Harold's professional forces formed a shield wall and held the high ground, but Harold was short of archers, and he had no cavalry. William had the advantage of a mixed force of infantry, cavalry, and archers.

Battle was joined with a Norman attack about 9:00 a.m. William's Breton left wing soon retreated in confusion, and there was a sense of panic in the army on false news that William had been slain. William did have three horses killed underneath him that day. Harold might have won the battle had he counterattacked at this moment of Norman vulnerability, but for some reason he did not, and the moment passed. William showed himself to his men, rallied them, and led his troops in cutting down the few Saxons who left the shield wall in the pursuit.

The battle raged for the remainder of the day and might have gone either way. The Normans mounted a series of attacks and feigned retreats but drew few of the Saxons from the protection of the shield wall. Had Harold been able to last the day, William's situation might have turned desperate, but William ordered high-angle arrow fire from his archers, followed by a last charge. Harold was struck in the eye with an arrow, probably in this barrage. In any case, the Norman horsemen and infantry managed to crack the shield wall. Harold was cut down fighting under his standard, and the English were soon in flight, pursued by the Normans. Harold's death made the battle decisive.

Following the battle William cautiously advanced on London, ravaging the countryside as he went. The death of Harold and his brothers in the battle created a leadership vacuum, and in mid-December most Anglo-Saxon nobles submitted to William. He was formally crowned king of England in Westminster Abbey on Christmas Day 1066, to be known to history ever since as William the Conqueror.

Significance

William then set out to pacify his new kingdom, building new castles and putting down revolts, sometimes with great ferocity. The most serious of these was that of Northumbria, led by Hereward the Wake and supported by the Danes, who sent a fleet in 1069. During 1069–1070 William proceeded north ravaging the countryside, including burning crops especially between York and Durham in what became known as the Harrying of the North. His brutal tactics worked, and England was largely pacified by 1071. William then invaded Scotland in 1072 and forced King Malcolm to pay tribute to him.

William parceled out land to his Norman followers and firmly established the continental feudal system in England. He reorganized England administratively, unifying the country under firm royal authority, and he also introduced Norman law and justice. William broke the long-standing Anglo-Saxon connection with Scandinavia, but this also ushered in a long period of confrontation with France, which would have terrible consequences, especially for France.

In 1086 William also ordered a full inventory of property, known as the Doomsday Book. Once this was ascertained, he insisted that taxes owed be paid directly to the king. This was of immense importance in strengthening England, especially in its later dealings with France, which was much wealthier than England but where the king enjoyed far less authority and the Crown was not able to utilize most of the available resources. In sum, William created the English nation and an effective, efficient state system centered on the king that was of tremendous advantage to England in the long run.

Further Reading

Bradbury, Jim. *The Battle of Hastings.* Stroud, Gloucestershire, UK: Sutton, 1998.

Freeman, Edward. *The History of the Norman Conquest of England.* Chicago: University of Chicago Press, 1974.

Howarth, David. *1066: The Year of the Conquest.* New York: Viking Penguin, 1977.

Morillo, Stephen, ed. *The Battle of Hastings: Sources and Interpretations.* Rochester, MN: University of Rochester Press, 1996.

Morris, Marc. *The Norman Conquest: The Battle of Hastings and the Fall of Anglo-Saxon England.* Cambridge, UK: Pegasus, 2013.

Crusades (1096–1291)

Dates	1096–1291
Location	Asia Minor, Syria, Palestine, Balkans
Combatants	Christian Europeans vs. Muslim Seljuk Turks
Principal Commanders	Papacy: Urban II, Clement III France: Godfrey of Bouillon, Louis VII, Philip II, Louis IX Germany: Conrad III, Frederick I Barbarossa, Frederick II England: Richard I, Edward I Muslim Seljuk Turks: Saladin
Principal Battles	Nicaea, Antioch, Jerusalem (first), Ramleh (first and second), Hattin, Jerusalem (second), Damietta, Mansura, Acre
Outcome	The Christians fail in their considerable effort to retake the Holy Land, with Muslim civilization proven to be as militarily capable and refined as Christian European civilization. The hold of the Catholic Church is lessened, and serfdom and the medieval age are dealt major blows. The Crusades can also be seen as a first step in the long history of European imperialism.

Causes

In the great age of faith there many military efforts said to be primarily motivated by Christian fervor and dubbed "crusades." These included the Reconquista in Spain of 722–1492, the Albigensian Crusade in France during 1209–1229, the Aragonese Crusade of 1284–1285, and the

Northern Crusade conducted by the Teutonic Knights in the Baltic region during the 12th and 13th centuries. But certainly the best-known, most ambitious, least successful, and yet most lastingly influential of military efforts cloaked in religion were those advanced by the Latin Roman Catholic Church and supported by the Latin West to wrest control from the Muslims of Jerusalem and the Holy Land of Palestine. The term "crusade" comes from the Spanish *cruzada,* meaning "marked by the cross."

Apart from the stated religious goals of spreading the faith and reclaiming the Holy Land from the "infidel," there were many purely secular motivations behind the Crusades. One was the advance of the Seljuk Turks. In 1070 they had captured Jerusalem, and palmers—those Christians who had undertaken a pilgrimage to Palestine and then wore crossed palm leaves as a sign of their accomplishment—began to tell of repression of Christians there. Reportedly, one Peter the Hermit brought a letter from Simeon, patriarch of Jerusalem, to Pope Urban II bearing witness to this.

The Byzantine Empire was then weak. This important Christian state guarded access to South-Central Europe and for seven centuries had held back would-be invaders from crossing the narrow straits that separated Asia from Europe. If Constantinople were to fall, this would open the floodgates to Muslim expansion into Europe, and the victory of Tours in 732 would be undone. The threat was such that Byzantine emperor Alexius I Comnenus (r. 1081–1118) sent emissaries to Pope Urban II urging that theological and political differences be set aside and that Latin Europe join him in driving back the Turks. Alexius argued that it would better to fight the Turks in Asia than in Europe.

There was also the ambition of the rising Italian city-states of Venice, Genoa, and Pisa. Their leaders sought to extend their commercial reach into the eastern Mediterranean, expanding trade and opening new markets and increasing their wealth and influence. Finally, there was also the quest for military glory and political advantage by kings and nobles.

The decision rested with Urban II. During March–October 1095 he toured northern Italy and southern France, meeting with leaders and enlisting support. Urban then called a church council at Clermont in France and, in what has been called the most influential speech in Medieval history, addressed the faithful and proclaimed a crusade to reclaim the Holy Land. Certainly personal ambition played a role, for Urban hoped thereby to unite the Christian West under his leadership.

Extraordinary inducements were offered to participants. These included a plenary indulgence remitting all punishment for sin to those who might fall in the war, remission of criminal punishments, and exemption from feudal dues and taxes. Religious frenzy now swept Christian Europe, unfortunately bringing with it the murder of thousands of Jews, chiefly in Germany.

Course of the First Crusade (1095–1099)

Urban set August 1096 as the date for the crusaders' departure. This was the age of faith, and many mostly unarmed peasants responded enthusiastically. In what became known as the People's Crusade or Popular Crusade—yet considered part of the First Crusade—some 40,000 people, including women and children, assembled. Alexius urged them to wait for the knights, but they crossed the straits into Asia Minor under the leadership of Peter the Hermit bound for the Holy Land. Their numbers soon dwindled to perhaps 20,000, and almost all of these were either killed or taken prisoner by the Seljuk Turks in battle in October near Nicaea. Perhaps only 3,000 returned to Constantinople.

Meanwhile, the various state military contingents, ultimately numbering as many as 50,000 men, moved largely by land toward the agreed-upon assembly point of Constantinople, arriving there in the autumn of 1096 and the spring of 1097. Alexius was interested only in securing his Asiatic objectives and not the crusader objective of capturing Jerusalem. Rightly fearful of their intentions, Alexius insisted that the crusaders camp beyond the city walls of Constantinople. Finally, with the arrival of the remaining contingents in the spring of 1097 and aided by bribes, Alexius secured the fealty of the crusaders and a pledge that they would help him recover Nicaea (Isnik) from the Seljuk Turks as well as hand over to him any other former Byzantine possessions they should conquer. Alexius then provided passage across the Bosporus as well as food and escorts to get the crusaders to the Holy Land and prevent plundering.

The crusaders and Byzantines laid siege to Nicaea during May 14–June 19. Alexius secured the surrender of the city to him and was able to keep the crusaders from sacking it. The crusaders then continued their march southeast. On July 1 in the Battle of Dorylaeum, Turkish cavalry under the personal command of Seljuk sultan of Rum Kilij Arslan attacked the outnumbered lefthand crusader column under Norman duke Bohemund of Taranto and was on the brink of destroying it when crusader heavy cavalry under Duke of Lower Lorraine Godfrey of Bouillon and Count Raymond

of Toulouse fall on the Turkish left and rear. About 3,000 Seljuk Turks and some 4,000 crusaders died in the fighting.

Continuing their advance, the crusaders captured Kilij Arslan's capital of Iconium (present-day Konya) while Alexius and the Byzantine forces reoccupied much of western Anatolia. Following the Battle of Heraclea (Eregh), the crusaders advanced on Antioch, winning a hard-fought battle at Tarsus on the way. A number of crusaders under Baldwin of Lorraine then left the main column to cross the Euphrates and take Edessa in Mesopotamia.

On October 21, the crusaders laid siege to Antioch. Emir Yagi Siyan mounted a skillful defense with skirmishing outside the walls. Twice the Christians drove off relief forces in battles at Harenc (December 31, 1097, and February 9, 1098). Close to starvation themselves, the poorly organized besiegers were saved only by the timely arrival of small English and Pisan supply flotillas and the capture of several small ports to allow access. Antioch fell on June 3, 1098, just before the arrival of a 75,000-man Seljuk relief force under Emir Kerboga of Mosul.

On arriving at Antioch, Kerboga commenced his own siege of the now Christian-controlled city. The Christians were cut off from their supply ports, and Yagi Siyan still held out in the city's citadel. Alexius was advancing with a Byzantine army on Antioch, but informed that the situation there was hopeless, he withdrew into Anatolia.

Spurred by the alleged sudden and miraculous appearance of the Holy Lance (the weapon used to pierce Jesus's side during the crucifixion), the crusaders risked everything in a sally from Antioch on June 25, 1098, by 15,000 men, only 1,000 of them mounted. The crusaders succeeded

THE CRUSADES

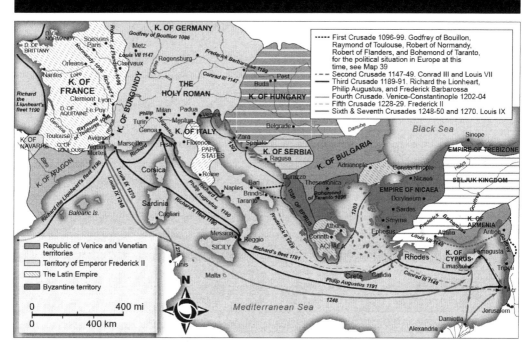

First Crusade 1096-99. Godfrey of Bouillon, Raymond of Toulouse, Robert of Normandy, Robert of Flanders, and Bohemond of Taranto, for the political situation in Europe at this time, see Map 39
Second Crusade 1147-49. Conrad III and Louis VII
Third Crusade 1189-91. Richard the Lionheart, Philip Augustus, and Frederick Barbarossa
Fourth Crusade. Venice-Constantinople 1202-04
Fifth Crusade 1228-29. Frederick II
Sixth & Seventh Crusades 1248-50 and 1270. Louis IX

Republic of Venice and Venetian territories
Territory of Emperor Frederick II
The Latin Empire
Byzantine territory

0   400 mi
0   400 km

in engaging the larger Muslim force where it could not maneuver and after repeated charges broke it, causing the Muslim besiegers to flee.

Most of the crusaders survived an outbreak of plague in Antioch during July and August 1098 (one notable victim was Bishop Adhemar du Pay, papal legate and nominal crusader leader), but the leaders argued among themselves as to their next course of action. Some chose to honor their oath to Alexius and returned to Constantinople, but the vast majority decided to continue on to Jerusalem, the most holy city for Christians, who believe it to be the site of Christ's death and resurrection. The city had been under Muslim control for 500 years and in 1099 was under the rule of the Fatimid Caliphate of Cairo.

The crusader advance began in mid-January 1099. The 400-mile march south

from Antioch along the eastern Mediterranean coast proceeded through Sidon, Acre, and Caesarea, with the crusaders arriving at Jerusalem on June 7, 1099. They then commenced a siege of that place. Duke Godfrey commanded the Christian force of some 13,000 men, including 1,300 knights. Fatimid governor of Jerusalem Emir Iftikhar ad-Dawla could count on 20,000 men.

With the defenders having poisoned the nearby wells and cisterns and with the heat oppressive, the crusaders knew that they had to work quickly. As early as June 12 they attempted an assault, but lacking sufficient scaling ladders and war machines, they were easily repulsed. Siege equipment came on June 17 when six supply ships arrived at Jaffa, which had been abandoned by the Egyptians. Within several weeks the crusaders had constructed a large number of mangonels and scaling ladders and two large wooden siege towers.

On the night of July 13–14 the crusaders braved defensive fire to push the towers against the city walls, and on the morning of July 15 Duke Godfrey led an attack from one of the towers by means of a wooden drawbridge, while other crusaders employed scaling ladders to enter the city. Many of the Muslims sought refuge in the al-Aqsa Mosque, where Tancred de Hauteville, one of the crusader leaders, promised that their lives would be spared. Once the Christian forces had taken the city, however, they embarked on an orgy of destruction, slaughtering all Muslims, including women and children, who could be found. This included those within the al-Aqsa Mosque. Estimates of the number of Muslims slain in Jerusalem reach as high as 70,000 people. The surviving Jews fared no better; the Christians herded them into a synagogue and then burned them alive. Their bloodlust spent, the victors proceeded to the Church of the Holy Sepulcher, the grotto of which they believed once held the body of the crucified Christ, and there gave thanks to the God of Mercies for their victory.

Learning of the advance on Jerusalem from Egypt of a 50,000-man Turkish army under Emir al-Afdal, Duke Godfrey led out some 10,000 crusaders against it. In the August 12, 1099, Battle of Ascalon, the Fatimids found themselves at great disadvantage against the more heavily armed and armored crusaders, who won a crushing victory.

Following the capture of Jerusalem, most of the crusaders still alive returned home. Those who remained set up small states in the Holy Land. Duke Godfrey died in July 1100, and Baldwin became king of Jerusalem. Near that city in 1101, Baldwin and only 1,100 men defeated an army from Egypt that may have numbered as many as 32,000. In the Second Battle of Ramleh in 1102, however, an overconfident Baldwin with only 200 men attacked some 30,000 Egyptians and was soundly defeated, although he managed to escape. Putting together a new army of 8,000 men, Baldwin was victorious over the Egyptians in the Battle of Jaffa and pursued them into Anatolia.

A protracted multifaceted struggle then ensued for control of Mesopotamia from among the crusaders, various Seljuk Turk sultanates, and other Muslim principalities. Kalij Arslan of the sultanate of Rum in Anatolia captured Mosul in 1102. He was subsequently defeated and killed in the Battle of the Khabur River of 1107 by forces led by Ridwan, emir of Aleppo. Although the crusaders continued to control the coast, they lacked the numerical strength to hold the interior.

During 1116–1117, King Baldwin of Jerusalem led a crusader expedition to the Gulf of Aqaba, where he built the fortress of Ailath (Eilat). In 1118 he led fewer than 1,000 men across the Sinai against Egypt but died during the campaign, and without its leader the expedition returned to Palestine.

Course of the Second Crusade (1147–1149)

The principal figures on the Christian side in the Second Crusade of 1147–1149 were Emperor Conrad III of Germany and King Louis VII of France. Proceeding by land, the Germans ran out of food near Dorylaeum and were overwhelmed by a Seljuk Turk attack. Conrad and a few followers managed to make it back to Nicaea and then proceed to the Holy Land by ship. The French, who took a longer route, were halted by the

Turks in battle near Laodicea. Louis and the cavalry then traveled to the Holy Land by ship. The infantry, continuing on by land, were annihilated by the Turks.

In 1148 the two Christian kings and their remaining men, joined by Baldwin III of Jerusalem, mounted an overland expedition against Damascus, which they invested. Dissension among the Christian forces led to abandonment of the siege, however. This ended the disastrous Second Crusade.

In 1153 Baldwin III captured Ascalon, bringing the entire coast of Palestine under his control. In 1169 King Amalric of Jerusalem led a joint crusader-Byzantine expedition against Egypt, which was repulsed. The Muslims had long fought among themselves, but in 1171 Seljurk Turk general Salah-al din Yusuf ibn Ayyūb, better known as Saladin, established the Ayyubid dynasty in Egypt. Thanks in large part to dissension among the crusaders, Saladin was able to expand his influence from Egypt into Syria and northern Mesopotamia. He eventually conquered all the territory once held by Nur-ed-din, atabeg of Mosul.

Crusader Reynald of Châtillon, lord of the castle at Kerak on the road between Damascus and Mecca, carried out a series of attacks on Muslim caravans and towns along the Red Sea. When King Guy de Lusignan of the Latin Kingdom of Jerusalem failed to punish his rival Reynald for these actions, Saladin vowed revenge. In June 1187 Saladin proclaimed a jihad (holy war) against the crusaders and mounted an invasion of Palestine.

On June 26, Saladin crossed the Jordan River at the head of some 20,000 men and laid siege to the crusader stronghold of Tiberias. King Guy's advisers called on him for an immediate effort to raise the siege. Count Raymond of Tripoli, the ablest of the crusader generals whose wife was then in Tiberias, nonetheless urged Guy to wait. Tiberias was well supplied, and Raymond argued that it would be to the crusader advantage to delay any relief effort until Saladin's forces had experienced supply problems in the countryside. The extreme heat of summer would also make campaigning difficult. Guy ignored this wise advice. Instead, he ordered Christian castles and strongpoints to contribute much of their garrisons and, in late June, led a relief force of approximately 1,200 mounted knights and 18,000 infantry toward Tiberias.

On July 2 the Christian force reached Sepphoris, about equidistant between Acre and Tiberias. Raymond again urged caution on Guy and again was rebuffed. Although Raymond warned Guy that there was only one spring accessible to the crusaders along the planned route of march, the army continued east. Saladin was pleased to learn of the crusader approach. He knew the impact of a lack of water on the heavily armored and armed crusader force.

Saladin immediately sent light cavalry to attack the Christians, bringing them to a halt on July 3 in the parched and barren land. The Muslim attack and the heat of the day forced the Christians to take up position near the village of Hattin, seven miles west of Tiberias and the Sea of Galilee and next to two mounds known as the Horns.

Saladin's men surrounded the crusaders and kept up constant arrow fire on their camp during the night of July 3–4. What little water the Christians had with them had by now been consumed. Saladin also had his men set fire to nearby brush upwind of the crusader camp, blowing smoke into it and making it even more difficult for the men and horses.

The next morning, July 4, Saladin still refused to close with the heavily armored Christians. Bringing up fresh stocks of arrows, he had his bowmen continue their harassing fire. In an effort to end this, the Christian cavalry charged the Muslims, but this action separated the cavalry from the infantry and enabled the Muslims to destroy the crusader forces piecemeal.

At the very end of the battle, Raymond and a small number of crusader horsemen succeeded in cutting their way out, but they were the only ones to escape. (Raymond later died of wounds sustained in the battle.) The remainder of the crusaders, out of water, their horses dying of thirst, and under constant harassing arrow fire, were forced to surrender. Guy was among the prisoners. Exact casualty totals in the Battle of Hattin are not known, but certainly the vast majority of the Christians were either taken prisoner or killed. While Saladin ordered Reynald executed, he treated Guy well and subsequently released him on the latter's pledge that he would not again take up arms against the Muslims.

Saladin's victory at Hattin had tremendous consequences. It led directly to the Muslim conquest of most of Palestine, the Christian garrisons of which had been badly depleted in putting together the expeditionary force. Only at Tyre, where Christian reinforcements arrived just in time by sea, did Saladin suffer repulse. Saladin then turned against Jerusalem. Laying siege to it on September 20, he took the city on October 2. Fighting then centered on Acre, to which the Christians laid siege. Although they were blockaded by Saladin from the land, the Christians were able to receive supplies from the sea and continue their siege operations. Nine major land battles and numerous other small engagements occurred in the vicinity between the crusader and Muslim forces.

Course of the Third Crusade (1189–1192)

The Muslim capture of Jerusalem shocked all Europe and led Pope Clement III to appeal for a new crusade in the Holy Land. Three of Europe's most powerful rulers answered the call: Emperor Frederick I Barbarossa of Germany, King Philip II Augustus of France, and King Richard I the Lion-Hearted of England. The Third Crusade lasted from 1189 to 1192.

Frederick led 30,000 men in a protracted march by land from Constantinople, but in June 1190 he was drowned in the Salef River in Cilicia, and his army soon disintegrated under his less capable son and successor, Frederick of Swabia. Little more than 1,000 men of the original force managed to join the Christian forces at Acre. Philip and Richard arrived in the Holy Land by sea, with Philip stopping en route to capture Cyprus, which he turned into a base for future military operations.

The central event of the Third Crusade was the great Siege of Acre (August 28, 1189–July 12, 1191). King Guy of the Latin Kingdom of Jerusalem, who had been freed by Saladin following the Battle of Hattin on a pledge that he would not again fight against the Muslims, secured a ruling by the Catholic Church that proclaimed his oath null and void. Guy, however, was now without a kingdom. But the Third Crusade brought to Palestine Christian reinforcements under Archbishop Ubaldo of Pisa as well as Sicilian mercenaries. Guy now took charge of them.

On August 28, 1189, Guy began an ineffectual siege of Acre. Following a failed assault several days later, he appealed to the Christian powers for additional assistance. In September a Danish fleet arrived and placed Acre under blockade from the sea. Ships from other European states also joined the effort. Conrad of Monferrat, who had established a Christian kingdom at Tyre, also landed troops. In October the reinforced crusaders again assaulted Acre but in bitter fighting were again repulsed.

Saladin sought reinforcements from other Muslim powers as far away as Spain. With this support, in October and December he was able to pass ships through the Christian naval blockade and bring supplies and men into Acre. He also began a land countersiege of King John's forces. Both sides constructed extensive trench systems and fortifications, with the crusaders having lines of both contravallation and circumvallation. Conrad was able to get past the Saracen fleet and deliver vital supplies to Guy.

Utilizing these supplies, during the winter of 1189 the Christians built three large siege towers and moved them against the city walls on May 1, 1190. On May 11, however, Saladin launched an attack on the Christian siege lines. The fighting was intense, and Saladin's attacks forced the crusaders to fight on both fronts, allowing the defenders of Acre to burn the crusaders' siege towers.

During the summer of 1190 more Christian reinforcements arrived, chiefly from France. The most important figure among them was Henry of Troyes, Count of Champagne, who took command of siege operations. In October the remaining Germans from Holy Roman emperor Frederick Barbarossa's forces arrived. The besieging crusaders now constructed both rams and trebuchets for another assault on Acre, but the defenders employed incendiary devices to destroy these siege engines

and beat back several major Christian assaults.

In November the crusaders succeeded in opening a land supply route, although Saladin was able that winter to close it off again and isolate the crusaders. The winter of 1190–1191 was especially severe and hard on the crusaders, who also suffered extensively from disease and famine. Among the victims were Guy's wife Sybelle and their daughters. The Christians would have broken off the siege had it not been for the hope of English and French reinforcements in spring.

As promised, additional Christian manpower, ships, supplies, and funds arrived on April 20, 1191, under French king Philip II Augustus and on June 8 under English king Richard I the Lion-Hearted. These created a new sense of hope and enthusiasm among the crusaders. With additional warships, the crusaders were at last able to cut off Acre entirely from the seaborne resupply. They also constructed a great many trebuchets and other artillery pieces as well as a large siege tower, then concentrated their attacks on one tower, known as The Accused.

With Acre in dire straits, on July 3 Saladin attempted to draw off the crusaders. The attack, led by his nephew, failed. The crusaders opened a number of breaches in the city walls, and although the defenders repulsed three assaults, Acre surrendered on July 12, 1191. The Christian success here helped ensure the survival of a truncated crusader kingdom in the Holy Land for another century.

Philip returned to France, although most of his forces remained behind. Richard was now in sole command of the crusader army. Saladin meanwhile began gathering resources to ransom the Acre garrison and conduct a prisoner exchange. Angered by the exclusion of certain Christian nobles, Richard refused Saladin's first payment and on August 20, believing that Saladin was delaying, ordered 2,700 Muslim prisoners executed. Saladin retaliated in kind, killing the Christian prisoners in his own possession.

Acre served as the chief military base for Richard in his effort to reconquer much of the coastal area of Palestine. Departing from there on August 22, Richard moved southward with fewer than 50,000 men intent on taking Jerusalem. A highly effective leader, Richard imposed considerable discipline on the unruly Christian commanders and their men.

The crusaders moved along the coast by easy marches, resupplied by sea. Saladin paralleled the march inland. Richard dispersed crossbowmen among his force to keep Saladin's horsemen at bay and prevent him from breaking apart the Christian column. He also ordered that the column not be drawn into battle with Saladin's harassing forces.

As the crusaders made their way down the coast, on September 7, 1191, Saladin ambushed them at Arsouf, opening with an attack on Richard's rear guard to try to get the Christians to retaliate so they could be cut off and destroyed. Richard refused battle until Saladin committed a larger force, then turned and mounted a coordinated cavalry charge that destroyed the Muslim force. On Richard's express command, the crusaders did not pursue. In the battle the Muslims suffered some 7,000 casualties against only 700 for the Christians. Saladin never again attempted to engage Richard in pitched battle.

After spending the winter of 1191–1192 at Ascalon, the crusaders resumed their advance on Jerusalem. Saladin initiated a scorched-earth policy and poisoned the wells. The shortage of provisions and always-present but growing dissension among the crusader leaders convinced Richard that he would not be able to take Jerusalem without risking the loss of his army, and he withdrew to the coast. Following numerous small engagements in which he distinguished himself militarily, Richard concluded a treaty with Saladin in 1192 that granted special rights and privileges to Christian pilgrims to Jerusalem. Saladin died the next year, ensuring the crusader states a short period of relief.

In 1197 Holy Roman emperor and king of Sicily Henry VI sent a preliminary small German force to the Holy Land. It captured Beirut and other coastal cities in 1198. Henry died in 1197, however, temporarily shelving plans for a larger effort.

Course of the Fourth Crusade (1202–1204)

In 1199 Pope Innocent III appealed for a new crusade to regain Jerusalem. Although the English and French kings did not participate, a crusader force assembled under Theobald III, Count of Champagne. Venice agreed to transport 25,000 crusaders to Egypt and maintain them there for three years in exchange for a cash payment and half of the crusader conquests. When Theobald died in 1201, Boniface of Montferrat became the new leader. In a meeting at Hagenau in December 1201, the crusaders decided to proceed to the Holy Land not by way of Egypt but rather via Constantinople.

This Fourth Crusade lasted from 1202 to 1204. When the crusaders assembled in the summer of 1202, they were unable to raise the sum promised to Venice and arranged to pay half the original sum in exchange for retaking the Venetian dependency of Zara. The pope condemned this attack on other Christians, but the crusaders captured and sacked Zara, bringing a papal excommunication.

The crusaders then intrigued with Alexius, son of deposed Byzantine emperor Isaac II. Most agreed that in return for a promised large cash payment, they would proceed to Constantinople and overthrow reigning emperor Alexius III. Some, notably Simon de Montfort of England, went on to Palestine instead.

Most of the crusaders now sailed into the Bosporus and set up camp ashore near Constantinople. Meanwhile, the Venetian fleet forced its way into the Golden Horn. On July 17, 1202, the crusaders attacked Constantinople. They were repulsed, but the Venetians captured a portion of the sea wall and secured part of the city. That night Alexius III fled; notables released former emperor Isaac II from prison and elected his son Alexius coemperor as Alexius IV. The new Byzantine leaders then attempted to raise the money promised by Alexius IV for a successful military effort.

In January 1204 resentment against both their new rulers and the crusaders produced a revolt in Constantinople led by Alexius Ducas Mourt-zouphlous, son-in-law of Alexius III. Isaac II was again imprisoned, and Alexius IV was executed. Alexius Ducas took the imperial throne as Alexius V.

This action, however, gave the crusaders the excuse to take Constantinople. They assaulted the city in early April 1204. Although the defenders, especially the Varangian Guard, fought well, catapults on the Venetian ships hurled incendiaries into the city, starting a major conflagration and causing the defenders to lose heart. After taking the city, the crusaders subjected it to rape and pillage. Many scholars believe that this first successful assault of Constantinople effectively signaled the end of the Byzantine Empire. Although it would continue in existence for another two centuries, the empire never really recovered from this blow inflicted by fellow Christians.

The empire's territory was now divided between Venice and the crusader leaders, with the establishment of the Latin Empire of Constantinople. On April 14, 1205, however, in the Battle of Adrianople, Czar Kaloyan of Bulgaria ambushed a Latin crusader army under new Latin emperor Baldwin I of Flanders. Kaloyan's Cuman allies feigned an attack on the crusader camp and then withdrew. The crusaders foolishly pursued the Cumans some distance, only to be ambushed by the main Bulgarian force. The Bulgarians killed some 300 crusader knights. Baldwin was taken prisoner and then blinded. He died in captivity. The Bulgarians overran much of Thrace and Macedonia.

Course of the Fifth Crusade (1218–1221)

Pope Innocent III urged a new military effort in the Holy Land, insisting that it proceed by way of Egypt. To win the support of the pope against his rival Holy Roman emperor Otto IV, Frederick II—king of Germany, Italy, and Burgundy—agreed to lead it. In 1218 the crusaders proceeded to Acre, where they joined contingents from Christian states in the Holy Land under John of Brienne, king of Jerusalem. They landed near Damietta, and while a Genoese fleet defeated an Egyptian fleet, the crusaders laid siege to the city, capturing it after a year and a half in November 1219. The crusaders rejected Egyptian peace offers, waiting for more than a year for the arrival of additional forces under Frederick II. He never appeared, but reinforcements finally arrived in early 1221.

Ultimately the crusaders fielded some 46,000 men, including 10,000 cavalry.

Sultan Malik al-Kamil had some 70,000 men. In June 1221 papal legate Cardinal Pelagius, who had insisted on taking command, ordered a crusader march on Cairo, which proceeded under difficult conditions. Al-Kamil offered to cede Jerusalem and other locations in the Holy Land in return for the crusader evacuation of Damietta. John urged acceptance, but Pelagius chose to reject the offer, insisting on an indemnity and other additional concessions. The crusaders then resumed their march but were repulsed in their attempt to cross the Ashmoun Canal.

At the same time, an Egyptian fleet cut off the crusaders from their base at Damietta. Facing starvation, Pelagius agreed to a face-saving arrangement whereby the crusaders would evacuate Damietta in return for safe passage home and some religious relics. The Fifth Crusade was a complete failure.

Course of the Sixth Crusade (1228–1229)

Holy Roman emperor Frederick II, under considerable pressure from Pope Gregory IX because of his failure to deliver on his promise to lead the Fifth Crusade, sailed from Sicily with a crusader force in 1227. Once at sea, however, Frederick and many of the crusaders fell ill with a fever, and the expedition returned to port. With relations already strained and assuming that this was simply a ploy to delay, Pope Gregory excommunicated Frederick.

Frederick II set out again in 1228, but Gregory reiterated the excommunication. He also declared Frederick's lands in southern Italy forfeit and proclaimed a Crusade against them. Mercenaries in the pay of Gregory then invaded and devastated Apulia.

In the Holy Land, Frederick discovered that the other crusaders would not cooperate with him because of the excommunication. Frederick nonetheless opened talks with Sultan al-Kamil and, through astute diplomacy, secured the cession of Jerusalem, Nazareth, and Bethlehem and a corridor connecting Jerusalem to the coast. Traveling to Jerusalem, he crowned himself king on February 18, 1229. Returning to Italy, Frederick drove out the papal forces from southern Italy in May and made peace with Pope Gregory that August. Despite the lack of fighting in the Sixth Crusade, Frederick II was more successful than any other crusader except Godfrey de Bouillon in the First Crusade.

Course of the Seventh Crusade (1248–1254)

The Seventh Crusade was sparked by the destruction of Jerusalem by the Khwarezmians in 1244. Endeavoring to escape the Mongols, who had taken their territory, the Khwarezmians took Jerusalem from the crusaders, sacked the city, and left it in ruins. The Khwarezmians then allied with Egypt against the crusaders, who themselves allied with the emir of Damascus. The two sides met in battle at Gaza later that same year, and the Khwarezmians and Egyptians were victorious, with Tatar Mamluke leader Baybars (Baibars) playing an important role.

King Louis IX of France (later canonized as Saint Louis) led the Seventh Crusade, departing France in 1248 with 1,800 ships carrying 60,000 troops (20,000 of them cavalry). After spending the winter in Cyprus, he occupied Damietta in Egypt in June 1249.

Not wishing to repeat the error of the Fifth Crusade by advancing on Cairo in summer, Louis delayed until autumn, which allowed Sultan Malik al-Salih time to prepare. The crusaders set out in November but advanced slowly and, as in the Fifth Crusade, were halted at the Ashmoun Canal by an Egyptian force commanded by Fakr-ed-din of perhaps 70,000 men centered on 10,000 Mamluks.

During December 1249–January 1250 the crusaders attempted to construct a causeway across the Ashmoun Canal to enable them to continue their drive on Cairo, but the Egyptians responded by widening the canal from the opposite bank at that point. After locating a ford near the causeway, Louis IX finally got his cavalry across, surprised the Egyptians, and won the Battle of Mansura on February 8, 1250. Emir Fakr-ed-din was among those killed.

The battle might have been decisive, but Robert of Artois threw away the possibility. Instructed to seize the canal bank and hold it for the main body of cavalry and the infantry, he instead chose to pursue the fleeing Egyptians into Mansura. In street fighting there, the Egyptians were able to offset the impact of the crusader heavy cavalry and almost annihilated Robert's force. Louis was saved only because the French infantry were able to cross to the opposite bank by utilizing a hastily constructed bridge from the end of the causeway.

On February 11 the crusaders withstood a large Egyptian attack against the bridgehead. By March, however, the crusader situation was desperate, and Louis ordered a withdrawal. Harassed by the Egyptians, the crusaders were decisively defeated in a pitched battle at Fariskur on April 8, 1250. Most of Louis's army was annihilated, and he was captured. Louis agreed to pay a ransom of 800,000 gold livres and to abandon Damietta. Sending most of the surviving crusaders home, he sailed to Acre. His

subsequent efforts in the Holy Land during 1250–1254 ended in failure.

Course of the Eighth Crusade (1270)

The Mongols, led by Hülegü, conquered most of Syria, and the Christian crusaders found themselves caught between the Mongols and Mamluks of Egypt. Although most of the other crusader leaders remained neutral, Bohemud VI of Antioch allied with Hülegü's general Kitbuqa and the Mongols against the Mamluks. The two sides came together in battle at Ain Jalut near Nazareth on September 3, 1260, which the Mamluks won. Kitbuqa was among the prisoners and was executed.

Baybars subsequently killed Qutuz and established himself as sultan. Although unsuccessful in his subsequent efforts to restore the Abbasid Caliphate in Baghdad, Baybars has been acclaimed as the greatest of the Mamluk sultans and recovered most of the crusader territory in Palestine and Syria.

The Christian reversals prompted King Louis IX of France to again take up the cross in 1270 in the Eighth Crusade. Intrigues by Baybars convinced Louis that he might convert the bey of Tunisia to Christianity, then proceed eastward to Egypt. Charles of Anjou, the new king of Sicily, reluctantly agreed to accompany his brother Louis to North Africa.

Meeting opposition, Louis commenced siege operations against Tunis. However, a plague swept the crusader camp, and Louis was among its victims. Charles then assumed command and negotiated an end to the crusade in return for tribute for both France and himself. Prince Edward of England (later king as Edward I) then arrived, only to find the Eighth Crusade at an end.

Course of the Ninth Crusade (1271–1272)

Edward campaigned in the Holy Land during 1271–1272. With some 1,000 crusaders, Edward mounted raids in Palestine, one of which reached Nazareth. Edward's forays had no major impact, however.

In 1289 Mamluk sultan Kala'un captured Tripoli from the crusaders, and two years later the final disaster occurred. After some Christian adventurers robbed a Muslim caravan in Syria, killed a number of Muslim merchants, and attacked several towns, Mamluk sultan Khalil demanded satisfaction. Receiving none, he marched against the Christian stronghold of Acre. Laying siege to it, he took Acre after 43 days and allowed his men to massacre or enslave the 60,000 prisoners. Tyre, Haifa, and Beirut soon fell, bringing finis to the crusader kingdoms of the Latin East.

Significance

In the two centuries of crusading effort, Muslim civilization had clearly proven superior to Christian civilization in war. While the Crusades in the Holy Land had failed in their religious purpose of securing that territory for Christianity, they nonetheless had major and far-reaching impact. They had, for example, helped delay the capture by the Turks of Constantinople. The Crusades also had a major role in bringing about the end of medieval Europe. Many knights had sold or mortgaged properties to take part in the Crusades, while peasants had secured remission of feudal dues and obligations. Serfs who participated had been able to leave the land, and many failed to return there afterward.

The coming together of two civilizations had profound impact on both. Muslims, once tolerant of religious diversity, were made intolerant by the Crusades, while the Christians discovered that another civilization could be as refined as their own. This certainly helped weaken the hold of the Catholic Church on the faithful. Certainly the power of the Catholic Church, enhanced by the First Crusade, was greatly diminished by those that followed.

Arabic words and Arabic science came to the West, as did probably the reintroduction of public baths and private latrines and a revival of the Roman custom of shaving the beard. Gunpowder, the compass, and printing were all known in the East and may have come to the West as a consequence of the Crusades. Certainly the crusaders brought back to Europe with them advanced glass-making techniques that would find their way into the stained glass of many Gothic cathedrals.

The Crusades brought home to Europeans the vastness of the world and the opportunities posed for trade. This led to the voyages of discovery and exploration. The crusaders may have lost the Holy Land, but the Italian cities greatly benefited from significantly increased trade in the eastern Mediterranean. This in turn influenced banking and produced the wealth that made possible the Renaissance.

Further Reading

Asbridge, Thomas. *The Crusades: The Authoritative History of the War for the Holy Land.* New York: Ecco, 2010.

Asbridge, Thomas. *The First Crusade: A New History; The Roots of Conflict between Christianity and Islam.* New York: Oxford University Press, 2005.

Findley, Carter Vaughan. *The Turks in World History.* New York: Oxford University Press, 2005.

Hillenbrand, Carole. *The Crusades: Islamic Perspectives.* Edinburgh, UK: Edinburgh University Press, 1999.

Hindley, Geoffrey. *A Brief History of the Crusades*. New York: Constable and Robinson, 2013.

Hindley, Geoffrey. *The Crusades: Islam and Christianity in the Struggle for World Supremacy*. New York: Carroll and Graf, 2004.

Hindley, Geoffrey. *Saladin: Hero of Islam*. Barnsley, South Yorkshire, UK: Pen and Sword Military, 2007.

Jackson, Peter. *The Seventh Crusade, 1244–1254: Sources and Documents*. Burlington, VT: Ashgate, 2007.

Madden, Thomas F. *The New Concise History of the Crusades*. Lanham, MD: Rowman and Littlefield, 2005.

Mayer, Hans Eberhard. *The Crusades*. 2nd ed. Oxford: Oxford University Press, 1988.

Nicolle, David. *The First Crusade, 1066–99: Conquest of the Holy Land*. New York: Osprey, 2003.

Nicolle, David. *The Fourth Crusade, 1202–04: The Betrayal of Byzantium*. New York: Osprey, 2011.

Phillips, Jonathan. *Holy Warriors: A Modern History of the Crusades*. New York: Random House, 2010.

Riley-Smith, Jonathan. *The Crusades: A Short History*. 2nd ed. New Haven, CT: Yale University Press, 2005.

Riley-Smith, Jonathan. *The First Crusaders, 1096–1131*. New York: Cambridge University Press, 1997.

Riley-Smith, Jonathan. *The Oxford History of the Crusades*. New York: Oxford University Press, 2002.

Runciman, Steven. *A History of the Crusades: The Kingdom of Acre and the Later Crusades*. 1951; reprint, New York: Cambridge University Press, 1977.

Tyerman, Christopher. *God's War: A New History of the Crusades*. Cambridge, MA: Belknap, 2006.

Vasil'ev, Aleksandr Aleksandrovich. *History of the Byzantine Empire, 324–1453*. Madison: University of Wisconsin Press, 1952.

Mongol Conquests (1206–1287)

Dates	1206–1287
Location	Asia, Russia, Eastern and Central Europe, the Middle East, Africa
Combatants	Mongols vs. virtually all Eurasian states
Principal Commanders	Mongols: Genghis Khan, Chepe, Ögödei, Jebe, Sübetai, Möngke Khan, Kublai Khan, Bayan, Güyük Xi Xai: Kusluk Khwarazm Empire: Alaud-Din Mohammed, Jellaluddin Principality of Kiev: Mstislav Poland: Bołeslav V Silesia: Prince Henry Bohemia: Wenceslas Hungary: Béla IV Mamluks: Saif ad-Fin Qutuz, Baybars, Kala'un
Principal Battles	Irtysh, Jand, Parwan, Indus, Kalka River, Huang He (Yellow River), Yinchuan, Hangzhou, Kraków (Cracow), Liegnitz (Legnica), Sajó River, Kosedagh, Ain Jalut, Hakata Bay (first and second), Homs
Outcome	The Mongols conquer most of Eurasia. The devastation wrought has major demographic consequences for both Europe and Asia.

Causes

Personal ambition and desire for territorial conquest lay behind the amazing expansion of Mongol landholdings, to include most of Asia, part of Southeast Asia, and much of Eastern Europe. Mongol military expansion was unlike almost any other. Remarkably well organized, it relied on an efficient intelligence service and a highly effective military. Its tactics were extremely violent and exacted a frightful toll on the peoples who were conquered, bringing with it widespread terror and population displacement on a heretofore unknown scale.

During a span of two centuries the Mongols conquered or pillaged much of the known world. As the largest contiguous land empire in history, the Mongol Empire was second in total area only to that of the British Empire at the end of the 19th century. At its greatest extent, the Mongol Empire embraced more than 12 million square miles and an estimated population of more than 100 million people. It extended from East Asia to Central Europe. Western Europe, however, remained apart from its control.

One man, Temujin, more readily known as Genghis Khan (Chingghis or Jenghis Khan), laid the foundation for and initiated this vast enterprise. Before he came to power the Mongols were a disparate group of tribes, warring largely with one another. They lived a nomadic, herding existence in Outer Mongolia, the Gobi Desert, and Inner Mongolia.

Temujin was born in the Gobi Desert region in 1162, the elder son of Yesügei (Yesukai) the Strong, chieftain of a sub-clan of the Great Mongols in north-central Mongolia. On the murder of his father in 1175, Temujin fled into the desert with the remainder of his family. By age 17, he was leading a band of followers in raids against his enemies. During years of fighting in the desert, Temujin gained a reputation for boldness, strong leadership, cunning, and astute diplomacy. His forces steadily grew in number, and by 1188 he probably had 20,000 men under arms. Temujin assembled a highly effective staff and gave considerable attention to improving weapons, equipment, tactics, and communication. His goal was to unify the diverse tribes of Mongolia and then conquer the neighboring non-Mongolian peoples.

In 1194 Temujin began a series of successful campaigns southwest of the Gobi Desert against the Tatars. During the next two decades he established an empire centered on the Gobi Desert, with his capital at Karakorum. By 1204 he had taken the name Genghis Khan (Supreme Ruler) and had unified the diverse tribes of Mongolia through a common-law system and the threat of military action. His administrative system was both efficient and fair, and he promoted toleration of all religions. Taking advantage of the skill in horsemanship instilled in every Mongolian male from youth, Genghis assembled a formidable and highly mobile military force, then prepared to use it to conquer much of Asia.

Course

Genghis Khan began the Mongol conquest of China by invading the Xi Xia (Western Xia or Tangut) Empire in late 1205. Frustrated in several campaigns by the Xi Xia defensive fortifications, he hired Chinese engineers to help him overcome these, and in 1209 the Xi Xias acknowledged his suzerainty. In 1208 he had crushed the last resistance to his rule in Mongolia, defeating Kushluk (Guchluk) of the Naiman tribe in the Battle of Irtysh. Granted refuge with the Kara-Khitai Tatars, in 1209 Kushluk seized control of the Kara-Khitais in a coup d'état. He then prepared to resume warfare against Genghis, whose spies kept him well informed of Kushluk's plans.

In 1211 Genghis invaded the Jin Empire of north China. Within two years his armies had conquered Jin territory as far as the Great Wall. He then sent his forces into the territory between the Great Wall and the Huang He (Yellow River), defeating the Jin armies there. Laying waste to much of northern China, in 1215 the Mongols finally captured and sacked the Jin capital at present-day Beijing and forced the Jin emperor to recognize Mongol suzerainty, although all China would not be conquered until 1234, after Genghis's death. Genghis acquired from the Chinese valuable military technology in tunnel engineering, siege engines, defensive armor, and, most important, the use of gunpowder.

In 1217 Genghis sent some 12,000 men under his brilliant young general Chepe (Jebei) against Kushluk in Kara-Khitai. Chepe defeated the Kara-Khitai army west of Kashgar, capturing Kushluk. Chepe then executed him.

Genghis then turned his attention to the Muslim Khwarazm Empire in the area between the Aral Sea and Afghanistan, ruled by Shah Alaud-Din Mohammed (Mohammed Shah). In 1218 Genghis had purchased stock in the goods of three Khiva merchants, and he dispatched with them Mongol representatives to obtain other products. Not unreasonably, Nasiruddin, governor of the frontier province of Otrar, believed that the Mongols were spies, but he rashly asked permission of the shah to execute them. Alaud-Din Mohammed gave him such authority, and the merchants were killed. Furious, Genghis sent an ambassador to Nasiruddin and demanded

retribution. Nasiruddin put the envoy to death. Genghis's response was war.

The word "horde," the usual descriptor for a Mongol field army, suggests that Mongol field forces were very large and unorganized and that they triumphed as a consequence of superior numbers. This is not true. The largest Mongol force assembled by Genghis Khan for a campaign was for the invasion of Persia and numbered fewer than 240,000 men. Indeed, most Mongol armies numbered fewer than 150,000 men. Mongol military success rested instead on superior homogenous organization, superb training, extraordinary discipline, excellent leadership, and speed of execution.

The Mongol Army was essentially a cavalry force. All males aged 15 to 60 and capable of undergoing rigorous training were eligible for conscription into the military. Raising the requisite forces was never a problem, however, because this was a source of honor in the tribal warrior tradition. Virtually all Mongols learned to ride from childhood. Reared in the harsh conditions of the Gobi Desert, they were accustomed to hardships and were generally in excellent physical condition. Commanders were selected on the basis of demonstrated leadership and courage in battle, and discipline was extraordinary, with complete obedience to orders.

The individual Mongol soldier was probably the best trained of his day in the world. Extensive drill allowed coordinated and complicated battlefield maneuvers, which were controlled by means of signal flags, whistling arrows, and fire arrows. All of this permitted great flexibility on the battlefield.

Winter was no barrier to Mongol movement, and the Mongols often utilized frozen rivers as ready-made highways. Unlike

ASIA, CA. 1330

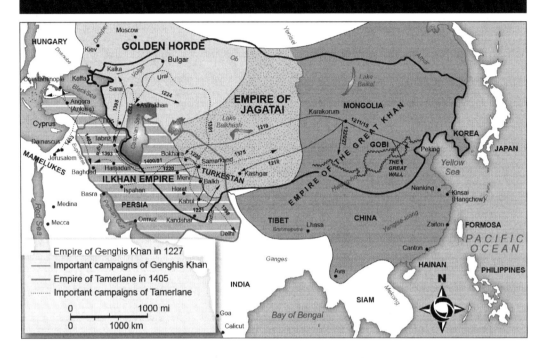

Empire of Genghis Khan in 1227
Important campaigns of Genghis Khan
Empire of Tamerlane in 1405
Important campaigns of Tamerlane

0   1000 mi
0   1000 km

the Huns or the Vikings, the Mongols were adept at military engineering and at siege warfare, including the construction of such artillery as the trebuchet. Mongol cavalry was generally more lightly armed and armored than its counterparts, allowing much swifter movement and maneuver. Each man was equipped with one or more spare horses, which were herded along behind the supply train. Mongol cavalrymen also carried sufficient basic equipment to maintain themselves in the field. Pillaging as they proceeded, Mongol forces were able to live off the land to a great degree, largely dispensing with supply trains.

Mongol field armies usually operated independently, which made it easier to live off the land. The Mongols employed a highly efficient courier system, enabling the field armies to keep in contact with each other and the Mongol leadership and

to coordinate their movements in order to concentrate resources at key locations. Most important, before they undertook a campaign, the Mongols devoted considerable attention to planning, including extensive intelligence collection on the enemy: his strengths and weaknesses and the disposition and size of forces.

The Mongols were particularly adept at siege warfare, which they learned during their early fighting in China. A large yet highly mobile siege train consisting of wagons and pack animals accompanied the field armies and was manned by highly efficient Chinese engineers. Mongol military engineers were among the best in the world. If a city could not be taken by storm, the siege train was brought forward and began operations, while the remainder of the army sought out the enemy field forces. The destruction of the latter generally brought the surrender of the town or city, in which case the besieged were treated with only moderate severity. If the besieged location resisted, once it was taken it would be given over to pillage and destruction. Oftentimes, the speed of the Mongol advance obviated the need for siege operations and saw towns and cities taken by surprise. On occasion, in an assault the Mongol forces would herd captives in front of their own assaulting troops, forcing the defenders to first kill their own countrymen in order to get at the attackers. The Mongols also employed fire arrows from horse archers as well as from siege engines. Mongol psychological warfare—in the form of the circulation of stories of what happened to a location when there was opposition and the Mongol willingness to treat leniently those who cooperated with them—often ended resistance before it had begun.

The Mongol invasion force of 1219 consisted of four main armies invading from the northeast under Genghis and his sons Juji, Jagatai, and Ögödei as well as a small force from Kara-Khitai under Chepe. With perhaps only 30,000 men between them, Juji and Chepe fought to a draw some 200,000 Khwarezmians in the Battle of Jand in the Ferghana Valley.

In 1220 the Mongol armies advanced into Transoxiana on a wide front, investing both Khojend and Otrar. Believing incorrectly that the converging Mongol armies outnumbered his own 500,000 men, Alaud-Din Mohammed panicked and fled. Genghis then captured Samarkand. Although he spared most of the inhabitants, Genghis killed all who took refuge in the citadel and the mosque. He then pillaged the city completely and conscripted some 30,000 young men into his army.

For five months Genghis's armies continued their pursuit of Alaud-Din Mohammed

all the way to the Caspian Sea, where he died in February 1221 on an island off the coast. Muslim resistance continued but was largely ineffective. Meanwhile, Alaud-Din Mohammed's son Jellaluddin (Jalal ad-Din Mingburnu) was busy raising a new army in Ghazni.

Commanding an army of about 120,000 men, Jellaluddin defeated some 30,000 Mongols in the Battle of Parwan (Pirvan) in the Hindu Kush. Jellaluddin's Afghan allies departed, however, and he withdrew with about 30,000 men into the northern Punjab, pursued by Genghis with some 50,000 Mongols. The next battle decided the campaign.

Jellaluddin had taken up an excellent defensive position along the Indus River, with one flank protected by a bend in the river and the other flank protected by mountains. The Mongols made the first charge in the 1221 Battle of the Indus, but the defenders halted it. A Muslim counterattack almost broke the center of the Mongol line, but Genghis was able to get some 10,000 men into the mountains and around the Muslim line. They now fell on the Muslim flank. Under attack from both front and flank, the Muslim defense collapsed, and the Mongols won the battle.

Jellaluddin rode his horse off a cliff into the river and managed to reach the other side. Genghis sent forces in pursuit, and they ravaged much of the rest of the Punjab but failed to locate the prince. Genghis Khan then broke off the pursuit and spent the next several years consolidating his hold over Ghazni.

At the same time that he was engaged with the Khwarezmian Empire, Genghis sent armies into the southern Caucasus. In 1221 he permitted Jebe and Sübetai (Subutai, Subodei) to conduct a reconnaissance in force through the Caucasus Mountains and into Southern Europe. Jebe apparently exercised overall command of the 40,000 Mongol forces. Advancing through Azerbaijan, they passed the winter of 1221–1222 in eastern Armenia. In the spring of 1222 they moved into present-day Georgia, defeating a Christian force that had assembled there to join the Fifth Crusade to the Holy Land. The Mongols then proceeded into southern Russia, defeating in detail the fierce tribes of the Russian steppes. Crossing the Don River, the Mongols entered the Crimean Peninsula, taking the Genoese fortress of Sudak before turning north into present-day Ukraine.

The Mongols passed the winter of 1222–1223 by the Black Sea. Believing that they had accomplished their mission, Jebe and Sübetai prepared to return home, but they also sent spies into Eastern and Central Europe to gather information regarding possible future campaigns. On May 31, 1223, a mixed force of some 80,000 men under Mstislav, the prince of Kiev, moved against the Mongols near the mouth of the Volga River. The two Mongol leaders sought a peaceful resolution, but when their envoys were murdered, they attacked and nearly annihilated the Russian forces in the Battle of the Kalka River, then raided several hundred miles northward before turning east on orders from Genghis. On the return trip, Jebe fell ill and died. After a march totaling some 4,000 miles, Sübetei and his men rejoined Genghis and the main Mongol armies.

The Xi Xia Empire had refused to aid the Mongols during Genghis's campaign against the Khwarezmian Empire. Indeed, the Tanguts had entered into an alliance with their former bitter enemy, the Jin Empire, against the Mongols. Genghis now prepared to invade both the Xi Xia and Jin Empires. During 1225–1226 he

designated his son Ögödei as his successor and assembled an invasion force of some 180,000 men.

The Mongols struck in late 1226 when the rivers were frozen. The Tanguts were prepared, and they met the Mongols with a numerically superior force of more than 300,000 men on the western banks of the frozen Huang He. Genghis Khan lured the Tanguts into attacking across the frozen ice, whereupon they came under assault by Mongol archers. Mongol cavalry and infantry then attacked the broken Tangut military formations as additional Mongol mounted forces swept around against the Tangut infantry on the other bank, annihilating it. The Mongol victory was complete. Reportedly, in the aftermath of the battle the Mongols counted some 300,000 Tangut dead.

Pursuing remaining Tangut forces, Genghis Khan's army killed the Xi Xia emperor, who had taken refuge in a mountain fortress. Part of the army then laid siege to the formidable walled city of Yinchuan, which had held out against the Mongols in the past, while Ögödei and the remaining forces moved against the Jins.

The Siege of Yinchuan lasted some six months. Genghis sent Chagaan to negotiate terms with new Western Xia emperor Mozhu, who agreed to surrender but asked for a month's delay to prepare suitable gifts. Genghis agreed, although Mongol military operations continued. Genghis rejected a peace offer from the Jins, however.

In August 1227 Genghis died. The cause of death remains unknown. It has been attributed to battle, illness, falling from his horse, or wounds sustained in hunting. Genghis had, however, shared his plans of campaign against the Jins with Ögödei, his son and designated successor. Meanwhile, in order not to jeopardize the ongoing campaign, Genghis's death was kept a secret. In September 1227, Mozhu surrendered and was promptly executed. The Mongols then mercilessly pillaged Yinchuan, slaughtering the city's population and effectively completing annihilation of the Western Xia state.

In 1231, the Mongols mounted their first invasion of Koryo (Korea). That same year after forming an alliance with the Songs, Ögödei implemented his father's plans for destruction of the Jin Empire. He sent a large army under Tolui south through Western Xia territory and the Song province of Sichuan. It then turned east and proceeded through Hanzhong into the territory of the Jin Empire. When Tolui died in 1232, Sübetei assumed command of the Mongol forces. He laid siege to the Jin capital of Pien-ching (present-day Kaifeng), which finally fell after a year. Sübetei then conquered the remaining Jin territory.

Ögödei refused to share his conquest of the Jin Empire with the Songs, leading the Songs in 1234 to seize the former Jin province of Henan. This in turn brought a protracted struggle (1234–1279) between the Mongols and the Songs. In 1235 Ögödei called a conference of key Mongol leaders to discuss options for future conquests. He presented four simultaneous military operations: Song China (where the campaign was already under way), Korea, Southeast Asia, and Europe.

Ögödei died in 1241, and the war against the Songs was won by his nephews Möngke Khan (r. 1241–1259) and Kublai Khan (r. 1260–1294) and their successors. Operating at first under the authority of his older brother, Kublai conquered Yunnan during 1252–1253 and a subordinate took Tonkin, capturing Thang Long (present-day Hanoi in northern Vietnam) in 1257. During 1257–1259, Möngke himself directed a

series of highly effective campaigns against the Songs, but his death from dysentery produced a dynastic struggle in the Mongol Empire and a temporary lull in fighting the Songs, allowing the latter a chance to rejuvenate. Not until 1268 was Kublai, having defeated his brother in a struggle for power, again able to direct full attention to the Songs.

Mongol general Bayan, grandson of Sübetei, played a key role in the Mongol success. The decisive battle was the capture of the Song capital of Hangzhou in 1276. It took three additional years of fighting, however, before the Mongols established complete control over the entire Song Empire.

Kublai was very much interested in the sea and, with the help of Song turncoats, built a large navy. It proved decisive in the Mongol victory over the Songs. Indeed, the culminating battle of the war occurred at sea in the Battle of Yamen in the Bay of Canton (Guangzhou). Although vastly outnumbered, the Mongol ships triumphed. The Song naval commander leapt into the sea with the boy Song emperor Huaizong in his arms, drowning both of them.

The fourth area that Ögödei had marked out for Mongol expansion was Europe, and during 1237–1238 the Mongols mounted invasions of eastern and northern Rus and in 1239–1240 southern and western Rus. In 1238–1239 they were in the North Caucasus, and in 1238–1240 they invaded Cumania and Alania in the western part of the Eurasian steppe. In 1240–1241 Mongol forces under Godan, son of Ögödei, conquered Tibet, and in 1241 the Mongols raided into the Punjab, capturing Lahore.

Having consolidated Mongol control over the loose federation of East Slavic tribes of Rus, Sübetei prepared to invade Central Europe. The states of Central and Western Europe knew little about Mongol conquests or intentions, but the Mongols had gathered accurate intelligence about the political situation to their west. Sübetei commenced his offensive in November 1240 with some 150,000 men. He began the campaign in winter in order to achieve maximum mobility on horseback in the marshlands and across frozen rivers. When Kiev rejected his surrender demands, Sübetei assaulted it, capturing Kiev on December 6.

Leaving behind 30,000 men to control the conquered territory and maintain his lines of communication, Sübetei invaded Central Europe with his remaining 120,000 men. The Mongol advance proceeded on four axes. Kaidu, grandson of Ögödei, commanded the northern flank; Batu, son of Jochi and grandson of Genghis, and Sübetei had charge of the two central forces; and Kadan, son of Ögödei, protected the southern flank. The two middle forces were to pass through the central Carpathian Mountains into Transylvania and then meet at Pest on the east bank of the Danube. Meanwhile, Kaidu proceeded into Silesia, defeating a Polish army under King Bołeslav V at Kraków (Cracow) on March 3, 1241.

To meet the Mongols under Kaidu, Prince Henry of Silesia assembled a mixed force of some 40,000 Silesians, Germans, Poles, and Teutonic Knights. At the same time, King Wenceslas of Bohemia marched north with 50,000 men to join them. Kaidu struck before the two could join. In the hard-fought Battle of Liegnitz (Legnica), also known as the Battle of Wahlstatt, on April 9, 1241, Kaidu smashed Prince Henry's army. Kaidu then halted, having achieved his aims of devastating north-central Europe and preventing its armies from moving southward.

The Mongol southern advance also went well. In mid-April the Mongols secured Transylvania, and Kadan drove northward through the Iron Gates to link up with Sübetei. On March 12, meanwhile, Hungarian king Béla IV had learned that the Mongols had taken the Carpathian passes. He immediately convened a conference of nobles at Buda, and on March 15 the conferees learned that the Mongol advance guard had already arrived at Pest, opposite Buda on the east bank of the Danube.

Béla was confident that the Pest defenses could hold against the attackers and so spent the next two weeks assembling an army of some 100,000 men. Believing that he had sufficient manpower to defeat the Mongols, at the beginning of April he departed Pest and moved east. The Mongols withdrew before Béla's cautious advance.

Late on April 10 about 100 miles northeast of Pest, the Hungarians encountered and defeated a weak Mongol force defending a bridge at Muhi on the Sajó River, a tributary of the Tisza. Béla then established a strong bridgehead on the east bank of the Sajó and camped for the night, with the bulk of his force on the west bank in a strong defensive position of wagons chained together.

The Mongols struck before dawn on April 11, attacking the Hungarian bridgehead with stones hurled by catapults and with an onslaught of arrows, followed closely by an infantry assault. The defenders fought fiercely, and the Hungarians sortied from the main camp to their aid, only to discover too late that the attack was only a feint. Sübetei had led 30,000 men to ford the river some distance south of the bridge and then came in from the south and rear of the Hungarians. Nearly surrounded, the Hungarians found themselves packed into a small area and were there destroyed by Mongol arrows, stones, and hurled burning naphtha.

Béla managed to escape with some of his men to the north toward Bratislava (Pressburg, Pozsony). Although Mongol losses in the Battle of the Sajó River were heavy, the Hungarian force was virtually destroyed, with between 40,000 and 70,000 dead, including much of the Magyar nobility. Only the Danube River prevented a further Mongol advance.

The Mongols now held all Eastern Europe from the Dnieper to the Oder and from the Baltic to the Danube. In a campaign of only four months, they had destroyed Christian forces numbering many times their own. Following the victory of the Sajó River, the Mongols now ravaged all eastern Hungary and Transylvania. In May 1241 Béla IV appealed in vain for aid to Pope Gregory IX and Holy Roman emperor Frederick II.

At the beginning of February 1242, Sübetei resumed the Mongol westward advance, crossing the frozen Danube. Although they laid waste to much of western Hungary, the Mongols were unable to take the fortified cities of Székesfehérvár and Esztergom. At the same time, other Mongol forces moved to the shores of the Adriatic in pursuit of Béla IV, who sought refuge on the fortified island of Trau, near Split (Spalato) in Croatia.

It was at this point that word arrived from Karakorum, 6,000 miles to the east, of the death of Ögödei on December 11, 1241. With all direct descendants required to be in Karakorum for the election of the new great khan, Sübetei reluctantly obeyed. In March 1242 the Mongol armies withdrew. Moving via the southeast, they ravaged present-day Serbia and Bulgaria. With a majority of its settlements having been destroyed and a large portion of the population slain during the Mongol occupation, the Hungarian state would have to be completely reconstituted.

Güyük, one of Ögödei's sons, was elected great khan in January 1246. Batu became khan of the western regions (Northwest Asia and Eastern Europe) known as the Kipchak Khanate and more usually the Khanate of the Golden Horde, perhaps for the gold color of their tents. Establishing his capital at Sarai (Zarev) on the lower Volga River, Batu secured the vassalage of Alexander Nevski, prince of Novgorod, who assisted him in securing Mongol control of all Russia. Batu and his descendants would rule Russia for the next 250 years. Batu also led the Mongols to victory over the Seljuk Turks in the June 26, 1243, Battle of Kosedagh, which brought Mongol control over Anatolia.

Güyük ordered a resumption of the Mongol offensives and accompanied the Mongol army sent against Eastern Europe but died en route to meet Batu. Batu declined the subsequent election as great khan, and Möngke (Mangu), son of Tolui, was selected in an assembly at Batu's camp. Confirmation by the obligatory full assembly was delayed by a conspiracy of other relatives who sought to overthrow Möngke. The plot was discovered, the conspirators were executed, and Möngke was reaffirmed as khan in 1251. He ruled until 1259.

In 1257 Mongol general Sogatu arrived in Annam (present-day central Vietnam) to conquer the Kingdom of Champa. The Mongol forces advanced easily through Annam, but the Chams took advantage of mountainous terrain to carry out a protracted guerrilla war.

In 1258 Mongol forces under Hülegü, grandson of Genghis, conquered southern Mesopotamia, taking Baghdad and ending the Abbasid Caliphate. By 1260 Hülegü had taken most of Syria, and the Christian crusaders found themselves caught between the Mongols and Mamluks of Egypt. Although most of the other crusader leaders remained neutral, Bohemud VI of Antioch allied with Hülegü's general Kitbuqa and the Mongols against the Mamluks. The two sides came together in battle at Ain Jalut near Nazareth on September 3, 1260. Each deployed about 20,000 men. Saif ad-Fin Qutuz and Baybars were the Mamluk commanders.

The Mamluks took a page from the Mongol book and drew out the Mongol cavalry by feigning retreat but then were almost overwhelmed by the furious Mongol charge. The Mamluks held, however, allowing their cavalry and infantry hidden in nearby valleys to fall on the Mongol cavalry and destroy it. The remaining Mongols were then forced to withdraw. Kitbuqa was among those taken prisoner and was executed. The Battle of Ain Jalut marked both the zenith of Mongol power and the first defeat from which they did not return and prevail. It served to shatter the myth of Mongol invincibility and has also been heralded as having prevented a Mongol invasion of Europe. Certainly, had the Mongols taken Egypt there was little to prevent them from sweeping across North Africa and then invading southern Spain.

In 1260 Kublai, fourth son of Toulai and grandson of Genghis Khan, was elected great khan. His brother Arigh Böke disputed the election, leading to a civil war (1260–1261) in which Kublai was victorious. In 1264 Kublai constructed a new Chinese-style capital known as Dadu on the site of present-day Beijing, and in 1271 he declared himself emperor, establishing a new Chinese dynasty, the Yuan. Conquering the Southern Songs in 1279,

he once again brought unity to northern and southern China and also proved to be one of China's most capable rulers.

Kublai's ambitions included not only the Eurasian landmass but also the Japanese archipelago. At first he tried diplomacy, sending five diplomatic missions to the Japanese court during the period 1268–1273. The Japanese killed some of the Chinese emissaries, and Kublai resorted to force.

The first invasion, in 1274, was most probably a reconnaissance in force. Kublai sent 25,000 soldiers to Korea and pressured the vassal Korean emperor to raise an army of 15,000 men and supply 900 ships to transport the 40,000 men, their horses, and equipment to Kyushu. The Mongols first took the islands of Tsushima and Iki, between Korea and Japan, as staging areas, then landed their army at Hakata Bay (Ajkozaki) on northern Kyushu. The Japanese hastily mobilized all available forces, but their generals had no experience in managing large bodies of troops, and the Mongols were both better armed and more effectively led. The Mongols were defeating the Japanese when a severe storm led the Mongol ship captains to call for the men to be reembarked or risk being marooned on Japanese soil. Although the majority of Mongol ships made it back to Korea, reportedly some 200 were lost at sea and others were taken by the Japanese, the invaders suffering some 13,000 men killed in the invasion attempt.

Kublai Khan then assembled a far larger expeditionary force in two separate contingents. The Northern Fleet sailed from ports in northern China; it numbered as many as 70,000 Mongol and Korean soldiers in perhaps 1,000 ships. The Southern Fleet was even larger. It numbered 100,000 men transported in perhaps 3,500 ships but was not yet ready when the Northern Fleet departed on May 22, 1281.

In early June, the Mongols again took Tsushima and Iki as staging areas. The expeditionary force then sailed to northern Kyushu, arriving in Hakata Bay on June 21. The Southern Fleet had not yet arrived, but troops from the Northern Fleet began to go ashore on June 23. This time the Japanese were better prepared. At sea they carried out nighttime harassing attacks against the Mongol ships and destroyed some of them. While the Japanese were unable to defeat the Mongols on land, they did check their advance inland.

The Southern Fleet began arriving in mid-July, and its deployment was complete by August 12. The Japanese appeared lost before such a large force, but on the night of August 14–15 a violent storm (the Kamikaze, or Divine Wind) blew in from the north and wrecked most of the Mongol ships in the bay. The Japanese claimed that only about 200 of the Mongol ships and 20 percent of the men survived the storm or the Japanese soldiers waiting for them when they swam ashore. Cut off from their supplies, those Mongols already ashore were easily defeated. Some 120,000 Mongols and Koreans may have perished in the invasion attempt, while the Japanese made slaves of some 12,000 others.

The indefatigable Kublai Khan made plans for yet another invasion of Japan, but unrest in China diverted him, and he never launched the third invasion. The Japanese retained their independence, and later a modernized Japan would seek to reverse the situation and itself control China.

The Mongols also suffered rebuff in Syria. In 1281 Mongol leader Abaqa Khan, at the head of perhaps 30,000–50,000 men, mounted an invasion of Syria. Aided by Christian crusaders, he reached as far south as Homs where, in the Second Battle of Homs, Mamluk sultan Kala'un with perhaps 100,000 men bested the Mongols and forced them back to the Euphrates River.

The Mongols continued their efforts to penetrate Southeast Asia. In 1277 forces from Burma (present-day Myanmar) invaded the bordering state of Kanngai, which owed allegiance to China. The Mongol governor of Yunnan responded by sending 12,000 Mongol troops to confront the 40,000 invading Burmese. In the Battle of Ngasaung-gyan, the Mongols were victorious. Their horses frightened by the Burmese elephants, the Mongols dismounted and used their bows and arrows to drive off the elephants, then remounted and made a decisive charge into the Burmese ranks. The Mongols then raided into Myanmar all the way to Bhamo. In 1283 following a new Burmese border raid, the Mongols again invaded. Defeating the Burmese at Kaungsin near Bhamo, the Mongols established a series of border fortresses along the upper Irrawaddy River, and in 1287 the Mongols conquered Myanmar and set up a puppet regime there.

The Mongols continued their attempt to secure present-day Vietnam. In 1781 they invaded the kingdoms of Annam and Champa in central Vietnam. In 1785 Toagau, son of Kublai Khan, led additional forces to Tonkin to assist Mongol general Sogatu, who was engaged in a protracted struggle to subdue Champa. Although Toagau captured Thang Long (present-day Hanoi), the Annamese resisted, and he was eventually defeated. Sogatu, marching north to assist him, was rebuffed by the Annamese and Chams. Returning to Champa, Sogatu was defeated there and killed, halting further Mongol advances southward.

The two sides then worked out an agreement whereby the Mongols withdrew in return for recognition by both Annam and Champa of Mongol suzerainty.

In 1294 the Mongol Empire split into separate provinces, or khanates. By the mid-14th century they were separate states: the Il-Khanate in Persia (present-day Iran), the Chagatai Khanate of Central Asia, the Yuaan dynasty of China, and the Golden Horde in present-day central and western Russia. Territorial gains of the Mongols persisted into the 14th century in China, Persia, and Russia and into 19th century in India in the Mughal Empire (Mughal being the Arabic word for "Mongol"). The longest lived of the successor states to the Mongol Empire was the Crimean Khanate; it was annexed by Russia only in 1783.

Significance

The Mongols had lasting impact. Their vast empire unified large areas of Asia and Eastern Europe. Some of this territory, including significant portions of Russia and China, remains unified today, although not under the Mongols. The Mongols were assimilated into the local populations.

Mongol conquest and rule also had pronounced demographic effects, although scholars disagree on the extent. Some hold that the Mongols caused depopulation on a massive scale and instituted major demographic shifts, such as the movement of the Iranian tribes from Central Asia into modern-day Iran. While the Mongols generally spared the lives of the populations of cities submitting to their rule, it was also common practice for them to slaughter all the inhabitants of those resisting. This, of course, encouraged enemies to surrender, but the effects of such policies could also be devastating. Hungary was said to have lost half of its population of 2 million, while the population of China also fell by half during its half century of Mongol rule. Russia also registered significant losses. Estimates of the number of people killed by the Mongols range from 30 million to 80 million people.

Some researchers also claim that the Black Death that devastated much of Europe in the late 1340s may have been the result of Mongol biological warfare. In 1347 the Mongols laid siege to Caffa, a Genoese trading outpost in Crimea. When plague infected the besiegers, they reportedly catapulted some of the corpses of those who had died of the plague over the walls of Caffa, infecting the inhabitants as well. When the Genoese departed by ship, they took the plague with them to Italy, where it rapidly spread. The Black Death claimed some 20 million people in Europe and perhaps 75 million worldwide.

Further Reading

Brent, Peter. *Genghis Khan: The Rise, Authority, and Decline of Mongol Power.* New York: McGraw-Hill, 1976.

Hartog, Leo. *Genghis Khan, Conqueror of the World.* Reprint ed. New York: I. B. Taurus, 1999.

Juvayni, 'Ala' al-Din, and 'Ala Malik. *Genghis Khan: The History of the World Conqueror.* Seattle: University of Washington Press, 1997.

May, Timothy. *The Mongol Art of War: Chinggis Khan and the Mongol Military System.* Yardley, PA: Westholme, 2007.

May, Timothy. *The Mongol Conquests in World History.* London: Reaktion Books, 2011.

Morgan, David. *The Mongols.* 2nd ed. Hoboken, NJ: Wiley-Blackwell, 2007.

Ratchnevsky, Paul. *Genghis Khan: His Life and Legacy.* Malden, MA: Blackwell, 1991.

Rossabi, Morris. *The Mongols: A Very Short Introduction.* New York: Oxford University Press, 2012.

Saunders, J. J. *The History of the Mongol Conquests.* Philadelphia: University of Pennsylvania Press, 2001.

Turnbull, Stephen. *Genghis Khan and the Mongol Conquests, 1190–1400.* New York: Routledge, 2003.

Hundred Years' War (1337–1453)

Dates	1337–1453
Location	France
Combatants	England vs. France and Scotland
Principal Commanders	England: Edward III, Henry V, John of Lancaster France: Philip VI, Charles V, Charles VI, Joan of Arc
Principal Battles	Sluys, Crécy, Poitiers, Agincourt, Orléans
Outcome	France is devastated, but the English are eventually expelled. The long war's legacy of hatred continues to fuel ongoing rivalry and enmity between France and England until 1904.

Causes

Actually a series of wars, the Hundred Years' War began in 1337 and lasted until 1453. The chief cause of the war was the desire of the English kings to hold on to and expand their territorial holdings in France, while the French kings sought to "liberate" territory under English control. King Edward III of England (r. 1327–1377) claimed to have better right to the French throne than did its occupant, King Philip VI (r. 1330–1350). Another factor was the struggle for control both of the seas and international trading markets. Finally, the English sought retribution for the assistance provided by the French to the Scots in their wars with the English.

In 1328, Philip VI marched in troops and established French administrative control over Flanders, where the weavers were highly dependent on English wool. Edward III responded to Philip's move by embargoing English wool in 1336. This led to a revolt of the Flemings against the French and their conclusion of an alliance with England in 1338. Edward III then declared himself king of France, and the Flemings recognized him as their king. Philip VI declared Edward's fiefs in France south of the Loire forfeit and in 1338 sent his troops into Guienne (Aquitaine). The war was on.

Course

The first phase of the war lasted from 1337 to 1396. It began with Edward dispatching raiding parties from England and Flanders to attack northern and northeastern France. In 1339 Edward invaded northern France but then withdrew before Philip's much larger army. Philip planned to turn the tables and invade England, ending Edward's claim to the French throne. Toward that end, French admiral Hughes Quiéret assembled some 200 ships, including 4 Genoese galleys, off the Flemish coast.

Already planning another invasion of France to secure the French throne, Edward III gathered some 200 ships at Harwich. Warned of the French invasion force assembly, Edward planned to strike first.

The English fleet sailed from Harwich on June 22, with Edward commanding in person, and arrived off the Flanders coast the next day. Fifty additional ships joined it, and Edward sent men and horses ashore to reconnoiter. The reconnaissance completed, he decided to attack the next day.

Sea battles of that day resembled fights on land and were decided at close range, often by boarding. Ships were virtually movable fortresses with temporary wooden structures known as castles added at bow (the origin of the term "forecastle") and stern of converted merchant ships in order to give a height advantage for bowmen or allow the opportunity to hurl down missiles against an opposing ship's crew. It has been claimed but not proven that some of the ships in the battle carried primitive cannon as well as catapults.

The battle occurred off Sluys (Sluis, Ecluse) on the Flemish coast. Quiéret had divided his 200 ships into three divisions. He ordered the ships of each division chained together side by side, with each ship having a small boat filled with stones triced up in the mast so that men in the tops could hurl missiles down on the English decks. The French were armed chiefly with swords and pikes but had little in the way of armor. Quiéret also had some crossbowmen. In effect, he planned to face the English with three large floating forts incapable of rapid movement. Estimates of the number of Frenchmen involved range from 25,000 to 40,000.

Edward had many archers and men-at-arms, the latter well armored. He placed the largest of his 250 ships in the van, and between every 2 ships filled with archers, he placed ships filled with men-at-arms. The smaller ships formed a second division with archers. The decisive weapon in this battle, as it would be on land, was the longbow, which outranged the crossbow.

Barbavera, the commander of the Genoese galleys in the French fleet, urged that they put to sea. He pointed out that failure to do so would yield to the English the advantages of wind, tide, and sun. Quiéret rejected this sound advice.

The Battle of Sluys opened at about noon on June 24, 1340. The English archers poured volley after volley of arrows into the French ships. Once they grappled a French vessel, the Englishmen boarded it and cleared its decks in hand-to-hand fighting. They then proceeded to the next ship, taking one after another under a protective hail of arrows.

Having secured the first division of French ships, the English moved on to the other two divisions. The action extended into the night. The French fleet was almost annihilated, with the English sinking or capturing 166 of their 200 ships. Estimates of casualties vary widely, but the French and their allies may have lost as many as 25,000 men killed, Quiéret among them. The English lost 4,000 men. Edward III now claimed the title "Sovereign of the Narrow Seas." His letter to his son about the battle is the earliest extant English naval dispatch.

The Battle of Sluys was the most important naval engagement of the Hundred Years' War, giving England command of the English Channel for a generation and making possible the invasion of France and the English victories on land that followed. Without the Battle of Sluys, it is unlikely that the war between England and France would have lasted long.

Edward then landed troops and besieged Tournai, but the French forced him to raise the siege and conclude a truce that same year. During 1341–1346 a dynastic struggle occurred in Brittany in which both Edward and Philip VI intervened.

To raise money, Philip had introduced the *gabelle* (salt tax), which led to increased dissatisfaction with his rule. In 1345 Edward began to raise an expeditionary force to invade Normandy, intending to assist his allies in Flanders and Brittany.

Edward landed at La Hogue near Cherbourg in mid-June with perhaps 15,000 men, including a heavy cavalry force of 3,900 knights and men-at-arms and a large number of archers. Most were veterans of the Scottish wars. Edward's army in France was experienced, well trained, and well organized; it was probably the most effective military force for its size in all Europe.

The fleet returned to England, and Edward marched inland. The English took Caen on July 27 following heavy resistance. Edward ordered the entire population killed and the town burned. Although he later rescinded the order, perhaps 3,000 townsmen died during a three-day sack of Caen. This act set the tone for much of the war.

Edward III then moved northeastward, pillaging as he went. For the next month, Philip chased Edward across northern France without bringing him to battle. Meanwhile, Philip's son, Duke John of Normandy, moved north against the English from Gascony, while Philip assembled another force near Paris. Edward III thus achieved his aim of drawing pressure from Guyenne and Brittany.

Reaching the Seine at Rouen, Edward learned that the French had destroyed all accessible bridges over that river except one at Rouen, which was strongly defended. Increasingly worried that he might be cut off and forced to fight south of the Seine, Edward moved his army rapidly along the riverbank southeast and upriver toward Paris, seeking a crossing point that would allow a retreat into Flanders if need be. At Poissy only a few miles from Paris, the English found a repairable bridge and, on August 16, crossed over the Seine there. Although Philip VI had a sizable force at St. Denis, he made no effort to intercept him.

Only after the English had crossed the Seine and were headed north did Philip attempt to intercept. Edward reached the Somme River on August 22, about a day ahead of the pursuing Philip, only to learn that the French had destroyed all the bridges over that river except those at heavily fortified cities. After vainly attacking both Hangest and Pont-Remy, Edward moved north along the western bank trying to find a crossing. On August 23 at Ouisemont, the English killed all the French defenders and burned the town.

On the evening of August 24 the English camped at Acheux. Six miles distant, a large French force defended the bridge at Abbeville, but that night the English learned of a ford only 10 miles from the coast that could be crossed at low tide and was likely to be undefended. Breaking camp in the middle of the night, Edward moved to the ford, named Blanchetaque, only to discover that it was held by some 3,500 Frenchmen under experienced French commander Godemar du Foy.

A now desperate supply situation and the closeness of the French army led Edward III to attempt to cross here. Battle was joined at low tide on the morning of August 1. Edward sent some 100 knights and men across the ford under the cover of a hail of arrows from his longbowmen. The English gained the opposite bank and were able to establish a small beachhead. Edward then fed in more men, and under heavy English longbow fire, the French broke and fled toward Abbeville. Soon the entire English army was across. So

ENGLAND AND FRANCE IN 1429

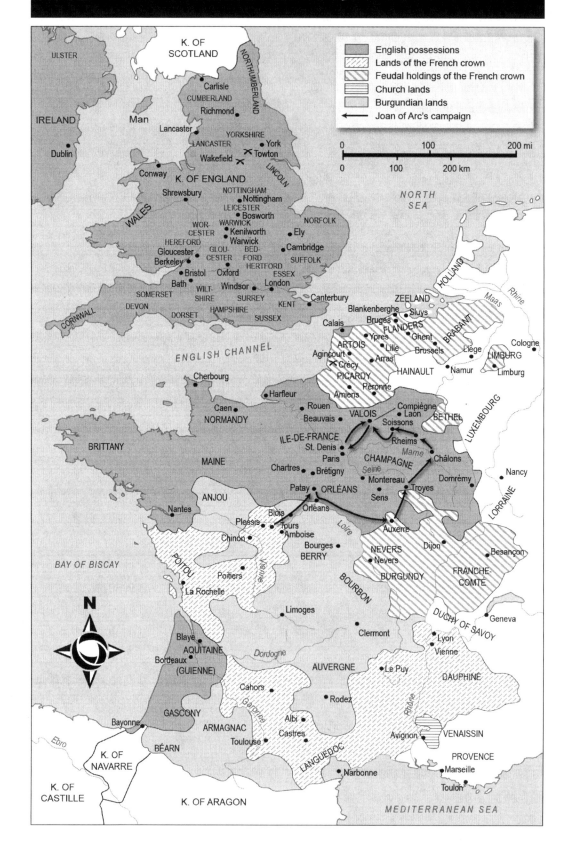

Legend:
- English possessions
- Lands of the French crown
- Feudal holdings of the French crown
- Church lands
- Burgundian lands
- → Joan of Arc's campaign

0   100   200 mi
0   100   200 km

confident was Philip VI that the English would not be able to cross the Somme that no effort had been made to clear the area on the east bank of resources, and the English were thus able to resupply, burning the towns of Noyelles-sur-Mer and Le Crotoy in the process.

Finally, having resupplied and reached a position where he could withdraw into Flanders if need be, Edward III decided to stand and fight. On August 25 he selected a defensive position near the village of Crécy-en-Ponthieu. High ground overlooked a gentle slope over which the French would have to advance. The English right was anchored by the Maye River. The left, just in front of the village of Wadicourt, was protected by a great wood 4 miles deep and 10 miles long.

Edward III commanded more than 11,000 men. He divided his forces into three divisions, known as "battles." Each contained a solid mass of dismounted men-at-arms, perhaps six ranks deep and about 250 yards in length. Edward positioned two of the "battles" side by side as the front line of his defense. The 16-year-old Edward, Prince of Wales (later known as the "Black Prince"), had nominal command of the English right, although Thomas de Beauchamp, 11th Earl of Warwick, held actual command. The Earls of Arundel and Northampton commanded the left "battle." The third "battle," under Edward's personal command, formed a reserve several hundred yards to the rear. Archers occupied the spaces between the "battles" and were echeloned forward in V formations pointing toward the enemy so as to deliver enfilading fire.

Edward located a detachment of cavalry to the rear of each "battle" to counterattack if need be. He also had his men dig holes on the slope as traps for the French

cavalry. The king used a windmill located between his own position and his son's right "battle" as an observation post during the battle.

It has been suggested that Edward may have had some gunpowder artillery at Crécy, but that is by no means certain. The year before he had ordered 100 *ribaulds,* light guns mounted on carts. If these were employed in the battle, it was the first European land battle for gunpowder artillery. In any case, they did not influence the outcome.

The French army at Crécy has been variously estimated at between 30,000 and 60,000 men, including 12,000 heavy cavalry of knights and men-at-arms, 6,000 Genoese mercenary crossbowmen, and a large number of poorly trained infantry. This French force, moving without a reconnaissance screen or any real order, arrived at Crécy at about 6:00 p.m. on August 26, 1346. Without bothering to explore the English position, Philip VI attempted to organize his men for battle. He positioned the Genoese, his only professional force, in a line in front. At this point a quick thunderstorm swept the field, rendering the ground slippery for the attackers.

The well-disciplined Genoese moved across the valley toward the English position, with the disorganized French heavy cavalry in a great mass behind them. Halting about 150 yards from the English "battles," the Genoese loosed their crossbow bolts, most of which fell short. They then reloaded and began to move forward again, only to encounter clouds of English arrows. The Genoese could fire their crossbows about one to two times a minute, while the English longbowmen could get off an arrow every five seconds. The English arrows completely shattered the Genoese, who were not able to close to a range where their crossbow bolts might have been effective.

The French knights behind the Genoese, impatient to join the fray, then rode forward up the slippery slope, over and around the crossbowmen, and encountered the same swarms of arrows. The shock of the French charge carried to the English line, however, where there was some hand-to-hand combat. The English cavalry then charged, and the remaining French knights were driven back. The French regrouped and repeatedly charged (the English claimed some 15–16 separate attacks throughout the night), each time encountering English arrows before finally breaking off contact. The battle was over. The French dead included some 1,500 knights and men-at-arms and between 10,000 and 20,000 crossbowmen and infantrymen in addition to thousands of horses. Philip VI was among the many Frenchmen wounded. English losses were only about 200 dead or wounded.

Crécy made the English a military nation. Europeans were unaware of the advances made by the English military system and were stunned at this infantry victory over a numerically superior force that included some of the finest cavalry in Europe. Crécy restored the infantry to first place. Since this battle, infantry have been the primary element of ground combat forces.

After several days of rest, Edward III marched to the English Channel port of Calais and, beginning on September 4, commenced what would be a long siege. Only in July 1347 did Philip VI make a halfhearted attempt to relieve Calais. The city fell on August 4. It turned out to be the sole English territorial gain of the campaign, actually of the entire Hundred Years' War. On September 28, 1347, the two sides concluded a truce that, under the impact of the plague known as the Black Death, lasted until 1354.

With the failure of negotiations for a permanent settlement, fighting resumed in 1355. The English mounted a series of devastating raids. King Edward III struck across the English Channel into northern France, his son Edward the Black Prince moved from Bordeaux into Languedoc, and Edward's second son John of Gaunt attacked from Brittany into Normandy.

The English did not seek battle with the far larger French army; their intent was simply to plunder and destroy. Edward III landed in France to strengthen the northern force but was forced to return to England on news that the Scots had taken Berwick. John was unable to cross the Loire and effect a juncture with his brother's force.

Edward the Black Prince had set out from Bergerac on August 4. Most of his men were from Aquitaine, except for a number of English longbowmen. He reached Tours on September 3 and there learned that French king John II (the Good, r. 1350–1364) and as many as 35,000 men had crossed the Loire at Blois on September 8. As he had only about 8,000 men, the Black Prince ordered a rapid withdrawal down the road to Bordeaux, but the English were slowed by their loot. The French succeeded in cutting off the raiders and reached Poitiers first, making contact on September 17 at La Chabotrie. The prince did not want to fight, but he realized that his exhausted men could go no farther without having to abandon their plunder, and he cast about for a suitable defensive position, moving to the village of Maupertuis some seven miles southeast of Poitiers.

John II wanted to attack the English on the morning of September 18, but papal envoy Cardinal Hélie de Talleyrand-Périgord persuaded him to try negotiations. The Black Prince offered to return towns and castles captured during his raid along with all his prisoners, to promise not to do battle with the French king for seven years, and to pay a large sum of money, but John II demanded the unconditional surrender of the prince and 100 English knights.

Edward refused. He had selected an excellent defensive site, and his men used the time spent in negotiations to improve their positions. Edward's left flank was protected by a creek and a marsh. Most of his archers were on the flanks, and his small cavalry reserve was on the exposed right flank.

John II's army greatly outnumbered his opponent. It included 8,000 mounted men-at-arms, 8,000 light cavalry, 4,500 professional mercenary infantry (many of them Genoese crossbowmen), and perhaps 15,000 untrained citizen militia. Rejecting advice to use his superior numbers to surround the English and starve them out or turn the English position, the king decided on a frontal assault. He organized his men into four "battles" of up to 10,000 men each. The men-at-arms in the French "battles" were to march the mile to the English lines in full armor.

The resulting Battle of Poitiers on September 19, 1356, was a repeat of the August 1346 Battle of Crécy. The footmen in the first French "battle" who had not fallen prey to English arrows reached the English defensive line at a hedge. The next French division, under the Dauphin Charles, moved forward and there was desperate fighting, with the French almost breaking through. Edward committed everything except a final reserve of 400 men, and the line held. The remaining French reeled back. The English were now in desperate straits, and if the next

French "battle" commanded by the Duc d'Orléans, the brother of the king, had advanced promptly to support their fellows or struck the exposed English right flank, the French would have won a great victory. Instead, on seeing the repulse of their fellows it withdrew from the field with them.

This produced a slight respite for the defenders to reorganize before the arrival of the last and largest French "battle" of some 6,000 men, led by John II in person. The French were exhausted by the long march in full armor, but the English were also at the end of their tether. Fearing that his men could not withstand another assault, the Black Prince ordered his cavalry and infantry, along with the archers who had used up their arrows, to charge the French. He also sent about 200 horsemen around to attack the French rear. Desperate fighting ensued in which John II wielded a great battle-ax.

The issue remained in doubt until the English cavalry struck the French rear. The French then fled; the English were too exhausted to pursue. "There were slain all the flower of France," says Jean Froissart in his chronicles. The French suffered perhaps 2,500 dead and a like number of prisoners, including King John II, his 14-year-old son Philip, and two of his brothers, along with a multitude of the French nobility, including 17 counts. The English may have sustained 1,000 killed and at least as many wounded.

Following the battle, the Black Prince withdrew to Bordeaux with both his booty and prisoners. Vast fortunes were made over the ransoming of the nobles. Meanwhile, there was chaos in France with the collapse of the central government.

The next 10 years saw the English raiding the French countryside almost at will, as did bands of freebooters known as *routiers.* Those French who could do so sought refuge in castles and fortified cities. In 1358 the peasants, who had been unable to defend themselves against their many attackers, rose up against the nobles in what is known as the Jacquerie. It was prompted by the heavy taxes levied on the peasants to pay for the war against England and the ransom of nobles taken in the Battle of Poitiers but also by anger regarding the pillaging of the countryside by the *routiers.* The Jacquerie was crushed by the nobles, led by Charles the Bad of Navarre.

In 1360 the Dauphin Charles signed the Treaty of Brétigny, ransoming John II in return for 3 million gold crowns. While Edward III gave up any claim to the throne of France, he received Guyenne in full sovereignty as well as the Limousin, Poitou, the Angoumois, the Saintonge, Rouerque, Ponthieu, and other areas. King Edward now possessed an independent Guyenne but also Aquitaine, representing one-third of the area of France. Edward set up the Black Prince at Bordeaux as the duke of Aquitaine.

John II was allowed to return home from England, but his three sons remained behind as hostages until the ransom was paid. When one son escaped, the good king returned of his own free will to take his place, dying in England in 1364. Incredibly, the lessons of the Battle of Poitiers seem not to have taken, it being said that the French remembered everything but learned nothing. Poitiers would be virtually replicated in form and effect at Agincourt in 1415.

Nominal peace was maintained from 1360 to 1368, although fighting continued in the successionist struggle in Brittany. There in 1364 the English drove off a French army attempting to relieve their siege of Auray and went on to take the town. Charles the Bad, ruler of Navarre,

took advantage of French weakness to seize territory in southwestern France.

In 1364 King Charles V came to the French throne. Known to French history as Charles the Wise, he was physically weak yet an able realist. He was probably responsible for saving France, rescuing it from the military defeats and chaos that occurred under his immediate predecessors Philip VI and John II. With the able assistance of the first great French military commander of the Hundred Years' War, constable of France Bertrand du Guesclin, Charles reformed the French military.

The two men created new military units and established the French artillery, along with a permanent military staff. They also reorganized the navy and ordered the rebuilding of castles and city walls (most notably in Paris). In addition, Charles managed to control the new financial arrangements established by the States General. In 1364, he dispatched du Guesclin and French troops to intervene in the civil war in Castilla (Castile).

In 1368 a revolt by the nobles of Gascony against Edward the Black Prince, Duke of Aquitaine, provided Charles the opportunity to test his new military. The French military intervention in Gascony, however, led King Edward III of England to again lay claim to the French throne.

Adopting a commonsense approach to warfare, du Guesclin employed such techniques as night attacks (despite English charges that these were unknightly). He also excelled in siege warfare, and one by one he captured castles held by the English. In 1370, however, Edward the Black Prince took and sacked the French city of Limoges, massacring many of its inhabitants.

The reformed French Navy met success when, off the southwest coast of France on

June 22–23, 1372, some 60 Castilian and French ships under Genoese admiral Ambrosio Bocanegra defeated an English fleet of 40 ships under John of Hastings, Earl of Pembroke, sent to relieve the French siege of English-held La Rochelle. The allies captured Pembroke, along with 400 English knights and 8,000 soldiers. This naval victory also gave the French control of the western French coast and of the English Channel for the first time since the Battle of Sluys in 1340.

In 1375 a formal truce went into effect between the two sides, lasting until 1383, although sporadic fighting continued. The principal figures in the war died during this period: Edward the Black Prince in 1376; his father, King Edward III of England, in 1377; Constable of France du Guesclin in 1380; and French king Charles V in 1380.

Richard II was only 10 years old when he became king of England in 1377. His uncle, John of Gaunt, Duke of Lancaster, exercised power as regent. The government was nearly overthrown in the Peasants' Revolt of 1381 led by Jack Straw and Wat Tyler. Then rebels under Thomas, Duke of Gloucester, defeated the royalists in the Battle of Radcot Bridge in 1387 and forced Richard to agree to their demands. Another dispute with his nobles led Richard to assume absolute power in 1397, producing yet another revolt and his forced abdication.

In 1386 the French began preparations for an invasion of England, but the plan was abandoned following an English naval victory in the Battle of Margate (March 24, 1387), when the English captured or destroyed some 100 French and Castilian ships. Another period of truce ensued during 1389–1396, nonetheless occasionally interrupted by fighting.

In 1396 Kings Richard III of England and Charles VI of France signed the Truce of Paris. Supposed to last 30 years, under it England retained in France only the port of Calais and Gascony in southwestern France between Bordeaux and Bayonne. The truce lasted only until 1415, however, and was, in any case, marked by intermittent warfare. In 1402, moreover, French troops had assisted the Scots in an invasion of England. The English also had to contend with a revolt in Wales during 1402–1409, led by the Prince of Wales Owen Glendower, who waged a highly effective guerrilla campaign against English rule. In 1403 English king Henry IV also faced a revolt of northern nobles led by Henry "Hotspur" Percy, who led some 4,000 men deep into central England with the aim of joining forces under Glendower. Henry, however, interposed his own army between them and defeated Percy in the Battle of Shrewsbury (July 21, 1403) before Glendower could arrive. Percy was among the dead.

With Henry IV preoccupied with these internal revolts, that same year the French raided the southern English coast, including Plymouth. In 1405 the French also landed troops to assist Glendower, but these accomplished little and were soon withdrawn. In 1406 the French mounted operations against English possessions in France, around Vienne and in Calais. In 1408 Hotspur Percy's father, Henry Percy, first Earl of Northumberland, rebelled against Henry IV but was slain in the Battle of Bramham Moor (February 19). The next year, 1409, Henry also defeated the revolt in Wales.

Louis, Duc d'Orléans, younger brother of French king Charles VI, and John I, Duke of Burgundy, had been at odds seeking to fill the power vacuum left by the increasingly mad Charles. Louis's assassination on November 24, 1407, brought war between the Burgundians and Orléanists, with each side seeking to involve England on its behalf.

In May 1413 new king of England Henry V (r. 1413–1422), seeking to take advantage of the chaos in France, concluded an alliance with Burgundy. Duke John promised neutrality in return for increased territory as Henry's vassal, at the expense of France. In April 1415 Henry V declared war on King Charles VI. Henry crossed the English Channel from Southampton with 12,000 men, landing at the mouth of the Seine on August 10.

On August 13, Henry laid siege to the channel port of Honfleur. Taking it on September 22, he expelled most of its French inhabitants, replacing them with Englishmen. Only the poorest Frenchmen were allowed to remain, and they had to take an oath of allegiance. The siege, disease, and garrison duties, however, reduced Henry V's army to only about 6,000 men.

For whatever reasons, Henry V decided to march overland from Honfleur to Calais. Moving without baggage or artillery, his army departed on October 6, covering as much as 18 miles a day in difficult conditions caused by heavy rains. The English found one ford after another blocked by French troops, so Henry took the army eastward, up the Somme, to locate a crossing. High water and the French prevented this until he reached Athies, 10 miles west of Péronne, where he located an undefended crossing.

At Rouen the French raised some 30,000 men under Charles d'Albert, constable of France. This force almost intercepted the English before they could get across the Somme. The trail was not hard to find, marked as it was by burning French farmhouses. (Henry once remarked that war without fire was like "sausages without mustard.")

D'Albert managed to get in front of the English and set up a blocking position on the main road to Calais, near the Château of Agincourt, where Henry's troops met them on October 24. Henry faced an army many times his own in size. His men were short of supplies, and enraged local inhabitants slew English foragers and stragglers. Shaken by his prospects, Henry V ordered his prisoners released and offered to return Honfleur and pay for any damages he had inflicted in return for safe passage to Calais. The French, with a numerical advantage of up to five to one, were in no mood to make concessions. They demanded that Henry V renounce his claims in France to everything except Guyenne, conditions he rejected.

The French nobles were eager to join battle and pressed d'Albert for an attack, but he resisted their demands that day. That night Henry V ordered absolute silence, which the French took as a sign of demoralization. Daybreak on October 25 found the English at one end of a defile about 1,000 yards wide and flanked by heavy woods. The road to Calais ran down its middle. Open fields on either side had been recently plowed and were sodden from the heavy rains.

Drawing on English success in the battles at Crécy and Poitiers, Henry V drew up his 800–1,000 men-at-arms and 5,000 archers in three "battles" of men-at-arms and pikemen in one line. The archers were located between the three and on the flanks, where they enfiladed forward about 100 yards or so to the woods on either side.

About a mile away, d'Albert also deployed in three groups, but because of French numbers and the narrowness of the defile these were one behind the other. The first rank consisted of dismounted men and some crossbowmen, along with perhaps 500 horsemen on the flanks; the second was the same without the horsemen; and the third consisted almost entirely of horsemen.

In the late morning of October 25, with the French having failed to move, Henry staged a cautious advance of about a half mile and then halted, his men taking up the same formation as before, with the leading archers on the flanks only about 300 yards from the first French ranks. The bowmen then pounded sharpened stakes into the ground facing toward the enemy, their tips at breast height of a horse to help protect against mounted attack.

Henry's movement had the desired effect, for d'Albert was no longer able to resist the demands of his fellow nobles to attack. The mounted knights on either flank moved forward well ahead of the slow-moving and heavily armored men-at-arms. It was Crécy and Poitiers all over again, with the longbow decisive. A large number of horsemen, slowed by the soggy ground, were cut down by English arrows that caught them en enfilade. The remainder were halted at the English line.

The cavalry attack was defeated long before the first French men-at-arms, led in person by d'Albert, arrived. Their heavy body armor and the mud exhausted the French, but most reached the thin English line and, by sheer weight of numbers, drove it back. The English archers then fell on the closely packed French from the flanks, using swords, axes, and hatchets to cut them down. The unencumbered Englishmen had the advantage, as they could more easily move in the mud around their French opponents. Within minutes, almost all in the first French rank had been killed or captured.

The second French rank then moved forward, but it lacked the confidence and cohesion of the first. Although losses were heavy, many of its number were able to retire to re-form for a new attack with the third "battle" of mounted knights. At this point Henry V learned that the French had attacked his baggage train, and he ordered the wholesale slaughter of the French prisoners, fearing that he would not be strong enough to meet attacks from both front and rear. The rear attack, however, turned out to be only a sally from the Château of Agincourt by a few men-at-arms and perhaps 600 French peasants.

The English easily repulsed the final French attack, which was not pressed home. Henry then led several hundred mounted men in a charge that dispersed what remained of the French army. The archers than ran forward, killing thousands of the Frenchmen lying on the field by stabbing them through gaps in their armor or bludgeoning them to death.

In less than four hours the English had defeated a force significantly larger than their own. The French lost at least 5,000 dead and another 1,500 taken prisoner. D'Albert was among those who perished. Henry V reported English dead as 13 men-at-arms and 100 footmen, but this is undoubtedly too low. English losses were probably on the order of 300 killed.

Henry V then marched to Calais, taking the prisoners who would be ransomed, and in mid-November he returned to England. The loss of so many prominent French nobles in the Battle of Agincourt greatly increased Duke John of Burgundy's influence, to the point that he was able to dictate French royal policy.

Henry V spent 1416 preparing his forces and putting together a powerful fleet, which turned back a Genoese effort to control the English Channel. He also secured the neutrality of Holy Roman emperor Sigismund, who had been allied with France. Returning to France in 1417, Henry conducted three campaigns in Normandy during 1417–1419. He successfully besieged Rouen during September 1418–January 1419 and secured all Normandy, except for the coastal enclave of Mont Saint-Michel.

Duke John of Burgundy was also actively campaigning. On May 29, 1418, his forces captured Paris. Installing himself there as protector of the insane French king Charles VI, John ordered the massacre of virtually all opposition leaders at court, although the Dauphin Charles managed to escape to the south.

With Duke John controlling Paris and the English having occupied northern France, the Dauphin sought a reconciliation with John. In July 1419 they met on the bridge of Pouilly near Melun. On the grounds that further discussions were required to secure the peace, Charles proposed another meeting, on the bridge at Montereay. There on September 10, John appeared with his escort for what he assumed to be negotiations, only to be killed by companions of the Dauphin. In consequence, Philip the Good, the new duke of Burgundy, and Isabeau de Bavière (Isabeau of Bavaria), queen consort of France, allied with the English against the Dauphin and his allies, the Orléanists and Armagnacs.

Henry V marched on Paris, forcing French king Charles VI to conclude the Treaty of Troyes on May 21, 1420. Charles agreed to the marriage of Henry to his daughter Catherine. The French king also disowned his son Charles as illegitimate and acknowledged Henry as his legitimate heir. Henry married Catherine of Valois on June 2, 1420, and was now ruler of France in all but name.

With the intention of invading southern France and defeating the Dauphin, Henry first consolidated his hold over French territory north of the Loire. In this connection he successfully besieged Meaux (October 1421–May 1422) but then became ill. On August 31, 1422, Henry V died of dysentery at Blois. The only child of Henry and Catherine, the nine-month-old Henry of Windsor, was crowned king as Henry VI, with Henry V's brother, John, Duke of Bedford, as regent.

French king Charles VI died in Paris on October 21, 1422. His supporters then crowned at Bruges the Dauphin as King Charles VII. Duke John of Bedford, regent for the boy-king Henry VI, meanwhile continued the English consolidation of northern France, completing it by 1428. Burgundy was increasingly restive in its alliance with England as John prepared to take the offensive against the Dauphin Charles south of the Loire.

In July 1423 a Burgundian-English force of some 4,000 men under Thomas Montacute, fourth Earl of Salisbury, met at Auxerre to intercept a Dauphinist French-Scottish army of 8,000 men under the Comte de Vendôme marching into Burgundy for Bourges. The two armies came together on July 31 at Cravant on the banks of the Yonne River, a tributary of the Seine. The Dauphinists were drawn up on the east bank, the Anglo-Burgundians on the west bank. Both were reluctant to attempt a crossing of the shallow Yonne, but after three hours Salisbury ordered his men to ford the waist-deep river, about 50 yards wide. English archers provided covering fire.

A second English force under Lord Willoughby de Eresby forced its way across a narrow bridge and through the Scots, cutting the Dauphinist army in two. The French then collapsed, although the Scots refused to flee and were cut down in large numbers. Reportedly, the French-Scottish army lost 6,000 dead and many prisoners, including Vendôme. This battle marked the zenith of English arms in the Hundred Years' War. The English and Burgundians now anticipated conquering the remainder of France.

In April 1424 John Stewart, second Earl of Buchan, arrived at the Dauphin Charles's headquarters at Bourges with an additional 6,500 troops from Scotland. In early August the Dauphinist forces departed Tours to join French troops under the Duke of Alençon and the viscounts of Narbonne and Aumale to relieve the castle of Ivry near Le Mans, under siege by the Duke of Bedford. Before the army could arrive, however, Ivry surrendered.

Following a council of war, the Dauphinists decided to attack English strongholds in southern Normandy beginning with Verneuil, which was secured by a ruse as Scots, pretending to be Englishmen escorting Scottish prisoners, were admitted to the fortified town. Learning what had transpired, John, Duke of Bedford, rushed with English troops to Verneuil.

The Scots persuaded the French to stand and fight, and battle was joined on August 17 about a mile north of Verneuil between 8,000–10,000 Englishmen and 12,000–18,000 French and Scottish troops. The battle was fought along the lines of Crécy and Agincourt, although this time French cavalry broke through. Instead of wheeling about and exploiting this situation, however, they continued on to the north to attack the English baggage train, and the French infantry were then defeated. Bedford had taken the precaution of protecting the baggage train with a strong force of 2,000 longbowmen, and they turned back the cavalry.

The battle was one of the bloodiest of the Hundred Years' War, but the English emerged victorious, with some 6,000 French and Scottish troops slain. Alençon was captured. The English paid a heavy price, however, with 1,600 of their own dead, far more than at Agincourt.

On March 6, 1426, Duke John of Bedford and an English army defeated a French army led by constable of France Arthur de Richemont at St. Jacques near Avranches. The battle forced Jean V, Duc de Brittany, the brother of de Richemont, to submit to the English.

Having consolidated his hold on northern France, Bedford launched a southern offensive. In September 1428 the Earl of Salisbury advanced from Paris with 5,000 men to secure the Loire River crossing at Orléans as the first step to taking the Dauphin's stronghold of Armagnac. Orléans was a large city and one of the strongest fortresses in France. Three of its four sides were strongly walled and moated, and its southern side rested on the Loire. The city walls were well defended by numerous catapults and 71 large cannon, and stocks of food had been gathered. Jean Dunois, Comte de Longueville, commanded its garrison of about 2,400 soldiers and 3,000 armed citizens.

Salisbury and his men arrived at Orléans on October 12, 1428, and commenced a siege. Because he had only about 5,000 men, Salisbury was unable to invest Orléans completely. Nonetheless, on October 24 the English seized the fortified bridge across the Loire, although Salisbury was mortally wounded. In December William Pole, Earl of Suffolk, assumed command of siege operations, with the English constructing a number of small forts to protect the bridge and their encampments.

On February 12, 1429, in the Battle of Rouvray, also known as the Battle of the

Herrings, an English supply convoy led by Sir John Falstaff transporting a large quantity of salted herrings to the besiegers was attacked by the Comte de Clermont and a considerably larger French force with a small Scottish contingent. Falstaff, who had about 1,000 mounted archers and a small number of men-at-arms, circled his supply wagons. Although greatly outnumbered, the English managed to beat back repeated attacks and then drove off the French.

Although the French in Orléans mounted several forays and were able to secure limited supplies, by early 1429 the situation in the city was becoming desperate, with the defenders close to starvation. Orléans was now the symbol of French resistance and nationalism.

Although the Dauphin Charles was considering flight abroad, the situation was not as bleak as it appeared. French peasants were rising against the English in increasing numbers, and only a leader was lacking. That person appeared in a young illiterate peasant girl named Jeanne d'Arc. Traveling to the French court at Chinon, she informed Charles that she had been sent by God to raise the Siege of Orléans and lead him to Rheims to be crowned king of France.

Following an examination of Jeanne by court and church officials, Charles allowed her, dressed in full armor and with the empty title *chef de guerre,* to lead a relief army of up to 4,000 men and a convoy of supplies to Orléans. The Duc d'Alençon had actual command. Word of Jeanne and her faith in her divine mission spread far and wide and inspired many Frenchmen.

As the French relief force approached Orléans, Jeanne sent a letter to the Earl of Suffolk demanding surrender. Not surprisingly, he refused. Jeanne then insisted that the relief force circle around and approach the city from the north. The other French leaders finally agreed, and the army was ferried to the north bank of the Loire and entered the city through a north gate on April 29.

Jeanne urged an attack on the English from Orléans, assuring the men of God's protection. On the morning of May 1 she awoke to learn of a French attack against the English at Fort St. Loup that had begun without her and was not going well. Riding out in full armor, she rallied the attackers to victory. All the English defenders were killed, while the French sustained only two dead. Jeanne then insisted that the soldiers confess their sins and that prostitutes be banned, promising the men that they would be victorious in five days. A new appeal to the English to surrender was met with derisive shouts.

On May 5 Jeanne led in person an attack out the south gate of the city. The French avoided the bridge over the Loire, the southern end of which the English had captured at the beginning of the siege, but crossed through shallow water to an island in the middle of the Loire and from there employed a boat bridge to gain the south bank. They then captured the English fort at St. Jean le Blanc and moved against a large fort at Les Augustins, close to the bridge. The battle was costly to both sides, but Jeanne led a charge that left the French in possession of the fort. The next day, May 6, Jeanne's troops assaulted Les Tournelles, the towers at the southern end of the bridge. In the fighting Jeanne was hit by an arrow and carried from the field. The wound was not major, and by late afternoon she had insisted on rejoining the battle.

On May 7 a French knight took Jeanne's banner to lead an attack on the towers. She tried to stop him, but the mere sight of the banner caused the French soldiers to follow it. Jeanne then joined the fray herself. Using scaling ladders, the French assaulted the walls, with Jeanne in the thick of the fight. The 400–500 English defenders attempted to flee by the bridge, but it was soon on fire and collapsed. On May 8 the remaining English forces abandoned the siege and departed.

In his official pronouncements Charles took full credit for the victory, but the French people attributed it to Jeanne and flocked to join her. Although the Hundred Years' War continued for another two decades, the relief of the Siege of Orléans was the turning point in the long war.

Following their defeat in the Siege of Orléans, the English dispatched an army from Paris under Sir John Falstaff. He joined his men with the remaining English defenders of the Loire battles, and they moved to join battle with the French in the vicinity of the small village of Patay. Falstaff and John Talbot, first Earl of Shrewsbury, had perhaps 5,000 men. French scouts discovered the English at Patay before the latter could complete their defensive preparations. Not waiting for the main body of the army under Jeanne d'Arc to arrive, the French vanguard of some 1,500 cavalry under Étienne de Vignolles, known as La Hire, and Jean Poton de Xaintrailles mounted an immediate charge. Many of the Englishmen with horses were able to escape, but the longbowmen were cut down. Unlike Crécy and Agincourt, for once a French cavalry frontal assault succeeded.

For perhaps 100 French casualties, the English suffered some 2,500 dead, wounded, or taken prisoner. Talbot was among those captured. Falstaff escaped but was blamed for the disaster and disgraced. The battle decimated the corps of seemingly invincible English longbowmen and did much to restore French confidence that they could defeat the English in open battle. The French peasants also took heart and began to engage the English in guerrilla warfare. Jeanne then led the army in the capture of territory controlled by the English, including the cities of Troyes, Châlons, and Reims. On June 26, 1429, Jeanne realized her goal of seeing Charles VII crowned king in the traditional manner at Rheims Cathedral. The ungrateful and lethargic Charles then denied Jeanne the resources to continue the struggle and, indeed, sought to discredit her.

Despite Charles VII's lack of support, Jeanne d'Arc was determined to liberate Paris. But English reinforcements arrived in the city in August, and Jeanne's attack on September 8, 1429, failed, and she was wounded. Still unsupported by King Charles VII, she led a small French force to Compiègne, which the English and Burgundians were besieging as part of the effort of English regent John, Duke of Bedford, to reestablish English control over the central Seine Valley, but on May 23, 1430, Jeanne was captured by the Burgundians, who turned her over to the English. Brought to trial by the English on charges of heresy, Jeanne was convicted and executed at Rouen on May 30, 1431. To his lasting shame, King Charles VII made no effort to save her. The English, however, created in Jeanne a martyr and ultimately a saint. French resistance to the English grew, although Duke John waged a skillful defense of the English holdings in France until his death on September 14, 1435.

In 1435 the English and French opened diplomatic talks. The English refused, however, to relinquish claims to the French throne and insisted on a marriage between the adolescent King Henry VI of England (crowned King Henry II of France in Paris at age nine in 1431) and a daughter of French king Charles VII. The English then broke off negotiations to deal with a French raid.

Meanwhile, Philip, Duke of Burgundy, agreed to join the negotiations. By the time the English returned to the talks, they discovered that Burgundy had in effect switched sides. Under the terms of the Treaty of the Peace of Arras of September 21, 1435, Philip agreed to recognize Charles VII as king of France. In return, Philip was exempted from homage to the French throne, and Charles agreed to punish the murderers of Philip's father, Duke John of Burgundy. The Treaty of Arras thus brought to an end the long Burgundian-Armagnac strife and allowed Charles VII to consolidate his position as king of France against the claim of Henry VI. With France already allied with Scotland, England was now largely isolated and vastly outnumbered in terms of population. Thereafter its position in France steadily eroded.

In 1436 French forces besieged Paris. With food in short supply, Parisians loyal to Charles VII allowed the besiegers entry to the city on April 13. The English then withdrew to the Bastille, where they were starved into submission and subsequently allowed to withdraw. This ended 16 years of English control of the city. A general amnesty followed.

On April 16, 1444, the English signed at the city of Tours a five-year truce, hoping that the demobilization of large numbers of French soldiers, many of whom would be roaming the countryside, would bring anarchy and strengthen their hand. The inept French king Charles VII, however, followed the advice of his principal ministers to the extent of authorizing the

creation of a standing professional army (the first in Europe since Roman times) to enforce the peace. This produced a well-trained force capable of contesting the English on an equal footing. With French resources so much greater than those of England, France's victory was now largely a matter of time.

With the expiration of the Truce of Tours in 1449, Charles VII had the forces ready to begin a campaign to retake Normandy. The French were led by Jean d'Orléans, Comte de Dunois, and had the benefit of a highly effective siege artillery train established by Jean Bureau, master of artillery, and his brother Gaspard Bureau. Facing the inept English commander Edmund Beaufort, Duke of Somerset, the French forced the surrender of Rouen on October 19, 1449. The French then besieged and quickly took Harfleur in December 1449 and Honfleur and Fresnoy in January 1450. They laid siege to Caen in March 1450.

The English assembled a small army of about 3,000 men under Sir Thomas Kyriell. It landed at Cherbourg on March 15, 1450. Instead of going to the aid of Caen, though, Kyriell diverted his force to capture Valognes. Although successful in this, the battle was costly in terms of casualties. At the end of March an additional 2,500 men arrived under Sir Matthew Gough, but Kyriell still had only about 4,000 men as he proceeded southward. Two French armies were just south of the Cotentin (Cherbourg) Peninsula in position to engage the English. The Comte de Clermont commanded 3,000 men at Carentan, 30 miles south of Cherbourg, while the Constable de Richemont had 2,000 more 20 miles farther south at Coutances and now hurried north to join Clermont.

On April 14 Kyriell was camped near the village of Formigny on the road to

Bayeux about 10 miles west of that city. Clermont was at Carentan, 15 miles west of Bayeux, while Richemont was moving through Saint-Lô, 19 miles southwest of Bayeux, hoping to link up with Clermont and prevent the English from reaching Bayeux. In midafternoon on April 15, Clermont approached the English camp. Alerted, Kyriell drew up his forces in the traditional English formation that had worked so many times in the past: some 600 men-at-arms in the center and close to 2,900 longbowmen *en echelon* on the flanks behind planted stakes and narrow trenches. The English formation was backed against a small tributary of the Aure River.

Clermont opened the Battle of Formigny with infantry attacks followed by cavalry. The English easily beat them back. Clermont then brought forward two cannon, which effectively harassed the English archers out of longbow range, leading the longbowmen to charge and capture the guns.

This inconclusive fighting lasted about three hours, sufficient time for the Constable de Richemont to arrive with his largely mounted force. He fell on the English left flank, forcing Kyriell to abandon part of his prepared position. In a series of charges, the French crushed the English for an overwhelming victory. The English sustained some 2,500 killed or seriously wounded, with another 900 taken prisoner, including Kyriell. The French suffered only about 500 casualties. The battle was one of the first in Western Europe in which cannon played a notable role. During the next several months, the French secured the remainder of Normandy. Caen fell on July 6, and Cherbourg surrendered on August 12.

In 1451, the French began the final chapter of the long Hundred Years' War

when Jean d'Orléans led some 6,000 men in an invasion of Guyenne in southwestern France. Benefiting greatly from their siege artillery train under Jean Bureau, the French captured the regional capital of Bordeaux on June 30 and Bayonne on August 20. Nonetheless, many Aquitaine nobles who—thanks to generations of English rule—identified with the English rather than the French continued to resist.

Although the French army in short order conquered Guyenne, resistance continued. Indeed, a number of the nobles and Bordeaux merchants sent a delegation to London that convinced King Henry VI to dispatch an army. It numbered some 3,000 men led by John Talbot, Earl of Shrewsbury. A veteran of much of the fighting in the war, he was now in his 70s. The English landed near the mouth of the Garonne on October 17, 1452, and the leaders of Bordeaux turned over the city to them. Other cities and towns of Guyenne quickly followed suit, effectively undoing the French conquest of 1451.

The French were caught by surprise, having expected the English expeditionary force to land in Normandy. Thus, it was not until the summer of 1453 that Charles VII had put together an invasion force. Three French armies sliced into Guyenne from different directions, and Charles VII followed with a reserve army. English reinforcements under Talbot's son, Lord de Lisle, arrived at Bordeaux, bringing total English strength up to about 6,000 men. Loyal Gascon forces supplemented this number.

In mid-July, the French eastern army laid siege to Castillon, west of Bordeaux on the Dordogne. Jean de Blois, Comte de Perigord and Vicomte de Limoges, was nominal head of the army, but actual command was held by master of artillery Jean

Bureau, assisted by his brother Gaspard Bureau.

In operations against Castillon, the French employed some 300 guns, most undoubtedly small. Up to 6,000 men were in the French camp, largely an artillery park beyond artillery range of Castillon and designed by Jean Bureau for defensive purposes. Another 1,000 French men-at-arms were in another camp about a mile to the north. Bureau placed some 1,000 French archers in the Priory of St. Laurent north of Castillon, where a relief force from Bordeaux might most logically be expected.

Talbot departed Bordeaux on the morning of July 16 with mounted troops followed by infantry and artillery. He had at least 6,000 English and Gascons. His men passed through St. Émillon on the night of July 16–17 and in the morning surprised the French archers in the priory, killing a number and scattering the remainder. Talbot allowed his men the opportunity to rest following their 30-mile march but then received a report that the French at Castillon appeared to be withdrawing. Wishing to strike his enemy at the most vulnerable, Talbot ordered an immediate attack without waiting for the arrival of his English-Gascon infantry.

Crossing the Lidoire River that joins the Dordogne from the north, Talbot paralleled the Dordogne to come in on the French artillery camp from the south. The French were prepared, and the English encountered a hail of gunfire from behind the earthen defenses. Talbot ordered his men to dismount and attack the French parapet on foot. Few reached it. With the English-Gascon infantry committed to the battle as they arrived, the French were able to defeat their enemy piecemeal. Breton cavalry then hit the English in the flank to cut off any retreat.

The attackers sustained some 4,000 casualties, including those captured. It was in effect Crécy and Agincourt in reverse, with the decisive element being cannon fire rather than archers. The French sustained perhaps only 100 casualties. The Battle of Castillon was decisive. With no field army left to support them, the remaining towns and cities of Guyenne quickly fell.

Bordeaux surrendered to Charles VII on October 10, 1453, following a three-month siege. Held by the English for three centuries, it was now definitively French. Bordeaux's capture effectively ended the Hundred Years' War, although coastal raids continued for the next four years.

Significance

Beginning as a feudal struggle between France and England, the Hundred Years' War came to assume a nationalist character. The war saw rapid military change, with the creation of a standing army and new weapons, technology, and tactics. The long struggle presaged the demise of the armored knight and the rise of the infantry as the dominant military arm. The fighting, coupled with the Black Death, devastated much of France. During the course of the war the total French population may have declined by as much as half, to 17 million. Normandy was particularly hard hit, losing perhaps three-quarters of its population.

Although the war created considerable wealth for many Englishmen through their ransom of captive French nobility, it also nearly bankrupted the English government and ultimately brought on a series of civil wars in England known as the Wars of the Roses (1455–1487). And although English monarchs continued to refer to themselves as king or queen of France until 1802, the English were obliged to give up all of their territory in France except for Calais, which itself was relinquished in 1558.

The establishment of professional armies late in the war also marked the end of feudalism. France was transformed from a feudal state to a more centralized state, with increasing power vested in the monarchy and where the people came to think of themselves as Frenchmen rather than, say, Normans or Bretons. The Hundred Years' War also created a strong enmity between England and France, leading to a rivalry that lasted until the Entente Cordiale of 1904.

Further Reading

Barber, Richard. *Edward Prince of Wales and Aquitaine.* London: Allen Lane, 1978.

Bourne, Alfred H. *The Crécy War.* Reprint ed. Westport, CT: Greenwood, 1976.

Clowes, William Laird. *The Royal Navy: A History from the Earliest Times to the Present,* Vol. 1. London: Sampson Low, Martson, 1897.

Froissart, Jean. *Froissart's Chronicals.* Edited by John Jolliffe. London: Harvill, 1967.

Gies, Frances. *Jean of Arc: The Legend and the Reality.* New York: Harper and Row, 1981.

Hewitt, H. J. *The Black Prince's Expedition of 1355–1357.* Manchester, UK: University of Manchester Press, 1958.

Hibbert, Christopher. *Agincourt.* New York: Dorset, 1978.

Keegan, John. *The Face of Battle: A Study of Agincourt, Waterloo & the Somme.* New York: Vintage Books, 1977.

Rodgers, William Ledyard. *Naval Warfare under Oars, 4th to 16th Centuries: A Study of Strategy, Tactics and Ship Design.* 1940; reprint, Annapolis, MD: Naval Institute Press, 1967.

Seward, Desmond. *The Hundred Years' War: The English in France, 1337–1453.* New York: Atheneum, 1978.

Sumption, Jonathan. *The Hundred Years' War: Trial by Battle.* Philadelphia: University of Pennsylvania Press, 1988.

Warner, Marina. *Joan of Arc: The Image of Female Heroism.* New York: Knopf, 1981.

Aztec-Spanish War (1519–1521)

Dates	1519–1521
Location	Mexico
Combatants	Spanish conquistadores and allied Tlaxcalan vs. Aztecs
Principal Commanders	Spain: Hernán Cortés Aztec Empire: Montezuma (Moctezuma) II, Cuitlahuac
Principal Battles	Cholula, La Noche Triste, Tenochtitlán
Outcome	The small Spanish military force and its Tlaxcalan allies are victorious. The mighty Aztec Empire is dissolved amid wholesale native deaths from European diseases to which they have no resistance, while Spain begins its march of conquest in Mesoamerica.

Causes

The Aztecs (or people from Aztlan, a mythological place), also known as the Mexicas, inhabited the area of present-day central Mexico and came to dominate much of southern North America. Their society was highly developed with a complex governmental structure and long-distance trade, but they had only limited scientific knowledge and no modern weaponry.

In the mid-14th century the Aztecs established their capital in the city of Tenochtitlán (today Mexico City), on an island on the western side of Lake Texcoco connected to the shore by long causeways. The Aztecs worshiped Huitzilopochtli (the god of the sun) and other deities. Believing that daily human sacrifices were necessary to keep the sun healthy and shining, they built altars to Huitzilopochtli and the other gods in the form of great pyramids that dominated the city. On special days, thousands of prisoners might be sacrificed. This practice did not endear the Aztecs to their conquered peoples and created ready allies for the Spanish.

Ultimately Tenochtitlán came to be a large and wealthy city of perhaps 60,000 buildings and 200,000 people, perhaps one-fifth of the total Aztec population. A million or so Aztecs ruled a subject population of perhaps 5 million.

In 1517, Spanish governor of Cuba Diego Velázquez de Cuéllar sent three ships under the command of Hernández de Córdoba to explore the Yucatán Peninsula. The Mayans at Cape Catoche invited the Spaniards ashore, whereupon the Spaniards offered the natives the protection of the king of Spain with the requirement that they submit to him. Mayans led by chief Mochcouoh (Mochh Couoh) then attacked the Spaniards at night, killing 20. Córdoba was among the mortally wounded. Few of the Spaniards returned to Cuba, but Velázquez sent a second expedition to the Yucatán of several hundred men in three ships under Juan de Grijalva.

Velázquez also sent a third expedition, this one to explore the Mexican coast. As its leader, he selected his brother-in-law Hernán Cortés (b. 1485) with orders to establish a coastal trading post. Cortés, however, was determined to explore "the mysterious land of the west," which was rumored to abound in gold, and he secured a clause in his orders that enabled him to take emergency measures without prior authorization if such were "in the true interests of the realm."

Velázquez was keenly aware that anyone able to secure the mainland for Spain would gain great fame and wealth beyond anything that could be found in Cuba, and as preparations went forward he began to fear that Cortés would use the expedition to establish himself as governor of the new territory independent of Velázquez's control. Although he was certainly correct in this assumption, Velázquez was not able to delay the expedition or replace Cortés before the latter sailed on February 18, 1519.

Course

The expeditionary force consisted of 11 ships carrying about 100 sailors, 530 soldiers (including 30 crossbowmen and 12 harquebusiers), a doctor, several carpenters, at least 8 women, and a few hundred Cuban natives and some Africans, both freedmen and slaves. The expedition also had 17 horses and 10 small cannon. Few of the men were trained soldiers, and Cortés himself had never commanded men in battle.

After first landing at and spending time on Cozumel Island and trying to convert the natives there to Christianity, Cortés learned of other Europeans on the Yucatán Peninsula and proceeded there. Landing at Potonchán, he discovered survivors of a Spanish shipwreck. He then defeated local natives in two small battles. Cortés also secured the assistance of a native woman, probably of noble birth and of Toltec or Tabascan origin. Known as Marina or La Malinche and sometimes called Malintzin or Mallinali, she knew the Aztec language. She soon also learned Spanish and became Cortés's primary interpreter, confidant, and mistress as well as the mother of his son Martin.

In April 1519 Cortés landed with his expeditionary force on the Mexican east coast in the present-day state of Veracruz. He then marched to the Totonac settlement of Cempoala and persuaded its chief to rebel against the Aztecs. Having disobeyed Velázquez's orders, Cortés now had no choice but to continue with his plans in the hopes that success would bring the approbation of the Spanish government.

Cortés ordered his men to establish a settlement called La Villa Rica de la Vera Cruz (this ultimately became the present-day city of Veracruz). Its legally constituted town council then conferred on Cortés the title of *adelantado.* Ironically, Velázquez had in fact employed this same legal mechanism to free himself from the authority of Diego Columbus in Cuba.

Not all of the expedition's members were pleased with this turn of events, and those still loyal to Velázquez plotted to seize a ship and return to Cuba. Learning of their plan, Cortés crushed the plot, ordered the two ringleaders hanged, and had several others lashed or maimed. To prevent such an event from occurring again, he ordered his ships sunk on the claim that they were no longer seaworthy. Cortés retained only one small vessel, which he then loaded with the 20 percent of the treasure obtained thus far, to which the king of Spain was entitled, in the hopes that this would enhance his chances at securing royal approval.

In August 1519 accompanied by several hundred natives who had rebelled against the Aztecs, Cortés began his march to the interior. During the next month he fought a series of battles with the Tlaxcalan people, the last one of which might have ended in defeat for Cortés had not the Tlaxcalans decided that rather than killing the Spaniards, it would be better to ally with them and defeat the Aztecs. Cortés and his men were then welcomed into the Tlaxcalan capital of Tlaxcala.

Aztec ambassadors, who had been present during the fighting between the Spaniards and the Tlaxcalans, urged Cortés to quit Tlaxcala and march on Cholula, which was under Aztec control and was then both the second-largest city of Mesoamerica and probably its most sacred, with a pyramid larger than those of Egypt. Cortés saw the city as a military threat to his rear in a march on Tenochtitlán and sent emissaries there to conduct talks. Tlaxcalan leaders, meanwhile, urged Cortés to proceed to the city of Huexotzingo, which was allied to Tlaxcala. In mid-October 1519, Cortés finally decided to send two men on foot as emissaries to Tenochtitlán while proceeding with his own men and a number of Tlaxcalan warriors to Cholula.

Accounts differ as to what occurred at Cholula, but apparently Aztec emperor Montezuma (Moctezuma) II had now decided to resist the Spanish advance and ordered the Cholulans, who had only a small military force, to do battle against them. Although Cortés and his men entered Cholula without resistance, no city leaders met with them, and they were not offered provisions. The Tlaxcalans warned that an Aztec army was marching on the city, and there was also a report that the Cholulans planned to attack the Spaniards while they slept. Whether this was true or not, Cortés, urged on by the Tlaxcalans, ordered a preemptive strike. The Spaniards seized and killed many of the leading city nobles, then

SIEGE OF TENOCHTITLÁN, MAY 26 – AUG 13, 1521

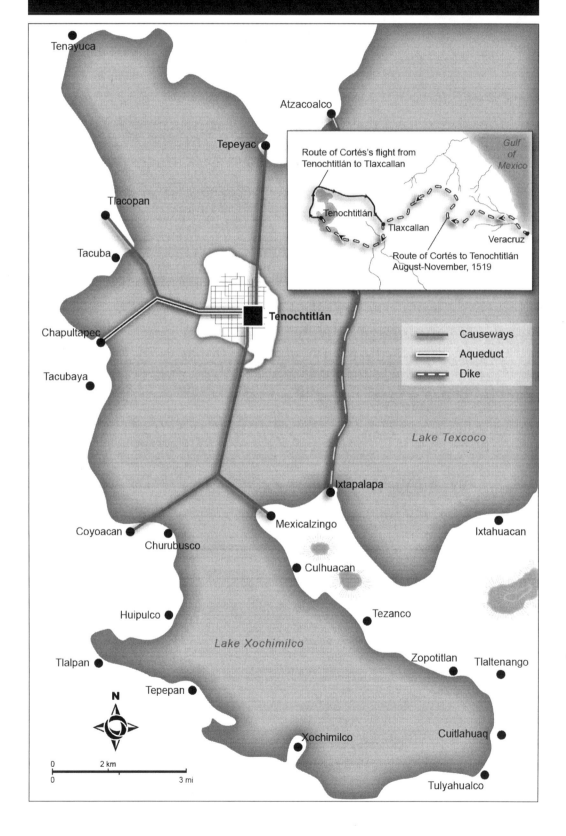

ordered the city fired. Cortés claimed that in three hours his troops and the Tlaxcalans killed 3,000 people and burned the city.

Cortés sent word to Montezuma that the people of Cholula had treated him with disrespect and that he had punished them accordingly. Cortés said that the Aztecs need not fear his wrath if they treated him with respect and gifts of gold. Montezuma then invited Cortés to visit the capital.

On November 8, 1519, Cortés and his men arrived at the fabled city of Tenochtitlán and were received there by Montezuma with all possible honors. The Spanish, who were dazzled by the gold and wealth of the capital, soon made clear their intention to rule. Cortés was able to capitalize in part on the Aztec belief in a great white god, Quetzalcoatl, whose return had been prophesied. With their horses, metal armor, and firearms, the Spanish could play the part.

Using the excuse of the death of some Spanish soldiers on the coast near Veracruz, Cortés took Montezuma captive and began to rule through him. This worked until Cortés sought to introduce Christianity. In the spring of 1520, Cortés departed Tenochtitlán to do battle with a rival Spanish force sent by Velázquez to punish Cortés for disobeying orders. Cortés defeated that force and added those of its members he captured to his own forces.

On his return to Tenochtitlán, Cortés discovered that his lieutenant Pedro de Alvarado, whom he had left in charge, was under siege by the Aztecs, who had revolted. While Cortés was able to reestablish his authority, the situation in the city soon deteriorated, and warfare resumed. Montezuma was killed, but his brother Cuitlahuac had already been elected emperor by chiefs determined to fight. Aztec

numbers now prevailed over Spanish firepower, and on the night of June 30–July 1 (La Noche Triste, meaning "The Sad Night") Cortés and many of his followers were forced to fight their way out of the city. They lost most of the gold they had hoped to bring out, along with 600 men and two-thirds of their 68 horses. The Aztecs harassed the Spanish in their retreat all the way to Tlaxcala.

Had Emperor Cuitlahuac continued guerrilla tactics, he might have been victorious. Instead, he chose to fight a set-piece battle in which the Aztec warriors came up against horse cavalry for the first time. At Otumba on July 7 the Spanish used their 28 horses to great advantage, driving against the conspicuously dressed Aztec leadership to win a victory in which thousands of Aztecs were killed.

Cortés then spent several months rebuilding his force. He sent ships to Jamaica to bring back replacement artillery and horses. At the same time, Cortés had his men construct 13 small brigantines in order to approach Tenochtitlán across Lake Texcoco. Each was manned by 12 native rowers and carried 25 Spanish soldiers.

Cortés was also aided by a surprise ally, for unwittingly the Spaniards had brought smallpox to the New World. The natives had absolutely no resistance to the disease, which wiped out much of the population. Cuitlahuac was among those who perished. Cuauhtemoc, a son-in-law of Montezuma, succeeded Cuitlahuac as emperor.

In early 1521, Cortés was ready to move. The Spaniards and their native allies began their approach to Tenochtitlán by taking control of towns around Lake Texcoco. By April this was complete. The Spanish had 184 harquebusiers, crossbowmen, and men-at-arms, along with 86 horsemen, perhaps 700 infantry, and 18 artillery pieces. They were also greatly aided by some 50,000 allied Tlaxcalans who opposed Aztec rule, led by Prince Xicotencatl II Axayacatl (Xicotencatl the Younger). Cortés divided his forces into three main groups under his lieutenants Alvarado, Gonzalo de Sandoval, and Cristóbal de Olid.

On May 26, forces under Sandoval and Alvarado destroyed the great aqueduct at Chapultepec, cutting off the water supply to Tenochtitlán. Five days later the Aztecs mounted an attack with hundreds of canoes across the lake. The Spaniards used cannon fire to destroy most of the canoes and win control of the lake. That same day Cortés launched an attack on Tenochtitlán. Some crossbowmen were able to land in the city but were soon driven out.

The fighting continued for 10 weeks, during which the Spaniards were able to view the sacrifice by the Aztecs atop the great pyramid of those they had taken prisoner. At night the defenders made fresh breaks in the causeways, providing access to the city, but the Spaniards and their allies were able to repair them. The Aztecs mounted human-wave attacks, which the Tlaxcalans defeated at heavy loss to themselves. Finally on August 13, Cortés launched an assault that brought victory the next day. Only a few Aztecs escaped in canoes. Reportedly, 150,000 people died in the city. One Spanish eyewitness said that it was impossible to walk in Tenochtitlán without stepping on corpses.

Following the capture of Tenochtitlán, Cortés set about completely dismantling Aztec society and replacing it with Spanish civilization. He was assisted in this by the continued ravages of smallpox that may have wiped out as much as 90 percent of the native population. Within a generation both the Aztec language and religion had disappeared.

Cortés subsequently led expeditions into present-day Guatemala and Honduras during 1523–1526. In 1528 he returned to Spain and successfully defended himself before Emperor Charles V against charges that he was setting up his conquests as his personal empire. Charles V confirmed him as the Marqués del Valle de Oaxaca and captain general of New Spain and the South Sea. In 1540 Cortés again returned to Spain to meet with Charles V. In 1541 he took part in a disastrous Spanish military expedition against Algiers. Retiring to his estate of Castilleja de la Cuesta near Seville, Spain, Cortés died in 1547.

Significance

The capture of Tenochtitlán was the principal event in the Spanish conquest of Mesoamerica. After their conquest of central Mexico, the Spaniards proceeded northward. It would be almost 60 years, however, before they were able to end resistance to their rule by the Indian population of Mesoamerica. The deaths of a majority of the native population from European diseases to which they had no immunity greatly facilitated the pacification. In 1535, meanwhile, Holy Roman emperor and king of Spain Charles V named Antonio de Mendoza the first viceroy of New Spain, a name suggested by Cortés. Spain's rule in Latin America lasted nearly three centuries.

Further Reading

Abbot, John S. C. *History of Hernando Cortez*. New York: Harper and Brothers, 1855.

Berdan, Frances F. *The Aztecs of Central Mexico: An Imperial Society*. New York: Holt, Rinehart and Winston, 1982.

Carrasco, David. *Montezuma's Mexico*. Niwot: University of Colorado Press, 1992.

Cortés, Hernán. *Letters from Mexico.* Translated and edited by Anthony Pagden. London: Oxford University Press, 1972.

Díaz del Castillo, Bernal. *The Discovery and Conquest of Mexico: 1517–1521.* Translated by A. P. Maudslay. New York: Farrar, Straus, and Cudahy, 1956.

Hassig, Ross. *Mexico and the Spanish Conquest.* New York: Longman, 1994.

Hassig, Ross. *Time, History, and Belief in Aztec and Colonial Mexico.* Austin: Texas University Press, 2001.

Johnson, William Weber. *Cortés.* Boston: Little, Brown, 1975.

León-Portilla, Miguel, ed. *The Broken Spears: The Aztec Account of the Conquest of Mexico.* Translated by Lysander Kemp. Expanded and updated ed. Boston: Beacon, 2011.

López de Gómara, Francisco. *Cortés: The Life of the Conqueror by His Secretary.* Berkeley: University of California Press, 1964.

Narrative of Some Things of New Spain and of the Great City of Temestitan. Translated by Marshall Saville. New York: Cortés Society, 1917.

Prescott, William H. *William H. Prescott's History of the Conquest of Mexico.* Edited by John H. Elliott. New York: Continuum, 2009.

Restall, Matthew. *Seven Myths of the Spanish Conquest.* New York: Oxford University Press, 2003.

Thomas, Hugh. *Conquest: Cortés, Montezuma, and the Fall of Old Mexico.* Reprint ed. New York: Simon and Schuster, 2013.

White, Jon Manchip. *Cortés and the Downfall of the Aztec Empire.* London: Hamish Hamilton, 1971.

Anglo-Spanish War (1585–1604)

Dates	1585–1604
Location	England, Spain, France, the Netherlands, Atlantic Ocean, English Channel, Caribbean, Ireland
Combatants	England vs. Spain
Principal Commanders	England: Elizabeth I; Charles Howard of Effingham; Sir John Hawkins; Sir Francis Drake; Robert Dudley, Earl of Leicester; Robert Devereux, Earl of Essex Spain: Philip II; Alessandro Farnese, Duke of Parma; Alonso Pérez de Guzmán, Duke of Medina Sidonia
Principal Battles	Cádiz (first), Channel Fight, Gravelines, Cádiz (second), Kinsale
Outcome	England retains its independence and goes on to challenge Spain in the New World and in Asia. The war marks the rise of England as the leading Protestant power in Europe and the beginning of the decline of Spain as a world power.

Causes

Although begun without formal declaration of war, the Anglo-Spanish War of 1585–1604 was immensely important in European and world history. Militant Catholic king Philip II of Spain (r. 1556–1598) was determined not only to uphold the Catholic Church but also to lead a great Catholic counteroffensive to roll back the tide of Protestantism. Into this vast effort he was prepared to pour all the blood and treasure of his kingdoms. Philip had a considerable personal interest in England. Although he had spent little time in that country, he had been comonarch of England because of his marriage to Queen Mary I of England (r. 1553–1558) until her death in 1558.

Philip II was determined to stamp out the Protestantism that had taken hold in his possession of the Netherlands. In 1566 William of Orange (also called William the Silent) led an open rebellion there against oppressive Spanish rule. Queen Elizabeth of England (r. 1558–1603) emerged as the Protestant champion, supporting the rebels, at first surreptitiously. Elizabeth girded her northern flank by concluding an alliance with King James VI of Scotland, ending warfare between their two countries.

Added to the religious issue and English support of the rebels in the Netherlands was a third cause of tension between England and Spain: the intrusion of English ships into Spain's empire in the New World. Beginning in 1562 under Sir John Hawkins and then Sir Francis Drake, English freebooters attacked Spanish shipping and engaged in the slave trade there in defiance of Spanish rule. Such activities proved immensely lucrative for the English Crown and came to have Elizabeth's support. By 1585, England and Spain were already at war to see which power would control the Atlantic Ocean.

Finally, the English supported the prior of Crato in his struggle with Philip II to secure the throne of Portugal. At the same time, the Spaniards began to support Catholic opposition in Ireland to the English rule there.

Course

The Anglo-Spanish War can be said to have commenced in August 1585 when Elizabeth actively intervened in the struggle in the Netherlands. When it appeared that Spanish troops under Alessandro Farnese,

better known by his later title of Duke of Parma, might capture the port of Antwerp, on August 10 Elizabeth concluded a treaty with the Dutch rebels, agreeing to provide men, horses, and subsidies. Elizabeth then sent some 6,000 English troops to the Netherlands under her favorite, Robert Dudley, Earl of Leicester. Dudley proved to be an inept field commander, however, and the troops were withdrawn in 1587.

With Philip having considered the Treaty of Nonsuch a declaration of war, Elizabeth ordered Drake to lead an expedition against Spain's colonies in the New World. Drake departed Plymouth in September 1585 with 21 ships and 1,800 soldiers under Christopher Carleill. Drake first proceeded against Vigo in Spain, which he held for two weeks. After plundering Santiago in the Cape Verde Islands, he sailed across the Atlantic to sack Santo Domingo and Cartagena de Indias in present-day Colombia. During his return voyage, on June 6, 1586, Drake raided San Augustín (St. Augustine) in Florida, then took off the English colonists from Roanoke Island and returned to England, arriving at Portsmouth in July 1586.

For Philip II the pivotal event in his decision to attack England directly was the execution of Mary, Queen of Scots. Mary was a Catholic and the former queen of France and then Scotland. Driven out of Scotland, she had sought refuge in England and had been placed under house arrest by Elizabeth. Mary had a claim to the English throne, and Philip was involved in a number of plots to overthrow Elizabeth and install Mary as queen. Fearful for her throne and indeed for her life, Elizabeth brought Mary to trial and had her executed on February 8, 1587. This action shocked all Catholic Europe, and Mary's claim to the English throne passed on, by her own deed

The Spanish Armada, 1588

of will, to Philip. With France distracted by religious civil war, Philip II now began planning his "Enterprise of England."

On July 29, Philip II secured authority from Pope Sixtus V to overthrow Elizabeth, Pope Pius V already having excommunicated her. Sixtus V authorized Philip to collect crusade taxes and promised additional funding of his own to the Spanish on their reaching England. He also gave Philip authority to place whomever he selected on the English throne.

Philip ordered the collection of a fleet of the largest naval and maritime vessels, intended for intimidation as much as outright invasion. Philip's strategy was to gain control of the English Channel and facilitate the passage of Parma's veteran Spanish army from the Netherlands to England. Philip appointed a distinguished Spanish seaman, Álvaro de Bazán, first Marquis of Santa Cruz, to command the Spanish Armada enterprise. Santa Cruz worked diligently, but he died suddenly in February 1588 and was replaced by a reluctant Alonso Pérez de Guzmán, Duke of Medina Sidonia, who had never before held command at sea. Meanwhile, Parma made preparations. He ordered a ship canal dug from Antwerp and Ghent to Bruges, assembled 28 warships at Dunkerque (Dunkirk), and ordered the construction of several hundred landing craft and barges to carry his men and horses across the channel to England.

The English were well aware of Spanish naval preparations, and during April–June 1587 Drake led 23 ships in a preemptive strike on the principal assembly point for the Spanish fleet at Cádiz, "singeing the beard of the King of Spain" as he put it. There the English destroyed 33 Spanish ships of all types along with a sizable number of seasoned staves that were necessary for the construction of barrels for the storage of provisions. This condemned the armada to rotting provisions in unseasoned barrels. Drake also attacked Spanish shipping and Lisbon Harbor and captured a large Spanish treasure galleon before returning to England.

In April 1588 the Spanish ships began to assemble. Delays led to refitting at the northern port of Carunna in June. Elizabeth resisted a call by her naval commander, Lord Charles Howard of Effingham, for another preemptive strike. In

June, however, she did authorize the calling up of about 60,000 men to resist any Spanish land invasion.

The armada of 124 ships, known as the Grande y Felicísima Armada or Armada Invencible (literally "Great and Most Fortunate Navy" or "Invincible Fleet"), finally set out on July 12. Manned by 8,500 seamen and galley slaves, it carried 19,000 troops. On July 19, the Spanish ships were sighted by the English off St. Michael's Mount, Cornwall, and the news was flashed to London by signal beacons across the southern coast of England. That evening the English fleet, having assembled at Plymouth, was trapped there by an incoming tide. The Spanish held a council of war to discuss the option of riding the tide into the harbor and attacking the English ships at anchor, but Medina Sidonia rejected it. That same night with the tide having turned, 55 English ships set out in pursuit of the Spanish. Admiral Lord Howard of Effingham had command with Drake as vice admiral and with Hawkins as rear admiral. Beginning on July 21, a running sea fight began as the Spanish ships swept east up the English Channel in a loose crescent-shaped formation.

To this point in history, battles at sea had been similar to those on land; the principal aim was to take enemy vessels by boarding. In the armada fight, a new form of battle at sea emerged because of the long-range guns employed by the English. In all the English had 172 warships, but 50 of these were only lightly armed and took little role in the battle. The English ships mounted a total of 1,972 guns, though, while the Spanish had only 1,124. The Spanish outnumbered the English in short-range cannon (163 to 55) and medium-range perriers (326 to 43), but this was reversed in long-range culverins (635 for the Spanish to 1,874 for the English). While the Spanish hoped to fight a traditional close-in engagement where they might grapple and board their opponents, the English planned to stand off and blast away at the Spanish ships beyond the range of the latter's guns.

The English early gained the weather gauge, establishing a position upwind and attacking the Spanish ships daily until the armada anchored at the French port of Calais on July 27. To this point, neither side had inflicted major damage on the other.

From Bruges, Parma sent word that he was under blockade by a Dutch fleet commanded by Justinus of Nassau. Then before dawn on July 28, the English sent eight fireships into the Calais anchorage, forcing the armada ships to cut their cables and put to sea. Medina Sidonia intended that his ships reanchor once the fireships had passed, but many of the Spanish vessels crashed together. Crews were unable to get at spare anchors, and the ships drifted northeastward along the coast. With the wind blowing out of the south-southwest, Medina Sidonia realized that his ships could not regain the harbor.

The Battle of Gravelines off the Flanders coast ensued, with the English engaging individual Spanish ships unable to establish a protective formation. The English maintained position to windward of the Spanish ships. The heeling hulls of the armada ships were thus exposed to possible damage below the waterline. The English were forced to break off the fight, however, and returned to port to replenish stocks of ammunition. Through a week of fighting the Spanish had expended upward of 100,000 rounds of shot, but no English ship was seriously damaged.

The famous storm known as the Protestant Wind now swept the Spanish ships into the North Sea, leaving their captains no choice but to continue on around the British Isles, then sail down the western coast of Ireland en route back to Spain. The ships limped in singly during August through September. Sixty-three of the Spanish ships, or half of the total, were lost, of which the English sank or captured 15. A major Atlantic storm drove many weakened ships and their exhausted crews ashore, and 19 Spanish ships are known to have been wrecked on the Scottish and Irish coasts.

After 1588, nothing went right for Philip II. He continued his plans to conquer England and his efforts to defeat the Dutch rebels. With the Spanish preparing a fleet at Cádiz for yet another naval expedition against England, in 1596 Queen Elizabeth authorized another raid on that port. It consisted of 17 English royal ships and 24 Dutch vessels, along with 100 transports and storeships and some private vessels, all commanded by Lord Howard of Effingham. Robert Devereux, Earl of Essex, had command of the troop contingent. The English offered not to burn the ships in the harbor in return for 2 million ducats, but Don Alonso Pérez de Guzmán el Bueno, seventh Duke of Medina Sidonia, refused, claiming that most of the cargoes were owned by foreign merchants. The English attacked on June 20, but the Spanish ships and shore batteries mounted a strong defense. The English only managed to capture 2 Spanish ships; the Spanish torched the remainder to prevent them from falling into English hands. Some 12 million ducats went to the bottom, but the Spanish recovered most of that treasure later.

English troops then went ashore and took Cádiz. Leaving it largely in ruins, they then moved on to Fairo, where they enjoyed less success. Although this operation forestalled any new Spanish assault on England, the English and Dutch incurred massive financial losses.

Philip added a new enemy when he intervened in the French religious wars of 1562–1598, going to war on the side of the Catholic League against the Protestant champion Henry of Navarre in 1595. This opened the possibility of another Spanish invasion of England across the English Channel, and Elizabeth concluded the Triple Alliance with the Dutch and the French under Henry. When Spanish troops captured Calais on April 24, 1596, Elizabeth sent 2,000 troops to France. Henry of Navarre triumphed over the Catholic League militarily, but Paris and many other places held out against him. Well aware that a considerable majority of the French population was Catholic and would remain thus, Henry converted to Catholicism, supposedly remarking that "Paris is well worth a mass." The war then came to an end with the Peace of Vervins (May 2, 1598). Philip II died on September 13 that same year, his grand design in ruins.

Meanwhile, English troops were fighting to put down a rebellion against their rule in Ireland. The Nine Years' War or Tyrone's Rebellion, named for Hugh O'Neill, Earl of Tyrone, had begun in 1594 and at its height during 1600–1602 became the largest English military effort of Elizabeth's reign with the dispatch to Ireland of some 18,000 troops.

Following a victory by the rebels in the Battle of Yellow Ford (August 14, 1598), Elizabeth sent out reinforcements under Robert Dudley, Earl of Essex, during 1599–1600. The Irish rebels easily outmaneuvered him, bringing Dudley's disgrace. The rebels appealed to Spain for help, and in 1601 King Philip III (r. 1598–1631) sent 4,000 troops under Don Juan de Águila.

The Spaniards landed in southern Ireland at Kinsale and captured it. Here, however, the Spaniards were checked by an English army of 6,500 men under Charles Blount, Lord Mountjoy. O'Neill then marched a rebel force of 12,000 men to Cork. He was attempting to link up with the Spaniards when on December 24, 1601, he was defeated in the Battle of Kinsale. Mountjoy then went on the offensive, raiding Ulster, which had been controlled by the rebels, and establishing forts. The rebellion was soon put down, and in 1603 O'Neill accepted the queen's pardon. In return for laying down his arms, he was allowed to retain his titles and lands.

King James VI of Scotland, son of Mary, Queen of Scots, succeeded to the throne of England as James I upon the death of Elizabeth on March 24, 1603. The official union of England and Scotland occurred on October 24, 1604. Meanwhile, the Treaty of London of August 28, 1604, restored the status quo ante bellum with Spain. James, a Protestant, rejected the Spanish demand for toleration of Catholics in England, but the English agreed to end their support for the Dutch rebellion against Spain. English trade with the entrepôt of Antwerp in the Spanish Netherlands was restored, while the English illegal trade with Spain's colonies in the New World came to an end.

Significance

The Anglo-Spanish War marked the beginning of the end of Spanish greatness and the rise of England. English privateering during the war destroyed much of Spain's merchant shipping, and increasingly Spanish goods came to be transported in Dutch and English ships. The armada battle of 1588 also had pronounced influence on the conduct of naval warfare. And, in an age in which religion was immensely important,

England's great victory over Spain in that battle seemed to many to be a sign that God favored Protestantism. One of the medals struck to celebrate the English victory bore these words in Latin: "He blew with His winds, and they were scattered."

Further Reading

Anderson David. *The Spanish Armada.* New York: Hempstead, 1988.

Beem, Charles. *The Foreign Relations of Elizabeth I.* New York: Palgrave Macmillan, 2011.

Fernadez-Armesto, Felipe. *The Spanish Armada: The Experience of War in 1588.* London: Oxford University Press, 1988.

Graham, Winston. *The Spanish Armadas.* New York: HarperCollins, 1972.

Hutchinson, Robert. *The Spanish Armada.* London: Orion, 2014.

Konstam, Angus. *The Spanish Armada: The Great Enterprise against England.* Oxford, UK: Osprey, 2009.

Lewis, Michael A. *Armada Guns: A Comparative Study of English and Spanish Armaments.* London: Allen and Unwin, 1961.

Martin, Colin, and Geoffrey Parker. *The Spanish Armada.* New York: Norton, 1988.

Mattingly, Garrett. *The Armada.* Boston: Houghton Mifflin, 1959.

McDowall, David. *The Spanish Armada.* London: Batsford, 1988.

Tinsey, John, and Richard Hook. *The Spanish Armada.* Oxford, UK: Osprey, 2000.

Williams, Jay. *The Spanish Armada.* New York: American Heritage Publishing, 1966.

Imjin War (1592–1598)

Dates	1592–1598
Location	Korean Peninsula
Combatants	Japan vs. Joseon Korea and China
Principal Commanders	Japan: Daimyo Toyotomi Hideyoshi, Konishi Yukinaga, Kato Kiyomasa, Konishi Yukinaga Korea: King Sonjo, Sin Nip, Yi Sun Sin China: Emperor Wanli (Zhū Yìjūn), Li Rusonh
Principal Battles	Ch'ungju, Hansan-do, Busan, Pyokchegwan, Haengju, Chinji, Ch'ilch'onnyang, Myongnyang, Noryang Strait
Outcome	Although Joseon Korea expelled the Japanese and remains independent, Korea itself is more devastated by the war than any other in its history. The roots of anti-Japanese sentiment in Korea are found in this war.

Causes

In 1590 Japanese daimyo and general Toyotomi Hideyoshi established himself as the power behind the throne controlling the entire nation. Toyotomi dreamed of making Japan the dominant power in East Asia and set the ambitious goal of conquering Ming dynasty China. Such an effort would have the advantage of diverting the energies of the ever-ambitious Japanese warlords from domestic affairs. To get at China, Toyotomi planned to first invade and secure Joseon (Choson) Korea, then a tributary state of China. Joseon Korea appeared weak and vulnerable to invasion. Having enjoyed two centuries of peace, its leaders had allowed the nation's military to deteriorate. The Korean military forces were small, disorganized, poorly equipped, and scattered around the country.

When the Koreans refused a Japanese demand for free passage to China, which would have meant Japanese occupation of their country, Toyotomi dispatched forces across Tsushima Strait (Korea Strait). The resulting first invasion is known in Korea as the Japanese Disturbance of Imjin (1592 being an *imjin* year in the Chinese sexagenary cycle).

Course

On May 23, 1592, Japanese ships carrying some 158,000 men crossed from Tsushima, easily brushed aside two Korean naval squadrons and landed at the port of Busan (Pusan) in southern Korea. The Japanese had the advantage of unity of command and superior weaponry in the form of matchlock firearms. Although the Koreans resisted the invasion, the Japanese soon secured Busan and, once they had reorganized, sent three columns northward. These met little resistance. In a major battle at Chungju (Ch'ungju) on June 7, the Japanese soundly defeated Korean Army forces under General Sin Nip. Several days later Korean king Sonjo fled north, first to Pyongyang, and then to Ŭiju on the Chinese border. Japanese forces entered the Korean capital of Seoul on June 9, only to discover much of the city burned and empty of inhabitants.

The Japanese expeditionary force then split into two main bodies: one under General Konishi Yukinaga proceeded north through western Korea to Pyongyang, while the other under General Kato Kiyomasa advanced up the eastern coast of Korea. Everywhere the Korean people paid a heavy price, with the Japanese killing many civilians as well as soldiers. (The Japanese kept a body count by routinely cutting off the ears of those slain.)

The Japanese military strategy called for the army to hold the southeastern and central regions of Korea, with the navy responsible for securing the rich rice-producing areas of Cholla (Chollq) and Chungcheong (Ch'ungch'ong) Provinces in order to secure a stable food supply for the occupying Japanese forces. This plan, however, rested on Japan maintaining control of the sea, also necessary in securing the lines of communication back to Japan, and that now came into question.

Korean admiral Yi Sun Sin (Yi Sun-sin), certainly one of history's most brilliant naval commanders, was one of the few Korean leaders to have taken meaningful steps to prepare for a Japanese invasion. On March 9, 1591, with the threat of Japanese invasion fully apparent, Yi had been appointed head of the left naval command of Cholla Province, along the southeastern coast. He then designed and caused to be built the famed *kobukson* (turtle ship), a new type of warship and in fact the world's first armored warship.

Sufficiently detailed descriptions of these vessels survive to provide a fairly complete picture of their appearance. They were about 116 feet in length and 28 feet in beam. They had a raft-like rectangular-shaped hull, a transom bow and stern, and a superstructure supporting two masts, each with a square rectangular mat sail. A carved wooden dragon head was set at the bow.

The ships were powered by both sail and oar, with openings for 8–10 oars on each side of the superstructure. The oars were to provide additional speed and maneuverability. The superstructure was

JOSEON NAVAL CAMPAIGNS, MAY – SEP 1592

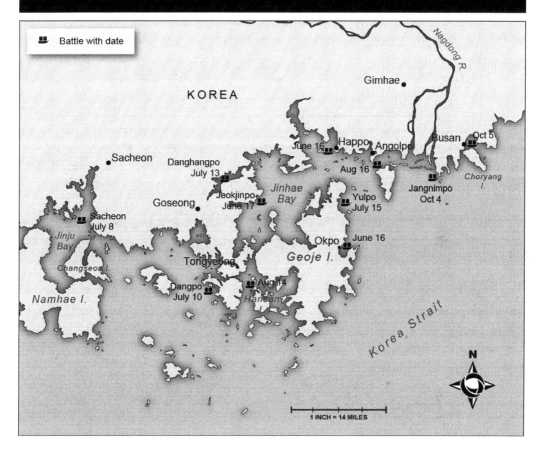

protected by a curved iron plated top that gave the vessel a turtle shell–like appearance. The iron plating had spikes set in it to prevent an enemy crew from boarding. The turtle ships mounted cannon: six on each side and several at the bow and stern.

The first of the turtle ships was launched just days before the Japanese invasion in May 1592. With the invasion, Yi collected 85 ships. These included two dozen galley battleships and 15 scout ships, with the remainder being fishing boat conversions. With this force, on June 16, 1592, Yi surprised and destroyed 26 Japanese ships off Okpo (Okp'o). The next day he sank

another 16 Japanese ships off Chokjinpo (Chokjinp'o).

Following repairs, Yi sailed with 26 ships, including 2 turtle ships, and destroyed 12 more Japanese ships off Sacheon (Sach'on) on July 8. On July 10 he sank 20 other Japanese ships off Dangpo (Tangp'o). Reinforced, on July 13 he sank the majority of 26 Japanese ships at Danghangpo (Tanghangp'o). These victories led the Japanese to send naval reinforcements. Yi, now with 55 ships, on August 13 discovered 75 Japanese ships at Kyonnaeryang (Kyonnaeryang) and sent a few of his own ships into the harbor in a successful effort to lure out the Japanese. The next day he captured 12 large Japanese ships and sank more than 40 others off Hanson Island (Hansan-do) in what is regarded as one of the most important Korean victories of the war. On August 16 he destroyed 30 or more of 40 Japanese ships at Angolpo (Angolp'o).

In September, Yi had at his disposal a fleet of 74 war galleys and 92 smaller vessels. He trained his men for three weeks and then set out for the principal Japanese base at Busan. Here the Japanese had 500 ships, 100 of them warships. On October 5 in the Battle of Busan, Yi attacked, destroying or capturing 100 Japanese vessels. He then scattered a large Japanese reinforcing convoy, sinking many of its ships.

The Japanese were now experiencing great difficulty ashore as well. Not only had Admiral Yi cut them off from resupply from Japan, but there was also a famine in Korea that reduced Japanese foraging, and the Japanese were under constant harassment from the increasing numbers of Koreans who joined insurgent militia forces known as *ŭibyong* (righteous warriors). Meanwhile, at the request of the vassal state of Korea, China intervened. In January 1593 Ming emperor Wanli (Zhū Yìjūn) sent a 40,000-man army commanded by General Li Rusonh into northern Korea, and on February 8 Chinese and Korean forces recaptured Pyongyang and pushed the Japanese forces southward. Chinese and Korean forces then prepared for a joint effort to retake Seoul. After they sustained heavy losses in a battle at Byeokjegwan (Pyokchegwan), however, the Chinese withdrew back to Pyongyang. This left the Korean forces vulnerable to an attack on their mountain fortifications north of the Han River at Haengju. Some 43,000

Japanese attacked, but after nine separate assaults and substantial casualties, the Japanese retreated southward. The Battle of Haengju of March 14, 1593, is celebrated in Korean history as one of the most important of the war.

With the principal Japanese generals, including Konishi Yukinaga, urging peace and the Chinese eager to return home, the two sides entered into talks. Japanese troops then withdrew from Seoul into an enclave around Pusan. The Japanese were determined, however, to secure the stronghold of Jinju (Chinji), which controlled access to the key rice-producing area of Cholla Province. Already in November 1592 a far smaller Korean force led by Kim Si-min had defeated a much larger Japanese army there, inflicting 30,000 casualties. Now in July 1593, the Japanese sent 79,000 men against Jinju and this time captured it on July 27, slaughtering many of its inhabitants.

Truce talks between China and Japan opened in April 1593 and went on for three years without resolution, with each side refusing to accept the demands of the other. Meanwhile, the Japanese withdrew most of their troops from Korea, and the Chinese removed all of theirs. On April 23, 1594, Yi attacked and sank 31 Japanese ships in actions around Danghangpo.

On March 1, 1597, General Toyotomi launched a new invasion from Japan, sending some 141,000 men by ship across the straits. Landing near Pusan, the Japanese forces again drove north, devastating much of the country and causing Ming China to again intervene militarily. The Koreans had been able to rebuild and improve their military, and this time the Japanese enjoyed less success on land and were held largely to Kyongsang Province.

The Japanese did, however, send out false information in an attempt to lure Admiral Yi into a trap. Aware of what the Japanese intended, Yi refused a royal order to attack, whereupon he was dismissed from command. His successor, Won Kyun, led the Korean fleet to destruction off Pusan in the Battle of Chilcheollyang (Ch'ilch'onnyang) on August 28, 1597. Won was among those killed, and the Koreans lost 157 of their 169 ships.

Following the disastrous Battle of Chilcheollyang, Yi was reinstated in command of the Korean Navy, now reduced to only 12 ships. Following a series of small victories, on December 4, 1597, in the Battle of Myeongnyang (Myongnyang), Yi employed his considerable experience and knowledge of Korean tides and currents to win his most brilliant victory over the Japanese. With only 12 ships of his own, he engaged 133 Japanese ships, although many of the latter were transport vessels. Yi sank 31 Japanese ships for no losses of his own before the remaining Japanese ships hauled off.

A lull in fighting of more than a year followed, giving Yi time to build up his naval strength. With some 150 ships, including 63 Ming warships led by Admiral Chen Lin, Yi attacked a Japanese fleet of equal size commanded by General Konishi Yukinaga. In the Battle of Noryang Strait of December 16, 1598, the Korean and Ming fleets captured or destroyed 200 Japanese ships. During the battle, however, Yi was struck and killed by a cannonball.

Again the Koreans and Chinese controlled the straits, and Japanese lines of communication to Korea were again effectively severed, cutting off their forces in Korea. Another motivation for peace was the death of Japanese general Toyotomi, the prime mover behind the invasion, on September 18, 1598. The new governing body of Japan, the Council of Five Elders, ordered the Japanese troops to evacuate Korea.

Significance

For Korea, the Japanese invasions were more devastating than any other war in their history including the 1950–1953 Korean War. The Koreans suffered tremendously from the Japanese presence but also at the hands of their allies, the Chinese. The decrease in the population had a tremendous effect on the agricultural economy, and the years that followed saw widespread famine, disease, and political upheaval. Certainly the Joseon dynasty never quite recovered from the shock of the war.

Korea also lost many priceless cultural treasures taken by the Japanese to Japan and never returned. The Japanese also took back to Japan tens of thousands of Koreans, most of them artisans and craftsmen, including highly skilled potters. (Korean pottery was then being highly prized and their work became the basis for much of subsequent Japanese pottery.) The departure of these skilled workers was a major blow to the Korean economy and greatly benefited that of Japan. Although some 7,000 Koreans were returned by Japan following the normalization of relations between the two countries in 1607, a large portion of the remaining captives were sold to European traders—mostly Portuguese—who then resold them in Southeast Asia. It is no wonder that Korean nationalists cited the war and its heroes in seeking to rally resistance to the Japanese occupation of 1910–1945. Certainly much of the present anti-Japanese sentiment in Korea stems from the Japanese-Korean War of 1592–1598.

In China, the war of 1592–1598 was used to fuel nationalistic fervor during the Japanese invasions of China in the 20th century. The war is also often cited by Chinese historians as proof of Chinese-Korean friendship.

The war also brought political upheaval in Japan and ultimately resulted in arguably its most important battle. Following the death of Toyotomi in 1598, a struggle ensued between his most powerful vassals for control, Toyotomi's son Hideyori then being only five years old. The leading nobles soon declared their allegiance to one side or the other, and on October 20, 1600, battle was joined at Sekigahara in what was probably both the largest and most important military engagement in Japanese history. Although fighting continued for some time thereafter, the victor at Sekigahara, Tokugawa Ieyasu, won out. Named shogun by Emperor Go-Yozei in 1603, Tokugawa moved the capital from Kyoto to Edo (Tokyo) and became de facto dictator of Japan. The Tokugawa shogunate lasted until the Meiji Restoration of 1868.

The war also had profound geopolitical significance in East Asia, as it weakened the Ming garrisons in Manchuria, making it far easier for the Manchus to attack there and ultimately bringing the military defeat of the Ming dynasty and the beginning of the Manchu dynasty.

Further Reading

Brown, Delmer M. "The Impact of Firearms on Japanese Warfare, 1543–1598." *Far Eastern Quarterly* 7(3) (May 1948): 236–253.

Galuppini, Gino. *Warships of the World: An Illustrated Encyclopedia.* New York: Military Press, 1989.

Hawley, Samuel. *The Imjin War.* London: Institute of East Asian Studies and the Royal Asiatic Society, Korea Branch, 2005.

Henthorne, William E. *A History of Korea.* New York: Free Press, 1971.

Kang, Ch'ol-won. *Songung Yi Sun-sin* [Yi-Sun-sin, a National Hero]. Seoul: Chisong Munhwa-sa, 1978.

Kim, Jinwung. *A History of Korea: From "Land of the Morning Calm" to States in Conflict.* Bloomington: Indiana University Press, 2012.

Park, Son-sik. *Yi Sun-sin.* Seoul: Kyujanggak, 1998.

Sansom, George. *A History of Japan, 1334–1615.* Stanford, CA: Stanford University Press, 1961.

Swope, Kenneth M. "Crouching Tigers, Secret Weapons: Military Technology Employed during the Sino-Japanese-Korean War, 1592–1598." *Journal of Military History* 69 (January 2005): 11–42.

Swope, Kenneth M. *A Dragon's Head and a Serpent's Tail: Ming China and the First Great East Asian War, 1592–1598.* Norman: University of Oklahoma Press, 2009.

Turnbull, Stephen R. *Fighting Ships of the Far East (2): Japan and Korea, 612–1639.* Buffalo, MN: Osprey, 2003.

Turnbull, Stephen R. *Samurai Invasion: Japan's Korean War, 1592–98.* London: Cassell, 2002.

Yi, Sun-sin. *Nanjung Ilgi: War Diary of Admiral Yi Sun-sin.* Edited by Sohn Pow-key and translated by Ha Tae-hung. Seoul: Yonsei University Press, 1977.

Thirty Years' War (1618–1648)

Dates	1618–1648
Location	Central Europe
Combatants	Protestant German princes, Danes, Swedes, French vs. Catholic German princes, Holy Roman Empire, Austria, Spain
Principal Commanders	Protestants: Palatinate, Frederick V; Denmark, Christian IV, Peter Ernst von Mansfield; Sweden, Gustavus II Adolphus, Johan Banér; France, Turenne, Louis d'Enghien, the Great Condé Catholics: Holy Roman emperor Ferdinand II, Count Johan Tserclaes Tilly, Albrecht Wenzel von Wallenstein
Principal Battles	White Mountain, Dessau Bridge, Lutter am Barenberge, Magdeburg, Breitenfeld (first), Lech River, Lützen, Nördlingen, Lens, Wittstock, Breitenfeld (second)
Outcome	The Thirty Years' War closes out the period of religious wars in Europe. The region is devastated by the fighting, and the Habsburgs are frustrated in their efforts to unify Germany, with it effectively atomized into some 350 sovereign political entities. Switzerland and the Netherlands are recognized as independent.

Causes

On October 31, 1517, Catholic theologian, professor, and parish priest Martin Luther nailed on the door of the Castle Church at Wittenberg in Electoral Saxony a declaration in Latin that challenged certain practices of the Catholic Church. Luther intended to begin a debate with other scholars, but the posting of this document, known as the Ninety-Five Theses, is usually given by scholars as marking the beginning of the Reformation. Within half a century what became known as Protestantism had spread across much of Europe. The so-called Reformation Era can be said to have ended in 1648. In it, England, France, Scotland, Scandinavia, Switzerland, Poland, Hungary, Ireland, Italy, the Slovene lands, and the Holy Roman Empire in Germany were all torn by conflict. While France, England, and other countries recovered, Germany did not.

Sparked by Luther's ideas, Germany experienced the Knights' Revolt of 1522 and the Peasants' Revolt of 1524. In 1531 wary of threats voiced against them by Holy Roman emperor Charles V, the German states favoring Luther's reforming ideas established the Schmalkaldic League, and in 1546 war began in Germany between the forces of the league, backed by France, and those of the Catholic states headed by the Habsburg Holy Roman emperor Charles V. Were it not for ineffective leadership, the Protestant states would have won.

The Peace of Augsburg of September 25, 1555, ending the war checked the expansion of Protestantism in Central Europe. The peace treaty banned all other religious practices from Germany except Catholicism and Lutheranism. The treaty also increased the power of the individual rulers of the German states and free cities in giving them the right to determine the religion of their peoples in the clause "cujus regio, ejus religio" ("whose region, his religion"). The Ecclesiastical Reservation also provided that if a Catholic spiritual prince (such as a bishop ruling a bishopric) became Protestant, he could not take his territory with him and it would remain with the church. In addition, all estates of the church confiscated after 1552 were to be returned to Catholic Church control. This compromise resolved nothing and only staved off war. Germany was now effectively divided into two hostile armed camps.

Calvinism spread in Germany, and although this was prohibited by the Peace of Augsburg, a number of states became Calvinist. Among these was the strategically important Palatinate, which lay on the middle Rhine. The Palatinate was also important politically, as its ruler, the elector palatine, was one of the seven men who selected the Holy Roman emperor. In 1608 urged by Elector Palatine Frederick IV, the Protestant states formed the Evangelical Union of the Protestant States. In order to strengthen their position, its member states sought alliances with the Dutch (who since 1588 had been at war with Catholic Spain in what would become known as the Eighty Years' War), with Protestant England, and with Catholic France (which, however, was ruled by the Huguenot-turned-Catholic King Henry IV and sought, as a matter of state policy, to weaken Germany). In 1609, the Catholic states of Germany formed their own counterpart, the Catholic League. It sought support from Spain.

The ensuing Thirty Years' War of 1618–1648 was extremely complex. It was a German civil war fought over the religious issue, but it was also a civil war over constitutional issues, especially the power of the Holy Roman emperor, who was seeking to centralize authority in his own hands at the expense of the princes and the free cities of the empire. These two did not coincide, for Catholic as well as Protestant princes were all determined to resist increased control by the emperor.

The war was also an international struggle that came to involve Spain, France, Transylvania, the ongoing struggle in the Netherlands, and the rulers of Denmark and Sweden. Most of the fighting, however, occurred in Germany. The war was also complicated in that it saw the rise of soldiers of fortune, military commanders with their own territorial aspirations. Although too complex to recount in full detail here, the Thirty Years' War was nonetheless the greatest of all of Europe's wars before those of the French Revolution and Napoleon and had a profound impact, especially on German history.

The immediate cause of the war was a revolt in Bohemia. The closing of a Protestant church in Braunau and the destruction of another in the archbishopric of Prague (Praha) greatly alarmed Protestants in Bohemia, as did the transfer of state administration to 10 governors, 7 of whom were Catholics. These events led Protestant Jindrich Matyas (Matthias), Count Thurn, to begin a revolt in Prague on May 23, 1618. In the so-called Defenestration of Prague, the rebels threw from a window in the chancellory two emissaries of Holy Roman emperor Marthias of Austria (r. 1612–1619) and their secretary. The three men fell 70 feet but survived (the Catholics claimed by divine intervention; the Protestants alleged that it was because they landed on a large manure pile). The rebels then established a provisional government, and Count Thurn proceeded to raise an army. These events mark the beginning of the Bohemian Phase (1618–1625) of the Thirty Years' War. Historians usually divide the conflict into four major phases: Bohemian (1618–1625), Danish (1625–1629), Swedish (1630–1634), and Swedish-French (1635–1648).

Course of the Bohemian Phase (1618–1625)

Fighting commenced in Bohemia in July 1618 when Count Thurn attacked and captured Krummau. In November, Count Ernst von Mansfeld and 20,000 mercenaries took Pilsen. The Catholics responded in the winter of 1618–1619 by assembling two armies—one from Flanders, financed by Spain, and the other from Austria. The Protestants held both at bay. Meanwhile, Prince Gábor (Gabriel) Bethlen of Transylvania took advantage of the preoccupation of the Habsburgs with Bohemia to reestablish the former Kingdom of Hungary. In 1618 he conquered northern (Royal) Hungary from the Habsburgs. Fighting in the east continued until 1620 and conclusion of an armistice.

On March 20, 1619, Holy Roman emperor Matthias died, opening up the succession to the imperial, Austrian, and Bohemian thrones. In May, Count Thurn marched on Vienna and was there joined by Bethlen and Hungarian forces. In the Battle of Záblatí (Sabalt, in the present-day Czech Republic) of June 10, 1619, however, imperial forces under Charles Bonaventure de Longueval, Comte de Bucquoi, defeated Protestant forces under Mansfeld, leading the Bohemian government to recall Thurn from Vienna. Prince Bethlen also departed, returning to Hungary.

Having already declared as invalid the March 1619 election of Ferdinand of Habsburg as their king, on August 26 the Bohemian Protestants chose the outspoken Calvinist Protestant elector palatine Frederick, head of the Protestant Union. He proceeded to Bohemia and took the title of Frederick V.

Meanwhile, on August 29 ardent Catholic Ferdinand of Habsburg was elected emperor by the electoral college at Frankfurt; he ruled as Ferdinand II until his death in 1637. During the next months in his bid to remove Frederick from the Bohemian throne, Ferdinand II received assistance not only from Catholic rulers Duke Maximilian of Bavaria and King Philip III of Spain but also from Lutheran duke John George of Saxony, who was wary of the growing power of Frederick V and the Palatinate. Frederick, meanwhile, received assistance from the Protestant Union, the Dutch, and the English.

On April 30, 1620, Emperor Ferdinand II issued an imperial mandate ordering Frederick to withdraw as king of Bohemia. Frederick's rejection of this amounted to a declaration of war. In July the Lutheran princes of the Protestant Union, jealous of Frederick's rising power and fearful of his Calvinism and of Emperor Ferdinand II, declared their neutrality. Meanwhile, Bohemian troops invaded Austrian territory, aided by an uprising of Austrian nobles against Ferdinand.

In late July acting in support of Ferdinand II, Duke Maximilian of Bavaria crossed into Austria with 25,000 Catholic League troops commanded by Johan Tserclaes, Count Tilly, who effectively restored order there. That same month, Spanish commander in the Netherlands Ambrosio Spinola, Marqués de Los Balbases, marched from Flanders with 25,000 troops, invading the Palatinate and capturing its cities. Frederick V was then in Bohemia and thus unable to protect his own lands.

GERMANY DURING THE THIRTY YEARS' WAR 1618–1648

Maximilian of Bavaria and Tilly joined imperial forces under Charles Bonaventure de Longueval, Comte de Bucquoi, for an invasion of Bohemia. Just west of Prague on November 8, 1620, their army of 27,000 men encountered some 30,000 poorly equipped and badly trained Protestant troops under Christian of Anhalt. This Battle of White Mountain lasted only an hour, with the Catholic side victorious. The Catholics sustained perhaps 700 casualties, the Protestants 5,000. The brevity of the battle and Frederick's precipitous flight from Prague upon Tilly's arrival there rendered his cause hopeless. Frederick became known as the "Winter King."

Now in possession of Bohemia, Ferdinand was crowned its king. He confiscated the estates of perhaps half of its nobles and distributed these among his supporters, who became the new nobility of Bohemia. Ferdinand then eradicated Protestantism in Bohemia and in Austria, where it had enjoyed some support. Catholicism seemed ascendant.

In the Netherlands, meanwhile, what came to be known as the Twelve Years' Truce ended in August 1621 with a renewal of warfare between the Spanish and Dutch. Prince Maurice of Nassau led the Dutch, while Spinola commanded the Spanish forces. In Central Europe, in August 1620 the Hungarians elected Gábor their king; believing that this might be premature, he refused to be crowned. The outcome of the Battle of White Mountain in Bohemia proved Gábor prescient, and on December 31, 1621, he and Emperor Ferdinand II concluded the Treaty of Nikolsburg, under which Gábor gave up the royal title in return for full sovereignty for Transylvania and religious freedom for Hungary. Northern Hungary also remained part of the Transylvanian state. Unfortunately for his now flourishing state, Gábor died in 1629, and the result was a year of anarchy until the election of György I Rákóczi.

In 1621 Count Mansfeld rallied to Frederick and raised an army from refugees of Bohemia and the Palatinate, which he financed by plundering much of the Rhineland. The Dutch also agreed to subsidize Frederick, and Duke Christian of Brunswick and Margrave George Frederick of Baden-Durlach lent their support. On April 27, 1622, some 14 miles south of Heidelberg in the Battle of Wiesloch (Mingolsheim), Mansfeld's Protestants defeated Tilly's Catholics. This rebuff delayed Tilly from effecting a juncture with Spanish forces from the Netherlands under Gonzalo Andrés Domingo Fernández de

Córdoba. On May 6, however, the combined Catholic armies of Tilly and Córdoba defeated Protestant forces under Margrave George Frederick in the Battle of Wimpfen. On June 20, 1622, in the Battle of Höchst, the combined Catholic armies numbering some 25,000 men under Córdoba and Tilly caught up with Duke Christian's Protestant army of only some 12,000 men at the Main River as it was attempting to link up with Mansfeld. Christian had no choice but to set up a bridgehead and force a crossing of the river. He accomplished this, but heavy artillery and musket fire cost him some 2,000 casualties and most of his baggage train, while the Catholic side sustained only minimal losses. Christian joined Mansfeld, but Höchst was the final battle for control of the Palatinate. Christian, Mansfeld, and Frederick withdraw first into Alsace and then into Lorraine, their men largely living off the land and destroying much of the countryside. Following a dispute with Christian and Mansfeld, Frederick revoked their commissions, whereupon they joined the Dutch.

Catholic forces were now everywhere on the offensive. Spanish troops in the Netherlands under Spinola invaded Holland and laid siege to Bergen-op-Zoom. Duke Christian and Mansfeld marched to the rescue but were intercepted en route on August 23 by Spanish general Córdoba at Fleurus in present-day Belgium. The Protestant side had 14,000 men and 11 guns, the Catholics only 8,000 men and 4 guns. In desperate fighting, however, the Protestants suffered perhaps 5,000 casualties (Christian was among the badly wounded) and the Catholics only 1,200. The remainder of the Protestant force escaped under Mansfeld and reached Bergen-op-Zoom, where they surprised Spinola and caused him to raise the siege.

Having already conquered most of the Palatinate, Catholic forces under Count Tilly initiated a siege of Heidelberg and took it on September 19 after nearly three months. Following all these Catholic successes, on February 23, 1623, Emperor Ferdinand pressured the electoral college of the Holy Roman Empire to depose Frederick as elector of the Palatinate and give that title to Ferdinand's ally, Duke Maximilian of Bavaria.

In the summer of 1623, Christian of Brunswick and a Protestant army of some 15,000 men departed East Friesland, but they were pursued by Tilly and a Catholic army of 25,000 men. On August 6, 1623, Tilly caught up with Christian about 10 miles from the Dutch border, near the village of Stadtlohn in Westphalia, and destroyed his army. Christian lost perhaps 13,000 men. Christian and the remainder escaped into Holland. Following these Protestant defeats and on the urging of his father-in-law King James I of England, Frederick of the Palatinate sought peace with Ferdinand II, leading to an armistice on August 27, 1623.

Despite the armistice, fighting soon resumed. Signaling the triumph of power politics and realpolitik over religious issues, French minister Armand Jean du Plessis de Richelieu (Catholic cardinal Richelieu) committed France to the Protestant side in the war by signing the Treaty of Compiègne with the Dutch against the Habsburgs on June 10, 1624. Within a month England, Sweden, Denmark, Savoy, and Venice all joined the alliance. France, Venice, and Savoy agreed to conduct operations in the Alps to disrupt Spanish lines of communication north from Italy to the Netherlands.

One of the major events of the war and of the long Dutch struggle for independence

was the August 28, 1624–June 5, 1625, siege of the fortified Dutch city of Breda in northern Brabant. Prominent officials in the Spanish court of King Felipe (Philip) IV (r. 1621–1665)—most notably the king's prime minister Gaspar Guzmán, the Duke of Sanlucar and Count of Olivares—were jealous of Spinola's military successes and may have attempted to set him up for failure. In any case, they persuaded Philip IV to order Spinola to lay siege to Breda, a stronghold that many considered unassailable.

Spinola moved against Breda with some 60,000 men. Prince Maurice of Nassau, stadtholder of Holland, had garrisoned Breda with about 9,000 troops, supported by artillery. The Dutch had also improved its defenses with moats, trenches, and revetments. Unlike previous Spanish sieges of Dutch towns (except for Jülich during 1621–1622), Spinola opted to starve out the city, and relieving the siege became the focus of all Dutch military efforts.

Spinola ordered construction of barricades to block major egress points from Breda so that his troops might defeat any sorties and also held back most of his cavalry and infantry as a mobile reserve to be able to counter anticipated Dutch relief operations. The Dutch did attempt sorties, while Maurice sought to get supplies into the city. All were rebuffed. At the same time, Maurice refused to be drawn into a pitched battle.

The winter of 1624–1625 was severe, and both sides, especially the Spanish in improvised field shelters, suffered greatly. With the arrival of spring, the Dutch, reinforced by German troops, mounted several unsuccessful attempts to break the siege. Maurice died in April 1625 and was succeeded as stadtholder of Holland by his younger brother Prince Frederick Henry.

He continued to refuse decisive battle with Spinola while ordering Mansfeld and 12,000 men on a fifth attempt to reach the city with supplies.

On May 12 Spinola defeated both Mansfeld and an attempted diversion in the form of a sortie from Breda, inflicting heavy losses on both. Utilizing heavy siege guns Spinola effected breaches in the walls, and on June 5, with all hope of relief gone and Spanish troops within the city, Breda surrendered. Spinola permitted the defenders to leave the city with their personal weapons, four artillery pieces, and such personal possessions as they could carry. Four thousand departed, leaving behind 5,000 dead; 8,000 civilians had also died in the siege, largely from disease and hunger.

The Spanish success at Breda was actually a detriment to their overall plans. The city had little strategic value, and the siege was financially costly. Its heavy drain on resources prevented the Spaniards from pursuing other goals.

Course of the Danish Phase (1625–1629)

With Protestant fortunes now at a low point, King Christian IV of Denmark entered the lists, initiating the Danish period (1625–1629). Christian was also the Duke of Holstein, a state in the Holy Roman Empire. He sought to curtail Habsburg influence and also to secure bishoprics in northern Germany as a kingdom for his younger son. A capable military commander, Christian would be overshadowed by Gustavus Adolphus of Sweden but, unlike Gustavus, was forced to fight largely alone, although he did receive limited financial support from the English, the Dutch, and the French. With Christian preparing to enter the war, Ferdinand II commissioned

mercenary captain Albrecht von Wallenstein, military governor of Prague, to raise an army. This force was, however, Wallenstein's personal instrument.

With some 20,000–25,000 men and only inadequately supported by his allies, Christian IV invaded northern Germany in May 1625. Imperial general Count Tilly moved to meet Christian, who advanced down the Weser River, seeking with only limited success to secure support from the German Protestant princes.

On April 25, 1626, some 12,000 Protestant troops under Mansfeld proceeding to Magdeburg were intercepted while attempting to cross the Elbe River at Dessau Bridge in Saxony-Anhalt by Wallenstein with 20,000 men. In the ensuing fighting, Mansfeld lost perhaps 4,000 men killed, wounded, or captured; Wallenstein's losses were negligible. Pursued into Silesia, Mansfeld made for the Dalmatian coast to offer his services to the Republic of Venice but died en route, and what remained of his army disbanded.

On August 27, 1626, in the Battle of Lutter am Berenberge in Brunswick, Count Tilly and some 20,000 imperial troops smashed Christian IV's army of 20,000 men. Christian lost some 6,000 killed and 2,500 taken prisoner against slight losses for Tilly. Wallenstein and Tilly then drove Christian's army back into Holstein. This one battle effectively ended whatever support there was among the northern German princes for Christian, compelled the withdrawal of Denmark from the war, and marked the end of Denmark as a major military power.

In 1628 Ferdinand II rewarded Wallenstein by giving him the duchies of Mecklenburg and Pomerania. This illegal step greatly alarmed the German princes and prompted their efforts to secure the removal of Wallenstein, which Ferdinand rejected. Endeavoring to secure the entire Baltic coast, during May 13–June 28, 1628, Wallenstein laid siege to the fortress of Stralsund, but following Swedish reinforcement of it and their threats of more active intervention, after a final unsuccessful assault he raised the siege on June 28. On August 3, 1628, Christian IV, having landed near Usedom, captured the city of Wolgast. On August 12, however, Wallenstein destroyed the invading Danes near Wolgast.

Following the success of his armies on the battlefield, on March 6, 1629, Emperor Ferdinand II issued the Edict of Restitution. Regarded as the high-water mark of the Catholic Counter Reformation, it restored to the Catholic Church all lands confiscated from it in violation of the Peace of Augsburg in 1555. Those lands taken from the church since 1552 were to be returned, and Calvinists were to be excluded from the privileges of peace. Strict enforcement of these provisions would have crushed Protestantism in Germany, but Ferdinand's ambitions aroused opposition of Catholic and Protestant princes alike and also alarmed the Catholic powers of Europe and even Pope Urban VII.

The Danish Period of the war ended with the Treaty of Lübeck of May 22, 1629. Although he was forced to give up many German bishoprics, Christian retained Holstein as well as Schleswig and Jutland. There also was no indemnity, Ferdinand being persuaded to grant lenient terms because of the growing threat posed by Sweden.

The Swedish Phase (1630–1635)

French chief minister Cardinal Richelieu, having worked to end Sweden's most recent war with Poland (1626–1629), now agreed to provide Swedish king Gustavus Adolphus (Gustav II Adolph or Gustavus Adolphus the Great) 1 million livres a year to maintain 40,000 men in Germany. The Dutch also agreed to help financially. On July 4, 1630, Gustavus, a staunch Lutheran whose armies went into battle singing hymns, landed in Germany to do battle with the Catholic imperial forces.

Meanwhile, opposition to imperial mercenary general Wallenstein had been steadily mounting among the German princes, Catholic as well as Protestant. Meeting at Regensburg (Ratisbon), they demanded that Ferdinand II dismiss Wallenstein, who had been building up his own forces at the expense of the other principal imperial field commander, Count Tilly. In order to secure German unity against Sweden, Ferdinand reluctantly agreed on August 24.

In November 1630 imperial forces besieged the great Protestant city of Magdeburg. Planned by Wallenstein, the siege was carried out by Count Gottfried H. zu Pappenheim and Tilly. Magdeburg, well supplied and fortified, resisted the attacks, and indeed that winter its people fared better than the besiegers.

Meanwhile, the alliance between France and Sweden was formalized in the Treaty of Bärwalde of January 23, 1631. In return for subsidies, Gustavus promised to permit freedom of worship for German Catholics and to conclude no separate peace for a period of five years. The Protestant German princes, emboldened by Sweden's entry into the war, met at Leipzig and on March 28 demanded that Ferdinand II address many problems, including the Edict of Restitution, depredations by imperial forces, Ferdinand's disregard of the imperial constitution, and difficulties facing the German people. The Protestant princes pledged to oppose Gustavus and the Swedes if Ferdinand would address these issues, but the crusading emperor rejected compromise, forcing the Protestant German princes to the Swedish side and causing them to establish in May an army under Hans Georg von Arnim.

Having secured his rear areas, Gustavus carried out a brilliant surprise strike against the city of Frankfurt (Frankfurt an der Oder), capturing it on April 13. Gustavus hoped that this would cause Tilly to raise the Siege of Magdeburg, but Tilly held on there, and Gustavus prepared to march against him. Before Gustavus could arrive, however, imperial troops stormed Magdeburg and sacked it. The city was burned to the ground, with only the cathedral left standing. Perhaps 5,000 of Magdeburg's 30,000 people survived. The event shocked Europe. Fear and anger combined to cause Protestant sentiment in Germany to move sharply to the side of Sweden and against Emperor Ferdinand.

France was not only allied with Sweden. In the Treaty of Fontainebleau (May 30, 1631) France concluded a secret defensive pact with Duke Maximilian of Bavaria. This forced Count Tilly to switch his allegiance from Maximilian to Emperor Ferdinand II.

During July–August 1631 inconclusive fighting occurred between Swedish forces led by Gustavus and imperial forces under Tilly. Suffering from a lack of supplies, Gustavus entrenched at Werben. Tilly twice attacked the Swedish camp but was each time repulsed with heavy losses. Tilly then marched into Saxony and laid waste to it. To save his state, Saxon ruler Elector John George concluded an alliance with Sweden on August 31, 1631, and placed his troops under Gustavus's command.

Warfare continued, meanwhile, between the Spaniards and the Dutch. The Spaniards planned to sail from Antwerp with 5,500 troops in 90 small ships to Goeree-Overflakkee island, presenting the Dutch with a fait accompli. Control of the two large fortresses on each side of the Volkerak Strait would enable the Spaniards to blockade the Dutch Hellevoetsluis naval base on Voorne Island and cut off Zeeland from the remaining Dutch provinces. Don Francisco de Moncada, Marquis of Aytona, had nominal command of the Spanish force, with Count Jan van Nassau Siegen actually in charge.

Discovering the Spanish plans, the Dutch sent out 50 small ships of their own under Vice Admiral Marinus Hollare. The Dutch intercepted the Spaniards in the eastern Scheldt. The subsequent Spanish attempt to capture the more southern island of Tholen was foiled by the timely arrival of 2,000 English mercenaries, who were able to wade there at low tide.

Van Nassau decided to try to pass through the Dutch fleet during the night of September 12–13. The Dutch discovered it. Allowing the Spanish ships to pass, they then attacked them from behind in the Slaak channel. Many Spaniards drowned, and more than 1,000 were taken prisoner. Van Nassau returned to Antwerp with only about a third of his ships.

In Germany meanwhile, Count Tilly, now with 36,000 men, captured Leipzig on September 15 as Gustavus's Swedish army of 26,000 men united with the 16,000-man Saxon army under Duke Johann George at Düben, 25 miles to the north. On the urging of his subordinate Count Pappenheim, Tilly abandoned Leipzig and took up position at Breitenfeld, four miles north of the city. The Battle of Breitenfeld (also known as the Battle of Leipzig) occurred on September 17, 1631.

Gustavus formed his men not in the traditional Spanish-designed *tercio* square of massed pikemen with harquebusiers or musketeers on its corners but instead in smaller, more mobile formations in which the musketeers, protected by pikemen, predominated. Gustavus thus enjoyed a considerable advantage in maneuverability over the bulkier massed imperial formations. His artillery was also lighter and more mobile than Tilly's heavier guns, and throughout the battle it exacted a heavy toll on the densely packed imperial formations.

The battle commenced with the imperial artillery opening up on Gustavus's force as it was still deploying. Artillery fire continued until midday, when the impetuous Pappenheim, acting without orders, attacked with his cavalry in an attempt to turn the Swedish right flank. Gustavus wheeled his cavalry reserve, catching Pappenheim between his two cavalry forces. Gustavus was also able to reposition his lighter guns and open up with grapeshot. These guns and the musketeers outranged the pistol fire of Pappenheim's cavalry and forced them to withdraw.

Tilly then advanced against the Saxons, whom he correctly believed to be the weakest Protestant element. Easily routing the Saxons, he then turned against Gustavus's now-exposed left flank. The more maneuverable Swedes countered that movement and held against Tilly's attack. Gustavus then led his own cavalry, the infantry closely following, against Tilly's left flank, retaking the artillery lost by the Saxons earlier and also securing many imperial guns. The Swedish and captured imperial artillery devastated the massed imperial formations.

After some seven hours of combat, the imperial forces fled the field that evening. The Swedes pursued until nightfall and a stand by Pappenheim's re-formed cavalry.

In the battle, Gustavus lost some 6,500 men killed or wounded. The imperial side suffered some 13,000 casualties: 7,000 dead and 6,000 taken prisoner. Tilly, badly wounded, was among those who escaped.

The Battle of Breitenfeld was the first major Protestant victory of the war and its turning point. The battle gave the initiative to the Protestants. Gustavus entered Leipzig the next day.

Uncertain of the loyalty of the German princes, Gustavus rejected a march on Vienna and instead moved to the Rhine. Within three months he controlled all northwestern Germany. At the same time, Saxon forces advanced on and captured Prague. On December 22, 1631, Gustavus secured the important city of Mainz in the Rhineland and wintered there. By now, the Protestants had some 80,000 men under arms. Given the disasters piling up for the imperial side, Emperor Ferdinand II in April 1632 recalled Wallenstein, who immediately began raising a new army of mercenaries.

In the spring, Gustavus advanced into southern Germany with 40,000 men. Crossing the Danube at Danauworth, he moved east into Bavaria, where Tilly awaited with an entrenched force of 25,000 men. Gustavus then crossed the Lech River near Rain on a bridge of boats. In the Battle of the Lech River (also known as the Battle of Rain) of April 15, 1632, Gustavus feigned a strong attack by part of his infantry with heavy artillery support against Tilly's strongly fortified center. With Tilly's forces and reserves committed, the outnumbered Swedes then fortified, repelling a series of fierce imperial counterattacks. The Swedish cavalry, meanwhile, crossed the Lech about six miles to the south. Gustavus planned for it to sweep in on the imperial left wing and outflank Tilly's entire army.

Before the Swedish cavalry could arrive, however, Tilly was mortally wounded by a cannonball (he died on April 30), and imperial resolve collapsed. Duke Maximilian of Bavaria then led a hasty imperial withdrawal, abandoning much of the army's artillery and baggage. Ironically, Tilly's wounding probably saved his army from complete destruction. Casualties totaled about 3,000 on the imperial side and 2,000 for the Swedes. Gustavus went on to occupy Augsburg, Munich, and all of southern Bavaria. The Austrian heartland appeared open.

On July 11, 1632, Wallenstein joined Duke Maximilian of Bavaria at Schwabach in northern Bavaria, entrenching his 60,000-man army near Fürth and Alte Veste. Gustavus, now with 20,000 men and entrenched near Nuremberg, sent for reinforcements. Their arrival gave him some 45,000 men.

During August 31–September 4 Gustavus repeatedly attacked the imperial camp, but Wallenstein's use of terrain and skillful dispositions prevented the Swedes from employing their excellent cavalry or artillery. Having suffered heavy losses, Gustavus then withdrew. With the surrounding countryside picked clean of supplies, in mid-September both armies moved northward.

Meanwhile, in the Netherlands on August 22, 1632, Dutch stadtholder Prince Frederik Hendrik captured Maastricht. Although the Dutch and Spaniards opened peace talks, nothing came of these.

In September 1622 Wallenstein took the offensive, invading Saxony and threatening the Swedish line of communications. Wallenstein had some 30,000 men, while Gustavus commanded about 20,000. Awaiting reinforcements, Gustavus entrenched at Naumburg while Wallenstein

set up his headquarters in Lützen, southwest of Leipzig.

On November 14 after holding his army at battle stations for two weeks, Wallenstein made the worst mistake of his military career. Believing that Gustavus had gone into winter quarters, Wallenstein ordered his own forces to disperse, sending a large number of men under Count Pappenheim to Halle. The next day, Wallenstein learned of Gustavus's approach. Immediately dispatching an appeal to Pappenheim to return, Wallenstein prepared to meet the Swedish attack, throwing up improvised defensive fortifications along a sunken road, with his right wing anchored on Lützen.

The battle occurred on November 16, 1632. Each side had about 19,000 men. Bernard of Saxe-Weimar commanded the Swedish left, Gustavus the right.

The battle was prolonged, with both sides suffering heavy casualties. Fortunately for Wallenstein, heavy fog delayed the Swedish attack until about 11:00 a.m. The Swedish right pushed back the cavalry on the imperial left, also driving in the musketeers and threatening the artillery. Pappenheim's men then arrived, just in time to stabilize that flank.

Wallenstein ordered his men to set fire to Lützen, and the smoke from the fires blew into the center of the Swedish line and blinded the men. Wallenstein further confused the Swedes by launching a cavalry attack there. Gustavus responded with a cavalry charge of his own, utilizing his left wing. Leading it in person and riding into an enemy formation, Gustavus was surrounded, shot three times, and killed. Bernard then assumed command of the Protestant forces.

News of the death of their king led the Swedes to attack with renewed fury and brought them victory. That night Wallenstein decamped, the imperial forces abandoning both their baggage and artillery and retreating to Leipzig before withdrawing entirely from Saxony into Bohemia. In the battle the Swedes suffered about 10,000 casualties, the imperial forces perhaps 12,000; Pappenheim was among the fatally wounded.

Although the Swedes were victorious and carried on under Gustavus's able lieutenant, Count Axel Oxenstierna, in the name of Gustavus's infant daughter Christina, the Protestant cause had lost its most notable champion. On April 23, 1632, Oxenstierna and the German Protestant princes formed the League of Heilbronn, ensuring a continuation of the Protestant alliance. Oxenstierna also renewed the French alliance, with the latter nation ultimately entering the war openly on the Protestant side.

Following the failure of peace efforts, in October 1633 Wallenstein conquered Silesia and then went into winter quarters in Bohemia. There he intrigued to become its king. On November 13 Bernard of Saxe-Weimar, now commanding Swedish forces in Germany, captured the city of Regensburg. His troops then occupied Bavaria.

The exact circumstances will never be known, but evidently Wallenstein hoped to restore peace to Germany based on toleration of the Protestants. Knowing that this would never have the approval of Ferdinand II, Wallenstein opened secret negotiations with the Protestant side, thus committing treason. Some of his aides betrayed the details to Ferdinand, who on January 21, 1634, secretly ordered the removal of Wallenstein as imperial generalissimo.

In mid-February several of Wallenstein's key lieutenants deserted him for Ferdinand, and on February 18 an order

dismissing Wallenstein was published. Wallenstein fled, but on February 25 at Eger (present-day Cheb) in Bohemia he was murdered by some of his staff officers, who were then lavishly rewarded by Ferdinand. The emperor's son, King Ferdinand of Hungary, assumed nominal command of the imperial forces, with Matthias Gallas, one of Wallenstein's chief lieutenants who had abandoned him in mid-February, as actual field commander.

In July 1634 a Swedish force of some 25,000 men under Bernard of Saxe-Weimar and Gustavus Horn pushed into Bavaria, hoping to divert the imperial forces under King Ferdinand of Hungary and Gallas who were moving on Regensburg. On July 22, however, imperial forces captured Regensburg. They also secured Donauworth and laid siege to Nördlingen in western Bavaria.

On August 23 the Swedes arrived near Nördlingen. On September 3 a Spanish army of 20,000 men under the young Cardinal Infante Ferdinand, brother of King Felipe IV (Philip IV) of Spain, joined the 15,000-man army of his cousin King Ferdinand of Hungary near Nördlingen.

The Battle of Nördlingen occurred on September 6, 1634, with the Protestants attacking. The outcome was influenced to some degree by feuding between Horn and Bernard. The Protestant plan called for Horn to attack the imperial right, while Bernard pinned the imperial left and prevented it from shifting resources to reinforce the right. Holding an excellent defensive position, the imperial and Spanish forces easily turned back the poorly coordinated Protestant attack. The imperial forces then counterattacked, routing the Protestant right, and wheeled into the Swedes. More than 6,000 Swedes died in the fighting, and only 11,000 men of the combined Protestant force escaped. The Catholic side sustained but 1,200 casualties.

The Battle of Nördlingen almost wiped out the army created by Gustavus and in effect reversed the Swedish victory of Breitenfeld. Following the battle, King Ferdinand of Hungary retook southern Germany for Catholicism. Immediate gains for the Catholic side included Göppingen (September 15), Heilbronn (September 16), Rothenburg (September 18), Stuttgart (September 20), Aschaffenburg (September 30), and Schweinfurt (October 15).

The situation appeared sufficiently dire that French chief minister Cardinal Richelieu brought his nation openly into the war on the Protestant side. In October 1634 under heavy French pressure, Colmar and other Alsatian cities agreed to admit French garrisons. On November 1, Richelieu negotiated the Treaty of Paris with the League of Heilbronn. Bernard and the Protestant princes agreed to surrender to France some lands in Alsace, to permit the Catholic faith in Germany, and to field 12,000 men in return for French payments of 500,000 livres a year. The Swedes, however, refused to ratify the treaty.

Course of the French-Swedish Phase (1635–1648)

Continuing their string of unbroken successes following the Battle of Nördlingen, imperial forces took Phillipsburg (January 24, 1635) and Speier (February 2). The French forces were driven back to the left bank of the Rhine. On April 30, 1635, Oxenstierna and Richelieu renewed the Swedish-French alliance, replacing the Treaty of Paris of the year before, which Sweden had refused to ratify. Sweden now recognized as French territory the left bank of the Rhine from Breisach to Strasbourg (Strassburg) in return for French recognition of Swedish control of Benfeld, Mainz, and Worms. France also agreed to declare war on Spain and not to conclude a separate peace. On May 19, France formally declared war on Spain.

In these circumstances, on May 30 Saxon and imperial negotiators hastily concluded the Treaty of Prague, under which Saxony received limited territorial concessions. The treaty also provided for amnesty, a common cause against Sweden, and freedom of religion for Lutherans (but not Calvinists). Brandenburg and many other German states accepted its provisions. From this point on, the war was a political rather than religious struggle.

In June 1635 French forces went on the offensive. French first minister Cardinal Richelieu had as his broad strategic goal the elimination of Spanish forces in what is now eastern France and western Germany. Five French field armies, totaling some 130,000 men, took the field. The first army was to secure Spanish-held Franche-Comté, the second was to occupy Lorraine, the third was to move across Switzerland and seize the key Valtelline Pass, the fourth was to operate with Duke Victor Amadeus of Saxony and invade Milan, and the fifth was to cooperate with Dutch leader Prince of Orange Frederik Hendrik to invade the Spanish Netherlands. The first three operations, solely French, were successful; the two allied operations failed.

In late July 1635 Bernard of Saxe-Weimar and his Protestant Weimar Army linked up with the French, assisting in the relief of Mainz on August 8; in mid-November they entered French service. On October 16 meanwhile, the Saxons, joined by other German signatories of the Treaty of Prague, now allied with Emperor Ferdinand II, declared war on their erstwhile ally of Sweden and attacked the smaller Swedish army under Johan Banér, who completely outgeneraled them. Receiving some limited reinforcements from Swedish forces fighting in Poland (the Poles having taken advantage of Swedish involvement in Germany to regain territory lost to Sweden earlier), the Swedes turned back Saxon attacks at Goldberg (December 7) and Kyritz (December 17).

Seeking to take advantage of the wide dispersion of French Army assets in the field and relative calm in central and eastern Germany, in 1636 Habsburg forces invaded France. Cardinal Infante Ferdinand of Spain commanded a combined Spanish-Bavarian force in an invasion of northeastern France, while Matthias Gallas led the main imperial army into Burgundy. The Spanish enjoyed success early on, crossing the Somme and advancing on Compiègne.

Refusing to panic, King Louis XIII and Richelieu raised a new army, mostly of militia and numbering some 50,000 men, and marched it to Compiègne, whereupon the invaders withdrew to the Netherlands to confront Prince Frederik Hendrik, who had resumed the offensive there. Meanwhile, Bernard entrenched at Dijon, blocking the advance of the main imperial army under Gallas, who also withdrew. On June 22, 1636, a combined French-Savoyard force under French marshal Charles de Créqui and Duke Victor Amadeus I of Savoy defeated the Spanish in the hard-fought Battle of Tornavento. The duke, however, rejected an advance on Milan.

In Germany near Wittstock in northwestern Brandenburg on October 6, 1636, a Swedish-Protestant force of 15,000 men under Johan Banér overwhelmingly defeated a combined Saxon-imperial army of 25,000 men commanded by Count Melchior von Hatzfeld and Elector John George. The Swedes sustained 3,100 casualties, while their opponents suffered 7,000 (including 2,000 captured).

Emperor Ferdinand II died on February 15, 1637. His eldest son Ferdinand, who as king of Hungary had been titular head of the imperial forces since the death of Wallenstein, became emperor as Ferdinand III. He ruled until 1657.

In May 1637 Swedish armies under Counts Lennart Torstenson and Banér reoccupied territory lost earlier, including Brandenburg. Threatening both Saxony and Thuringia, they were halted by the arrival in Saxony of imperial forces under Count Gallas. In the Netherlands on October 11, 1637, Dutch forces under Frederik Hendrik took Breda after a prolonged siege. The Spaniards were allowed to withdraw from the city, which had been under their control since 1625.

French military operations in 1638 were largely unsuccessful. The French suffered rebuffs in the Spanish Netherlands, in northern Italy, and in a march on Madrid in Spain. Only in Alsace did the French enjoy success. The Swedes fared no better in eastern Germany. Bavarian general Gottfried von Geleen forced Banér's far smaller Swedish army back from the Elbe to the Oder, where Banér anticipated being reinforced by Carl Gustav Wrangel. Cut off by the main imperial army under Gallas, Banér managed to escape and joined Wrangel in Thuringia, where they passed the winter.

In Alsace, Bernard of Saxe-Weimar was with his advance guard moving to cross the Rhine near Basel when he was cut off by a surprise imperial forces attack. Managing to withdraw, he then crossed the Rhine again and, joining the remainder of his army, moved on Rheinfelden, where during February 28–March 1 he defeated imperial forces under Count Savelli. In the Battle of Wiitenweier (August 18), Bernard defeated imperial forces attempting to end his siege of the great fortress of Breisach on the Rhine. Breisach was the key to control of Habsburg lands along that strategic waterway. It was starved into surrender on December 17, 1638. During February–July 1639, Bernard completed the conquest of all Alsace and demanded to be made duke of Alsace. Richelieu refused, and Bernard died of a fever (some contend that he was poisoned) at Neubourg on July 11, 1639. Jean de Guébriant succeeded him in command.

In 1639 Spain dispatched to Flanders a great armada of 70 ships under Don António Oquendo with the plan to engage and destroy the Dutch fleet, recently reorganized under Admiral Maarten Harpertszoon Tromp. Oquendo also escorted 50 transports with up to 24,000 infantry intended for service in the Netherlands. On September 16 Tromp met the Spanish with only 17 ships and, in fighting during the next three days, forced them to withdraw without having reached the Netherlands. The Spaniards then anchored in English waters in the Downs roadstead off Kent.

English king Charles I attempted to deal. He offered the French access to the Spanish fleet in return for the restoration of the Palatinate, while to the Spanish he offered protection in return for a substantial cash payment. An English fleet under Admiral John Pennington sought to prevent the Dutch from attacking. In the meantime Tromp built up his strength, while Oquendo managed to get a dozen of his transports across to the Netherlands.

On October 21 Tromp attacked the Spanish fleet in English waters, detaching some of his ships under Admiral Witte Corneliszoon de Wit to prevent the English

from interfering. Oquendo decided to try to reach Dunkerque, but only 16 of his ships made it. The Battle of the Downs claimed the lives of some 7,000 Spaniards, ended what remained of Spanish naval power, seriously weakened the Spanish military position in Flanders, and gave the Dutch undisputed naval supremacy in their conflict with Spain.

In 1639 the French had only mixed success in fighting in the Netherlands and little in northern Spain, although they did advance into Roussillon. French forces enjoyed some success in northern Italy, but Savoy switched to the imperial side. In eastern Germany, Swedish general Banér, having been reinforced, advanced and defeated a Saxon-imperial army at Chemnitz on April 14, 1639, giving the Swedes control of western Saxony. Banér then invaded Bohemia but was repulsed in his effort to capture Prague. After devastating the area for supplies, he went into winter quarters in the Erzgebirge (Ore Mountains).

There were no major military campaigns or battles in 1640, and Germany remained largely quiet. In northern Italy, French forces under Cadet la Perle, Duke of Harcourt, defeated Spanish forces under Marquis Leganez in the Battle of Casale (April 29), then besieged another Spanish force that was itself besieging the citadel of Turin. Reinforced, Leganez attempted to invest Harcourt's besiegers, but Harcourt defeated Leganez (July 11) and took Turin. The French also captured Arras in the present-day Nord-Pas-de-Calais region of northern France on August 8.

On July 22, 1640, a naval engagement occurred off Cádiz, Spain. A French fleet under Armand de Maillé-Brézé, Duc de Fronsac, was attempting to intercept a Spanish convoy from Cádiz sailing to the Indies. On encountering the French,

Spanish commander Don Gomez de Sandoval ordered the merchant ships to return to port, shielding them with his 12 galleons. Fortunately for the Spanish, the French attacked without plan, and the Spanish lost only a single galleon.

Holy Roman emperor Ferdinand III, now anxious to secure peace, convened a diet at Regensburg during September 13, 1640–October 10, 1641, and offered terms on the basis of the Peace of Prague of 1635 and a general amnesty. Meanwhile, Swedish commander in chief in Germany Banér died of natural causes in May 1641. Torstenson replaced him.

Fighting at sea continued, and during June 30–July 2, 1642, off Barcelona, French admirals Armand de Maillé-Brézé and the Chevalier de Cangé, with 44 warships and 14 fireships, attacked a Spanish fleet under the Duke of Ciudad Real with 36 sailing warships, 6 fireships, and several galleys. The running Battle of Barcelona was indecisive. The Spaniards lost 2 galleons, and the French lost 1 ship, that commanded by the able Cangé. Badly wounded, he elected to go down with his ship.

In the spring of 1642 Swedish general Torstenson took the offensive. Crossing the Elbe, he laid siege to Leipzig and overran much of Saxony. The approach of imperial forces under Archduke Leopold William, brother of Holy Roman emperor Ferdinand III, and Ottavio Piccolomini, however, caused Torstenson to raise the siege and withdraw some four miles northeast to Breitenfeld.

The Second Battle of Breitenfeld (also known as the First Battle of Leipzig) of November 2, 1642, began with Torstenson attacking as the imperial forces formed for battle and ended in a crushing Swedish victory. The imperial side sustained some 15,000 casualties, including 5,000 killed

and an equal number captured. Some 4,000 Swedes were killed or wounded. The battle was the nadir of imperial fortunes in the later stage of the war. Following it, Swedish forces occupied Saxony.

Unrest in Spain and in France handicapped general military operations by these two leading powers along the Flemish border and in northern Italy during 1641 and 1642. In Paris, Richelieu put down a revolt sponsored by the Spanish. Louis XIII then accompanied a French army that conquered Roussillon on the Spanish frontier, while another French army aided rebels in Catalonia.

In May 1643 Francesco de Mello led a 26,000-man Spanish army from the Netherlands through the Ardennes region toward Paris. En route he laid siege to Rocroi. Twenty-two-year-old French Army general Louis II de Bourbon, Duc d'Enghien, advanced with 23,000 men to meet the Spaniards along the Meuse River.

Enghien came on the Spaniards besieging Rocroi on May 18. Knowing that 6,000 Spanish reinforcements were en route, Enghien rejected the advice of his older, experienced subordinate commanders and decided on an immediate attack, sending his men forward through the only approach to Rocroi, a defile between woods and marshes. That afternoon the French took up position on a ridge overlooking Rocroi. The Spanish then formed up between the French and Rocroi.

The Battle of Rocroi began shortly after dawn on May 19 when Enghien personally led a French cavalry attack on the Spanish left. Defeating the Spanish cavalry, Enghien then moved against the Spanish infantry. At the same time and against Enghien's orders, the French cavalry on the left attacked the Spanish right and were repulsed. The Spanish then mounted a counterattack but were halted by French reserves. Enghien managed to get his cavalry in behind the center of the Spanish infantry, smashing through to attack from behind the Spanish right-flank cavalry engaging his reserve and scattering it. This left the 18,000 Spanish infantry isolated. Long regarded as the finest in Europe, their square formations repulsed two French attacks before Enghien massed his own artillery and guns captured from the Spaniards and hammered the Spanish formations.

The Spaniards asked for quarter, and Enghien rode forward to take the surrender, but some of the Spanish infantry, apparently believing that this was the beginning of a French cavalry charge, opened fire on him. Angered by this seeming treachery, the French attacked the Spaniards, without quarter and with devastating result, virtually destroying them. Spanish losses in the battle totaled some 8,000 killed and another 7,000 taken prisoner. French losses were 4,000. The important Battle of Rocroi is often regarded as marking the end of Spanish military greatness.

Enghien then secured Lorraine and the Rhine Valley. On June 18 he laid siege to the fortress city of Thionville, taking it five days later. During August–November French marshal Jean-Baptiste Budes, Comte de Guébriant, crossed the Rhine with his Weimar Army and advanced into Württemberg. He captured Rottweil on November 19 but was mortally wounded in the siege. Josias von Rantzau succeeded him. The Weimar Army was then surprised and largely destroyed by a Bavarian imperial army under Baron Franz von Mercy. Henri de la Tour d'Auvergne, Viscount of Turenne, who had been commanding in Italy, succeeded Rantzau and withdrew into Alsace what remained of the Weimar Army. The Bavarians retook Rottweil on December 22.

The French no longer had the support of the Swedes, who had been ravaging much of Bohemia and Moravia. In September 1643 war began between Sweden and Denmark. Torstenson then quit Bohemia and marched his army north. That December his forces invaded the Danish Jutland Peninsula.

Also in September a naval battle occurred in the Mediterranean. Spanish admiral Martin de Mencos was proceeding toward Cartagena with 25 warships to join another Spanish fleet there in hopes of driving the French from the Mediterranean. On September 24 they encountered 24 French warships under Admiral Armand de Maillé-Brézé off Cape Gata, Spain. The Spanish ships became scattered, and the French were thus able to swarm single vessels. No French ships were lost, but the Spaniards lost a half dozen ships sunk or captured and many others badly damaged.

In mid-April 1644, Bavarian forces under Baron Mercy advanced through the Black Forest toward the French. Mercy captured Uberlingen on May 11 and French-held Freiburg on July 28. Facing Mercy's numerically superior army, French marshal Turenne withdrew his Weimar Army to Breisach, there to await reinforcements under the Duc d'Enghien, who arrived on August 3, 1644, and assumed command of the combined French armies, now numbering 17,000 men and equaling that of Mercy.

In the ensuing Battle of Freiburg, the French advanced on that city and recaptured it from Mercy in a series of sanguinary battles on August 3, 5, and 10. The Bavarians then withdrew, leaving the French in possession of the Rhine Valley. Both sides had lost as much as half of their strength. Enghien then secured the fortresses of the middle Rhine Valley.

On October 13, 1644, in the Fehmarn Strait in the North Sea, a combined Swedish-Dutch fleet under Karl Gustav Wrangel of 37 ships destroyed a Danish fleet under Pros Mund of only 17 ships. Only 3 Danish ships escaped. Apart from a large number of killed (including Mund) or wounded, some 1,000 Danes were taken prisoner. That same year Swedish general Torstenson outmaneuvered both Danish and imperial forces under Count Gallas, who then withdrew into Bohemia, pursued by Torstenson.

Torstenson launched a surprise winter campaign, marching up the Danube toward a virtually undefended Prague. A combined imperial-Bavarian force under General Johann von Werth intercepted him. Each side had about 15,000 men, but the Swedes had 60 guns to only 26 for the imperial side. The ensuing Battle of Jankau, fought southeast of Prague on March 6, 1645, ended in a decisive Swedish victory. The imperial side lost its artillery and half its force. Emperor Ferdinand III and his family fled to Graz.

By the end of the month Torstenson had taken Krems, and the Swedes had a bridgehead across the Danube. Torstenson's subsequent five-month siege of Brno (Brünn) in southern Moravia ended in failure on August 18, however. Crippled by gout, Torstenson was forced to resign in December and was replaced by Wrangel, who withdrew into Hesse.

In the spring of 1645, a French army under Marshal Turenne invaded central Germany but was badly defeated by a Bavarian army under Baron Mercy at Mergentheim on May 6. Swedish forces and a French army under the Duc d'Enghien rushed to Turenne's aid. That summer the combined forces of Turenne and Enghien invaded Bavaria with about 12,000 men and on August 3 defeated a Bavarian army of approximately the same size under Baron Mercy. Each side suffered some 5,000 casualties in this Second Battle of Nördlingen (Allerheim). Mercy was among the dead. Their own heavy casualties prevented the French from following up their victory, but the battle helped persuade the Bavarians to open peace negotiations with the allied side.

In 1644, Prince of Transylvania György I Rákóczi had reentered the war against Austria to secure those parts of northern Hungary that had reverted to the Habsburgs on the death of Prince Gábor Bethlen. The Treaty of Linz of December 16, 1645, restored the lands in question to him and reconfirmed religious freedom in Habsburg Hungary.

In 1646 in Hesse, the Swedish army under Wrangel and the imperial army under Archduke Leopold William maneuvered without decisive contact. Turenne also avoided contact. Meanwhile, foraging by all the armies devastated Germany. That August, Turenne and Wrangel joined forces near Giessen. Leopold William, wary of being cut off by the 19,000-man allied force, withdrew to Fulda. In September the allied army invaded Bavaria and ravaged the countryside. Duke Maximilian, outraged at the lack of imperial support, opened negotiations with the allies, concluding the Truce of Ulm with them on March 15, 1647.

French forces in Flanders under Gaston de Orléans and Enghien meanwhile captured a number of fortresses, including the important port of Dunkerque. In northern Italy the French met little success in an invasion of Tuscany, however. The French were also largely rebuffed in Spain. At the end of the year Enghien, on the death of his father now the Prince de Condé (and known as the Great Condé), assumed command of French forces in Spain.

On June 14, 1646, an inconclusive naval battle occurred off Orbetello in Tuscany when a French fleet under Admiral Armand de Maillé-Brézé taking part in the siege was attacked by a Spanish fleet under Don Francisco Pimiente of 25 sailing warships and 20 galleys. The French had 16 sailing warships, 20 galleys, 8 fireships, and some transports. Losses were slight and both sides claimed victory, but the capable Maillé-Brézé was killed, and shortly thereafter the French raised their siege.

There was little military action in 1647. The German countryside had been so devastated by warfare and foraging that it was difficult to keep troops in the field. Wrangel raided Bohemia from Hesse, but Turenne had to put down a revolt by his Weimar Army, which he then disbanded. He then moved into Luxembourg to meet a Spanish invasion from the Netherlands. In the autumn, Duke Maximilian of Bavaria made peace with Emperor Ferdinand III and again fielded an army against France and Sweden but too late for operations before winter. In Flanders and in the Meuse area there was scant activity, and in Italy and Spain there was little change.

On January 30, 1648, in the Treaty of Münster, the Spanish and the Dutch concluded peace, bringing to a close the long Dutch Revolt (1568–1648). Spain recognized the independence of the United Provinces of the Netherlands. Warfare in Germany continued, however, as other negotiations proceeded.

In the spring of 1648, Turenne and Wrangel joined forces at Ansbach and marched into and ravaged Bavaria. Bavarian general Peter Melander withdrew his 10,000-man army behind the Danube. On May 17 at Zusmarhausen, 14 miles west

of Augsburg, the allies caught up with Melander and inflicted a crushing defeat; Melander was among the dead. The Bavarian and imperial forces then withdrew, first to Augsburg and then beyond the Inn River. Recalled from Spanish service, General Ottavio Piccolomini assumed command of the remaining imperial forces and held the allies at the Inn, although beyond that line the allies largely devastated Bavaria. In July, Wrangel and Turenne moved against Munich. With peace negotiations nearing completion, however, French first minister Cardinal Jules Mazarin, who had replaced Richelieu on the latter's death in 1642, ordered them to withdraw into Swabia.

Prior to his invasion of Bavaria, Swedish commander Wrangel had detached a force under Hans Christoffer, Count von Königsmarck, to invade Bohemia. Cutting a path of destruction through the Upper Palatinate into Bohemia, on July 26, 1648, Königsmarck arrived at Prague. Thanks to a betrayal, he was able to secure about a quarter of the city. Despite this and later reinforcements, the Swedes were unable to take the remainder of Prague. The siege ended in November with news of peace.

Seeking to take advantage of the Fronde, a civil war in France led by much of the nobility against the Crown, the Spaniards mounted what would be their final invasion of France during the war. Archduke Leopold William had command. Condé rushed up from Catalonia to Flanders to take command of the French forces, and battle occurred on August 20, 1648, at Lens, a fortified city in the Hainaut region of present-day Belgium that had been captured by the French the year before. Condé had cobbled together some 16,000 men (more than half cavalry) and 18 guns. Leopold William had 18,000 men (more than half of them cavalry) and 38 guns. Condé won a smashing victory in what was the last major battle of the war. French casualties are unknown, but Spanish losses totaled some 10,000 men, including 6,000 taken prisoner.

With the French and Swedes everywhere victorious, Emperor Ferdinand III was more than ready to negotiate. So too was Mazarin, whose hold on power had been badly shaken by the Fronde. The Swedes were also weary.

The parties reached agreement in October 1648 in the Treaty of Münster and the Treaty of Osnabrück. France and the Holy Roman Empire signed the Treaty of Münster, while Sweden and the Holy Roman Empire signed the Treaty of Osnabrück. The two treaties are collectively known as the Peace of Westphalia.

It was a compromise agreement. To some extent Ferdinand III was able to play the Swedes against the French. The primary part of the settlement involved a complex series of land transfers within the Holy Roman Empire. The Swedes received the western half of Pomerania along with a part of eastern Pomerania, notably the city of Szezecin (Stettin) and the island of Rügen; the port of Wismar; and the bishoprics of Bremen and Verden (taken from the Danes in the 1643–1645 Danish-Swedish War). This led to a complex chain reaction of land transfers chiefly consisting of the resecularization of bishoprics returned to the Catholic Church under the Edict of Restitution of 1629. This arrangement ended the effort of the Catholic Church to reestablish its paramount position in northern Germany.

Brandenburg was enlarged significantly and came to overshadow Saxony, long the leading state of northern Germany. Brandenburg received farther (western) Pomerania. In recompense for its loss of the other half of Pomerania (all of Pomerania should have passed to it upon the death of the last duke in 1637), Brandenburg received the large archbishopric of Magdeburg and the smaller bishoprics of Halberstadt, Minden, and Kammin. Saxony secured part of Magdeburg and was confirmed in its control of Lusatia.

Bavaria was also increased in size and stature. It retained the Upper Palatinate, while the Lower Palatinate passed to Carl Ludwig, son of the dispossessed Frederick V. At the same time, Ludwig was recognized as the eighth elector of the empire.

France secured Alsace and Breisach and the right to garrison Phillipsburg. France also secured confirmation of its rights to the bishoprics and cities of Metz, Toul, and Verdun in Lorraine, which it had held since the mid-16th century, as well as recognition of its rights to Pinerolo in Savoy.

The Peace of Westphalia in effect ended the Catholic Counter Reformation in Germany. The treaty not only reconfirmed the terms of the Peace of Augsburg of 1555, which gave each prince the right to determine the religion of his state, but also added Calvinism to Lutheranism and Catholicism as acceptable religions. Despite strong efforts, Sweden was unable to secure any guarantees that Protestants in the Habsburg lands would be able to practice their religion. This meant that the many Protestant exiles from Bohemia would not be returning home.

Another pressing problem was the disposition of Catholic Church lands seized in defiance of the Peace of Augsburg. Here the Protestants scored a clear victory, with the lands to remain with those who held them on January 1, 1624. This did, however, sanction the Catholic Reformation carried out in Bohemia after 1620.

Important changes also occurred in the composition of the Holy Roman Empire in that the Dutch and the Swiss were confirmed as independent of it. The Dutch secured control of both banks of the Scheldt and the closure of that river to oceangoing vessels. This provision meant the commercial destruction of Antwerp in the Spanish Netherlands. The Dutch also received from Portugal the right to maintain outposts in Brazil and Indonesia.

There were also dramatic and far-reaching changes in the constitution of the empire that prevented the formation of a strong German state until the late 19th century and invited outside interference in German affairs. In fact, it was in the constitution of the empire that the French, Swedes, and Dutch secured their greatest victory. Each of the more than 300 German states was declared virtually sovereign, free to conduct its own foreign policy, and make treaties and military alliances, and wage wars, with the sole proviso that these not be directed against the emperor. Finally, there was a full amnesty within the empire with the exception of Austria and Bohemia, where it was to apply only to those who had risen in rebellion after 1630.

Significance

The Thirty Years' War resulted in the effective atomization of Germany. While other areas of Europe were coalescing into large unified nation-states, Germany was moving in the opposite direction. Its population reduced by a third to a half, physically devastated by 30 years of war, and now divided into many small states, Germany ceased to play a major role in world affairs. That place was now taken by the Atlantic powers of the Dutch Republic, England, and France. France and Sweden were made guarantors of the peace, and although Sweden became too weak to exercise that right effectively, the French used it as a legal excuse to intervene in Central Europe during the next century and a half. The Thirty Years' War was thus a major watershed in world history. With it also, the European wars of religion came to an end.

Further Reading

Benecke, Gerhard. *Germany in the Thirty Years War.* London: St. Martin's, 1978.

Bonney, Richard. *The Thirty Years' War, 1618–1648.* London: Osprey, 2002.

Cooper, J. P. *The New Cambridge Modern History,* Vol. 4, *The Decline of Spain and the Thirty Years War, 1609–48/59.* Cambridge: Cambridge University Press, 1970.

Cramer, Kevin. *The Thirty Years' War & German Memory in the Nineteenth Century.* Lincoln: University of Nebraska, 2007.

Gutmann, Myron P. "The Origins of the Thirty Years' War." *Journal of Interdisciplinary History* 18(4) (1988): 749–770.

Helfferich, Tryntje, ed. *The Thirty Years War: A Documentary History.* Indianapolis: Hackett, 2009.

Kennedy, Paul. *The Rise and Fall of the Great Powers: Economic Change and Military Conflict from 1500 to 2000.* New York: HarperCollins, 1988.

Langer, Herbert. *The Thirty Years' War.* Poole, UK: Blandford, 1980.

Mitchell, John. *Life of Wallenstein, Duke of Friedland.* Westport, CT: Greenwood, 1968.

Oakley, Stewart. *War and Peace in the Baltic, 1560–1790.* London: Routledge, 1992.

Parker, Geoffrey. *The Thirty Years' War.* London: Routledge and Kegan Paul, 1984.

Prinzing, Friedrich. *Epidemics Resulting from Wars.* Oxford, UK: Clarendon, 1916.

Rabb, Theodore K. "The Effects of the Thirty Years' War on the German Economy." *Journal of Modern History* 34(1) (1962): 40–51.

Roberts, Michael. *Gustavus Adolphus.* New York: Addison Wesley, 1992.

Rogers, Clifford, ed. *The Military Revolution Debate.* Boulder, CO: Westview, 1995.

Wedgwood, C. V. *Thirty Years War.* New York: New York Review of Books, 2005.

Wilson, Peter H. *Europe's Tragedy: A History of the Thirty Years War.* London: Allen Lane, 2009.

Great Northern War (1700–1721)

Dates	1700–1721
Location	Northern and East Central Europe
Combatants	Sweden and Ottoman Empire vs. Russia, Denmark, Saxony, and Poland
Principal Commanders	Sweden: Charles XII, Carl Gustaf Reinskiöld Russia: Peter the Great, Boris Sheremetiev Poland/Saxony: Augustus II (also known as Frederick Augustus I, elector of Saxony), Stanisław I Leszczyński
Principal Battles	The Sound, Narva (first), Dünamünde, Hummselsdorf, Narva (second), Fraustadt, Holowczyn, Lesnaya, Poltava, Storkyro, Gangut
Outcome	Sweden loses its position as the dominant power on the Baltic coast, and Peter the Great secures for Russia his "windows on the Baltic." The war marks the decline of Sweden and the arrival of Russia as a major European power.

Causes

The Great Northern War of 1700–1721 was the struggle for control of the Baltic region of Europe. It was caused by the determination of the rulers of Poland, Russia, and Denmark to end Sweden's domination there. Augustus II the Strong, elector of Saxony (r. 1694–1733), king of Poland and grand duke of Lithuania (r. 1697–1706), and king of Poland (1709–1733), was the prime mover in the alliance; he sought to reunite Livonia with Poland. Czar Peter I (Peter the Great) of Russia (r. 1682–1721) desired to regain Russian access to the Baltic, which had been lost to Sweden as a result of the 1617 Treaty of Stolbovo following the Time of Troubles. Peter also wanted to make his country a major naval power. Danish king Frederick IV (r. 1699–1730) sought to retake territory lost earlier in wars to Sweden and to secure Scandinavian dominance.

Between 1560 and 1658, Sweden had created a considerable empire in the Baltic. Centered on the Gulf of Finland, this territory included the provinces of Karelia, Ingria, Estonia, and Livonia. As a consequence of its participation in the Thirty Years' War (1618–1648), Sweden also secured territory in northern Germany, including Western Pomerania, Wismar, the Duchy of Bremen, and Verden. At the same time Sweden defeated Denmark in a series of wars (1643–1645, 1657–1658, and 1658–1660), adding Danish and Norwegian territory north of Øresund (the Sound, the strait separating the Danish island of Zealand from the southern Swedish province of Scania).

Peter, Alexander, and Frederick sought to take advantage of the youth and inexperience of young Swedish king Charles XII. Born in 1682, he had become king three months shy of his 15th birthday in April 1697 on the death of his father, Charles XI. Johann Parkul, a noble, politician, and adventurer who greatly resented Sweden's control of his native Livonia, brought together the rulers of Russia, Denmark, and Saxony in a secret treaty signed at Preobrazhenskoye (now a part of Moscow), a favorite residence of Peter I, on February 22, 1700. It established the Northern Union, an alliance with the goal of wresting control of the Baltic from Sweden.

Course

Augustus II sent a small Saxon army across the Dvina River to seize Dünamunde in Livonia (in present-day Latvia) from Sweden, which it accomplished on March 23, 1700. Meanwhile, on March 17, 1700, Denmark formally entered the war when its army attacked across ducal Schleswig and invaded the duchy of Holstein-Gottorp, allied with Sweden. The immediate Danish goal was to recover Scania. In June, Polish-Saxon forces laid siege to Riga. With King Charles XII preparing to attack, Augustus II raised the siege on September 29.

Charles now demonstrated the considerable military abilities that would earn him the sobriquet "Alexander of the North." Against the advice of his advisers, he decided to attack Denmark. Swedish admiral Hans Wachmeister's fleet of 38 ships of the line and 10 frigates joined a combined Anglo-Dutch fleet off Denmark under English admiral Sir George Rooke numbering 23 ships of the line, 5 frigates, and 11 other ships. The English and Dutch decided to intervene in order to ensure a supply of naval stores from the Baltic. Their aim was to aid Sweden while seeing to it that the Danes were not unduly hurt.

The Danes removed navigational markers, and some of the larger Swedish ships grounded before being refloated. The two fleets made contact in the Sound on July 6, 1700. Seeing that his 29 ships of the line were badly outnumbered, Danish admiral Ulrik Christian Gyldenløve withdrew to Copenhagen and positioned his ships behind hulks and booms in the harbor. The allies did not attempt to force the harbor and were unable to effect any major damage to Copenhagen through long-range shelling.

On August 4, however, Charles XII arrived in Zealand with a sizable land force and commenced preparations for a land siege of Copenhagen. Before this could commence, however, Danish king Frederick IV agreed to peace in the Treaty of Travendal (August 18, 1700). Denmark returned Schleswig to the Duke of Holstein-Gottorp and pledged not to fight against Sweden. (The Danes reentered the war after Charles's disastrous defeat at Poltava in 1709, however.)

Meanwhile on August 20, 1700, Russia joined the war with an invasion of Ingria. In October some 37,000 Russian troops laid siege to Narva in eastern Estonia, defended by only 1,800 men. On October 16 Charles XII landed at Pärnu, Livonia (present-day Pernau, Estonia), with a small force intending to aid Riga, then besieged by Polish-Saxon forces. While awaiting reinforcements, he decided to march to the relief of Narva. Departing on November 23 and aided by General Carl Gustav Reinskiöld but only having some 10,500 men, on November 28 Charles easily defeated Russian troops seeking to block his approach. Peter I then departed Narva, leaving command there to Field Marshal Charles Eugène de Croy.

The Battle of Narva on November 30, 1700 (November 20 according to the

Swedish transitional calendar; all dates here are new style), was fought in a snowstorm that blew in the direction of the Russians, obscuring their vision. The Russians were also handicapped in that many of their officers were foreigners, so commands had to be translated and then relayed in Russian. The Swedes broke through and virtually destroyed the Russian force, nearly four times their own in size. Charles lost only 667 dead, while Russian losses were estimated at 15,000 killed in the fighting or drowned and many others captured. The Swedes also secured more than 20,000 muskets.

Rightly considered one of the greatest victories in Swedish history, Narva was a painful lesson for Peter on the need to improve his army. He now hired increasing numbers of Western military advisers to train his military and also purchased Western weapons.

Following his victory at Narva, Charles turned to relieve the Polish-Saxon siege of Riga and concentrate on Poland rather than following up with Russia. This decision has been criticized by some military historians, but an invasion of Russia immediately after the Battle of Narva would have left strong Polish-Saxon forces in his rear. In December Charles relieved Riga, but Polish-Saxon forces soon resumed the siege, and he had to return there and again relieve Riga on July 17, 1701.

On July 9, 1701, Charles carried out a surprise crossing of the Daugava (Western Dvina) River to attack Russian and Saxon forces at Dünamünde. Under cover of a smoke screen, boats carried 6,000 Swedish troops across the river. The men were protected from small-arms fire by bales of straw and raised wooden landing ramps lowered on reaching the opposite bank. Charles also utilized to good effect floating batteries of cannon. In the ensuing battle, he defeated the Russo-Saxon force commanded by Saxon field marshal Adam Heinrich von Steinau. The only part of the Swedish plan that went awry was that the force of the river prolonged assembly of an elaborate pontoon bridge, constructed in sections, delaying the Swedish pursuit and allowing most of the allied force to escape. The Swedes sustained 500 dead or wounded, the Saxons some 800; 700 other Saxons were taken prisoner. This victory gave Charles all Courland.

With Charles occupied against Poland, Peter I reorganized his army and prepared to invade Ingria. Charles had left only 15,000 men to defend that considerable area against the numerically far stronger Russian forces. Charles had also taken his best troops with him and had ordered the Swedish government not to send reinforcements to the Baltic while he was still fighting Poland. Peter's main concern was that Poland not sign a separate peace with Charles. In a meeting with King Augustus II of Poland at Birse, Peter secured a pledge that Poland would remain in the war in return for 20,000 Russian troops, 100,000 pounds of gunpowder, and a subsidy of 100,000 rubles per year for three years.

Russian forces then invaded Ingria. Russian general Boris Sheremetiev defeated Swedish general Wolmar Anton von Schlippenbach at the Battle of Errestfer (Erastfer) on January 9, 1702, with the Swedes losing 3,000 killed or wounded and 350 taken prisoner. A delighted Peter made Sheremetiev a marshal. Sheremetiev continued his offensive and with 30,000 men again defeated Schlippenbach, with 8,000 Swedes, in the Battle of Hummselsdorf on July 19. The Swedes sustained some 5,500 casualties, almost 70 percent of their force. By the end of the year, Russian forces had secured much of the Neva River Valley.

Charles meanwhile was preoccupied with Poland. Following his invasion of Lithuania, he advanced on and occupied the undefended city of Warsaw on May 14, 1702. He then moved westward in hopes of a decisive engagement with Polish king Augustus II. At Klissow (Kiszow) on July 19 Charles, with some 12,000 men, attacked and defeated a Saxon army of 16,000. The Saxons suffered 4,000 casualties, the Swedes only 900. Augustus, however, was able to extricate the remainder of his force. Charles marched on and occupied Kraków (Cracow), then consolidated his control of Poland.

On May 1, 1703, Charles and some 3,200 men defeated a Saxon force of some 3,500 men under General Adam Heinrich von Steinau at Pułtusk in Poland. At a cost of 18 dead, the Swedes killed some 200 Saxons and captured another 800. Charles went on to besiege and take Thorn in December.

Meanwhile, Peter was busy securing his "windows on the Baltic." On May 1, 1703, Russian troops under Sheremetiev captured the small Swedish fortress of Nyen (Nyenskans, renamed Slottburg) at the mouth of the Neva River. On May 27, the Russians commenced construction on the north side of that river of a town that would grow into the city of St. Petersburg. To assist in its defense, the Russians began construction on a nearby island of what would become the fortress of Kronstadt.

Charles meanwhile forced the Poles to depose Augustus II as king of Poland and on July 6, 1704, secured the election of his own candidate, Stanisław I Leszczyński. (Officially crowned king on October 4, 1705, Leszczyński's first official act was

to conclude a formal alliance with Sweden, promising to assist Sweden against Russia.) Meanwhile, Poland was suffering greatly under the Swedish occupation, and fighting occurred between partisans of Augustus and Leszczyński. In August, taking advantage of Charles's temporary absence, Augustus briefly recaptured Warsaw.

In the spring of 1704 having acted on Czar Peter I's orders and destroyed Ingria as a Swedish supply area, Russian forces laid siege to the two great Swedish fortresses in Estonia: Tartu (Dorpat) and Narva. Marshal Sheremetiev besieged Tartu with 20,000 men in June, forcing its surrender on June 24. Scottish mercenary General George Ogilvy and Sheremetiev then laid siege to Narva, held by a small Swedish garrison under General Henning Horn.

Narva fell on August 20, and the Russians then massacred its Swedish inhabitants, including women and children. Peter arrived in person several hours after the fall of the fortress and, in an effort to restore order, killed a number of the Russian plunderers himself. The Russian victory at Narva, while tarnished by the behavior of the Russian troops, revenged Peter's humiliating defeat there in 1700 and strengthened Russia's hold on the Baltic.

Anxious to keep Augustus II in the war against Sweden, Peter increased his subsidies to the Saxon king. In a new treaty of August 30, Peter promised to provide 12,000 Russian troops, to pay for the maintenance of 47,000 Polish troops, and to furnish a subsidy of 200,000 rubles a year until the end of the war. A Russian effort to bring Brandenburg-Prussia into the war failed, however, owing to Prussian king Frederick I's fear of the Swedes and his concern about Russian gains in the Baltic.

Peter detached Sheremetiev and ordered him to reconquer Courland, but

BATTLE OF POLTAVA, JULY 8, 1709

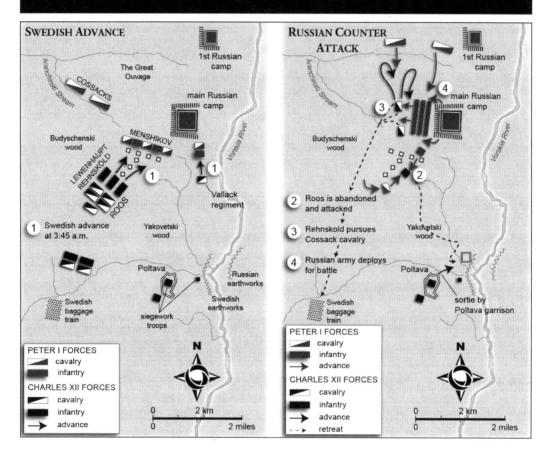

SWEDISH ADVANCE

Ivanchinsii Stream

COSSACKS

The Great Ouvage

1st Russian camp

Budyschenski wood

MENSHIKOV

main Russian camp

LEWENHAUPT
REHNSKOLD

ROOS

Vorskla River

Vallack regiment

1 Swedish advance at 3:45 a.m.

Yakovetski wood

Poltava

Russian earthworks

Swedish earthworks

Swedish baggage train

siegework troops

PETER I FORCES
cavalry
infantry

CHARLES XII FORCES
cavalry
infantry
advance

N

0   2 km
0   2 miles

RUSSIAN COUNTER ATTACK

Ivanchinsii Stream

1st Russian camp

4

3

main Russian camp

Budyschenski wood

Vorskla River

2

2 Roos is abandoned and attacked

3 Rehnskold pursues Cossack cavalry

4 Russian army deploys for battle

Yakovetski wood

Poltava

sortie by Poltava garrison

Swedish baggage train

PETER I FORCES
cavalry
infantry
advance

CHARLES XII FORCES
cavalry
infantry
advance
retreat

N

0   2 km
0   2 miles

Swedish general Adam Loewenhaupt defeated Sheremetiev in the Battle of Gemaurhof (June 16, 1705), whereupon Peter hurried to Sheremetiev's assistance, and Loewenhaupt fell back on Riga. The Russians conquered Courland and then went into winter quarters.

In January 1706 Charles suddenly moved into eastern Poland in an effort to clear it of supporters of King Augustus II and to attack Russian forces under General George Ogilvy entrenched at Grodno. Unable to tempt Ogilvy into leaving his defenses to fight, Charles had to content himself with severing the latter's supply route to Russia. Former Polish king

Augustus hurried to Warsaw to join his Russian and Polish troops with Saxon forces under General Johann Matthias von der Schulenburg, hoping to crush the Swedes between his own troops and those of Ogilvy. This plan was frustrated by Swedish general Carl Gustaf Reinskiöld's brilliant victory with 9,400 men (5,700 cavalry) over Schulenburg with 18,000 men (2,000 cavalry) in the Battle of Fraustadt (present-day Wschowa) on February 13, 1706. The Swedes lost only 424 killed and 760 wounded; the allied force was virtually annihilated, with some 7,300 killed and 7,600 captured. Reinskiöld ordered the execution of some 500 Russians taken during the battle in retaliation for widespread Russian atrocities in Courland.

Fearing for the safety of his army at Grodno, Peter ordered Ogilvy to abandon his artillery and immediately withdraw to Russia. Ogilvy protested the order and was replaced. Split into small detachments, the bulk of the Russians then escaped, aided by spring floods on the Niemen River that held up the pursuing Swedes, who gave up the chase at Pinsk.

Much to the relief of Peter, Charles turned to deal with Augustus instead of continuing against Russia. In August, Charles began an invasion of Saxony. He easily captured Leipzig, and Augustus sued for peace. In the ensuing Treaty of Altranstädt (September 24, 1705), Augustus agreed to abdicate the throne of Poland and to recognize Stanisław I Leszczyński as king. Augustus was also forced to renounce all anti-Swedish alliances and to assist Sweden against Russia. (Augustus renounced the treaty and reclaimed the Polish throne following Charles's defeat in the Battle of Poltava in 1709.)

Fearful of a Swedish invasion of Russia, Peter attempted to come to terms with Charles, offering to surrender all his Baltic possessions except St. Petersburg. If Charles had been capable of moderation and had seized this opportunity, he would have achieved a stunning success against overwhelming odds. But ambition overcame judgment, and he rejected the Russian overtures. Peter now prepared for a guerre à outrance (war to the utmost, fight to the finish). Charles also began preparations for an invasion of Russia. Peter decided not to contest the inevitable Swedish invasion but instead to withdraw his forces and practice a scorched-earth policy, drawing the Swedes deep into Russia while harassing and wearing them down.

Charles's planned invasion was delayed for a year by conflict with Holy Roman emperor Leopold I, mostly on religious grounds. Charles demanded compensation for the depredations committed by imperial troops against Protestants in Silesia, which was in direct contravention of the Treaty of Osnabrück of May 15, 1648 (one of the treaties ending the Thirty Years' War), of which Sweden was a guarantor. Leopold prepared for war, but other considerations intervened. Fearful that Sweden would join France in the War of the Spanish Succession (1701–1714), the Western allies prevailed on Leopold to yield to Charles's demands in August 1707.

Delayed by the tardy arrival of reinforcements, Charles was unable to take the field until November, a factor of incalculable value to Peter, who was forced to deal with a Bashir uprising in the Volga region followed by a rebellion of the Don Cossacks. Charles ultimately assembled 44,000 men (24,000 cavalry and 20,000 infantry), two-thirds of them veteran troops, the largest force he ever commanded. Peter concentrated his forces at Grodno and Minsk. Charles arrived at the Vistula River on December 25, 1707, and crossed it into Russia, despite dangerous ice floes, on January 1, 1708.

Moving rapidly east, Charles entered Grodno on January 26, 1708, only two hours after Peter had departed. Charles now faced the choice of recovering the Baltic provinces lost previously to the Russians or pursuing Peter's forces into the heart of Russia and dictating peace. Charles's generals urged the former, but the headstrong Charles opted for the far more difficult choice.

Crossing the Berezina and Drucz Rivers without problem, the Swedes reached the Wabis, where they discovered a strong

Russian army commanded by Shere-metiev on the other side of the river near the small town of Holowczyn (Golovchin). Detecting the one vulnerable point in the six-mile-long Russian line, Charles concentrated his forces against it and attacked. Charles had some 20,000 men, Peter perhaps 38,000.

Charles was victorious in this Battle of Holowczyn on July 14. The Swedes suffered 1,265 dead and 1,028 wounded while inflicting 3,000 casualties on the Russians and scattering the remainder of Sheremetiev's army. The engagement was the last pitched battle won by Charles in Russia and opened up his approach to the Dnieper River, with the Swedes reaching Mogilev on the Don River on July 18.

Charles halted his army for a month while awaiting reinforcements. Peter would not risk another general engagement and slowly withdrew before the Swedish advance, destroying everything in a scorched-earth policy. The Swedes thus began to suffer serious supply shortages, both in food for the men and in fodder for the horses. Russian forces also struck at vulnerable Swedish units along the route of march.

Awaiting a large supply train under Swedish general Adam Loewenhaupt, Charles held his first council of war in early October but rejected suggestions that he withdraw northward into Livonia and winter in his own territory. Instead, he decided to move southward to join Cossack leader Ivan Mazepa in Ukraine, ordering Loewenhaupt to meet him there. This was perhaps Charles's worst military decision. He should have waited for Loewenhaupt's arrival with supplies and then consolidated before pushing deeper into Russia. Meanwhile, to the north another Swedish force under General Georg Henrik Lybecker

was rebuffed by the Russians at St. Petersburg and forced to withdraw into Finland.

As Charles moved south with the main Swedish army to Ukraine, the first in a chain of disasters struck the invaders. During October 9–10 at Lesnaya (present-day Lyasnaya in Belarus), just east of the Dnieper River, General Loewenhaupt with 11,000 Swedish reinforcements and a substantial supply train were attacked and savaged by a much larger Russian force. Loewenhaupt was forced to burn the supply train to keep it from falling into Russian hands. In all the Russians lost 4,000 men, but Swedish losses totaled 8,000 men killed or wounded, 16 guns, and 2,000 wagons of provisions. Loewenhaupt and 6,000 exhausted and hungry Swedish survivors of the battle joined Charles and the main Swedish army on October 21. Czar Peter had already crushed Mazepa's revolt in Ukraine (Mazepa joined Charles at Horki in Severia on November 6), so the move southward had been pointless.

The winter of 1708–1709 was the coldest in Europe in a century, and the Swedes suffered terribly. Charles accomplished wonders in merely holding his army together. At Crekova with only 400 men, he drove back 7,000 attacking Russians; at Opressa with only 800 men, he defeated 5,000 Russians.

Nonetheless, by the spring of 1709 Charles's army had dropped to half its invasion size of 41,000 men. Charles had about 20,000 men capable of battle and only 34 guns and little powder. Communications with Sweden had been severed. Charles nonetheless remained confident.

On May 2 Charles laid siege to the small Russian fortress of Poltava on the Vorskla River in Ukraine. Peter immediately marched to Poltava with 80,000 men and more than 100 guns. Aware of Peter's approach, Charles should have broken off the siege and withdrawn east into Poland. This did not suit his aggressive nature and disdain for the Russian soldier, and he foolishly decided to stand and fight.

Extensive maneuvering followed Peter's arrival, during which Charles was badly wounded in the foot on June 27 while making a reconnaissance, forcing him to move about by litter. Informed of this fact, Peter resolved not to refuse battle if offered. Indeed, in order to provoke Charles to attack him, Peter ordered a fortified Russian camp constructed several miles north of Poltava. Its eastern flank rested on the Vorskla, its southern flank on a marsh and small stream.

Charles was equally ready for battle, for his supply situation would not allow long delay. He attacked Peter's position early on the morning of July 8, 1709. The initial Swedish assault was successful, but there was scant coordination between the major elements of the army, and Peter was able to rally his forces to meet the final Swedish attack by 7,000 men against frightful odds.

The Russians had 40,000 fresh troops and a crushing superiority in artillery (most of Charles's far fewer guns were still involved in the Siege of Poltava). Peter assumed personal command of an infantry division, riding among the men and shouting encouragement. Charles's wound prevented him from doing the same.

In their final attack, the Swedes were cut down in large numbers by Russian artillery fire. Over by noon, the Battle of Poltava claimed some 3,000 Swedish dead and a like number captured. Russian losses were given as 1,345 killed and 3,290 wounded. Charles fled by horse with Mazepa and about 1,500 Cossacks and Swedes into Turkish Moldavia. General Adam Loewenhaupt surrendered the remaining 12,000 Swedes at Perevolchina on June 30. Total Swedish losses were thus 9,234 killed or wounded and 18,794 taken prisoner.

The Battle of Poltava marked the turning point in the Great Northern War and the end of Swedish domination of the Baltic shore. The battle's immediate impact was to revive the coalition of powers against Sweden. Already the same day as the battle, Peter concluded an alliance with Denmark "to restore the equilibrium of the north." On learning of Poltava, King Augustus II also revived his alliance with Russia. In a treaty of October 17, 1709, Peter promised to assist Augustus in regaining the throne of Poland, although in a secret article Augustus agreed that Livonia would henceforth belong to Russia.

Support for Charles XII's puppet ruler in Poland, Stanisław I Leszczyński, immediately vanished as, reflecting the new reality, the Polish nobles rallied to their former ruler, Augustus II. With Russian troops marching west and occupying Poland, Peter was in effect the real master of that country.

Concern over the attitude of the Western powers, which favored Sweden as long as the War of the Spanish Succession continued, led Peter to proceed cautiously. Efforts by Denmark and Russia to secure the adherence of Prussia were limited by the cautious approach of Prussian king Frederick I. The Danes took Schleswig, Bremen, and Verden. The latter two were then ceded to Hanover in order to secure its entry into the war. The Russians occupied Carelia, Livonia, Estonia, and what remained of Ingria.

Despite the opposition of the maritime powers of England and the Netherlands, the Danes attacked Sweden itself. Some 15,000 Danish troops under Christian

Ditlev Reventlow landed in Skania in southern Sweden to virtually no resistance and soon controlled most of central Skania.

The Swedes were still a formidable military power, and they frantically assembled and trained 16,000 men under Count Magnus Stenbock, who quickly marched to cut the Danish supply lines. Reventlow turned to meet the Swedes but suddenly fell ill and was replaced by Jorgen Rantzau. The two sides then raced to secure the important city of Helsingborg. The Swedes and Danes were of about equal strength of 14,000 men, although the Swedes had more cavalry and fewer infantry.

In the Battle of Helsingborg on March 10, 1710, Rantzau sacrificed overall direction of the battle to take personal part in the fighting and was wounded. The Danes were defeated, and much of their army took refuge in Helsingborg. The Danes refused to surrender, and because their own force was too small to take the city by storm, the Swedes laid siege to and commenced shelling the city. Much of Helsingborg was destroyed before the Danes evacuated. The battle claimed 7,500 Danish killed, wounded, or captured; the Swedes sustained 2,800 casualties.

The Battle of Helsingborg, although a major loss for the Danes, proved to be of great advantage to Czar Peter, for it prevented the Swedes from sending reinforcements to the Baltic provinces, ensuring Peter a near free hand there. He laid siege to Riga and forced its surrender in July 1710. The Russians had already invaded Finland and taken Vyborg in June.

The Ottoman Empire now unexpectedly entered the war on the Swedish side. Following the Battle of Poltava, the Russians had demanded that the Ottomans surrender Charles XII and Ukrainian Cossack leader

Mazepa. Forced into diplomacy for the first time in his reign, Charles had skillfully exploited Sultan Ahmed III's fears that Russia, once victorious in the north, would turn south against the Ottoman Empire. The Russian fortification of Azov and the construction of a Black Sea fleet fueled this apprehension, as did Peter's threats of invasion. The Porte formally declared war on November 20, 1710, initiating the Russo-Turkish War of 1710–1711. Grand Vizier Baltaji Mehmet led an Ottoman army of nearly 200,000 men northward to the frontier.

Seeking to counter the Ottoman move, Peter concluded a new alliance with Augustus II and a secret treaty with Demetrius Cantemir, *hospodar* (lord) of Moldavia. The anticipated uprising of Serbs and Bulgars against the Ottomans failed to materialize, however, and Peter's army, reduced to 38,000 men by mid-July 1711, was outmaneuvered and driven back to the Pruth by the vastly superior Ottoman and Tatar force of 190,000 men with 300 guns. Had the Ottomans delayed, they would have destroyed the now-starving Russian force, which was without hope of relief, but they opted for negotiations, which had tremendous future consequences.

Although Peter was prepared to concede much more, including the surrender of all his Baltic holdings except St. Petersburg, the restoration of Stanisław I Leszczyński as king of Poland, and a sizable indemnity, his negotiator succeeded in reaching an amazingly favorable settlement. In the Treaty of the Pruth of July 21, 1711, the Russian army was allowed to depart in return for Peter's pledge to return Azov to Ottoman control and to dismantle Taganrog and other fortresses on the Sea of Azov, to withdraw from Poland and end Russian interference in Polish affairs, and to grant Charles XII free passage back to Sweden.

Two days after the Russians left the Pruth, Charles arrived there to receive the unwelcome news that peace had been concluded. Outraged, he spent the next three years in the Ottoman Empire trying in vain to get the Ottomans to resume war with Russia. As it worked out, Peter was forced to give up Azov and dismantle the Black Sea fortresses only upon a new Ottoman declaration of war on Russia, and he did not honor his pledges regarding Poland.

Charles's stay at Bender led to unsettled debts with local merchants, and mobs supported by a larger number of Janissaries attacked his unfortified residence. Charles and some 40 of his followers reportedly killed 200 Turks before he was taken and placed under house arrest, first at Dimetoka (present-day Didimoticho) and then at Istanbul.

The war now shifted to a struggle over Swedish possessions in Germany. Charles foolishly rejected overtures from the maritime powers of England and the Netherlands, which were sympathetic to Sweden and hostile to Russia, to mediate an end to the war. Despite the presence of a large Danish fleet in the Baltic, Swedish general Magnus Stenbock succeeded in transporting nearly 10,000 men and some artillery to Rügen. Counting the Stralsund garrison, he had 17,000 men.

Wisely refusing to invade Poland as Charles wanted, Stenbock proceeded to Wismar to protect Sweden's German possessions. With the Russians and Saxons moving against him from the southeast and the Danes moving from the southwest, he sought to prevent their union by first engaging the weaker foe of the Danes with a force about his own in size.

On December 20, 1712, at Gadebusch, about 20 miles south of Lübeck, Stenbock employed his artillery to good advantage and defeated the Danes and some Saxon troops under King Frederick IV and General Jacob Heinrich von Flemming. The Swedes suffered only about 500 dead and 1,100 wounded for 3,250 Danes and Saxons killed or wounded and 2,600 captured. Charles elevated Stenbock to field marshal, but the battle had little strategic impact.

Hoping to drive Denmark from the war by occupying Jutland, Stenbock crossed the Holstein frontier on January 1, 1713. Burning the city of Altona, which he later sought to justify as retaliation, he marched north, pursued by Peter with Russian, Polish, and Saxon forces. Cut off from Jutland, in early February Stenbock sought refuge in the fortress of Tönning in Holstein-Gottorp. After the failure of an attempted breakout, Stenbock surrendered at Oldensworth on May 16, 1713. He secured honorable terms for his army but was himself kept a prisoner in Denmark until his death in 1717.

Relations remained tense between the Ottoman Empire and Russia until the Treaty of Adrianople (Edirne) of June 5, 1713, resolved differences between the two states. Sultan Ahmed III regained Azov. Peter also agreed to demolish the fortress of Taganrog and others in the area and to halt all interference in the affairs of the Polish-Lithuanian Commonwealth.

Fighting continued between Sweden and Russia, however. In the Battle of Storkyro (also known as the Battle of Napue) near the village of Napue on March 2, 1714, some 4,000 untrained Finnish levies under Karl Gustaf Armfeit suffered defeat by a Russian force at least twice as large under

Mikhail Golitsyn. The Swedes suffered perhaps 2,500 dead or wounded; the Russians lost 3,000.

Peter now decided to invade Finland. Preparations included a substantial increase in the size of the Russian Navy through new construction (chiefly galleys) and the purchase of a number of 44- to 50-gun ships from England, France, and the Netherlands. The Russian fleet sailed in late May 1714. On August 7, 1714, the Russians especially employed their galleys to good advantage in the Battle of Gangut, fought in Riilahti Bay north of the Hanko Peninsula near present-day Hanko, Finland. Here Russian admiral Fyodor Apraksin, with a vastly superior number of vessels, won a resounding victory over the Swedes under Vice Admiral Gustaf Wattrang in what the Russians remember as their first major naval victory.

The Swedish Navy conceded control of the Gulf of Finland to the Russians, who were now able to block Swedish ships from entering waters east of the Sea of Åland and could easily supply their own forces in Finland. The Swedish Navy remained a powerful regional force; the Russian Navy was not yet ready to challenge it for control of the Baltic. Nonetheless, Russian forces now occupied all Finland (1713–1721), a time of hardship remembered in Finland as the Greater Wrath.

Finally convinced that the Ottoman Empire was not going to reenter the war, in late September 1714 Charles XII departed the Ottoman Empire and, accompanied by a single aide, made his way incognito across Europe by a circuitous route. In November he arrived in Stralsund, which along with Wismar was all that remained of Swedish territory in Germany. Unwisely rejecting negotiations that might have brought Sweden considerable concessions, Charles

remained determined to carry the long war forward to complete victory.

The accession to the throne of England of elector of Hanover Georg Ludwig as King George I following the death of Queen Anne in August 1714 resulted in a third coalition against Sweden. By the end of the war, with Sweden fast approaching exhaustion, a series of partition treaties produced an alliance against Sweden of Great Britain (Hanover), Russia, Prussia, Saxony, and Denmark.

For 12 months Charles, with almost superhuman heroism, defended Stralsund against the allies, driving them from Usedom Island until it was finally taken by Denmark and Prussia at heavy cost. On December 23, 1715, Stralsund, now virtually destroyed, surrendered to the allies, Charles having escaped to Sweden by sea two days before.

It had long been obvious to the allies that the war would continue until they actually invaded and defeated Charles in Sweden itself. The allies were deeply suspicious of one another and especially of Russia, now actively intervening in German affairs; however, the participation of Russia was essential for the success of any invasion. Charles meanwhile revitalized the Swedish military effort. Raising an army of 20,000 men, he moved into Skania, forestalling the allied plan to invade Sweden.

The allies then prepared to attack Charles in Skania. A force of 30,000 Russians and 28,000 Danes assembled in Zealand, but in September, having found the Swedes firmly entrenched, Peter, now suddenly cautious, withdrew his troops, bringing an end to the Skania expedition.

Apparently hoping to trade the duchies of Bremen and Verden for part of Norway, Charles laid siege to the Danish fortress of Fredriksten (present-day Halden, near

Oslo) and was on the point of capturing it when he was shot and killed on November 30, 1718, while he was in the trenches observing preparations for the final assault.

In March 1720 King Charles XII's surviving sister, Ulrica Leonora, was elected queen of Sweden. Negotiations for peace resumed with Russia, but the Swedish delegates declared that they would rather continue the war than surrender all the Baltic provinces, as the Russians demanded. In July the Russians mounted a devastating naval raid against the Swedish coast, destroying considerable property. The Swedish government was not intimidated and indeed broke off negotiations with Russia and opened negotiations with Hanover, Prussia, and Denmark.

In the Treaty of Stockholm of November 20, 1719, Sweden ceded Bremen and Verden to Hanover. In a second Treaty of Stockholm of February 1, 1720, Sweden ceded to Prussia Szczecin, Swedish Pomerania south of the Peene River, the islands of Usedom and Wollin, and the towns of Damm and Gollnow. In the Treaty of Frederiksborg of July 3, 1720, Sweden came to terms with Denmark. Sweden agreed to pay an indemnity of 600,000 riksdalers, end its alliance with Holstein, and forfeit its right to duty-free passage of the Sound.

In 1720 the Russian Navy again mounted large-scale raids on the Swedish coast, laying waste to towns, villages, and farms. Sweden, effectively isolated, was forced to come to terms with Russia. In the Treaty of Nystad of September 10, 1721, which was concluded without the participation of Poland, Sweden was forced to cede to Russia the eastern coast of the Baltic, including Livonia, Estonia, Ingria, the province of Keksholm, and the fortress of Vyborg. In return, Russia retroceded to Sweden Finland west of Vyborg and north of Keksholm, an indemnity of 2 million thalers, and free trade in the Baltic.

Significance

The 21-year-long Great Northern War was a catastrophe for Sweden, ending its tenure as the dominant power on the Baltic coast. That place was now taken by Russia, which also came to be recognized as a major European power.

Further Reading

Bengtsson, Frans Gunnar. *The Life of Charles XII, King of Sweden, 1697–1718.* Translated by Naomi Walford. Stockholm: Norstedt, 1960.

Englund, Peter. *The Battle That Shook Europe: Poltava and the Birth of the Russian Empire.* London: I. B. Tauris, 2013.

Frost, Robert I. *The Northern Wars: War, State and Society in Northeastern Europe, 1558–1721.* New York: Longman, 2000.

Hatton, Ragnhild Marie. *Charles XII of Sweden.* New York: Weybright Talley, 1974.

Lisk, Jill. *The Struggle for Supremacy in the Baltic, 1600–1725.* New York: Funk and Wagnalls, 1967.

Moulton, James R. *Peter the Great and the Russian Military Campaigns during the Final Years of the Great Northern War, 1719–1721.* Lanham, MD: University Press of America, 2005.

Roberts, Michael. *From Oxenstierna to Charles XII: Four Studies.* Cambridge: Cambridge University Press, 2003.

Starkey, Armstrong. *War in the Age of the Enlightenment, 1700–1789.* Westport, CT: Praeger, 2003.

Stiles, Andrina. *Sweden and the Baltic, 1523–1721.* London: Hodder and Stoughton, 1992.

Voltaire. *Voltaire's History of Charles XII, King of Sweden.* Translated by Winifred Todhunter. London: Dent and Sons, 1915.

Wolf, John B. *The Emergence of the Great Powers, 1685–1715.* New York: Harper, 1951.

War of the Spanish Succession (1701–1714)

Dates	1701–1714
Location	The Netherlands, Spain, Germany, Italy, North and South America, Mediterranean Sea, Atlantic Ocean, Caribbean
Combatants	England, the Netherlands, Austria, Spain, Portugal, Savoy, and Prussia vs. France, Spain, and Bavaria
Principal Commanders	England: William III; Queen Anne; John Churchill, First Duke of Marlborough Austria: Leopold I, Prince Eugène of Savoy France: Louis XIV; Louis Josef, Duc de Vendôme; Claude Louis Hector de Villars; Camille d'Hostun, Comte de Tallard Spain: Philip V Bavaria: Duke Maximilian
Principal Battles	Vigo, Höchstädt, Blenheim, Gibraltar, Ramillies, Turin, Oudenarde, Malplaquet, Denain
Outcome	The Bourbon dynasty is confirmed on the throne of Spain, but French territorial aspirations are arrested. The English and Dutch gain commercial advantage, marking the rise of England as the preeminent European power, while Spain is no longer regarded as a major power.

Causes

The War of the Spanish Succession, fought from 1701 to 1714 not only on battlefields in Europe but across the globe, might best be described as the first world war. It was also the last of French king Louis XIV's wars of territorial expansion. Its root cause was the matter of who would inherit the Spanish throne and Spain's territories in Europe and Asia. Indeed, one of the reasons Louis XIV had been willing to conclude peace at Ryswick in 1697, ending the Nine Years' War (War of the Grand Alliance, also known as King William's War in America) that had pitted France against the Grand Alliance powers of England, Spain, the Holy Roman Empire, and the United Provinces, was the developing situation in Spain.

The prematurely senile king of Spain Charles II (r. 1665–1700) was childless. At stake was the inheritance not only of

Spain but the Spanish throne's vast holdings elsewhere in Europe as well as in the Americas and Asia. The two major contenders for the throne were the rulers of France and Austria. Louis XIV of France was the son of the elder daughter of Spanish king Philip III and was married to the elder daughter of King Felipe IV (Philip IV). Holy Roman emperor Leopold I of Habsburg was the son of the younger daughter of Felipe III (Philip III) and was married to the younger daughter of Felipe IV. Louis claimed the Spanish throne for his second grandson, Philippe, Duc d'Anjou, while Leopold claimed it for his second son, Archduke Charles.

A third possible heir existed in electoral prince Joseph Ferdinand of Bavaria. Born in 1692, he was the grandson of Leopold I although in the female line and thus a member not of the Habsburgs but of the Wittelsbach family. His mother was

Leopold's daughter by his first marriage to the younger daughter of Felipe IV. Prince Joseph would have been the lawful heir under Felipe IV's will. The maritime powers of Britain and the United Provinces (the Netherlands) favored Prince Joseph because he was unlikely to attempt to merge Spain with either Austria or France.

With the end of the War of the Grand Alliance in 1697 and with both sides exhausted and Charles II's death looming, France and England reached agreement on what became known as the First Partition Treaty. In it they recognized Joseph Ferdinand as the legitimate heir to the Spanish throne. France and the Austrian Habsburgs would then divide Spain's holdings in Italy and the Netherlands. The Spaniards, who were not consulted in these discussions, were understandably angry regarding the result. Charles agreed to name Joseph Ferdinand his heir but specified that he was to receive the entire inheritance and not just those holdings chosen by England and France.

Leopold died of smallpox in 1699, however. England and France then drew up the Second Partition Treaty whereby Archduke Charles would inherit the Spanish throne, with France receiving all of Spain's Italian possessions. Leopold, who was not consulted, was displeased, for he sought the Spanish holdings in Italy as both the easiest and most desirable to hold. In Spain there was considerable opposition to the treaty and to any plan of partition, but the leading nobles were divided between Charles and Philippe, Duc d'Anjou, the grandson of Louis XIV, as to who should inherit the empire. Following considerable bribes disbursed by Louis XIV's agents in Spain, the pro-French faction at court came out on top.

In October 1700 Charles II agreed to bequeath the entire Spanish holdings to the Duc d'Anjou. To prevent the union of France and Spain, should Philippe inherit the French throne the Spanish throne would go to his younger brother, the Duc de Berri. Next in succession was Archduke Charles.

Advisers to Louis XIV were divided. Most believed that it would be safer for France to accept the Second Partition Treaty than to risk a general European war by attempting to take the entire Spanish inheritance. But others suggested that even the Second Partition Treaty would still probably mean war with Austria, which was not a party to it. Besides, Charles II's will specified that the inheritance could not be broken. If the Duc d'Anjou were to reject the inheritance in its entirety, it would go to Charles, Duc de Berri, and if he should also refuse, it would pass to Archduke Charles. Fully aware that England and the United Provinces of the Netherlands would not join France against Austria and Spain to impose a partition treaty, Louis XIV took the fateful decision to accept the entire inheritance on behalf of his grandson. Even then Louis XIV hesitated, for this would undoubtedly mean a long and costly war.

Charles II died on November 1, 1700, and on November 24 Louis XIV accepted the entire Spanish inheritance on behalf of his grandson. This decision touched off the long-feared general European war. The new king of Spain, Philip V (Felipe V), born on December 19, 1683, and the first Bourbon monarch of Spain, was king from 1700 until his death on July 9, 1746.

Course

The War of the Spanish Succession lasted from 1701 to 1714. It pitted France, Spain, Bavaria, and Köln (Cologne) against

Austria, England, the United Provinces of the Netherlands, and most of the German states (notably Prussia and Hanover). Portugal and Sardinia, which first sided with France and Spain, subsequently switched sides.

The war began slowly, but in the spring of 1701 the French took fortresses in the Spanish Netherlands. There was little support in England for war, but when Louis XIV cut off Britain and the United Provinces from Spanish trade, this angered powerful commercial interests in both countries and fueled sentiment in England for war.

On September 7, 1701, English king William III concluded a treaty with the United Provinces and Austria against France. The three powers recognized Philip V as king of Spain but awarded Holy Roman emperor Leopold Spanish possessions in Italy. The treaty also obliged Austria to take the Spanish Netherlands, which forced it to defend this area (and thus the United Provinces) from French attack. England and the Netherlands secured a pledge that they would retain their special trading privileges with Spain. Although William died the next year, he had forged the alliance that would prevent Louis XIV from dominating Europe. William's successor, Queen Anne (r. 1702–1714), prosecuted the war vigorously.

In late May 1701, Prince Eugène of Savoy secretly moved an Austrian army from the Tirol (Tyrol, Tirolo) to Vicenza in Italy. This caught off guard French marshal Nicolas de Carnat, who had moved a French army into the defile of Rivoli, and forced the withdrawal of the French westward from the Duchy of Milan. During May–August Eugène, with forces inferior numerically to those of his enemy, outmaneuvered Carnat and forced the

French back to the Oglio, a tributary of the Po River in Lombardy. In August Louis XIV replaced Carnat with Marshal François de Neufville, Duc de Villeroi, who led his army against Eugène's army at Chiari. Although Eugène's force was smaller, his camp was well fortified, and the French suffered a rebuff with heavy losses on September 1, 1701. Both sides then went into winter quarters, the Austrians to the east of the French, blockading the French and Spanish garrison at Mantua.

On February 1, 1702, Eugène mounted a surprise attack on the French at Cremona on the Po River. Aided by confederates in the city, Eugène sent some 400 men into Cremona through a large sewer pipe during a period of several days. On the night of January 31–February 1 this force attacked, immediately followed by an assault by the principal Austrian force. Perhaps 1,000 French soldiers were killed, many as they slept, and Villeroi was taken prisoner while trying to rally his men. What seemed to be a stunning Austrian victory turned against Eugène by evening, however. With a relieving French army approaching Cremona, the Austrians withdrew. Louis XIV then replaced Villeroi with Marshal Louis Josef, Duc de Vendôme.

On May 15 England formally declared war on France and Spain, and Queen Anne appointed John Churchill, Earl of Marlborough, to command the land forces of England and the United Provinces. In June 1702 Marlborough invaded the Spanish Netherlands. Commanding 50,000 men, 12,000 of whom were English, Marlborough endeavored to bring the French under Marshal Louis François, Duc de Boufflers, to battle. The Dutch commissioners with the allied army had a veto over the use of their troops, and they refused on four separate occasions to allow Marlborough

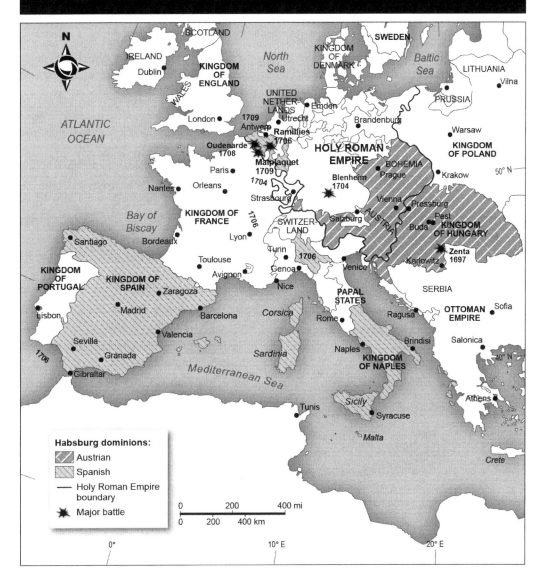

EUROPE IN 1701, THE SPANISH SUCCESSION

N

SCOTLAND

IRELAND
Dublin

KINGDOM
OF
ENGLAND

WALES

London

SWEDEN

KINGDOM
OF
DENMARK

North
Sea

Baltic
Sea

LITHUANIA
Vilna

PRUSSIA

ATLANTIC
OCEAN

1709
Antwerp

UNITED
NETHER-
LANDS

Emden

Utrecht

Ramillies
1706

Brandenburg

Warsaw

KINGDOM
OF POLAND

Oudenarde
1708

Malplaquet
1709

HOLY ROMAN
EMPIRE

BOHEMIA
Prague

Krakow

50° N

Paris

1704

Blenheim
1704

Vienna

Pressburg

Nantes

Orleans

Strasbourg

Bay of
Biscay

Santiago

KINGDOM OF
FRANCE

Bordeaux

1706

SWITZER-
LAND

Salzburg

AUSTRIA

Pest
Buda

KINGDOM
OF HUNGARY

Lyon

Turin

1706

Venice

Karlowitz

Zenta
1697

KINGDOM
OF
PORTUGAL

KINGDOM OF
SPAIN

Zaragoza

Toulouse

Avignon

Genoa

Nice

PAPAL
STATES

SERBIA

OTTOMAN
EMPIRE

Sofia

Lisbon

Madrid

Barcelona

Corsica

Rome

Ragusa

Salonica

Sevilla

Valencia

1706

Granada

Gibraltar

Sardinia

Naples

KINGDOM
OF NAPLES

Brindisi

40° N

Mediterranean Sea

Tunis

Sicily
Syracuse

Malta

Athens

Crete

Habsburg dominions:
- Austrian
- Spanish
- Holy Roman Empire boundary
- Major battle

0   200   400 mi
0   200   400 km

0°   10° E   20° E

to engage the French with the combined force. Marlborough did take a number of fortresses in the Spanish Netherlands, including Venloo (September 15), Roermond (October 7), and Liège (October 15). These successes led Queen Anne to elevate him to Duke of Marlborough.

Meanwhile Prince Louis, margrave of Baden, led an Austrian army across the Rhine at Spires, the French sending reinforcements under Marshal Nicolas de Catinat to protect Strasbourg. During July 29–September 12, Prince Louis besieged Landau (then French but today part of Germany) in the Palatinate. Taking the city, he threatened to invade Alsace, but Bavaria entered the war on the French side in September and captured Ulm. This forced Prince

Louis to withdraw back across the Rhine to defend his own country, and with 14,000 men he was defeated by French marshal Claude Louis Hector de Villars and 17,000–20,000 men at Friedlingren on October 14.

In Italy, French forces under Vendôme took Guastalla and then proceeded northward, planning to besiege Borgoforte. Learning of this, Prince Eugène abandoned his siege of Mantua and moved against the French, camped near Luzzara on the right bank of the Po. Vendôme occupied an excellent prepared position, with the Po on his left. Eugène struck on August 15 with some 25,000 men against about 30,000 French, but the French turned back several attacks by the better-trained Austrians. Although Eugène ultimately drove the French from the field, that was all he gained. The Austrians sustained some 2,500 casualties, while French losses were perhaps 4,000. Both sides faced one another until November when the French went into winter quarters, ending the 1702 campaign in Italy.

Meanwhile, the English and the Dutch had sent out a powerful fleet of some 160 warships (including 30 English and 20 Dutch ships of the line) intending to open a campaign in Spain with the seizure of the port of Cádiz. English admiral Sir George Rooke had overall command, with General James Butler, Duke of Ormonde, having charge of 4,000 ground troops. The fleet arrived at Cádiz on August 23, and with little opposition the allied troops went ashore both here and at Rota and Puerto Santa Maria. With Rooke and Ormonde quarreling, the Spanish now fully aroused, and little accomplished after a month ashore, in late September the troops were reembarked, and the fleet sailed away.

On the return voyage to England, Rooke learned of the arrival at Vigo Bay on the northwestern Spanish coast of 22 Spanish treasure ships and a French naval escort of 34 warships under Admiral François de Rousselet, Marquis de Châteaurenault. The treasure ships, with a cargo of some £4.5 million in gold and silver, the richest ever to reach Spain from the Americas, lay at anchor, with the French warships forming a protective barrier and the narrow harbor entrance guarded by a floating boom and two shore forts.

Rooke arrived off Vigo on October 22 and landed Ormonde's troops. The allies broke through the protective boom and bombarded the Spanish shore fortifications, capturing the Spanish forts and 18 French warships. The remainder were burned. Much of the gold and silver had already been offloaded or went down with the treasure ships, but the attackers secured something less than half of it.

In May 1703 Marlborough captured Bonn but failed in efforts to take Antwerp. Meanwhile, the French enjoyed success in Germany, where Villars joined with Duke Maximilian of Bavaria. Villars wanted an immediate descent on Vienna, but Maximilian rejected this.

Seeking to take advantage of the preoccupation of the Austrians, in May 1703 Hungarian nobleman Ferenc II Rákóczi led a revolt against Austrian rule. Not only the peasants but also a large number of large landowners and a majority of the nobility joined this struggle for Hungarian independence. Duke Maximilian of Bavaria was a close ally. By the end of 1704, Emperor Leopold I controlled only the westernmost regions of Hungary and some of the Saxon districts. Unfortunately for the Hungarians, however, the English-Habsburg victory in the Battle of Blenheim (also known as the Second Battle of Höchstädt) of August 1704 made the defeat of Leopold almost impossible. The price of war also became too high, and peace was concluded at Szatmár on April 30, 1711. New emperor Charles VI agreed to grant a general amnesty and promised to respect the privileges of the Hungarian nobility, including tax exemption. Rákóczi fled abroad.

In July 1703, meanwhile, Bavarian forces under Duke Maximilian occupied the Tirol, while French forces under Marshal Villars in the Danube Valley held at bay two imperial armies under Otto Ernst Leopold zu Limburg-Styrum and Prince Louis of Baden. Marshal Vendôme was slow to move his army from Italy, and Austrian forces in the Tirol, supported by the local population, drove out the Bavarians in August. Vendôme, who had been moving to the Brenner Pass, remained in Italy.

Imperial armies under Limburg-Styrum and Prince Louis marched against the French under Villars, but the latter was able to concentrate against each in turn. Villars defeated Louis's effort to secure Augsburg in the Battle of Munderkingen on July 31, 1703, then joined Maximilian of Bavaria. On September 20, Villars and Maximilian with 24,000 men met and decisively defeated Limburg-Styrum's 20,000 imperial troops near Höchstädt in Bavaria. The French and Bavarians lost only 1,000 dead or wounded, while the imperial side lost some 5,000 dead, wounded, or taken prisoner along with 37 guns and the entire supply train. Villars again urged an immediate attack on Vienna, then under pressure from the Hungarians from the east. The timorous Maximilian again refused, and following a confrontation, Villars resigned his command and returned to France, replaced by Marshal Ferdinand de Marsin.

In order to ensure effective communications with their army in Bavaria under Marsin, the French had meanwhile created a new army under Marshal Camille d'Hostun, Comte de Tallard, to operate in the Palatinate. On September 6, 1703, French marshal Sébastien le Prestre de Vauban captured Alt Breisach, the powerful imperial fortification on the right bank of the Rhine River south of Kehl. Tallard then cleared the Palatinate, recapturing Landau on November 12 and defeating the allies at Speyer on November 15.

The French now contemplated a French-Bavarian drive on Vienna for 1704, but their position was weakened by the defection to the imperial side of Savoy in October and Portugal in December. In November 1703 also, Emperor Leopold I, his southern flank now shored up by the defection of the Savoy side, recalled Prince Eugène of Savoy from Italy with the assignment of protecting Vienna against the anticipated Franco-Bavarian attack of the spring of 1704. The French campaign plans were an open secret. They called for Villeroi to contain Anglo-Dutch forces in the Netherlands while Tallard joined French and Bavarian forces under Marshal Marsin and Maximilian for a drive on Vienna. Prince Eugène and Marlborough countered with their own plan.

In late February 1704 an Anglo-Dutch expedition under Admiral Rooke landed at Lisbon with Archduke Charles, the Habsburg candidate for the Spanish throne, in an invasion of Spain. Rooke was then to attack Toulon, the major French naval base on the Mediterranean, and aid Huguenot rebels in southern France. At the same time, Marlborough planned to lead forces south from the Netherlands and achieve a concentration of Anglo-Dutch forces with those of Prince Eugène to confront the French in the Danube Valley. The allied goal here was to prevent the

French-Bavarian thrust against Vienna, drive the French from Germany, and force Bavaria from the war.

In April 1704 French marshal Marsin and Duke Maximilian of Bavaria commanded some 55,000 men concentrated around Ulm. Tallard, preparing to move east, had 30,000 men at Strasbourg, and Villeroi commanded 46,000 men confronting Marlborough in the Spanish Netherlands. Marlborough assumed (correctly, as it turned out) that Villeroi would be drawn south after him and away from the Netherlands. Marlborough had some 70,000 men, Prince Eugène commanded 10,000 men south of Ulm, and the Austrians had perhaps 30,000 men defending Vienna. Prince Louis of Baden had 30,000 men on the Rhine at Stollhofen.

Leaving some 50,000 men to defend the Netherlands, Marlborough set out on May 19, 1704, without informing the Dutch government (which most certainly would not have agreed) and marched southward with 21,000 men, approximately 14,000 of them British troops. This force was augmented by German soldiers as it moved south. In early June, Marlborough met with Prince Eugène and Prince Louis of Baden. Marlborough and Louis continued their march south toward Donauwörth, while Eugène returned to Stollhofen to prevent French forces under Villeroi (now at Strasbourg and shadowing Marlborough's movements in the anticipation that he might turn west for a campaign on the Moselle) and those under Marshal Tallard (now at Landau) from reinforcing French and Bavarian forces under Marsin and Maximilian.

Marlborough approached the Danube crossing point at Donauwörth and on July 2 mounted an attack on French forces under Marsin defending the Schellenberg, a hill commanding Donauwörth. Catching the French by surprise but sustaining heavy casualties, Marlborough took the hill and the French pulled back, allowing him to secure Donauwörth without a siege and cross the Danube uncontested.

Marsin and Duke Maximilian of Bavaria marched to Augsburg to prevent a move by Marlborough against Munich, but they refused battle until they could be reinforced, allowing Marlborough and Prince Louis time to lay waste to much of western Bavaria. On July 29 Marshal Tallard, who had succeeded in eluding blocking imperial forces, moved east and reached Ulm, then joined Marsin and Maximilian south of the Danube. Prince Eugène and 20,000 men meanwhile marched to link up with Marlborough. Not knowing where Eugène had gone, Marshall Villeroi elected to remain in the vicinity of Strasbourg to protect against a possible allied invasion of Alsace. With a major confrontation now near, Marlborough, who had a low military regard for Prince Louis, detached him and a small force to besiege Ingolstadt while Marlborough prepared with the rest of his force to join Eugène.

Matters in southern Germany now came to a head. Informed of the arrival of Prince Eugène and his 20,000-man army near Donauwörth just north of the Danube, Tallard marched against him. Eugène at once informed Marlborough and called on him to come up as soon as possible. The two allied armies met at Donauwörth on August 12.

Rather than stand on the defensive, Eugène and Marlborough decided to attack the French and Bavarians under Tallard. Beginning at 2:00 a.m. on August 13, Marlborough and Eugène moved with their combined force of some 52,000 men and 60 guns from Donauwörth five miles to the southeast to attack the combined Franco-Bavarian force of 56,000 men with 90 guns situated on the west bank of the Danube. Tallard was caught by surprise, having not believed that the allies with a presumed force far inferior in numbers to his own would attack him. The French and Bavarians were camped just across the Nebel River, a small tributary of the Danube.

Prince Eugène commanded the allied right against the Bavarians, while Marlborough had charge of the allied left against the French. Marlborough had the larger force and was to make the major effort while Eugène fixed the Bavarians (who outnumbered his own force three to two) in place with an aggressive holding attack.

The battle commenced about 7:00 a.m. on August 13, 1704, when Marlborough opened artillery fire on the surprised French, but a delay in Eugène's arrival until about 12:30 allowed the French and Bavarians time to deploy. The extreme right flank of the French infantry was at the village of Blenheim on the banks of the Danube. The wide center of the allied French-Bavarian line was along a ridgeline overlooking the Nebel. It then extended northwest about two miles to the village of Oberglau.

On Eugène's arrival, both he and Marlborough's men attacked simultaneously. Marlborough sent 10,000 infantry forward across the Nebel against Blenheim, while Eugène attacked at Oberglau and to the northwest. The French repulsed the attack on Blenheim with heavy losses. Tallard then committed his reserves to the threatened flanks, enabling them to turn back a second attack on Blenheim by Marlborough, again with heavy losses for the attackers.

With 11,000 French now relatively isolated on the flank at Blenheim, Marlborough made his major effort in the center of the line with his remaining infantry and cavalry. Crossing the Nebel, these forces came under a French cavalry attack but repulsed it. A second French cavalry attack, had it been accompanied by infantry and artillery, might have won the battle, but Tallard did not order it. Thanks to the timely intervention of Eugène's cavalry, Marlborough was able to repulse the French cavalry alone that struck the right flank of his advancing troops.

Marlborough then re-formed his forces in the center of the line and again ordered them forward. At 5:30 his cavalry broke through the center of the French line, causing the Bavarian right wing to withdraw back to the north on the remainder of the Bavarian army. Marlborough's infantry then poured into the gap and, swinging left, cut off the French at Blenheim and pursued the remaining fleeing French troops, hundreds of whom drowned trying to cross the Danube. Tallard and two of his generals were among the many prisoners. After several failed attempts to break free, the French at Blenheim also surrendered. The Bavarians were, however, able to retreat in good order from their numerically inferior foe.

The Battle of Blenheim resulted in allied losses of 4,500 killed and 7,500 wounded, while the French and Bavarians sustained 18,000 killed, wounded, or drowned and 13,000 taken prisoner. This battle was the most important of the war; it shattered French military prestige and completely reversed the military balance. The battle cemented the Anglo-British-Austrian alliance against France, saved Vienna from attack, and removed Bavaria from the war. Duke Maximilian was forced to flee his country, which was annexed by Emperor Leopold I. Marlborough now returned to the Netherlands, while Prince Eugène departed for Italy.

On July 31, 1704, meanwhile, a powerful Anglo-Dutch fleet under Admiral Rooke landed some 1,800 troops at Algeciras, Spain, for an attack on Gibraltar, then held by only some 250 men. Gibraltar surrendered on August 4. The only major fleet engagement of the war, the Battle of Vélez-Málaga, occurred in the Mediterranean on August 24 about 80 miles northeast of Gibraltar. It was fought between an Anglo-Dutch fleet commanded by Rooke, with 53 ships of the line and 13 other ships, and a French fleet under Admiral Louis Alexandre de Bourbon, Comte de Toulouse, with 50 ships of the line and 43 other ships, who had the mission of recapturing Gibraltar. No ships were lost in the engagement, but the English and Dutch suffered some 787 killed and 1,931 wounded. The French lost 1,585 killed (including 3 admirals) and about the same number wounded. The battle was an allied strategic victory, for they had blunted this French effort to recapture Gibraltar.

The French did not give up trying to retake Gibraltar. During August 1704–March 1705, French marshal René de Froulay, Comte de Tessé, led French and Spanish ground forces in an unsuccessful siege of Gibraltar. Following the French defeat at sea in the Battle of Marbella of March 10, 1705, in which the French lost three ships captured and two driven ashore and burned, Tessé ended the siege, however.

The year 1705 saw stalemate on the major fighting fronts of the Netherlands, the Rhine, and Italy. In Spain, allied forces landed at Barcelona in late August, capturing that city on October 9. French and Spanish troops were forced to break off a countersiege in April 1706 to meet an allied invasion from Portugal under

Portuguese general Marquês des Minas with Portuguese and English forces. Heavily committed elsewhere, the French were unable to reinforce, and allied troops under Henri de Massue, Earl of Galway (a Huguenot who had left France following the revocation of the Edict of Nantes and was now in English employ), captured Madrid on June 27, 1706. The allies then proclaimed Habsburg claimant Archduke Charles as king of Spain.

In the long run this worked to the advantage of Bourbon king of Spain Philip V, however, for the Portuguese and Protestant invasion rallied the Spanish people. King Philip and the Duke of Berwick (the illegitimate son of James II of England, now in French employ) and their Franco-Spanish forces were thus able to recover Madrid on October 4. The Portuguese forces returned to their own country, while Charles and the other allied troops withdrew into Valencia.

Marlborough meanwhile was enjoying success in the Netherlands. In May 1706 French marshal Villeroi, believing correctly that Marlborough intended to seize Namur in the Spanish Netherlands, moved there with about 60,000 men but was intercepted north of Namur at Ramillies by Marlborough's slightly more numerous allied force of about 62,000 British, Dutch, and Danish troops. The French took up position on high ground and partially entrenched. Their lines, however, were dangerously overextended.

The Battle of Ramillies was joined on May 23. Marlborough feinted an attack on the French left, causing Villeroi to shift his reserves and pull some units from his right wing, whereupon Marlborough launched his main attack on this weakened French sector. Although the French on the right flank fought hard, they were outnumbered and were soon overwhelmed.

Sensing that the entire French line was near collapse, Marlborough ordered a general advance, and under aggressive action by Danish cavalry, the French fled in great disorder. The subsequent aggressive allied pursuit ended some 20 miles from Louvain (Leuven). Total French casualties in the battle were some 13,000 killed or wounded along with 6,000 captured. Allied losses were only 1,066 dead and 3,633 wounded.

The Battle of Ramillies had major consequences, for it allowed the allied forces to overrun the Spanish Netherlands. During June–October, Marlborough captured a dozen important fortresses in the Netherlands and northeastern France. These included Louvain (May 25), Ghent (May 31), Odenard (June 3), Antwerp (June 6), Ostend (July 4), Dunkerque (Dunkirk, July 6), Menin (August 22), and Dendermonde (September 5). Ath, under siege from September 16, surrendered on October 2. The allies also captured some 14,000 French soldiers in these operations and now controlled most of the Spanish Netherlands in the name of Austrian archduke Charles. These operations led Louis XIV to recall Vendôme, his best general, from Italy to replace Villeroi and also forced the reallocation of French assets to the Netherlands front, rendering circumstances easier in Italy for Prince Eugène. The French king also put out tentative peace feelers.

On the Italian front in the spring of 1706, Vendôme, with 100,000 men against 70,000 allied troops (30,000 Savoyards and 40,000 Austrians), divided his army and on the night of April 18–19 launched a surprise attack on the Austrians in the area between Montichiari and Calcinato. In this Battle of Calcinato, Vendôme routed the imperial army, inflicting casualties of 3,000–6,000 men and causing the Austrians to withdrew

east of the Adige River. On April 22 Prince Eugène of Savoy arrived from Vienna and assumed command, halting the withdrawal at the Adige and maneuvering against Vendôme. On May 22, meanwhile, French marshal Louis d'Aubusson de la Feuillade laid siege to Turin, the capital of Savoy.

The Austrians reinforced Prince Eugène along the Adige, bringing his strength up to about the equal of Vendôme, now with some 40,000 men. Answering appeals from ruler of Savoy Duke Victor Amadeus II to relieve the Siege of Turin, Eugène fixed the French in place with 18,000 men and then marched south with the remainder around the French right, threatening Vendôme's lines of communication and obliging him to fall back, beginning on July 13. Having been recalled by Louis XIV, Vendôme departed on July 18. Young Philippe II, Duc d'Orléans, succeeded him in command, assisted by Marshal Marsin.

Eugène, in a highly unorthodox move, now suddenly moved westward, abandoning his lines of communication and living off the land. He captured Parma on August 15 and affected a juncture with Duke Victor Amadeus II on August 31. The allies now had some 36,000 men along with some 6,000 Savoyards east of Turin and perhaps 15,000 within Turin itself. These 57,000 allied troops faced some 80,000 French troops involved in operations against Turin holding strong lines of circumvallation against Savoyard forces east of the city, along with 20,000 in various fortresses in northern Italy. Nonetheless, Eugène decided to attack.

Eugène struck on September 7, selecting a relatively isolated part of the French line of contravallation between the Dura and Stura Rivers, two tributaries of the Po. The attacking Savoyard and Austrian troops enjoyed initial success, but the Duc d'Orléans was able to reinforce and halt the incursion.

Eugène then re-formed and launched a second attack, this one supported by a sortie of Savoyard troops from within Turin. Caught between the two attacking forces, the French collapsed. Orléans was wounded, but his second-in-command, Marshal Marsin, mortally wounded, was taken prisoner. In the course of its precipitate flight, the French army abandoned all its equipment, supplies, and 100 pieces of artillery. In the debacle the French suffered some 2,000 killed, 1,200 wounded, and 6,000 taken prisoner. The allies sustained only 950 killed and 2,500 wounded. The arrogant and largely incompetent Marshal Feuillade, who had been directing the siege, was made the scapegoat.

The Turin Campaign, perhaps the most brilliant of the war, was decisive as far as Italy was concerned. During September–December 1706 Eugène's forces drove the French from Italy entirely, ending fighting on that front for the remainder of the war.

In Spain in the spring of 1707, the Earl of Galway led an allied army of 22,000 Portuguese, British, and Dutch troops from Valencia toward Madrid. They were met on April 25 at Almansa by a Franco-Spanish army of some 25,000 men commanded by the Duke of Berwick, which inflicted a decisive defeat on Galway. Almansa is sometimes noted as the only battle between the English and French in which the English army was commanded by a Frenchman and the French army was led by an Englishman. The Spanish and French forces suffered some 3,500 killed or wounded, while the allies sustained 5,000 dead or wounded, along with 12,000 captured.

The destruction of the principal pro-Habsburg army in Spain allowed Bourbon king Philip V to take the initiative and recover Valencia. Both sides then went into winter quarters. Soon support for Archduke Charles, the Habsburg claimant to the throne, was limited to Catalonia and the Balearic Islands. Philip's government also gained increasing support from the Spanish people for its efficiency and effective administration.

In July and August 1707, Eugène invaded southern France from northern Italy in conjunction with an English fleet, but this attempt to capture Toulon was repulsed. In May 1708 Vendôme seized the initiative in Flanders, capturing both Ghent (July 4) and Bruges (July 5). On July 11, however, Marlborough and Eugène met the French in the Battle of Oudenarde with about 100,000 men on each side. Thanks to disastrous decisions by the Duc de Burgundy overruling Marshal Vendôme, the French were driven from the field. Allied losses were some 2,000 dead and 5,000 wounded, while the French suffered 4,000 dead, 2,000 wounded, 9,000 taken prisoner, and 3,000 missing. Vendôme was able to rally the retreating French forces and indeed repulse the pursuing allied troops at Ghent, ensuring French control of western Flanders. Although Louis removed his grandson from command, the damage had been done. The allies took Lille in December. Refusing to go into winter quarters, in January 1709 Marlborough captured Ghent and Bruges.

With these defeats and a hard winter that killed large numbers of livestock and destroyed the spring wheat crop, in April 1709 Louis XIV opened negotiations at The Hague. Confident of total victory, the allies insisted on harsh terms, demanding that Louis surrender Spain and all its territories to Archduke Charles as well as all border fortresses in the Spanish

Netherlands to the Dutch and that France yield much of Alsace and the city of Strasbourg.

Louis was willing to accept these terms, but the allies also demanded that he employ the French Army to expel his grandson Philip V from Spain. The last was too much, and Louis appealed directly to the French people who, convinced that the war was now a struggle for national survival, united behind the war effort.

The period of negotiations had given France time to regroup. Several months of maneuvering in the Spanish Netherlands followed, during which the allies captured Tournai and besieged Mons. After taking Mons, Marlborough and Eugène planned to invade France, drive on Paris, and end the war.

Ordered to hold Mons, Villars concentrated 90,000 men at Malplaquet, threatening the siege of Mons and bringing on the largest battle of the war. Marlborough and Eugène left about 20,000 men to continue the siege and advanced with some 90,000 troops against Villars. As at Blenheim and Oudenarde, Marlborough commanded the allied left and Eugène the right. They planned for holding attacks by each flank, with the main attack to be launched by Marlborough against the French center once the French reserves were committed to shore up the flanks hit earlier. This was the first time Marlborough and Eugène had faced Villars, a general equal in ability to themselves.

At Malplaquet both sides fought well. The French were dug in, but the strength of the initial allied flanking attacks forced Villars to weaken his center, mainly to meet Eugène's attack on the French left. Twice wounded, Eugène refused to retire. Villars was also badly wounded while personally leading a French counterattack

and was forced to yield command to his equally able subordinate, Boufflers.

In early afternoon Marlborough launched his tried-and-true infantry-cavalry attack against the French center and indeed managed to break through. In accordance with Villars's plan, however, Boufflers committed his last reserves and counterattacked to reestablish the French line. Marlborough responded by committing his remaining reserves, again attacking the French center and forcing Boufflers to order a general retirement, which the French carried out in good order. The allies were unable to pursue.

Casualty figures for the battle vary widely, but there was no mistaking the fact that the allies had lost many more men than the defending French. French casualties numbered between 11,000 and 15,000 men, while the allies lost 18,000 to 24,000 men. Although counted as an allied victory, the battle proved costly to them in many ways. In the short run, the allies were able to intensify their siege of Mons, which surrendered to them on October 20. The Battle of Malplaquet, however, rendered it impossible for the allies to continue with their planned invasion of France. Indeed, during the winter of 1709–1710 the French constructed formidable defenses along their northwestern frontier.

In Spain, Philip V rejected efforts to get him to give up his kingdom for limited compensation in Italy. Imperial forces under Guido Starhemberg defeated him at Almenara on July 27, 1710, and at Saragossa (Zaragoza) on August 20. Philip V abandoned Madrid, and Archduke Charles entered the capital on September 28. But imperial forces lacked the numbers to pacify Spain, the country's population was largely hostile, and Louis XIV aided his grandson by dispatching Vendôme there.

In November 1710 the allies evacuated Madrid and withdrew toward Catalonia. Vendôme forced the English under James Stanhope to surrender at Brihuega (December 9). While Starhemberg defeated Vendôme at Villaviciosa (December 10), he was forced to continue his withdrawal to Barcelona.

Philip V was finally secure as king of Spain when Charles departed that country in April 1711 to become Holy Roman emperor on the death of his older brother Joseph I. Since a Habsburg occupying both the imperial and Spanish thrones would upset the European balance of power and be unacceptable to the major European states, this brought additional pressure for a negotiated settlement.

The alliance against France and Spain now began to crumble, aided by Marlborough's departure. In Britain, the close friendship between Queen Anne and Sarah Churchill, Duchess of Marlborough, came to an end and with it the duke's political influence. At the same time, the Whig ministry that supported the war was replaced by the Tories, who opposed it. Blamed for the heavy casualties at Malplaquet and falsely charged with padding his accounts, Marlborough was removed from his command in December 1711, bringing to a close his brilliant military career. In effect the Tories ended British participation in the war.

Peace negotiations commenced in earnest at Utrecht. Eugène returned to the Spanish Netherlands but was unable to persuade the Dutch to agree to offensive action. Nonetheless, in May 1712 he crossed the Scheldt hoping to do battle with Villars. But with English forces in his army under strict orders not to fight, Eugène was forced to retire. On July 24, Villars attacked and soundly defeated part of his army at Denain, and Eugène withdrew across the Scheldt. Villars's recapture of a number of fortifications strengthened the French position in the peace negotiations.

Holy Roman emperor Charles VI continued the war against France, but he failed to adequately supply Eugène in the Spanish Netherlands, who was heavily outnumbered by the French. After Villars captured Landau and Freiburg, Charles agreed to peace.

The War of the Spanish Succession also saw fighting in the Caribbean and in South America, but this was largely limited to indecisive naval actions. In September 1711 French forces briefly seized Rio de Janeiro from the Portuguese, while the war marked the beginning of the struggle between France and Britain for control of the Indian subcontinent.

The fighting in America was known by English colonists as Queen Anne's War. In late 1702 Governor James Moore of Carolina led an unsuccessful expedition to take St. Augustine from the Spanish. Colonial and allied Native American raids into northern Florida followed, as did numerous raids along the northeastern frontier between New England and Canada, many by Abenaki native allies of the French against New England. The English retaliated with operations in Acadia. In 1704 and 1707 the English tried and failed to take Port Royal, from which French privateers were operating against New England shipping and fishing. In October 1710, New England colonists and English warships captured Port Royal. In 1711, a major operation to take Quebec involving the largest armed force of the English North American colonies turned back when a number of its ships struck rocks and sank in foggy conditions in the St. Lawrence River.

After a dozen years of war, on April 11, 1713, all of the principal warring powers except Austria, which continued to fight against France, concluded peace at Utrecht in the Netherlands. The Peace of Utrecht was actually a series of separate treaties among the various powers.

Under the peace terms, French king Louis XIV secured his principal war aim in that his grandson was confirmed as ruler of Spain and its colonies as Philip V. The British were major winners in the war, however. Great Britain (the Act of Union of England and Scotland during the war on May 1, 1707, had established the United Kingdom of Great Britain) secured recognition by France of the Protestant succession in England as well as a guarantee that the thrones of France and Spain would never be united. France also ceded to Britain important possessions in the New World, including Newfoundland, Nova Scotia (Acadia), and Hudson Bay. France, however, retained New France (Quebec). Spain ceded Gibraltar and the island of Minorca to Britain, and Britain also secured important trading concessions in the Asiento, the contract to supply the Spanish colonies with African slaves as well as give them the right to send one 500-ton ship per year with British-manufactured goods.

The United Provinces of the Netherlands secured the Spanish Netherlands, which was then handed over to the Austrians with the conclusion of a barrier treaty concerning the French frontier fortresses from Furnes to Namur, which the Dutch were to be allowed to garrison. The city of Lille was returned to France, and the fortifications of Dunkerque were to be demolished.

The duchy of Savoy received the island of Sicily as a kingdom and a slight favorable modification in its Italian border. In return for renouncing all claims to the throne of Spain, the kingdom secured the right of inheritance in the event that the Bourbon line should die out. Prussia also received recognition as a kingdom and secured Neuchâtel and part of Guelders. Portugal gained advantage from a change in the boundaries in South America.

Reservations in the peace, as Austria was not a participant, included the transfer to the emperor of Spain's appendages of the Spanish Netherlands, Milan, Naples, and Sardinia but not Sicily. The empire was also to be assured of the status quo of the Treaty of Ryswick.

Holy Roman emperor Charles VI continued the war against France, but his principal general, Prince Eugène of Savoy commanding in the Spanish Netherlands, was poorly supplied. He had available only some 60,000 men against French marshal Claude Louis Hector de Villars with 120,000 men. Even the capable Eugène could not overcome such odds.

French marshal Villars captured Landau and Freiburg, after which Charles agreed to peace with France in his own name in the Treaty of Rastatt (Rastadt) of March 7, 1714, and in the name of the empire in the Treaty of Baden in Switzerland on September 7, 1714. Under the terms of these treaties, Charles took possession of the Spanish Netherlands (now known as the Austrian Netherlands) as provided in the 1713 Treaty of Utrecht, but France retained Landau. Charles also secured Naples, Sardinia, and Milan. The electors of Bavaria and Cologne, who had been under the ban of the empire, were reinstated in their lands and titles. The peace settlement of 1713–1714 did not include any treaty between Spain and the emperor, as Charles VI refused to recognize Philip V as king of Spain.

Significance

With these settlements, warfare to contain French hegemony in Europe came to a close for the time being. In the so-called Family Compact France and Spain aligned their policies in the decades to come, but Spain, stripped of its possessions in the Netherlands and Italy, was no longer regarded as a major European power.

Further Reading

Chandler, David. *The Art of Warfare in the Age of Marlborough*. New York: Hippocrene Books, 1976.

Chandler, David. *Marlborough as Military Commander*. 1973; reprint, New York: Penguin, 2000.

Crouse, Nellis M. *The French Struggle for the West Indies, 1665–1713*. New York: Columbia University Press, 1943.

Frey, Linda, and Marsha Frey. *The Treaties of the War of the Spanish Succession: An Historical Critical Dictionary*. Westport, CT: Greenwood, 1995.

Hattendorf, John. *England in the War of the Spanish Succession*. New York: Garland, 1987.

Jongste, Jan A. F. de, and Augustuus J. Veenendaal Jr. *Anthonie Heinsius and the Dutch Republic 1688–1720: Politics, War, and Finance*. The Hague: Institute of Netherlands History, 2002.

Lynn, John. *The Wars of Louis XIV, 1667–1714*. New York: Longman, 1999.

Mckay, Derek. *The Rise of the Great Powers, 1648–1815*. New York: Longman, 1983.

Ostwald, James. *Vauban Under Siege: Engineering Efficiency and Martial Vigor in the War of the Spanish Succession*. Boston: Brill Academic Publishers, 2006.

Symcox, Geoffrey. *War, Diplomacy, and Imperialism, 1618–1763*. New York: Harper Torchbooks, 1973.

Wolf, John B. *The Emergence of the Great Powers, 1685–1715*. New York: Harper and Row, 1962.

War of the Austrian Succession (1740–1748)

Dates	1740–1748
Location	Europe, North America, India
Combatants	Austria, England, Piedmont-Sardinia, Saxony, and the United Provinces vs. Prussia, Sweden, France, Spain, and Bavaria
Principal Commanders	Austria: Maria Theresa, Prince Charles Alexander of Lorraine Prussia: Frederick II France: Louis XV; Maurice, Comte de Saxe
Principal Battles	Mollwitz, Chotusitz, Fontenoy, Hohenfriedberg, Soor, Louisbourg
Outcome	Prussia secures Silesia, marking its arrival as a major European power.

Causes

In 1740, the House of Habsburg had recovered from the humiliation in the Peace of Westphalia of 1648 ending the Thirty Years' War. It had the Austrian Netherlands (present-day Belgium) and substantial holdings in Italy, but its chief power base was the central Danube region, where its lands included not only Austria but also Hungary and Bohemia. An Austrian Habsburg was also Holy Roman emperor as Charles VI (r. 1711–1740).

But Charles had no male heir. This was the same problem that had confronted that Spanish branch of the Habsburgs and that had prompted the War of the Spanish Succession (1701–1714) and the end of Habsburg rule in Spain. Although the Salic Law of Succession prevented a woman from heading the Holy Roman Empire, Charles hoped to secure guarantees that his daughter Maria Theresa could rule the House of Austria's territories. Toward that end, Charles drew up the Pragmatic Sanction in 1713. Eventually he was able to secure pledges from all member states of the empire that they would abide by it. He also won the support by treaty of the major European powers, including Britain and Prussia.

The year 1740 saw two new rulers in Europe. Prussian king Frederick William I died on May 31, 1740, and was succeeded by his 28-year-old son, Frederick II (r. 1749–1786). Thanks to his father's energetic efforts, Frederick inherited the fourth-largest and most efficient army in Europe as well as a full treasury. Because Frederick was interested in the arts, European observers assumed that he would end the military, autocratic rule of his father. In this they were sadly mistaken, for Frederick was also a great militarist and was determined to challenge Austria for leadership in the Germanies, expand Prussia's territory, and make Prussia a Great Power in Europe.

The second change occurred in the Habsburg lands with Charles VI's death on October 20. Twenty-three-year-old Archduchess Maria Theresa now inherited the Austrian holdings. There were other rulers who coveted the Habsburg lands—including elector of Bavaria Duke Charles Albert, king of Spain Philip V, and king of Poland and elector of Saxony Augustus III. While they held back, Prussian king Frederick II had no hesitation. Although Frederick recognized Maria Theresa's accession to the Austrian throne and offered Prussian military assistance against other claimants, he also announced that Prussia would occupy Silesia pending settlement of an old Brandenburg claim to that rich province. Maria Theresa rejected this proposal, and on December 16, 1740, the Prussian army invaded Silesia, then part of Bohemia. Frederick did not shrink from the use of force or the immorality of the action. This began what is known in German history as the First Silesian War (1740–1742), which became part of the larger War of the Austrian Succession (1740–1748). It also initiated what would turn out to be a 120-year struggle between Prussia and Austria over which power would dominate the Germanies, not to be resolved until the Battle of Königgrätz (Sadowa) in 1866.

Frederick's bold gamble, a clear act of aggression undertaken without declaration of war, offered the promise of doubling Prussia's population (to 6 million people) and providing valuable natural resources and industry. Maria Theresa, unschooled in the art of government by her father and with Austria weak militarily, appealed to the other powers that had guaranteed the Pragmatic Sanction but initially received no support. Guided by principle, she was determined to contest Frederick's action. She knew the value of Silesia, the loss of which would sharply diminish the German portion of the Habsburg holdings and increase the influence of the Slavic lands.

Course

During December 1740–February 1741, Frederick consolidated Prussian control of Silesia, overrunning all that province except for some Austrian-held garrison towns. Meanwhile, Austrian field marshal Wilhelm Reinhard Count von Neipperg assembled an army in Bohemia. Catching much of Frederick's army still in winter quarters, Neipperg entered Silesia and retook most of it in March and April.

The two armies came together on April 10, 1741, at Mollwitz (now Małujowice, Poland) near the Oder River. Neipperg had 16,600 men, and Frederick had 23,400. Morning fog allowed Frederick and Prussian field marshal Count Kurt Christoph von Schwerin to advance their forces close to the Austrians. Instead of ordering an immediate attack on the surprised Austrians, who now had to deploy, the inexperienced Frederick formed in line of battle, significantly reducing his numerical advantage.

The Austrian cavalry forced in the Prussian right wing and drove the Prussian cavalry from the field. Schwerin persuaded Frederick to flee (perhaps so he could have a free hand to win the battle, although this brought the lifelong enmity of Frederick). Meanwhile, the death of the Austrian cavalry commander threw his men into confusion. Schwerin rallied the disciplined and well-trained Prussian infantry, halted the Austrian cavalry, and drove the Austrian infantry from the field. The fighting claimed 3,900 dead or wounded and 700 captured; the Austrians sustained 2,500 dead or wounded and 1,500 captured.

The Battle of Mollwitz again gave Frederick possession of Silesia. It also led to a widened war, as Frederick's success encouraged Duke Charles Albert of Bavaria. Hoping to secure the imperial crown for himself, Charles Albert sent his army into Bohemia. France, allied with Bavaria, also entered the war. The French hoped to secure the Austrian Netherlands (present-day Belgium). French king Louis XV dispatched Marshal François Marie, Comte de Broglie, and an army into southern Germany to support the Bavarians. In July 1741 the Bavarians captured Passau in Upper Austria, but the French and Bavarians rejected suggestions by Frederick for a joint attack on Vienna.

Saxony and Savoy also joined the struggle against Austria. Britain and the Netherlands supported Maria Theresa, not because of Prussia's seizure of Silesia but in order to check growing French power in Europe. Britain and the Netherlands both extended financial subsidies to the Austrians.

Sweden allied with Prussia and, seeking to gain back some of its Baltic territories lost in the Great Northern War, attacked Russia, which upheld the Pragmatic Sanction. The Russo-Swedish War was easily dealt with. Swedish timing could not have been worse. The Swedish Army was small, and its galley fleet was still building. The Russians had also concluded their war with the Ottoman Empire in 1739, and their entire army was now free to act against Sweden.

The fighting took place in Finland. The Swedes threatened St. Petersburg, setting the stage for a coup d'état against the pro-Austrian Russian regime of Anna Leopoldovna. The coup of December 6, 1740, brought Elizabeth I to the Russian throne, but she reneged on her pledge to return the Baltic provinces to Sweden, and Russia continued its support of Austria.

The Russians ended the threat to St. Petersburg with a victory at Lappeenranta on September 3, 1741. Then in the spring of 1742, they invaded Finland. In August after a string of smaller victories,

WAR OF AUSTRIAN SUCCESSION, 1740 – 1748

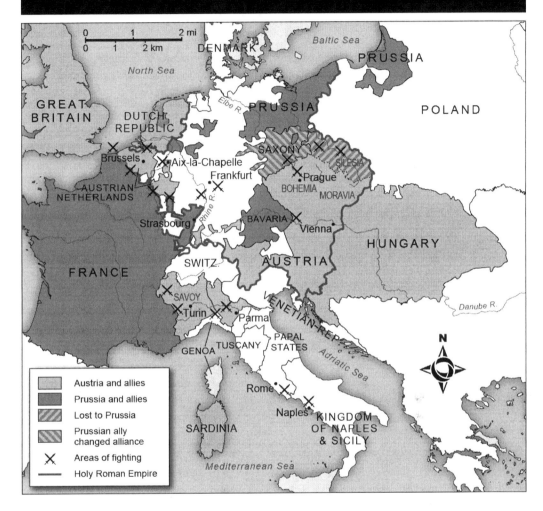

Russian field marshal Peter Lacy encircled the Swedish army near Helsinki and forced it to surrender on September 4. This ended fighting on land. With the Russian fleet approaching Umeå and Denmark threatening to enter the war against Sweden, Sweden concluded peace at Åbo on August 7, 1743. Sweden ceded to Russia a strip of Finland northwest of St. Petersburg with the towns of Lappeenranta (Villmanstrand) and Hamina.

On October 9, 1741, meanwhile, Maria Theresa concluded with Frederick the secret Truce of Klein Schnellendorf. This understanding ceded Silesia to Frederick, provided he would not mount further operations against the Austrians. The truce allowed the Austrians to concentrate against the Bavarians and French.

Austrian commander in Silesia Field Marshal Wilhelm Reinhard, Count von Neipperg, then withdrew his army from

Silesia and joined the fighting in Bohemia, where French and Bavarian armies had invaded with the objective of capturing Prague (Praha). While an army under Maria Theresa's consort, Grand Duke Francis of Lorraine, ineptly opposed the allied invasion, she traveled to Budapest. There as queen of Hungary, she rallied the Hungarian nobles, who pledged substantial manpower in return for political concessions.

While the principal Austrian army, commanded by Field Marshal Ludwig Andreas von Khevenhüller, Count von Aichelberg-Frankenburg, prepared to invade Bavaria, a second Austrian force under Field Marshal Prince Charles Albert of Lorraine (younger brother of Francis and thus brother-in-law of Maria Theresa) prepared to assist Bohemia. With the Austrians still marshaling their forces, the allies captured Prague on November 26, then consolidated their control over western and central Bohemia. Charles Albert of Bavaria was crowned king of Bohemia on December 19.

That December also, fighting resumed in Silesia. Believing Austria now sufficiently militarily strong to recover Silesia and also defeat the French and Bavarians, Maria Theresa revealed the terms of the truce with Prussia to embarrass Frederick with his allies. Frederick then dispatched Field Marshal Count Kurt Christoph von Schwerin to Bohemia to cooperate with the allies, and Frederick soon followed.

During 1741–1743 Spanish and Neapolitan forces failed in their effort to conquer the Austrian duchy of Milan. In 1742 the Kingdom of Sardinia joined the Austrian side, while at the same time a British amphibious threat forced Neapolitan troops to abandon operations against Milan and return home.

In January 1742 Maria Theresa ordered her principal field army, under Aichelberg-Frankenburg, into Bavaria. On January 24, Charles Albert of Bavaria was crowned Holy Roman emperor as Charles VII (r. 1742–1744), the first time in 300 years that the imperial dignity was held by a non-Habsburg. That very day, however, the Austrians captured his capital of Munich.

Austrian success in Bavaria forced Charles Albert to cancel plans for a joint operation with the French and Prussians in Bohemia. With only relatively weak French forces remaining in the vicinity of Prague, Austrian field marshal Prince Charles Alexander of Lorraine left a small covering force to watch the French there and moved the bulk of his army against Prussian forces under Frederick II ravaging Moravia. This threat to his lines of communication and a Hungarian invasion of Silesia forced Frederick to withdraw to Silesia. The Austrians pursued, and the two armies came together at Chotusitz (Chotusice) in Bohemia on May 17, 1742.

The Austrians had about 24,000 men, the Prussians perhaps 28,000. The battle was a bloody one and ended with an Austrian withdrawal in good order and the Prussians in no condition to pursue. The Austrians lost about 1,000 killed and 6,000 wounded, the Prussians some 1,000 killed and 4,000 wounded. Meanwhile, French forces in Bavaria took advantage of the departure of most of the Austrian forces to defeat the remaining weak covering force near Prague at Sahay on May 25.

Under heavy pressure from the British government, which demanded that she concentrate her resources against France, Maria Theresa came to terms with Frederick. In the Treaty of Breslau of June 11, 1742, that ended the First Silesian War, she agreed to the cession to Prussia of almost all Silesia, although fully expecting this to be temporary. A Habsburg army under Prince Charles Alexander of Lorraine then laid siege to French forces occupying Prague.

Although Frederick's aggression had succeeded and Silesia was now Prussian, it was also clear that Austria was much stronger than its opponents had assumed. The war continued another six years, but these fundamental facts held true.

Austria's military situation improved in 1743. The Pragmatic Army of British, Hanoverian, Dutch, and Austrian troops formed in the Austrian Netherlands. Commanded by British king George II, also elector and ruler of Hanover, this army of some 40,000 men advanced up the Rhine. In the Battle of Dettingen near the Main River on June 27, 1743, the Pragmatic Army defeated a French force of 30,000 men under Marshal Adrien-Maurice, third Duc de Noailles. The battle is noteworthy in being the last commanded by an English king. George II actually led the key counterattack in person. In the fighting the allies suffered some 2,500 casualties, the French perhaps 4,000. A new Austrian invasion of Bavaria swept the French from that state.

With English Jacobite leaders formally requesting that France mount an invasion to restore the Stuarts to the British throne, in November 1743 Louis XV authorized an invasion for February 1744 from the port of Dunkerque, hopefully catching the English by surprise and bringing Charles Edward Stuart (known as the "Young Pretender" and "Bonnie Prince Charlie") to power.

The French sent out from Brest 19 ships of the line under Admiral Jacques, Comte de Roquefeuil, to secure the channel. The British Channel Fleet under admiral Sir John Norris was closing on the French when on February 24 one of the worst storms of the century intervened and scattered de Roquefeuil's squadron, sinking 1 ship and disabling 5 others. Most of the warships managed to regain Brest during the next several days, albeit in damaged condition. The French barges had begun embarking some 10,000 troops when the storm struck, wrecking the troop and equipment transports and sinking some with the loss of all hands. The French then called off the invasion plans. Although France officially declared war against England on March 20 (Britain reciprocated on March 31), it gave no more support to a Stuart restoration.

With France and Britain now officially at war, France undertook major offensive operations in the Austrian Netherlands and along the Rhine. Louis XV assumed personal command of a large army of 90,000 men for an invasion of the Austrian Netherlands, although Marshal Maurice, Comte de Saxe, held actual field command. Another French army was to oppose Austrian forces in the Middle Rhine, while a third army would join Spanish forces against the Austrians in northern Italy.

In June 1744 Frederick II, alarmed by Austrian military successes and correctly convinced that Maria Theresa planned to annex at least part of Bavaria and regain all Silesia, concluded a new treaty with France. This began the Second Silesian War (1744–1745). A Prussian army of 80,000 men was to invade Bohemia and take Prague, while a French army under Marshal de Coigny and an imperial army under Marshal Friedrich Heinrich, Count von Seckendorff, invaded and occupied Bavaria.

Meanwhile, the fighting in northern Italy, heretofore largely desultory, intensified in the spring of 1744 when Prince Louis François de Bourbon-Conti attempted to move his army from Dauphiné to join Spanish forces under Captain General John, Count de Gages, on the lower Po River and seize the Duchy of Milan from Austria. Assisted by Austrian forces, King Charles Emmanuel III of Sardinia held up Conti's advance. At the same time, some 6,000 Austrian troops under Prince Johann G. Lobkowitz drove the main Spanish army in northern Italy southward, seizing Valletri but then suffering defeat in fighting outside the city with some 10,000 combined Spanish-Neapolitan troops under King Charles. In the Battle of Madonna del Olmo on September 30, the Sardinian king again attacked the Franco-Spanish forces but was again defeated. The French and Spaniards went into winter quarters without having linked up with the Spanish armies to the south and with the Austrians and Sardinians retaining control of the Po Valley.

In August 1744, Prussian troops moved on three axes into Bohemia, converging and capturing Prague following a brief siege (September 2–6, 1744). Frederick then pressed southward, threatening Vienna. Maria Theresa rallied her people as able field marshal Otto Ferdinand, Count von Abensperg und Traun, took command of Vienna's defense and, with some Saxon units, held Frederick and the Prussians in check.

Habsburg forces under Prince Charles Alexander of Lorraine now hastily moved east across the Rhine toward Bohemia. With the French doing nothing to assist him and with his own army about to be caught between two large Habsburg armies, Frederick quit Bohemia and Moravia and withdrew into Silesia. On January 7, 1745, the Austrians caught the Bavarians in their winter quarters at Amberg and defeated them. The Austrians then overran much of Bavaria, including Munich.

Holy Roman emperor Charles VII had died on December 27, 1744. On April 22, 1745, his son, young elector of Bavaria Maximilian Joseph, having been driven from his lands, concluded peace with Austria in the Treaty of Füssen. Maximilian Joseph received recognition of his hereditary claim to his ancestral lands in return for renouncing any claims on the Austrian throne and agreeing to support the election of Duke Francis of Lorraine, consort of Austrian archduchess Maria Theresa, as Holy Roman emperor; he was elected as Emperor Francis I on September 13, 1745. All this left Frederick II of Prussia isolated, as the French seemed interested only in operations in the Austrian Netherlands.

Despite operating largely alone and having to deal with insurgent forces in Silesia, Frederick continued to register victories. Austrian prince Charles Alexander of Lorraine, commanding some 59,000 Saxon and Habsburg forces, invaded Silesia. Not realizing that Frederick was marching against him, he moved his army toward Wrocław (Breslau) and camped near Hohenfriedberg, only to be caught largely unawares by Frederick early on June 4, 1745. The Austrians and Saxons lost in the battle some 4,000 killed or wounded and 7,000 prisoners, along with 66 guns. Prussian losses were only 2,000 men. Frederick's masterful victory soon caused him to be known by contemporaries as "Frederick the Great." He pursued the withdrawing Austrian and Saxon forces with only about half of his own army, while the remaining Prussian troops dealt with the Austrian and Hungarian irregulars.

Following three months of indecisive maneuvering in northeastern Bohemia, in September 1745 Frederick began the withdrawal into Silesia of his army, now down to about 18,000 men. Charles Alexander of Lorraine, commanding some 39,000 Habsburg troops, followed. Frederick, aware of the Austrian pursuit, halted at Sohr (Soor) only to discover that Charles had carried out a night march and gotten in behind his army, blocking the Prussian route to Silesia.

Under heavy Austrian fire, Frederick carried out a great wheeling movement to bring his army into position. Much to the surprise of the Austrians, who had not expected the heavily outnumbered Prussians to attack, the Prussian pivot suddenly advanced against the Austrian left wing. The Austrians were thrown back in disorder and forced to retreat to the southwest, leaving Frederick free to return to Silesia. The Prussians lost 900 dead and 2,700 wounded. Austrian losses were on the order of 7,000, including more than 3,000 prisoners. The Austrians also abandoned 22 guns.

With the warring powers all nearly bankrupt, peace negotiations went forward at Dresden. With Frederick threatening to leave his army in occupation of Saxony, the French successful in the Austrian Netherlands, and much of the English Army having departed the continent to deal with the large Jacobite Uprising of 1745 in Scotland, Maria Theresa had little choice but to agree to peace on Frederick's terms. Under the Treaty of Dresden signed on December 25, 1745, that ended the Second Silesian War, Maria Theresa confirmed the Treaty of Breslau and the cession of Silesia to Prussia. She received in return only recognition by Frederick of her remaining territories and of her husband as emperor

of the Holy Roman Empire. Saxony was forced to pay Prussia an indemnity of 1 million thalers. This treaty did not, however, end the Austrian war with France.

The war continued for another three years, with considerable fighting in Italy and in the Austrian Netherlands, but these had little effect on Germany, and the French were unsuccessful in their efforts to get Frederick to rejoin the war. Led by Marshal Saxe, the French won a number of victories in the Austrian Netherlands, including Raucoux (Rocour) near Liège (October 11, 1746), giving them possession of that long-coveted territory. The French were, however, discouraged by Austrian victories in Italy, British victories at sea, the fighting in India, and the British capture of the French fortress of Louisbourg on Cape Breton Island. Also, Czarina Elizabeth brought Russia into the war as an ally of Austria and sent troops to the Rhine.

The warring sides finally agreed to peace, concluded at the imperial free city of Aachen (Aix-la-Chapelle) on October 18, 1748. The treaty provided for the reciprocal restitution of all conquests. Thus, the French returned the Austrian Netherlands and the Dutch barrier towns; they also restored Madras in India to the British. The British returned Louisbourg to the French.

Austria, however, was obliged to cede the northern Italian duchies of Parma, Piacenza, and Guastalla to Spanish infante Duke Don Philip and various territories in western Lombardy to its ally, the Kingdom of Sardinia. The Duchy of Modena and the Republic of Genoa were both restored to independence. Both the Asiento contract and the right of the English to send an annual trading ship to the Spanish colonies, guaranteed by the 1713 Treaty of Utrecht, were reconfirmed. The treaty also provided guarantees that Silesia belonged to Prussia, that the Pragmatic Sanction applied to Austria, and that the House of Hanover would retain succession in its German states and in Great Britain.

Significance

Prussia was the great winner in the war, which also marked the arrival of Prussia as a Great Power. Silesia was almost entirely German, as populous as the Dutch Republic, and the most industrially advanced state east of the Elbe River. In acquiring it, Frederick II doubled Prussia's population and more than doubled its resources. Indeed, by 1752 Silesia was producing more than one-quarter of Prussia's state revenues.

The war, which was more than anything an effort to partition the Austrian Empire, had failed in that regard, however. Hungary had clearly cast its lot with Austria, and a Habsburg had been restored to the imperial throne. The war also had done nothing to diminish the Austrian determination to reverse its outcome. Nor did the conflict end the rivalry between Britain and France overseas. The war had, however, clearly revealed the problem faced by France as an Atlantic power in having to maintain both a strong army and a strong navy, while Britain could have the luxury of concentrating on its navy. In France, there was a general resentment of the treaty having forced it to surrender its brilliant conquest of the Austrian Netherlands. There was also considerable resentment of the treaty among the British in New England in North America because of the return of Louisbourg to France.

Both Austria and Prussia were soon preparing for a new round in their struggle to see which would dominate the Germanies. Fighting broke out again eight years later. The same broad antagonisms of Prussia versus Austria and France versus England remained, but in the Seven Years' War (1756–1763) Britain and France switched sides.

Further Reading

Anderson, M. S. *The War of Austrian Succession, 1740–1748.* New York: Longman, 1995.

Asprey, Robert B. *Frederick the Great: The Magnificent Enigma.* New York: Ticknor and Fields, 1986.

Black, Jeremy. *America or Europe? British Foreign Policy, 1739–63.* London: University College London Press, 1998.

Browning, Reed. *The War of the Austrian Succession.* New York: St. Martin's, 1993.

Chandler, David. *The Art of Warfare in the Age of Marlborough.* New York: Hippocrene Books, 1976.

Clowes, William Laird. *The Royal Navy: A History from the Earliest Times to 1900,* Vol. 3. 1898; reprint, London: Chatham, 1996.

Duffy, Christopher. *The Military Experience in the Age of Reason.* New York: Atheneum, 1988.

Harding, Richard. *Seapower and Naval Warfare, 1650–1830.* London: UCL Press, 1999.

Luvaas, Jay, *Frederick the Great on the Art of War.* New York: Free Press, 1966.

Mahan, J. Alexander. *Maria Theresa of Austria.* New York: Thomas Y. Crowell, 1932.

Skrine, Francis Henry. *Fontenoy and Great Britain's Share in the War of the Austrian Succession 1741–48.* London: William Blackwood and Sons, 1906.

Smith, Rhea Marsh, *Spain: A Modern History.* Ann Arbor: University of Michigan Press, 1965.

Starkey, Armstrong. *War in the Age of Enlightenment, 1700–1789.* Westport, CT: Praeger, 2003.

Carnatic Wars (1746–1748, 1749–1754, and 1757–1763)

Dates	1746–1748, 1749–1754, and 1757–1763
Location	Southern India
Combatants	British East India Company vs. French East India Company
Principal Commanders	Britain: Robert Clive, Sir Eyre Coote, Edward Peyton, Edward Boscawenn, Sir George Pocock France: Joseph François Dupleix, Bernard Mahé de La Bourdannais, Charles Godeheu Indian States: Anwaruddin, Chanda Sahib, Nasir Jung, Muzaffar Jung, Siraj-ud-Daulah
Principal Battles	Negapatam, Madras, St. Thome, Ambur, Arcot, Plassey, Negapatam (second), Pondicherry
Outcome	The British East India Company becomes the dominant force in India.

Causes

The Carnatic (Karnatic) Wars were a series of conflicts fought between Britain and France and allied Indian states for control of the Indian subcontinent. The wars occurred during the decline of the Moghul Empire (1526–1857), itself accompanied by invasions of northern India from Afghanistan. Several territories, including the Carnatic (Karnataka) in southern India, achieved autonomy within the empire. The death of Dost Ali Khan, nawab of the Carnatic, in 1740 led to a successionist struggle between his son-in-law Chanda Sahib and Anwaruddin Muhammed Khan, the son of the nizam of Hyderabad and natural heir to the throne.

French administrator in India Joseph François Dupleix played a key role in the ensuing Carnatic Wars. Arriving in India in 1715, Dupleix became head of the French Compagnie des Indes (India Company) in 1742. Since the establishment of their trading stations on the Indian subcontinent in the 16th and 17th centuries, the European powers all resorted to employing native Indians to help maintain their forts. Following the establishment of the Compagnie des Indes in 1719, Dupleix took the lead in the creation of wholly native Indian infantry units. These native troops became known as sepoys. With few French troops available, Dupleix hoped to be able to use the sepoys to expand French holdings in India, then limited largely to a few coastal trading posts, of which the principal one was Pondicherry on the southeastern coast of the subcontinent.

Course of the First Carnatic War (1746–1748)

During the War of Austrian Succession in Europe (1740–1748) there was fighting between the British and French in India. Britain and France did not formally go to war against one another until March 1744, and Dupleix was instructed not to initiate hostilities. The British in India were under no such restriction, and they were encouraged to take action on the arrival there in 1745 of a Royal Navy squadron commanded by Commodore Curtis Barnett that cleared French merchant shipping from the Bay of Bengal. With the French squadron withdrawn and fearing a British attack on Pondicherry, Dupleix appealed for assistance to able French admiral Bernard Mahé de La Bourdannais, who was at Île de France (present-day Mauritius). La Bourdannais secured seven armed merchantmen to add to his single ship of the line *Achille* (70 guns), then had the ships painted and armed with numerous fake cannon to mask their weakness. In July 1746 he set sail for the Coromandel coast with 1,200 troops.

In the meantime, Commodore Barnett died of illness and was succeeded by the less aggressive Commodore Edward Peyton, who nonetheless had at his disposal seven ships of the line, manned by veteran crews. On July 25, 1746, the two squadrons came in sight of one another. Bluffing the British, La Bourdannais deployed as if for a close action with a view toward boarding. Peyton, perceiving himself outnumbered, commenced a long-range cannonade. Although the French ships sustained some damage in this Battle of Negapatam, the distance mitigated the effect, and the French maintained their formation.

Dawn found La Bourdonnais downwind in formation, supposedly awaiting battle. Peyton met with his captains, who agreed that they should break off the action and return to Tricomalee for repairs. British losses were 14 killed and 46 wounded, while the French lost 27 killed and 53 wounded. As a consequence of the battle, La Bourdonnais was able to reinforce Pondicherry and went on to invest Madras, the principal British base in India, without interference. Peyton was recalled to England and died a broken man the next year.

With La Bourdonnais blockading it from the sea, Dupleix laid siege to Madras

from the land side. Following brief resistance during September 2–10, Madras surrendered. This victory encouraged Dupleix in his belief that he could establish a French empire in southern India. Dupleix had led Anwaruddin, first nawab of Arcot, to believe that Madras would be his, but he now withdrew this pledge, and the nawab sent 10,000 men to take Madras from the French. The French sortied from Madras on September 21 with a far smaller force but easily defeated the nawab's army.

Dupleix planned to take the British base at Cuddalore, but the arrival of British reinforcements prevented this. Dupleix then sent Colonel Paradis, his engineer and ablest military commander, with 300 French troops and 700 sepoys against 10,000 troops under Anwaruddin, who was moving against Madras. Although the exact circumstances of the ensuing Battle of St. Thome of November 3 remain in dispute (particularly whether the French had artillery), Paradis ordered his men to fire one volley and then charge with the bayonet. This unexpectedly bold attack routed the nawab's army. Dupleix then declared Madras to be French and appointed Paradis to command it. The Battle of St. Thome set a pattern in India whereby small numbers of European troops, assisted by European-trained native soldiers, laying down rapid fire could defeat large indigenous armies and especially their vaunted cavalry. This helped transform the balance of power in India. The British East India Company now responded to Dupleix's success by raising 3,000 sepoys of its own.

During August–October 1748, British forces under Rear Admiral Edward Boscawen laid siege to the French base at Pondicherry, ably defended by Dupleix. Boscawen had six ships of the line and a number of smaller warships as well as

3,240 land troops, including sepoys and another 2,000 native cavalry. In the ensuing siege, generally regarded as one of Dupleix's most brilliant military exploits, the British side suffered 1,065 men killed and the French only some 200. Sickness and the coming of the monsoon season forced Boscawen to abandon the siege in early October, a week before the Treaty of Aix-la-Chapelle ending the War of the Austrian Succession was known in India. The treaty restored Madras to the English in return for Fort Louisbourg in North America to the French. Each side in India now maintained some 10,000 sepoys.

Course of the Second Carnatic War (1749–1754)

The Second Carnatic War was touched off by a successionist struggle following the death in 1748 of nizam of Hyderabad Nizam-ul-Mulk, Asaf Jah I. Two individuals sought the throne: his son, Mir Ahmad Ali-Khan (Nasir Jung), and his grandson, Hidayat Muhi ud-Din Sa'adu'llah Khan (Muzaffar Jung). Seeking to take advantage of the turmoil to become nawab of Arcot, Chanda Sahib supported Muzaffar Jung and intrigued against Nawab Anwaruddin Muhammad Khan in Arcot (the Carnatic). The French chose to support Muzaffar Jung and Chanda Sahib, hoping to bring both to power in their respective states. The British responded by supporting their two opponents against the French. With Britain and France officially at peace, the troops fighting in India were those of their respective East India Companies.

Initially the French enjoyed success. In the struggle as to who would rule the Carnatic, the combined forces of Chanda Sahib, Muzaffar Jang, and the French under Charles Joseph Patissier, Marquis

de Bussy-Castelnau, defeated Anwaruddin in the Battle of Ambur on August 3, 1749. This battle demonstrated convincingly the superiority of European arms and warfare. Anwaruddin was among those killed in the fighting, and Chanda was proclaimed nawab, although Dupleix was the power behind the throne. This did not end the successionist struggle, however, for the British supported Muhammed Ali Khan Walajah, son of Anwaruddin, who controlled Trichinopoly (Tiruchirappalli).

During 1749–1751 there was fighting in the Carnatic as Nasir Jung, supported by the English under Robert Clive, campaigned there. Nasir Jung was assassinated in December 1749, however, and his son Muzzafar Jung (probably responsible for the deed) succeeded him as ruler. From September to October 1751, French puppet ruler in the Carnatic Nawab Chandra Sahib besieged the British garrison at Trichinopoly. Departing Madras with only 500 men and three guns, Clive captured Chandra Sahib's capital of Arcot on September 12. Rajib Shah, the nawab's son, then marched from Trichinopoly to retake Arcot.

Following a 50-day siege and with Clive's forces reduced to only 120 Europeans and 200 sepoys, Rajib Shah launched an assault with elephants to batter down the walls; however, the defenders' musket fire stampeded the elephants. Following three desperate assaults, Rajib Shah withdrew, his forces having suffered 400 casualties to only 6 for his opponents. This exploit greatly enhanced both Clive's reputation and that of the British in India. The war was ended by the 1754 Treaty of Pondicherry. It recognized Muhammad Ali Khan Walajah as nawab of Arcot. Dupleix, who had not been adequately supported by the French government, was recalled to France, and French efforts in

BATTLE OF PLASSEY, JUNE 23, 1757

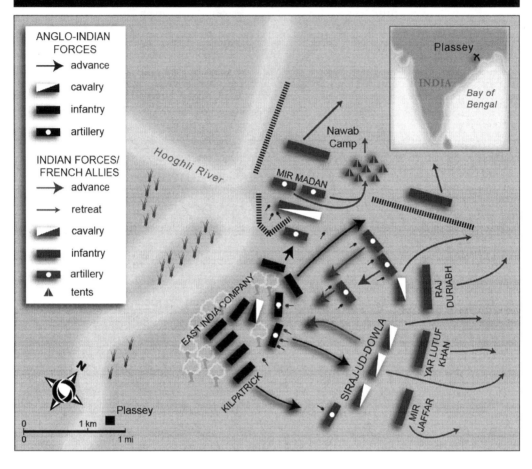

India suffered. Charles Godeheu replaced Dupleix.

Course of the Third Carnatic War (1757–1763)

The Third Carnatic War spread from southern India into Bengal. In June 1756 Muhammad Siraj-ud-Daulah, nawab of Bengal, marched on Calcutta and captured it. The so-called Black Hole of Calcutta (a subterranean prison in which 146 British soldiers were allegedly imprisoned in one room 18 feet square with but a single window for ventilation, where a day later only 23 of the men were alive) shocked the British

into action. Historians now cast doubt on the numbers involved and even whether the Black Hole incident occurred at all. Certainly the British manipulated news of the event to discredit Siraj-ud-Daulah.

Clive, now a lieutenant colonel and governor of Fort St. David, was ordered to recapture Calcutta. With only 900 British troops and 1,500 sepoys, Clive retook the city on January 2, 1757. Following an inconclusive battle with Siraj-ud-Daulah, Clive signed a treaty with him under which the British were allowed to reoccupy Calcutta and were indemnified by Siraj-ud-Daulah for their losses.

Siraj-ud-Daulah soon opened negotiations with the French. Learning of this, Clive conducted secret negotiations with Siraj-ud-Daulah's uncle, Mir Jaffar, who assured Clive of his support in unseating the nawab. Siraj-ud-Daulah had insisted that the British and French not fight each other in India, even though war had broken out between the two powers in Europe (the Seven Years' War of 1756–1763).

Clive now provoked a confrontation with Siraj-ud-Daulah by mounting an attack on a French settlement not far from the nawab's capital of Mursidabad. Siraj-ud-Daulah responded by assembling a Bengali force estimated to number as many as 35,000 infantry, 15,000 cavalry, and 10,000 militiamen. He also had 53 artillery pieces manned by French crews. Siraj-ud-Daulah then moved this large force toward Calcutta.

Clive had only 3,200 men (1,100 Europeans and 2,100 sepoys) as well as eight small cannon and two howitzers. Instead of remaining in the strong defensive position of Fort William, however, Clive took the offensive. Mir Jaffar assured him that when the battle began he would withhold his troops, who constituted perhaps three-quarters of Siraj-ud-Daulah's force, and then turn them against the nawab.

On the evening of June 22, 1757, Clive set up camp in a mango grove south of Calcutta and north of the town of Pelasi, known to the English as Plassey. Clive anchored his western flank on the Bhagirathi-Hooghli River. Siraj-ud-Daulah's army took up position in a great semicircle facing west toward the British positions and the Bhagirathi-Hooghli. With his back against the river, Clive was almost surrounded.

The battle opened on the morning of June 23 when the French artillery opened up against the English. This fire was ineffective, because Clive's men were positioned on the reverse slope of a hill next to the mango grove. Much of the morning was consumed in an artillery duel, but the British fire was far more effective because Siraj-ud-Daulah's troops were in the open. At noon a monsoon rain began. The powder for the French artillery became soaked and useless. Mir Mudin Khan, the nawab's field commander, assumed that the same had happened to the British powder and ordered an immediate attack. Clive, however, had covered his powder supply.

Siraj-ud-Daulah launched a large-scale cavalry attack on the British position, but Clive's guns cut down large numbers of them and broke up the attack; Mir Mudin Khan was among those killed. Mir Jaffar withheld his 45,000 men, although he did not, as promised, turn them against Siraj-ud-Daulah.

Sensing defeat, Siraj-ud-Daulah fled the scene with his 2,000-man bodyguard. Those of the nawab's troops who continued to fight were overwhelmed by British artillery fire, and by late afternoon the battle was over. Clive's casualties totaled 23 killed and 49 wounded. Siraj-ud-Daulah may have lost upward of 1,000 men. Siraj-ud-Daulah was captured a few days later and executed. Mir Jaffar replaced him as nawab and lavished considerable sums on Clive and his officers. London appointed Clive the governor of Bengal. He left India in 1760.

Fighting between the French and British continued, and on April 29, 1758, in the Bay of Bengal, British vice admiral Sir George Pocock, with seven ships of the line, was endeavoring to relieve the British garrison at Fort St. David just south of Pondicherry, which had come under siege in March by French troops under Irish-born Thomas Arthur, Comte de Lally, when Pocock sighted, pursued, and engaged a French squadron of eight ships of the line under French admiral Anne Antoine, Comte d'Aché de Serquigny. The ensuing battle was indecisive, but the French ships, which were transporting troops to Pondicherry, suffered disproportionately higher casualties, for the English as usual aimed for the hulls of their opponents. The British lost 29 killed and 89 wounded, the French 162 killed and 360 wounded. D'Aché then proceeded to Pondicherry, but Pocock was unable to relieve Fort St. David, which surrendered to the French on June 2.

In July, Pocock with seven ships of the line took up station off French-held Pondicherry. This prompted a sortie, on July 28, by French admiral d'Aché and nine ships of the line, which sailed southward and declined to engage the British. Several days of pursuit and maneuvers followed before Pocock brought d'Aché to battle off Cape Negapatam on August 3. A number of the French ships sustained significant damage—two in a collision—before d'Aché judged the battle lost and signaled a withdrawal. The French ships escaped the pursuing British, and d'Aché then returned to Pondicherry, having lost some 250 killed and 600 wounded; the British suffered only 31 killed and 166 wounded. The encounter off Negapatam, while indecisive, heavily damaged the French squadron. D'Aché concluded that he could no longer support land operations at Madras, and he sailed to Mauritius to refit.

Commencing in December 1758, French forces under Lally laid siege to Madras, but the British held out, able to resupply Madras from the sea. A British relief force under Francis Forde arrived by sea and on January 25, 1761, defeated Lally, forcing him to raise the siege. With Clive ill and having returned to Britain, General Sir Eyre Coote assumed command of Clive's troops and on December 6, 1760, completed the investment of the French stronghold of Pondicherry. The British siege went forward despite a typhoon that threatened the British naval blockade. On January 15, 1761, Lally was forced to surrender Pondicherry.

Significance

By the terms of peace that ended the Seven Years' War in 1763, the French regained Pondicherry and Chandernagor, but the Carnatic Wars had in effect ended their hopes of being a major power on the Indian subcontinent. French influence in India was now greatly diminished, and the French Compagnie des Indes was dissolved in 1769. The Carnatic Wars in effect made Britain the dominant power on the subcontinent.

Further Reading

Bruce-Jones, Mark. *Clive of India.* New York: St. Martin's, 1975.

Clowes, William Laird. *The Royal Navy: A History from the Earliest Times to 1900,* Vol. 3. 1898; reprint, London: Chatham, 1996.

Dull, Jonathan R. *The French Navy and the Seven Years' War.* Lincoln: University of Nebraska Press, 2005.

Edwards, Michael. *Clive: The Heaven-Born General.* London: Hart-Davis, 1977.

Keay, John. *The Honourable Company.* New York: Macmillan, 1994.

Mason, Philip. *A Matter of Honour.* London: Jonathan Cape, 1974.

McLeod, John. *The History of India.* Westport, CT: Greenwood, 2002.

Robert, P. E. *History of British India.* London: Oxford University Press, 1952.

Stein, Burton. *A History of India.* Oxford, UK: Blackwell, 1998.

French and Indian War (1754–1763)

Dates	1754–1763
Location	North America
Combatants	France and allied Native Americans vs. Britain and allied Native Americans
Principal Commanders	Britain: Edward Braddock; John Campbell, fourth Earl of Loudon; Jeffrey Amherst; James Wolfe France: Louis Joseph, Marquis de Montcalm
Principal Battles	Jumonville Glen, Monongahela, Fort William Henry, Fort Carillon, Louisbourg, Quebec
Outcome	France loses virtually all its North American territory to Britain and is bent on revenge for its losses here and failure in the Seven Years' War.

Causes

The French and Indian War of 1754–1763 was the last in a series of conflicts between English and French colonists in North America for control of the continent. The earlier struggles were King William's War (1688–1697), mirroring the War of the European struggle of the War of the League of Augsburg; Queen Anne's War (1702–1714) during the War of the Spanish Succession; and King George's War (1740–1745) during the War of the Austrian Succession. Unlike these three previous conflicts, the French and Indian War began first in America and was then subsumed by the wider European conflict of the Seven Years' War (1756–1763).

The English colonies were located along the Atlantic seaboard from Nova Scotia in the north to Georgia in the south. The English numbered some 1.5 million settlers. The population of New France was concentrated in the St. Lawrence River Valley, while some French also inhabited Acadia (present-day New Brunswick and parts of Nova Scotia, including Île Royale, present-day Cape Breton Island). Some Frenchmen also lived in New Orleans and in small settlements along the east side of the Mississippi River and in the Illinois Country. With a total population of only some 75,000, however, the French were at a great demographic disadvantage. They did have the support of the majority of the Native Americans, for unlike the English, many French trappers and fur traders lived among the Indians and often married Indian women. Native American support for the English was largely limited to the Iroquois Confederation and, in the South, the Catawbas and Cherokees.

The cause of the war was the growing rivalry between the French and British for control of the Ohio River Valley. On August 28, 1753, Robert d'Arcy, Earl of Holdernesse, British secretary of state for the Southern Department (which included North America) authorized Britain's North American colonial governors to demand that the French withdraw from several disputed territories and, failing that, to employ colonial militiamen to force them out.

The colony of Virginia claimed the Ohio Valley region and, on receipt of this order, Virginia Lieutenant Governor Robert Dinwiddie dispatched 21-year-old Major

George Washington and some dozen men to the French outpost of Fort Le Boeuf (in present-day Waterford in northwestern Pennsylvania). Washington arrived there on December 16, 1753 and met with fort commander Jacques Legardeur de St. Pierre, who received Dinwiddie's order and forwarded it on to his superiors in Quebec.

That the French were not prepared to accede to the British demand became apparent on April 16, 1754, when some 500 men under French captain Claude Pierre Pécaudy, Seigneur de Contrecoeur, forced to depart 40 Englishmen working for the Ohio Company, a Virginia company, who were constructing a trading post at the confluence of the Allegheny and Monongahela Rivers. The French then began turning it into a military post, known as Fort Duquesne. Meanwhile, Washington returned to the frontier with 150 Virginia militiamen and some native allies under orders to dislodge the French. Contrecoeur, commanding Fort Duquesne, ordered Ensign Joseph Coulon de Villiers de Jumonville and 35 men to discover the whereabouts of the English.

Course

Dividing his force into smaller scouting parties, Washington and approximately 47 men caught up with Jumonville in the Allegheny foothills near present-day Uniontown, Pennsylvania, on May 28, 1754. The ensuing skirmish claimed 1 Virginian dead and 2 wounded. Most of the Frenchmen were either captured or killed. Washington's native allies killed Jumonville, who had been wounded and taken prisoner. This engagement, known as the Battle of Jumonville Glen, began the French and Indian War.

Washington consolidated his force and, knowing that the French would soon be looking for him, commenced construction of the aptly named Fort Necessity (near present-day Uniontown, Pennsylvania). Jumonville's brother, Captain Louis Coulon de Villiers, led some 600 French Canadians and 100 native allies from Fort Duquesne against the British colonials. Following a brief battle at Fort Necessity on July 3, 1754, Washington and about 450 colonial militiamen surrendered, the French allowing them to return to Virginia with the honors of war. Both sides now began mobilizing for full-scale war.

With the commencement of hostilities, both France and Britain sought to send reinforcements in the form of regular troops. With the French assembling a large supply convoy, the British ordered Vice Admiral Sir Edward Boscawen with 17 ships of the line to seek out and intercept the French before they could reach the St. Lawrence River. French admiral Emmanuel Auguste de Cahideuc, Comte Dubois de la Motte, commanded 16 French ships of the line escorting the convoy.

The English ships failed to locate the French before they arrived at Quebec, but the British subsequently sighted several French ships of the line in the Strait of Belle Isle, which separates the Labrador Peninsula from Newfoundland. The British captured two of the French warships on June 8, 1755, marking the beginning of an undeclared naval war between the two powers (war was not formally declared until May 17, 1763, upon news in London of the French invasion of Minorca). The British also began to seize French ships on the high seas wherever they could be found. Admiral Edward Hawke put to sea with the plan to intercept the French convoy homeward bound from North America, but the latter returned safely to Brest.

In 1755 English North American colonial officials put into motion a series of small offensives. During June 2–26, Nova Scotia lieutenant governor Charles Lawrence and British colonel Robert Mockton sailed with 250 British regulars and some 2,000 provincial troops to the Bay of Fundy and there captured French Forts Beauséjour and Gaspéreau on the isthmus connecting Nova Scotia to the mainland. With the area firmly under their control, the British then expelled the French Acadians. In all, some 11,500 were deported.

Also in 1755, William Johnson, an English civilian with wide experience among the natives and now a commissioned brigadier general, led some 3,500 British colonists and 300 natives from Albany, New York, against French Fort St. Frédéric on Lake Champlain. To defend that place, French maréchal de camp Baron Jean-Armand Dieskau proceeded up the Richelieu River with a mixed force of some 2,000 French regulars, Canadian militia, and natives, and on September 8, 1755, they attacked Johnson's camp at the southern end of Lake George. The French were defeated and Dieskau taken prisoner, but Johnson halted his advance and ordered his men to construct Fort William Henry. The French countered by building Fort Carillon (later known as Fort Ticonderoga) to the north.

In a third expedition by English provincial forces, Massachusetts governor William Shirley led some 2,500 men, including British regulars, from Albany, New York, up the Mohawk Valley toward Fort Niagara. After reaching Oswego, with many of his men ill and supplies short and upon learning of the British defeat in the Battle of the Monongahela, Shirley withdrew.

The major British effort in 1755 was by new commander in North America major general Edward Braddock, who had arrived in Virginia in April with two British regiments. His goal was to take French Fort Duquesne. Braddock planned a slow-moving road-building project through the wilderness followed by a European-style siege. En route, he split his force of about 2,100 men into two bodies: the first of some 800 men with the baggage and artillery and the other a flying column of 1,300 men to prepare for the siege.

Aware of the dangers of wilderness warfare, Braddock employed more than a third of his advance force on screens and patrols, but he eschewed long-range patrolling. On July 9 about 10 miles short of his goal and with his screening force smaller than usual and close to the main body, Braddock was ambushed just west of the Monongahela by French captain Daniel Liénard de Beaujeu with some 900 men, two-thirds of them natives.

With the French and Indians firing from cover and concealment, the British vanguard fell back and became entangled with the main body, which Braddock had ordered to advance. The battle lasted three hours, but discipline ended when Braddock was shot from his horse, mortally wounded. Virginia Militia colonel Washington, along without official status as an observer, helped organize the wild British retreat. In the battle, the French and Indians lost 23 killed and 16 wounded, while the British suffered 456 killed and 521 wounded.

In 1756 fighting began in Europe in what became the Seven Years' War when King Frederick II of Prussia invaded

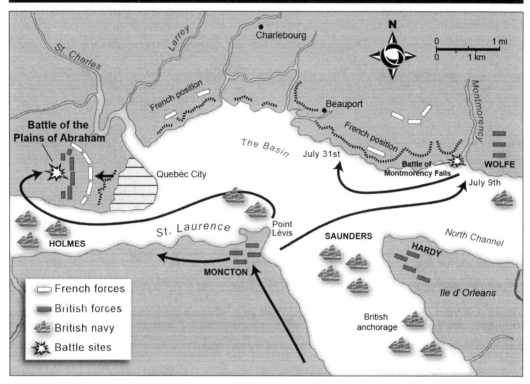

BATTLE OF QUEBEC (PLAINS OF ABRAHAM)
SEPTEMBER 13, 1759

Saxony in a preemptive attack against the powerful coalition formed by Austria to reverse the results of the War of Austrian Succession (1740–1748). That same year saw new commanders sent out to North America. British major general John Campbell, fourth Earl of Loudon, arrived in July and began reorganizing his men, while French major general Louis Joseph, Marquis de Montcalm, had arrived with reinforcements in May. Fearing British attacks from Oswego, New York, on Lake Ontario's southeastern shore and from the Champlain Valley against Montreal and the St. Lawrence River Valley, New France governor-general Pierre de Rigaud de Vaudreuil ordered an attack on the vulnerable British outposts.

The able Montcalm, who had favored a more cautious policy, crossed Lake Ontario with some 3,000 men in hundreds of small craft and commenced a bombardment of Fort Ontario, taking both it and Fort Oswego, across the Oswego River, on August 13 and 14. In these twin victories the French captured nearly 1,600 British troops and camp followers, 6 ships, 77 artillery pieces, 12 tons of gunpowder, 200 tons of provisions, and more than sufficient specie to pay for the cost of the expedition. After demolishing the fortifications, Montcalm withdrew. The French had secured Lake Ontario and removed the British threat to their western outposts' supply line. The victories also caused many natives to rally to the French.

Both sides then went into winter quarters, the French maintaining a strong garrison at Fort Carillon, the British at Fort William Henry.

In 1757 the British planned to take the important French fortress of Louisbourg on Cape Breton Island. Guarding the mouth of the St. Lawrence River, the lifeline of New France, Louisbourg was also a haven for French privateers operating against the New England fishing industry. At the end of June 1757, Loudon arrived at Halifax from New York to lead an expedition of 12,000 men against Louisbourg, but the French garrison had been reinforced, and a French naval squadron had arrived there. A major storm on September 24 scattered the British squadron under Vice Admiral Francis Holborne, assigned to operate in conjunction with Loudon's land force, forcing Holborne to return to Britain for repairs. The expedition was then called off.

Taking advantage of the draining off of British troops for the operation against Louisbourg, Montcalm had advanced from Fort Carillon with 6,000 French troops and militia and almost 2,000 allied natives to attack British Fort William Henry at the head of Lake George. Lieutenant Colonel George Monro commanded some 1,500 regulars and militia and 18 heavy cannon at the fort. The reduced British garrison was still undertaking repairs to the fort, which had been damaged in a surprise winter attack that also destroyed British ships protecting its water approaches. Montcalm was thus able to transport his siege cannon via Lake George. The siege commenced on August 3, 1757.

With the fort's walls crumbling under French fire and informed that he could not expect reinforcement, Monro surrendered on August 9 under terms providing safe passage to Fort Edward and the retention of personal effects. Many of the natives allied with the French saw these terms as a betrayal by Montcalm and a conspiracy between whites. Following the British evacuation, some natives entered the fort and scalped most of the British wounded and ill left behind as unable to travel. Then as the British column set out for Fort Edward, the natives demanded the personal possessions of the British, and panic set in. The few French military escorts were powerless to intervene; between 69 and 184 British died in the ensuing confusion. Hundreds made their way to Fort Edward, where their exaggerated stories stunned and aroused the British.

Instead of proceeding to Fort Edward, Montcalm, who was personally dismayed by the violation of the surrender terms by his native allies, burned Fort William Henry and returned northward. Both sides then went into winter quarters.

British prime minister William Pitt was determined to defeat the French in North America. His three-pronged strategy included the taking of Louisbourg, Fort Duquesne, and Fort Carillon. These accomplished, the British would then move against both Montreal and Quebec. In March 1758 Pitt named Major General James Abercromby to replace the ineffective Loudon. Recognizing Abercromby's limitations, however, Pitt sent out Major General Jeffery Amherst as the new British commander in North America.

In late June, Abercromby led a 13,000-man force down Lake George toward Fort Carillon. His forces outnumbered at least three to one, Montcalm ordered his men to construct a stacked-log wall about six feet tall with firing steps and loopholes across the western approaches a half mile from the fort. Montcalm positioned most of his 4,200 defenders along this line.

On July 8 Abercromby ordered at least six assaults against this line, but the attacking troops became entangled in the abatis before the French wall. Inexplicably, Abercromby never brought up artillery. Having sustained almost 2,500 casualties to only 400 for the defenders, Abercromby then withdrew.

Meanwhile, the British prepared another attempt to capture Louisbourg, essential for future British operations against Quebec. French forces there were severely handicapped by serious shortages of weapons, supplies, and even food. Anticipating a new English assault on the fortress, Montcalm increased the size of the French squadron at Louisbourg to 5 ships of the line and 6 other warships. Including seamen and militiamen, Louisbourg was defended by some 6,000 men. Meanwhile, the British naval blockade of French ports prevented effective resupply. Of 23 French ships sent to Louisbourg, only 7 arrived, and a major French fleet appeared too late.

In March 1758 Amherst assumed command of the British invasion force. Admiral Edward Boscawen commanded the naval escort of 39 warships manned by 14,000 officers and men. The expeditionary force of 167 ships carrying 13,200 troops arrived on June 8 and began coming ashore in a hotly contested landing that almost failed some four miles southwest of the fortress. Governor of Louisbourg Augustin de Boschenry de Drucour carried out a capable defense, but once the British were ashore it was largely a matter of time. In the ensuing fighting, young Brigadier General James Wolfe particularly distinguished himself.

The British set on fire or captured the French ships of the line, and on July 26 Drucour surrendered. The siege cost the British 195 men killed and 363 wounded. French losses were 400–800 killed. The British took 3,600 prisoners, including 1,400 wounded, and they secured 216 guns and some mortars. New France never recovered from this blow.

Meanwhile, British colonel John Bradstreet led 3,000 provincial troops up the Mohawk River to capture French Fort Frontenac (present-day Kingston, Ontario), at the entrance to the St. Lawrence River on Lake Ontario, on August 27. In July, British brigadier general John Forbes departed Carlisle, Pennsylvania, with some 7,000 men, 5,000 of them provincial troops, for Fort Duquesne. Forbes devoted considerable effort to construction of a road with strategically placed forts. On September 14, 1758, an advance force of 800 men engaged the French at Duquesne. The British sustained a severe reverse and the loss of 300 men, but this did not deter Forbes. Abandoned by their native allies, cut off from Canada by the destruction of Fort Frontenac, and with Forbes's main body less than a day's march away, the French quit their position and burned Fort Duquesne on November 24. The British occupied what remained the next day.

Pitt's strategy for 1759 involved the capture of Fort Niagara to cut off western Canada from the St. Lawrence, an offensive up the Lake Champlain Valley to the St. Lawrence, and an assault on the French capital and stronghold of Quebec. On the Niagara front, Brigadier General John Prideaux led 2,000 British regulars up the Mohawk Valley to reoccupy Fort Oswego. They then moved by water along the south shores of Lake Ontario against Fort Niagara, commanded by French captain Pierre

Pouchot who hoped to hold off the British until a relief force could arrive from Fort Machault. With the defeat of the relief force in the Battle of La Belle Famille on July 24, however, Pouchot surrendered Fort Niagara the next day. Prideaux was killed during the siege.

At the same time, Amherst and 11,000 British regulars were proceeding against Fort Carillon. Amherst captured it on July 26 and took Crown Point, farther north on the lake, on July 31. His men then wintered at Crown Point.

The centerpiece of Pitt's strategy to win the war in America in 1759 was the capture of Quebec. This task was entrusted to young Major General James Wolfe with some 9,000 men. Rear Admiral Charles Saunders commanded the naval component. The British expeditionary force departed Louisbourg at the beginning of June, and on June 26 Saunders landed Wolfe's men on Orléans Island in the St. Lawrence River, just below Quebec.

Quebec is located on the northern shore of the St. Lawrence at the point where the river widens to nearly two miles across. Enclosed by walls, the Upper Town was situated at the top of steep bluffs overlooking the St. Lawrence River and the much smaller St. Charles River that flows into it. There were few possible means to assault the city from the river itself. Below the town the St. Charles and Montmorency Rivers presented formidable obstacles. West of Quebec farmland flattened into a plateau known as the Plains of Abraham, named after an early settler. Montcalm commanded the French garrison. He had 12,000 regular troops and militia, assisted by some Indians, to defend what appeared to be an almost impregnable fortress. Unfortunately for the French cause, Montcalm was subject to the authority of his rival, Governor-General Vaudreuil.

The eastern (downstream) approach to Quebec appeared to be the least formidable, and Wolfe first tried it. However, Montcalm had strongly fortified here, and the British effort failed. At the same time, British attempts to draw the French troops out of Quebec and their entrenchments into a pitched battle were unsuccessful. The British cut off the city from Montreal, lobbed shells into Quebec, and raided nearby French settlements with a view toward demoralizing the Quebecois, but into early September all of Wolfe's efforts to gain a foothold to attack Quebec had failed. Wolfe also fell sick with a fever, and many of his men believed him to be dying. Saunders, fearing that his ships would become trapped in winter ice in the St. Lawrence, threatened to depart. Wolfe realized that if he could not bring Montcalm to battle by the end of September, he would have to abandon the campaign.

Wolfe sought the advice of British Army captain Robert Stobo, who had been held prisoner in Quebec earlier and knew the city well. Stobo informed Wolfe of a narrow footpath angling up the steep cliffs just north of the city. Determined to try this approach, Wolfe managed to get troops up the footpath on the night of September 12–13. The French pickets assumed that the British boats were part of a French supply convoy due from Montreal. Not informed that this resupply effort had been canceled, they failed to give the alarm. British colonel William Howe's light infantry gained the top and captured the French positions overlooking the landing site below. Wolfe and the main body followed.

By dawn on September 13, some 4,500 British troops were drawn up on the Plains of Abraham. Montcalm carried out a personal reconnaissance of the British position and decided on an immediate attack with what forces were available before Wolfe could solidify his position and construct field fortifications. Had he waited, Montcalm would have had a far better chance of defeating the British.

By midmorning on September 13, Montcalm had assembled a mixed force of 4,500 French regulars and poorly trained militiamen to face the equal number of well-trained British regulars. Montcalm had no artillery, Vaudreuil having stupidly insisted on retaining it for the defense of the city.

The battle commenced about 10:00 a.m., with Montcalm attacking. The French militia fired too early, and there was little cohesion in the French force. The British, however, demonstrated excellent fire discipline, standing and firing in volleys when the French reached 60 yards' range. With the French at 40 yards, the British fired a devastating volley and then began to move forward. The French broke and fled back into the fortress. The battle had lasted little more than half an hour.

Casualties were comparable—some 644 French to 658 British—but the French never recovered from the psychological shock of the defeat. Both commanders were mortally wounded in the battle, but Wolfe at least had the satisfaction of knowing that he had triumphed. Vaudreuil now abandoned Quebec, leaving it to the city's mayor to surrender the city on September 18.

The Battle of the Plains of Abraham (also known as the Battle of Quebec) must be counted as the most important military engagement in the history of North America, for it broke the back of French resistance in Canada and secured British control of the continent. The British victory was sealed by the Battle of Quiberon Bay on November 20, when British admiral Hawke's ships defeated the French Brest Squadron, ensuring that the French would not be able to resupply North America.

Most remaining French troops gathered at Montreal under Montcalm's replacement, Major General François Gaston de Lévis. The British naval squadron departed Quebec in October, but 7,300 men under Brigadier General James Murray remained. This number was, however, quickly halved by hunger, scurvy, and unusually cold weather. Had the French attacked that winter, they would have had an excellent chance of retaking Quebec.

Because of the earlier ice melt at Montreal, Lévis departed Montreal in mid-April and moved down the St. Lawrence River toward Quebec with some 6,900 men. On April 24 they came ashore and moved inland. On the evening of April 27 they skirmished with British troops at the parish church at Sainte Foy, about five miles west of Quebec. The next day Murray marched out of Quebec with some 3,800 men, perhaps half of them militiamen, and in the Battle of Sainte Foy (also known as the Second Battle of Quebec) the French were victorious. The French suffered 833 casualties, the British 1,124. Lévis then laid siege to Quebec, but the British navy reestablished its blockade of the mouth of the St. Lawrence, and the next month a British supply ship arrived at Quebec, breaking the siege. French forces then withdrew to Montreal.

Three British columns now converged on Montreal. British brigadier general James Murray proceeded up the St. Lawrence from Quebec, arriving at Varenne downstream from Montreal on August 31. Colonel William Haviland led another British force up the Lake Champlain Valley, driving the French from Isle-aux-Noix by August 25. And General Amherst proceeded down the St. Lawrence River on August 10. Amherst forced the surrender of Fort Lévis by August 25 and arrived at Montreal by September 6. Vaudreuil capitulated on September 8, ending French rule of Canada.

In the Treaty of Paris of February 10, 1763, Britain, France, and Spain concluded peace. The treaty formalized a substantial exchange of territories, most of which was to British advantage. As far as North America was concerned, all of New France was ceded to British control except the small fishing islands of Saint-Pierre and Miquelon as well as Louisiana, which France had ceded to Spain. Britain also acquired Florida from Spain.

Significance

Great Britain was now the world's chief colonial power, its primary goal in the war. Humiliated, French leaders looked for revenge. Meanwhile, Britain grappled with the difficulties of administering their vast new North American holdings, including the toleration of Catholicism in New France, which was strongly opposed by the Puritan colonists of New England, and the setting of territorial boundaries.

British politicians also endeavored to find some means for the colonists to help pay for the defense of North America, which was immediately racked by an Indian uprising in Pontiac's War (1763–1766). British efforts to try to find an acceptable tax led to a full-scale revolt by the American colonists in 1775, which gave the French their opportunity for revenge.

Further Reading

Anderson, Fred. *Crucible of War: The Seven Years' War and the Fate of the Empire in British North America, 1754–1766.* New York: Knopf, 2000.

Black, Jeremy. *Pitt the Elder: The Great Commoner.* Cambridge: Cambridge University Press, 1992.

Clowes, William Laird. *The Royal Navy: A History from the Earliest Times to 1900,* Vol. 3. 1898; reprint, London: Chatham, 1996.

Corbett, Julian S. *England in the Seven Years' War.* London: Greenhill Books, 1992.

Dull, Jonathan. *The French Navy and the Seven Years' War.* Lincoln: University of Nebraska Press, 2005.

Fowler, William, Jr. *Empires at War: The French and Indian War and the Struggle for North America, 1754–1763.* New York: Walker, 2004.

Frégault, Guy. *Canada: The War of the Conquest.* Translated by Margaret M. Cameron. London: Oxford University Press, 1969.

Jennings, Francis. *Empire of Fortune: Crowns, Colonies and Tribes in the Seven Years' War in America.* New York: Norton, 1990.

Kennedy, Paul. *The Rise and Fall of British Naval Mastery.* New York: Penguin, 1976.

Leach, Douglas E. *Arms for Empire: A Military History of the British Colonies in North America, 1607–1763.* New York: Macmillan, 1973.

Middleton, Richard. *The Bells of Victory: The Pitt-Newcastle Ministry and the Conduct of the Seven Years' War, 1757–1762.* Cambridge: Cambridge University Press, 1985.

Parkman, Francis. *Montcalm and Wolfe.* 1884; reprint, New York: Crowell-Collier, 1962.

Warner, Oliver. *With Wolfe to Quebec: The Path to Glory.* Toronto: William Collins and Sons, 1972.

Seven Years' War (1756–1763)

Dates	1756–1763
Location	Principally Europe but also North America, South America, Africa, India, Philippine Islands
Combatants	Prussia, Great Britain, Hanover, Portugal vs. Austria, France, Russia, Saxony, Spain, Sweden
Principal Commanders	Prussia: Frederick the Great, Duke Ferdinand of Brunswick Britain: George II; George III; William Augustus, Duke of Cumberland; Sir Edward Hawke Austria: Maria Theresa, Maximilian von Browne, Leopold Joseph von Daun, Prince Charles of Lorraine, Ernst von Laudon (Loudon) France: Louis XV; Louis Charles César Le Tellier, Duc d'Estrées; Louis François Armand du Plessis, Duc de Richelieu; Charles de Rohan, Prince de Soubise Russia: Elizabeth I, Peter III, Catherine the Great, Count Wilhelm Fermor
Principal Battles	Prague, Kolin, Rossbach, Leuthen, Krefeld, Zorndorf, Hochkirch, Minden, Kunersdorf, Quiberon Bay, Torgau, Liegnitz, Wilhelmsthal, Lutterberg
Outcome	Prussia retains Silesia and its status as a major European power. France is determined to exact revenge.

Causes

Following the War of Austrian Succession (1740–1748), Archduchess Maria Theresa of Austria unbent every effort to reverse its outcome and recover Silesia from Prussia. Her army, although still inferior to that of Prussia, had nonetheless performed well late in the war, and her resources were still formidable. The limitations of the British and Dutch alliance were evident, however, as the British saw Austria chiefly as an auxiliary against France, and Britain and the Dutch had contributed little military assistance to Austria. Maria Theresa now engineered what became known as the Diplomatic Revolution of the Eighteenth Century, dispatching Wenzel Anton Count Kaunitz as ambassador to France (1750–1753) with the assignment of breaking the French-Prussian alliance.

In 1754 fighting had broken out in America and on the high seas between the British and French, and there was danger of this spreading to Britain's German possession of Hanover. Still, it is doubtful that France would have allied with Austria without an action taken by King Frederick II of Prussia. Frederick was greatly alarmed by the general international situation. His seizure of Silesia ensured permanent Austrian hostility. Russia was also anti-Prussian. To counter a September 1755 treaty between Russia and Britain to protect Hanover against Prussia, Frederick signed with Britain the Statute of Westminster on January 16, 1756. In it he agreed to neutralize Germany and remove it from fighting between Britain and France.

This limited step had disproportionate results. At the French court there was considerable anger concerning Frederick's demarche toward Britain. There was also a sense that Prussia had become too powerful. The misogynist Frederick had also offended in well-publicized remarks not only Czarina Elizabeth of Russia but also Madame de Pompadour, influential mistress to Louis XV. On May 1, 1756, therefore, Louis XV concluded with Austria the First Treaty of Versailles. It bound each power to supply the other, if attacked, with an army of 24,000 men or its money equivalent. One consequence of this alliance was the marriage of the future French king Louis XVI to Marie Antoinette, daughter of Maria Theresa. Thus, whereas in 1740 Prussia and France had allied against Austria and Britain, in 1756 Prussia and Britain were allied against Austria and France. Nonetheless, the two major rivalries of Britain against France and Prussia against Austria continued.

Frederick was well aware of the formation against him of what was arguably the most powerful military coalition of the century. Unwilling to wait until his enemies of Austria, France, Russia, and Saxony were ready to strike, he decided on a preemptive attack, beginning what would be the Seven Years' War (1756–1763). Ultimately involving all the leading European powers, the conflict saw fighting across the globe: in North America, the Caribbean, and India as well as on the high seas. It also initiated for Prussia what would turn out to be the most desperate struggle for survival in 18th-century Europe.

Course

As noted, fighting had already begun between Britain and France in 1754. When the French invaded Minorca, Britain formally declared war on May 17, 1756. The two powers fought an inconclusive naval battle off Minorca on May 20 that led to a British naval withdrawal and British surrender of the island.

The Seven Years' War and the Third Silesian War formally began on August 29, 1756, when Frederick mounted without declaration of war a preemptive strike against Saxony with 70,000 men. He captured the Saxon capital of Dresden on September 10 and then extracted large cash payments and drafted Saxons into his army, two practices he continued throughout the war. Frederick maneuvered brilliantly, moving rapidly and often surprising his opponents. His military genius was barely enough, however, as Prussia had as ally only Britain, which provided mainly financial subsidies.

Austrian marshal Maximilian von Browne advanced with 34,500 men to relieve some 14,000 Saxons trapped at Pirna on the Elbe. Frederick moved into Bohemia to oppose him with 28,500 men. The two armies met along the Elbe near Lobositz (Lovosice) on October 1. The battle began badly for Frederick but ended with an Austrian withdrawal. The Prussians suffered perhaps 700 killed and 1,900 wounded; Austrian losses were about 3,000. The Saxons at Pirna surrendered, and Frederick incorporated them into his army.

In April 1757 Frederick invaded Bohemia in force. He had some 175,000 men, half of them along the Bohemian frontier; the remainder were in defensive postures against France, Russia, and Sweden. Austria was then the only allied power ready militarily, and Maria Theresa had some 132,000 troops in northern Bohemia. In a risky maneuver, Frederick split his forces, sending some of his men across the mountains east of the Elbe and moving with the

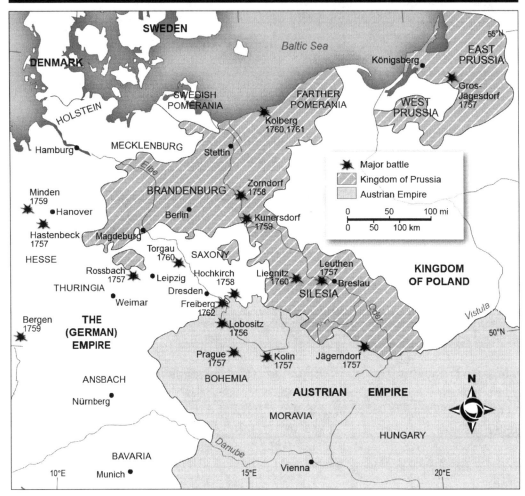

CENTRAL EUROPE IN THE SEVEN YEARS' WAR 1756 – 1763

largest body from Pirna against Prague (Praha), where the Austrians had 55,000 men under Prince Charles of Lorraine.

On May 1, meanwhile, in the Second Treaty of Versailles, France agreed to a substantial increase in its military commitment. France pledged to maintain an army of 105,000 men in Germany as well as 10,000 German mercenaries and to pay Austria a large annual subsidy of 12 million florins. In return, France was to receive four cities in the Austrian Netherlands,

with the remainder of the Austrian Netherlands going to Don Philip, the Duke of Parma and Louis XV's son-in-law. The cession of the Austrian Netherlands was, however, conditional on the Austrian recovery of all Silesia.

On May 6, Frederick with some 56,000 men faced 55,000 Austrians under Prince Charles and Marshal Browne near Prague and forced their withdrawal back into Prague. The fighting claimed some 13,400 Austrians and 14,300 Prussians.

His resources insufficient to storm Prague, Frederick hoped to starve it into submission. Marshal Leopold von Daun now moved with an Austrian relief force toward Prague. Taking 32,000 men from his forces besieging Prague, Frederick moved to block Daun with 44,000 men. The two armies met at Kolín (Kolin) in Bohemia on June 18. Daun had established a strong defensive position, and Frederick's attack was poorly coordinated. After five hours of fighting Frederick withdrew, having sustained some 13,800 casualties, while Daun lost 9,000. This battle was Frederick's first defeat of the war, and it forced him to abandon both his siege of Prague and plans to march on Vienna. Now facing some 110,000 Austrians, he had to abandon all Bohemia.

Austrian forces under Prince Charles and Marshal Daun crossed the Elbe on July 14. Frederick had not expected an attack from this direction and had given his brother Prince August Wilhelm command of forces on the east bank of the river. Advancing rapidly, on July 23 the Austrians captured the Prussian supply base of Zittau in Saxony and there secured substantial provisions. Furious, Frederick relieved his brother of command.

As the Austrians drove north into Saxony, Marshal Louis Charles César Le Tellier, Duc d'Estrées, invaded Hanover with a French army of 100,000 men in an effort to draw Prussian resources from the east. A second French army of 24,000 men under Marshal Charles de Rohan, Prince de Soubise, and 60,000 Austrians under Prince Joseph of Saxe-Hildgurhausen moved northeast into Franconia to join d'Estrées. Concurrently, Marshal Stepan Apraksin and a Russian army of 100,000 men invaded East Prussia, and 16,000 Swedes landed in Pomerania.

Pinned down in the east, Frederick was unable to assist in the west. This was left to the 40,000-man Hanoverian Army of Observation that included a majority from Hanover as well as men from Hesse and some Prussians. Duke William Augustus of Cumberland, son of King George II of Britain, had command. Cumberland refused to defend the Rhine. His chief objective being to prevent the French from occupying Hanover, he concentrated behind the Weser River at Hamelin, hoping to prevent a French crossing.

The French took Emden on July 3 and Kassel (Cassel) on July 15. On July 16 they crossed the Weser in force, obliging Cumberland to do battle at Hastenbeck on June 26, 1757. D'Estrées had some 65,000 men, and the outnumbered Cumberland was forced to withdrew. The allies suffered 1,300 casualties, the French 2,600. This battle brought the French occupation of Hanover.

In the east, meanwhile, Field Marshal Stepan Fedorovich Apraksin and 75,000 Russians captured Memel. It became the principal Russian base for the invasion of East Prussia. The Russians then crossed the Pregel River. On August 30 Prussian field marshal Hans von Lehwaldt led 15,500 men in a surprise attack on a Russian corps, but other Russian forces quickly came up, forcing Lehwaldt to withdraw. While the Russians lost more than 5,400 men, Prussian casualties of 5,000 men and 28 guns lost were far heavier in percentage of forces engaged. The way to Berlin appeared open, and it was widely expected that Apraksin would move against Königsberg (present-day Kaliningrad) and overrun all East Prussia, but he soon halted and then withdrew back into Russia. This was to support Peter III as heir to the throne but also because of a major outbreak of smallpox in the army and the collapse of the primitive Russian logistical system.

Leaving a small Prussian force in Silesia under August Wilhelm, Duke of Brunswick-Bevern, Frederick rapidly marched westward with only 23,000 men to meet the most serious of the immediate allied military threats to his regime: the principal French army under Marshal Louis François Armand du Plessis, Duc de Richelieu, who had replaced Marshal d'Estrées; a second army of French forces under Soubise; and Austrian/imperial forces under Prince Joseph Friedrich von Sachsen-Hildburghausen. Richelieu remained stationary, however, and Soubise and Hildburghausen, who had captured Magdeburg, withdrew to Eisenach on Frederick's approach. Frederick then shifted direction to try to halt the Austrians under Prince Charles and Marshal Daun. On October 16, however, Austrian troops raided Berlin.

Learning that French forces under Soubise and Austrian-imperial forces under Sachsen-Hildburghausen had resumed their eastward movement, Frederick again marched westward. Departing Dresden on August 31 with 22,000 men, he covered 170 miles in only 13 days by arranging ahead for supplies and doing away with supply wagons. Crossing the Saale River, he drew the allies into battle in the vicinity of the village of Rossbach, west of Leipzig.

In the Battle of Rossbach of November 5, 1757, the two allied armies had together perhaps 66,000 men, Frederick only 22,000. The allies, moreover, occupied commanding terrain. Given their crushing numerical advantage, the allied commanders decided to envelop the Prussian east flank and sent three columns of 41,000 men south to accomplish this.

Guessing their intention, Frederick feinted a withdrawal eastward while slipping most of his forces south to his own left, a move concealed from allied observation by a line of hills. When the enveloping force completed its movement and swung northward, it met heavy Prussian artillery fire and the repositioned German infantry. At the same time, Prussian cavalry swung wide to the east and struck the right flank of the advancing allied columns. The Prussian infantry then smashed into the allied troops *en echelon* (in overlapping succession), completely routing them in less than an hour and a half. The Prussians suffered only 169 dead and 379 wounded. Allied losses were some 10,000, about half of them prisoners. Some 25,000 allied troops had not fought in the battle. Frederick's brilliant victory removed the immediate threat to Prussia from the west and allowed him to shift his resources eastward to confront the Austrian armies advancing on Prussia from the south.

On November 22, Prince Charles of Lorraine and Marshal Leopold von Daun with 84,000 men encountered a Prussian army of 28,000 men at Wrocław in Silesia under August Wilhelm, Duke of Brunswick-Bevern, forcing it to withdraw west of the Oder after having sustained 6,000 casualties that included August Wilhelm, taken prisoner, to 5,000 for the Austrians. Wrocław surrendered on November 25.

Having marched eastward 170 miles in only 12 days, Frederick joined what remained of Brunswick-Bevern's force near Liegnitz (Legnica). With about 33,000 men, he moved east to meet the Austrians. Informed of Frederick's approach, Prince Charles took up position with his 65,000 men near the village of Leuthen, a few miles from Wrocław.

The Battle of Leuthen occurred on December 5, 1757. Frederick and his commanders were well familiar with the area, the site of Prussian military maneuvers. Outnumbered two to one, Frederick feinted a major attack on the Austrian right while he took advantage of a low range of hills to shift the bulk of his attacking force to the left. Charles took the bait, shifting reserves from his left front to his right to meet the threatened attack. Frederick's infantry then struck the Austrian left. Charles endeavored to shift resources but was forced to withdraw. Nightfall ended the battle and rendered impossible any Prussian pursuit. The bulk of the Austrian forces escaped to Wrocław.

The Battle of Leuthen shattered Charles's army, which lost 6,750 killed or wounded, more than 12,000 captured, and 116 guns. Prussian losses were 6,150 killed or wounded. Frederick retook Wrocław five days later, capturing another 17,000 Austrians. Both armies then went into winter quarters. Only half of the Austrian force that had begun the campaign remained.

In fighting in the west in 1758, on June 23 an allied German force of 32,000 men from Hanover, Hesse, and Brunswick under Duke Ferdinand of Brunswick attacked and defeated a 50,000-man French army commanded by Marshal Gaspard, Duke of Clermont-Tonnerre, at Crefeld (Krefeldt) in the Rhineland, northwest of Düsseldorf. The French withdrew to Cologne (Köln).

In yet another military embarrassment for the French, in August 1758 the British sent troops across the English Channel and destroyed port facilities at Cherbourg. Not satisfied, in September the British sought to attack St. Malo. Finding it too well fortified they withdrew, only to suffer more than 800 casualties while reembarking their raiding force.

In the east, in January 1758 Russian forces, now commanded by General Count Wilhelm Fermor, again invaded East Prussia but were brought to a halt by terrible road conditions. That spring Frederick campaigned in Moravia against the Austrians. In May he besieged Olmütz (Olomouc) on the Oder, defended by Marshal Daun. Frederick broke this off on July 1 on learning of the Russian approach. Carefully maneuvering to deceive the Austrians as to his real intent, he marched rapidly against the Russians.

Frederick arrived at the Oder across from Küstrin with 25,000 men and 167 guns as General Fermor and 43,000 Russians with 210 guns were laying siege to Küstrin, less than 100 miles from Berlin. Feinting a crossing of the river there, Frederick instead moved north in a night march, crossed the river, and in a wide turning movement threatened Fermor's lines of communication back to Russia. Learning of the Prussian moves, Fermor lifted the siege and took up a defensive position facing north at the Prussian village of Zorndorf (now Sarbinowo, Poland), about 6 miles southeast of Küstrin.

The August 25 Battle of Zorndorf has sometimes been referred to as the bloodiest battle of the century. The Russian infantrymen doggedly refused to withdraw, and large numbers were cut down where they stood. Fighting continued until nightfall. The Prussians lost 12,797 men, the Russians some 18,500. The battle was a draw, although Fermor's withdrawal two days later allowed Frederick to claim victory. The battle was strategically important, as it prevented the Russians from linking up with the Austrians and perhaps defeating Frederick once and for all.

This was not the end of fighting in the east that year. Learning that Austrian forces under Marshal Daun were threatening those under his brother Prince Henry of Prussia near Dresden, Frederick II hurried there with his part of the army, arriving on September 12. The Austrians then withdrew. Now having 31,000 men, Frederick commenced offensive operations, only to be surprised and surrounded by a secret night march by Daun and 80,000 Austrians at Hochkirch, about five miles east of Bautzen in Saxony.

Daun attacked at dawn on October 14, employing his own oblique attack. Despite a nearly threefold disadvantage in manpower, the Prussians fought hard, and their cavalry managed to open an escape route through the Austrian lines. Most of the army escaped but at the cost of 9,097 dead, wounded, or captured. The Austrians also secured 101 Prussian guns. Austrian casualties totaled 7,587.

Daun then laid siege to Dresden. Learning that Frederick had reconstituted his army and was marching against him, Daun raised the siege and retired into winter quarters at Pirna. The end of the year saw Frederick in firm control of both Silesia and Saxony. Both the Russian and Swedish forces had evacuated Prussian territory. The year 1758 had nonetheless been costly for Frederick. Although he could still field 150,000 men, the campaigns of 1758 had cost him 100,000 of his best-trained men, and the army was no longer the quality of the year before.

In western Germany in 1759, April 13 saw an allied force of 35,000 men under Duke Ferdinand of Brunswick attack at Bergen near Frankfurt-am-Main a French force of 28,000 men commanded by Marshal Victor François, Duc de Broglie. Rebuffed, the allies withdrew in good order. The French then seized the bridges over the Wesel and advanced to Minden. On July 25, French forces under General Louis de Brienne de Conflans, Marquis of Armentières, captured Münster in present-day Rhine-Westphalia, taking 4,000 allied prisoners.

The French then concentrated some 60,000 men near Minden under Marshal Louis Georges, Marquis of Contades. On August 1, 1759, Duke Ferdinand of Brunswick led 45,000 allied troops, including 10,000 Britons, against the French, driving them off. The Battle of Minden cost the allies some 2,800 casualties; the French sustained 10,000–11,000 as well as the loss of 115 guns. Ferdinand pursued the French almost to the Rhine, halting only when Frederick ordered him to send men east. The Duc de Broglie replaced Contades, who was sacked.

In the east, in July 1759 Russian general Pyotr Saltykov led 47,000 men from Posen along the Oder River toward Crossen. Frederick II ordered Prussian lieutenant general Karl von Wedel and 28,000 men to stop the Russian advance. Saltykov defeated Wedel on July 23 in the Battle of Kay (Paltzig, now in Poland). The Prussians suffered 8,300 casualties to 6,000 for the Russians. Saltykov then crossed the Oder and occupied Crossen.

Frederick was determined to prevent the Russians from joining the Austrians. Before he could carry this out, however, some 18,500 Austrians under Lieutenant Field Marshal Ernst von Laudon (Loudon) joined Saltykov's 41,000 men east of Frankfurt an der Oder. Frederick, with 50,900 Prussians, crossed the Oder and on August 12 attacked the entrenched allies in hilly terrain at Kunersdorf (present-day Kunowice, Poland).

Frederick attempted a simultaneous double envelopment. Owing to his men's inadequate training and woods that imposed delay, the attacks occurred piecemeal, but Frederick insisted on continuing the attacks and was defeated. Frederick himself barely escaped capture. Shocked by their own heavy casualties, however, the allies failed to exploit their victory. Russian and Austrian losses totaled 15,700 men (5,000 killed), but the Prussians suffered 19,100 casualties (6,000 dead) and lost 172 guns. Much of what remained of the Prussian army was scattered; indeed, immediately after the battle, Frederick had only 3,000 men under his direct command. Kunersdorf was the worst defeat of Frederick's military career.

Within a few days most of Frederick's scattered forces rejoined him, bringing his strength to 32,000 men and 50 guns. Receiving reinforcements from Duke Ferdinand of Brunswick, Frederick regained his determination. The Russians, having exhausted forage and other area resources, retired to the frontier. Frederick therefore decided to move against Marshal Daun's Austrians, who had captured Dresden on September 4.

Frederick sent 14,000 men under General Friedrich August von Finck to cut the Austrian lines of communication with Bohemia. Frederick expected Daun to withdraw once this occurred, but Daun trapped Finck. Outnumbered 42,000 to 14,000, Finck surrendered his entire force on November 21. Both sides then went into winter quarters.

The French had hoped to invade the British Isles in 1759, but to accomplish this they would have to join their Mediterranean and Channel Fleets. British admiral Sir Edward Hawke commanded the Channel Fleet confronting the French Brest squadron. Admiral Sir Edward Boscawen,

charged with containing the French Toulon Squadron, defeated it in the Battle of Lagos (August 18, 1759). The Brest Squadron remained a major threat, however.

On November 14 a storm drove the British blockaders off station, and French admiral Hubert de Brienne, Comte de Conflans, sortied from Brest with 21 ships of the line. Hawke was soon in pursuit with 24 ships of the line. Surprised by Hawke on November 20 southeast of Belle Isle on his way to escort transports carrying troops to Scotland, Conflans was unable to form a line of battle and tried to escape into the Vilaine estuary, utilizing pilots familiar with the coast to take him into the wind-swept and rocky lee shore. In terrible conditions Hawke signaled a general chase, and his ships followed the French into Quiberon Bay. In the ensuing battle fought in high winds and torrential rain, the French lost 4 ships of the line and 1,300 men killed.

Hawke anchored for the night, intent upon destroying the remaining French ships come daylight. In the dark, however, eight French ships escaped to Rochefort, where they remained for the rest of the war. Seven others lightened ship and entered the Vilaine estuary, where they were stranded for a year. Conflans was forced on the morning of November 21 to run his own ship on the rocks rather than have it taken by the British.

The Battle of Quiberon Bay cost the French six ships of the line wrecked or sunk and 1 captured, along with 2,500 dead. The British lost two ships of the line wrecked and 400 dead. The battle ended any French threat of invasion of the British Isles for the rest of the war. It also prevented the French from resupplying or augmenting their forces in North America. Although French privateers continued to enjoy success against British merchant shipping, the French Navy was largely swept from the seas.

During the winter of 1759–1760 the allies planned for a series of coordinated attacks in the spring to destroy Frederick. The Austrians concentrated 100,000 men under Marshal Daun in Saxony and 50,000 men under Marshal Laudon in Silesia. Laudon was to cooperate with 50,000 Russians in East Prussia under Marshal Saltykov. If Frederick turned on any one of these, the others were to move against Berlin. Frederick was on the Elbe with 40,000 men facing Daun, Prince Henry was in Silesia with 34,000 men, and an additional 15,000 Prussians opposed other Russian and Swedish forces ravaging Pomerania. In the west, Duke Ferdinand of Brunswick commanded an allied army of 70,000 men in Hanover opposing some 125,000 French troops.

The Prussians suffered their first reverse on June 23, 1760, when Marshal Laudon with some 28,000 men defeated Prussian general Henri de la Motte Fouqué with 11,000–12,000 men at Landshut in Silesia. During July 13–22 Frederick attempted to engage both Laudon, besieging the Prussian fortress of Glatz (now Kłodzko in Lower Silesia, Poland), and Daun. When Frederick threatened Laudon, Daun marched to his assistance. Frederick then quickly countermarched and attempted to recapture Dresden. The Prussians shelled the city, inflicting considerable damage, but failed to bring about an Austrian surrender. On July 21 Daun reinforced Dresden, obliging Frederick to abandon his operations there. Then on July 26, Laudon's Austrians captured Glatz.

Laudon next moved against Wrocław, held by 4,000 Prussians under General Bogislav von Tauentzien with 9,000 Austrian prisoners. Laudon laid siege to Wrocław

on July 30 but, facing the imminent arrival of Prussian reinforcements under Prince Henry, raised it on August 5. Salykov's Russians were still five days' march away.

Calling on Prince Henry to join him, Frederick II led 30,000 men into Silesia. Laudon with 24,000 men and Daun with 36,000 pursued, and the chances appeared good that Count Zacharias Chernyshev would join them near Wrocław with 25,000 Russians.

The Prussians and Austrians met near the large Silesian city of Liegnitz. The Austrians planned a double envelopment, with Laudon taking a blocking position to hold Frederick in place. On the night of August 14–15 in a brilliant march, however, Frederick shifted position so that when Laudon launched his attack before dawn on the morning of August 15, it was the Prussians who enveloped and defeated him before Daun could come up. Frederick then cut his way out, having inflicted some 8,500 Austrian casualties and captured 80 guns for losses of only 3,394 men. Although his men were fresh, Daun decided not to attack on his own, missing an excellent opportunity to destroy Frederick with superior forces. A false report by Frederick led Chernyshev to believe that the Austrians had been totally defeated, causing him to withdraw. Frederick then maneuvered against Daun.

During October 9–12, 1760, meanwhile, 20,000 Russians under General Gottleb Tottleben and 15,000 Austrians under Marshal Franz Moritz Lacy briefly occupied Berlin. On October 9 also, Russian troops ambushed Prussians retreating from Berlin to Spandau, killing or capturing 3,300. The allied occupation of Berlin was mild, no doubt because Tottleben was carrying on a treasonous correspondence with the Prussians. Although private residences were sacked and the occupiers secured a ransom of 1.5 million thalers, the only significant damage to the Prussian war effort was destruction of the city's gunpowder plant. With Frederick hurrying there, the allies evacuated Berlin.

Learning that Daun was concentrating some 52,000 men near Torgau, Frederick assembled 44,000 men and moved against the entrenched Austrians, attacking on November 3. Concentrated Austrian artillery fire claimed 5,000 Prussian grenadiers in only one hour, and Frederick called off the assault, believing the battle lost. Marshal Lacy replaced Daun, wounded in the foot, and the battle turned that evening when Prussian general Hans von Zeiten attacked and captured much of the Austrian artillery, then turned these guns against the Austrians. That night Lacy withdrew toward Dresden. This Prussian victory came at heavy cost, however: 16,670 casualties against Austrian losses of 15,000 (7,000 of them prisoners) and 43 guns. Both sides then went into winter quarters.

In western Germany in 1760, Duke Ferdinand of Brunswick sought to emulate Frederick with a series of rapid marches and maneuvers to keep French forces separated and allow him to defeat them in detail. In the Battle of Warburg in present-day North Rhine–Westphalia on July 31, 1760, Ferdinand and some 16,000 men defeated French lieutenant general Chevalier du Muy with 20,000 men. The French suffered between 6,000 and 8,000 casualties and lost 12 guns. The allies sustained 1,200 casualties. French marshal de Broglie took advantage of Ferdinand's absence to seize Kassel (Cassel), however.

In early autumn with the French threatening to invade Hanover, Duke Karl Wilhelm Ferdinand and some 20,000 men marched against the French-held fortified town of Wesel at the juncture of the Rhine and Lippe Rivers. The French defenders destroyed key bridges, and Lieutenant General Charles Eugène Gabriel de La Croix de Castries, Marquis de Castries, moved to relieve Wesel but then decided to await additional reinforcements before attacking.

Determining that he could not take Wesel by storm, Duke Ferdinand ordered up heavy siege and bridging equipment. In the meantime, he planned to attack de Castries with a movement around the French left flank at Kloster Kamp during the night of October 15–16. The allied assault early on October 16 enjoyed initial success, but de Castries rushed up reserves and counterattacked, carrying the day. Ferdinand then fell back toward the Rhine, but the bridge of boats he had ordered constructed there was swept away by the fast-flowing river, stranding his army on the west bank for two more days. De Castries chose to await reinforcements and failed to exploit the situation. The French suffered 3,123 casualties, while the allies lost 1,615. The battle ended the Siege of Wesel, and the opposing western armies then went into winter quarters.

In the summer of 1761, Frederick learned that Austrian forces under Marshal Laudon and Russians under General Aleksandr Buterlin had joined near Liegnitz. Frederick then dug in at Bunzelwitz in Silesia some 20 miles east of Glatz in the Eulen Gebirge (Owl Mountains). In only 10 days and nights, Frederick's men turned this natural fortress on the northern frontier of today's Czech Republic into a formidable defensive position. Still, Frederick had only 53,000 men against some 130,000 for the allies.

Laudon drew up a detailed plan for a massive attack that had an excellent chance of success, but Buterlin rejected it, his caution the result of two factors: Russian empress Elizabeth had sent a message in June during the army's march through Poland indicating that she would like to see it return to Russia intact, and Elizabeth was in failing health, with the heir apparent an unabashed admirer of the Prussian king. The inability of the allies to agree on a plan of action in addition to an unusually hot summer and a near total lack of forage for the horses led the Russians to withdraw back to the Oder beginning on September 9.

Laudon was able to salvage something from the frustrating 1761 Silesian campaign, however. Acting on information provided by an escaped Austrian prisoner, Laudon moved against the important Prussian-held fortress of Schweidnitz in late September, storming and capturing it on September 30 without preliminary bombardment, taking 3,800 Prussians prisoner, and depriving Frederick of his best-placed and most important Silesian supply depot. For the first time in the war Austria held significant areas of Silesia during the winter, forcing Frederick to remain in Silesia instead of wintering in Saxony as he desired.

In the west in 1761, two French armies totaling 92,000 men under Marshal de Broglie and Marshal Soubise, attempted to force the allies from Lippstadt. On July 15 the French attacked an entrenched allied force of 65,000 German and British troops under Duke Ferdinand at Villinghausen, near Hamm in present-day North Rhine–Westphalia. With the two French commanders of equal rank and each reluctant to take orders from the other, the French withdrew. The allies suffered some 1,400 casualties, the French 5,000. By October, however, the French had pushed allied forces east to Brunswick.

Winter set in early that year, and morale was low among the Prussian forces, with soldiers deserting in large numbers. There was even a plot to assassinate Frederick. In Saxony, Prussian prince Henry was holding his own against the Austrians under Marshal Daun, but in western Germany the situation appeared precarious. British king George II died on October 15, and his successor, George III, began withdrawing some British troops from the continent and threatened an end to subsidies to Prussia. Frederick now had only 60,000 men, and the end appeared near.

The war had also expanded that fall. France and Spain concluded a pact against Britain in August 1761, and Spanish and French troops invaded Portugal in October. Britain came to the assistance of Portugal and declared war on Spain in January 1762.

With the end for Frederick apparently near, on January 5, 1762, there occurred the so-called Miracle of the House of Brandenburg. Czarina Elizabeth I died. Her successor, the mad Peter III, an unabashed admirer of Frederick, immediately withdrew Russia from the war. On May 15 in the Treaty of St. Petersburg, Russia concluded peace with Prussia and agreed to evacuate East Prussia. Czar Peter even loaned Frederick a Russian army corps.

Russia's decision to withdraw from the war caused Sweden to follow suit. In the Treaty of Hamburg of May 22, Prussia and Sweden concluded peace on the basis of status quo ante bellum. Frederick was now free to concentrate against Austria, while Duke Ferdinand held the French at bay in the west.

On June 24, 1762, at Wilhelmsthal in Westphalia, Duke Ferdinand's allied army of 50,000 men defeated a French army of 70,000 commanded by Marshal Louis Charles d'Estrées and Marshal

Soubise. The allies almost encircled the French before they escaped and withdrew across the Fulda River. The French suffered some 3,500 casualties, while the Allies suffered 700.

Taking advantage of anger over Czar Peter III's pro-Prussian policies and fearful that he intended to divorce her, Peter's wife Catherine and her lover Grigori Orlov led a conspiracy that deposed Peter on July 9 and brought his murder on July 18. Although new czarina Catherine II ended the alliance with Prussia, she did not resume Russia's involvement in the war, and without this Maria Theresa had no realistic hopes of holding Silesia.

Catherine ordered the return to Russia of General Count Zacharias Chernyshev's corps sent by Peter to aid Frederick. Realizing the necessity for prompt action, Frederick convinced Chernyshev to postpone his departure for three days in order to influence Austrian marshal Daun's decisions. Frederick then moved against Daun, entrenched at Burkersdorf.

The Russians and some Prussians to the northwest convinced Daun that the attack would come from that direction, while on July 21 Frederick and the bulk of the Prussian forces attacked from the northeast. Daun had perhaps 30,000 men at Burkersdorf, but Frederick enjoyed local superiority with perhaps 40,000, and that afternoon Daun withdrew. The Prussians suffered 1,600 casualties, while the Austrians lost at least that number dead or wounded and another 550 taken prisoner. The Russians then returned home. The battle, while not particularly bloody, was decisive in that Frederick now gradually regained control of Silesia.

Meanwhile on October 29, 1762, at Freiburg in Saxony, a 30,000-man Prussian army under Prince Henry defeated an Austrian, imperial, and Saxon army of 40,000 men under Austrian marshal Giovanni Serbelloni in the final major action of the war between Prussia and Austria. In the west, Duke Ferdinand of Brunswick, commanding more than 12,000 allied troops and 70 siege guns, captured Kassel (Cassel) in Hesse on October 12, taking 5,300 Frenchmen prisoner, and in November he drove French forces back across the Rhine.

The Seven Years' War also saw major fighting overseas. Here the British capitalized on their control of the seas. Fighting in America, which had begun earlier and was known as the French and Indian War (1754–1763), saw the English conquer New France and also secure Florida from Spain. (On November 13, 1762, in the Treaty of Fontainebleau, French king Louis XV compensated King Charles III of Spain by secretly ceding to Spain all Louisiana west of the Mississippi, including New Orleans.) In the Third Carnatic War (1757–1763) the British cemented their position in India against the French.

The British also triumphed in the Caribbean. In a bid to acquire some of the rich French sugar islands, the British invaded Martinique in January 1759. Rebuffed here by a sizable French garrison, the British moved against Guadeloupe instead. Landing there on January 23, the British captured it on May 1. The British returned to Martinique in January 1762 with a large force, and this last French stronghold in the West Indies surrendered on February 12. The British also captured St. Lucia (February 25) and Grenada (March 4).

Following Spain's entry into the war on the side of France, British forces moved against Cuba. Admiral Sir George Pocock commanded an armada of some 200 ships carrying 15,500 ground troops, many of them provincials, under Lieutenant General George Keppel, Earl of Albemarle. The troops landed near Havana beginning on June 7, 1762, and following a siege, Havana surrendered on August 13. The British secured some £3 million in specie and important stores as well as 9 Spanish ships of the line. British casualties totaled 1,790 killed, wounded, or missing, but many others fell prey to disease.

British forces also moved against the Philippines. On September 23, 1762, a British expeditionary force of some 2,300 men under Brigadier General Draper lifted by the ships of Rear Admiral Sir Samuel Cornish's East India Squadron and two East Indiamen arrived in the Philippines, much to the surprise of the Spanish. On October 5, Spanish authorities surrendered not only Manila but also the entire Philippine Islands. Manila was to be ransomed for 4 million Spanish dollars, although only half this sum was ever paid. The Philippines and the prize money were handed over to the East India Company. In all, the operation cost the British 150 casualties.

All participating states were now thoroughly exhausted by the fighting, and serious peace talks began in November 1762. In the Treaty of Paris of February 10, 1763, Britain, France, and Spain concluded peace. France ceded to Britain both New France and Cape Breton Island; both sides recognized the Mississippi River as the boundary between the British colonies and French Louisiana (secretly ceded to Spain). France also ceded to Britain Grenada in the West Indies and its possessions on the Senegal River in Africa.

One of the biggest issues of the peace was whether Britain should retain the rich sugar island of Guadeloupe or New France

(Canada). There were strong voices in Britain for Guadeloupe, which offered the promise of helping to offset the tremendous financial cost of the war. Besides, it might be wise to keep the French threat to ensure the loyalty of the North American English colonists. In the end, however, London kept Canada and returned Guadeloupe, with tremendous consequences for American history. France regained Martinique, Goree in Africa, and the island of Belle-Isle off the French coast. France also regained Pondicherry and Chandernagor in India, but the British were now clearly dominant there. Spain lost Florida to Britain, but Britain returned to the Spanish its conquests in Cuba, including Havana, as well as the Philippines.

On February 15, 1763, Austria, Prussia, and Saxony concluded peace in the Treaty of Hubertusburg. It reconfirmed the previous treaties of Breslau, Berlin, and Dresden in that Prussia kept possession of Silesia. Saxony was restored, and all three nations retained their antebellum boundaries. Prussia agreed to support Archduke Joseph (the future Joseph II) as Holy Roman emperor.

Significance

Prussia emerged from the war with its prestige much enhanced and confirmed as a major European power, although the rivalry with Austria remained. Internationally, Britain was clearly the world's chief colonial power. France and Spain had been humiliated, and French leaders yearned for revenge, the opportunity for which came during the American Revolutionary War.

Further Reading

Anderson, Fred. *Crucible of War: The Seven Years' War and the Fate of the Empire in British North America, 1754–1766.* New York: Knopf, 2000.

Black, Jeremy. *Pitt the Elder: The Great Commoner.* Cambridge: Cambridge University Press, 1992.

Clowes, William Laird. *The Royal Navy: A History from the Earliest Times to 1900,* Vol. 3, *1898.* Reprint ed. London: Chatham, 1996.

Corbett, Julian S. *England in the Seven Years' War.* London: Greenhill Books, 1992.

Dull, Jonathan. *The French Navy and the Seven Years' War.* Lincoln: University of Nebraska Press, 2005.

Kennedy, Paul. *The Rise and Fall of British Naval Mastery.* New York: Penguin, 1976.

Middleton, Richard. *The Bells of Victory: The Pitt-Newcastle Ministry and the Conduct of the Seven Years' War, 1757–1762.* Cambridge: Cambridge University Press, 1985.

American Revolutionary War (1775–1783)

Dates	1775–1783
Location	North America, Caribbean, Atlantic Ocean
Combatants	Britain, German auxiliaries, and allied Native Americans vs. North American colonists and Native American allies, France, Spain, and the Netherlands
Principal Commanders	Britain: George III, Lord George Germain, Sir William Howe, Sir Henry Clinton, Lord Charles Cornwallis. John Burgoyne, Earl Richard Howe America: George Washington, Nathanael Greene, Benedict Arnold, Horatio Gates French: Jean-Baptiste Donatien Vimeur, Comte de Rochambeau; François-Joseph-Paul, Comte de Grasse
Principal Battles	Lexington and Concord, Bunker Hill, Quebec, Long Island, White Plains, Trenton, Princeton, Brandywine, Germantown, Saratoga, Monmouth, Savannah, Charles Town (Charleston), Camden, King's Mountain, Cowpens, Guilford Court House, Second Battle of the Chesapeake, Yorktown, Gibraltar, Saintes
Outcome	The United States wins its independence, although Britain retains Canada. Despite its considerable effort, France gains little except a mammoth debt, leading to the French Revolution of 1789.

Causes

Separated by both 3,000 miles of ocean and dissimilar circumstances, it was inevitable that differences in outlook would arise between the ruling class in Britain and the inhabitants of British North America. Statesmen in London did not understand this, and even when they did, they made little or no effort to reconcile the differences. The communities on each side of the Atlantic had been growing apart for some time, but the crushing British victory over France in the French and Indian War (1754–1763) removed the French threat and gave free play to the forces working for separation.

Almost immediately after the war, in 1763 Chief Pontiac of the Ottawa Indians led an intertribal Native American alliance in a rebellion along the western frontier. British regulars put it down, but in these circumstances London decided to station 10,000 regulars along the frontier and require the Americans to pay part of their upkeep. The plan seemed fair, especially as the mother country was hard-pressed for funds following the heavy expenditures of the French and Indian War and the concurrent Seven Years' War (1756–1763) and because the soldiers would be protecting the colonials both from Indian attack and any French resurgence. This decision, however, ignited a long controversy about Parliament's right to tax. Apart from import duties (much of which were evaded through widespread smuggling), Americans paid only those few taxes assessed by their own colonial legislatures. By the same token, Americans did not have any direct representation in the British Parliament.

Parliament's effort began with the American Duties Act of April 1764, commonly known as the Sugar Act. Although it lowered the duty on foreign molasses, the act imposed the duty on all sugar or molasses regardless of its source. The Stamp Act of 1765 was a levy on all paper products. Reaction was such that the act was repealed the next year, as was the Sugar Act. Generally unnoticed in the excitement over the repeal was the Declaratory Act of March 1766. It asserted Parliament's right to bind its American colonies "in all cases whatsoever."

The next effort by Parliament to find some tax that the colonials would pay came in the Townshend Acts of 1767. These imposed customs duties on glass, lead, paint, paper, china earthenware, silk, and tea imported from Britain into the colonies. According to chancellor of the exchequer Charles Townshend, the revenues raised would be applied to help pay the salaries of royal governors and judges as well as the cost of defending the colonies. But the act was clearly an attempt to make British officials independent of colonial legislatures to enable them to enforce parliamentary

authority. It too was repealed after colonial protests, in March 1770, except for the tax on tea. The colonists' primary complaint was that Parliament had no right to levy internal taxes against them because they had no representation in that body.

Tensions between colonists and British soldiers also had been rising. This was in part for economic reasons (many British soldiers had, out of need, taken part-time jobs away from Bostonians). Another problem was the Quartering Act, by which Bostonians were forced to house and feed British troops. These factors led to a bloody confrontation on March 5, 1770, known as the Boston Massacre.

The prolonged British effort to bring the colonies to heel and colonial resistance to it ended with the so-called Boston Tea Party. In May 1773, Parliament attempted to rescue the financially strapped yet politically well-connected British East India Company. The government authorized the company to sell its considerable surplus of tea directly to its own agents in America. The tea would actually be cheaper, even with the tax in place, than smuggled Dutch tea, but the arrangement would cut out colonial middlemen, establishing a monopoly on what was the principal colonial drink and ending a major element of the smuggling trade. Public meetings in New York, Philadelphia, and Boston all condemned the act.

On the evening of December 16, some 8,000 people in Boston met in protest of the arrival there of three ships carrying East India Company tea. Afterward a number of the men, in the guise of Mohawk Indians, boarded the ships and, working throughout the night, emptied them of 342 large chests of tea, which were dumped into Boston Harbor. Further disorders against the landing of tea followed.

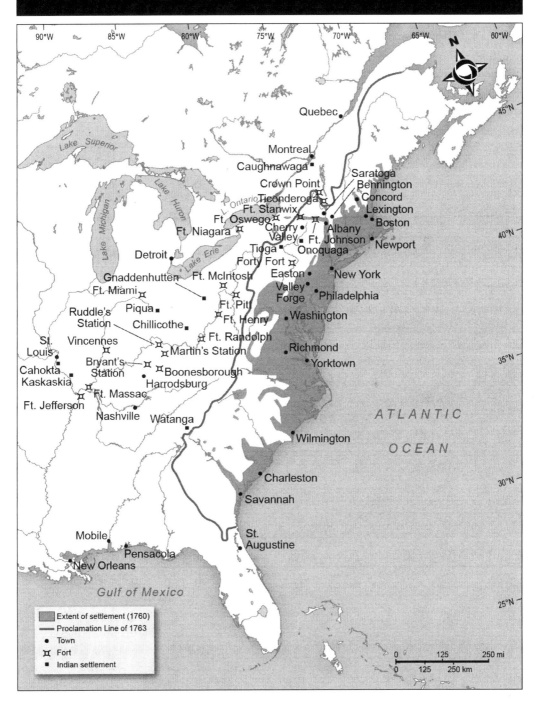

THE AMERICAN REVOLUTION, 1775 – 1783

Quebec

Montreal
Caughnawaga
Crown Point
Saratoga
Bennington
Ticonderoga
Ft. Stanwix
Concord
Lexington
Ft. Oswego
Cherry
Boston
Ft. Niagara
Valley
Albany
Tioga
Ft. Johnson
Newport
Onoquaga
Detroit
Forty Fort
Gnaddenhutten
Ft. McIntosh
Easton
New York
Ft. Miami
Valley
Forge
Philadelphia
Ruddle's
Station
Piqua
Ft. Pitt
Chillicothe
Ft. Henry
Washington
Ft. Randolph
St.
Louis
Vincennes
Martin's Station
Richmond
Bryant's
Station
Yorktown
Cahokta
Boonesborough
Kaskaskia
Harrodsburg
Ft. Massac
Ft. Jefferson
Nashville
Watanga
Wilmington

Lake Superior
Lake Michigan
Lake Huron
L. Ontario
Lake Erie

ATLANTIC

OCEAN

Charleston
Savannah

Mobile
St.
Augustine
Pensacola
New Orleans

Gulf of Mexico

Extent of settlement (1760)
Proclamation Line of 1763
• Town
⊠ Fort
■ Indian settlement

0   125   250 mi
0   125   250 km

90°W   85°W   80°W   75°W   70°W   65°W   60°W

45°N

40°N

35°N

30°N

25°N

This event ended the period of British government patience. Frustrated by its fruitless decade-long effort to tax the colonies and by colonial intransigence and lawlessness, London now adopted a harder line. Determined to teach the rebellious American subjects a lesson, in March 1774 King George III, who was determined to exercise his royal prerogatives, and his ministers pushed through Parliament the first of what became known as the Coercive Acts, measures known in America as the Intolerable Acts. The first of these, the Boston Port Bill, closed the port of Boston, threatening the colony with economic ruin. Other legislation suspended the Charter of Massachusetts, placed that colony under martial law, and gave the new government extensive new powers over town meetings. The Quartering Act required colonial authorities to provide housing and supplies for British troops. If the colonists would make restitution for the destroyed tea, the restrictions would be lifted. Nonetheless, this strong action against a colonial government and the colony's economic livelihood created a firestorm in America, lending credence to arguments by New England's radical leaders that the British were out to crush American liberties.

At the same time, although not part of the coercive program, the Quebec Act of May 1774 seemed a gratuitous British insult and one of the "intolerable" measures. Actually one of the most enlightened pieces of imperial legislation of its day, it sought to reconcile the large number of French Catholics to British rule by granting full civil rights and religious freedom to Canadians. This was anathema to many Protestants in New England. More important for the seaboard colonies, the act defined the borders of the former New France as the French had drawn them, cutting them off from further westward expansion.

After the Intolerable Acts and the Quebec Act, self-authorized groups met in several colonies and sent delegates to the Continental Congress in Philadelphia in September 1774. The delegation adopted the so-called Continental Association that called for nonimportation of English goods after December 1. North American lieutenant general Thomas Gage reported to London that the situation was dangerous and that he lacked sufficient manpower to deal with events if fighting were to break out. This did not affect George III and his ministers, who were determined to pursue a hard line. In February 1775, Parliament declared Massachusetts to be in rebellion.

Gage strongly disagreed with London's approach. In a report sent to London but not shared with Parliament, he estimated that in the event of fighting, it would take a year or two and 20,000 men just to pacify New England. If these men could not be supplied, Gage advocated a naval blockade and economic pressure as the best approach. The ministry in London disagreed. It held that 10,000 troops, supported by Loyalists, would be sufficient. Surely Gage was a defeatist or worse. London was convinced that the vast majority of Americans were loyal to the Crown, that any problems were the work of only a few agitators, and that a show of force and the arrest of the troublemakers would restore order; all would then be well.

The war that London now entered into so blithely caught Britain unprepared. Troops would have to be raised, the navy rebuilt, and men and supplies shipped across the Atlantic Ocean. While the Royal Navy, once rebuilt, could enforce a blockade and land troops at any point on the American seaboard and extract them again, campaigning in the interior in a land without adequate roads or strategic centers would be difficult indeed.

Course

Fighting began on April 19, 1775, when Gage sent troops from Boston to destroy stores of arms that the radicals had been stockpiling at Concord. He had carried out similar operations in the past, but this time the militia were alerted. At Lexington, the soldiers encountered a hastily assembled small militia force but, in a brief skirmish, easily brushed them aside. The British then marched on to Concord and completed their mission. The withdrawal to Boston became a nightmare, however, for the local militia was then out in force, and the militiamen sniped at the British from cover along the route. In all, the operation claimed 273 British casualties of some 1,800 engaged and 95 Americans. Some 15,000 New England militiamen then closed around Boston. Commanded by Major General Artemus Ward, they commenced the Siege of Boston (April 19, 1775–March 17, 1776).

On the outbreak of fighting, perhaps a quarter of Americans counted themselves as Patriots, another quarter remained loyal to Britain, and half of Americans were neutral. The Patriots were highly motivated, however, and they secured control of most of the local militia formations, using these throughout the war to control local Loyalists (Tories) and the countryside as well as to assist Continental Army formations in combat. In the latter role, however, the poorly trained militiamen often broke and ran. On May 10, 1775, Patriot forces totaling 83 men and led by Connecticut colonel Ethan Allen and Massachusetts colonel Benedict Arnold surprised and seized poorly garrisoned British Forts

Ticonderoga and Crown Point on Lake Champlain, securing 78 serviceable cannon as well as other military supplies.

In late May, British major generals John Burgoyne, Henry Clinton, and William Howe arrived at Boston with 3,500 troops, bringing British strength there to 6,500 men. They carried orders to impose martial law throughout Massachusetts, and they pressed Gage to undertake offensive action. At the same time, the British government was scouring the German states to hire troops to augment its own very small professional army. These auxiliaries, numbering in all some 30,000 men, came to be known collectively as Hessians, as perhaps half of them were from Hesse-Kassel (Hesse-Cassel).

The Second Continental Congress, having in mid-May urged all 13 colonial governments to undertake military preparedness, nonetheless recognized the need for a regular military establishment, and in June it authorized the establishment of 10 rifle companies for the Continental Army (Army of the United Colonies) and named Virginian George Washington as general and its commander. Washington took up his duties at Cambridge, Massachusetts, in early July.

On October 30, Congress also voted to establish a navy. A number of its ships were conversions and some were secured abroad, although Congress approved construction of 13 frigates. A number of states also raised navies, and Washington authorized armed schooners to disrupt British supplies into Boston. The main Patriot effort at sea during the war was by privateers, however. They captured some 3,087 British ships. A number of these were retaken, leaving 2,208 in American hands. The Americans also captured 89 British privateers, of which 75 remained in American hands. (British privateers captured 1,135 American merchantmen, of which 27 were retaken or ransomed. The British also captured 216 privateers.) These figures compare with a total of 196 ships captured by the Continental Navy. The captures of merchantmen drove up insurance rates and helped turn many in the British merchant class against the war. American privateers and Continental Navy ships may also have taken prisoner as many as 16,000 British seamen. This compares to 22,000 British soldiers taken by the Continental Army during the war.

On June 17, 1775, during the Siege of Boston, General Howe led an amphibious operation in Boston Harbor to seize high ground fortified by the Patriots on the Charlestown Peninsula. Instead of simply cutting off the rebel force by taking Charlestown Neck, however, Howe opted for a frontal assault. The ensuing Battle of Bunker Hill was a British victory, but at terrible cost. Of 2,400 British troops engaged, 1,054—including 92 officers—were casualties and 226 were dead. Probably some 1,500 Americans were engaged; of these 140 were killed, 380 were wounded, and 39 were captured. In terms of percentage of casualties to force engaged, it was one of the most sanguinary battles of the entire century. The battle shook Howe and may well have contributed to his later failure while commander in chief to press home attacks.

Fighting worked against reconciliation. At the end of July, the Continental Congress rejected a plan put forward by British prime minister Frederick, Lord North, second earl of Guilford, for reconciliation. It called for an end to taxes on all colonies that raised money to pay for British officials and military personnel. The Continental Congress continued to insist that

colonial legislatures alone should determine how monies raised might be spent. King George III's Royal Proclamation of Rebellion issued in late August, which promised severe punishment for all officials deemed treasonous, in effect ended the possibility of reconciliation.

On June 1, the Continental Congress had voted to dispatch expeditionary forces to Canada to seal the back door to America. There were to be two separate forces: the first would take Montreal, then join the second in capturing Quebec. The first force, initially under Major Philip Schuyler, stalled in a poorly conducted Patriot siege of St. Johns on the Richelieu River, while Colonel Benedict Arnold led a second force through the Maine wilderness to Quebec. With St. Johns finally taken and Montreal seized, Brigadier General Richard Montgomery joined Arnold at Quebec. With enlistments expiring and supplies running out, the Americans attempted a desperate attack on December 31, 1775, in the midst of a snowstorm. The attack was a complete failure. Montgomery was killed, and Arnold was wounded. The British captured 426 Americans; another 50 were killed or wounded but not captured. British losses were only 5 killed and 13 wounded. Arnold attempted to maintain a siege with his few remaining men, but in May 1776 this was broken with the arrival of a British supply ship. In the spring of 1776, British reinforcements drove the Americans, belatedly reinforced, from Canada. The Americans were not wrong in attempting the Canadian expedition. The failure was in not adequately supporting it from the start.

During the winter of 1775–1776, the Americans transported cannon from Fort Ticonderoga to Boston. In March 1776 they seized undefended Dorchester Heights and fortified it, then placed the cannon there. Howe, who had replaced Gage as British commander in North America, withdrew his men from Boston, sailing to Halifax, Nova Scotia. Washington permitted the British to depart unmolested on Howe's pledge not to destroy the city.

The Patriot side rightly feared a British invasion of New York down Lake Champlain that would cut off New England from the rest of the colonies. To counter this, Arnold, now a brigadier general, oversaw the building of a small flotilla of gondolas and galleys. In the Battle of Valcour Island on October 11–13, 1776, a more powerful British flotilla destroyed the American vessels, but Arnold had imposed delay on the British, and Major General Sir Guy Carleton, British commander in Canada, judged it too late in the season and called off the planned invasion that year. Meanwhile on June 28, 1776, Patriot forces repulsed a British attempt under Major General Henry Clinton to take Charles Town (Charleston), South Carolina, in the Battle of Sullivan's Island (June 28, 1776), the British losing several warships in the effort. The Continental Congress now voted on July 4 to approve the Declaration of Independence, proclaiming the United States a free and independent nation.

That same month, Howe arrived by sea at New York with 33,000 British and German troops. Washington had anticipated this move but had rejected mounted formations, and his defensive dispositions were not the best, although Howe showed little imagination and lacked drive. The British defeated the Americans in the Battle of Long Island (August 27, 1776), then crossed to Manhattan and in a series of battles pushed Washington's forces northward, taking New York City and then defeating the Americans at Harlem Heights (September 16) and White Plains (October 28).

Washington was able to extract his forces except for a large garrison, subsequently reinforced, but he foolishly left a sizable garrison under Colonel Robert Magaw at Fort Washington on the east bank of the Hudson on the assumption that if necessary it could be evacuated across the Hudson. It was now reinforced to nearly 3,000 men. Howe, however, sent ships up the river and then 10,000 men against the fort from the land side on November 16, taking it by assault the same day. The British actually lost more killed and wounded in the fighting: 78 killed and 374 wounded, while 59 Americans died and another 96 were wounded. But American losses in prisoners and supplies were staggering. The British captured 230 officers and 2,607 soldiers. They also secured 146 cannon, 2,800 muskets, 12,000 shot and shell, and 400,000 musket cartridges. The action here was second only to the surrender of Charles Town in 1780 as the worst Patriot defeat of the entire war.

The same thing almost happened to Fort Lee, across the Hudson from Fort Washington, but its garrison was forewarned and the men got away, although they were forced to abandon military stores. Washington now withdrew across New Jersey, leisurely pursued by Howe. In December the British occupied the port of Rhode Island, securing there a major anchorage for the British navy, and after setting up a string of outposts in western New Jersey, Howe went into winter quarters.

It looked as if the war was about over and the British had won. With most Continental Army enlistments set to expire at the end of the year, Washington embarked on a daring gamble. He planned to cross the Delaware River early on December 26 with some 5,500 men in three bodies and attack the Hessian garrison at Trenton of some 1,600 men commanded by Colonel Johann Rall. A storm swept through the area, and only Washington's group of 2,400 made it across in time for the attack. But Washington was determined to proceed, and surprise was complete. Artillery, in which the Americans had a considerable advantage, was a major factor in the outcome. The Hessians had 22 killed, 92 wounded (Rall mortally), and 948 captured. The remaining Hessians would also have been taken had the other columns gotten into position in time. The Americans sustained only 2 men frozen to death and 5 wounded. On December 27 the Continental Army was back across the Delaware.

The Battle of Trenton changed the entire campaign. It helped end Continental Army fear of Hessian troops and added immensely to Washington's prestige, at such a low point a month before. The battle also restored Patriot morale, which had been at its lowest point since the start of the war. Washington had snatched victory out of the jaws of death and fanned the dying embers of American independence into flame again.

Washington recrossed the Delaware for an attack on Princeton on January 3, 1777, and was again victorious. He then went into winter quarters at Morristown, New Jersey. During the early months of 1777, Patriot forces harried British communications in New Jersey with guerrilla attacks.

France, meanwhile, was providing valuable military assistance to the Patriot side. Pushed by his foreign minister Charles Gravier, Comte de Vergennes, who was anxious to weaken France's rival Britain but also to avenge France's humiliating defeats of the French and Indian War and the concurrent Seven Years' War, King

Louis XVI agreed in 1776 to extend secret aid to the American rebels. This assistance ultimately included more than 200 cannon, 20–30 mortars, 30,000 small arms, 100 tons of gunpowder, and clothing and tents sufficient for 25,000 men. Its importance cannot be overstated.

Meanwhile, British secretary of state for the American Department Lord George Germain, the man actually running the war for the British, approved two entirely different, even opposing, plans for the 1777 campaign. The first would see Howe move against Philadelphia. Howe believed that this would force Washington to defend the Patriot capital and give Howe the chance to destroy him.

In the second plan, Lieutenant General John Burgoyne would push south from Canada along the Lake Champlain corridor to Albany, New York, where he expected to meet part of Howe's army driving north from New York City up the Hudson. Burgoyne also planned a secondary campaign in conjunction with allied Native Americans in the Mohawk Valley to force a dispersion of American resources. British control of the Hudson would cut off New England from the rest of the colonies, but Burgoyne's polycentric plan failed to take into account the considerable logistical considerations, problems of coordination and timing, and Howe's own plan, which meant that few men would be available to move up the Hudson from New York City.

Leaving Clinton in command at New York, Howe set sail on July 23 with some 16,000 men in 267 ships protected by 16 warships. The troops began coming ashore at the head of the Chesapeake Bay on August 25, then moved toward Philadelphia. On September 11, Howe defeated Washington's army of 11,000 men drawn up along Brandywine Creek. Howe fixed the

Americans in place with part of his army and then marched with the majority around the American right, attempting to get in behind Washington and bag his entire force. Howe was again slow in execution, and Washington was able to withdraw in good order. American casualties were some 200 killed, 700–800 wounded, and almost 400 prisoners; the British lost 99 killed, 488 wounded, and 6 missing. Howe occupied Philadelphia on September 26.

On October 4, Washington with 11,000 men attempted a complicated multipronged night march against the British encampment at Germantown near Philadelphia. It met failure, thanks to poor coordination of the attacking columns and the timely arrival of British reinforcements from Philadelphia. American losses were 152 killed, 521 wounded, and about 400 taken prisoner; the British lost 71 killed, 450 wounded, and 14 missing.

In a series of hard-fought actions and heavy casualties on both sides, Howe took the American forts on the Delaware River and opened a supply line for the Royal Navy to Philadelphia. He then settled in at Philadelphia for the winter. Washington also went into winter quarters, at nearby Valley Forge, during which German volunteer Wilhelm von Steuben became the drillmaster of the Continental Army. He subsequently instilled both order and discipline, enabling the Continentals to fight on equal footing with their British counterparts.

Although Howe informed Burgoyne of his plans and there was little chance of major assistance, Burgoyne pressed ahead with his own campaign, starting out in June 1777 with some 10,500 men. All went well at first. In early July Burgoyne easily recaptured Fort Ticonderoga, forcing its defenders to hastily abandon the fortress. But Burgoyne's advance then slowed. In part it was the terrain and in part the highly effective scorched-earth policy practiced by American commander Major General Schuyler. At the same time, Burgoyne's secondary effort met rebuff in the Siege of Fort Stanwix (August 2–23, 1777).

With his supply situation becoming desperate, Burgoyne dispatched a foraging expedition of Hessians into Vermont. On August 16, Brigadier General John Stark and some 2,200 militiamen defeated this force and a reinforcing unit in the Battle of Bennington. In all, the Hessians sustained 207 killed and 700 captured for American casualties of only 30 killed and 40 wounded. The Patriot side also secured much-needed military supplies and weapons.

Refusing suggestions that he withdraw, Burgoyne crossed the Hudson River on September 15 and advanced to Bemis Heights, where he came upon defensive works ordered by new American commander Major General Horatio Gates. On September 19 in the Battle of Freeman's Farm (First Battle of Saratoga), the American force of some 8,000 men rebuffed a British attack. Burgoyne attacked again on October 7 and in the Battle of Bemis Heights (Second Battle of Saratoga) was again halted. Too late, Burgoyne then tried to withdraw but was forced to surrender his army of 5,895 officers and men on October 17.

The surrender of an entire British army was decisive, for it convinced French leaders that the Patriot side could indeed win the war, and on February 6, 1778, the French government signed a treaty of alliance with the United States. Britain declared war on France in June. Spain followed France into the war the next year, hoping to secure Gibraltar, and the Dutch Republic joined the fray when Britain declared war on it in late 1780. The war for American independence had become a world war.

Recognizing the changed situation, London now offered the United States all except for independence. The offer came too late and was spurned. Howe resigned his command in the spring of 1778 and was replaced by Clinton, now a lieutenant general. Clinton withdrew British forces from Philadelphia across New Jersey to be conveyed by ship to New York.

Determined to attack Clinton en route, Washington broke camp and fell on Clinton's rear elements. The Battle of Monmouth on June 28 was the last major engagement of the war in the North. Major General Charles Lee badly managed the Continental attack (he was later court-martialed and dismissed from the army), and Washington ended up taking command himself and fighting against a British counterattack. American losses were 152 killed and 300 wounded versus British losses of 290 killed, 390 wounded, and 576 captured. Clinton was able to return to New York City, however, while Washington took up station at White Plains.

Washington could do little to halt subsequent British raids on Connecticut and New Jersey coastal towns, and he was keenly disappointed that a newly arrived French fleet under Vice Admiral Jean-Baptiste, Comte d'Estaing, with 4,000 ground troops, was unable to attack British ships in New York Harbor, largely thanks to Vice Admiral Lord Richard Howe's skillful ship dispositions.

Washington then agreed to a plan for a joint attack by d'Estaing and Patriot ground forces against the British garrison of some 3,000 men at Rhode Island, commanded by Major General Robert Pigot. Major General John Sullivan had command of the Patriot ground element, increased by militia to some 10,000 men, while d'Estaing provided naval support and also was to land French troops. D'Estaing secured control of Narragansett Bay, costing the British 5 frigates, 2 sloops, and several galleys, although their guns and ammunition were offloaded and added to the British land defenses. Howe sailed from New York with 13 ships of the line to engage d'Estaing with 12, but the anticipated major naval confrontation did not occur, thanks to a hurricane on August 11 that damaged both fleets. Despite Sullivan's pleas to remain even for a few days, d'Estaing insisted on removing his ships to Boston to effect repairs. Sullivan then continued on alone. Sullivan might still have won a victory, but with d'Estaing's departure most of the American militiamen lost heart and decamped. Pigot then sortied from Newport to attack the Americans on August 28–29.

In what became known as the Battle of Newport, some 5,000 Americans held off an attack by 3,000 British troops. Sullivan then withdrew northward, removing his men from the island on the night of August 30. It was a wise decision, for the next day 4,000 British reinforcements arrived. Sullivan openly attacked d'Estaing for his role, but Washington was able to smooth the ruffled feathers.

Thereafter the war in the northern states was largely a stalemate. The British raided New England coastal towns, and the Americans attacked isolated British garrisons. In one spectacular raid, Brigadier General Anthony Wayne attacked the strong British outpost at Stony Point, New York, held by 700 regulars, capturing it with the bayonet alone on July 15, 1779. The Americans lost 15 killed and 80 wounded, but British losses were 63 killed, more than 70 wounded, and 543 captured. Although Wayne was forced to abandon the post several days later, the attack secured much-needed arms, including 15 cannon, as well as supplies. In October 1779, the British evacuated Rhode Island.

In 1780 Major General Arnold, who had sought command of West Point, turned traitor and endeavored to surrender to the British that key fortification on the Hudson and perhaps Continental Army commander General Washington as well. The plot was discovered in late September, but Arnold was able to flee to the British, where he accepted a commission as a brigadier general and subsequently campaigned in Virginia. In July 1781, French Army lieutenant general Comte de Rochambeau arrived in America with 5,000 French troops to cooperate with Washington against the British.

As the war for independence wore on, America's economic situation, never robust, sharply deteriorated. With wealth mostly in land and with Congress unable to tax, the central government resorted to printing paper money to pay its bills, and this led to rampant inflation and currency that was all but worthless. Among the consequences of this were several mutinies in the Continental line.

Fighting had now largely shifted to the American South. Germain and other British leaders in London concluded that the South, with a perceived larger Loyalist population, might be more easily conquered than the North. They planned to secure an area, then raise Loyalist militias to control it. In December 1778, Clinton sent a military force to secure the important seaport of Savannah, Georgia. It fell to the British on December 29. American losses were some 550, including 450 captured; the British suffered only 9 men killed and 4 wounded. The British also secured numerous weapons as well as ships in the harbor.

In early September 1779, d'Estaing arrived off the mouth of the Savannah River with 20 ships of the line, 13 smaller warships, and 3,900 ground troops, but he was slow to move against the British. Finally disembarking his ground troops, on September 12 he invested Savannah, being joined during the next week by Continental Army commander in the South Major General Benjamin Lincoln with more than 2,000 Continentals and militia from Charles Town. British commander at Savannah Major General Augustine Prevost had 3,500 men. The city's defenses were strong, and he quickly improved them to withstand a lengthy siege. Unwilling to wait too long lest his fleet encounter the hurricane season, d'Estaing insisted on an assault, but the British were alerted by a deserter as to the exact point of the attack and repelled the allied assaults of October 9. In what was the most desperate fighting since Bunker Hill, the assaults cost the allies 244 killed, 584 wounded, and 120 captured. British losses were only 40 killed, 63 wounded, and 52 missing or deserted. Refusing to remain longer, d'Estaing embarked his troops and sailed away, while Lincoln returned to Charles Town.

Clinton now prepared a major seaborne assault from New York City on Charles Town by 8,000 British regulars and Loyalist militia. Charles Town's leaders insisted that Lincoln fight for the city, and he allowed his forces to be bottled up there. When the British began shelling the city during the resultant siege of March 29–May 12, 1780, the same city leaders insisted that Lincoln surrender. It was the greatest Continental Army defeat of the war. The siege itself claimed 89 Americans killed and 138 wounded, while the British lost 76 killed and 189 wounded. At Charles Town, however, the British captured 5,466 officers and men (including 7 generals), 400 cannon, and 6,000 muskets. They also secured several Continental Navy frigates. British forces soon moved into interior South Carolina, cooperating with Loyalist militias to set up military outposts there. Clinton meanwhile returned to New York, leaving Lieutenant General Lord Charles Cornwallis as British commander in the South.

Named to replace Lincoln, Major General Gates collected all the forces he could and rashly marched southward from Hillsborough, North Carolina. Cornwallis rushed northward, and the two forces came together at Camden, South Carolina, on August 16. The Continentals fought well, but the militiamen broke and ran, and Gates was routed. The British suffered 68 killed, 245 wounded, and 11 missing; American losses were some 900 killed or wounded and 1,000 captured. The British also secured seven guns, numerous small arms, and all the American stores and baggage. Gates escaped capture, but Washington replaced him with Major General Nathanael Greene.

After Camden, Cornwallis moved northward toward Charlotte, North Carolina, where he hoped to find strong Loyalist support. A virtual civil war now raged in the South between Patriots and Loyalists in which both sides committed atrocities. One large encounter between the two militias, the Battle of King's Mountain on October 7, brought a resounding Patriot victory. British major Patrick Ferguson's Loyalist force of 1,125 men suffered 1,105 dead or captured (Ferguson refused surrender and was among those killed). Patriot losses were only 40 killed. This defeat of his western flanking force

caused Cornwallis to suspend his efforts to secure all North Carolina, and he fell back to Winnsboro, South Carolina, for the winter. The British suffered another stinging defeat on January 17, 1781, when Lieutenant Colonel Banastre Tarleton's legion charged without reconnoitering a Continental Army and militia force under Brigadier General Daniel Morgan at Cowpens, South Carolina. Although Tarleton escaped, he lost 90 percent of his force: 100 dead, 229 wounded, and 600 unwounded prisoners. Morgan's losses were only 12 killed and 60 wounded. Morgan also secured some 800 muskets, 2 cannon, 100 horses, and all the British supplies and ammunition. Patriot morale soared.

Cornwallis was determined to bag Morgan and now moved against him in force. Morgan was soon joined by Greene and the main Continental force in the South, and a race northward ensued. Greene won the so-called Race to the Dan (the river separating North Carolina and Virginia) during January 19–February 15, 1781, in what is regarded as one of the most masterly withdrawals in U.S. military history. Greene reorganized his forces and again advanced into North Carolina in early 1781.

On March 15, the two sides again came together in the Battle of Guilford Courthouse. On paper Greene had the superior force—4,404 men—but only 1,490 were Continental troops, and only about 500 of these were trained veterans. The great majority of Greene's men were unreliable militia. Cornwallis had only 1,900 men, but all were regulars and almost all were disciplined veterans. The battle was hard-fought, but Greene was unwilling to hazard his forces and withdrew. Cornwallis trumpeted a victory, but it was a costly one indeed. The Americans sustained 264 casualties: 79 killed and 185 wounded, more than half of them militia. Another 160 Continentals were missing, along with several hundred militia, most of them having simply returned home. British casualties were, however, a quarter of their force: 93 killed and 439 wounded, a number of these mortally.

After retiring to Wilmington to regroup, Cornwallis decided to move northward with the bulk of his army into Virginia in order to cut the flow of supplies southward to Greene. Lieutenant Colonel Francis, Lord Rawdon, assumed command of British forces in South Carolina. Greene, choosing not to follow Cornwallis, began driving British forces from inland North and South Carolina and securing that territory. Although Greene sustained defeats in the battles at Hobkirk's Hill (April 25) and Eutaw Springs (September 8, 1781), his masterful Southern Campaign secured virtually all North Carolina, South Carolina, and Georgia, forcing the British into coastal enclaves at Charles Town and Savannah.

Meanwhile, following raids in the Virginia interior, Cornwallis withdrew his forces to the tobacco port of Yorktown shadowed by a smaller American force under Major General Marie Joseph du Motier, Marquis de Lafayette, that was shadowing Cornwallis. Washington had hoped that he and Rochambeau might mount an attack on New York City but then learned that French vice admiral François-Joseph-Paul, Comte de Grasse, planned to avoid hurricane season in the West Indies by sailing northward with a powerful fleet and 3,300 ground troops for Chesapeake Bay and that he would remain there until October. Seeing the possibility of entrapping Cornwallis, Washington and Rochambeau sent 7,000 men southward toward Yorktown. On August 30, meanwhile, de Grasse arrived in the Chesapeake with 28 ships of the line and commenced landing his ground forces.

At the same time, Rear Admiral Thomas Graves with 5 ships of the line, reinforced by 14 ships of the line under Rear Admiral Samuel Hood, just arrived from the West Indies, sailed from New York in August in an effort to intercept 8 ships of the line and 18 transports under French commodore Jacques Comte de Barras, which had sailed from Newport and were correctly presumed to be heading for Chesapeake Bay.

Sailing faster than Barras, Graves arrived in Chesapeake Bay first on September 5 and there discovered de Grasse's ships. Instead of swooping down on the more powerful but unprepared French fleet, Graves formed his ships into line ahead and waited for de Grasse to come out. Shorthanded with many of his men occupied in ferrying French and American troops down the bay, de Grasse nonetheless stood out with 24 ships of the line to meet the British. The resulting engagement was a draw. The British sustained 336 casualties, the French 221. No ships were lost on either side.

Several days of inconclusive maneuvering followed, during which Barras arrived with his ships. Graves then decided to return to New York to gather additional ships. This tactically inconclusive Second Battle of the Chesapeake doomed Cornwallis at Yorktown and thus deserves to be ranked among the most important strategic victories in world history.

On September 28, the allies laid siege to Yorktown. Following some fighting and with his garrison running out of food, Cornwallis surrendered on October 19, 1781. A total of 8,077 British surrendered—840 seamen, 80 camp followers, and 7,157 soldiers. During the siege the

British lost 156 killed and 326 wounded; the allies suffered only 75 killed and 199 wounded (two-thirds of these French). When Parliament learned of this dire event, it voted on March 4, 1782, to end offensive war in America, and peace negotiations began in earnest between American and French envoys in Paris.

Fighting continued in America, of course, including operations in the Ohio country that helped secure that vast territory for the United States in the peace settlement, but most of the warfare was of low intensity. Overseas, there was fighting in India. The British withstood a long siege by the Spaniards and French at Gibraltar (1779–1783), and in the West Indies the French, Spaniards, Dutch, and British all sought to capture islands of the other side. Any French advantage here, however, was lost late in the war with the British naval victory of the Battle of the Saintes (April 12, 1782).

On March 20, 1782, rather than lose a vote of no confidence, Lord North resigned as prime minister. Peace talks finally bore fruit with the signing on November 30, 1782, of the Treaty of Paris between the representatives of the United States and the British government. The Americans signed the treaty in violation of their alliance with France that stipulated that neither was to sign a separate peace, and they ignored protests by Spain concerning lands east of the Mississippi River. The treaty was not to take effect, however, until the ongoing fighting between Britain and France and Spain was also resolved.

The most important article of the peace treaty was, of course, that granting independence to the United States. The Americans also secured territory as far west as the Mississippi River, free navigation of the Mississippi, fishing rights off the Grand Banks, and the removal of British troops from American soil. The treaty was most generous, with the British endeavoring, successfully, to wean the United States from France.

The British evacuated Charles Town on December 14, 1782, and the French departed America six days later. Britain, France, and Spain agreed to peace terms on January 20, 1783. On February 4, 1783, King George III declared a formal end to hostilities with America, and on January 14, 1784, the Confederation Congress ratified the Treaty of Paris, officially ending the American Revolutionary War. Estimates vary, but perhaps 100,000 Loyalists left the territory of the United States during 1775–1783, most of them settling in the maritime provinces of Canada.

Significance

The United States had secured its independence. With the Articles of Confederation governing the new nation having proved ineffective, a new Constitution was written and approved in 1787 that gave more powers to the central government, including the right to impose taxes. The United States soon became a beacon of hope for the oppressed of much of the rest of the world, who wished that their own nations might be more like it.

For Native Americans, the war proved disastrous. Without a European power to act as a counter to the triumphant Americans, the Indian nations had little leverage against continued white encroachment of their ancestral lands. A vicious war between the Indians and the American military occurred in the Old Northwest Territory between 1785 and 1795, ending in a Native American defeat. A relentless westward expansionism by settlers resulted in a string of Indian Wars that did not end until 1890, at which time most remaining Native Americans had been herded onto reservations.

Britain suffered little from the loss of its major colonies, as trade promptly resumed and at greater volume than before. France, for all its considerable efforts and expense, gained virtually nothing except a crushing increase in the national debt that would force the Crown to consider taxing the nobles and the church. This led to the so-called Aristocratic Reaction and the calling of the States General, whereby the leaders of the Third Estate (with 97 percent of the nation's population), buoyed by the ideas of popular sovereignty and democracy embodied in the American Revolution, stood firm and produced the French Revolution of 1789.

Further Reading

Alden, John R. *A History of the American Revolution.* New York: Knopf, 1969.

Black, Jeremy. *War for America: The Fight for Independence, 1775–1783.* Phoenix Mill, Far Thrupp, Stroud, Gloucestershire, UK: Alan Sutton, 1991.

Heimert, Alan. *Religion and the American Mind, from the Great Awakening to the Revolution.* Cambridge, MA: Harvard University Press, 1966.

Higginbotham, Don. *The War of American Independence: Military Attitudes, Policies, and Practice, 1763–1789.* New York: Macmillan, 1971.

Middlekauff, Robert. *The Glorious Cause: The American Revolution, 1763–1789.* New York: Oxford University Press, 2005.

Miller, John C. *Triumph of Freedom, 1775–1783.* Boston: Little, Brown, 1848.

Ward, Christopher. *The War of the Revolution.* Edited by John Richard Alden. New York: Skyhorse Publishing, 2011.

Wood, Gordon S. *The Creation of the American Republic, 1776–1787.* Chapel Hill: University of North Carolina Press, 1969.

French Revolutionary Wars (1792–1802)

Dates	1792–1802
Location	Western and Central Europe, the Middle East, India, Caribbean
Combatants	France vs. Prussia, Austria, Britain, Dutch Republic, Sardinia, Spain, Portugal, Russia, Ottoman Empire
Principal Commanders	France: Louis XVI, Charles François Dumouriez, Lazare Carnot, Jean-Baptiste Jourdan, Jean Victor Moreau, Napoleon Bonaparte, André Masséna Britain: Lord Richard Howe; Sir John Jervis; Frederick, Duke of York and Albany; Sir Hyde Parker; Horatio Nelson Prussia: Karl Wilhelm, Duke of Brunswick Austria: Marshal Dagobert Sigismund, Count Wurmser; Karl Mack von Leiberich; Archduke Charles Russia: Aleksandr Suvorov
Principal Battles	Valmy, Jemappes, Neerwinden, Glorious First of June, Fleurus, Mantua, Rivoli, Texel, Pyramids, Nile, Acre, Aboukir, Marengo, Zurich (third), Copenhagen
Outcome	France secures its long-held goal of natural frontiers in the northeast and is recognized as the most powerful state in Europe, but Bonaparte will not permit the Peace of Amiens to last.

Causes

In 1792 France declared war on Austria and Prussia, beginning the decade-long Wars of the French Revolution (April 20, 1792–May 27, 1802), to be followed by yet another round of warfare during 1803–1814 and again briefly in 1815. The first decade of warfare is usually divided into the wars of the First Coalition (1792–1797) and the Second Coalition (1799–1801), although France and Britain were continually at war during the period 1793–1802.

The wars were a direct result of the French Revolution of 1789. Many assumed at the time and since that the French Revolution was caused by Enlightenment ideas and the "wind from America," but the prime mover was in fact a financial crisis brought on by France's participation in the American Revolutionary War (1775–1783). Bad weather and poor harvests abetted the situation. Although France was actually Europe's richest country, the church (the First Estate, with perhaps 1 percent of the population) and the nobility (the Second Estate, with 2 percent) were exempt from taxes, which were paid by everyone else (the Third Estate). As the First and Second Estates together possessed some half of the land of France, the government was chronically poor.

The decision of the Crown to tax those previously exempt led to the so-called Aristocratic Reaction (1787–1789) in which the nobles, who also controlled the First Estate, demanded the calling of the States General, the national representative body that had last met in 1614. The nobles expected to have to pay some taxes but to secure a degree of control over the Crown. The success of the nobles in forcing the meeting of the States General, however, led leaders of the Third Estate to rebel in turn. With the Third Estate having 97 percent of the population, its publicists demanded it be allowed to elect more representatives, and the government agreed to the "doubling of the Third," giving it the number of representatives equal to those of the clergy and nobility combined. This did not seem to be a major concession, as voting was to be by order, and the first two estates could outvote the Third Estate two to one.

When the States General met at Versailles in May 1789, however, representatives of the Third Estate refused to transact business until there was a vote by head, and supported by nonnoble members of the clergy and some liberal nobles, they stood firm in this demand. King Louis XVI, who had initially sided with the nobles, finally yielded, and the National Assembly came into being, with major changes enacted into law. Although the revolution continued to evolve and become more radical, throughout representatives of the middle class remained solidly in charge.

On April 20, 1792, however, revolutionary France declared war on Austria and Prussia, beginning the War of the First Coalition. There was little external threat to France, despite the loud posturing of the nobles who had fled abroad and even the Declaration of Pillnitz of August 27, 1791. Intended as a warning to the revolutionaries, it was issued by Habsburg Holy Roman emperor Leopold II and King Frederick William II of Prussia. They declared their support for Louis XVI and called on the European powers to intervene if the French king was threatened.

The French declaration of war was the result of many factors. French leaders believed that they had to export the revolution as the new regime, and they would not be safe until there were similar neighboring regimes. The French people were then badly divided over the course of the revolution, especially regarding the new Civil Constitution of the Clergy that regulated the church. A foreign war could unite the French people behind the government. Personal ambition also played a role. Ironically, Louis XVI supported a declaration of war because he believed that the conflict would go badly for France and strengthen his own hand. To hasten this, he shared French military plans with the Austrians. What the French moderate leaders behind the declaration of war could not see, however, was that their decision would bring their own downfall, a radicalization of the revolution, and its eventual sublimation to the ambition of one man.

The timing seemed propitious; the Austrians and Prussians were preoccupied with partitioning Poland and kept their best troops in the East, more afraid of each other and Russia than of revolutionary France. Indeed, the French Revolution was saved at the expense of Poland. The Russians invaded Poland anew in May 1792, followed by the Prussians, and Poland underwent a second partition in January 1793, followed by a third and final partition in 1795.

Course of the War of the First Coalition (1792–1797)

The war opened with a French invasion of the Austrian Netherlands (present-day Belgium), but following several years of political unrest and the emigration of many officers, the French army was hardly ready. Only 28,000 men were on hand when the invasion began on April 28, 1792, and the initial fighting went badly for France. The Austrians easily defeated French forces around Lille and then laid siege to that French city. French marshal Jean-Baptiste Donatien de Vimeur, Comte de Rochambeau (a hero of the American Revolutionary War), resigned as commander of the Army of the North, replaced by another American Revolutionary War stalwart, Marie Joseph Paul Yves Roch Gilbert du Motier, Marquis de Lafayette. Stung by the military reversals, on June 20, 1792, a mob invaded the Tuileries Palace in Paris, confronting and threatening King Louis XVI before withdrawing.

In July 1792 some 84,000 coalition forces assembled at Coblenz (Koblenz) in the Rhineland under Karl Wilhelm, Duke of Brunswick. On July 25 he issued what became known as the Brunswick Manifesto, threatening France with destruction should any harm come to King Louis XVI or if there was resistance to the allied invasion. Intended to intimidate the revolutionaries and protect the king, it had the opposite effect. Known in Paris on August 3, it triggered an insurrection there on August 10. A crowd attacked the Tuileries Palace. The king fled to the National Assembly, then ordered his loyal 950-man Swiss Guards and some supporters who were holding off the attackers to lay down their arms, condemning most of them to death at the hands of the mob.

The storming of Tuileries ushered in the radical period of the revolution (August 10, 1792–July 28, 1794). The king was "suspended" from office, then imprisoned. Lafayette considered a march on the capital but, fearing arrest by the new radical government in Paris, fled across the border and was taken prisoner by the Austrians. French foreign minister Charles François Dumouriez, a prime mover behind the war, replaced him.

On August 19, Brunswick's troops crossed the French frontier and captured the fortresses of Longwy (August 23) and

BATTLE OF VALMY, SEPTEMBER 20, 1792

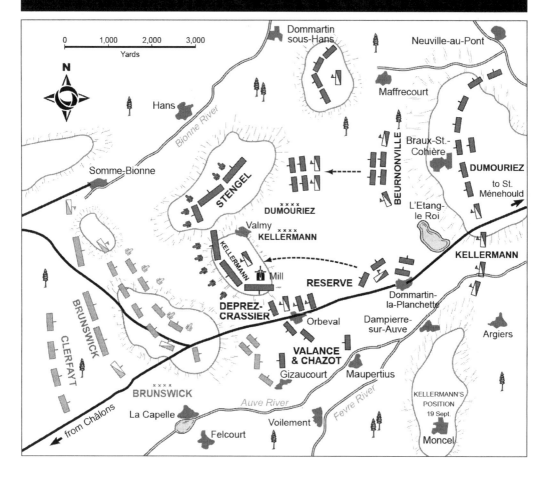

Verdun (September 2), then moved slowly through the Argonne Forest toward Paris. On September 2–6 with news of Brunswick's approach and rumors widespread of a royalist uprising, radical leaders of the Commune of Paris organized a massacre of some 1,000 people in the city's prisons aimed at influencing voting for the new National Convention and securing political control of the city.

At Valmy on September 20, General François C. Kellermann's Army of the Center blocked Brunswick's advance in what was little more than an artillery duel. Brunswick called off two infantry

advances short of the French lines when the French troops failed to bolt. Personnel losses on both sides were slight, but Brunswick then withdrew back across the French border.

The cannonade of Valmy saved the French Revolution, at least to the extent of ending allied hopes of crushing it in 1792. It also marked the end of the age of dynastic armies and the arrival of the new age of patriotic "national" armies. On September 21 in Paris, the new National Convention met for the first time and that same day voted to abolish the monarchy. A day later it proclaimed France a republic.

In the southeast, French forces invaded Piedmont, overran Savoy, and, on September 29, secured Nice. The National Convention declared Savoy a French department. French forces under General Adam Philippe Custine invaded Germany, capturing Mainz (October 21) and reaching as far as Frankfurt. Dumouriez forced the Austrians to raise their siege of Lille and withdraw from France, then invaded the Austrian Netherlands and defeated the Austrians under Marshal Duke Albert of Saxe-Teschen in the Battle of Jemappes near Mons (November 6). Dumouriez went on to capture Brussels (Bruxelles) on November 14. French forces also besieged the port of Antwerp. The Duke of Brunswick, however, enjoyed success against the French forces in Germany, retaking Frankfurt (December 2) and driving Custine's army back to the Rhine. Custine then went into winter quarters at Mainz.

Meanwhile, deposed king Louis XVI was placed on trial before the National Convention, convicted of a variety of crimes, and sentenced to death. He was publicly guillotined on January 21, 1793. This event brought the expulsion from Britain of the French ambassador. Already at war with Austria, Prussia, Spain, and Piedmont, Britain and the United Netherlands (Dutch Republic) now joined the coalition against France.

In this period of crisis for France, in February 1793 the National Convention created the Revolutionary Tribunal to try those accused of antirevolutionary crimes. In March, however, counterrevolutionary armed revolts began in the Vendée region of south-central France, and on April 6 the National Convention created the Committee of Public Safety—eventually numbering 12 men—to provide temporary strong leadership to meet the foreign and domestic threats. Maximilian Robespierre came to dominate it.

In late April the so-called Federalist Revolt spread to Marseille and to other major cities by June. In Paris the revolution became more radical. On June 2 the National Convention purged its more moderate revolutionary leaders, the so-called Brissotins or Girondins who had begun the war. The radicals, known as the Montagnards (Mountain), who were only a minority of the population and centered in Paris, ruled France until July 27, 1794.

With the French government having declared the annexation of the Austrian Netherlands, it ordered Dumouriez to invade the Dutch Republic. During the winter of 1792–1793, however, the allies had built up their strength. Brunswick attacked Custine at Coblenz, and Prince Josias of Saxe-Coburg invaded the Austrian Netherlands, engaging and defeating Dumouriez and the French at Neerwinden on March 18, 1793. Dumouriez carried out a skillful withdrawal, but the Austrians recaptured Brussels and the southern Netherlands.

Falsely accused of treason by the radicals in Paris, Dumouriez tried to engineer a march on Paris to overthrow the government. When this failed, on April 5 he deserted to the Austrians. Custine, who took over Dumouriez's command, was defeated near Valenciennes (May 21–23), leading to his execution by order of the Committee of Public Safety. The allies captured Condé (July 10) and Valenciennes (July 29); the Army of the North, now commanded by General Jean Nicolas Houchard, withdrew to Arras.

France appeared on the brink of defeat. The Vendée was in full revolt, both Lyon and Marseille had also rebelled against the central government, and a British-Hanovarian army under Frederick

Augustus, Duke of York, laid siege to Dunkerque (Dunkirk).

On August 23 the National Convention ordered a *levée* en masse, or national conscription. This made every able-bodied male of military age liable for army service and produced more than 600,000 recruits in 14 field armies. Former French Army captain Lazare Carnot, a member of the Committee of Public Safety, developed tactics that took advantage of élan and numbers, and on August 25 Marseille was recovered by revolutionary forces just as it was about to be handed over by royalists to the English.

In July, Toulon had overthrown its Jacobin government and then invited in the British and Spanish. They arrived on August 27 and landed men. In September, French Republican forces arrived and invested Toulon from the land, but little was accomplished until December, when young artillery captain Napoleon Bonaparte convinced his superiors to employ land artillery from high ground that forced the British from the port on the night of December 18–19, but not before burning and destroying 19 French ships (11 of them ships of the line); the Spanish took off 3 small French warships and the British 15, including 3 ships of the line.

News of the loss of Toulon, known in Paris on September 4, had led to the decision of the National Convention to resolve "Let terror be the order of the day." Supposedly to protect the republic from its many enemies, the Reign of Terror was also an instrument by the radical minority to remain in power. As many as 40,000 people died until it was shut down on July 27, 1794, with the overthrow of the radicals.

The first major victories for Carnot's new armies came in northeastern France against the British in the Battle of Hondschoote (September 6–8, 1793) and against the Dutch at Menin (September 12–13). The victor in the latter battle, Jean Nicolas Houchard, failed to drive back the Austrians, however, and was arrested and guillotined in November. General Jean-Baptiste Jourdan replaced him. Carnot ordered Jourdan to relieve Maubeuge, then besieged by the Austrians under the Count of Saxe-Coburg. In the ensuing Battle of Wattignies near Lille (October 15–16), the French were successful, forcing Saxe-Cobourg to lift the siege of Maubeuge and withdraw.

During October–December 1793 the revolt in the Vendée was largely quelled. Lyon was retaken by revolutionary forces on October 9, and Toulon was retaken on December 19. Along the Rhine after being defeated by allied forces under the Duke of Brunswick at Kaiserslautern (November 28–30), French forces under General Louis Lazare Hoche were victorious at Fröschwiller (December 22). Four days later, Hoche also defeated an Austrian army under General Dagobert Sigmund von Wurmser at Geisberg in Alsace. By year's end, the French had retaken Mainz and pushed the allies back across the Rhine.

There was also sporadic but indecisive fighting in northwestern Italy and along the frontier with Spain. Fighting also spread to the West Indies, where British forces captured Martinique in March 1794 and St. Lucia and Guadeloupe in April. The French, however, retook all Guadeloupe by December. There was also inconclusive fighting involving British, French, and Spanish forces in Santo Domingo, and each side attacked the other's merchant shipping.

In Europe in the spring of 1794, French forces went on the offensive in Flanders.

The French Army of the North, now under General Charles Pichegru, seized Menin and Courtrai. Dutch and Austrian troops under Austrian field marshal Charles de Croix, Count von Clerfayt, forced the French from Courtrai, however. The French counterattacked and forced Clerfayt to withdraw.

In fighting near Tourcoing just north of Lille, the Army of the North defeated the Austrians, British, and Hanovarians on May 18. This battle halted the allied advance into northeastern France and forced the Austrians onto the defensive. On May 22, Pichegru attacked Tournai but was defeated there by a larger allied force.

At sea there was a major battle on June 1, known to the British as the Glorious First of June and to the French as the Battle of 13 Prairial (for that date in the new revolutionary calendar). Admiral Louis Villaret-Joyeuse had sortied from Brest with the Atlantic Fleet, hoping to link up with and bring safely into port some 170 merchant vessels loaded with grain from the United States, and expected to arrive in late May. British admiral Lord Richard Howe appeared with the Channel Fleet. In the battle the French had 26 ships of the line, the British 25. Howe won a resounding victory by turning into the midst of the French line, piercing it in a half dozen places, and forcing a melee battle. The French lost 7 ships, the British none. Villaret-Joyeuse returned to Brest on June 11, but there was no sign of the grain ships. With the fleet preparing another sortie, the convoy arrived safely on June 12 with 24 million pounds of flour, escaping British detection by mere chance.

At the end of June, the French won the most important land battle of the War of the First Coalition. Following an earlier unsuccessful effort, on June 25 Jourdan captured Charleroi in the Austrian Netherlands before Saxe-Coburg arrived on June 26. In the ensuing Battle of Fleurus, 82,000 French defeated a force of 70,000 allies, who then withdrew across the Meuse.

Fleurus dealt a crushing blow to Austrian hopes of retaining the Austrian Netherlands. French forces then took Brussels (July 10) and Antwerp (July 27). By the end of the year, the French controlled the entire Austrian Netherlands. Fleurus also had important political repercussions. Easing the military threat to France, it ended justification for the Reign of Terror and was thus a major impetus behind the July 27 overthrow of the radicals. This ushered in that period of the revolution known as the Thermidorean Reaction, during which the instruments of the Reign of Terror were shut down.

In August–December 1794 Jourdan cleared the left bank of the Rhine. General Jean Victor Moreau took command of the new French Army of the Rhine and Moselle and laid siege to Mainz, while Pichegru crossed the Meuse in October, took Nijmegen, and drove the Austrians beyond the Rhine. Other French troops crossed the Pyrenees into Spain and forced the allies from Savoy.

Instead of going into winter quarters after taking Nijmegen, Pichegru carried out a winter campaign facilitated by one of the coldest winters on record, which enabled his cavalry to cross frozen rivers and lakes. Pichegru captured Utrecht (January 19, 1795) and then Amsterdam (January 20). On January 23, French hussars took the surrender of the Dutch fleet, frozen in the ice at Den Helder. Pichegru then secured the entire Dutch Republic. Renamed the Batavian Republic, in May it concluded a defensive alliance with France.

In June the British landed some 2,500 French émigrés and a considerable quantity of weapons in Quiberon Bay, Brittany. Although thousands of Bretons joined, this effort was hampered by divided command, and French general Hoche sealed off the peninsula and by late July defeated the royalists. British ships rescued only 2,000 of some 17,000 royalists. Hoche also captured arms sufficient for 40,000 men. Then on July 22 in the Treaty of Basel, Spain concluded peace with France, ceding to France Santo Domingo, the eastern portion of the island of Hispaniola.

In August 1795 France received its third constitution, that of the Year III. It created the Directory, named for its five-man executive. There was also a legislature of the Council of Elders and the Council of Five Hundred, but the framers, fearful of their own position and lives, rigged it so two-thirds of the members of the new government came from the National Convention.

Widespread opposition to this new government and the two-thirds decree led to an uprising in Paris on October 5, 1795 (13 Vendemaire). Forewarned, the government placed General of Brigade Napoleon Bonaparte in charge, and he employed artillery—the "whiff of grapeshot" (a phrase coined by 19th-century historian Thomas Carlyle in *The French Revolution: A History*)—to kill perhaps 200 people and crush the uprising. Bonaparte's reward was promotion to general of division and command of the French Army of Italy in March 1796.

Meanwhile, French forces were active in the Rhineland. Jourdan's Army of the Sambre and Meuse operated west of Coblenz against the Austrians under Clerfayt. Pichegru's Army of the Rhine and Moselle in Alsace and the Palatinate confronted allied troops under Marshal Dagobert Sigismund, Count Würmser. The French took Luxembourg on June 15, 1795. In early September, Jourdan invaded Germany but was outmaneuvered by Clerfayt near Höchst in early October. Pichegru, meanwhile, lost Mannheim before concluding a general armistice on December 21.

In northern Italy General Barthélemy Schérer, commander of the French Army of Italy, fought a series of engagements with Austrian and Piedmontese troops, the principal battle being a French victory at Loano (November 23). It consolidated French control of western Liguria and the Maritime Alps.

French plans for 1796 called for Jourdan's Army of the Sambre and Meuse to advance and draw the Austrians north. Moreau's Army of the Rhine and Moselle would then push into Bavaria. The two would then join for an advance on Vienna, with the Army of Italy coming up from the south.

On March 1796 Bonaparte assumed command of the Army of Italy, then holding a line from Nice almost to Genoa. Opposing him were Piedmontese under Baron Michelangelo Colli and Austrians under General Jean Pierre Beaulieu. Bonaparte took advantage of the fact that his enemies were both extended and separated. Bonaparte's subordinate General André Masséna surprised 4,500 Austrians at Montenotte (April 12). Other French victories followed at Colli (April 13), Dego (April 14–15), and Ceva (April 18). After his defeat at Mondovi (April 21) in Piedmont, Colli withdrew to Turin. King Victor Amadeus of Piedmont-Sardinia concluded that further resistance was futile and on April 26 concluded an armistice with the French that effectively ended Piedmontese participation in the war.

Bonaparte then advanced to the Po River against the Austrians, crossing at Piacenza and causing Beaulieu to withdraw eastward and abandon both Pavia and Milan. Bonaparte defeated the Austrian rear guard at Lodi (May 10), then entered Milan (May 15). Victor Amadeus II concluded formal peace with France on May 21, surrendering Nice and Savoy to France outright and allowing France to garrison Piedmont.

Austrian field marshal Archduke Charles, younger brother of Emperor Francis II, now commanded allied forces in Germany. On June 10, 1796, Jourdan crossed the Rhine at Düsseldorf. Reaching Wetzlar, he was repulsed there by Charles (June 16) and withdrew back across the Rhine. Moreau, meanwhile, crossed the Rhine at Strasbourg during June 23–27 and pushed Charles's southern forces back to Neresheim, where the two sides fought an indecisive action (August 1–3). Marching rapidly north, Charles defeated an outnumbered Jourdan at Amberg (August 24). Learning that also on August 24 Moreau had defeated Austrian forces at Friedberg, Jourdan regrouped near Würzburg in northern Bavaria. Archduke Charles pursued and defeated Jourdan there on September 3. Jourdan then withdrew on the Rhine, engaging in a series of running battles with the Austrians until Charles broke off the pursuit and moved south. Moreau, learning of Jourdan's defeat, also withdrew, crossing the Rhine on October 26.

Meanwhile, Bonaparte captured Paschiera, Legnago, and Verona. Beaulieu withdrew into the Tyrol (Tirol), leaving some 14,000 men behind at Mantua, the strongest fortress of the so-called Quadrilateral. For the next seven months, Mantua was the centerpiece of the struggle for control of northern Italy. Bonaparte blockaded it in June and by July 15 had it fully invested. In the meantime, his forces ranged over much of Italy, and his

emissaries secured peace with the papacy and with Naples. The papacy ceded Bologna and Ferrara to France as well as a sizable indemnity and important works of art; Naples made a large financial contribution.

Marshal Wurmser, having replaced Beaulieu as Austrian commander in Italy, in July 1796 moved south to relieve the siege of Mantua but made the fatal error of dividing his army, not once but twice. Bonaparte was victorious at Losano (August 3) and Castiglione (August 5). Wurmser then withdrew to the Adige River.

On August 24 Bonaparte restored the siege of Mantua. The Directory, however, ordered him to join Moreau for a drive on Vienna. The Austrians were aware of the French plans, and Wurmser hoped to surprise the French by moving with superior numbers to Mantua. Wurmser, however, again divided his forces, this time into three groups, each unable to support the other. Bonaparte defeated one Austrian force at Caliano on the upper Adige on September 2. On September 8, Masséna and General Pierre Augereau caught half of Wurmser's army at Bassano and routed it.

Wurmser surprised Bonaparte, however, by continuing south and entered Mantua on September 12. The next day he attacked the besieging French forces and drove them northward, then on September 14 smashed a French corps advancing on Mantua from the east. On September 15 he again sortied. Bonaparte, having united his forces, drove Wurmser back into Mantua, where he remained bottled up until he surrendered in February 1797.

With Wurmser and 25,000 men besieged at Mantua, Vienna appointed Baron Jozsef Alvinczy von Bøtberek to command in Italy. As with his predecessors, he had more men than Bonaparte—some 50,000 to 30,000—but demonstrated the same fatal propensity of dividing his forces. Had he not done so, he might have been able to defeat Bonaparte, whose own men were also badly divided, violating what later became an ironclad rule of having forces march dispersed but within mutually supporting distance. Alvinczy hoped to unite with a force from the Tyrol, then drive on Mantua.

Bonaparte was determined to prevent the Austrian juncture. On November 12 he attacked Alvinczy's advance guard at Caldiero, but Alvinczy rapidly brought up reinforcements, and Bonaparte withdrew to Verona. Bonaparte now conceived a bold plan. Leaving only a small force to hold Verona while making it appear that his entire army was there, he consolidated the remainder and attacked and defeated Alvinczy at Arcole (Arcola) during November 15–17. The Austrians then withdrew northward.

In 1796 Irish nationalist leader Wolfe Tone convinced the French government to send an expeditionary force to Ireland, claiming that this would enjoy widespread support. The French sailed from Brest on December 16 with 43 ships, 17 of them ships of the line, and 15,000 French troops under General Hoche. At sea the French split into squadrons to avoid detection, but in increasingly bad weather only a few of their ships reached the rendezvous point of Bantry Bay, on December 21. None of the French troops went ashore, as continued bad weather caused a return to France on December 30. Five of the French ships were lost at sea, and the British captured 6 others.

In continued fighting in Italy, Bonaparte was at Bologna when he learned on January 10, 1797, that Alvinczy was on the move with a sizable force. Bonaparte hastily concentrated at Rivoli and was in position

there when the Austrian arrived on January 14. Bonaparte hoped to hold off Alvinczy until he could bring up reinforcements. Fortunately for Bonaparte, Alvinczy had sent most of his men in a sweep around the French to take them from the rear. Still, the battle was going badly for the French until Masséna arrived with reinforcements and broke through into the Austrian rear. Alvinczy's detachments sent to surround the French were also defeated, and the Austrians then withdrew northward.

The Battle of Rivoli was the last and most important battle of Bonaparte's Italian campaign. Following it, Vienna replaced Alvinczy with Archduke Charles, who was promised 90,000 men, evidence that Vienna recognized that Italy was now the decisive theater of war and that Bonaparte had to be defeated there.

While Bonaparte was fighting at Rivoli, other Austrian troops moved toward Verona and Mantua. Some 9,000 reached the outskirts of Mantua on January 16 and attempted to gain the fortress but were surrounded and forced to surrender, while Wurmser's simultaneous sortie was beaten back. On February 2, 1797, Wurmser surrendered. During the six-month siege the Mantua garrison had been reduced from 25,000 to 16,000 men through malnutrition and disease. The siege also resulted in 6,000 civilian deaths.

Meanwhile, Spain had switched sides in the Treaty of San Ildefonso of August 19, 1796. The French and Spanish planned to combine their navies in an invasion of Britain. On February 1, 1797, Spanish admiral José de Córdoba y Ramos departed Cartagena with 27 ships of the line, 12 frigates, and some smaller vessels and sailed into the Atlantic, planning to put in at Cádiz, where he would take on supplies and sail for Brest to rendezvous with the

French and Dutch fleets for the invasion of England.

British admiral Sir John Jervis was then off Portugal with 15 ships of the line, 5 frigates, and several smaller vessels seeking to prevent just such a concentration. Had not a gale driven the Spanish ships well to the west, Córdoba would have gained Cádiz, and Jervis would have been forced to resort to a blockade. Informed of the presence of the Spanish ships, Jervis sailed south and met them off Cape St. Vincent on February 14.

After an hour of fighting it looked as if Córdoba might be able to escape, when Jervis signaled for each ship to act on its own. Already Captain Horatio Nelson had taken the initiative and broken from the line-ahead formation and turned into the path of the advancing Spanish line. Other ships followed. In the ensuing melee battle, the British took four Spanish ships (two by Nelson). Although the remaining Spanish ships escaped to Cádiz the next day, the Battle of Cape St. Vincent ended the threat of an allied invasion of Britain.

In the spring of 1797, Bonaparte invaded Austria from Italy. Archduke Charles had discovered on taking command of Austrian forces there that he had some 60 percent of the men promised, and half of these were in the Tyrol. The rest were under his own immediate command along the Tagliamento River, where Bonaparte outnumbered him two to one.

Leaving Joubert with a small force to operate in the Tyrol, Bonaparte moved against Charles and defeated him along the Tagliamento River in the Battle of Valvasone (March 16). Charles retired behind the Isonzo but again had to withdraw to prevent encirclement. Bonaparte then crossed the Julian and Carnic Alps, moving toward Vienna. Covering 400 miles in only 30 days, his forces united at Klagenfurt in Carinthia. Charles, now with only 10,000 men, attempted to stop the French there but was again defeated.

On April 6 Bonaparte reached Leoben, only 95 miles from Vienna. Joubert had been successful in the Tyrol and was en route to join him at Vienna. On April 7 recognizing the hopelessness of his situation, Charles requested an armistice, which Bonaparte granted, resulting in the Preliminary Peace of Leoben of April 17. With Venetia in open rebellion against the French and with the Tyrol a threat, Bonaparte was also anxious for peace.

In May, using the pretext of an uprising in Verona, French troops invaded and occupied Venetian territory, including the Ionian Islands. Then on July 9 the French proclaimed establishment of the Ligurian Republic, the former Republic of Genoa. It too was firmly under French control.

In April 1797 French forces had renewed operations across the Rhine. New French commander of the Army of the Meuse and Sambre General Hoche and French forces under Moreau both crossed the river. General Maximilian Anton Carl, Count Baillet de Latour, commanded Austrian forces opposing Moreau, while his subordinate General Baron Werneck defended the lower Rhine. Hoche crossed the Rhine at Neuwied and defeated Werneck (April 18). Moreau crossed the river two days later, and the French forced the Austrians back to Rastatt.

In France, a royalist plot brought a coup d'état. Following elections in the spring of 1797, a royalist conspiracy developed, led by Pichegru in the Council of 500 and one of the five directors, François-Marie Barthélemy. Three of the other five directors were opposed, and the fifth, Lazare Carnot, attempted to heal the breach. When this failed, the three appealed to Bonaparte in Italy, who dispatched General Augereau to Paris.

Appointed to command the National Guard, Augereau set up a camp of 30,000 men on the outskirts of Paris. On September 4, 1797 (18 Fructidor by the revolutionary calendar), Augereau's men invaded the Tuileries and seized control of the government. The elections of some 200 councilors were annulled, and more than 50 individuals, including Barthélemy and Carnot, were deported. Although the royalist threat was ended and the republic was preserved, the constitution had been violated and the first free elections in the history of the French republic quashed. More than ever, the republicans were dependent on the army.

Meanwhile at sea, British vice admiral Adam Duncan had blockaded Dutch warships in the Texel. In early October 1797, however, Duncan departed with most of his ships for repairs and reprovisioning, leaving only a small squadron to continue the blockade. The Dutch government ordered Admiral Jan Willem de Winter to engage the blockaders. Informed of Dutch preparations, Duncan immediately returned with his ships on October 11, just as the Dutch fleet sortied. The British had 16 ships of the line while de Winter had 15, all of which were smaller. The two fleets came together northwest of the village of Kamperduin (Camperdown). Duncan had several ships severely damaged but captured 11 Dutch ships, 7 of them ships of the line.

On October 17, 1797, on his own authority Bonaparte dictated the final peace settlement with Austria. Austria was forced to cede the Austrian Netherlands. It received the territory of Venetia as far as the Adige, including the city of Venice, and also Istria and Dalmatia. France retained the Ionian Islands. Austria also recognized the French

Italian satellite state of the Cisalpine Republic. In secret provisions, Austria promised to cede to France the left bank of the Rhine from Basel to Andernach, including Mainz; princes who lost territory there were to be compensated with German territory on the right bank of the Rhine. The treaty ended the war of the First Coalition, although France remained at war with Britain.

In December Bonaparte returned to Paris, a national hero in France and *stupor mundi* (the wonder of the world) elsewhere. In only one year he had defeated five opposing armies, each larger than his own, and taken 160,000 prisoners. He had also sent millions of francs in precious metals and artworks to Paris.

Having subdued their continental adversaries, the French now made preparations to invade Britain. In January 1798 Bonaparte assumed command of the French Army of England. It is doubtful whether he believed success was possible; indeed, he reported to the Directory that the forces assigned him were totally inadequate. Bonaparte proposed several alternative plans, including seizing Egypt in order to be able to threaten British India by land.

In April 1798 the Directory approved Bonaparte's suggestion and appointed him to command the French Army of Egypt. Certainly the members of the Directory were anxious to have their overly popular general out of France. The assembly of troops at Dunkerque continued in order to prevent the British from shifting naval assets to the Mediterranean.

In February 1798, meanwhile, French forces occupied Rome, taking Pope Pius VI captive and proclaiming a Roman Republic, and in April they occupied Switzerland. France annexed Geneva and proclaimed the remainder the Helvetic Republic.

On May 19, 1798, Bonaparte sailed from Toulon with 34,000 troops in 400 transports, escorted by 13 ships of the line and many smaller warships. On June 12 he scooped up Malta, defended by only 300 Knights Hospitalers, adding some 6 million francs in treasure to his coffers. The armada sailed again on June 19.

Bonaparte's luck held. Learning of the French plans, in April the British had dispatched 14 ships of the line to the Mediterranean under Rear Admiral Horatio Nelson. Lacking scouting vessels, Nelson narrowly missed his quarry. Moving at twice the speed of the French, the British passed the French only a few miles distant on a foggy night. Guessing that Alexandria was the French objective, Nelson arrived there on June 29 but, with no French there, immediately departed. That evening an advance French frigate anchored, followed by the entire French fleet on July 1.

Fearing Nelson's imminent return, Bonaparte immediately sent his troops ashore. They captured Alexandria, then marched to the Nile, where on July 13 they defeated a force of Egyptian Mamluks. A week later on July 21 south of Cairo and near the great pyramid of Khufu (Cheops), Bonaparte defeated up to 40,000 Mamluks commanded by Murad Bey, styling it the Battle of the Pyramids (although the latter were not in sight). The French captured Cairo the next day.

After weeks of searching, on August 1 Nelson located the French ships at Abu Qir (Aboukir) Bay, a few miles east of Alexandria. Nelson had 13 ships of the line and 2 smaller ships. French vice admiral François Brueys d'Aigalliers had 13 ships of the line, 4 frigates, and a number of smaller vessels. Many of the French ships of the line were larger than those of the English, but many crewmen were sick and others were ashore; some of the French ships were also weakly armed. Certainly the French were unprepared for battle.

Brueys had anchored his ships in a single line, protected by shoals, but had failed to order cables strung between the ships to prevent penetration by opposing ships; nor did his ships have springs attached to their anchor cables to prevent an opposing vessel from engaging them stern to stern. The nearest French land batteries were also three miles distant and thus unable to support the fleet.

Nelson attacked immediately. The Battle of Aboukir Bay, which the British remember as the Battle of the Nile, was a disaster for the French. The French ships had been anchored so as to allow them sufficient room to swing with the current. Guessing that the French ships were unprepared to fight on their port sides, Nelson sent his leading ships in from that direction. The first British ship grounded, but three others managed to get in between the French battle line and the shore.

The remaining British ships moved down the outside of the French line. Brueys's ships now came under attack from two sides, a serious disadvantage for the shorthanded French. The British doubled up on one French ship after another. Battle continued well into the night. The 120-gun flagship *Orient* caught fire and its magazine exploded, with Brueys among the many dead. It went down with most of Bonaparte's treasury, some £600,000 in gold and diamonds alone. By dawn only two French ships of the line remained; the rest had been burned, sunk, or captured.

Bonaparte's army was now cut off in Egypt. The battle also led to the formation of a new coalition against France, adding Russia, Austria, the Italian states, and the Ottoman Empire. Britain and Portugal had remained at war with France.

Meanwhile, disaffection in Ireland, nurtured by the French, led the Directory to send another expeditionary force there in

August 1798. There were two independent expeditions. The first, from Rochefort, landed some 1,150 men, but Irish support was lacking, and the French surrendered on September 8. The second, from Brest, counted 4,000 troops, but it was discovered, shadowed, and its ships engaged in mid-October. The French lost 7 of 10 ships, and no French troops from it landed in Ireland.

During July 1798–September 1800 France was also embroiled in an undeclared war with the United States, what was known as the Quasi-War. It grew out of French seizures of American merchant ships trading with Britain. The war was fought entirely at sea and took place off the American coast but primarily in the West Indies. The fighting involved ships of the U.S. Navy and the French Navy as well as privateers on both sides. By early 1799, the French ships were driven from the American coast and largely eliminated from the Caribbean. Fearful of driving the United States into active collaboration with Britain, Bonaparte agreed to negotiations in March 1800 that resulted in the Convention of Mortefontaine (or Convention of 1800) of September 30, 1800, that ended hostilities.

Course of the War of the Second Coalition (1798–1802)

With the French now cut off in Egypt, Ottoman forces assembled to defeat them. Achmed Pasha assembled one army in Syria; another assembled on Rhodes to be escorted to Egypt by a British naval squadron.

At the same time fighting occurred in Italy, where French troops under Joubert overran Piedmont in November and early December, forcing King Charles Emmanuel IV to flee to Sardinia. Concurrently, a Neapolitan army under Austrian general

Karl Mack von Leiberich marched into the Roman Republic and captured Rome on November 29, only to be driven out on December 15 by French forces under General Jean Etienne Championnet.

Allied plans called for a three-pronged assault on France. An Anglo-Russian army under the Duke of York was to force the French from the Netherlands, an Austrian army under Archduke Charles would push them from Germany and Switzerland, and Austro-Russian forces under Russian general Aleksandr Suvorov were to expel the French from Italy. Not counting the unreliable Neapolitan forces, the allies outnumbered the French some 300,000 to 200,000.

In Italy, Neapolitan forces under Austrian general Mack had retaken Rome from the French, but under attack by Championnet's French troops, they mutinied and forced Mack to flee for his life. The French then took Capua as well as the city of Naples. King Ferdinand IV fled to Sicily, and on January 23, 1799, the French established at Naples the satellite Parthenopean Republic.

In Egypt on February 10, Bonaparte led 13,000 men in an invasion of Syria. Capturing Jaffa on March 3, he learned that many of the 2,000–2,500 prisoners had earlier been released on parole. Unable to spare troops to guard them, Bonaparte ordered the prisoners shot—a decision made easier by the Ottomans having tortured and killed French prisoners.

On March 17, Bonaparte laid siege to the fortress city of Acre on the eastern Mediterranean. Acre had massive stone walls and some 250 cannon. Unfortunately for Bonaparte, he had sent his siege guns by sea, and they were intercepted by British warships, then brought into Acre and employed against him. Bonaparte's field guns could not inflict material damage, and his only recourse was costly infantry assaults. When these failed and with the spread of plague and reports of a large Ottoman force massing against him, Bonaparte ended the siege on May 20 and withdrew back to Egypt.

In fighting in Europe in March 1799, General Jourdan's Army of Mayence (Mainz) crossed the Rhine at Kehl and commenced operations against Archduke Charles's Austrians. Rebuffed at Ostrach on March 21, Jourdan caught Charles at Stockach on March 25 with part of his army and enjoyed success until Charles was able to bring up the remainder. Now outnumbered, Jourdan had to withdraw. This ended major military action in Germany for the remainder of the year. Disappointed at the outcome of the campaign and in poor health, Jourdan resigned his command.

Concurrent with Jourdan's advance, Masséna had moved from central Switzerland to cover Jourdan's right flank. Crossing the upper Rhine, Masséna captured an Austrian force near Chur in the Grisons but failed twice (March 18 and 23) to take Austrian-held Feldkirch and halted his advance, then sent General Claude Lecourbe and his men into the Tyrol. Part of the French Army of Italy joined Lecourbe there, and together they wreaked considerable havoc.

Fighting also occurred in Italy. In northern Italy, French general Barthélemy Scherer took the offensive against an Austrian army under Paul Kray von Krajova, hoping to defeat them before the arrival of Austrian reinforcements and Russian troops under Aleksandr Suvorov. Kray defeated Scherer in the Battle of Magnano, April 5, 1799, forcing him to withdraw. Moreau then replaced Scherer.

Shortly after the Battle of Magnano, Suvorov arrived and assumed command in northern Italy. Heavily outnumbering Moreau, he drove the French back. Detaching Kray to besiege Mantua and Peschiera, Suvorov defeated Moreau at Cassano (April 27). Two days later Suvorov entered Milan, bringing an end to the French-sponsored Cisalpine Republic. On May 27, he occupied Turin and blockaded what was left of Moreau's army at Genoa. Following differences with the Austrians, however, Suvorov scattered his men to take the remaining French garrisons. In May also, a Russian-Ottoman fleet in the eastern Mediterranean captured the Ionian Islands from France. The Russians held the islands until 1807.

In May, Masséna assumed command of Jourdan's army in addition to his own. Masséna's Army of the Danube was responsible for the defense of both Switzerland and the Rhine south of Mainz. He withdrew slowly back on Zurich, followed by the Austrians under Archduke Charles and General Friedrich von Hotze.

In the First Battle of Zurich (June 4–6), Masséna repulsed the Austrians. Superior Austrian numbers and the questionable loyalty of the Swiss, however, led him to withdraw farther west on June 7. Archduke Charles did not believe he had sufficient numerical advantage to press the issue.

In August, Masséna resumed the offensive. Defeating Charles's left wing in rugged territory of the upper Rhine and Rhône River Valleys, Masséna advanced on Zurich but was repulsed there on August 14. Two days later, he blunted an Austrian attack at Dottingen.

In fighting in northern Italy in June 1799, French general Etienne Jacques Joseph Alexandre MacDonald hurried up from southern Italy with his army. In the hard-fought Battle of the Trebbia (June 17–18), Suvorov defeated MacDonald, who then managed to join Moreau with part of his men at Genoa. King Ferdinand IV meanwhile returned to Naples, where he ended the Parthenopean Republic and carried out savage reprisals. The French-established Roman Republic suffered the same fate. Suvorov then drove the French back to the Riviera, causing the Directory in Paris to replace Moreau with Joubert.

Advancing from Genoa, Joubert attacked Suvorov's Russians and Austrians at Novi on August 15, only to be decisively defeated. Joubert was among the dead. Suvorov pursued the French, forcing them back across the Apennines.

Suvorov halted his pursuit on learning that French general Championnet's Army of the Alps had entered Italy via Mt. Cenis Pass. Suvorov moved north to engage Championnet, but before he could accomplish this he received orders to join his army with that of Russian general Alexander Korsakov, who had taken over from Archduke Charles in Switzerland.

New allied plans called for Charles to march north and join his army to the British and Russian forces under the Duke of York and drive the French from the Netherlands. The combined Russian armies of Suvorov and Korsakov would then expel Masséna from Switzerland. Obedient to orders, Suvorov left allied operations in Italy to Austrian marshal Michael Melas. On November 4 at Genoa, Melas defeated Championnet, driving the French back across the Alps.

In Egypt, an Ottoman army under Mustafa Pasha, supported by the Royal Navy, landed on July 10, 1779, and captured Aboukir fortress, then dug in there. Although Bonaparte had only 7,700 men and 17 guns, he attacked and won a resounding victory in the Battle of Aboukir (July 25). During negotiations regarding the return of Ottoman prisoners, British commodore

Smith provided Bonaparte with copies of the London *Times* revealing French military setbacks elsewhere. Without having received orders to do so, Bonaparte then decided to abandon his command in Egypt. On August 24 he and key aides sailed aboard two French frigates. Bonaparte's luck held, and after a stop at Corsica he landed in France at Fréjus on October 9.

The 1799 allied offensive in the Netherlands had begun in August when a British expeditionary force under Prince Frederick, Duke of York and Albany, landed in Holland. On August 30 the Dutch fleet in the Texel surrendered to a British squadron without a fight. Now reinforced by Russian troops, Frederick took the offensive. On September 19 in the First Battle of Bergen, French general Guillaume Marie Anne Brune with French and Bavarian troops met the advancing British and Russians. Taking advantage of poor allied coordination, Brune halted their advance.

Prince Frederick was successful against Brune in the Second Battle of Bergen on October 2, however. But in the Battle of Castricum (October 6) along the North Sea coast, Brune was again able to take advantage of poor allied cooperation. Realizing that he lacked the strength to drive the French from the Netherlands and having accomplished his goal of securing the Dutch fleet, York withdrew. On October 18 he concluded with the French the Convention of Alkmaar. The British returned some 8,000 French and Dutch prisoners held in England in exchange for their own unhindered evacuation from the Netherlands. They also kept the Dutch ships taken earlier.

Meanwhile, Korsakov and Suvorov were preparing to invade France from the southeast. Archduke Charles had marched northward but left behind some Austrian troops under Hotze. Seeing an opportunity to attack before the allies could concentrate against him, Masséna advanced with his Army of the Daunbe against the remaining allied forces in Switzerland. Masséna and most of his men attacked Korsakov near Zurich and were victorious in this Third Battle of Zurich (September 25–26). Korsakov withdrew in some disorder toward the upper Rhine. Masséna's victory here helped save France and gave the Directory a brief respite.

Suvorov, meanwhile, had fought his way through the St. Gotthard at considerable cost but arrived at Zurich too late. He then managed to extricate his army, although with great hardship, across the Alps to Ilanz on the upper Rhine, only to learn that Czar Paul I had removed him from command. Indeed on October 22 Paul, disgusted with his allies, withdrew Russia from the war.

The Directory did not have much longer to live. On his return to France, Bonaparte trumpeted his successes in Egypt and was greeted as a conquering hero. Arriving in Paris on October 15, he allied himself with Directors Emmanuel Siéyès and Roger Duclos. With the assistance of Napoleon Bonaparte's brother Lucien, president of the Council of 500, on November 9, 1799, the three men overthrew the government in what was known as the Coup of 18 Brumairet. It was actually two coups, as Bonaparte secured practical power for himself. In the new government known as the Consulate, he controlled the state as first consul for 10 years. Ducos and Siéyès refused subordinate roles and were bought off and replaced by two others as second and third consuls.

The Constitution of the Year VIII, overwhelmingly approved by popular vote in late December, had only a window dressing of representative institutions. Bonaparte, meanwhile, reformed the state administration and introduced a more efficient tax collection system.

In Egypt, meanwhile, General Jean Baptiste Kléber assumed command in Egypt. Following the failure of the British to ratify the Convention of El Arish that would have repatriated the French Army of Egypt, on March 20, 1800, Kléber attacked a British-supported Ottoman force at Heliopolis. Although he had no more than 10,000 men against a reported 60,000 Ottomans, Kléber was victorious. He then retook Cairo, which had revolted against French rule.

Bonaparte then took the field himself. Joining the French Army of the Reserve at Dijon in early March 1800, he sought to emulate Hannibal in a crossing of the Alps, hoping to cut off Austrian forces in Italy, where Masséna opposed Field Marshal Melas. Masséna personally commanded 10,000 men besieged at Genoa by Austrian general Karl Ott. Melas and the remaining Austrians campaigned against the rest of Masséna's men beyond Nice in the Var Valley.

Bonaparte crossed the Alps in May and reached the Lombard Plain. Moving rapidly, on June 2 he captured Milan. Restoring the Cisalpine Republic, he advanced against Lodi to prevent the Italians from reaching Mantua. On June 4, however, Masséna was forced to surrender Genoa. His men were starving, and he was granted favorable terms that allowed his army to quit the city under arms. Only 6,500 of his men had survived, however. Melas had extended these terms so that he could concentrate on defeating the remaining French forces in Italy.

At Montebello in Lombardy on June 9, French general Jean Lannes unexpectedly encountered Ott's army moving north from Genoa. Joined by men under General Claude Victor, Lannes defeated Ott and drove him toward Alessandria.

Bonaparte had hoped to catch the Austrians between his own army and that of Masséna, but although he made a valiant effort, Masséna was unable to deliver his half-starved men. Undeterred, Bonaparte moved against Melas alone, seeking a quick, decisive victory to cement his political control of France. Melas, meanwhile, left some men to garrison Genoa and concentrated the remainder at Alessandria, about halfway between Genoa and Milan.

Thinking that Melas was at Turin, Bonaparte separated his forces, sending some men to prevent the Austrians from escaping to Genoa (where they might be supplied by the British fleet) or to the Quadrilateral fortresses. He himself stumbled into Melas's numerically superior force at Alessandria on June 14.

Bonaparte was slow to realize the threat but then sent urgent appeals for his detached units to return. By 5:00 p.m. the Austrians had driven Bonaparte back some five miles. Melas had sustained a minor wound early and, believing the battle won, retired to Alessandria and gave command to General Anton Zach. The Austrians were now strung out in pursuit formation.

At this point, French general Louis Charles Desaix arrived with his corps and led an attack on the middle of the overconfident and disorganized Austrians near the village of Marengo, panicking and routing them but at the cost of his own life.

Melas requested an armistice, which Bonaparte granted on June 15. Bonaparte then turned over command to Masséna and returned to Paris. The fighting in Italy was over. In September 1800, however, the British captured Malta following an uprising there against the French.

Things also went well for the French in Germany, where Moreau proved to be a brilliant commander. With his Army of the Rhine, he forced Austrian general Kray back into Bavaria. Moreau won victories at Stockach (May 3), Möskirch (May 5), Ulm (May 16), and Hochstadt (June 19). Kray retired behind the Inn River, and Moreau took Munich in July. The two commanders then concluded an armistice. The Austrians rebuilt their forces and, encouraged by a British subsidy, refused to negotiate a settlement.

At the beginning of December, Moreau was in Bavaria with his army widely dispersed over a 30-mile front when it came under attack from Austrian archduke John's army and was forced into a fighting withdrawal from Ampfling on December 1. Believing the French to be in full retreat, Archduke John ordered his forces to continue toward Munich and concentrate near Hohenlinden. The archduke's forces advanced in parallel columns, with the principal column under Johann Kollowrat proceeding down a hard-surface road through the Forest of Hohenlinden. The Battle of Hohenlinden opened on the morning of December 3 when French troops concealed along the road fired on the Austrians. Moreau was able to concentrate the bulk of his forces, whereas Archduke John was unable to do the same in timely fashion. The more numerous Austrians then withdrew, having sustained far heavier losses than the French.

Moreau then moved against Vienna, while another French force under Macdonald advanced from Switzerland on the Tyrol and Brune moved up from Italy with a third army. Under these circumstances, on December 25 Austria sued for peace, in effect ending the War of the Second Coalition. The formal treaty was concluded at

Lunéville on February 9, 1801. It reconfirmed the provisions of the earlier treaties of Leoben and Campo Formio in 1797 and also practically dissolved the Holy Roman Empire. Austria ceded the left bank of the Rhine to France, the boundary being the middle of the river. The princes who lost lands here were to be compensated elsewhere in Germany. Austria also agreed to recognize the Batavian, Helvetian, Cisalpine, and Ligurian Republics.

In December 1800 Czar Paul, having learned of the British seizure of Malta, to which he had pretensions, embargoed all British ships and signed a naval convention with Sweden in which the two powers revived the League of Armed Neutrality of 1780 that would have allowed noncontraband goods, including timber and flax, to pass to France. In February 1801 after the Treaty of Lunéville, Russia expanded the league to include Denmark and Prussia. The British had long relied on the Baltic region for grain imports, but the Royal Navy was dependent on it for timber and naval stores. London thus regarded the league as a direct threat.

The immediate problem was with Denmark and its claimed right to convoy its merchant shipping through the British blockade without being subject to search. On July 25, 1800, a small British squadron brought a Danish convoy into port to search it for contraband. Pressured by the presence of a British squadron off Copenhagen, the Danes agreed to allow their convoys to be searched, but the event pushed Denmark closer to Russia, and Denmark embargoed British shipping. London now decided on force and, if necessary, a preemptive strike to break up the League of Armed Neutrality.

Admiral Sir Hyde Parker commanded the Baltic expedition, with Vice Admiral Horatio Nelson second-in-command. The question was whether to descend on Denmark or to move against the source of the problem and attack the Russian fleet at Reval (Tallinn), while the remainder of the Russian ships were icebound at Kronstadt. This would be the boldest, most certain course. Nelson wanted it, but Parker decided on a descent on Denmark.

The British sailed on March 12 with 53 ships—20 of them ships of the line—and nearly two regiments of ground troops. They had sent a diplomatic mission ahead, so the Danes had some warning. Parker also delayed for a week upon his arrival, giving the Danes additional time.

Nelson led the April 2 assault on Copenhagen with 30 ships, including 10 smaller ships of the line and 7 bomb vessels. Parker remained some four miles offshore with the larger ships of the line. Danish commodore Johan Fischer had 18 warships, armed hulks, and floating batteries moored paralleling the shore and supported by shore batteries.

Things went badly for Nelson from the start when several of his ships grounded. A long, slow slugfest ensued, with superior British gunnery finally beginning to tell. But Parker signaled a recall. Nelson ignored the order, which had it been carried out would probably have turned victory into disaster, for the only way for to withdraw was up the channel and across the undefeated northern Danish defenses. Nelson's captains copied him and also refused to disengage.

By afternoon several British ships were flying distress signals, but Nelson had disabled a dozen Danish ships and overwhelmed the southern shore defenses. He was thus in position to bring up his bomb vessels to shell the city. The Danes then agreed to a cease-fire, and then, under

Nelson's threat to bombard Copenhagen, agreed to a truce and to take no action under the Treaty of Armed Neutrality.

The Battle of Copenhagen was unnecessary. Had the British proceeded to Tallinn, leaving only a squadron at Copenhagen to keep the Danes in check, they would have discovered that Czar Paul had been assassinated on March 24 and that his successor, Alexander I, had changed policies. The armed neutrality was over by June, and British trade in the Baltic was flowing freely without threat of hindrance.

Meanwhile on March 18, 1801, in the Treaty of Florence, the Kingdom of Naples surrendered the island of Elba and territory in central Italy to France. Naples also agreed to the stationing of French troops in a number of Italian towns and to close its harbors to British and Ottoman shipping.

On March 2, 1801, the British landed some 16,000 troops under Lieutenant General Sir Ralph Abercromby in Aboukir Bay and defeated the small French force there. On March 12 the British began an advance on Alexandria, defeating a smaller French force at Mandora (March 13). French reinforcements under General Jacques Menou arrived at Alexandria from Cairo, but the British repulsed his effort on March 21 to take Alexandria, although Abercromby was mortally wounded.

During March–September 1801, British and Ottoman forces conquered the rest of Egypt. Kléber, stabbed to death by a Syrian student in Cairo on June 14, was succeeded by Menou. The British took Cairo on June 27. Only after additional bloodshed and the surrender of Alexandria on September 2 did Menou agree to accept the accord signed by Kléber 19 months earlier and to which the British were now prepared to agree. The French survivors were repatriated in cartels sent from France. Of Bonaparte's original force of some 50,000 army and naval personnel in Egypt, only half returned to France. Egypt was restored to Ottoman control.

On July 15, 1801, meanwhile, Bonaparte concluded a concordat with the Catholic Church. This helped heal the major breach caused by the Civil Constitution of the Clergy. The concordat did much to bridge the religious divide in France and bring to an end most counterrevolutionary agitation.

On March 27, 1802, the Wars of the French Revolution officially came to end with the conclusion of the Treaty of Amiens between France and Britain. There was to be a full exchange of prisoners, and Britain returned to France and its allies all territories it had taken except for Trinidad, ceded by Spain, and Ceylon (Sri Lanka), ceded by the Batavian Republic (the Netherlands). France was to withdraw its troops from the Papal States and the Kingdom of Naples. Malta was to be restored to the Knights of Malta. At the same time, peace was concluded between France and the Ottoman Empire.

Significance

The French Revolutionary Wars left France enjoying a paramount place in Europe. Its centuries-long effort to secure natural frontiers in the northeast had been at last achieved. France now controlled the Rhineland and had satellite kingdoms in the Low Countries and in Italy. Neither side fully lived up to the terms of the Treaty of Amiens, however. The British, for example, failed to turn over Malta, while the French continued to meddle in Italy. Bonaparte would have done well to have given Amiens a chance. Unfortunately for France and for Europe, he put his own ambition ahead of the interests of his countrymen. War formally resumed in May 1803.

Further Reading

Attar, Frank. *Aux armes citoyens! Naissance et fonctions du bellicisme révolutionnaire.* Paris: Éditions du Seuil, 2010.

Attar, Frank. *La Révolution française déclare la guerre à l'Europe: L'embrasement de l'Europe à la fin du XVIIIe siècle, 1792.* Bruxelles: Editions Complexe, 1992.

Bertaud, Jean-Paul. *The Army of the French Revolution: From Citizen-Soldiers to Instrument of Power.* Princeton, NJ: Princeton University Press, 1988.

Black, Jeremy. *British Foreign Policy in an Age of Revolutions, 1783–1793.* Cambridge: Cambridge University Press, 1994.

Blanning, T. C. W. *The French Revolutionary Wars, 1787–1801.* London: Arnold, 1996.

Blanning, T. C. W. *The Origins of the French Revolutionary Wars.* London: Longman, 1986.

Clowes, William Laird. *The Royal Navy: A History from the Earliest Times to 1900,* Vol. 4, *1899.* Reprint ed. London: Chatham, 1996.

Connelly, Owen. *The Wars of the French Revolution and Napoleon, 1792–1815.* New York: Routledge, 2006.

Crawley, C. W., ed. *The New Cambridge Modern History,* Vol. 9, *War and Peace in an Age of Upheaval, 1793–1830.* Cambridge: Cambridge University Press, 1965.

Doughty, Robert Allan. *Warfare in the Western World,* Vol. 1, *Military Operations from 1600 to 1914.* Boston: Houghton Mifflin, 2007.

Esdaile, Charles. *The French Wars, 1792–1815.* London: Routledge, 2001.

Forrest, Alan A. *The Soldiers of the French Revolution.* Durham, NC: Duke University Press, 1990.

Fremont-Barnes, Gregory. *The French Revolutionary Wars.* Oxford, UK: Osprey, 2011.

Gardiner, Robert. *Fleet Battle and Blockade: The French Revolutionary War, 1793–1797.* Annapolis, MD: Naval Institute Press, 1996.

Griffith, Paddy. *The Art of War of Revolutionary France, 1789–1802.* Mechanicsburg, PA: Stackpole Books, 1998.

Napoleonic Wars (1803–1814, 1815)

Dates	1803–1815
Location	Europe
Combatants	France vs. Britain, Prussia and other German states, Austria, Spain, and Russia
Principal Commanders	France: Napoleon I, Pierre-Charles de Villeneuve, Joachim Murat, Michel Ney, Auguste Marmont, Louis Davout Britain: Horatio Nelson; Arthur Wellesley, Duke of Wellington Prussia: Frederick William III, Gebbard Leberecht von Blücher Austria: Baron Karl Mack von Leiberich; Archduke Charles, Duke of Teschen; Karl Philipp, Prince of Schwarzenberg Russia: Alexander I, Mikhail Illarionovich Kutuzov
Principal Battles	Ulm, Trafalgar, Austerlitz, Jena and Auerstädt, Eylau, Friedland, Bailén, Essling, Wagram, Vitoria, Borodino, Retreat from Moscow, Leipzig, Waterloo
Outcome	Far from defeating Britain, the wars end with the British Empire as the world's strongest. Napoleon's continental empire is dismantled, but the nationalism and reforms unleashed by the French Revolution and spread by Napoleonic conquest have a profound effect on Europe and the world.

Causes

The French Revolutionary Wars of 1792–1802 had ended with the Treaty of Amiens between France and Britain on March 25, 1802. Although there had been great rejoicing in both France and Britain, the peace did not last. First Consul Napoleon Bonaparte continued significant administrative reforms and helped heal the wounds inflicted on France by the revolution, but at the same time he was preparing to renew war with Britain. British leaders were all too well aware that France was growing steadily stronger.

Both sides failed to live up to the treaty's provisions. Britain refused to evacuate Malta, as provided by Amiens. Peace might not have lasted in any case, but Bonaparte gave it no chance by refusing any concessions. Indeed, although the treaty had recognized France in possession of the long-sought natural frontiers in the northeast, Bonaparte put personal ambition first, annexing Piedmont in Italy, Elba, and part of Switzerland. Perhaps most important to the British, he refused to implement his pledge in the Treaty of Amiens to negotiate a trade agreement with Britain. Bonaparte also alarmed the British by sending troops to Haiti, although his plans for a new empire in America went awry and ended with the sale of Louisiana to the United States in 1803.

Ambition was certainly a strong motivator for Bonaparte, but it was not the only factor. Opportunities presented themselves and he took advantage, even when national interests should have dictated refusal. Some historians have seen him as the defender of the revolution against old monarchical Europe. Others have credited him with a grand unifying scheme for Europe, although one in which France enjoyed

primary place. Others see the resumption of war as simply a continuation of the long struggle between Britain and France.

In any case, in April 1803 the British withdraw their ambassador from Paris and resumed warfare at sea. Formal declaration of war came on May 16, 1803.

Course of the War between Britain and France (1803–1805)

French troops responded by occupying British king George III's family possession of Hanover in Germany, which they ravaged. Bonaparte also gathered shipping and at Boulogne created a camp for the 200,000-man Army of England (the future Grande Armée) and a supposed invasion. On October 2, 1804, Royal Navy captain Sidney Smith led a fireship raid against the mouth of the Rhine and destroyed a number of these vessels, while other British ships sought to prevent a concentration of French naval assets for an attempt across the English Channel.

On December 2, 1804, Bonaparte was crowned emperor as Napoleon I. Pope Pius VII was summoned to France for the ceremony, but in a fitting gesture Bonaparte crowned himself, his elevation confirmed by a subsequent overwhelming popular vote. In effect, royal absolutism had returned to France but in greatly more efficient form.

Course of the War of the Third Coalition (1805)

In January 1805, Spain joined France in the war. In April, meanwhile, Britain entered into a formal alliance with Russia, initiating the Third Coalition against France. Austria and Sweden joined in the next several months. The allies planned for Habsburg archduke Charles, their top field commander, to advance with 90,000 men against French marshal André Masséna's 50,000-man Army of Italy, then drive against the French Army of England.

Napoleon meanwhile hoped to concentrate French and Spanish naval assets for a brief mastery of the English Channel and an invasion of England by his Army of England. He planned a deception that he hoped would cause the British to leave the channel unprotected. Admiral Pierre Charles Villeneuve's fleet at Toulon and allied Spanish ships under Admiral Federico Carlos de Gravina were to sail to the West Indies. At the same time, Admiral Honoré Ganteaume and his 21 ships were to break out from Brest and release Spanish ships at El Ferrol in northwestern Spain. French hopes rested on British warships pursuing west. The French fleets would unite at Martinique under Ganteaume, elude their pursuers, and make for the channel. Napoleon assumed that he would then have available 60–70 ships of the line and at least a dozen frigates to provide a brief period of naval mastery sufficient to convoy a host of small vessels ferrying an invading army across the channel to England.

British vice admiral Horatio Nelson had been carrying out a loose blockade of Toulon in the hope of enticing out his opponent. On March 30 Villeneuve indeed escaped Toulon and sailed west into the Atlantic, where he reached Cádiz and linked up with Gravina. Their combined 20 ships of the line, 8 frigates, and some smaller vessels then sailed for the West Indies with Nelson's 10 ships in pursuit. Napoleon's orders were for Villeneuve to wait at Martinique no longer than 35 days. If Ganteaume was unable to break free of Brest, Villeneuve was to proceed to El Ferrol and then on to Brest to release Spanish and French ships for the invasion attempt.

After inconclusive maneuvering, on June 8 Villeneuve panicked on the news that Nelson was in pursuit and departed Martinique for Europe. Nelson followed and returned to Gibraltar on July 20. Two days later Admiral Sir Robert Calder, with 15 ships of the line and 2 frigates, clashed with Villeneuve's combined fleet off Cape Finisterre. The Spanish ships bore the brunt of the attack, and the British took 2 of them as prizes, along with 1,200 seamen as prisoners. Poor visibility allowed the remainder of the combined fleet to escape, but 5 other Spanish vessels, including a frigate, were so badly damaged that they had to go into dry dock for repairs. Calder had won a nominal victory, but it was by no means decisive.

Villeneuve meanwhile proceeded to El Ferrol, and then on August 13, taking advantage of a loophole in his orders, he proceeded south to Cádiz, leading Napoleon to abandon any hopes of an invasion of England. The British soon had the combined French and Spanish naval force at Cádiz under blockade. British prime minister William Pitt insisted that Nelson, then in England, take command from Vice Admiral Lord Cuthbert Collingwood.

Arriving on station, Nelson rejected Collingwood's more cautious close blockade in favor of a loose arrangement that kept his fleet out of sight of Cádiz. Nelson employed a line of frigates to signal the main body of the fleet over the horizon, some 50 miles out. Nelson hoped that this would entice out the French and Spanish. A loose blockade was risky because his enemies might get away. Nelson, however, preferred it to no action at all.

Napoleon meanwhile left Marshal Guillaume Marie Anne Brune and 30,000 men at Boulogne to continue the invasion charade and to protect against any

EUROPE IN 1810

British invasion. Marshal André Masséna and 50,000 men held Italy, and General Laurent Gouvion Saint-Cyr marched to Naples with 20,000 more. On August 24 Napoleon ordered the Army of England, now renamed the Grande Armée, to march eastward to defeat the Austrians, and the Russians should they arrive in time, before they could organize.

On September 13, Austrian general Karl Mack von Leiberich invaded Bavaria with 70,000 men. On September 26 unknown to Mack, Napoleon crossed the Rhine. Mack's army was in present-day Baden-Württemberg on the Danube. The Russians had dispatched 95,000 men, and its advance force of 35,000 men under Field Marshal Mikhail Kutuzov was to link up with Mack at Ulm by October 20.

On October 6 Napoleon reached the Danube, and his army then crossed the river. Napoleon was unaware of Mack's precise location. Mack wanted to cut through the French rear and join the Russians at Regensburg (Ratisbon). Had this occurred, the Austrians would have caught the French artillery and ammunition trains and army treasury virtually unprotected, but Archduke Ferdinand, who was with Mack, refused to authorize this. On the night of October 12–13 Napoleon learned of Mack's location and ordered the army back across the Danube with a concentration at Ulm.

Although some of Mack's army escaped ahead of time, Napoleon surrounded the remainder at Ulm by October 15 and opened a bombardment. On October 20

Mack surrendered his 27,000-man army and 65 guns.

The next day, the most important naval battle of the Napoleonic Wars occurred in the Mediterranean. In mid-September Napoleon ordered the combined French and Spanish fleet to the Mediterranean to support French operations in southern Italy. Villeneuve knew that his ships were not ready, and his Spanish colleagues urged him not to sail on grounds of approaching bad weather. Yet Villeneuve, stung by Napoleon's charges of cowardice and news from Madrid that he was to be ordered back to Paris to explain his conduct, now risked all.

On October 19, Villeneuve's 18 French and 15 Spanish ships of the line exited Cádiz. Nelson soon learned of this via his frigate lookouts. Outnumbered by his opponents 33 ships of the line to only 27, Nelson planned to split off the enemy center and rear from the van by attacking in several columns. With the French and Spanish ships running before the wind, the van would find it difficult to tack back and rejoin the action, which hopefully would be decided before they could do so.

On October 21 when Nelson's ships appeared, Villeneuve ordered a return to Cádiz. This caused great confusion in the five-mile-long already irregular allied line as Nelson's ships drove directly into its center. The British ships were outgunned, and the French and Spanish had some 30,000 men to slightly more than 17,000 for the British. But Nelson's ships were far superior in both gunnery and seamanship. These factors and superior leadership more than compensated for any numerical deficiencies.

In the ensuing five-hour Battle of Trafalgar the British captured 19 allied ships, and another blew up. No English ship was lost, but human casualties were heavy, and Nelson was mortally wounded by a French sharpshooter. Then shortly after the battle a great storm blew in, and most of the prizes were lost as victor and vanquished worked together to save their ships and themselves. Although no British ship was lost, of the original 19 prizes, excluding 4 taken to Gibraltar, 4 were scuttled, and 2 others escaped to Cádiz. The remainder either sank in the storm or were dashed on the rocks, with heavy personnel losses. Although 13 French and Spanish ships made it back to Cádiz, 3 broke up on the rocks. The battle thus claimed 23 capital ships. Then on November 5 in the Battle of Cape Finisterre, 4 French ships of the line that had survived Trafalgar were also taken.

Napoleon dismissed the Battle of Trafalgar in a single sentence: "Some ships have been lost in a gale following an unwisely undertaken engagement." In truth, the battle shattered the French Navy and firmly established Britain as mistress of the seas, not to be seriously challenged until the end of the 19th century. The battle also confined Napoleon to the land. To get at the British thereafter, he resorted to a trade war by denying British goods entry into Europe, which alienated many Europeans and brought the overextension of French military commitments.

Following the Battle of Ulm, Napoleon sent some forces south to delay Austrian troops crossing the Alps from Italy while he drove east with the Grand Armée. Kutuzov had reached the Inn River with 38,000 Russians, but on news of Napoleon's advance he burned bridges over the Inn and withdrew eastward. Napoleon ordered his cavalry under Murat to pursue. The Russians carried out effective delaying actions at both Dürnstein (November 11) and Hollabrünn (November 15–16). On November

12 Murat and Marshal Jean Lannes entered Vienna, which had been declared an open city. The Austrians and Russians now had some 86,000 men.

Leaving 20,000 men to garrison Vienna, Napoleon turned north into Moravia with 70,000 men. Archdukes Charles and John in Italy attempted to reach Austria with their 80,000 men. They, however, came under attack by a total of 55,000 French troops under Marshal Michel Ney, General Auguste Marmont, and Marshal Masséna.

As Napoleon advanced toward the Russian frontier, he found himself at a decided disadvantage in troop strength and facing increasingly long and vulnerable supply lines. On November 28 Russian and Habsburg forces at Olmütz moved south against him. Napoleon was confident. Selecting the ground for the battle, he planned to bait his opponents by withdrawing before them from the advantageous high ground of the Pratzen Heights. Carefully concealing his own numbers, he would extend his right flank to invite an allied attack there.

Supposedly impressed by his own troops marching in review, Czar Alexander I, who was with the army, overruled Kutuzov and ordered the allied troops forward to attack the seemingly weak French right wing. Had the czar but waited, Napoleon would have been far more vulnerable, and Prussia might also have joined the allied coalition.

The ensuing battle of December 2, 1805, is called the Battle of Austerlitz for the small nearby village but is also known as the Battle of the Three Emperors because Emperor Francis II was also present.

The timely arrival of 6,000 French reinforcements from Vienna under Marshal Louis Nicolas Davout halted the Russian attack on the French right, and Napoleon then sprang his trap, sending Marshal Nicolas Jean de Dieu Soult's corps to retake the high ground of the Pratzen Heights abandoned earlier, cutting off the allied left, and then turning to the right and rolling up the Russians on the French right. Other French forces cut off and shattered the Russian left. By nightfall the allied army had ceased to exist as a fighting force. Napoleon's losses were some 9,000 killed or wounded, while the Russians and Austrians sustained 12,000 killed or wounded, along with 15,000 captured. Napoleon caused the 180 allied guns taken to be melted down to form the column to the Grand Armée that still stands in the Place Vendôme in Paris.

Alexander refused to make peace and simply withdrew his forces back to Russia. French foreign minister Maurice de Talleyrand-Périgord urged Napoleon to conclude a generous peace with Austria in order to win its friendship. Talleyrand understood that lasting peace rested on French hegemony over Europe rather than trying to conquer all of it. Napoleon ignored this sound advice, now more convinced than ever that he could not be beaten on the battlefield.

Peace was concluded on December 26 at Pressburg (today Bratislava, Slovakia). France received Piedmont, Parma, and Piacenza. The Kingdom of Italy gained all the territory Austria had received from the 1797 Treaty of Campo Formio as well as Venetian Istria and Dalmatia. Austria also agreed to recognize Napoleon as king of Italy. Bavaria secured from Austria territories of the Tirol and the free city of Augsburg. Baden and Württemberg were given the remaining Austrian territory in western Germany. Austria received Salzburg, Berchtesgaden, and the estates of the Teutonic Order, which were secularized.

France now controlled western and southern Germany.

Britain meanwhile employed its sea power to strengthen its blockade of territory held by France and to assist its allies fighting on land. In January 1806 the British took the Cape Colony, belonging to the Batavian Republic, a French satellite. They continued to capture French ships on the high seas, and in July they captured Buenos Aires.

On July 12, 1806, Napoleon announced formation of the Confederation of the Rhine. All German princes, except for the rulers of Austria, Prussia, Brunswick, and Hesse, joined it in alliance with France. Recognizing the inevitable, on August 6 Holy Roman emperor Francis II, already calling himself Francis I, emperor of Austria, abdicated the throne of the Holy Roman Empire, officially bringing it to an end.

Course of the War of the Fourth Coalition (1806–1807)

Prussian king Frederick William III, who had held back joining Austria and Russia in 1805 when such a step could easily have brought Napoleon's defeat, now stupidly embarked on war. Frederick William was angered by Napoleon's reorganization of Germany and the French violation of the Prussian territory of Ansbach in 1805. In June 1806, Frederick William also learned that Napoleon was considering taking Hanover from Prussia and returning it to Britain in order to secure peace. Napoleon would have compensated Prussia elsewhere, but Frederick William began preparations for war. This Fourth Coalition allied Prussia with Britain and Russia, which had remained at war with Napoleon, and also ultimately included Saxony and Sweden.

Prussia had about 150,000 troops, and Russia began assembling two armies of 60,000 men each. Napoleon had some 200,000 men in his Grande Armée. Well aware of his adversaries' scarcely concealed plans and unwilling to wait to be attacked on their terms, Napoleon rapidly and secretly massed men in northeastern Bavaria for an invasion of Prussia.

Napoleon took personal command of some 180,000 French troops and could call on 100,000 allied Germans. With Prussian forces already advancing, on October 8 Napoleon began his own movement north from Bavaria in parallel columns on a front of about 30 miles, preceded by a cavalry screen.

Although Frederick William III accompanied the army in the field, 71-year-old Karl Wilhelm Ferdinand, Duke of Brunswick, held actual field command. Brunswick had three armies: 75,000 men under himself, 38,000 under Friedrich Ludwig Prince von Hohenlohe, and 30,000 under General Ernst Rüchel.

On October 14 the French came on the Prussians unawares. Hohenlohe encountered Napoleon at Jena, while 15 miles north at Auerstädt it was Brunswick and the king against Davout. Napoleon with 90,000 men (40,000 actually engaged) defeated Hohenlohe with 38,000 men (33,000 engaged). Hohenlohe called on Rüchel to join him, but the latter arrived late and had to fight a separate battle. In the two battles at Jena, the French sustained 5,000 casualties for 26,000 Prussians (15,000 prisoners).

The major battle took place at Auerstadt. Here Davout with only 27,000 men engaged and defeated Brunswick with 63,000. Brunswick was blinded and mortally wounded, and the king dithered over a replacement with the result that substantial portions of the Prussian forces were not committed to battle. After six hours of heavy fighting, the Prussians broke. Davout achieved a complete victory but at the cost of 8,000 casualties; Prussian losses were 15,000. In the wild retreats that followed, the two Prussian armies merged, heightening both confusion and panic.

This single day virtually ended Prussian resistance to the French. Murat took Erfurt (October 15), Davout captured Berlin (October 24), and Murat bluffed Hohenlohe into surrendering his larger force at Prenzlau (October 28). Most Prussian fortresses and their garrisons, including Magdeburg, fell with little resistance. The last major Prussian force, under General Gebhard Leberecht von Blücher, surrendered at Ratekau near Lübeck on November 24. Frederick William III fled to Königsberg.

From Berlin on November 21, Napoleon issued the Berlin Decree instituting the Continental System. The decree prohibited trade between the French Empire, including the German states, and Britain. Napoleon's intention was to disrupt British trade and force that country into ruinous inflation. He also hoped that this would stimulate continental, especially French, industry.

Britain responded with its Orders in Council of January 1807. These prohibited neutral ships from trading between French-controlled ports and those of its allies. Britain insisted that neutral ships bound for a French or French-held port first discharge their cargoes in Britain before obtaining an export license.

At the end of November Napoleon moved into Prussian Poland, up to the line of the Vistula (Wisła) River, and occupied Warsaw (Warszawa). Calling on the Polish people to ally themselves with France, he created the Duchy of Warsaw. No doubt Napoleon intended to re-create the Kingdom of Poland, but the right moment for this never came. In December Elector Frederick Augustus of Saxony abandoned Prussia and allied himself with France. Napoleon rewarded him with the title of king and shortly thereafter made him ruler of the new Duchy of Warsaw.

In late December French forces began to clash in Poland with Marshal Count Alexander Kamenski and the Russians and remaining Prussian troops. Heavy fighting occurred at Pultusk and at Golymin on December 26. With the weather already very cold, both sides then went into winter quarters.

In January 1807 Russian general Levin August Gottlieb Theophil, Count von Bennigsen, who had taken command from Kamenski and was aware from captured French orders of troop dispositions, surprised Napoleon by taking the offensive. Marshals Jean Baptiste Jules Bernadotte and Michel Ney south of Königsberg (today Kaliningrad) fell back, but when Napoleon ordered a rapid concentration and pursuit, Bennigsen withdrew.

Napoleon caught up with Bennigsen at Eylau-Preussisch (Bagrationowski), but only Davout was sufficiently close to be able to answer the emperor's orders to reinforce. Disdainful of the Russians, on February 8 Napoleon attacked with only 50,000 men and 200 guns. (Davout's 15,000 did not arrive until the afternoon.) Bennigsen had 67,000 men and 460 guns and was reinforced during the battle to 75,000 men by the arrival of a Prussian corps. Fought in occasional snow squalls, the battle saw one of the great cavalry charges in history when Napoleon, close to defeat, ordered Murat against the Russian center. Davout had almost turned the Russian flank when the arrival of the Prussians prevented disaster. The battle ended in a draw at nightfall, though Bennigsen withdrew. Napoleon suffered close to 25,000 casualties, Benningsen more. Both armies then went into winter quarters.

In February 1807, the British employed their sea power to capture Montevideo and then again took Buenos Aires (July 5), although they soon abandoned it. The British also sought to employ their navy against the Ottoman Empire, for at the end of 1806 the Ottomans, encouraged by Napoleon's victory at Austerlitz, had renounced their alliance with Britain and Russia and declared war on Russia in what would be a relatively low-intensity struggle in Moldavia, Wallachia, Armenia, the Caucasus, and the Dardanelles, until 1812.

Fearful that Ottoman naval resources would join those of France, the British dispatched a large squadron to the Dardanelles under Vice Admiral Sir John Duckworth to sail to Istanbul (Constantinople) and there demand surrender of the Ottoman fleet. Should negotiations fail, Duckworth was to bombard Istanbul and capture or destroy the Ottoman ships.

Duckworth set out on February 11 with eight ships of the line, two frigates, and two bomb vessels but lost one of the ships of the line to a fire and explosion. Sultan Selim III rejected the British ultimatum, and Ottoman guns ashore sank two British ships and badly damaged others. This British naval foray, at least, was a total failure.

The British then attempted to open another front against the Ottomans, this time in Egypt where Muhammad Ali had established himself as ruler under Ottoman suzerainty. In mid-March 1807, 5,000 troops under Major General A. Mackenzie Fraser came ashore at Alexandria and soon captured it. Fraser's effort to capture Rosetta met rebuff, however. Their situation

steadily deteriorating, the British evacuated Egypt in mid-September.

Napoleon meanwhile took the offensive against Bennigsen. He built the Grand Armée to 200,000 men. Bennigsen also rebuilt his forces, to 90,000 men. Hoping to catch the French by surprise, on June 5, 1807, Bennigsen moved against Marshal Ney, a week before Napoleon's planned advance. Ney withdrew, and Napoleon then attacked Bennigsen in strong defensive positions in Heilsberg on the Alle (Lyna, or Lava) River. The French took Heilsberg (June 10), and Bennigsen then withdrew. Both armies were moving on opposite sides of the Alle River in the direction of Königsburg. Learning that a French unit, presumed to be a division, was widely separated from the rest of army, on June 13 Bennigsen ordered his troops across the river. The unit in question turned out to be Jean Lannes's corps of 18,000 men on the right French flank. Convinced early on June 14 that this was indeed Bennigsen's main element, Napoleon ordered his entire army to mass at Friedland.

The Battle of Friedland of June 14 pitted Napoleon with 80,000 men against Bennigsen, with only 60,000. Lannes had been forced back some three miles before Napoleon attacked. Using his superior numbers, he crushed the Russians against the river, driving Bennigsen into Friedland and, by nightfall, back across the river.

The battle was decisive. The Russians suffered 30,000 casualties, half of them killed or drowned, and 80 guns lost. French casualties totaled 11,400. On June 19 Napoleon occupied Tilsit (Sovetsk), and the Russians requested a truce, which Napoleon granted.

The War of the Fourth Coalition effectively came to an end with the Treaties of Tilsit of July 7 and 9 between France and Russia and France and Prussia. Napoleon met with Czar Alexander I on a raft in the Niemen River, the boundary between Prussia and Russia. Russia agreed to recognize the Grand Duchy of Warsaw, formed of territory taken from Prussia, under the king of Saxony. Russia received part of East Prussia (Bialystock). Alexander agreed to recognize Napoleon's siblings as monarchs and also recognize the Confederation of the Rhine. He also accepted French mediation to end the war between Russia and the Ottoman Empire, while France accepted Russian mediation to end its war with Britain. In secret articles, Alexander agreed to an alliance with Napoleon against Britain should the British reject proffered peace terms.

Tilsit cost Russia little, but Prussia lost nearly half its territory. It ceded to France all territory east of the Rhine and that west of the Elbe to Saxony, while the Grand Duchy of Warsaw secured all territory taken by Prussia in the partitions of Poland since 1772. Prussia also gave up Danzig (Gdansk), taken by the French and now made a free city. Prussia recognized Napoleon's siblings and agreed to close its territory to British goods. The Prussian Army was restricted to 42,000 men, and Prussia had to pay an indemnity, subsequently set at 120 million francs (raised in 1808 to 140 million). Until this was paid, Prussia had to support a French occupation army of 150,000 men.

In many ways, Tilsit was the height of Napoleon's rule. He now controlled virtually all of Western and Central Europe and commanded allied forces of 800,000 men, a size without parallel in European history. Only Britain opposed him.

Following Tilsit, the British government feared that Denmark might join its fleet to those of France and Russia and decided to reprise its action of 1801 by striking first. Admiral James Gambier sailed for Copenhagen with 29 ships of the line and 53 frigates and smaller warships. Lieutenant General Lord Cathcart commanded the land contingent of 29,000 men in 380 transports. The Danes had 20 ships of the line, 27 frigates, and 60 smaller ships, but the British caught them by surprise with none of their ships ready for combat.

When the Danes refused to negotiate, the British troops landed north of Copenhagen. Hostilities commenced on August 17, and on September 2 the British began a bombardment of Copenhagen. With parts of the city soon in flames, the Danes surrendered on September 6 and agreed to hand over the entire fleet as well as all cannon in the arsenal. After destroying those they did not want, on October 21 the British departed with 79 Danish ships, including 16 ships of the line. The military booty amounted to some 3 million thalers. Severe storms on the return trip to Britain caused the loss of 25 ships, and only 4 Danish ships of the line were actually taken into the Royal Navy. On September 5 also, the British also took the small Danish island of Heligoland (Helgoland) in the North Sea. It remained in their hands until 1890.

In August 1807 largely as a result of French mediation called for by the Treaty of Tilsit, Russia and the Ottoman Empire concluded an armistice. Russia removed its forces from Wallachia and Moldavia, and Ottoman forces retired to Adrianople. Desultory fighting resumed in 1809, however. The conflict was not resolved until the Treaty of Bucharest in May 1812.

Now allied to France, Russia called on Sweden to renounce its alliance with Britain. When the Swedes refused, in February 1808 Russian troops invaded Finland. The Swedes evacuated Finland in December, and in September 1809 they concluded the Treaty of Fredrikshamn, ceding all Finland and part of Lapland to Russia. On January 6, 1810, Sweden signed the Treaty of Paris with France, joined the Continental System, and regained Pomerania.

Meanwhile, in Milan on December 17, 1807, Napoleon issued another decree tightening the Continental System, in effect closing the entire European continent to British goods. The decree also authorized French warships and privateers to capture neutral ships sailing from any British port or from any country occupied by the British. Ships submitting to search on the high seas by the Royal Navy would be considered lawful prizes if captured by the French. Napoleon's effort to close off British goods from Europe now led him into perhaps the most disastrous decision of his career: the intervention in the Iberian Peninsula. This "Spanish ulcer," as Napoleon came to call it, would cost him 300,000 casualties in five years of fighting.

On November 19, French and Spanish troops invaded Portugal. At first all went well. French forces under General Jean Andoche Junot captured Lisbon on December 1. Then in March 1808, Napoleon sent 100,000 troops into Spain under Marshal Murat on the pretext of guarding its coasts against the British. Spanish king Charles IV abdicated in favor of his son Ferdinand VII, but Napoleon then had both men renounce the throne.

On May 2, however, an uprising known as El Dos de Mayo (The Second of May) against French rule occurred in Madrid. The French put it down with great savagery. Indeed, Napoleon welcomed this as a means of securing Spanish submission to his authority. He then sent his elder brother Joseph, currently the king of Naples, to Spain as king, whereupon Murat took Joseph's place at Naples. Meanwhile, a guerrilla war began in Spain (the word "guerrilla" in fact comes from the Spanish word *guerra* and is the diminutive, meaning "small war"). The fighting often saw no quarter given by either side. Typical of the desperate nature of the struggle were two French sieges of Zaragoza (Saragossa) during June 15–August 17, 1808, and December 20, 1808–February 20, 1809, the second of which claimed 54,000 Spanish lives. The British provided arms and assistance to insurgents in both Spain and Portugal, then dispatched an expeditionary force to Portugal.

On July 19, 1808, General Pierre Dupont and some 20,000 French troops were surrounded and forced to surrender at Bailén (Baylen) by 30,000 Spanish troops under General Francisco Castaños. Dupont's men were mostly inexperienced raw recruits, but their surrender, the first of a French army under Napoleon, sent shock waves across Europe, invigorating opposition to French rule in other countries, especially Austria. It was also a great boost to the continued Spanish resistance and to British hopes for it.

At the end of July, King Joseph panicked and decided to evacuate Madrid, withdrawing his forces north of the Ebro River. A furious Napoleon decided to go to Spain in person. Then on August 1 a British expeditionary force commanded by Lieutenant General Sir Arthur Wellesley landed north of Lisbon. Junot marched from Lisbon with 13,000 men to engage Wellesley's 17,000 men at Vimeiro (August 21). Devastating British musket fire against dense French attack formations gave the British victory. Junot's position was now completely untenable, but the elderly and inept commanders of the British expeditionary force in Portugal,

Lieutenant Generals Hew Dalrymple and Harry Burrard, granted Junot generous terms. In the Convention of Cintra of August 30, 1808, the French army in Portugal was transported back to France by British navy ships, with all its weapons, equipment, and the loot acquired in Portugal. A storm of protest in Britain over this led to the recall of the senior British officers in Portugal, although Wellesley, who had opposed the terms, was exonerated. Lieutenant General Sir John Moore then assumed command of British forces in Portugal.

British forces in Portugal were reinforced to 35,000 men. Moore left 12,000 men there and invaded Spain with the remainder to assist some 125,000 Spanish Army and irregular forces. Napoleon also reinforced in Spain.

Buoyed by events in Spain, Austrian leaders considered resuming war with France. To prevent this, Napoleon met with Russian czar Alexander I at Erfurt during September 27–October 14, 1808, seeking to secure a pledge that war between Austria and France would necessarily mean war between Austria and Russia. This undoubtedly would have prevented Austria from going to war, but at night Alexander met secretly with Napoleon's chief negotiator, Talleyrand, who was working against his master in the hopes of restoring a balance of power in Europe. Talleyrand persuaded Alexander against extending the guarantee and thus was probably more responsible for the war in 1809 between Austria and France than any other individual.

In early November, Napoleon arrived in Spain. Moving south of the Ebro River with nearly 200,000 men, he entered Madrid on December 4. Napoleon then abolished monastic orders and the Inquisition, confiscated rebel property, and ordered the sequestering of goods deemed necessary to France. After restoring Joseph to power, he departed Madrid on December 22 to deal with Moore.

Taking advantage of his great numerical advantage, Napoleon attempted to destroy Moore's force, but the latter hurriedly withdrew to La Coruña (Corunna), where his men might be evacuated by the Royal Navy. Messages from Paris that the Austrians were mobilizing led Napoleon to quit Spain. On January 16, 1809, Soult attacked Moore at La Coruña but was repulsed (Moore was mortally wounded). The next day, the Royal Navy evacuated the British force.

The British continued to employ their sea power to advantage. During 1808–1809 they abetted a revolt in Santo Domingo against French-speaking blacks in Haiti. In January 1809 British and Portuguese forces took possession of Cayenne, capital of French Guiana (Guyane), and the next month the British secured Martinique. In July they occupied the island of Gorée (now considered part of Dakar) in Senegal, and in February 1810 they captured Guadeloupe in the West Indies. In July and December, respectively, they occupied Réunion (then known as Bourbon) and Mauritius, two French islands in the Indian Ocean used for commerce raiding.

In Spain following the Battle of La Coruña, French forces under Soult invaded Portugal, but British forces there, now under Wellesley, had been reinforced. Wellesley surprised Soult at Oporto on May 21, forcing him back to Spain.

Meanwhile, deteriorating relations between Napoleon and Pope Pius VII, driven by Napoleon's high-handed measures in dealing with the church in France and his seizure of some papal territories, led Pius to remain outside the Continental System.

On February 2, 1809, French troops had occupied Rome, and on May 17 Napoleon ordered the Papal States incorporated with France. On June 10 Pius VII excommunicated Napoleon, and on July 6 the emperor ordered the pope arrested and held.

Archduke Charles had rebuilt the regular Austrian Army to 300,000 men and the Landwehr to some 150,000, but the troops were still poorly trained, and Charles opposed war. He was overruled, however. In March 1809 the Austrians proclaimed a German war of liberation, beginning the War of the Fifth Coalition.

Course of the War of the Fifth Coalition (1809)

Austrian leaders were disappointed by the response in Germany to their declaration of war. Prussia had yet to recover from its defeat in 1806–1807, and most of the major German princes had benefited greatly from Napoleon's rearrangement of territory and had no incentive to join a war against him. Only in the Tirol, where the peasants wanted to return to Habsburg rule, was there widespread support, and it was crushed by February 1810. Russia remained on the sidelines.

On April 9, 1809, Archduke Charles invaded Bavaria with 209,000 men, moving against Regensburg (Ratisbon). Archduke John also commanded some 72,000 men for operations in Italy. Detaching 10,000 to support rebels in the Tirol, he sent another 12,000 into Croatia, then invaded Italy across the Julian Alps with the remaining 50,000.

Prince Eugène de Beauharnais, Napoleon's stepson, commanded the French Army of Italy of 37,000 Italians and 15,000 French. With some 35,000 men, Eugène attacked the Austrians at Sacile (April 16) but was rebuffed in the first defeat of the French by the Austrians since 1800. Eugène withdrew behind the Piave River.

On April 17, Napoleon took command at Donauwörth of what he called the Army of Germany. Numbering 200,000 men, it included 50,000 German troops; half the French soldiers had never experienced combat. Crossing the Danube to strike the center of the extended Austrian forces, Napoleon won a minor victory at Abensberg (April 20), then split the Austrian army in two. Pursuing what he believed to be the main Austrian force south toward Landshut, Napoleon left Marshals Davout and François Lefebvre to deal with the "rear guard" near Eggmühl, actually the main Austrian force under Archduke Charles. Davout's repeated appeals finally brought Napoleon to Eggmühl on April 22, forcing Charles to withdraw across the Danube at Regensburg.

To cover his withdrawal, Charles left a strong force to defend Regensburg. Napoleon ordered Marshal Jean Lannes to storm the walls. This succeeded, but most of Charles's army escaped. Charles reached the vicinity of Vienna with 100,000 men on the north bank of the Danube across the river from Napoleon.

Violating his usual rule to pursue armies rather than to capture cities, Napoleon now moved on Vienna, hoping this would cause the Austrians to sue for peace. He took the city on May 13, but no peace emissaries met him.

With the permanent bridges across the Danube north of Vienna destroyed, Napoleon looked for a way to cross. He seized Lobau Island, five miles downstream from Vienna (May 18), and engineers began building pontoon bridges to span the river there. Unaware how close the main Austrian army was, Napoleon failed to mass his forces on the island before crossing, putting the crossing in jeopardy. Napoleon had only 82,000 men. Charles 100,000 just north of Lobau Island and another 16,000 north of Vienna.

Napoleon was able to cross only 66,000 men before the bridging collapsed under the swollen waters and floating mines and other objects were launched by the Austrians upstream. Unable to reinforce, Napoleon was defeated in the Battle of Essling (May 21–22). The Austrians suffered 23,000 casualties, the French 25,000, including Marshal Lannes killed. It was Napoleon's first personal military defeat.

Archduke John meanwhile had been withdrawing his forces over the Alps from Italy to join Archduke Charles at Vienna. Prince Eugène pursued the Austrians northward, inflicting large losses as they crossed the Piave and Tagliamento. Napoleon reinforced Eugène and ordered him to prevent Archduke John from joining Archduke Charles. On June 14, Eugène caught up with Archduke John and defeated him in the Battle of Rabb. Archduke John was unable to join Archduke Charles in time, while Eugène reinforced Napoleon with his 30,000 men.

Napoleon now had some 198,000 men and 480 guns, Archduke Charles 140,000 men and 450 guns. Napoleon made meticulous preparations, including the erection of additional bridges spanning the Danube, determined to attack before Archduke John could arrive. Expecting Napoleon to again cross at the same point, Archduke Charles positioned some 25,000 men to defend north of the Danube and Lobau Island. Napoleon feinted there but crossed downstream to outflank the defenders. Charles's delaying force, too small to delay the French, was quickly lost.

Napoleon crossed the Danube on the night of July 4–5 and the next day attacked the Austrian eastern (left) wing. The Austrians held. Knowing that the bulk of Napoleon's forces were on the French right flank, Archduke Charles planned a major stroke against the French western (left) flank on July 6. General Klaus von Klenau was to cut Napoleon off from his Danube bridgehead, destroy the bridges, and envelop the French. This attack was initially successful, with Klenau apparently having clear access to the French rear, but indecision ruined the effort. Masséna halted and drove back the Austrians, who were also under flanking fire from French artillery on Lobau Island.

Meanwhile, Davout's attack on the Austrian left made steady progress. At the same time Napoleon massed artillery and troops under General Macdonald on the Austrian center. Following the greatest concentration of artillery fire to that point in history by 112 guns, Macdonald's infantry charged, and the Austrians gave way. The Austrians withdrew in reasonably good order but were nonetheless decisively defeated in what had been a near-run thing for Napoleon.

With some 340,000 men engaged, Wagram was the largest of any Napoleonic battle to that point. In the sense of numbers of men and firepower, Wagram presaged the later battles of the American Civil War and World War I. The cost of victory was nonetheless high. The French sustained 32,000 casualties and the Austrians 40,000, with the difference primarily in prisoners taken by the French.

The Austrians had no choice but to request an armistice and conclude peace. Although the House of Habsburg survived a fourth defeat at the hands of the French without internal revolution, the peace treaty concluded at the Schönbrunn Palace outside of Vienna on October 14,

1809, was nonetheless harsh. Austria was forced to cede Salzburg, Berchtesgaden, the Inviertel, and part of the Hausrückviertel to Bavaria. Napoleon's Grand Duchy of Warsaw gained western Galicia (which had been taken from Poland in the course of the earlier partitions). Russia secured Tarnopol in eastern Galicia. Austria also yielded to France Dalmatia, Slovenia, and Croatia, which Napoleon then organized, along with the Ionian Islands (taken earlier), into a new state known as the Illyrian Provinces. The French inroads in Poland and in the Balkans were nonetheless alarming to Czar Alexander of Russia.

In all, Austria ceded some 32,000 square miles of territory and 3.5 million people. It was also forced to join the Continental System, pay an indemnity of 85 million francs, and reduce its armed forces to no more than 150,000 men. Austria joined Prussia as a second-rate power.

In the Iberian Peninsula in June 1809, Wellesley invaded Spain from Portugal with 45,000 men. In July King Joseph devised a plan that, had it been forcefully executed, might have trapped and destroyed Wellesley. It called for 60,000 men to move south from Salamanca and get in behind Wellesley. But the French troops from Salamanca were slow to arrive, so Joseph, Marshal Claude Victor, and troops from Madrid met Wellesley alone.

The ensuing Battle of Talavera, fought some 70 miles southwest of Madrid on July 27–28, was indecisive. Warned of the approach of the Salamanca force, Wellesley retired, forced to withdraw back to Portugal. Shortly thereafter Wellesley was ennobled as Viscount Wellington of Talavera.

Meanwhile, another British force invaded the Low Countries. Planned to assist Austria, this effort to seize the port of Antwerp should have been abandoned upon news of that Austrian defeat. Rear Admiral Sir Richard John Strachan commanded what was the largest task force to that point in British history: 245 warships, 37 of them ships of the line, escorting nearly 400 transports with nearly 40,000 troops (3,000 of them cavalry) and 206 artillery pieces. Lieutenant General John Pitt, Earl of Chatham, commanded the land force. The British planned to attack up the West Scheldt estuary.

The first troops came ashore on July 19, but the expedition proved to be a dismal failure not from significant fighting but instead from poor army-navy cooperation and heavy casualties from disease in the Scheldt islands. The British withdrew in December. The attack did have one positive for the British war effort, as it led them to concentrate their land efforts in the Iberian Peninsula.

From Milan on November 23 and December 17 Napoleon expanded the Continental System, authorizing the seizure of any ships that had called at British ports and the confiscation of cargoes not certified as originating outside of Britain or its colonies. London responded that the Royal Navy would seize any ship that dared sail directly for a European port controlled by Napoleon. These policies directly affected international trade and were a chief cause of war between Britain and the United States in 1812.

The Continental System was not only a failure but was also a major factor in Napoleon's defeat. It caused him to spread thin his limited resources and also angered Europeans, including the French middle class, who desired trade with Britain and British goods. Exports to Britain were especially important to Russia. Meanwhile, the British did everything they could to pry open the blockade. Some trading continued, sometimes with Napoleon's approval.

In Spain, meanwhile, insurgent Spanish forces suffered their worst defeat of the Peninsular War, routed by Soult's cavalry at Ocaña near Madrid (November 19, 1809). Soult then conquered all Andalusia except Cádiz, site of the Spanish naval base and the capital of the free Spanish government, defended by ships of the Royal Navy. On February 5, 1810, Marshal Victor commenced a siege of Cádiz; it lasted until August 24, 1812. French general Louis Gabriel Suchet meanwhile established French control over Aragon and Valencia. Spanish guerrillas continued operations in remote regions of Spain, however, attacking small French garrisons and supply columns but not seriously challenging French rule.

Napoleon believed that the key to stabilizing the situation in Spain was to drive the British from Portugal. He gave Masséna command of the 60,000-man Army of Portugal and ordered him to clear the British from Iberia. Following a 24-day siege, Masséna captured Ciudad Rodrigo in Salamanca Province (July 10), then invaded Portugal on September 15. Wellington withdrew before him.

With 25,000 British and a like number of Portuguese troops, Wellington established a strong defensive position at Bussaco, near Luso. Masséna attacked Wellington on September 27. Because Wellington had positioned his men on the reverse slope of a long ridge, Masséna was uncertain as to his strength and dispositions. With their artillery fire largely ineffective, the French were driven off.

Wellington then continued his withdrawal into Portugal, occupying the prepared Torres Vedras line before Lisbon on October 10. Testing the allied position and finding it too strong to attack, Masséna remained in place until, his army starving, he had to withdraw. Deprived of food and harried by British hit-and-run tactics, he lost 25,000 men before regaining Spain early in 1811. Virtually all Portugal was now free of French control.

In November 1810, French marshal Bernadotte became crown prince of Sweden with the full support of Napoleon. Bernadotte, now known as Karl Johan, was soon the most powerful man in Sweden, directing both its military and political affairs but to the benefit of Sweden rather than France. This would have profound impact later.

On December 31, 1810, Czar Alexander I announced that Russia was withdrawing from the Continental System. Napoleon's ambiguous plans regarding Poland, his annexation of Oldenburg without consultation with Alexander and compensation, and French troop movements in Europe all alarmed Alexander. But Alexander's chief concern was the Continental System, which had caused great unrest among the Russian nobility by cutting off long-standing and important Russian trade with Britain. The nobles also strongly opposed the Westernizing influences introduced by the French alliance. Alexander was well aware that his father Paul I had been assassinated in a noble conspiracy. Napoleon rejected the repeated appeals from French ambassadors to Russia Armand Augustin Louis de Caulaincourt and Jacques Lauriston for a few minor concessions to preserve the alliance. He now decided on military action, a course that Caulaincourt strongly opposed.

This decision was taken with sizable French forces still fighting in the Iberian Peninsula. Masséna attempted to relieve a British siege of Almeida but was rebuffed by Wellington in the Battle of Fuentes de

Oñoro (May 3–5, 1811). But following a siege of nearly three months, Suchet took the port of Tarragona. Then in the Battle of Albuera (May 16), Soult was prevented from raising the allied siege of Badajoz.

Napoleon now assembled in eastern Germany and Poland a vast force of 611,000 men, 250,000 horses, and 2,000 guns—the largest army under one command to that point in history. The first wave numbered 490,000 men, with 121,000 to follow. More than 130,000 other men remained in the Germanies. The Grand Army of Russia was a truly European force. Only some 200,000 came from the France of 1789 (i.e., born citizens of France); another 100,000 were from the new departments of France. There were also 130,000 Germans from the Confederation of the Rhine, 90,000 Poles and Lithuanians, 30,000 Austrians, 27,000 Italians and Illyrians, 20,000 Prussians, 9,000 Swiss, 5,000 Neapolitans, and units from Spain and Portugal.

Although on a scale unprecedented in his previous campaigns, Napoleon's supply preparations fell short. His army entered Russia with but three weeks of supplies, for he planned to live off the land and win one big battle in western Russia that would bring the czar to his senses and restore the Russian alliance. Napoleon failed to anticipate Alexander withdrawing deep into the vast stretches of Russia or embarking on a scorched-earth policy. Napoleon also did not take into account the likely difficulties of securing adequate supplies for his men and fodder for the horses, nor did he take into account problems of sickness, stragglers, and the indiscipline of the allied contingents. In the end it was matters of supply, rather than Russian winter and the Cossacks, that destroyed him.

Meanwhile, British sea power continued to register successes. British authorities in India mounted an attack on the Dutch in Java, taking Batavia in August 1811. In September the Dutch ceded Java, Palembang, Timor, and Macassar.

In the Iberian Peninsula in early January 1812, Wellington again invaded Spain and laid siege to Ciudad Rodrigo, taking it after a 12-day siege (January 19). For his success, Wellington was elevated to earl. He then moved against Badajoz and, in its third siege of the war (March 17–April 6), took it also. On July 22 in his most brilliant victory to that point, Wellington defeated Marmont, who had replaced Masséna in command of French forces in Spain, in the Battle of Salamanca. The French sustained 13,000 casualties, including 7,000 prisoners; allied casualties were only about 4,800. This crushing victory opened the way for Wellington to Madrid, and King Joseph fled to Ocaña. Wellington entered Madrid (August 12) to general popular enthusiasm, securing some 180 guns and substantial quantities of military stores.

Moving northward, Wellington hoped to destroy the French Army of Portugal, shattered at Salamanca. Its new commander, French marshal Bertrand Clausel, had reconstituted it and on August 13 began a counteroffensive, relieving a number of French garrisons. Wellington then advanced on Burgos but failed to take it in siege operations during September 19–October 10.

The French, having built up their forces to 110,000 men, forced Wellington with 73,000 to withdraw. The British abandoned Madrid on October 31 and retreated to Salamanca and then across the Huebra River, where the French abandoned the pursuit. Wellington then went into winter cantonments near Ciudad Rodrigo, receiving reinforcements from Britain, an enhanced subsidy, and appointment as general in chief of the Spanish Army and allied commander in the peninsula (a position previously denied him by his stubborn and on occasion difficult Spanish allies).

Course of the War of the Sixth Coalition (1812–1814) and the Invasion of Russia

On June 24, 1812, Napoleon crossed the Niemen River into Russia with some 490,000 men. Czar Alexander had about 450,000 men, but only 130,000 of these, under Prince Mikhail Barclay de Tolly, were in position to contest the French advance. Russian forces facing Napoleon would have been even smaller but for an alliance with Sweden, which allowed Alexander to remove 30,000 men from Finland, and the end of war with the Ottoman Empire.

With so few troops initially available, however, the Russians simply withdrew, and Napoleon occupied Vilna (Vilnius) on June 26. Napoleon tarried there for three weeks, turning it into a major base that could be supplied from Königsberg (Kaliningrad) and Danzig on the Baltic by way of the Niemen River.

Marshal Murat led the allied advance with his cavalry. With no sense of the limits of men and horses, his pace condemned to exhaustion those who followed. At the time, the price seemed acceptable to Napoleon in the expectation of catching and destroying the Russians. Napoleon inserted his own forces between the two Russian armies, hoping to destroy each in turn, but Prince Pyotr Ivanovich Bagration was able to join Barclay near Smolensk on the Dnieper.

Napoleon expected the Russians to fight for Vitebsk. They did not. It fell on July 29, but Napoleon stayed there for two weeks. Despite the fact that there had been very little fighting, the Grand Armée had already lost some 100,000 men through hunger, heat, disease, desertion, and straggling. Losses were particularly heavy among the cavalry and draft horses.

At Smolensk for the first time since the invasion, the Russians stood and fought. On August 17 the French stormed that fortified city and, at considerable cost, breached its walls. That night the Russians withdrew in good order across the Dnieper, setting the city on fire as they did so.

Napoleon had planned to winter at Smolensk and organize his conquests, but the ease and speed of his advance led him to decide to proceed to Moscow that autumn, convinced that taking that city would force Czar Alexander I to treat with him. Murat resumed the advance, again with a killing pace that had devastating effects on the rest of the army. Alexander now replaced Barclay with old Field Marshal Mikhail Kutuzov, who had originally urged withdrawal and a scorched-earth policy. Now ordered to stand and fight, he planned a defensive battle behind well-fortified positions at Borodino, the last natural defense before Moscow.

Napoleon, who relied primarily on mobility, would be forced to attack a well-entrenched enemy. Because he had lost so many men on the march, the two armies were approximately equal in size: 130,000 in the Grande Armée and about 120,000 Russians. Kutuzov had 640 guns, Napoleon 587.

Impressed with the strength of the Russian position, the prescient Davout urged Napoleon to turn it by attacking around the southern flank. Fearing that the Russians would simply slip away, Napoleon rejected this sound advice in favor of a frontal assault. Massed artillery fire would destroy the Russian redoubts, which would then be taken by infantry assault.

The Battle of Borodino began early on September 7, but the French artillery fire failed to destroy either the redoubts or their artillery. Successive French ground assaults against the Russian positions on high ground overlooking the battlefield gained ground only slowly and at heavy cost. At last the attackers forced the defenders from their redoubts in the late afternoon, only to see them re-forming.

It was one of Napoleon's principles to throw in his reserves at the decisive moment of battle. Murat and Ney urged him to do so, but here so far from home the emperor refused to commit the Imperial Guard, his personal reserve, and the battle ended without decisive tactical result. The next day Kutuzov withdrew off toward Moscow, enabling Napoleon to claim victory.

Borodino claimed 28,000–31,000 casualties (including 47 generals) in the Grande Armée and upward of 45,000 Russians. Napoleon trumpeted a great victory, but he and his men knew better. Borodino was a hollow victory, for the Russian Army was still largely intact.

Kutuzov withdrew back into Moscow and then to the south, followed by much of the city's population. Napoleon entered Moscow on September 14 with 95,000 men. That night Moscow, largely of wood, was in flames. The conflagration was set by the Russians, who also disabled much of the firefighting equipment. For the next five days the French army was occupied fighting the flames, and they saved the Kremlin.

Napoleon waited for Alexander to come to terms. Kutuzov sent messages that made Napoleon believe that the Russians would treat with him, but Alexander delayed. Fearful of the reaction of Europe should he withdraw without being able to claim victory, Napoleon rejected the advice of those who knew the nature of Russian winter and delayed a decision.

Finally after five weeks of waiting in Moscow, on October 17 Napoleon ordered the withdrawal. It began on October 19. The French made use of every available vehicle, and had it been in normal weather conditions, might have been able to pull it off. Moving southwest from Moscow, for five days there was little opposition. Then on October 24 at Maloyaroslavets, the Russians appeared in force behind the Luzha River.

The ensuing battle was hard fought, with the town changing hands nearly a dozen times before the French secured it. Napoleon then took the fateful decision to turn back to the northwest and follow the same route by which he had advanced to Moscow. While more secure, it had been stripped bare of resources and was thus totally unable to sustain the army. With no forage available, the French army's logistical system collapsed.

The Russians refused to engage the French in pitched battle, instead attacking isolated units. Winter set in early and was unusually severe, for which the French were utterly unprepared. Mud turned to snow and ice, and men and horses slipped, starved, and froze to death. Discipline collapsed. On November 13 some 50,000 Frenchmen—all that were left of the 100,000 who had departed Moscow—straggled into Smolensk. Perhaps a third were capable of combat.

Napoleon found his way blocked at Krasnoi (Kransny) by Kutuzov. In a half dozen actions during November 15–18 collectively known as the Battle of Krasnoi, most of the French managed to cut their way through. At Orsha, Napoleon ordered the remnants of his army to take a more southernly approach to Vilna, even though this meant they would have to cross the Berezina River near Borisov because of the threat of a 30,000-man Russian army commanded by General Ludwig Adolf Peter Wittgenstein. Kutuzov was two days' march to the southeast with 80,000 men; Admiral Pavel Chichagov, with 35,000, was to the west at Borisov. Napoleon then had only about 25,000 men with as many or more stragglers and perhaps only a dozen guns.

As the French approached the Berezina the weather turned, and an early thaw melted the ice and transformed the river into a formidable obstacle. Napoleon was, however, reinforced by troops under Oudinot and Victor, bringing his effective strength to some 48,000 men. Russian forces still vastly outnumbered his own, had far more artillery, and were better provisioned. Probably only Napoleon's presence saved the army, for the Russian commanders were wary of attacking him.

The bridge at Borisov had been destroyed, but fortunately for Napoleon, his chief engineer General Jean Baptiste Eblé had retained crucial forges and tools and needed only protection from Chichagov's troops on the west bank to bridge the river. Napoleon ordered Oudinot to draw off Chichagov by feinting southward against Tshetshakov. This worked, and Eblé's engineers braved the frigid water to construct a bridge.

Napoleon's few cavalry crossed over, followed by infantry to hold the bridgehead. A second bridge was then thrown up, and the few French guns remaining went across it to reinforce the bridgehead. Too late, Chichagov rushed north to attack the 11,000 French troops holding the bridgehead.

By midday on November 27, the French rear guard east of the river was battling Wittgenstein's arriving army. Davout and Prince Eugène crossed with their men, leaving only Victor's corps to hold off Wittgenstein's Russians on the east bank. Victor's men crossed after midnight on November 28. Wittgenstein then closed in, and on the morning of November 29 his artillery opened fire on the bridges. Eblé continued to hold so that as many French stragglers as possible could cross. By 9:00 a.m., however, he withdrew his last defenders and destroyed the bridges. A few hundred men were caught on the bridges and died. Another 10,000 on the east bank fell to the Cossacks.

What remained of the Grande Armée pushed Chichagov aside and continued the withdrawal. The crossing of the Berezina had claimed some 15,000 French and 13,000 Russian casualties, not counting those caught on the east bank, but Napoleon had escaped with 100,000 men—half of them stragglers. The road to Vilna and safety was open. On December 5 at Smorgoniye, Napoleon left the army to return to Paris. Traveling incognito by both sleigh and carriage, he arrived there early on December 19, having covered 1,300 miles in less than 15 days.

Elements of the Grand Armée reached Vilna on December 8, but not until they crossed the Niemen River did they find refuge. Of the some 460,000 men who had entered Russia in June, only as many as 100,000 returned. A like number were prisoners in Russia. The same number perished in battle, while the remainder were lost to disease, starvation, and the elements. Of the 50,000-man Imperial Guard who had entered Russia, fewer than 500 survived. Napoleon has been unable to conquer all Europe. Now it would be seen if all of Europe could conquer Napoleon.

On December 30, Prussian general Hans David Ludwig, Count Yorck von Wartenburg, commanding the Prussian detachment in Napoleon's Grande Armée, on his own initiative signed a truce with the Russians at Tauroggen (present-day Tauragė, Lithuania), agreeing to await orders from the Prussian king but in any case not to fight against Russia for the next two months. Yorck in effect made the decision for the vacillating Frederick William. Although the king officially repudiated the Convention of Tauroggen, it irretrievably compromised Prussian policy, and when Russian troops crossed the Oder River on February 28, he concluded an alliance with Czar Alexander. Russia pledged to continue the war against France until all of Prussia's former territory was restored.

On March 16, 1813, Prussia formally declared war on France. The Prussian Army was vastly improved from that of 1806–1807, thanks largely to the extensive reforms of minister of war General Count Gerhard von Scharnhorst. A wave of anti-French sentiment swept the Germanies, beginning the so-called German War of Liberation.

Course of the German War of Liberation (1813)

Also identified as part of the War of the Sixth Coalition (1813–1814), the War of German Liberation pitted Russia, Britain, and Prussia against France and its allies. Austrian field marshal Prince Charles Philip of Schwarzenberg had also defected from the Grand Armée with his corps and withdrawn into Bohemia. The Austrians rejected suggestions that they join Napoleon and, for the moment, remained neutral. On March 3, 1813, after the United Kingdom agreed to Swedish claims to Norway, Sweden entered an alliance with the United Kingdom and declared war against France and in June entered the coalition.

Napoleon replaced the impetuous Murat as commander in Germany with the steadier Prince Eugène. Although many of Napoleon's top commanders had lost confidence in him, support remained strong in France, where he assembled 200,000 men, almost all untrained. Particularly grievous was the loss in Russia of skilled junior officers and noncommissioned officers as well as trained horses. Equipment and arms were also in short supply. Meanwhile, the allies assembled some 100,000 well-trained veterans, and on March 27 the Russians occupied Dresden.

Napoleon might have minimized his army's shortcomings by standing on the defensive behind the Rhine, but true to form, he took the offensive. In Saxony on April 30 he took command of the new Grand Armée. Altogether, he had some 300,000 men in Germany. All major battles of the German War of Liberation occurred in Saxony.

On May 1 with about 120,000 men, Napoleon crossed the Saale River toward Leipzig. The allies were caught by surprise, but Napoleon was unaware of their exact dispositions. Marshal Kutuzov had died in April, and Alexander had not yet named a successor, but Russian general Wittgenstein commanded some 110,000 allied troops facing Napoleon.

Battle was joined at Lützen near Leipzig on May 2. Wittgenstein and Prussian general Blücher with 73,000 men caught Napoleon with his own army widely separated and only 45,000 men initially available. Napoleon held off the attackers until evening, when he gained the numerical advantage (ultimately 110,000 men) and was able to defeat his enemy, although he lacked the cavalry to follow up the victory.

Each side sustained about 20,000 casualties. An exuberant Napoleon proclaimed, "I am again the master of Europe."

Napoleon captured Dresden during May 7–8 and, with reinforcements from France, then had 250,000 men. Detaching Ney with four corps totaling 85,000 men to march on Berlin, Napoleon pursued the allies with his main force. Learning that they were at Bautzen on the Spree River, Napoleon hurried there and ordered Ney to redirect two of his corps south. Fortunately for Napoleon, Ney misunderstood the orders and marched south with all his men. Late on May 19 Napoleon had 115,000 men at Bautzen. Wittgenstein had 96,000 men in well-prepared defensive positions east of the Spree. Napoleon planned to attack the Russians along the Spree front while Ney took them from the rear.

Battle was joined at noon on May 20. Napoleon concentrated his artillery fire on the center of the allied line and, throwing up bridges, sent men across the Spree under fire. By 6:00 p.m. the French had taken Bautzen and the first allied line. Both sides reorganized.

Battle resumed the next day. By midafternoon, Napoleon had pushed back Blücher about a mile, but the attack stalled. Ney was slow to arrive and failed to cut the allied line of retreat, and the Russians and Prussians were able to escape. Napoleon again lacked cavalry to pursue. Each side sustained about 20,000 casualties.

Although Marshal Davout captured Hamburg and secured the lower Elbe, Napoleon's problems were increasing. Cossacks were raiding the French rear areas, disrupting and destroying supply trains, and a great many French were sick and stragglers. Allied strength was also increasing. Swedish crown prince Karl Johan was moving into northern Germany

with 120,000 men, and the Austrians were mobilizing 240,000 men in northern Bohemia. Thus on June 2 when the allies requested an armistice, Napoleon agreed.

Both sides planned to use the Armistice of Poischwitz, to last from June 4 through July 20, to reinforce. The allies also hoped to convince Austria to join the war on their side. On June 14 Czar Alexander, inspired by Austrian foreign minister Clemens von Metternich, proposed a peace conference at Prague. On June 24 Metternich concluded with Prussia and Russia the Treaty of Reichenbach, pledging to put demands to Napoleon and, if he failed to agree, to bring Austria into the war.

Metternich met with Napoleon at Dresden on June 26. Napoleon foolishly rebuffed Metternich, claiming that Austria would not dare go to war against him. That same evening, the Austrian decision to go to war was sealed by news of a British victory at Vitoria in Spain, virtually ensuring an invasion of southern France from Spain.

Despite the failure of the Napoleon-Metternich meeting, both sides agreed to extend the armistice to August 16, and peace talks opened at Prague. Napoleon sent Caulaincourt as his representative but refused any meaningful concessions. The allies demanded that the Grand Duchy of Warsaw be ceded to Russia, that Austria receive back the Illyrian Provinces, that Prussia be restored to its 1805 territory, and that the Confederation of the Rhine be dissolved. With no agreement, both sides returned to the battlefield.

On August 12, Austria declared war on France. The allies put in the field four major armies totaling 515,000 men, soon to be 600,000. Napoleon could count on only 370,000.

Napoleon's best course was to preserve his strength, concentrate his resources, and await an allied move; instead, his three armies operated independently, and that of Marshal Oudinot sent against Berlin to destroy the Swedish Army was beyond supporting distance. Giving command to Oudinot instead of the more reliable Davout may have cost Napoleon the campaign.

Meanwhile, Napoleon and Ney prepared to operate in Silesia against the Prussians under Blücher and in Bohemia against the Austrians under Field Marshal Prince Charles Philip von Schwarzenberg. At Trachtenberg the allies adopted a plan to avoid battle if Napoleon was present while seeking to isolate and destroy his subordinates. Far superior allied numbers eventually rendered this unnecessary. On August 23, Oudinot was defeated at Grossbeeren by Prussian forces under Friedrich Wilhelm Baron von Bülow.

Napoleon, having left a corps under Marshal Laurent Gouvion Saint-Cyr at Dresden, set out after Prussian and Russian forces under General Blücher, who withdrew. Saint-Cyr soon came under attack by Austrian forces from Bohemia, however, and Napoleon turned back with the Imperial Guard to assist, giving command of his remaining forces to Marshal Macdonald. Blücher then turned, and on the Katzbach River near Liegnitz with 115,000 men, on August 26 he engaged and defeated Macdonald's 102,000-man army. The French suffered 15,000 casualties along with 100 guns lost; Prussian casualties were only about 4,000. Austrian forces under Schwarzenberg, accompanied by Austrian emperor Francis I and Prussian king Frederick William III, shortly joined by Russian czar Alexander I, meanwhile attacked Saint-Cyr, joined by Napoleon, at Dresden.

Both sides built up their resources at Dresden, and by August 27 the allies had 170,000 men and 400 guns, while Napoleon had 120,000 men and 250 guns. Although outnumbered, Napoleon attacked both allied flanks and turned their left. While he failed to achieve the double envelopment that might have brought strategic result, he won a brilliant tactical victory. By the time Schwarzenberg broke off the battle, it had claimed 38,000 allied casualties and 40 guns, for French casualties of some 10,000. On the night of August 27–28 the allies withdrew. Dresden was, however, Napoleon's last victory on German soil.

Napoleon ordered General Dominique Vandamme to cut off the Austrians' retreat and destroy their supply trains. On August 29 Vandamme encountered an Austrian corps under Alexander Ivanovich Ostermann-Tolstoy near Kulm in northern Bohemia and, having superior numbers, engaged it. On August 30, however, a Prussian corps under General Friedrich von Kleist arrived. Outnumbered 32,000 to 54,000, the French fought well but were defeated. The allies suffered 11,000 casualties, but half of the French force were casualties including Vandamme, who was captured.

Having replaced Oudinot with Ney, Napoleon ordered Ney to resume the offensive against the Swedes and Prussians under Swedish crown prince Karl Johan and Prussian general Bülow at Dennewitz in Brandenburg. The allies were victorious, however. Bavaria now switched sides. In the Treaty of Ried of September 8 between that country and Austria, King Maximilian I of Bavaria agreed to fight against Napoleon on condition of a guarantee of his state's independence and territorial integrity. On October 14, Bavaria formally declared war on France.

The allies were now closing in on Napoleon from the north, east, and south.

Fearful that the allies might sever his communications to France, Napoleon left Saint-Cyr to defend Dresden (surrendered on November 11) and on September 14 ordered a withdrawal west of the Elbe. By mid-October Napoleon's main army was being driven toward Leipzig.

Numbers heavily influenced the outcome of the Battle of Leipzig of October 16–19, also known as the Battle of the Nations. Initially Napoleon had 177,000 men in the vicinity, the allies more than 254,000. Two days later, Napoleon had 195,000 men and 734 guns, but the allies had 410,000 men and 1,335 guns. In terms of sheer numbers, Leipzig was probably the largest battle until the 20th century.

The battle opened on October 16, with Napoleon attacking the Austrians under Schwarzenberg south of Leipzig. Although the French infantry were able to advance, Napoleon lacked the cavalry to support them. That same day Blücher attacked Marmont north of Leipzig, forcing the French there to withdraw toward Leipzig.

On October 17 there was only light action. Napoleon made a tentative attempt, without result, to negotiate, and both sides received reinforcements. Napoleon gained 17,000 men, but the allies secured 70,000 Russian troops and 85,000 Swedes.

Napoleon knew that he had to withdraw westward. Pulling his men in tightly around Leipzig, he secured his avenue of retreat. The allies attacked all along the line, but the French managed to hold, despite the defection of the Saxons and some other German troops. That night the French began withdrawing.

On October 19 the allies again attacked, storming Leipzig. The French were withdrawing in good order over the Elster River bridge until the span was prematurely blown, trapping four corps on the Leipzig side. They fought desperately but were driven into the river.

In the Battle of Leipzig the French sustained 38,000 killed or wounded and another 30,000 prisoners. They also lost 325 guns. The allies suffered about 54,000 casualties. As Napoleon withdrew to the Rhine, his German allies defected and threw off the rulers imposed by Napoleon. The liberation of Germany was complete, and the allies were in position to invade France from the northeast, while British forces invaded southwestern France from Spain.

Napoleon returned to Paris on November 9. The day before over British objections, the allies again offered Napoleon generous peace terms. Austria and most of the German rulers feared the expansion of Russian influence into Central Europe and were content solely to end French rule in Germany and Italy. They were willing to see Napoleon remain in power so that France would be a strong counterweight to Russia, which had already taken Poland. Under the peace terms, France was to have its natural boundaries of the Rhine and the Alps.

Napoleon foolishly rejected the offer, claiming it was a trick. Therefore, on December 1 the allies resolved to continue the fight. On December 21, their armies crossed the Rhine at both Mannheim and Coblenz.

Meanwhile, 1813 saw British and allied Spanish forces successful in Spain. Having reorganized his forces, in the spring of 1813 Wellington took the offensive. He now commanded some 172,000 men against 200,000 French and, in a series of maneuvers, forced the French back. On Napoleon's orders, King Joseph again abandoned Madrid (May 17). Napoleon ordered him to concentrate at Valladolid.

Joseph moved too slowly, however, and was outflanked there and forced north of the Ebro River.

With some 60,000 men, Joseph established defensive positions south and west of Vitoria. Outnumbered by Wellington's 80,000 men, Joseph and his chief of staff, Marshal Jean Baptiste Jourdan, compounded the numerical disadvantage by widely dispersing their men. They did, however, have more guns: 150 to 90.

On June 21, Wellington attacked simultaneously in four columns. Exploiting gaps in the allied line, he won a complete victory. The allies sustained 5,000 casualties, the French 8,000, but in a precipitous retreat Joseph abandoned 143 guns, baggage, his treasury, vast amounts of stores, and even his crown. Fortunately for the French, the allies were not prepared for a rapid pursuit.

The Battle of Vitoria was decisive. It marked the end of Napoleonic rule in Spain and enabled Wellington to invade France and, as already noted, had a profound effect on the vacillating Austrians and the war in Germany.

Wellington now moved against the strategically important port of San Sebastián on the French border but was forced to break off siege operations there on news that French forces, now under Marshal Soult, had returned to Spain and were proceeding against Pamplona. In the Battle of Sorauren (July 27) northeast of Pamplona, Soult had a considerable numerical advantage but delayed attacking for a day, giving Wellington time to reinforce and rebuff the French, who withdrew.

Following smaller inconclusive battles, Soult withdrew to France to prepare defenses against the anticipated allied invasion. Wellington then resumed operations against San Sebastián, taking it on August 31 in hard house-to-house fighting. The troops then went on a rampage, destroying most of the city. Fighting also occurred to the east when Soult attempted to relieve San Sebastián but was defeated by a largely Spanish force in the Battle of San Marcial (August 31).

Beginning on October 7, Wellington led 24,000 allied troops across the Bidassoa River into France. By early November he had 82,000 men against only 62,000 French, many of them raw conscripts. Soult could only hope to delay the allies. On November 10 along the lower Nivelle River, Wellington breached Soult's defensive positions.

On December 10 having secretly concentrated his forces, Soult opened the Battle of Nivelle. Although the French achieved surprise and forced the British back, Soult mismanaged the fighting and, lacking resources to exploit the situation, finally withdrew. Deteriorating weather conditions then drove both sides into winter quarters.

Hostilities resumed in February 1814. Wellington advanced beyond Bayonne, leaving 31,000 men to encircle the city and its 17,000-man French garrison while he drove Soult's remaining men northward.

Wellington and Soult clashed again in the hard-fought Battle of Orthez (February 27). The British won, and Soult executed a fighting withdrawal on Toulouse. Wellington then broke off the pursuit to take the important port city of Bordeaux, which surrendered without a fight on March 12.

Meanwhile, the allies invaded France from the east. At the beginning of 1814 Napoleon commanded 118,000 men on French soil west of the Rhine. Utilizing the advantage of interior lines, he sought to get between the allied forces, attack them at their most vulnerable points, and destroy them piecemeal. The numbers were heavily against him, however, and his troops were largely young and untrained. His was a risky strategy indeed, and it was much to Napoleon's military acumen that he was able to accomplish so much with so few resources.

The allies were in three main armies. Swedish crown prince Karl Johan commanded 100,000 men proceeding through the Low Countries. Prussian general Blücher and 110,000 men were moving through the Moselle Valley, and Austrian field marshal the Prince of Schwarzenberg commanded 210,000 Austrian and Russian troops advancing through Switzerland and the Belfort Gap. The allied objective was Paris.

On January 29 at Brienne, Napoleon and 30,000 men surprised and defeated Blücher, caught with only part of his force. Blücher reorganized, with Schwarzenberg reinforcing him to 110,000 men. Napoleon also reinforced to 40,000. Napoleon attacked on February 1 but withdrew on discovering Blücher's far greater strength. Blücher then proceeded down the Marne Valley and Schwarzenberg down the Seine Valley, both toward Paris.

Napoleon then surprised Blücher. In the battles at Champaubert (February 10), Montmirail (February 11), Château-Thierry (February 12), and Vauchamps (February 14) Napoleon inflicted four defeats on the Prussians, who lost about 9,000 men for only 2,000 French. Blücher then withdrew north of the Marne.

Napoleon then turned south against the Austrians and Russians. Leaving 12,000 men on the Marne, he gathered 70,000 and moved against Schwarzenberg. On November 17 Napoleon defeated Wittgenstein at Nangis (February 17), and the next day he defeated the Prince of Württemberg

at Montereau. Shaken, Schwarzenberg withdrew southward.

Having regrouped, Blücher resumed his drive on Paris and by February 27 was only 25 miles from the capital. Leaving Macdonald with 40,000 men to continue the pursuit of allied forces under Schwarzenberg, Napoleon turned north with 30,000 men to confront Blücher. This, however, allowed Schwarzenberg to turn back and defeat Macdonald at Bar-sur-Aube (February 27).

With their field armies in some disarray, the allied leaders met in the Congress of Châtillon during February 5–March 19 and offered Napoleon's representative Caulaincourt the French frontiers of 1792 if the emperor would agree to peace. Buoyed by his recent battlefield successes and against the advice of Caulaincourt, Napoleon refused in perhaps the best example of his irresponsibility as a national leader.

On March 9 at Chaumont the allies concluded a number of treaties, arranged by British foreign secretary Robert Stewart, Viscount Castlereagh, that finally forged the grand alliance the British had so long sought. The four Great Powers (this descriptor now made its way into diplomatic parlance) of Britain, Russia, Austria, and Prussia all pledged to continue the war until their policy objectives were achieved. These were identified as a confederated Germany, an enlarged and independent Holland, an independent Switzerland, a restored Spain under a Bourbon king, and the restoration of the states of Italy.

Castelreagh promised the allied leaders that Britain would expend on the war double the sum provided by any other power. The allies agreed that the alliance would remain in effect for 20 years after the end of the fighting and that they would work to prevent any disruption of the terms agreed to at a forthcoming general peace conference. Chaumont was in effect the cornerstone for the alliance system that would maintain the balance of power in Europe for decades thereafter.

At Laon on March 9–10 Napoleon with only 37,000 men attached Blücher, reinforcing to 85,000 men, and was defeated. Marmont, with 9,000 men, had attempted to join Napoleon but was driven off in a separate engagement. Napoleon ordered him to take up the defense of Paris while he himself withdrew to Soissons.

In a bold but dangerous move, Napoleon marched 40 miles across the front of Blücher's army to defeat an isolated Russian corps at Rheims. Napoleon captured Rheims, losing only 700 men; the Russians suffered 6,000 casualties. His confidence restored, Napoleon moved rapidly south against Schwarzenberg to Arcis-sur-Aube, reportedly held by a small allied force. Unknown to him, however, Schwarzenberg had concentrated his forces between Troyes and Acris for a major offensive. Although the ensuing Battle of Arcis-sur-Aube (March 20–21) opened on near equal terms (20,000 French to 21,000 allies), by the second day of fighting Schwarzenberg had 80,000 men. Napoleon had only 28,000 and was forced to withdraw eastward. More important, Schwarzenberg and Blücher continued their drives west.

Napoleon then developed a new plan to operate against the allied rear areas in hopes of cutting their supply lines and causing them to turn back from Paris. He moved his own forces and those of Marshal Macdonald to establish a line east of Vitry and ordered Marshals Marmont and Edouard Mortier to join him. This, however, placed the latter in the direct path of the vastly larger allied army under Schwarzenberg. Outnumbered five to one,

in the Battle of La Fère-Champenoise on March 25, Marmont and Mortier were driven back in the direction of Meaux and Paris. Napoleon now could no longer prevent the allies from attacking Paris, nor could he reach there before them, although he moved in that direction with what remained of his army.

On March 28, Schwarzenberg united his army with that of Blücher at Meaux near Paris as the court and most of the government quit the city for the south.

On March 30 Marshals Marmont and Mortier, with only about 22,000 men between them, tried to halt the 110,000-man allied assault on Paris from the north. They were driven back to Montmartre, bringing allied artillery within range of the capital. On March 31 the allied troops entered Paris. Having put up a valiant fight for the capital and sustaining 4,000 casualties for allied losses of 8,000, Marmont and Mortier surrendered the city.

Napoleon was then at Fontainebleau south of Paris with 60,000 men. Encouraged by their cheers and their calls for a march on Paris, Napoleon prepared such an operation. In Paris, however, Talleyrand met with allied leaders and persuaded the French Senate to depose Napoleon. Then on April 4, Napoleon's marshals confronted him and told him the fight was over. Napoleon reluctantly yielded and that same day agreed to abdicate in favor of his three-year-old son Napoleon François Joseph Charles, the king of Rome. Such an option was unacceptable to the allied leaders, and on April 11 Napoleon abdicated unconditionally in the Treaty of Fontainebleau. He and his wife, former Austrian archduchess Marie Louise, were allowed to keep the courtesy titles of emperor and empress, and Napoleon was granted full sovereignty of the island of Elba off the west coast of Italy. Marie Louise was to receive the Duchies of Parma, Placentia, and Guastalla. The French government was to pay Napoleon an annual subsidy of 2 million francs. Some fighting continued to southward until April 26, when all of the French forces under Soult opposing Wellington were appraised of events.

On May 26 the allies imposed on France the remarkably lenient First Treaty of Paris. The allied leaders had claimed all along that Napoleon, not France, was the enemy, and the treaty was designed both to preserve a strong France and to get new Bourbon king Louis XVIII (r. 1814–1824) off to a good start. France was reduced to its frontiers of 1792, which included Avignon, Venaissin, parts of Savoy, and some border strongholds in the northeast, none of which had belonged to France in 1789. France agreed to recognize the independence of the Netherlands, the German and Italian states, and Switzerland. There was no indemnity.

Given the complexity of territorial settlements elsewhere, the allied leaders agreed to a general peace conference to meet at Vienna. Britain simply announced that it would return the Netherlands Indies but retain Malta, Helgoland, Trinidad, the Cape of Good Hope, and Ceylon (Sri Lanka), and Britain subsequently secured a protectorate over the Ionian Islands. Britain agreed to return to France its overseas colonies except for Tobago, St. Lucia, and Mauritius.

In September 1814 representatives of virtually all European states—and those of a number of states no longer existing—began gathering at Vienna in what was one of the most important diplomatic assemblies of modern times. Emperors Alexander I of Russia and Francis I of Austria were present, along with the kings of

Prussia, Bavaria, Württemberg, and Denmark, but the real work of the congress was carried on by their first ministers. The key players here were Count Metternich of Austria, Viscount Castlereagh of Britain, Prussian chief minister Prince Karl August von Hardenburg, and Talleyrand of France.

A serious split developed at Vienna between Austria and Britain on the one hand and Prussia and Russia on the other. Russia wanted all Poland in a reconstituted Kingdom of Poland, with Alexander as its ruler. Prussia, supported by Russia, sought all Saxony. Austria and Britain feared the increase in Russian and Prussian influence. The controversy almost brought war and enabled Talleyrand to play a key role, supporting Austria and Britain. Metternich proposed a defensive alliance of Austria, Britain, and France, and this secret treaty was signed on January 3, 1815. This discord encouraged Napoleon to try one final toss of the dice, whereupon the allies quickly composed their differences. Indeed, on news of the secret treaty, Russia and Prussia backed down. Russia received most of Poland, and Prussia received part of Saxony.

Napoleon had been well informed of events at Vienna. Seeking to take advantage of the allied divisions and dissatisfaction in France with the return of the Bourbons, he decided to return to France. (As he put it, "the illness and cure were in accord.") Napoleon believed that he was absolved from terms of the Treaty of Fontainebleau because of the failure of the French government to pay the annual subsidy promised to him. Departing Elba with several hundred followers in a brig, he landed at Fréjus in France on March 1.

Napoleon made his way north to Paris. Marshal Ney, dispatched by Louis XVIII to arrest Napoleon, was unable to hold back his men, who rallied to their former commander, along with Ney. On March 19 Louis XVIII fled to Ghent, and the next day Napoleon entered Paris, beginning the brief period of rule generally referred to as the Hundred Days.

There was, however, no enthusiastic general welcome from among the French population. To secure their assistance, Napoleon ordered a new more representative constitution drawn up, but he knew that his survival rested not on constitutions but on the battlefield. In Vienna, the leaders of Europe resolved to crush Napoleon; on March 13, 1815, they declared him an outlaw. They quickly gathered their armies while Napoleon put together his own makeshift military force.

Austria, Britain, Prussia, and Russia each pledged to field 180,000 men against France. Most other European powers joined but not Sweden, which was then involved in the takeover of Norway. The initial allied forces against Napoleon numbered 400,000 men, with Wellington receiving their command.

Napoleon meanwhile assembled an army of 300,000 regulars, but his field army, the Army of the North, numbered only 125,000. Many of his marshals either fled abroad or refused to join him. Facing formidable odds, Napoleon's only hope was to strike first and defeat the allies singly before they could concentrate against him. He planned to move first against the 110,000-man Anglo-Dutch force under Wellington at Brussels, then turn and deal with the 120,000 Prussians under Blücher at Liège. Napoleon hoped that once he had bested these two, the allies would treat with him.

Napoleon departed Paris on June 11, secretly concentrating his forces near Charleroi in Belgium and hoping to strike before his opponents realized he had left Paris. On June 15 Napoleon seized Charleroi. Blücher reacted by assembling his forces 10 miles north of Charleroi, while Wellington began his own slower concentration 15 miles to the west. The key point was Quatre Bras, a small crossroads town that linked the two allied armies.

On June 16 Napoleon ordered Ney and 24,000 men of the French left wing to take Quatre Bras, while he himself led 71,000 men against 84,000 Prussians under Blücher at Ligny. Napoleon defeated Blücher but expected Ney to fall on the Prussian right flank and complete the French victory. Ney, however, had been slow to move and was held up at Quatre Bras until afternoon by forces under the Prince of Orange, one of Wellington's subordinate commanders. Wellington and British reinforcements then came up, achieved numerical superiority, and threw Ney back. Because of confusing orders from Ney, a French corps of 20,000 men moved back and forth between the two French armies and was unable to aid either. Blücher was thus able to withdraw from Ligny toward Wavre in good order. In the two battles combined, the allies lost about 21,400 men, the French some 16,400.

Belatedly, on the morning of June 17 Napoleon made what turned out to be a fatal error, detaching Marshal Emmanuel de Grouchy and 33,000 men to pursue Blücher and the Prussians. Napoleon and Grouchy assumed that the Prussians would retreat back on their base of Namur. Napoleon then turned with the main body to assist Ney, planning to drive toward Brussels along the Charleroi road.

Wellington meanwhile was withdrawing north and concentrating at the small village of Waterloo, north of Quatre Bras on the Charleroi-Brussels road. Wellington appealed to Blücher to send him at least one corps; Blücher promised to come to his assistance with two corps or more. Wellington later called this "the decision of the century."

Napoleon joined Ney at Quatre Bras and, on the afternoon of June 17, set out after Wellington. Steady rain, quagmires of mud, and the superb hit-and-run tactics of British horse artillery delayed Napoleon's arrival at Waterloo until midnight. Both sides were arrayed along ridgelines about a mile apart. Wellington planned to fight a defensive battle until Blücher and the Prussians could arrive. Wellington made his dispositions carefully, confident in his superb well-trained veterans of the Peninsular War. Still, Wellington knew that an allied victory depended on whether the Prussians could arrive in time.

Napoleon was certain that the Prussians would not come to the aid of Wellington. He therefore overruled his staff and did not recall Grouchy. This meant that Napoleon had just 72,000 troops at Waterloo against 68,000 British and Dutch. Had he recalled Grouchy, Napoleon would have had more than 100,000 men. If Blücher were able to join Wellington, however, the allies would have an overwhelming advantage of nearly 140,000 men.

The heavy rains had made the battlefield soggy. Napoleon had expected to open the battle at 6:00 a.m. on June 18, but on the advice of his artillery commander, who wanted firmer ground for movement of the guns, he delayed the attack. Battle was not joined until near noon, and it was after 1:00 p.m. when the grand battery of 80 French guns opened up. The first French infantry attack did not occur until about 1:45. Had the ground been firmer, Napoleon might well have destroyed Wellington's forces and reached Brussels that evening.

The battlefield at Waterloo measured only about three square miles. Napoleon was confident that massed artillery fire followed by a frontal infantry assault would carry the day. Wellington, however, positioned the bulk of his forces on the reverse slope of the ridge, protected from direct French artillery fire. The French infantry attack was launched against the center of the allied line, but the English hollow squares withstood repeated French infantry attacks. Napoleon's younger brother Jérôme, moreover, disobeyed orders only to occupy the approaches to the château of Hougoumont, wasting an entire division in repeated unsuccessful charges against the building's thick walls. French infantry and cavalry attacks were not coordinated, and Ney, whose courage was unquestioned, led his troops into battle piecemeal.

Despite savage fighting, British and Dutch forces managed to hold long enough to allow Blücher's Prussians to join them and save the day. Grouchy meanwhile was held up by the Prussian rear guard at Wavre and chose to continue his attack there rather than march to the sound of the guns at Waterloo, audible less than 14 miles distant. The retreat of the Imperial Guard—the first time this had occurred—signaled the end of the battle. When word went out of this, the retreat became a rout. Casualties totaled 35,000 for the French (9,000 captured), 15,000 for the British-Dutch forces, and 7,000 for the Prussians.

Napoleon fled the field, his escape purchased with the lives of two regiments of his Old Guard. He first went to Paris, where he found that Joseph Fouché had seized power in the name of the recently deposed Bourbons. On June 22 he abdicated in favor of his son and then went to Rochefort, where on July 15 he surrendered to the British and went aboard a British ship of the line. The British sent him to the small remote island of St. Helena in the windswept South Atlantic.

The Battle of Waterloo is rightly regarded as one of the most important battles in world history, but it is significant only in that it marked the end of Napoleon's rule. What if the battle had gone the other way? Given the general lassitude of the French people and the determination of the allies to defeat him, it seems certain that Napoleon would have been beaten in another subsequent battle of the nations.

Napoleon's Hundred Days were costly for France. In the Second Treaty of Paris of November 20, 1815, France lost additional territory (being restricted to the borders of 1790 rather than 1792 under the First Treaty of Paris) and had to pay an indemnity of 700 million francs, support an allied army of occupation until the indemnity was paid, and return all captured artworks to their countries of origin. Concurrent with the First Treaty of Paris, the major powers agreed to the Quadruple Alliance. Britain, Austria, Prussia, and Russia pledged to maintain for 20 years the arrangements they had made at Vienna and Paris. They also agreed to meet periodically in order to discuss problems of common interest and to maintain the peace of Europe, establishing what became known as the Concert of Europe. The British government, however, served notice that it did not regard this as a license to meddle in the internal affairs of other states and that it would intervene only to maintain the territorial boundaries agreed to.

Significance

In the Final Act of the Congress of Vienna of June 8, 1815, Austria received Lombardy and Venetia, the Illyrian Provinces (former French kingdoms of Illyria and Dalmatia), and Salzburg and the Tirol, both from Bavaria. Austria, however, gave up the Netherlands.

Prussia gained two-fifths of Saxony, Posen and Danzig (Gdansk), and Swedish Pomerania and Rügen (for which Denmark received Lauenburg). Prussia also secured territory in Westphalia as well Neuchâtel. In return, Prussia yielded Ansbach and Baireuth to Bavaria, East Friesland to Hanover, and part of its Polish territory before 1807 to Russia.

To offset any future French threat to the northeast, the Dutch Republic secured the former Austrian Netherlands (Belgium), the new enlarged state being known as the Kingdom of the Netherlands. Metternich hoped this step would enhance the possibility of future cooperation between France and Austria. The Netherlands, however, was sharply divided along religious and linguistic lines.

One of the most difficult problems to resolve was that of the German states. Napoleon had consolidated some 350 of them into a tenth that number. German nationalism, so evident in the German War of Liberation of 1813, was now deliberately set aside in favor of a loose-knit German Confederation of 39 states, including 5 free cities, with Austria as its permanent president. The Act of Confederation was signed on September 8, 1815.

The new Polish state, Congress Poland, encompassed much the same territory as Napoleon's former Grand Duchy of Warsaw. Its king, Czar Alexander, granted Poland a liberal constitution (which Russia did not have), with Polish as the official language and its own army. Kraków (Cracow) became a free state under the protection of Russia, Austria, and Prussia.

Sweden was confirmed in possession of Norway (acquired in the Treaty of Kiel of

January 14, 1814), with Norway receiving a guarantee of its rights and a separate constitution. In the Act of Union of 1815, Norway was confirmed as an independent kingdom, merely united with Sweden under the same ruler. Denmark was compensated by receiving Lauenburg.

Switzerland was reconstituted as an independent confederation of 22 cantons. Spain, Sardinia (which secured Genoa), Tuscany, Modena, and the Papal States were all reconstituted. The duchies of Parma, Modena, Lucca, and Tuscany were given to members of the Habsburg family. The Bourbons were not reestablished in the Kingdom of Naples until 1815 (then the Kingdom of the Two Sicilies). In Italy as in Germany, nationalism was deliberately stymied, with Habsburg predominance reestablished.

Although Napoleon Bonaparte had been defeated, France had been stripped of its conquests, and the European balance of power had seemingly been restored, the French Revolution and Napoleonic eras resulted in the spread of nationalism throughout continental Europe but also in Latin America, where independence movements against Spanish and Portuguese rule flourished and a number of states took advantage of the fighting in the Iberian Peninsula to declare their independence from Spain. Napoleonic imperialism and the example of French nationalism also had a profound impact on other would-be nation-states, such as Belgium and Poland. Napoleon's consolidation of the many small German and Italian states into far fewer but larger entities, coupled with the powerful example of French nationalism, also had a profound impact. For good reason, Napoleon has been called the step-father of modern Italy and Germany. This worked its way out in both revolution and war. Russian influence also now extended 250 miles farther west into Europe.

Of all former European colonial empires, the Napoleonic Wars ended with the British Empire by far the largest and most dynamic. Britain also led in the new Industrial Revolution, held a prime place in world trade, and maintained the world's largest navy. Far from defeating what he called "the nation of shopkeepers," Napoleon had strengthened it.

Further Reading

Bell, David A. *The First Total War: Napoleon's Europe and the Birth of Warfare as We Know It.* Boston: Houghton Mifflin, 2008.

Chandler, David G. *The Campaigns of Napoleon.* New York: Macmillan, 1968.

Chandler, David G., ed. *Napoleon's Marshals.* New York: Macmillan, 1987.

Clowes, William Laird. *The Royal Navy: A History from the Earliest Times to 1900,* Vol. 5, *1900.* Reprint ed. London: Chatham, 1996.

Connelly, Owen. *The Wars of the French Revolution and Napoleon, 1792–1815.* New York: Routledge, 2006.

Crawley, C. W., ed. *The New Cambridge Modern History,* Vol. 9, *War and Peace in an Age of Upheaval, 1793–1830.* Cambridge: Cambridge University Press, 1965.

Doughty, Robert Allan. *Warfare in the Western World,* Vol. 1, *Military Operations from 1600 to 1914.* Boston: Houghton Mifflin, 2007.

Dwyer, Philip. *Citizen Emperor: Napoleon in Power.* New Haven, CT: Yale University Press, 2013.

Elting, John R. *Swords around a Throne: Napoleon's Grande Armée.* New York: Free Press, 1988.

Esdaile, Charles. *The French Wars, 1792–1815.* London: Routledge, 2001.

Forrest, Alan I. *Napoleon's Men: The Soldiers of the Empire Revolution and Empire.* New York: Hambledon Continuum, 2006.

Hall, Christopher D. *British Strategy in the Napoleonic War, 1803–15.* New York: St. Martin's, 1992.

Harvey, Robert. *The War of Wars*. London: Constable and Robinson, 2013.

Haythornthwaite, Philip J. *Napoleon's Military Machine*. London: Hippocrene, 1988.

Lefebvre, Georges. *Napoleon: From 18 Brumaire to Tilsit, 1799–1807*. Translated by Henry Stockhold. New York: Columbia University Press, 1969.

Lefebvre, Georges. *Napoleon: From Tilsit to Waterloo, 1807–1815*. Translated by J. E. Anderson. New York: Columbia University Press, 1969.

Ross, Steven T. *European Diplomatic History, 1789–1815: France against Europe*. New York: Anchor Books, 1969.

Rothenberg, Gunther E. *The Art of Warfare in the Age of Napoleon*. Bloomington: Indiana University Press, 1978.

Rothenberg, Gunther E. *Napoleon's Great Adversaries: The Archduke Charles and the Austrian Army, 1792–1814*. Bloomington: Indiana University Press, 1982.

Greek War of Independence (1821–1832)

Dates	1821–1832
Location	Greece, Macedonia, Crete, Cyprus
Combatants	Greeks, Britain, France, and Russia vs. Ottoman Turks
Principal Commanders	Greece: Lazaros Kondouriottis Russia: Nicholas I, Prince Alexander Ypsilanti Britain: Sir Edward Codrington Ottoman Empire: Mahmud II, Ibrahim Ali, Reshid Pasha
Principal Battles	Dragashani, Tripolitsa, Messolonghi, Athens, Navarino Bay
Outcome	Greece becomes independent in a significant victory for nationalism, with a profound impact for Southern Europe.

Causes

The 11-year-long Greek War of Independence, which lasted from March 21, 1821, to July 21, 1832, was a watershed event in European history. In February 1821, an insurrection in Wallachia in present-day Romania against the Ottoman Empire precipitated a similar revolt against Ottoman rule by the Greeks. Numerous factors were at play here. Although Greece had been part of the Ottoman Empire since the mid-15th century, the Greeks had retained their national identity under loose Ottoman rule. The nationalism born of the French Revolution of 1789 inspired the Greeks, but they had seen their appeal for self-determination rejected by the Great Powers meeting in the Congress of Vienna of 1814–1815.

In 1814, therefore, Greeks in Odessa, Russia, founded the Hetairia Philike (Association of Friends) with the avowed aim of expelling the Ottomans from Europe. These nationalists received aid from Greeks living abroad and from Russia. Czar Alexander I was much interested in the establishment of an independent Greece under Russian protection as a means to secure access to the Mediterranean, and Russia had long used its claim to protect the rights of Greek Orthodox Christians to intervene in the Ottoman Empire. Alexander Ypsilanti (Ypsilantis), a general officer in the Russian Army from a powerful Greek family in Moldavia, headed the Association of Friends. He hoped to establish a Greek empire embracing other Ottoman territories in Europe, including modern Romania.

Course

The Greek War of Independence began on March 21, 1821, when Ypsilanti led an armed force from Ukraine into Moldavia and then appealed to Russia for assistance in a war to free Greece from Ottoman rule. Influential Austrian first minister Klemens von Metternich strongly opposed outside interference. The revolt, he said, should be allowed to "burn itself out beyond the pale of civilization." Czar Alexander was then under Metternich's influence, and the Russians disavowed Ypsilanti.

Ottoman sultan Mahmud II was thus able to crush the uprising easily in the Battle of Dragashani (June 19, 1821) in Wallachia. Ypsilanti fled across the border into Austria, where he was arrested and imprisoned until 1827. (Released at the insistence of Russian czar Nicolas I [r. 1825–1855], Ypsilanti retired to Vienna, where he died in poverty in 1828.)

Inspired by Ypsilanti's rising against the Ottomans, however, Greeks in the Morea (Peloponnese) of southernmost Greece rebelled, besieging the Ottoman garrison at Tripolitsa, then the largest city of southern Greece. The attackers stormed the city on October 5, 1821, however. Over the next several days the Greeks massacred some 10,000 Turks, including women and children. Many were tortured to death. Savage Ottoman reprisals followed, and all Greece then rose against Ottoman rule. On January 13, 1822, Greek independence was proclaimed at Epidauros.

In March 1822, several hundred armed Greeks from the nearby island of Samos landed on the island of Chios (Scio) off western Anatolia and attacked Turks living there. While some of the local Greeks joined, most realized the precariousness of their position and refused to participate.

A powerful Ottoman naval squadron under Captain-Pasha Kara Ali soon arrived at Chios in response to events. The Ottomans then killed outright or starved to death some 42,000 Greeks. Another 50,000 were enslaved, and perhaps 23,000 were exiled. Fewer than 2,000 Greeks on the island survived. The event was subsequently immortalized in a famous painting by French artist Eugène Delacroix.

The plight of the Greeks led to a wave of sympathy for them in Europe. Known as Philhellenism, it was in part based on the democratic and artistic legacy of ancient Greece. Many Europeans, especially in Britain, France, and Germany, took up the Greek cause, the best known of them being British poet George Gordon, sixth Baron Byron, who died of a fever there in 1824. Ultimately, the foreigners included the able British naval officer Lord Thomas Cochrane, who commanded the Greek Navy, and British general Sir George Church. The foreign officers, however, often found their efforts foiled by Greek infighting.

In July 1832 two Ottoman armies invaded and soon overran all Greece north of the Gulf of Corinth. The Ottoman army under Omar Vrioni was halted before the strategically located Greek fort of Messolonghi (Missolonghi) that guarded the entrance to the Gulf of Corinth. Beginning on October 25, 1822, the Ottomans opened siege operations. Both sides then reinforced. A final Ottoman attack on January 6, 1823, was beaten back, and the Ottomans then raised the siege and retired. The Greeks, however, failed to take advantage of the respite and dissipated their energies in leadership struggles as Theodoros Kolokotronis opposed

BATTLE OF NAVARINO BAY, OCTOBER 20, 1827

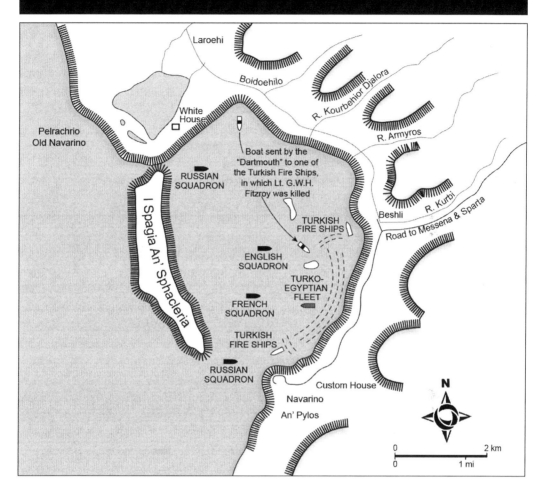

Lazaros Kondouriottis. This flared into civil war in 1824, during which Kolokotronis was defeated.

With the Ottoman military intervention in Greece going badly, however, Sultan Mahmud II appealed for assistance to his powerful vassal, Muhammad Ali of Egypt, who then dispatched a powerful fleet and army to Greece under his son Ibrahim Ali. The Egyptian expeditionary force landed in Greece on February 24, 1825, and soon subdued virtually the entire peninsula. As a result of this intervention, Egypt secured Crete.

In the spring of 1524, an Ottoman army under Reshid Pasha drove from the north and on April 7 opened a second siege of the strategically important Greek stronghold of Messolonghi, which guarded access to the Gulf of Corinth. The defenders held out for an entire year, rejecting Ottoman offers of honorable terms. Prolonged resistance was possible only because the Greeks were able to resupply the fortress from the sea. When the besiegers closed this off, starvation and disease took their toll. A final Ottoman assault occurred on the night of April 22. A few defenders managed to reach the forests of Mount Zygos, but most who did so perished there.

Following his victory at Messolonghi, Reshid Pasha led his army to Athens and laid siege to the Acropolis in May. Accorded the honors of war, the Greek garrison surrendered on June 5.

With the Ottomans controlling virtually all Greece, Greek nationalists appealed to Britain. The British government, worried that Russia might intervene unilaterally and end up dominating Greece, sought to work out a solution acceptable to all the Great Powers.

Czar Nicholas I now took up the Greek cause. The devout Nicholas believed it his duty to answer the call of his orthodox coreligionists in Greece against the Ottomans. He was joined by the British and French governments, which became involved in large part to forestall Russian expansion into the Mediterranean. On April 5, 1826, the Russian government demanded that the Sublime Porte return to the status quo in the Danubian principalities and also dispatch a special envoy to St. Petersburg to discuss relations. Pressed by France and Austria, the Ottomans agreed.

With Ottoman and Egyptian forces now fully in control of Greece, representatives of the French, British, and Russian governments on July 6, 1827, concluded the Treaty of London. It called on the Ottomans to agree to an armistice and on the Egyptians to withdraw. Should the Porte refuse, the three powers pledged to come to the aid of the Greeks with their naval forces. In the meantime, the British made a strong but ultimately unsuccessful diplomatic effort to get Muhammad Ali to remove his forces from Greece.

On August 16 the same three powers sent a note to the Porte demanding an armistice, which the Ottomans rejected on August 29. With that, the British, French, and Russian governments issued orders to their naval commanders in the Mediterranean to sever waterborne Ottoman and Egyptian resupply to Greece. In late August 1827 despite warnings from the European governments not to do so, Egypt dispatched a large naval squadron with troop reinforcements to Navarino Bay (present-day Pylos) on the west coast of the Peloponnese. On September 8 it joined several Ottoman ships already there.

Four days later, a British squadron under Vice Admiral Sir Edward Codrington arrived off the bay. The French and Russian governments also had dispatched squadrons to Greece. Codrington's instructions called on him to try to secure an armistice and to use force only as a last resort. Codrington strongly supported Greek independence and had been freed to use force because the Ottoman government had rejected the allied conditions.

On September 25 Codrington and French admiral Henry Gauthier de Rigny met with Egyptian commander in Greece Ibrahim Pasha to discuss a mediation arrangement already accepted by the Greeks. Ibrahim agreed to an armistice while awaiting instructions from the sultan. Leaving a frigate at Navarino Bay to watch the Egyptian and Ottoman ships there, Codrington then withdrew to the British-controlled Ionian island of Zante (Zakynthos).

Ibrahim learned that while he was expected to observe a cease-fire, Greek naval units under British mercenary commanders were continuing operations in the Gulf of Corinth, at Epirus, and at the port of Patras. Then during September 29–30, a Greek steamer warship, the *Karteria,* sank nine Ottoman ships off Salona (Split) in Dalmatia. Codrington sent messages to warn these British officers, who were not under his command, to desist from such operations; this had little effect, however. Ibrahim duly protested and, when nothing changed, decided to act.

On October 1, Ibrahim ordered ships from Navarino Bay to assist the Ottoman garrison at Patras. Codrington's squadron intercepted them and forced the ships to return to Navarino. On the night of October 3–4 Ibrahim personally led another relief effort. Although they managed to avoid detection by the British picket ship at Navarino Bay in the darkness, a strong lee wind prevented Ibrahim's ships from entering the gulf. Ibrahim was forced to anchor off Papas and await the storm's end. This allowed Codrington time to come up with his squadron. Firing warning shots, he forced Ibrahim to return to Navarino Bay.

Ibrahim continued land operations, which included the wholesale burning of Greek villages and fields, the fires from which were clearly visible from the allied ships. A British landing party also reported that the Greek population of Messenia was close to starvation.

On October 13 Codrington was joined off Navarino Bay by the French squadron under de Rigny and a Russian squadron under Admiral Count L. Heidin (Heyden). Both of these commanders were inferior in rank to Codrington, who also had the most ships, and they agreed to serve under his command.

On October 20, 1827, following futile attempts to contact Ibrahim, Codrington consulted with the other allied commanders and made the decision to enter Navarino Bay with the combined British, French, and Russian squadrons. The allies had 11 ships of the line and 15 other warships. Codrington flew his flag in the ship of the line *Asia* (84 guns). He also had 2 74-gun ships of the line, 4 frigates, and 4 brigs. French admiral de Rigny had 4 74-gun ships of the line, 1 frigate, and 2 schooners. Admiral Count Heidin's Russian squadron consisted of 4 74-gun ships of the line and 4 frigates. The Egyptians and Ottomans had 65 or 66 warships in Navarino Bay: 3 Ottoman ships of the line (2 of 84 guns each and 1 of 76), 4 Egyptian frigates of 64 guns each, 15 Ottoman frigates of 48 guns each, 18 Ottoman and 8 Egyptian corvettes of 14 to 18 guns each, 4 Ottoman and 8 Egyptian brigs of 19 guns each, and 5–6 Egyptian fire brigs. There were also some Ottoman transports and smaller craft.

Around noon on October 20, the allied ships sailed in two lines into Navarino Bay. The British and French formed one line, the Russians the other. The Ottomans demanded that Codrington withdraw, but the British admiral replied that he was there to give orders, not receive them. He threatened that if any shots were fired at the allied ships, he would destroy the Turko-Egyptian fleet.

The Egyptian-Ottoman ships were lying at anchor in a long crescent-shape formation, with their flanks protected by shore batteries. At 2:00 p.m. the allied ships began filing into the bay. They then took up position inside the crescent. The British ships faced the center of the Ottoman-Egyptian line, while the French were on the Ottoman left and the Russians were on the Ottoman right. The shore batteries at Fort Navarino made no effort to contest the allied movement. Still, Codrington's plan appeared highly dangerous, for it invited the Ottomans to surround the allied ships, which with the prevailing wind out of the southwest carried the risk of being trapped. The plan simply revealed the complete confidence of the allies in their tactical superiority.

Codrington dispatched the frigate *Dartmouth* to an Ottoman ship in position to command the entrance of the bay with an order that it move. The captain of the *Dartmouth* sent a dispatch boat to the Ottoman ship, which then opened musket fire on it, killing an officer and several seamen. Firing immediately became general, with shore batteries also opening up on the allied ships.

The ensuing four-hour engagement, essentially a series of individual gun duels by floating batteries at close range without overall plan, was really more of a slaughter than a battle. Three-quarters of the ships in the Ottoman-Egyptian fleet were either destroyed by allied fire or set alight by their own crews to prevent their capture. Only one, the *Sultane,* surrendered. Allied personnel losses were 177 killed and 469 wounded; estimates of the Ottoman and Egyptian killed or wounded are in excess of 4,000 men.

News of the allied victory was received with great popular enthusiasm in virtually all of Europe. The Porte, furious at what had happened, demanded reparations. Recalled to Britain, Codrington was subsequently acquitted on a charge of disobeying orders.

The Battle of Navarino Bay removed any impediment to the Russian Black Sea Fleet, and in April 1828 Russia declared war on the Ottoman Empire. The battle also led directly to Egypt's withdrawal from the war and to Greek independence. Navarino Bay is also noteworthy as the last major battle by ships of the line in the age of fighting sail.

On August 9, 1828, the British and French governments concluded a convention with Muhammad Ali in which the Egyptian leader agreed to withdraw his forces from Greece. The French dispatched an expeditionary force, and under its supervision the Egyptians evacuated during the winter of 1828–1829. This action virtually ended the war.

In the London Protocol of May 22, 1829, the ambassadors of the Great Powers decided that Greece south of a line from the Gulf of Volo to the Gulf of Arta, with Negroponte (Euboea) and the Cyclades (without Crete), was to be an autonomous tributary kingdom of the Ottoman Empire, with a ruling prince not to be chosen from the royal families of Britain, France, or Russia. In March 1832, the Great Powers agreed on Prince Otto of Bavaria as the ruler of Greece. They also extended the frontiers of Greece to a line between Volo and Arta.

Significance

The Greek War of Independence led to the establishment of a fully independent Greek state, but many problems confronted it, including the destruction of more than a decade of war. Its population of only some 800,000 was less than a third of the 2.5 million Greeks living in the Ottoman Empire, and for a century thereafter the Greek government sought to gather in "unredeemed" Greeks into a larger Greek territorial entity.

The successful Greek revolt was the first great triumph for nationalism in Europe following the French Revolutionary and Napoleonic periods. The revolt not only had profound influence in the Ottoman Empire, where other subject peoples such as Armenians, Bulgars, Romanians, and Serbs all yearned for freedom, but also resonated in Poland and elsewhere in Europe.

Further Reading

Anderson, R. C. *Naval Wars in the Levant, 1559–1853.* Liverpool: University Press of Liverpool, 1952.

Brewer, David. *The Greek War of Independence: The Struggle for Freedom from Otto-*

man Oppression and the Birth of the Modern Greek Nation. Woodstock, NY: Overlook, 2001.

Bridge, F. R., and Roger Bullen. The Great Powers and the European State System, 1814–1914. London: Longman, 1980.

Clogg, Richard. A Concise History of Greece. 2nd ed. Cambridge: Cambridge University Press, 2002.

Crawley, C. W. The Question of Greek Independence: A Study of British Policy in the Near East, 1821–1833. New York: H. Fertig, 1972.

Dakin, Douglas. The Greek Struggle for Independence, 1821–1833. Berkeley: University of California Press, 1973.

Howarth, David Amine. The Greek Adventure: Lord Byron and Other Eccentrics in the War of Independence. New York: Atheneum, 1976.

Jelavich, Barbara. History of the Balkans: Eighteenth and Nineteenth Centuries. New York: Cambridge University Press, 1983.

Koliopoulos, John S. Brigands with a Cause: Brigandage and Irredentism in Modern Greece, 1821–1912. Oxford, UK: Clarendon, 1987.

Ortzen, Len. Guns at Sea: The World's Great Naval Battles. London: Cox and Wyman, 1976.

Phillips, W. Alison. The Greek War of Independence, 1821–1832. New York: Scribner, 1897.

Sayyid-Marsot, Afaf Lutfi. Egypt in the Reign of Muhammad Ali. Cambridge: Cambridge University Press, 1984.

Stavrianos, Leften Stavros. The Balkans since 1453. New York: Rinehart, 1953.

St. Clair, William. That Greece Might Still Be Free: The Philhellenes in the War of Independence. New York: Oxford University Press, 1972.

Woodhouse, C. W. The Greek War of Independence: Its Historical Setting. London: Hutchinson's University Library, 1952.

Opium Wars (1839–1842, 1856–1860)

Dates	1839–1842, 1856–1860
Location	China
Combatants	China vs. Britain and France
Principal Commanders	China: Emperor Daoguang, Lin Zexu, Yeh Ming-ch'en Britain: Sir James John Gordon Bremer, Charles Elliot, Sir Michael Seymour, Sir James Hope France: Charles Guillaume Marie Apollinaire Antoine Cousin-Montauban
Principal Battles	Boque Forts, Ningpo, Shanghai, Canton, Baihe (Taku or Peiko) Forts, Peking
Outcome	A major blow to the Qing dynasty, the wars open China to exploitation by Britain and France in concessions and outright loss of territory, forced acceptance of the opium trade, and indemnities.

Causes of the First Opium War (1839–1842)

The two Opium Wars (1839–1842 and 1856–1860) resulted from trade disagreements between Chinese Qing dynasty officials and British merchants trading in Canton (present-day Guangzhou), the only port allowed to foreign merchants by the Qing dynasty. The British imported from China vast quantities of tea as well as silk goods and fine porcelain. The British, however, had little that the Chinese wanted in return except silver, which the British were forced to acquire elsewhere at considerable expense.

In an effort to offset the adverse trade balance with China and the outflow of silver, the British embarked on the widespread smuggling of opium into China. The opium was produced in India under special government monopoly on condition that it be sold in China. The trade was illegal under Chinese law and carried out in defiance of efforts by Qing officials to end it. This and the foreigners' defiance of Chinese law brought war.

Lin Zexu headed the Qing government's attempt to end the opium trade. He eventually forced British chief superintendent of trade in China Charles Elliot to hand over to Chinese authorities some 20,000 chests of opium, each containing about 120 pounds of the drug. In July 1839, rioting British sailors destroyed a Chinese temple near Kowloon and killed a man who tried to stop them. British authorities rejected a Qing demand to hand the sailors over for trial. The British themselves subsequently tried six of the men in Canton but immediately released them on their return to Britain.

Meanwhile in an effort to end the opium trade, Qing authorities insisted that all merchants sign a bond agreeing to obey Chinese law and place themselves under its jurisdiction. They also had to promise, on pain of death, not to smuggle opium. Elliot then ordered the British community to withdraw from Canton and prohibited trade with the Chinese, but some merchants who did not deal in opium were willing to sign the bond and remain.

With war between Britain and the Chinese central government now looming, on August 23, 1839, the British seized the trading outpost of Hong Kong as a base for military operations.

Course of the First Opium War (1839–1842)

Fighting in the First Opium War (also known as the First Anglo-Chinese War) began on November 3, 1839, and on January 14 Qing emperor Daoguang called on all foreigners in China to end assistance to the British in China. Seeking to force the Qing government to terms, the British government and the British East India Company agreed to mount an expedition against Canton. The expeditionary force departed Singapore under Captain Sir James John Gordon Bremer in June 1840. It consisted of 1 British ship of the line and 5 smaller warships, 2 Indian steam warships, and 26 transports and storeships lifting about 3,600 troops. Other British warships subsequently joined.

On arrival, Bremer first attacked and seized Chusan Island, then blockaded the Ningpo (Ningbo) and Canton (Pearl) Rivers. British emissary Captain Charles Elliot then demanded compensation for losses suffered by the British from interrupted trade. The Qing government refused, and on February 26, 1841, the British attacked and seized the Bogue Forts defending the entrance to the Pearl River, the waterway between Hong Kong and Canton. Then on May 24 a successful amphibious assault brought the British capture of Canton.

A lull in the fighting ensued. During August–December 1841, however, the British carried out a number of amphibious operations along the China coast. They captured Amoy (Xiamen) on August 26 and Ningpo on October 13.

Recommencing major military operations in the spring of 1842, British forces

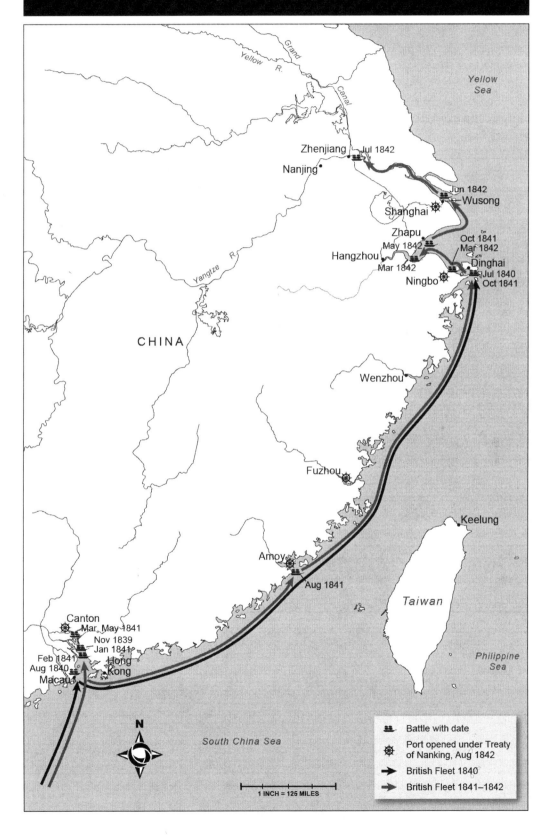

captured Shanghai on June 19, then moved up the Yangzi (Changjiang) River to take Chenkiang (Zhenjiang) on July 21. With this success threatening Nanking (Nanjing), the Qing government sued for peace.

Under the unequal Treaty of Nanking of August 29, 1842, that ended the war, the Qing government ceded Hong Kong Island to the British; agreed to fixed tariffs on British goods; opened the ports of Guangzhou (Canton), Xiamen, Fuzhou, Shanghai, and Ningbo to British merchants; and agreed to pay a heavy indemnity of $20 million for seized British opium and war costs. In the separate Treaty of the Bogue (October 1843), the Qing government extended to Britain most favored nation status and agreed that British subjects were to enjoy extraterritorial privileges in the treaty ports. In 1844, the Qing government concluded similar treaties with France and the United States.

The First Opium War was a heavy blow to the Qing dynasty. The ease with which the British and their modern weapons had defeated the far more numerous Chinese forces sharply undermined the government's authority and contributed substantially to the great Taiping Rebellion (1850–1864).

Causes of the Second Opium War (1856–1860)

On October 8, 1856, Chinese officials seized the Chinese-owned *lorcha* the *Arrow* and arrested its crew on smuggling charges. The *Arrow* was registered in Hong Kong and flew the British flag. Thus, this Chinese action brought an immediate British demand for the return of the ship and its crew.

On October 14, Yeh Ming-ch'en (Ye Mingchen), the Chinese imperial governor of Kwangtung (Guangdong) and Kwangsi (Guangxi) Provinces at Canton and also the imperial commissioner in charge of barbarian (non-Chinese) affairs, released a few members of the crew but also asserted that the British lacked jurisdiction. Indeed, the *Arrow*'s right to fly the British flag was questionable because its Hong Kong registry had expired.

British officials consulted with Rear Admiral Sir Michael Seymour, commanding the British squadron in Chinese waters, who wanted to employ force.

Course of the Second Opium War (1856–1860)

The British decided on an ultimatum with a 24-hour deadline. Despite last-minute concessions by Yeh, on October 23, 1856, Seymour's men stormed ashore and captured the barrier forts, Canton's main defenses located on both sides of the Pearl River some 12 miles from the city proper. This action began the Second Opium War (also known as the *Arrow* War). The British spiked the forts' guns and burned their interior buildings. Seymour then proceeded to Canton.

On October 27, British ships opened fire on the city, battering its walls and opening a breach through which British seamen entered to sack Commissioner Yeh's residence. Lacking sufficient resources to remain, the British then withdrew. Yeh then ordered all foreigners to leave Canton.

French forces joined the British against the Qing, using the excuse of the murder of French missionary Auguste Chapdelaine. On May 20, 1858, British and French forces operating under the command of Seymour attacked the Baihe (Taku or Peiko) Forts on the Baihe (Hai) River about 36 miles from Tientsin (Tianjin). Some 1,200 men went ashore to spike the guns and destroy Chinese shore installations.

Beginning on May 29, 1858, the Chinese government negotiated with the British, French, U.S., and Russian governments. On June 25, the two sides reached agreement in the Treaty of Tientsin. It involved the opening of treaty ports; the establishment of Western embassies in Peking (Beijing), then closed to foreigners; and other concessions. The Qing government then refused to ratify the treaty, however, and the war continued. The Russians were also active, and in May the local governor of Aigun signed the Treaty of Aigun, which assigned all the land north of the Amur to Russia and declared the land east of the Ussuri River and south of the Amur (northern Primorye) to be a Russo-Chinese condominium until its status could be resolved by additional negotiations.

Fighting resumed in 1859 after the Qing government refused to permit the establishment of a British embassy in Peking as promised in the 1858 Treaty of Tientsin. On June 25, 1859, British and French naval forces, now commanded by Rear Admiral Sir James Hope, again attacked the Chinese Beihe Forts near Tientsin. These works, destroyed in 1858, had been rebuilt by the Chinese.

The Chinese put up an effective defense and forced the landing parties to retire. U.S. Navy Asiatic Squadron commander Commodore Josiah Tattnall declared that "blood is thicker than water" and provided covering fire to the withdrawing allied force. In the fighting the British lost three gunboats as well as 89 men killed and 345 wounded. French losses were 4 killed and 10 wounded. Chinese casualties are unknown.

The British and French governments committed additional resources to the fighting. In May 1860 they assembled at Hong Kong 11,000 British troops under Lieutenant General Sir James Hope Grant and 7,000 French troops under Lieutenant General Charles Guillaume Marie Apollinaire Antoine Cousin-Montauban. These forces then moved north and landed at Pei Tang (Beitang) on August 1. On August 21, they assaulted and successfully captured the Tagu or Peiho forts. They then marched on Peking, pushing aside en route a Qing army of some 30,000 men. The allied troops arrived at the imperial capital on September 26, assaulting and capturing the city by October 6. Following considerable looting, the troops then set fire to the Summer Palace and the Old Summer Palace. General Grant ordered the burning in reprisal for the ill-treatment of British diplomat Sir Harry Smith Parkes and his party when they had attempted to negotiate an end to the fighting and had been seized and tortured in September.

With the capture of Peking, the Qin dynasty sued for peace. In the Treaty of Beijing of October 18, 1860, China ratified the earlier Treaty of Tianjin (1858). The Treaty of Beijing also legalized the import of opium. Britain, France, Russia, and the United States received the right to legations in Peking, then a closed city. The Chinese also agreed to open 10 additional ports for foreign trade, including Niuzhuang, Danshui, Hankou, and Nanjing. Foreign ships received the right to free navigation on the Yangtze River, and foreigners were allowed to move freely inside China for travel, trade, and missionary activities. Western citizens residing in China, including those of the United States, were also granted extraterritorial protections from Qing civil and criminal law. The Qing government was forced to pay an indemnity of 3 million ounces of silver to Britain and 2 million to France. The Qing government also had to surrender to the

British the territory of Kowloon on the Chinese mainland opposite Hong Kong and also grant special rights to the French.

Significance

The Opium Wars in effect fully opened China to economic exploitation by the Great Powers. The Russians also took advantage of Qing weakness to seize the left bank of the Amur River and the Maritime Provinces. The Russo-Chinese Convention of Peking of November 14, 1860, saw the Chinese forced to agree to the cession to Russia of all land north of the Amur River and east of the Ussuri River. During 1860–1861 the Russians established there the port of Vladivostok (meaning "Ruler of the East").

Further Reading

Chang, Hsin-Pao. *Commissioner Lin and the Opium War.* Cambridge, MA: Harvard University Press, 1964.

Fairbank, John King. *Trade and Diplomacy on the China Coast: The Opening of the Treaty Ports, 1842–1854.* Cambridge, MA: Harvard University Press, 1953.

Fay, Peter Ward. *The Opium War, 1840–1842: Barbarians in the Celestial Empire in the Early Part of the Nineteenth Century and the Way by Which They Forced the Gates Ajar.* Chapel Hill: University of North Carolina Press, 1975.

Greenberg, Michael. *British Trade and the Opening of China, 1800–42.* Cambridge: Cambridge University Press, 1951.

Lin, Manhong. *China Upside Down: Currency, Society, and Ideologies, 1808–1856.* Cambridge, MA: Harvard University Asia Center, 2006.

Lovell, Julia. *The Opium War: Drug, Dreams and the Making of China.* London: Picador, 2011.

Polachek, James M. *The Inner Opium War.* Cambridge, MA: Council on East Asian Studies, Harvard University, 1992.

Waley, Arthur. *The Opium War through Chinese Eyes.* London: Allen and Unwin, 1958.

Mexican-American War (1846–1848)

Dates	April 25, 1846–February 2, 1848
Location	Mexico
Combatants	United States vs. Mexico
Principal Commanders	United States: James K. Polk, John C. Frémont, Robert Field Stockton, Stephen Watts Kearny, Zachary Taylor, Winfield Scott Mexico: Mariano Arista, Pedro de Ampudia, Antonio López de Santa Anna
Principal Battles	Palo Alto, Monterrey, Buena Vista, Veracruz, Cerro Gordo, Contreras and Churubusco, Molino del Rey, Chapultepec
Outcome	The United States annexes considerable Mexican territory, but the dispute over whether it will be slave or free helps bring on the American Civil War.

Causes

The war between the United States and Mexico during April 25, 1846–February 2, 1848, is known by a number of different names, including the Mexican-American War, the Invasion of Mexico, the U.S. Intervention, and the United States War against Mexico. The basic cause of the war was the determination of U.S. leaders, specifically President James K. Polk, to acquire the Mexican frontier provinces of Texas, California, and New Mexico (which then included Arizona).

Americans began to settle in Texas in the 1820s. It was never part of Louisiana, and President James Monroe had agreed that the Sabine and Red Rivers formed the southwestern boundary of the United States. Yet subsequent presidents pressed the Mexican government to sell Texas to the United States, causing considerable resentment in Mexico.

Paradoxically, Mexico, which had secured its independence from Spain in 1821, encouraged U.S. citizens to settle in Texas, as Mexican citizens were reluctant to move there because of frequent raids by Comanche Indians. In 1820 the Mexican government granted Moses Austin of Missouri a large tract of land in Texas, hoping thereby to form a barrier against the Comanches. Moses Austin soon died, but his son Stephen F. Austin brought 300 families there. The new settlers did not, however, take up residence where the Mexican government had intended. A steady stream of immigrants followed, and by 1834 some 20,000 Anglos in Texas outnumbered the native Mexicans there four to one.

Many factors estranged Texas from Mexico. Mexico had formally abolished slavery, yet it existed in Texas. All settlers were supposed to be Roman Catholic, yet few were. There were also differences concerning Mexican Army garrisons, political representation, the tariff, and Mexico's efforts to impose property taxes and close Texas to further immigration (which continued illegally).

In 1834 Mexican general Antonio López de Santa Anna became dictator of Mexico. Abandoning the federal system,

he proclaimed a unitary constitution and soon moved against semi-independent Texas. Fighting began, and Texas declared its independence in 1836. Santa Anna led 3,000 troops into Texas and defeated the 200 Texan defenders of the Alamo fortress in San Antonio (February 23–March 6). But Texas generalissimo Sam Houston held the army together and caught the Mexicans by surprise, defeating them in a 10-minute battle at San Jacinto (April 21, 1836). Captured after the battle, Santa Anna was forced to sign a treaty recognizing Texas independence.

Texas secured recognition as an independent republic from Britain, France, and the United States. Although Texas now had an Anglo population of only about 50,000 people and Mexico had some 6–7 million, the Mexican government made no effort to reconquer Texas. Most Texans wanted to join the United States, but they also insisted on maintaining slavery. This was a barrier and imposed delay on annexation in the U.S. Congress, with the Whig Party largely opposed. On December 29, 1845, however, Texas joined the United States by joint resolution of Congress, which did not require a two-thirds vote and was of dubious legality. Mexico broke diplomatic relations with the United States in protest but also made no overt move to try to regain Texas.

On March 4, 1845, James K. Polk became U.S. president. He had campaigned largely on manifest destiny: the notion that America had the right to expand west to the Pacific and south to at least the Rio Grande. What Polk really wanted was California, known to be rich in natural resources and with only a small Mexican population. Polk was in part prompted by real concerns that if the United States did not acquire California, Britain or France

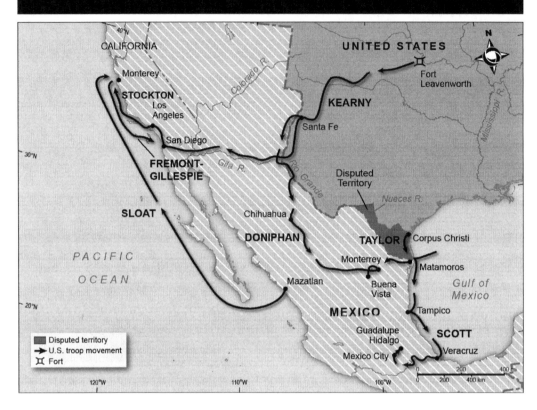

MEXICAN WAR CAMPAIGNS, 1846 – 1848

might seek to do so. Polk first tried to purchase California from Mexico, and when that failed he goaded Mexico into a war with the United States, the primary goal of which was to secure California.

In July 1845, Polk ordered Brigadier General Zachary Taylor and an "Army of Observation" of some 3,500 men (about half of the regular U.S. Army) to take up position along the Nueces River, the southwestern border of Texas, supposedly to protect Texas from Mexican attack. Meanwhile, Polk sought to encourage revolt in California, sending Corps of Topographical Engineers captain John C. Frémont and 55 men on an exploring expedition to "map the source of the Arkansas River" but with the real and secret goal of stirring revolt against Mexico in sparsely populated Alta (Upper) California.

At the same time, Polk made another effort to buy California from Mexico. In 1843 Mexico had agreed to pay the United States for claims by American citizens regarding property damaged and destroyed in civil unrest but made only several installments before financial exigencies forced their suspension. Mexico did not, however, repudiate the indebtedness. In November 1845 Polk sent John Slidell as his diplomatic agent to inform the Mexicans that the U.S. government would assume the unpaid claims in return for Mexican recognition of the Rio Grande boundary for Texas. Polk also authorized Slidell to offer Mexico between $25 million and $30 million for the cession of New Mexico and Alta California. As a matter of national honor, Mexican leaders refused to receive Slidell. Indeed, rumors that the government was about to do so brought yet another Mexican revolution.

On January 15, 1846, the day after Polk learned of the Mexican government's refusal to receive Slidell, he ordered General Taylor to cross the Nueces River and advance to the Rio Grande. Although the Mexican government had not given up and indeed had reiterated its claims to Texas, it had made no military threats against it, and Polk's action was in effect an act of war. The Nueces had been the recognized southern boundary of Texas for a century. (Texas had claimed the Rio Grande as its southern boundary as a result of the 1836 Treaty of Velasco, but this treaty had never been ratified by the Mexican government.)

On March 23, Taylor's men occupied the left bank of the Rio Grande and established Fort Texas (later known as Fort Brown and today Brownsville) opposite the Mexican town of Matamoras. The Mexican commander there ordered him back to the Nueces, but Taylor refused. On April 25 Polk began preparing a message to Congress urging a declaration of war on the basis of the Mexican government's refusal to receive Slidell and the unpaid claims.

On May 9, however, dispatches from Taylor provided Polk a better excuse for war. On April 25 a 2,000-man Mexican cavalry unit had crossed the Rio Grande and skirmished with a troop of 70 U.S. dragoons, killing 16 of them. Polk promptly sent Congress a war message, with documents enumerating the "wrongs and injuries" suffered by the United States from Mexico. Polk's war message concluded that "the cup of forbearance has been exhausted" and stated that Mexican forces had "invaded our territory and shed American blood upon the American soil." On May 13, 1846, Congress declared war. The vote was 40 to 2 in the Senate and 174 to 14 in the House of Representatives.

Course

Support for the war among Americans varied according to region. In the southern and western regions sentiment was strongly in favor of the war, while the war was unpopular among the eastern states. Those opposing slavery, particularly in the Northeast, viewed the war as a southern conspiracy to secure more slave territory. Although the war enjoyed support in the South, some elder statesmen there expressed concern—correctly, as it turned out—that the acquisition of additional territory would upset the sectional balance and revive the issue of slavery in the territories.

In 1846 the United States had a population of 17 million people, Mexico only 7 million. The regular Mexican Army was, however, a large European-style force numbering 32,000 men, while the regular U.S. Army numbered only 8,000. Mexico had virtually no navy, however; the U.S. Navy of 70 warships soon established control of the seas, which proved of great advantage logistically to army operations.

Americans expected a quick victory. Congress authorized an increase in the size of the regular army to 15,000 men and eventually to 32,000, but the war was to be fought mainly with volunteers, of which Congress initially authorized 50,000. A total of 104,000 American troops served: 60,000 volunteers, 32,000 regulars, and 12,000 militiamen. More than half of the men served only 12 months or less. The constant turnover proved to be a major problem in conducting campaigns, and

Polk made a number of poor appointments of generals.

Mexicans were confident, and there was talk of their forces invading the American South and freeing the slaves. The unsettled Oregon boundary question that threatened war between the United States and Britain also suggested that Mexico might gain a powerful ally, but to forestall this possibility Polk negotiated the Oregon Treaty with Britain (signed on June 15, 1846). The treaty divided that territory.

There were three major theaters of war: California, northern Mexico (the Rio Grande), and central Mexico. A fourth theater of Baja (Lower) California and the Pacific coast was largely conducted by U.S. naval forces. California saw a number of relatively small engagements. Frémont, who had entered California in December 1845, rushed about and ultimately supported a small number of American settlers in the Sacramento Valley who carried out what became known as the Bear Flag Revolt. On June 14, 1846, they took possession of Sonoma. Commodore John D. Sloat of the Pacific Squadron secured the capital of Monterey on July 7 and declared California annexed to the United States. San Francisco (then known as Yerba Buena) was taken on July 9. On July 15 Commodore Robert Field Stockton took command from Sloat, who promoted Frémont to major but also placed his "California Battalion" of about 160 men under his own orders. Stockton quickly took control of such key locations along the California coast as Santa Barbara, San Pedro, and Los Angeles.

While northern California was relatively quiet, Mexican forces did recapture parts of southern California. Brigadier General Stephen Watts Kearny moved with a number of his men to California from Santa Fe, New Mexico, which Kearny had taken upon marching from Fort Leavenworth, Kansas. Learning that Stockton had secured California, Kearny sent the majority of this force back to Santa Fe, an action that would have negative consequences.

In the meantime, native Mexican Californians in southern California had succeeded in recapturing parts of the region. When Kearny arrived, he had to fight his way into southern California. On December 5, 1846, his forces encountered a large Mexican force at San Pascual. The battle there was inconclusive, but it forced Kearny to wait for reinforcements, the first of which arrived on December 11 in the form of sailors and marines dispatched by Stockton.

After Stockton and Kearny joined forces, they defeated the Mexicans in the Battle of San Gabriel (January 8, 1847) and the Battle of La Mesa the next day. On January 10 U.S. forces moved into Los Angeles, and on January 13 Frémont signed the Treaty of Cahuenga, or the capitulation of Cahuenga, formally ending hostilities in California.

In the Rio Grande theater of war, Mexican forces opened a siege of Fort Texas (May 3–9, 1846), but only two Americans were killed in the subsequent Mexican artillery bombardment, one of whom was fort commander Major Jacob Brown. General Taylor, moving to raise the siege with 2,300 men, was intercepted by Mexican general Mariano Arista with 2,700 men. The ensuing Battle of Palo Alto (May 8) saw few casualties on both sides and was decided largely by highly effective American flying artillery (horse artillery). Another American victory the next day at Reseca de la Palma saw hand-to-hand combat and more casualties (122 Americans and 515 Mexicans). Although

Taylor relieved now-renamed Fort Brown, he refused to advance until he received reinforcements and supplies. (Polk had assumed that Taylor's men could simply live off the land.) After these had arrived, Taylor moved but failed to take heavy siege guns with him. He first occupied Matamoros and then Camargo before moving toward Monterrey, where he arrived in late September.

The ensuing Battle of Monterrey of September 21–24 pitted 6,200 Americans against 7,300 Mexicans under General Pedro de Ampudia. Taylor planned to circle around the city and cut the Mexican supply lines. This went well, but Taylor's dispatch of infantry into the city was mishandled, and the fighting there saw heavy losses on both sides and the American attack on a key fortress repulsed. Subsequent American attacks made better progress, whereupon Ampudia requested an armistice, which Taylor accepted. It was to last for eight weeks and allowed the Mexican forces to evacuate Monterrey. The battle itself claimed 531 American casualties and 367 Mexicans.

Taylor's decision greatly angered Polk, who now saw the general, who had embarked on a public relations campaign apart from official channels, as a possible political rival. Polk now reluctantly turned to Major General Winfield Scott, who proved to be an extraordinarily good choice. Never really popular like Taylor, who incurred heavier casualties, Scott was a great strategist, tactician, and logistician who planned campaigns carefully and secured his military objectives with little loss of life. In the meantime, General Santa Anna, who had been in exile at Havana, returned to Mexico City in September 1846 and assumed the presidency, taking direction of the Mexican war effort.

Scott stripped Taylor of the bulk of his best troops, with most who remained being untrained volunteers. The Mexicans had captured one of Scott's couriers. With knowledge of the American strategic plan, Santa Anna saw a chance to destroy Taylor and then Scott in detail. Taking 20,000 largely untrained men, Santa Anna marched up from Mexico City against Taylor. Forewarned of Santa Anna's approach, Taylor selected an excellent defensive position on high ground to help offset the effect of Santa Anna's 6,000 cavalry. Additional U.S. forces under Brigadier General John E. Wool arrived in time, while many of Santa Anna's men failed to complete the grueling march from Mexico City.

The Battle of Buena Vista (February 22–23, 1847) thus saw some 4,700 Americans against 15,000 Mexicans. Although greatly outnumbered, Taylor won the battle, the key being U.S. mobility and the rapid fire of U.S. light artillery. Casualties were 660 Americans and some 1,500 Mexicans (killed or wounded); another 1,500 Mexicans were missing in action. The Battle of Buena Vista ended the fighting in northern Mexico. Santa Anna now withdrew southward to raise more troops and march to oppose Scott's march on Mexico City.

Scott's plan to win the war was made possible by the U.S. Navy control of the Gulf of Mexico. The plan called for a landing at Veracruz and a march 260 miles overland to Mexico City. Utilizing 65 surfboats carried in transports, on March 9, 1847, the American expeditionary force began coming ashore three miles south of Veracruz. Within 24 hours Commodore David Conner's ships had put ashore Scott's entire army of 12,000 men with artillery, horses, vehicles, and supplies in what was the first large amphibious operation in American military history. Siege guns manned by sailors came ashore to bombard Veracruz, which surrendered on March 27. At the same time, Mexico City was undergoing another revolution. Mexican internal discord greatly assisted the Americans throughout the war.

Scott conducted a brilliant campaign with a field force of only some 10,000 men (only about half what he had requested), hampered by jealous subordinates—including a number of political appointees—and often short of supplies. Scott completed the march to Mexico City in six months, without military reverse. His insistence on amicable relations with the Mexicans, with his men paying for horses and food, greatly assisted in securing his march route.

Santa Anna's effort to keep the Americans within the yellow fever belt failed, with Scott constantly turning strong Mexican positions by outflanking them. In the Battle of Cerro Gordo (April 17–18), Corps of Engineers captain Robert E. Lee found a path to outflank 12,000 entrenched Mexicans, forcing Santa Anna to withdraw. The army then pushed on to Puebla, Mexico's second-largest city, where it remained for three months, building up its strength as volunteer forces replaced those whose terms of enlistment had expired. Scott now had 11,000 men against 30,000 Mexican troops defending Mexico City. With his supply lines now under constant attack by Mexican guerrilla forces, Scott left only a weakened force to defend Puebla and, in a daring maneuver, cut himself off from his base and advanced on Mexico City by living off the land.

On August 10 U.S. troops reached the continental divide and then on the Mexico City outskirts engaged and defeated the Mexicans at Contreras and Churubusco. At Contreras during August 19–20, 10,700

Americans engaged 11,000 Mexicans and sustained only 60 casualties for some 1,800 on the Mexican side (nearly half of them prisoners). Churubusco was much more sanguinary for the Americans; here on August 20, 8,500 Americans sustained some 1,000 killed or wounded against a Mexican force of only 3,800, which, however, occupied a strongly fortified position. Mexican losses were 721 killed or wounded and 1,821 captured. The Americans lost 177 killed or missing and 879 wounded. Most of the American casualties were inflicted by the artillery of the San Patricio battalion, made up of Irish and other deserters from the U.S. Army. About 80 of these were taken in battle, and 51 were subsequently hanged.

Scott then granted Santa Anna an armistice, instructing Department of State chief clerk Nicholas Trist, who had been attached to Scott's command and was fluent in Spanish, to open negotiations with the Mexican side. Mexican officials so objected to the American terms that Santa Anna decided to try another military test of strength. On September 8 in the Battle of Molino del Rey, the U.S. Army encountered 8,000 entrenched Mexicans. U.S. casualties totaled 788, while the Mexican side lost around 2,000 killed or wounded and 700 captured.

Scott had 7,180 men for the final assault on the Mexican capital against an estimated 15,000 Mexicans. Swinging around the principal Mexican defenses, he attacked Mexico City from the southwest, and on September 13 U.S. forces stormed the fortified hill of Chapultepec, heroically defended by 100 boy cadets of the Mexican military school. Mexico City surrendered on September 17.

In late September, Santa Anna endeavored to cut Scott off from the coast by sending General Joaquín Rea against Puebla. Santa Anna then joined him, but Puebla held. Santa Anna moved to attack the American relief column from Veracruz under Brigadier General Joseph Lane but was defeated by Lane in the Battle of Huamantla (October 9). Lane then relieved Puebla (October 12). A new Mexican government ordered Santa Anna to give up command of the army, while Scott carried out a largely antiguerrilla pacification campaign.

Months passed before any Mexican government was willing to negotiate, however. Polk chose to blame Scott and Trist and actually ordered the latter home and Scott to resume military operations. Trist and Scott, then in serious negotiations, ignored Polk's orders.

Utilizing his considerable diplomatic skills and liberal bribes, Trist negotiated the Treaty of Guadalupe Hidalgo of February 2, 1848. In it, Mexico ceded Texas with the Rio Grande boundary, New Mexico (including Arizona, Colorado, Utah, and Nevada), and Upper California to the United States. The U.S. government assumed the $3.25 million in unpaid claims owed to its citizens and paid Mexico $15 million—half the amount Slidell had been authorized to offer for the same territory in 1846. After the Senate approved the treaty, Polk did his best to humiliate Scott, who had won the war, and Trist, who had won the peace. Polk replaced Scott and dismissed Trist from the Department of State.

Significance

At minimal cost of 1,733 killed in battle or dead of wounds and 11,550 deaths from other causes, chiefly disease, the United States largely completed its continental area except for Alaska. (The Gadsden Purchase, completed in 1854, added from Mexico 29,640 square miles in present-day southern Arizona and southwestern New Mexico.) However, the matter of whether this new territory would be slave or free led to an intensified national debate over slavery that brought about the American Civil War of 1861–1865.

Further Reading

Bauer, K. Jack. *The Mexican War: 1846–1848.* Lincoln: University of Nebraska Press, 1992.

Bauer, K. Jack. *Surfboats and Horse Marines: U.S. Naval Operations in the Mexican War, 1846–48.* Annapolis, MD: United States Naval Institute, 1969.

Bauer K. Jack. *Zachary Taylor: Soldier, Planter, Statesman of the Old Southwest.* Baton Rouge: Louisiana State University Press, 1985.

Clary, David A. *Eagles and Empire: The United States, Mexico, and the Struggle for a Continent.* New York: Bantam Books, 2009.

Eisenhower, John. *So Far from God: The U.S. War with Mexico.* New York: Random House, 1989.

Fowler, Will. *Santa Anna of Mexico.* Lincoln: University of Nebraska Press, 2007.

Greenberg, Amy S. *A Wicked War: Polk, Clay, Lincoln, and the 1846 U.S. Invasion of Mexico.* New York: Knopf, 2012.

Henderson, Timothy J. *A Glorious Defeat: Mexico and Its War with the United States.* New York: Hill and Wang, 2007.

Johnson, Timothy D. *A Gallant Little Army: The Mexico City Campaign.* Lawrence: University Press of Kansas, 2007.

Johnson, Timothy D. *Winfield Scott: The Quest for Military Glory.* Lawrence: University Press of Kansas, 1998.

Meed, Douglas. *The Mexican War, 1846–1848.* New York: Routledge, 2003.

Merry, Robert W. *A Country of Vast Designs: James K. Polk, the Mexican War and the Conquest of the American Continent.* New York: Simon and Schuster, 2009.

Pinheiro, John C. *Manifest Ambition: James K. Polk and Civil-Military Relations during the Mexican War.* Westport, CT: Praeger Security International, 2007.

Pletcher, David M. *The Diplomacy of Annexation: Texas, Oregon, and the Mexican War.* Columbia: University of Missouri Press, 1973.

Price, Glenn W. *Origins of the War with Mexico: The Polk-Stockton Intrigue.* Austin: University of Texas Press, 1967.

Singletary, Otis A. *The Mexican War.* Chicago: University of Chicago Press, 1960.

Smith, Justin Harvey. *The War with Mexico.* 2 vols. New York: Macmillan, 1919.

Winders, Richard Price. *Mr. Polk's Army: The American Military Experience in the Mexican War.* College Station: Texas A&M Press, 1997.

Wars of Italian Unification (1848–1870)

Dates	1848–1870
Location	Italy and Sicily
Combatants	Sardinia (Piedmont-Sardinia) and France vs. Austria; Italy vs. Austria
Principal Commanders	Sardinia/Italy: King Charles Albert; King Victor Emmanuel II; Camillo Benso, Count of Cavour; Giuseppe Garibaldi; Enrico Cialdini; Count Carlo Pellion di Persano France: Napoleon III, Nicolas Oudinot, Patrice de MacMahon Naples: Francis II, Ferdinando Lanza Austria: Franz Joseph I, Count Joseph Radetzky, Count Franz Gyulai, Archduke Albrecht, Wilhelm von Tegetthoff
Principal Battles	Custoza (first), Novara, Venice, Magenta, Solferino, Calatafimi, Custoza (second), Lissa
Outcome	The states of the Italian peninsula and Sicily are unified as the Kingdom of Italy, and statesmen have to take into account a new major European state.

Causes

When the wars of the French Revolution and the Napoleonic era commenced in 1792, Italy was little more than a geographical expression—a patchwork of 15 small states, each in rivalry with, if not openly hostile to, the others. Not since the days of the Roman Empire had the Italian peninsula been united politically.

The wars of the period 1792–1815 had profound impact on Italy. Napoleon Bonaparte had conquered much of the peninsula and introduced a uniform system of laws and administration. He had also reduced the number of states to three. Part of northwestern and east-central Italy was incorporated into France, with the Kingdom of Italy in the northeast and the Kingdom of Naples in southern Italy. Napoleon, the great practitioner of French nationalism, had also declared at St. Helena that "Italy is one nation."

The example of what the French had accomplished with a more effectively administered nationalist state was not lost on the Italians. The Congress of Vienna of 1814–1815 had, however, resurrected the old Italy of many different monarchial states dominated in the north by Austria. Small nationalist uprisings in the immediate aftermath of the Napoleonic Wars by the so-called Carbonari had been easily crushed. Nonetheless, a new spirit of what came to be called the Risorgimento (Resurgence) swept the peninsula.

Three men played key roles in the unification of Italy to follow. They were Giuseppe Mazzini (1805–1872), Count Camillo Benso di Cavour (1810–1861), and Giuseppe Garibaldi (1807–1882). Mazzini devoted his life to the cause of Italian independence and unity, which he believed should be entrusted to the young. In 1832 Mazzini organized among Italian exiles in Marseille, France, the first lodge of Young Italy. First established in Italy at Genoa, this organization soon spread throughout northern and central Italy and then the entire peninsula. The banner of the organization had the words "Unity and Independence" on one side and "Liberty, Equality, Humanity" on the other. Members agreed to promote the national ideal, regardless of personal cost.

Mazzini believed strongly that all states should be organized on the basis of nationality and that, in keeping with the dignity of the individual, the only acceptable form of government was a republic. Not all Italian nationalists favored this, however. A number wanted to see Italy united under a limited monarchy; they looked to the Kingdom of Sardinia (most often known at the time and since as Piedmont-Sardinia or Sardinia-Piedmont for its two component territories). Other Italian nationalists favored a federation of states under the presidency of the pope.

Mazzini's plan for revolution in northern Italy was discovered by the authorities in 1833 before it could be carried out. Many of Mazzini's followers were arrested, and a dozen were executed. Mazzini himself was tried in absentia and sentenced to death. Despite this setback, he tried again the

next year. The revolt was in Piedmont, and among its participants was Italian sailor Giuseppe Garibaldi, who had recently joined the movement at Genoa. Piedmontese authorities easily crushed the revolt during January 31–February 1, 1834.

In 1846 Giovanni Maria Mastai-Ferretti became pope as Pius IX. The Papal States of central Italy were notorious in their poor government, and Pius IX was soon hailed as a reformer. He released numerous political prisoners, permitted freedom of the press, allowed Rome to have its own city government, and carried out a number of other reforms that endeared him to liberals. Also regarded as an Italian nationalist, Pius IX arranged a customs treaty with Piedmont and Tuscany that could have been the start of political unification for all Italy, and he adopted a hostile stance toward Austria. Pius began to backtrack, however, when he realized the full implications of the reform movement, which were at sharp variance with papal sovereignty.

In Vienna there was great concern over the evolutionary agitation in Italy. Old Field Marshal Joseph Radetsky von Radetz, viceroy of Lombardy-Venetia, then part of the Austrian Empire, favored a strong stance, and in July 1847 following revolutionary agitation and disorders there, Austrian troops occupied Ferrara, one of the papal legations in which Austria had garrisoning rights. This action, however, greatly inflamed Italian nationalism.

Revolutionary agitation in Italy nonetheless continued. In late 1847, Grand Duke Leopold of Tuscany and King Charles Albert of Piedmont-Sardinia were both forced to grant constitutions. In January 1848 the people of Palermo, Sicily, rioted against their reactionary ruler, King Ferdinand II; he too was forced to grant a constitution. Then on March 18 revolt broke out in Milan, capital of Lombardy. In the so-called Five Days of Milan, Radetsky was forced to withdraw Austrian troops from the city. They retreated to the stronghold at the foot of the Alps, known as the Quadrilateral, comprising the cities of Mantua, Verona, Peschiera, and Legnago.

Course

With the unrest and seeming success of revolutionaries in various parts of Italy, on March 22, 1848, King Charles Albert of Piedmont-Sardinia declared war on Austria in what he expected to be a war of national liberation by Italians, boasting that "Italia fera da se" ("Italy will do it by itself"). Thousands of volunteers from other parts of Italy, including troops from the Papal States, joined the 60,000-man Sardinian Army. On March 26, 1848, fortified by what had happened in Milan, revolutionaries seized control of the arsenal in Venice and organized both a civic guard and a provisional government. Austrian forces evacuated Venice on March 26, and it was declared a republic under the leadership of revolutionary Daniele Manin. In mid-June, however, Radetzky assumed the offensive and soon reestablished Austrian control in Lombardy and in most of Venetia, except Venice.

Charles Albert's troops, however, proved to be poorly trained and equipped and ineffectively led. Sharp divisions also developed among the allied Italian contingents, and under heavy Austrian pressure, Pope Pius IX withdrew papal forces and announced his neutrality in a war with another Catholic power. Radetzky's men were not only better trained but also enjoyed the advantage of numbers (33,000 to 22,000).

The two sides joined battle at Custoza near Verona during June 24–25. The fighting was fierce and casualties were heavy on both sides, but the Austrians triumphed. King Charles Albert now appealed to France for assistance, but the new republican government in Paris was dealing with the massive worker uprising in Paris known as the June Days and was in no position to intervene.

Radetsky drove Charles Albert's troops from Lombardy, and on August 9 Sardinian Army chief of staff General Carlo Canera di Salasco concluded a six-month armistice, expecting to resume the struggle at its end. On their part, the Austrians needed to concentrate on crushing the revolution that had swept Hungary.

In November 1848, papal prime minister Pellegrino Rossi, a liberal whose reforms were nonetheless insufficient for many, was assassinated in Rome. A revolt occurred, and Pius IX fled to Gaeta. On February 9, 1849, a constituent assembly declared Rome a republic. The effects of this were great especially in northern Italy, where Charles Albert, under considerable pressure from radicals in Piedmont, renounced the Armistice of Salasco and again took up arms against Austria.

Assembling an army of 75,000 men and 141 guns, Radetzky invaded Piedmont and defeated Charles Albert's army of 87,500 men and 109 guns in the Battle of Novara during March 22–23, 1849. The Sardinian side suffered some 2,000 casualties, the Austrians a bit more. Charles Albert was forced to sign a second armistice and abdicate the throne in favor of his son, Victor Emmanuel II. Sardinia did, however, retain its liberal constitution of 1848.

In northern Italy, only the city of Venice held out against the Austrians. His victory also allowed Radetzky to send part of his forces north to assist in the fight against the Hungarians. Peace with

THE UNIFICATION OF ITALY, 1848 – 1870

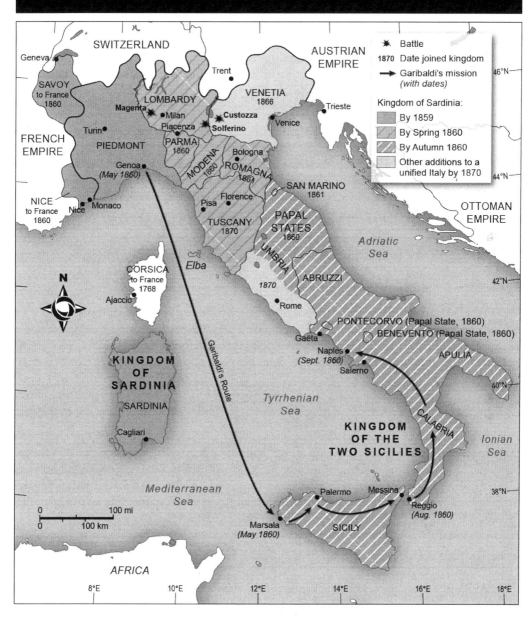

Piedmont-Sardinia was formally concluded on August 9, with the latter forced to pay an indemnity of 65 million francs. Although Charles Albert's efforts had failed completely, Italian patriots now looked to the Kingdom of Sardinia for leadership in the unification struggle.

The news of the defeat of Italian forces at Novara led revolutionaries in Rome at the end of March to reorganize their government along more moderate, conciliatory lines. Mazzini was the best-known figure in the new government. Despite this, the new leaders of Austria (Emperor Franz

Joseph I) and France (President Louis Napoleon Bonaparte) each considered sending troops to restore Pius IX to power. With the Austrian Army still heavily engaged against the Hungarians, Bonaparte moved first. In April 1849 the French Assembly voted funds for a military expedition, supposedly to forestall Austrian intervention but in reality prompted by Bonaparte's hopes of winning the political support of French Catholics.

On April 24, French marshal Nicolas Oudinot and some 8,000 men landed at Città Vecchia, Italy, and then moved against Rome. Believing that the republicans enjoyed only limited support, Oudinot ordered an assault. The defenders, commanded by Garibaldi, repulsed the French attacks of April 29–30. The republicans also deflected attacks by the Neapolitan Army at Palestrina (May 9) and at Velletri (May 19).

French government emissary Ferdinand de Lesseps (later the builder of the Suez Canal) reached an understanding with the republican government that would have allowed French troops into the city in return for French acceptance of the new republic and a guarantee to protect Rome against other foreign intervention. Bonaparte, however, disavowed it and then reinforced Oudinot and ordered him to take Rome by force.

On June 3, French troops again assaulted and, in desperate fighting, were again repulsed. Oudinot was then forced to commence siege operations. At the request of Pius IX, Spain also sent some 9,000 troops. Realizing that the situation was hopeless, on June 30 Garibaldi came to terms with Oudinot. Garibaldi and some 4,000 volunteers were allowed to march out of the city on July 2. They hoped to join the defenders of the Republic of Venice but were soon

pursued by French, Austrian, Spanish, and Italian loyalist forces, and most were captured, killed, or dispersed. Garibaldi was among those escaping; he ended up in exile in the United States.

Although republican Venice had come under blockade by the Austrians months earlier, on May 26, 1849, the defenders were forced to abandon Fort Marghera. Food was soon scarce. On June 19 the powder magazine blew up, and the next month cholera broke out. The Austrians then began to shell the city, and when the Piedmont-Sardinian fleet withdrew from the Adriatic, the Austrians were also able to attack by sea.

On August 24, 1849, with food and ammunition exhausted, Manin negotiated the city's capitulation, securing amnesty for all except himself and a few others who were nonetheless allowed to go into exile. Manin departed Venice three days later in a French ship; he died in exile in France.

The lessons of 1848–1849 were clear. First, the unification of Italy would not be achieved around the papacy, for when Pius IX returned to Rome it was as a confirmed reactionary. Second, Italy could not "do it by itself." Outside assistance, most likely that of France, would be necessary in throwing off the Austrian yoke. Third, Italian nationalists now regarded Piedmont-Sardinia, which had demonstrated its steadfastness by twice going to war against Austria, as the natural leader in the unification struggle.

Piedmont-Sardinia was now widely regarded as a progressive state. As minister of commerce and agriculture during 1850–1852, Camillo Benso, Count of Cavour (generally known as Cavour), had done much to transform the state economically, and in 1852 he was rewarded with appointment as prime minister. Displaying extraordinary political and diplomatic skills, Cavour became the real power in the state and directed the unification struggle until his death in 1861.

Cavour embarked on a series of political, social, and economic reforms to make the kingdom a model of parliamentary monarchy and an exemplar for the rest of Italy. In January 1855 he took his country into the Crimean War (1854–1856) to gain the support of Britain and France, and he used the Congress of Paris at the end of that conflict to present the problems of Italy.

In 1856, leading Italian nationalists formed the National Society to support the unification of Italy under the Kingdom of Sardinia. Then on January 14, 1858, Italian nationalist Felice Orsini, angered by the failure of Napoleon III (a participant in his youth in the Italian revolutionary movement) to support the present unification movement, attempted to assassinate the now emperor of France. This seems to have prompted Napoleon to act, for on July 20, 1858, he met with Cavour at Plombières in southeastern France and there concluded a secret agreement.

The Pact of Plombières called for the two powers to goad Austria into war against Piedmont-Sardinia, at which point France would come to its assistance with 200,000 men. The two would then fight until Italy was "free from sea to sea" and they had established a kingdom of northern Italy consisting of Piedmont-Sardinia, Lombardy, Venetia, Parma, Modena, and the Papal Legations of Ravenna, Ferrara, and Bologna. Napoleon wanted a federation of Italian states under French influence to include the new kingdom of northern Italy as well as a kingdom of central Italy (Tuscany with Umbria and the Marches), Rome and its surrounding territory, and the Kingdom of Naples. All

these would be under the presidency of the pope. In return for its aid against Austria, Piedmont-Sardinia would then cede Nice and Savoy to France.

To cement the pact, Princess Clotilde, daughter of King Victor Emmanuel II, was betrothed to Prince Joseph Charles Bonaparte, cousin of Napoleon III. (They were married in January 1859.) The formal treaty was signed on December 10, 1858, after Napoleon assured himself of the goodwill of Russian czar Alexander II.

In January 1859 Napoleon III publicly complained about the plight of Italy and unsatisfactory relations with Austria, while articles in the official French press attacked Austrian rule there. Many ardent French Catholics also expressed alarm over the direction of events and possible threats to the papacy. Finding his Italian policy opposed by his wife Eugénie and a majority of his cabinet ministers, Napoleon wavered.

On March 9 Cavour mobilized the Sardinian Army, calling up reserves and also recruiting volunteers, many of whom were from Lombardy, in a direct provocation to Austria. On April 9 Emperor Franz Joseph I authorized mobilization of the Austrian Army. Then with Napoleon backtracking, on April 20 the Austrian government made a fatal error in sending an ultimatum to Piedmont-Sardinia, giving it three days to demobilize. Cavour, believing the opportunity for war lost, had on April 19 already ordered demobilization, but with no direct telegraph link between Turin (Turnio) and Vienna, Austrian leaders were unaware of this. The Austrian ultimatum appeared to be an act of diplomatic bullying and provided Cavour with the excuse he needed for war. Piedmont-Sardinia rejected the ultimatum, and on April 29 Habsburg forces invaded Piedmont.

On May 3, 1859, France declared war on Austria. The ensuing conflict is known as the Franco-Austrian War, the Second War of Italian Independence, and the Austro-Sardinian War. For three weeks inept Austrian commander Field Marshal Count Franz Gyulai marched and countermarched, failing to take advantage of his superior numbers and allowing French troops to come up. Napoleon III arrived at Genoa by sea on May 12 to take personal command.

In the first real engagement of the war, Gyulai, perhaps under prodding from Vienna, ordered General Count Stadion to mount a reconnaissance in force with his corps toward Voghera in Lombardy on May 20. This Habsburg force of some 27,000 men encountered near Montebello a French infantry division and some Piedmontese cavalry, totaling perhaps 8,000 men. French division commander General Elias Forey audaciously attacked. Only a portion of the Habsburg force took part, and after two hours of fighting the French drove the Austrians from Montebello.

Stadion, having sustained 1,300 casualties, withdrew all the way to Stradella. Allied casualties totaled 730. Assuming that the rest of Gyulai's force would resume the attack the next day, Forey also withdrew. Although not a major battle, Montebello brought great prestige to the French and was a major morale boost for the allies and a corresponding depressant for the Austrians.

With all the French troops and their equipment having arrived, the allies now took the offensive, planning to advance on Novara and then to Milan. Part of the Piedmontese army advanced to Robbio, where on the morning of May 30 it crossed the Sesia River and, following hard fighting, captured Palestro, Confienza, and Vinzaglio. The next day, Habsburg general Fredrick Zobel counterattacked at Palestro with some 14,000 man and 42 guns against the Piedmontese under King Victor Emmanuel II. The previous night, the king had called up reinforcements in the form of a French Zouave regiment so that the allies had 21,000 men and 36 guns.

In the Battle of Palestro the allies repulsed the Austrians, suffering some 600 casualties against Austrian losses of 1,600. The allies, however, had 50,000 men within several hours' march and had failed to use these superior resources; nor did they pursue the retreating Austrians.

On June 4, the two sides clashed at Magenta in one of the two major engagements of the war. This battle pitted 54,000 French troops against 58,000 Austrians. Napoleon III planned a pincer movement against the Austrians by maneuvering General Marie Edme Patrice Maurice de MacMahon's II Corps on the left bank of the Ticino while the Imperial Guard and III and IV Corps crossed the stream farther south. The French did not expect the Austrians to react prior to the closing of the pincers.

The Austrians, however, had already decided to retreat to the northeast. They were even slower in their withdrawal than MacMahon was in his advance, and the two sides clashed on the morning of June 4. MacMahon's corps managed to break through and win the battle, mainly because of the élan of the French infantry, the highly effective fire of French rifled artillery, and the inept performance of Habsburg commander Gyulai. The Austrians, however, withdrew in good order, unmolested, to Robecco. French casualties totaled 4,515, while the Austrians lost 10,406 (including 4,500 prisoners). On June 8, Napoleon III and Victor Emmanuel II made a triumphal entry into Milan.

Napoleon III then ordered Marshal Achille Baraguay d'Hilliers, supported on his right by General Adolphe Niel's IV Corps and on his left by MacMahon's II Corps, to attack Austrian forces 18 miles southeast of Milan at Melegnano. Battle was joined in the early evening of June 8.

Poor tactics denied the French the opportunity to trap the isolated Austrians. Failing to wait for MacMahon's corps to arrive, Baraguay d'Hilliers immediately launched an infantry attack without adequate artillery support. Habsburg general Ritter Ludwig August von Benedek's VIII Corps was heavily entrenched and barricaded in the small medieval town. Their rifle fire exacted a heavy toll on the attackers. The French II Corps did not arrive in time for the battle, which ended at nightfall with the Austrians withdrawing in good order. The French sustained 948 casualties, the Austrians 1,480. The French then returned to Milan.

Austrian emperor Franz Joseph I dismissed Gyulai. Assuming personal command himself, he moved against the French and Piedmont-Sardinian forces. Thanks to poor reconnaissance, the ensuing battle and culmination of the war came as a surprise to both sides. As with other battles of the war, the Battle of Solferino of June 24 saw little recognition on the part of the generals of the tremendous defensive firepower of the rifled musket behind field entrenchments. It was also marked by poor coordination of forces; men were committed to battle en masse as they arrived, charging in large frontal assaults with the bayonet.

The forces involved were quite large; indeed, Solferino was the biggest battle in Europe since Leipzig in 1813. The French and Piedmontese had some 138,000 men and 366 guns, while the Austrians committed 129,000 men and 429 guns. The allies enjoyed superiority in numbers and in cavalry. The Austrians had the advantage of fighting from defensive positions and greater numbers of artillery. The battle was concentrated along the Mincio River, centered on the town of Solferino. MacMahon commanded the French forces. Napoleon III, King Victor Emmanuel II, and Franz Joseph I were all present.

Fighting began at 4:00 a.m. when the advance elements on each side stumbled upon the other. Much of the ensuing combat was hand to hand, with the battle decided by the bravery of the attacking French and Piedmontese infantry. The fighting lasted until about 8:00 p.m. with the collapse of and subsequent general withdrawal by the Austrian center, saved from a rout only by the effective leadership of General Benedek.

Although the allies trumpeted a great victory, it was a hollow one. The allies had suffered 17,191 casualties, the Austrians 22,097. The suffering of the wounded was made all the more horrible from totally inadequate ambulance services. Many lay for days under a hot sun until they were attended to. Swiss businessman Henri Dunant witnessed the battle and its aftermath, and in 1862 he published a small book about his experiences and efforts to tend to the wounded. Dunant suggested that each country form societies to care for those wounded in battle, and this led in 1864 to the formation in Geneva of the International Committee of the Red Cross.

The bloodshed of Solferino caused Napoleon misgivings. He was also concerned about a mobilization of forces by Prussia and possible military intervention by that country on the Rhine while his best troops were committed in Italy. Habsburg troops also now occupied strong defensive positions in the Quadrilateral. It was also apparent that Napoleon III had misread the strength of the Italian unification movement, and the likely result of a total Austrian defeat would be a unitary Italian state rather than the loose confederation under French influence that he had envisioned. Finally, French public opinion was now against the war.

In light of all of this, Napoleon III abandoned his ally Piedmont-Sardinia and his pledge to free Italy "from sea to sea" and unilaterally concluded an armistice with the Austrians on July 8, 1859. He then met with Franz Josef I at Villafranca on July 11. The Austrian emperor agreed to turn over to France all Lombardy, except for the fortress cities of Mantua and Peschiera, with the understanding that France would then cede the territory to Piedmont-Sardinia. Austria would retain control of Venetia. The rulers of Modena, Parma, and Tuscany—all unseated by nationalist uprisings during the war—were to be returned to their thrones. The terms were formally ratified by the Treaty of Zurich on November 10, 1859. Italian nationalists were outraged by events, and Cavour foolishly urged Victor Emmanuel II to continue the war alone. When the king refused, Cavour resigned.

In the late summer of 1859, popularly elected assemblies in Parma, Modena, Tuscany, and the Romagna called for union with Piedmont-Sardinia. The Sardinian government was, however, reluctant to agree without the approval of Napoleon III. In January 1860 Cavour returned as prime minister and negotiated the annexation of these states. Napoleon III insisted on in return, and received from Piedmont, both Nice and Savoy. In early March, plebiscites in Parma, Modena, Tuscany, and the Romagna duly approved annexation to

Piedmont. Another plebiscite on March 24 confirmed the transfer of Nice and Savoy to France in the Treaty of Turin.

Meanwhile, following an abortive uprising led by Rosolino Pilo in Sicily against King Francis II on March 4, 1860, Garibaldi handpicked a force of some 1,150 volunteers to continue the work of Italian unification. It was known as the Mille (One Thousand) and also, for their makeshift uniforms, the Red Shirts. Most had served under Garibaldi in the war against Austria and respected his leadership.

Having received secret financial support and arms from Cavour, Garibaldi sailed from Genoa in two steamers, arriving at Marsala in western Sicily on May 11. Several Neapolitan Navy gunboats appeared and, although delayed by the presence of several British warships, sank one of the steamers and captured the other. Garibaldi, however, was able to get all his men ashore and march inland.

Garibaldi announced that he was assuming the dictatorship of Sicily in the name of Victor Emmanuel II, "King of Italy." Although Bourbon king of the Two Sicilies (Naples and Sicily) Francis II had an army of some 100,000 men, he was unpopular with his subjects, and Garibaldi gathered recruits as he proceeded toward Palermo.

At Calatafimi on May 15, Garibaldi did battle with General Francisco Landi and 2,000 men of the Neapolitan Army. In this sharp action, Garibaldi recklessly exposed himself to enemy fire in rallying his men, but the One Thousand were victorious. They suffered some 30 dead and 150 wounded, 100 of them so badly that they could not proceed, but the Neapolitan forces fled to Palermo.

Increasing numbers of Sicilians rallied to Garibaldi, who advanced on the

Sicilian capital of Palermo, held by some 22,000 Neapolitan troops under General Ferdinando Lanza. On May 27 although he had only about 750 men able to fight, Garibaldi attacked. A significant portion of Palermo's 180,000 residents rallied to Garibaldi, including some 2,000 prisoners liberated from the local jails, and on the first day of fighting the Neapolitan forces were driven back from a number of key positions. Lanza then shelled that part of the city that had been lost, leading to some 600 civilian deaths during a three-day span. By May 28, though, Garibaldi controlled much of Palermo, and on May 29 the One Thousand defeated a Neapolitan counterattack, and Lanza requested a truce.

With the arrival of two battalions of well-trained and well-equipped Bavarian mercenaries in the employ of the Bourbons, however, the situation looked bleak for Garibaldi, whose men were almost out of ammunition. He was saved by Lanza's decision to surrender on May 30. An armistice was hastily arranged by British admiral George Rodney Mundy, and a convention on June 6 provided for the withdrawal by sea from Palermo of some 22,000 royal troops, to be effected by June 19.

In late June in a bid to win moderate support for his regime, Francis II formed a liberal ministry and adopted the liberal constitution of 1848. It was too late. With the fall of Palermo, only Syracuse, Augusta, Milazzo, and Messina remained under Bourbon control. Cavour, now worried by the pace of Garibaldi's victories and unsure of his intentions, sent an envoy calling for the immediate annexation of Sicily to Piedmont, but Garibaldi rejected this, pending completion of his mission.

Garibaldi then created the Southern Army, reinforced by volunteers from throughout Italy and some regular Piedmontese troops sent by Cavour. Against these, Francis II mustered 24,000 men at Messina and the other fortress cities. Garibaldi also had to contend with lawlessness as peasants revolted against the landowners.

On July 20 Garibaldi and 4,000 of his men attacked Milazzo, held by perhaps 3,000 Bourbon troops under General Bosco. The attackers suffered 750 killed or wounded, while the Neapolitan troops, fighting from cover, sustained only 150 casualties, although they were eventually forced to surrender. Under terms of the capitulation, the defenders were allowed to depart on July 24 with the full honors of war, leaving Garibaldi the fortress guns, munitions, and stores. Shortly thereafter, Messina surrendered. All remaining Sicilian strongholds capitulated by the end of September.

Not content to rest on his laurels, Garibaldi was adamant about crossing into southern Italy and defeating the remaining Neapolitan forces. Cavour at first opposed this, then agreed. On August 22, Garibaldi crossed the narrow Straits of Messina with some 4,000 men. He faced in southern Calabria perhaps 20,000 well-equipped Neapolitian Army troops. Apart from some relatively minor battles, Garibaldi's progression to Naples was an easy one, however.

King Francis II still had some 40,000 men. Plans to block Garibaldi on the plain between Eboli and Salerno evaporated, however, and on September 5 the entire Neopolitan cabinet resigned. Two days later, Garibaldi entered Naples in triumph. Francis II fled to the fortress of Gaeta. Garibaldi planned to defeat the remaining Neapolitan troops, then march on Rome and conquer Venetia.

Although Garibaldi had always professed loyalty to King Victor Emmanuel II, Cavour was worried about the international impact of Garibaldi's future plans. He feared that a march on Rome would bring French intervention, while a march on Venetia would assuredly mean a new war with Austria. An uprising in the Papal States on September 8, 1860, however, gave Cavour the opportunity to take leadership of the campaign for Italian unification out of Garibaldi's hands.

When the papacy rejected Cavour's demands that it disband its foreign military force, on September 10 Cavour sent Piedmontese forces south into papal territory. The British government supported the move, fearing a Muratist (French) restoration in Naples. There was other fighting, but the principal battle occurred on September 18 at Castelfidaro, a dozen miles south of Ancona. Although overall the Piedmontese forces were considerably larger than those of the papacy, at Castelfidaro each side deployed only about 3,000 men. The Piedmontese were commanded by General Enrico Cialdini, the papal side by expatriate French general and commander of the papal army Louis Christophe Léon Juchault de Lamorcière.

The Piedmontese lost several dozen dead and about 140 wounded. Papal losses were not much greater, but the battle was decisive, as the papal forces dissolved virtually overnight. Piedmontese forces then advanced into Neapolitan territory and linked up with Garibaldi.

King Francis II hoped that with his sizable remaining Neapolitan forces he could defeat Garibaldi before the Piedmontese army could arrive. Battle was joined north of Naples in northern Campania between Capua and Maddaloni, along the Volturno River. General Giosuè Ritucci commanded

31,200 Neapolitan troops; Garibaldi had only about 20,000 men.

Ritucci attacked at dawn on October 1. The battle raged most of the day and ended in a Neapolitan defeat. Garibaldi sustained 2,017 casualties. Bourbon losses are not known with any certainty but were probably no fewer than 1,000 killed or wounded, with 2,000 taken prisoner the next day.

During October 21–22, Naples and Sicily voted by plebiscite to join Piedmont-Sardinia. Similar favorable votes occurred in the Marches (November 4) and Umbria (November 5). On October 26 at Teano in northern Campania, Garibaldi met with King Victor Emmanuel II. Garibaldi requested that he be allowed to remain for one year as dictator of the former Kingdom of the Two Sicilies and that his officers be absorbed into the new Italian Army. Victor Emmanuel, however, refused both requests, whereupon Garibaldi returned to his home at Caprera.

Beginning on November 3, 1860, Piedmontese forces laid siege to Gaeta, where former Neapolitan king Francis II had taken refuge with his remaining forces. The siege was protracted by actions undertaken by the French. Emperor Napoleon III ordered French Mediterranean Squadron commander Vice Admiral Marie Charles Adelbert Le Barbier de Tinan to position his own ships between the Piedmontese ships and the shore forts. Under growing British diplomatic pressure, however, the French withdrew their ships on January 10. Gaeta surrendered on February 14, and Francis II went into exile in Austria.

On March 17, 1861, King Victor Emmanuel of Piedmont-Sardinia became King Victor Emmanuel I of Italy under a constitution based on that of Piedmont-Sardinia from 1848. Italy was now united except for Rome and the territory around it held by the pope and Venetia, which was still under Austrian control. Unfortunately for Italy, its brilliant statesman Cavour died on June 6 at age 51, just when his wise stewardship was most needed.

Agreement was reached between Italy and France on September 15, 1864, regarding the status of Rome. The Italian government promised to protect the Papal States against external menaces (i.e. Garibaldi's nationalists), and the French government promised to withdraw its troops from Rome within two years, allowing sufficient time for the creation of an effective papal army.

Prussian minister president Otto von Bismarck, confident in the military reforms enacted in his country, was now actively planning for war against Austria to bring about the unification of Germany under Prussian leadership. He first had to isolate Austria, however. To secure French neutrality in any war with Austria, Bismarck traveled to Biarritz and on October 4, 1865, met with Napoleon III. Napoleon pledged French neutrality in return for unspecified "compensation" on the left bank of the Rhine. He was hardly the innocent in this. Napoleon expected a protracted struggle (after all, the last war between Austria and Prussia lasted for seven years, during 1756–1763) whereby France would be able to step in and dictate a settlement.

To encourage the war, Napoleon urged Bismarck to make an ally of Italy. In return for its participation in a war against Austria, Italy would receive compensation in the form of Venetia. On April 8, 1866, Prussia and Italy concluded a secret alliance whereby Italy promised to join Prussia if war were to begin between Prussia and Austria within three months, with the promise of Venetia as a reward.

With war between Prussia and Austria now looming, on June 12 Napoleon III signed a secret treaty with Austria. France promised to remain neutral in the forthcoming conflict as well as to work for Italian neutrality. (Napoleon had, of course, already encouraged Italy to conclude a treaty with Prussia.) In return Austria agreed to cede Venetia to France, which would then hand it over to Italy whether or not Austria won the war. If Austria were to win the war and its reorganization of Germany upset the balance of power, as was bound to be the case, Vienna promised not to object to the organization of a buffer state under French influence in the Rhineland. Napoleon stupidly assumed that he could not lose.

War between Prussia and Austria commenced on June 14, and six days later Italy declared war on Austria in accordance with its secret treaty with Prussia. Italy's strategic plan called for an invasion of Austrian Venetia along the Mincio and Po Rivers by some 200,000 men and 370 guns, an area defended by the Austrian South Army of 75,000 men and 168 guns. The critical battle of the campaign occurred at the old battlefield of Custoza, southwest of Verona. In a major tactical blunder, Italian general Alfonso Ferrero di La Marmora, unaware of the South Army's strength and dispositions, managed to get only 65,000 troops and 122 guns across the Mincio. They confronted virtually the entire Austrian South Army under Field Marshal Archduke Albrecht.

In the daylong Battle of Custoza on June 24, the Austrians defeated the Italian columns piecemeal and drove them back across the Mincio into Lombardy. Albrecht did not pursue. The Italians sustained 3,800 killed or wounded and 4,300 prisoners. Austrian casualties totaled 4,600 killed or wounded and 1,000 missing. On July 3, Emperor Napoleon III arranged the transfer of Austrian-held Venetia to France, then ceded it to Italy.

During July 3–21 Garibaldi, given a general's commission and command of 10,000 men and a flotilla on Lake Garda, fought a series of small indecisive engagements with the Austrians: Monte Asello (July 3), where he was among the wounded; Lodorone (July 7); Darso (July 10); Candino (July 16); Ampola (July 19); and, in the largest engagement of the campaign, Bezzecca (July 21). Garibaldi was about to attack Trent when he was ordered to withdraw. Bismarck had made it clear that he would not permit the Italians to hold part of the Trentine Tirol (Tyrol).

The only naval battle of the war occurred on July 20, 1866, in the Adriatic between Italy and Austria. Italy had built up its navy before the war, adding ironclads acquired from Britain and the United States. Unfortunately for Italy, at the insistence of King Victor Emmanuel II the incompetent Admiral Count Carlo Pellion di Persano commanded the Italian fleet. Energetic young Rear Admiral Wilhelm von Tegetthoff commanded the Austrian fleet. Ordered to sea, Persano sortied on July 15 with virtually the entire Italian Navy but did not sail to Pola, where the Austrian Navy was located; instead, he sought an easy victory against the Austrian Adriatic island of Lissa. For two days the Italian fleet bombarded Lissa with little effect, while the Italian ironclad capital ship *Formidabile* of 20 guns was badly damaged by shore fire and suffered 60 casualties.

News of the Italian attack reached Pola, and on July 19 Tegetthoff sortied for Lissa with 21 warships, his flag in the ironclad frigate *Erzherzog Ferdinand Maximilian.* In all, his ships, 7 of which were ironclads, displaced 57,300 tons, mounted 532 guns, and carried 7,870 men. Persano commanded 31 ships, 12 of them ironclads. They displaced 86,000 tons, mounted 645 guns, and carried 10,900 men. The Italians had the advantage in all except leadership and discipline.

The Austrians were sighted at dawn on July 20. Persano had no contingency plan and was engaged in landing troops on Lissa, but by 10:00 a.m. the Italian ships were under way. Tegetthoff ordered his armored ships to charge the Italian vessels and attempt to ram and sink them. Both sides also fired on the other, and some of the Italian ships also attempted to ram the Austrian vessels. Persano then broke off the action. The Italians lost two ships (one to a ram), and four others were badly damaged. They also suffered 619 dead and 39 wounded. Later another Italian ship foundered in a squall off Ancona, largely because of damage sustained at Lissa. Austrian losses were only several ships damaged and 38 men killed and 138 wounded.

Lissa was notable as the first battle between oceangoing ironclad fleets at sea. It was also the only major fleet encounter between ironclads, in which the principal tactic was ramming. Even though only one ship was sunk by this method during the battle, for the next three decades the world's navies made the ram standard equipment in battleship construction. Unfortunately for the Austrians, however, their victory at sea went for naught. The Prussian triumph on land over the Austrians in the Battle of Königgrätz (Sadowa) in Bohemia decided the war.

The Treaty of Vienna of October 12, 1866, that formally ended the Austro-Prussian War confirmed Italy's annexation of Venetia. That December the last French troops were withdrawn from Rome and returned to France.

Concerned about open preparations by Garibaldi to raise 10,000 volunteers to march into papal territory and capture Rome and about the effect this would have on his support in France, in October 1867 Napoleon III ordered French troops to return to Rome to preserve the remaining papal territory. Garibaldi had indeed planned both an uprising in Rome and a march on the city. The uprising occurred on October 22, when the rebels seized part of the city but were then defeated by papal forces. The last group of rebels was captured on October 25.

Meanwhile, the French 2,000-man expeditionary force, commanded by General Pierre Louis Charles de Failly, arrived at Civitavecchia on October 26 and prepared to do battle with Garibaldi's ragtag force of some 8,000 men, which had arrived on the outskirts of Rome after defeating a papal force, mostly of foreign volunteers, sent against them at Monte Rotondo on October 24.

On November 3 near the village of Mantana, northeast of Rome, Garibaldi's men joined battle with the French and some 3,000 papal troops under General Hermann Kanzler. Garibaldi was defeated, in part because of the excellent French chassepot rifle, here making its first battlefield appearance. The allies took some 800 prisoners. Garibaldi and 5,100 men returned to the Kingdom of Italy, where they were arrested.

Rome was added to the Kingdom of Italy in 1870, however. Taking advantage of the withdrawal of French troops on August 19, 1870, as a consequence of the Franco-Prussian War, General Raffaele Cardona led 60,000 Kingdom of Italy troops to invest the city. On September 20 following a short bombardment, his forces effected a breach in the walls at Porta Pia and entered the city. Pope Pius IX then ordered his troops to lay down their arms.

On October 2 following a plebiscite, the Kingdom of Italy annexed Rome. Italy was at last reunited, and Rome became the capital. Pius IX shut himself up in the Vatican; not until 1929 would the papacy recognize the loss of Rome and be content with Vatican City.

Significance

A new major power had come into being in Europe, but the high hopes of the Risorgimento were slow to be realized, for the history of Italy in the decades after 1871 is one of political squabbling, parliamentary infighting, regional factionalism, and inattention to national welfare. The differences between the urban, industrialized, and generally prosperous north and the rural, impoverished, and agricultural south were particularly pronounced. It would be generations before this situation was even partially addressed and Italy was able to realize its potential. Regardless, European diplomatic calculations had to take a new populous nation state into account, and Italy would play an important role in World War I.

Further Reading

Beales, Derek Edward Dawson. *The Risorgimento and the Unification of Italy.* New York: Barnes and Noble, 1971.

Coppa, Frank J. *Pope Pius IX: Crusader in a Secular Age.* Boston: Twayne, 1979.

Davis, John A., ed. *Italy in the Nineteenth Century, 1796–1900.* Oxford: Oxford University Press, 2000.

Hibbert, Christopher. *Garibaldi and His Enemies: The Clash of Arms and Personalities in the Making of Italy.* Boston: Little, Brown, 1966.

Holt, Edgar. *The Making of Italy 1815–1870.* New York: Atheneum, 1971.

Idley, Jasper. *Garibaldi.* New York: Viking, 1976.

Mack Smith, Denis. *Cavour.* New York: Knopf, 1985.

Mack Smith, Denis. *Mazzini.* New Haven, CT: Yale University Press, 1994.

Mack Smith, Denis. *Modern Italy: A Political History.* Ann Arbor: University of Michigan Press, 1997.

Matin, George. *The Red Shirt & the Cross of Savoy: The Story of Italy's Risorgimento (1748–1871).* New York: Dodd, Mead, 1969.

Thayer, William Roscoe. *The Life and Times of Cavour.* 2 vols. New York: Houghton Mifflin, 1911.

Trevelyan, George Macaulay. *Garibaldi and the Making of Italy.* London: Longmans, Green, 1911.

Turnbull, Patrick. *Solferino: The Birth of a Nation.* New York: St. Martin's, 1985.

Taiping Rebellion (1851–1864)

Dates	1851–1864
Location	China
Combatants	Taiping vs. Imperial Chinese government
Principal Commanders	Taiping: Hong Xiuquan, Yang Xiuqing Imperial Chinese: Lu Jianying, Li Hongzhang, Frederick Townsend Ward, Charles George Gordon, Zeng Guofan
Principal Battles	Wuchang, Nanjing (first), Suzhou, Nanjing (second)
Outcome	The bloodiest war of the entire 19th century, the Taiping Rebellion sparked widespread unrest against the imperial Chinese government.

Causes

The Taiping Rebellion in China (1851–1864) was sparked by agrarian unrest during the reigns of Qing dynasty emperors Daoguang (Tao-kuang, r. 1821–1850) and Xianfeng (Hsien-feng, r. 1851–1861). This was largely the consequence of a decline in arable land per capita of population, absentee landlordism, and natural disasters. The leader of the revolt was Hong Xiuquan (Hung Hsiu-ch'üan), a failed civil service examination candidate from Kwangtung (present-day Guangdong) Province. Hong claimed that the ruling Manchus had lost their mandate from heaven following the defeat by Britain of the Chinese in the First Opium War of 1839–1842. Hong vowed to end Manchu rule and establish a new government responsible to the people, to be known as the Taiping Tianguo (Heavenly Kingdom of Great Peace).

A self-proclaimed Christian, Hong borrowed from that religion certain teachings, including the Ten Commandments. He held that he had divine authority to regulate all earthly affairs. The Taipings banned gambling and the consumption of alcohol and opium. Because the latter was so important in their trade with China, the Western governments supported the imperial government in its efforts to crush the Taipings.

Course

In January 1851 Hong formally proclaimed the Taiping revolt against the Manchu dynasty. It began in Kwangsi

BATTLE OF NANJING, MARCH 20, 1853

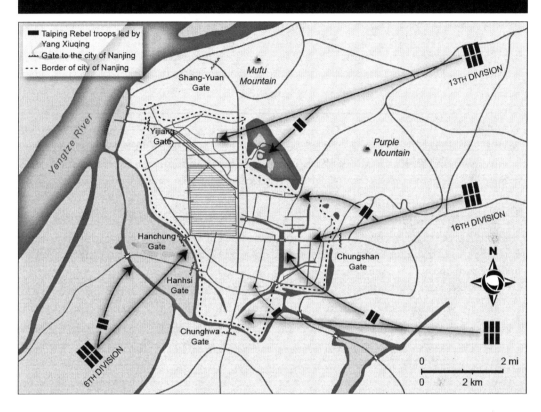

(Guangxi) Province and expanded into Hupei (Hubei) and Hunan Provinces. Many Chinese were sympathetic with the Taiping goals, and Hong soon had at his disposal a well-trained and highly motivated army of 50,000 people. The army included women as well as men, for an important element of Taiping teaching was gender equality. Later, the army grew to upward of a half million.

Taiping army strength rested on its high morale, strict discipline (the troops had to obey a set of 62 rules), and religious conformity. The Taipings also had effective military commanders, especially Yang Xiuqing (Yang Hsiu-ch'ing), who led rebel military forces against the Imperial Army in the Yangtze River (Changjiang)

Valley. The central government was seriously handicapped in dealing with the Taiping Rebellion by having to fight simultaneously against inroads in China by the Western powers led by Britain as well as other internal unrest.

In late December 1852, Taiping forces laid siege to Wuchang in Hupei Province. Following a 20-day siege, they took that city on January 12, 1853. The Taipings now controlled the upper Yangtze River and its trade, enabling them to cut off the interior from the coast. Despite this success, the Taipings committed a major strategic error. Instead of moving against the imperial capital of Beijing in Hopeh (Hebei) Province, they proceeded down the Yangtze against Nanking (Nanjing), capital city of Kiangsu

(Jiangsu) Province. This decision cost them their best chance of taking Peking (Beijing) and overthrowing the Manchus. The Taipings apparently decided on this course of action because of reports of large imperial forces protecting Peking.

In early February 1853 some 500,000 Taipings departed Wuchang, crossed the Yangtze River, and burned their floating bridges behind them in order to delay advancing imperial forces. While part of the army moved on the north side of the river by land, the majority traveled toward Nanjing by water in some 20,000 requisitioned watercraft. The Taipings easily captured Kiukiang (Jiujiang) in western Jiangxi Province and Anking (Anqing), the capital of Anhwei (Anhui) Province. After securing provisions from storehouses in these locations, the Taipings continued on to Nanjing, arriving there on March 6.

With word of the Taiping approach, people in the surrounding area sought refuge in Nanjing, the population of which swelled to some three-quarters of a million. Although ill-prepared for a siege, the defenders managed to hold the Taipings at bay for 13 days. On March 19, however, the Taipings deployed hundreds of horses carrying effigies of soldiers bearing torches before the west wall. Expecting an attack from that quarter, the defenders rushed there. Too late they discovered that this was a ruse, as two large Taiping mines exploded elsewhere, breaching the city wall. Although a third mine exploded late, killing many of the attacking troops, the Taipings secured access to the city. The Taipings may also have been aided by spies. Reportedly, they had sent some 3,000 of their number into the city disguised as Buddhist monks.

News of the death of Lu Jianying (Lu Chien-ying), the imperial commander in Nanjing, demoralized the defenders, many of whom then abandoned their posts. On March 20 the Taipings assaulted the inner Imperial City, defended by 40,000 Manchu troops. The Taipings captured it in costly human-wave assaults, then massacred some 30,000 of the defenders who had refused to surrender.

Having secured Nanjing, the rebels made it their capital and there proclaimed a new dynasty, the Taiping Tianguo (T'ienkuo, Heavenly Kingdom of Great Peace). Hong was the ruler. However, he never rigorously implemented the egalitarian social programs that had drawn so many poor Chinese to the cause. Furthermore, the revolutionary nature of the Taiping policies and religion proved repugnant to the Chinese landholding elite, who supported the Qing government. These factors and endemic, bloody infighting among the Taiping leadership doomed their regime to eventual failure. Despite its promises of reform, the Taiping regime also became increasingly repressive. This was probably the key factor in its subsequent demise.

With the end of the Second Opium War (the *Arrow* War) in 1860, Viceroy Zeng Guofan (Tseng Kuo-fan) and Li Hongzhang (Li Hung-chang) worked to reform and revitalize the imperial government and to subdue the Taipings.

In 1860 with the Taipings threatening Shanghai, wealthy Chinese merchants in that city financed a mercenary army. It was initially composed of foreigners and commanded by American Frederick Townsend Ward, who had arrived in Shanghai with his brother that same year. A merchant marine officer and soldier of fortune from Salem, Massachusetts, Ward had been a filibuster in Mexico and had also fought as a French Army officer in the Crimean War (1853–1856). His Foreign Arms Corps, which began with only about 100 men and a military reverse, steadily grew in size and came to be known as the Ever Victorious Army for its series of successful military campaigns.

In 1861 Ward was made a brigadier general in the Imperial Army. During a four-month span he and his army, assisted by British and French forces returning from their operations at Beijing, won 11 victories and cleared a swath of territory about 30 miles wide around Shanghai. On August 20, 1862, however, Ward was mortally wounded while leading an assault on the walled city of Tzeki (Cixi) in Chekiang (Zhejiang).

In 1863 at the request of the Chinese imperial government, the British government assigned Captain Charles George Gordon of the Royal Engineers to succeed Ward. Hereafter known as "Chinese" Gordon, Gordon led the Ever Victorious Army south along the Grand Canal and captured Soochow (Suzhou) in Jiangsu Province on December 4, 1863. Gordon then proceeded to lay siege to Nanking.

Taiping ruler Hong Xiuquan declared to his followers that God would not let Nanjing fall. In June 1864, however, with imperial forces approaching, Hong died of food poisoning. Meanwhile Gordon, disgusted by the Qing government's execution of prisoners, gave up command of the Ever Victorious Army. Chinese imperial forces under Viceroy Zeng Guofan (Tseng Kuo-fan) nevertheless ended the rebellion when they breached the Nanjing walls and took the city on July 19, 1864.

The imperial troops executed most of the Taiping leaders. Imperial forces exhumed Hong Xiuquan's body to verify his death, then cremated it and fired the ashes from a cannon to ensure that his remains had no resting place.

Although the Taiping Rebellion is usually said to end with the capture of Nanjing, isolated Taiping detachments continued to resist. A large Taiping force was destroyed in February 1866, and the last Taiping units were not defeated until 1871. Regional revolts continued into 1881.

Significance

However measured, the Taiping Rebellion was the most destructive war of the entire 19th century. The casualty totals were far greater than those of the contemporaneous bloody American Civil War (1861–1865). Most estimates place the number of dead from the rebellion, directly or indirectly, at 20 million people. Some estimates range as high as 30 million dead.

The Taiping Rebellion was the first total war in China. Both sides waged war on civilians as well as the opposing armies. Agricultural areas were devastated as each side sought to deprive the other of resources. Indeed, most of those who perished in the war died of famine or disease. Some 600 cities were destroyed in the fighting, which also saw the widespread massacres of their populations. Women were also sold into concubinage.

The Taiping Rebellion fanned widespread regional unrest in China. The apparent collapse of imperial authority during the rebellion encouraged unrest throughout China.

Further Reading

Gray, Jack. *Rebellions and Revolutions: China from the 1800s to the 1980s.* New York: Oxford University Press, 1990.

Heath, Ian. *The Taiping Rebellion, 1851–1866.* London: Osprey, 1994.

Hsü, Immanuel C. Y. *The Rise of Modern China.* New York: Oxford University Press, 1999.

Jian, Youwen. *The Taiping Revolutionary Movement.* New Haven, CT: Yale University Press, 1973.

Michael, Franz H., ed. *The Taiping Rebellion: History and Documents.* 3 vols. Seattle: University of Washington Press, 1966.

Porter, Jonathan. *Tseng Kuo-fan's Private Bureaucracy.* China Research Monographs. Berkeley: Center for Chinese Studies, University of California Press, 1972.

Spence, Jonathan D. *God's Chinese Son: The Taiping Heavenly Kingdom of Hong Xiuquan.* New York: Norton, 1997.

Spence, Jonathan D. *The Search for Modern China.* New York: Norton, 1999.

American Civil War (1861–1865)

Dates	April 12, 1861–May 9, 1865
Location	North America
Combatants	United States of America (North) vs. Confederate States of America (South)
Principal Commanders	United States: Abraham Lincoln, Winfield Scott, George B. McClellan, Ulysses S. Grant, William T. Sherman, David Farragut, David Dixon Porter Confederate States: Jefferson Davis, Robert E. Lee, Joseph E. Johnston, Braxton Bragg
Principal Battles	Fort Sumter, Bull Run (first), Fort Donelson, Shiloh, Seven Pines, Seven Days' Campaign, Bull Run (second), Antietam, Perryville, Corinth, Fredericksburg, Chancellorsville, Stones River, Vicksburg, Gettysburg, Chickamauga, Chattanooga, Overland Campaign, Wilderness, Spotsylvaniua Court House, Cold Harbor, Petersburg, Atlanta, Nashville, Savannah
Outcome	Slavery is abolished and the Union is preserved, with the latter having immense consequence for world affairs.

Causes

The United States underwent great territorial expansion during the first half of the 19th century as a consequence of the Louisiana Purchase (1803), the acquisition of Florida (1819), and the Mexican-American War (1846–1848). The country also experienced rapid population growth from both a high birthrate and immigration. By 1860 with some 31 million people, the United States was more populous than Great Britain and almost as large as France.

By 1860, however, the United States was coming apart. North and South were entirely estranged. The South had an agricultural economy based on the production of cotton, tobacco, rice, sugarcane, and naval stores. It was the world's largest producer of raw cotton, but seven-eighths of it was exported, chiefly to the United Kingdom. Southerners therefore sought a low tariff in order to be able to purchase cheaper manufactured goods from Britain, then leading the Industrial Revolution. The North, on the other hand, had a balanced economy. It was rapidly industrializing, and northern business interests sought a high tariff to protect their finished goods against cheaper British manufactures. Capital also tended to multiply in the North, and banking, insurance companies, and railroads all concentrated there. Increasingly the railroads were tying the West to the North. There was also a large and growing population imbalance between North and South; new immigrants could not compete with free slave labor in the South and settled primarily in the North. Most whites in the South were also hurt economically by the slavery system.

The Mexican-American War set up the American Civil War, for the chief issue regarding the newly acquired territories was whether they would be slave or free. The Missouri Compromise of 1820 provided that new states would be admitted to the Union on the basis of one slave and one free in order to maintain rough parity in the U.S. Senate and in presidential elections. But California was admitted singly as a free state in 1850. In the ensuing Compromise of 1850 the North agreed to enforce laws on runaway slaves. This, however, ran counter to increasing abolitionist sentiment in the North that fueled violence in the territories, especially Kansas.

As abolitionism gained strength in the North, white southerners increasingly saw their way of life threatened. Political parties and even churches split along regional lines. Increasingly there was talk of secession; most southerners believed that a state had the right to secede from the Union, whereas northerners rejected this notion.

In October 1858 militant abolitionist John Brown led a raid on the federal arsenal at Harpers Ferry, Virginia (now West Virginia), with the intention of setting up a base in the Appalachian Mountains for fugitive slaves and using arms from the arsenal to raid the South. The raid was easily put down and Brown was tried and hanged, but the event greatly alarmed southerners, who saw in it true northern sentiment, and led to increasing numbers of state militia units in the South.

In November 1860, Republican Party candidate Abraham Lincoln was elected president of the United States with a plurality of the vote and largely because the Democratic Party split on the issue of slavery. The Republican platform called for no more slavery in the territories but promised no interference with slavery in the states. Nonetheless, many southern leaders refused to accept a "Black Republican President," and on December 24, 1860, South Carolina voted to secede from the Union. State conventions in Alabama, Georgia, Florida, Mississippi, Louisiana, and Texas followed South Carolina's lead. On February 8, 1861, representatives from the seven seceded states met at Montgomery, Alabama, and formed the Confederate States of America. The next day the Confederate Congress elected Jefferson Davis president.

U.S. president James Buchanan's Democratic administration had almost a month to go, but Buchanan was afraid of using force and alienating the border states, chiefly Virginia, and took no action. But after taking office, Lincoln also did nothing for six weeks. In his March 4, 1861, inauguration, Lincoln renewed his promise to respect slavery where it existed and to enforce the fugitive slave laws but said that he would not countenance secession.

The Confederates had now taken control of all federal forts and navy yards in the seceded states except the key installations of Fort Pickens at Pensacola, Florida, and Fort Sumter in Charleston Harbor, South Carolina. Lincoln reluctantly concluded, against the advice of a majority of his cabinet, that he had to send relief expeditions to these two installations even though this would probably cause Virginia to secede as well. Lincoln informed Davis that this would be only for provisioning, but Davis ordered Major General P. G. T. Beauregard at Charleston to demand the surrender of Fort Sumter. If refused, he was to reduce the fort. Following an unsatisfactory reply from fort commander Major Robert Anderson, Beauregard ordered fire opened on Fort Sumter before the Union relief expedition could arrive.

Shelling commenced at 4:30 a.m. on April 12, 1861. After 34 hours of bombardment and short of ammunition and provisions, Anderson surrendered. The only casualty in the shelling was a horse.

A whirlwind of patriotic fervor swept the North, and on April 15 Lincoln called for 75,000 volunteers to serve three months, limited constitutionally to the 90-day term for militia in federal service. Claiming that Lincoln's call for volunteers was an act of war against the South, Virginia seceded. This was a major blow to the North, for it gave the South the important Tredegar Iron Works at Richmond, the largest such enterprise in the South, and the largest prewar navy yard (at Norfolk) as well as many of the South's best officers, including General Robert E. Lee. Virginia was closely followed in secession by Arkansas, Tennessee, and North Carolina. In a major blow to the Confederacy, however, Kentucky declared its neutrality.

Course

The North enjoyed tremendous advantages. The population of its 23 states was 22 million, a figure that continued to increase during the war thanks to ongoing immigration. (Some 400,000 foreign-born soldiers served in the Union Army during the war.) The North also had a well-balanced economy with some 90 percent of the prewar manufacturing facilities. Its superior rail network proved to be of immense logistical advantage during the war. The North also had a large merchant marine. Its population was better educated, and it enjoyed superior managerial systems essential in waging modern war. At the start of hostilities the U.S. Army numbered only some 25,000 men, but its 90 ships (40 in commission at the start of hostilities) completely eclipsed the navy of the South, which had only a handful of ships.

The 11 seceded states had only 9 million people, but 3.5 million of these were slaves. Although the South's abundant natural resources had not been developed and its manufacturing resources were severely limited, it had only 29 percent of the 1860 railroad track, and this steadily deteriorated during the course of the war owing to the Union blockade. The South was also plagued by states' rights. Having protested federal power, the seceded states were now reluctant to yield authority to the Confederate government. The South also had a much higher rate of illiteracy, which adversely impacted war management.

Despite the great advantages lying with the North, the secessionists were convinced that the North would not fight to maintain the Union and that if it did Great Britain and France, dependent on southern staples, would recognize the Confederacy and provide material assistance. To encourage this, at the beginning of the war Davis embarked on so-called cotton diplomacy of withholding the southern cotton crop from shipment in order to force European intervention. This did not have the desired result.

Southerners also believed that the Confederacy could simply stand on the defensive and wear down the North, which in

CIVIL WAR, 1861 – 1862

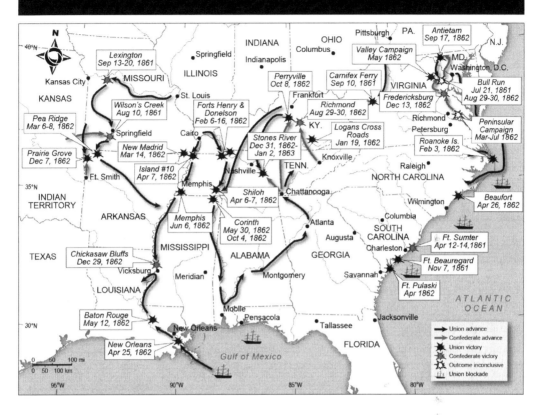

order to win would have to physically invade and conquer the South. Southerners also believed that their greater emphasis on outdoor living, familiarity with firearms, and inclination for military service would give them an advantage.

Southerners sought recognition of independence. The Northern war aim was restoration of the Union until after 1862 when abolition became a secondary objective. Yet in proclaiming a blockade of the South on April 19, 1861, and forbidding trade with the seceded states (August 16), Lincoln recognized a state of war.

Lincoln was a superb war leader. Although he had scant military experience, he understood the strategic picture clearly and had an excellent sense of what needed

to be accomplished and how to go about it. He proved singularly adroit at communicating his war aims and the importance of adroit diplomacy. He also understood the importance of sea power and a naval blockade and determined that the chief military goal would be the destruction of Confederate armies rather than controlling territory. His problem was in finding the right leaders to carry out his plans.

Jefferson Davis was an interesting study in contrast. Aloof and inflexible, during the Mexican-American War he had commanded a regiment with great distinction, and he had been an excellent secretary of war (1853–1857). Based on his supposed expert knowledge, he insisted on intervening in military decisions and made a number of very poor personnel appointments and strategic choices.

U.S. Army commanding general Brevet Lieutenant General Winfield Scott developed the war plan that would defeat the South. Dubbed the "Anaconda Plan" for the South American snake that strangles its victim to death, Scott planned to blockade the Confederacy, build up and train a large Union Army, and then invade and bisect the South via its great rivers. Although Scott soon retired, Lincoln basically followed his plan.

There were three major theaters of war: the eastern theater, the western theater (from the Appalachian Mountains to the Mississippi River), and the Trans-Mississippi West. The eastern theater has received the most attention, in part because of the proximity of the two capital cities, the fame of the generals who fought there, and the concentration of newspapers in the East. Also, some 60 percent of all Civil War battles occurred in Virginia. The western theater, with its abundant natural resources and major rivers, deserves to rank in importance with the eastern theater, but the Trans-Mississippi theater was of little importance, especially after Union forces gained control of the Mississippi River.

Early fighting occurred in Kentucky and western Virginia (soon to secede from the rest of Virginia as the new state of West Virginia) during April 15–July 20, 1861. Major General George B. McClellan, a West Point–trained officer who was in the railroad business when the war began, led some 20,000 Union troops in securing this area for the Union, with the notable battles being those of Philippi (June 3, 1861) and Rich Mountain–Carrick's Ford (July 11–14). Skirmishing between the two sides also occurred at Big Bethel (June 10) near Union-held Fort Monroe in far eastern Virginia.

With the Northern public and press demanding military action and a quick end to the rebellion and the 90-day enlistments in some volunteer regiments about to expire, Lincoln overruled Scott, who wanted more time to train the men, and ordered Brigadier General Irwin McDowell to advance from southwest of Washington westward with 30,000 men and defeat Confederate brigadier general Beauregard's forces at Manassas Junction, Virginia. Once this had been accomplished, McDowell was to turn south and march on Richmond, now the Confederate capital. Brigadier General Patterson and another Union force were to prevent Confederate brigadier general Joseph E. Johnston from bringing 10,000 Confederates from the Shenandoah Valley to Manassas.

The Battle of Bull Run, also known as the Battle of Manassas (the Union named battles for the nearest body of water, the Confederates for the nearest telegraph station), began before dawn on July 21. McDowell attacked and seemed to have carried the day by midafternoon. But his plan proved overly complicated for the largely untrained Union troops, and Johnston eluded the inept Patterson and brought his men to Manassas Junction by rail just in time to prevent disaster. A magnificent stand by Confederates under Brigadier General Thomas J. Jackson (now dubbed "Stonewall") turned an apparent Southern rout into victory. McDowell's men began a withdrawal back toward Washington that soon became a rout. The Confederates were equally disorganized, however, and incapable of a pursuit into Washington. Confederate casualties totaled 1,982; the Union lost 2,896 (nearly half of them captured or missing). The Confederates also secured substantial amounts of weapons and supplies.

The battle ended any illusions about the war and brought home to both sides a realization of the resources that would be required to win it. Convinced of the need for more thorough training for the army, Lincoln replaced McDowell with McClellan; upon Scott's retirement, on November 1 McClellan became Union general in chief.

On April 19, Lincoln had proclaimed a naval blockade of the South. U.S. secretary of the navy Gideon Welles requisitioned merchant ships in Northern harbors for conversion into warships, and he commenced a massive naval construction program. This included many steam warships and soon also ironclads.

It took time to establish an effective blockade of the nearly 3,500 miles of Confederate coastline. To run the blockade, the Confederates counted on speedy, stealthy ships, most of them built in England. Nassau in the Bahamas became a major supply port, with European cargoes offloaded there and at other points in the West Indies for transshipment to the South. Some 800 ships passed through the blockade in its first year of operation, but in 1860 some 6,000 ships had entered and cleared Southern ports. At first the Confederacy did not restrict cargoes, and most blockade-runners carried nonmilitary goods, as the financial return on these was much greater. Joint Union naval and military expeditions secured bases for the North and helped tighten the blockade. Chances of capture of blockade-runners were estimated at 1 in 10 in 1861 but 1 in 3 in 1864. By 1865 also, the Union Navy, with 700 vessels of all types including 60 ironclads, was the second largest in the world behind only the Royal Navy in Great Britain. During the war, the vast majority of Union ships were employed in blockade duties. Confederate secretary of the navy Stephen R. Mallory sought to break the Union blockade by the construction of ironclads, sending raiders to sea against Union merchant shipping and, as the war continued, employing new technology in the form of mines and submarines.

Europeans were divided about the Civil War. Generally speaking, the upper classes favored the South while the lower classes identified with the Union. Businessmen saw in the South a lucrative market for finished goods. Yet the British government, followed by France and other nations, dashed Southern hopes by declaring neutrality. This move angered Washington but prohibited the armed ships of either side from bringing their prizes into British ports. This was a particularly heavy blow to Confederate privateers and government commerce raiders.

As McClellan repeatedly ignored orders by Lincoln for offensive action in Virginia, the Union scored victories early in 1862 in Kentucky and Tennessee. Confederate major general Leonidas Polk's mistaken decision to invade Columbus, Kentucky, in September 1861 ended that state's neutrality and turned Kentucky against the Confederacy. Union brigadier general George H. Thomas decisively defeated the Confederates under Major General George B. Crittenden in the Battle of Mill Springs (January 19–20) in Kentucky.

In the Battle of Pea Ridge fought in Benton County, Arkansas, during March 7–8, 1862, U.S. major general Samuel R. Curtis with 10,500 men won a major victory against 16,500 Confederates under Major General Earl Van Dorn. Union losses were

1,384 against as many as 4,600 Confederates. It was the first major Union victory in the Trans-Mississippi West theater and ensured Union control of Missouri for more than two years.

In early February 1862, Union brigadier general Ulysses S. Grant and a gunboat flotilla with the first ironclads of the war under Commodore Andrew H. Foote moved against Confederate fortifications on the Tennessee and Cumberland Rivers. Foote captured Confederate-held Fort Henry on the Tennessee (February 6), but most of its garrison marched the short distance to Fort Donelson on the Cumberland. Confederate commander of the Western Department General Albert S. Johnston regarded Donelson as the major defense of Nashville, and he now reinforced it to buy time for his flanking garrisons to withdraw from Bowling Green and Columbus, Kentucky. Grant soon besieged Fort Donelson, and following a failed attack by Foote's gunboats and an unsuccessful effort by the Confederates to break free, Donelson surrendered on February 16. The Union took some 15,000 prisoners plus substantial equipment and supplies. The Confederates suffered some 1,500–3,500 killed or wounded in the battle; Union casualties totaled 2,832.

The capture of Forts Henry and Donelson were the first two significant Union victories of the war and gave it access to middle Tennessee and its abundant natural resources. Nashville fell to the Union on February 25, the first Confederate state capital in Union hands.

Grant was prevented from moving immediately against the Confederate key railhead of Corinth, Mississippi, when his superior, Major General Henry W. Halleck, diverted 25,000 men in the Army of Mississippi under Brigadier General John Pope to expel Confederate forces from the upper Mississippi. Pope and Foote's gunboat flotilla besieged Island No. 10 in the Mississippi River on March 16. The Confederates surrendered on April 7, but the delay allowed Johnston time to bring up reinforcements at Corinth. Grant marched with 36,000 men to Pittsburg Landing just across the Tennessee border from Corinth, ordered to wait there for 20,000 reinforcements under Major General Don Carlos Buell. But Buell was delayed, and Grant, who was always offensively minded, chose to drill Union reinforcements rather than erecting fortifications.

Johnston was determined to attack. His 40,000 men struck before dawn on April 6, taking the Union troops by surprise in what became known as the Battle of Shiloh, for the Baptist church there. Confusion reigned on both sides, and Johnston was mortally wounded. The hungry Confederate troops, seemingly on the verge of success, stopped to loot the Union camps, and a fierce Union stand imposed further delay. But with Union troops close to defeat, Beauregard broke off the assault to reorganize.

That night Buell's Army of the Ohio arrived, and the next day the stronger Union forces attacked. By evening the Confederates were in retreat to Corinth, with Union forces too exhausted to pursue. The battle cost the Union 13,038 casualties of some 63,000 men engaged, while the 40,000 Confederates suffered 10,694. The grim tally of 23,732 casualities from this single battle was more than the United States had suffered in all of its previous wars combined.

While Union forces were steadily working their way southward along the northern Mississippi, other Union forces secured its mouth. Following a two-day largely ineffective bombardment of Confederate forts on the lower river by 13-inch mortars aboard specially constructed river craft, Flag Officer David Farragut ran his squadron past the forts and on April 26 took the surrender of New Orleans. Union troops under Major General Benjamin F. Butler then occupied the city.

By now Lincoln had lost confidence in McClellan for his inaction and on March 11, 1862, removed him from command of the entire army, leaving McClellan with its chief field force, the Army of the Potomac (Halleck became general in chief in July). Lincoln ordered McClellan to commence immediate operations against Richmond, but McClellan planned an advance not south from the Washington area, as Lincoln desired, but instead from the east by way of the peninsula between the James and York Rivers. McClellan's opponents persuaded Lincoln to withhold General McDowell's strong corps to protect Washington.

The water route to Richmond up the James as well as Union transports at Hampton Roads now came under threat from the Confederate ironclad ram *Virginia,* formed from the hull of the scuttled U.S. Navy steam warship *Merrimack* at the Norfolk Navy Yard. On March 8 the *Virginia* sallied and sank the Union frigate *Cumberland* and burned the sloop *Congress.* Other Union wooden warships, including the flagship *Minnesota,* ran aground endeavoring to escape. That evening the *Virginia* retired, its crew confident of completing the destruction of the Union ships the next day. That same evening, however, the revolutionary Union ironclad *Monitor* arrived in Hampton Roads and took up position near the *Minnesota.* The next day the two ironclads did battle in the first clash between such ships in history. It seemed an unequal match, with the much

larger *Virginia* mounting 10 guns to only 2 for the *Monitor.* The *Monitor,* however, proved far more nimble, and its turret revolved (the first such use in actual warfare), enabling the gun ports to be moved away from enemy fire while its 2 11-inch Dahlgren smoothbore guns were being reloaded. The battle lasted four hours. Although the *Monitor* got off far fewer shots, most of these told, while most of the shells from the *Virginia* failed to register. The battle ended in a draw with both vessels retiring, but the *Virginia* had been hit 50 times and was leaking. The *Monitor* had sustained only 21 hits and was virtually undamaged.

Both sides now pushed construction of ironclads. Of 40 ironclads laid down by the North during the Civil War, 35 were of the turreted *Monitor* type. The South continued to construct casemated ironclads of the *Virginia* type. The battle also led to an effort on both sides to manufacture more powerful guns capable of penetrating the new iron plating.

On March 17 McClellan's army began its movement south by water from Alexandria, Virginia, to Fort Monroe, and then marched west toward Richmond in the March–August 1862 Peninsula Campaign. McClellan's advance was glacial. On April 5 McClellan began a siege of Yorktown but, despite a sevenfold manpower advantage, did not take it until May 4 upon the Confederate withdrawal. A stubborn Confederate rearguard action at Williamsburg (May 5) prevented McClellan from confronting the bulk of Joseph Johnston's army and its supply train. By May 14, however, the Army of the Potomac had reached the Pamunkey River, some 20 miles from Richmond. Despite his overwhelming numerical advantage (100,000 Union troops to 60,000 Confederates), McClellan halted the advance to await arrival of McDowell's 40,000-man corps from Fredericksburg, south of Washington.

General Robert E. Lee, then military adviser to President Davis, recommended that Major General Thomas E. Jackson in the Shenandoah Valley be reinforced and mount an operation to divert as many Union reinforcements from McClellan as possible. Davis agreed. Union major general Nathaniel P. Banks was supposed to clear the valley as part of McClellan's Richmond campaign. Upon defeating Jackson, Banks would then cover Washington, releasing McDowell to join McClellan.

Jackson's ensuing Valley Campaign (March 23–June 9, 1862) was one of the most brilliant in military history. Commanding no more than 18,000 men, he parlayed excellent intelligence and rapid movement (his infantry were known as foot cavalry) to tie down more than 64,000 Union troops. Jackson engaged three Union armies under Banks, Major General John C. Frémont, and Brigadier General James Shields in a series of battles (Kernstown, March 23; McDowell, May 8; Front Royal, May 23; First Winchester, May 25; Cross Keys, June 8; and Port Republic, June 9) and numerous other actions. The Union suffered some 8,000 casualties, the Confederates fewer than 2,500.

Although Jackson did not have the means to attack Washington, fears of this led Lincoln to detach 20,000 men from McDowell and rush them to the Shenandoah. Jackson meanwhile had left the valley for the critical battles before Richmond.

At the end of May, troops of the Army of the Potomac occupied both sides of the Chickahominy River, with their northern elements reaching out to meet McDowell and the lower part only some five miles from Richmond, just beyond Fair Oaks

Station. In the Battle of Seven Pines (Fair Oaks, May 31–June 1), General Johnston and 39,000 men attacked two Union corps isolated on the south bank by the flooded river from the main part of McClellan's army. The passage of a third corps across the river prevented a Union defeat. Union casualties were under 6,000; Confederate casualties were almost 8,000 including Johnston, severely wounded.

On June 1, President Davis replaced Johnston with Lee in command of the Army of Northern Virginia. During June 12–15, Lee sent his cavalry commander Major General James E. B. Stuart and 1,200 men in a ride entirely around McClellan's army, destroying Union supplies and rattling the Union commander, now firmly convinced that he was outnumbered.

Determined to drive McClellan from the peninsula, Lee assembled some 97,000 men (the largest force he would ever command) and sent them against McClellan in what became known as the Seven Days' Campaign (June 25–July 1). Jackson had just arrived, and Lee planned to send Jackson's corps in a flanking attack against Union major general Fitz John Porter's corps on the north side of the Chickahominy, with most of the army under Lee west of Mechanicsville moving against McClellan's center.

The operation was poorly handled. Jackson, physically spent from the Shenandoah Valley Campaign, failed to exercise effective command and moved too slowly, never getting into the fight in the Battle of Mechanicsville on June 26. Porter turned back the Confederate assaults and, learning of Jackson's approach, retired to Gaines' Mill.

Lee again attacked Porter on June 27 in the Battle of Gaines' Mill. Jackson was again late and failed to get in behind

Porter's right flank as Lee had planned. Lee managed to penetrate Porter's left, however. In danger of a double envelopment with the approach of Jackson, Porter managed to withdraw in good order thanks to the arrival of Union reinforcements. That night on McClellan's order, Porter withdrew to the south bank of the Chickahominy. Ignoring appeals from his subordinates that Richmond was his for the taking, McClellan withdrew to the James River and the protection of Union gunboats.

During June 29–30 Lee pursued, suffering sharp rebuffs in battles at Peach Orchard, Savage's Station, White Oak Swamp, and Glendale-Frayser's Farm. Jackson again failed to envelop the Union right flank. In the Battle of Malvern Hill on July 1 Porter, in the absence of McClellan, exercised command, and the Army of the Potomac, supported by the heavy guns of the Union James River squadron, turned back Lee's desperate attacks, with the Confederates suffering more than 5,000 casualties. Although this was a clear Union victory, an unnerved McClellan ordered an immediate retreat to Harrison's Landing. The next day, the Confederates withdrew toward Richmond. In the Seven Days' Campaign the Union suffered nearly 16,000 casualties, but Confederate losses were more than 20,000.

McClellan had fumbled away victory. He informed Washington during the campaign that he was outnumbered two to one when the reverse was true. A little more energy on his part and the war might have been ended or drastically shortened. On August 3 Lincoln ordered McClellan to return with his army to Washington.

Halleck now consolidated the Armies of Virginia under General Pope. Major General Ambrose E. Burnside was to march north from Fortress Monroe to Falmouth, and McClellan would bring his army to Alexandria and there join Pope for an overland march south to Richmond. Determined to strike while the Union forces were still divided, Lee ordered Jackson to attack Pope's rear and destroy his headquarters and supply base at Manassas Junction (August 26). Pope then moved to attack Jackson in the belief that he was isolated from the main Confederate army. This led to the Second Battle of Bull Run (August 29–30). Confederate general James Longstreet hit Pope in the flank and sent the Union forces reeling back toward Bull Run. Major General Fitz-John Porter, who had refused to throw his corps into action the first day, was made the scapegoat for Pope's defeat and was cashiered, but McClellan also had failed to reinforce Pope in time.

Pope withdrew to the defenses of Washington, and Lincoln reluctantly replaced him with McClellan as commander of the Army of the Potomac. McClellan then reorganized his forces and moved to meet Lee, who in mid-August had begun an invasion of the North in the hope of cutting rail lines and isolating Washington, with Harrisburg as his probable ultimate objective. Again overestimating Confederate strength, McClellan proceeded in customary slow fashion. A fluke brought McClellan to Antietam, Maryland. Lee's entire operational plan had fallen into Union hands. Incredibly, McClellan was slow to take advantage, and it took him two days to cover the 10 miles to the South Mountain passes. On September 14 Confederate forces fought small, intense engagements for the passes, buying precious time for Lee to bring his scattered troops together. Lee ordered his men to concentrate at Sharpsburg.

On the afternoon of September 15, McClellan and some 55,000 men of the Army of the Potomac were within easy striking distance of Lee, just east of Sharpsburg with only 18,000 men. Hilly terrain allowed Lee to conceal his inferior numbers, but had McClellan moved that afternoon he would have enjoyed an overwhelming victory. McClellan delayed, and Jackson arrived in midday on July 16, having the day before taken the surrender of Harpers Ferry. That action netted the South 12,419 prisoners, 13,000 small arms, 73 cannon, 200 wagons, and considerable stocks of military equipment in what was the largest Union surrender of the war. Even with Jackson's corps, however, Lee was still outnumbered more than two to one: 41,000 to 87,000.

The battle began on the morning on September 17. McClellan threw away his great advantage of vastly superior numbers, holding an entire corps in reserve and employing a piecemeal rather than simultaneous form of attack, which was mirrored by subordinate units. McClellan also failed to utilize his cavalry to cut Confederate lines of communication and prevent reinforcements from reaching the battlefield from the south. Even a delay of an hour or two would have changed the battle, as Lee's remaining three divisions arrived on the battlefield in late morning, with the fighting already under way.

The Battle of Antietam was the bloodiest single day of the war. Union casualties totaled 2,108 dead, 9,540 wounded, and 753 captured or missing. Confederate losses were 1,546 dead, 7,752 wounded, and 1,018 captured or missing. These were fewer than those of the Union but nearly twice as great as a percentage of total force: 26 percent to 15 percent. Lee waited a day and then pulled back into Virginia with his prisoners and booty. McClellan trumpeted a victory but failed to pursue Lee effectively.

The Battle of Antietam, while inconclusive, was nonetheless one of the most important engagements of the war. Lee's defeat weakened Confederate hopes of securing recognition from Britain and France. Never again was the Confederacy this close to winning foreign diplomatic recognition. The Union victory also helped ensure that the Democrats did not win control of the U.S. House of Representatives in the November congressional elections. A single percentage's shift in the vote would have brought Democratic control and a push for a negotiated end to the war. Antietam also gave Lincoln the opportunity to issue the Preliminary Emancipation Proclamation, which he did on September 22. This freed all slaves in areas of the South still in rebellion as of January 1, 1863. The proclamation effectively gave the Union the moral high ground and greatly lengthened the odds against foreign recognition of the South. Lincoln, angered by Lee's escape, McClellan's procrastination in pursuing him, and a daring cavalry raid by General Stuart into Pennsylvania around Gettysburg (October 10–12), replaced McClellan with General Burnside on November 7.

Now under General Burnside, the Army of the Potomac advanced against Lee, arriving at the Rappahannock across from Fredericksburg on November 19, 1862. Pontoon bridges for the crossing had not arrived, but instead of immediately crossing in boats, Burnside elected to wait for the bridges. When they did arrive on November 27, the Confederates had reinforced. The crossing, which did not begin until very early on December 11, came under heavy Confederate rifle fire, but with massed Union artillery fire and the engineers using the pontoons as makeshift boats, bridges were placed, and the army

CIVIL WAR, 1863 – 1865

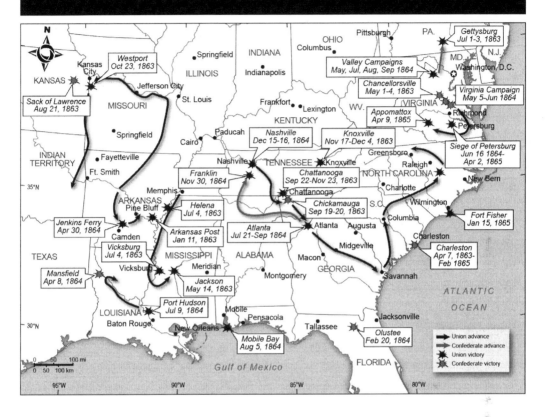

crossed by nightfall. Burnside spent the next day organizing the attack. Lee's army was now entirely in place and occupying excellent well-prepared defensive positions on high ground just west of the city. Burnside commanded some 120,000 men, Lee 78,000.

On December 13 Burnside ordered two attacks. The first was by Major General G. Gordon Meade on the Confederate right, commanded by Jackson. Meade achieved some success before his men were driven back by Confederate reinforcements, sent by Lee. The second attack, on the Confederate left, came against the heart of Lee's defenses on Marye's Heights directly behind Fredericksburg, where a shoulder-high stone wall ran for some 400 yards

and was defended by Confederate infantry two ranks deep. Six hundred yards of open field stretched between the Confederate position and the town, where the Union soldiers were located.

Burnside's assault on Marye's Heights began at noon and promptly came under devastating Confederate artillery fire. Lee also reinforced the defenders at the wall to four ranks deep, allowing the Confederates there to lay down a continuous hail of fire against 14 separate Union attacks, which ended only at nightfall. No Union soldier ever reached the wall, and few got within 50 yards.

The Battle of Fredericksburg was Lee's most lopsided victory of the war. The Union side suffered 12,653 casualties to only

4,201 for the Confederates. The Confederates also recovered 11,000 Union firearms.

On January 25, 1863, Lincoln replaced Burnside as commander of the Army of the Potomac with Major General Joseph Hooker, who accomplished much in retraining the army and building esprit de corps.

With the increasing need for manpower, both sides resorted to conscription. The Confederacy was first, in April 1862, followed by the North in March 1863. Individuals could avoid service by providing a substitute or making a cash payment. In the South, those owning 20 or more slaves were exempt. Whereas 20 percent of the Confederate Army was conscripted, only 6 percent of the Union Army was. Blacks also fought for the North; some 200,000 served, mostly in labor units, and under white officers, but black infantry regiments distinguished themselves in many battles.

On April 27, 1863, Hooker crossed the Rappahannock to the west of Fredericksburg with 130,000 men to attack Lee, with fewer than 60,000 men, at Chancellorsville. Seeking to take advantage of his greatly superior numbers, Hooker planned a double envelopment with the eastern pincer at Fredericksburg. But then Hooker suddenly halted to see what Lee would do. Hooker also erred in sending 10,000 cavalry in a wide sweep south well below Fredericksburg to destroy Confederate supply depots and lines of communication; this action uncovered the Union right wing and denied Hooker intelligence regarding Lee's intentions.

Lee now staged a double envelopment of a double envelopment, endeavoring with his far smaller force to surround a much larger one. Lee would demonstrate with about 17,000 men in front of the Union line while sending Jackson and 26,000 men in a movement around the Union right flank.

Success rested on Hooker's continuing failure to exploit the Confederate separation or determine Jackson's intentions.

Jackson struck on May 2. Although his force had been detected moving off, it was thought that it was retreating; indeed, Union major general Daniel Sickles advanced his men to attack, weakening the Union line. Jackson's attack was a complete surprise and enfiladed the Union lines. Union troops were sent reeling back in confusion. Increasing Union resistance, darkness, and the loss of Confederate unit cohesion in the heavily wooded Wilderness all prevented a Union catastrophe. That evening Jackson was shot by his own men in front of his own lines while reconnoitering and subsequently died of complications. On May 3, however, Stuart, who replaced Jackson, resumed the Confederate attack, further constricting Hooker's lines.

Another part of the battle, often known as the Second Battle of Fredericksburg, occurred on May 3. Major General John Sedgwick and 25,000 men advanced from Fredericksburg against 10,000 Confederates at Salem Church. Lee now feinted again. Leaving just a small force against Hooker, Lee turned east to deal with Sedgwick. Hooker did nothing, and Sedgwick, surrounded on three sides and unaided, retired back across the Rappahannock during the night of May 4.

On May 5 Hooker pulled his battered army back across the Rappahannock. The May 2–4 Battle of Chancellorsville was a military masterpiece but also the South's costliest victory. Union casualties were far higher than those for the Confederates—17,197 to 12,764—but the Union losses were 13 percent of effectives, while the Confederate casualties counted 21 percent. Particularly grievous was the loss of

Jackson. The Army of Northern Virginia was never quite the same without him.

Meanwhile, Union forces in the western theater were endeavoring to take the Confederate fortress of Vicksburg on the Mississippi. Attempts by the navy in May and June 1862 had met rebuff. Grant took command of the Army of the Tennessee in October 1862 and attempted a land assault (October 16–December 20) that had to be called off following a successful Confederate assault on his major supply base. Subsequent joint army-navy efforts to approach Vicksburg from the north via rivers and bayous during early 1863 were also unsuccessful.

Vicksburg, commanded by Lieutenant General John C. Pemberton, was ideally situated for defense and strongly fortified. It was most vulnerable from the south and east, but these were remote from Grant's supply base to the north at Memphis.

On March 29, 1863, Grant cut loose from his base, crossed the Mississippi above Vicksburg, and marched down the Louisiana shore of the river to a point south of the city where Rear Admiral David Dixon Porter's Mississippi Squadron, which ran the Vicksburg batteries on the night of April 16–17, ferried his men across the river (April 30). Grant planned to attack Vicksburg from the rear. Gambling boldly, he ignored Halleck's instructions to await reinforcements, which would also give the Confederates time to reinforce and fortify, and abandoned his river base at Grand Gulf and marched inland, carrying supplies in wagons and living off the land as much as possible.

Grant planned to place his own force between the Confederate forces at Vicksburg and Jackson, Mississippi, then destroy the latter and turn on the former. Following a series of small victories he took Jackson,

held by 6,000 Confederates, on May 14. Soon abandoned by Grant, the Confederates reinforced there, but Grant had destroyed it as a transportation and logistics center for Vicksburg. Pemberton now came out of Vicksburg to engage Grant. In a hard-fought battle at Champion's Hill (May 16), Grant with 32,000 men defeated Pemberton with 25,000. Pemberton then retired back into Vicksburg. Outnumbered at the outset although his opponents were divided, Grant had marched 200 miles in less than three weeks, won five battles, and inflicted 8,000 casualties.

After two futile assaults (May 19 and 22) against Vicksburg, Grant began a siege (May 22–July 4). With food running out and after a six-week bombardment, on July 4 Pemberton surrendered the city and more than 30,000 men. The remaining Confederate Mississippi stronghold, Port Hudson, surrendered on July 9. The entire river was now under Union control, and the Confederacy was split north to south.

At the same time as the Siege of Vicksburg was occurring, the most important of Civil War battles took place in the eastern theater. After considerable discussion and Lee's opposition, President Davis dropped plans to reinforce Vicksburg and accepted Lee's plan to invade Pennsylvania. This was not to relieve pressure on Vicksburg or to support a Southern peace offensive. It was, rather, a spoiling attack designed to give Virginia a reprieve, disrupt Northern war plans, and delay the next Union invasion.

At the end of May 1863, Lee's army was south of the Rappahannock River in and near Fredericksburg; Hooker's army was just north of the river. Hooker had some 85,000–90,000 men, and Lee had about 70,000. On June 3 Lee began moving west. He planned to move beyond the

Blue Ridge, march north and cross the Potomac River, and then threaten Philadelphia and Baltimore, cutting communications to Washington and putting pressure on Hooker to attack him in circumstances of Lee's choosing. Hooker meanwhile moved parallel to Lee, keeping his own army between Lee and Washington.

By the end of June, Lee's infantry and artillery crossed the Potomac. Lee, however, had heard nothing from his cavalry. Stuart, charged with screening the Confederate right flank and keeping Lee informed of Hooker's movements, had been forced farther east than planned, and as a result Hooker was able to get his entire army north of the Potomac unreported to Lee. Lee assumed that the Army of the Potomac was still in Virginia. Lee's own army was spread over 45 miles when on the evening of June 28 Lee learned that Hooker's entire army was in the vicinity of Frederick, Maryland, and much closer to the separate pieces of his army than those were to each other.

Lee ordered an immediate concentration at the road hub town of Gettysburg. The leading divisions of the Army of the Potomac were also headed there, but Hooker no longer had command. In what seemed a dangerous move with a major battle looming, on June 28 Lincoln named General Meade as the fifth commander of the Army of the Potomac in 10 months. Meade was solid and dependable, unlikely to be rattled by Lee.

Preliminary contact between the two armies occurred on June 30 at Gettysburg, with both sides rushing men forward. Lee was not happy that battle had been forced on him here by a premature engagement with Union troops. He had hoped to fight from prepared defensive positions at Cashtown to the northwest.

The Battle of Gettysburg, probably the most famous battle in American history, lasted three days (July 1–3). The two sides were about evenly matched. The Army of the Potomac had an advantage in manpower (some 94,000 to 72,000), but the men were exhausted and hungry after their forced marches to the battlefield. Meade also had an edge in artillery.

On July 1 the Confederates drove Union forces back through Gettysburg to strong positions on Culp's Hill and Cemetery Hill, themselves occupying Seminary Ridge, a long partially wooded rise running north and south paralleling Cemetery Hill. Although Union forces had purchased valuable time, this came at high cost; of 18,000 Union troops who fought that day, two-thirds were casualties.

July 2 saw the heaviest fighting. Union forces had the advantage of interior lines about three miles in length in what came to be called the Fishhook, for its shape. The Confederate positions around them were about six miles long. Meade could thus shift troops and supplies more quickly than Lee and was also able to communicate more effectively than his Confederate counterpart. Stuart, however, now arrived with his cavalry. Longstreet urged Lee to secure the two Round Tops at the southern extremity of the Union line and then swing in behind the Union forces, cutting them off from the rear. Lee, however, decided on a two-prong attack on the Union flanks. They were to be semisimultaneous, but Longstreet's orders reached him late, and much time was lost maneuvering to avoid Union lookouts on Little Round Top.

As it worked out, the Confederate attack on the two Round Tops to the south came two to three hours before that of Lieutenant General Richard Ewell on Culp's Hill on the Union right. Lee gave his corps commanders great discretion, but Ewell was no Jackson, and this was the first time he had commanded a corps in battle. Longstreet took Round Top but failed to take Little Round Top, which would have enabled him to enfilade the Union line. His men were turned back here by Colonel Joshua Chamberlain's badly outnumbered 20th Maine Regiment. Ewell's attack on Culp's Hill was also turned back, while Major General Jubal Early's men were driven off Cemetery Hill. The latter attack occurred at 8:00 p.m. in a desperate after-dark assault.

On July 3 Lee, having tested the Union flanks, proposed a massive frontal assault on the Union center, which was commanded by Major General Winfield Scott Hancock, perhaps the best Union general on the field. At the same time, Lee ordered Stuart and his cavalry to sweep around the Union positions from the north, then close on the center from the east. But Stuart's cavalry never got into the fray; they were halted five miles east of the battlefield and defeated there by Union cavalry.

At about 1:00 some 160 Confederate guns on Seminary Ridge opened fire, answered by more than 100 Union guns on Cemetery Ridge. The firing went on for two hours in the largest artillery duel in the history of North America. The Confederate guns largely overshot, with most of their damage coming in rear areas. The guns then fell silent, and the Confederate assault began across open ground a mile away on Seminary Ridge in ranks a mile wide with battle flags flying. Three divisions took part, but the other two melted away, and only that of Major General George Pickett remained, giving the name to Pickett's Charge. The Union guns

opened up when the attackers were about a half mile distant. Only several hundred Confederates reached the Union line, where there was hand-to-hand combat in what is often referred to as the "high-water mark of the Confederacy." Out of about 12,000–13,500 men, Pickett lost 8,000–10,000 that day.

Lee hoped that Meade would try to attack him the next day. Lee kept his defensive line, although shortening it from six to four miles. Meade rejected this course out of hand. He had sustained 23,000 casualties. Lee's losses, however, were at least as great and possibly as many as 28,000. When Meade failed to attack, on the night of July 4 Lee decamped, taking advantage of darkness and torrential rain to withdraw back down the Cumberland Valley. The Potomac was up, and for a time it looked as if Meade might catch Lee and pin him against the river, but the river went down, and Confederate engineers were able to construct a bridge so that Lee crossed over it on July 14 with his equipment, booty, and 6,000 Union prisoners. The South claimed Gettysburg a victory, but Lee and his men knew better. Gettysburg and Vicksburg decisively tipped the diplomatic balance in favor of the North. Confederate hopes of foreign recognition were gone.

In the western theater, General Braxton Bragg's second Confederate invasion of Kentucky brought victory over Buell in the Battle of Perryville (October 8, 1862), but a lack of support for the Confederacy in Kentucky soon forced Bragg to withdraw. Union major general William Rosecrans and his 60,000-man Army of the Cumberland then maneuvered Bragg's 43,000 Confederates out of Tennessee, defeating Bragg in the Battle of Stones River (December 31, 1862–January 2, 1863). The

Union suffered 12,906 casualties, the Confederates 11,739.

The prize was Chattanooga, a key rail center and gateway to the heart of the Confederacy. Bragg withdrew to Lafayette, Georgia, about 26 miles from Chattanooga, where he was reinforced to about 66,000 men. Rosecrans now blundered. Tricked into believing that Bragg was in full retreat, Rosecrans pushed ahead, with elements of his army sufficiently separated that they could not support each other.

Lying in wait along Chickamauga Creek, Bragg's men struck on September 19. Heavy fighting occurred along a four-mile front, but the Union lines held. On September 20 Bragg again attacked, trying to drive between the Union forces and their base at Chattanooga. The Union side held until misinformation led to a mistaken order by Rosecrans to shift an entire division, opening a gap in the Union line into which the Confederates poured and routed half the Union army. But Union general George Thomas ("the Rock of Chickamauga") took charge of the remaining Union troops and held, preventing catastrophe. Chickamauga was one of the most costly battles of the war. The Union reported 16,160 casualties, but Confederate losses were 18,454. Although Bragg could claim victory, he failed to mount a credible pursuit, dithering for four days and then deciding to take Chattanooga by siege. Meanwhile, Union reinforcements poured into that town.

Thomas now replaced Rosecrans in command of the Army of the Cumberland, while Grant took overall command of Union armies in the western theater on October 16. On November 23–25 Grant took the offensive in the Battle of Chattanooga (Lookout Mountain–Missionary Ridge), with Union forces under Generals Hooker, Thomas, and William T. Sherman defeating the Confederates under Bragg. With Union forces now in control of Chattanooga and key mountain passes, they were poised to bisect the upper and lower South by marching across Georgia to the sea. On December 3 Longstreet abandoned his siege of Union-held Knoxville, Tennessee, and ordered a retreat.

In March 1864 Grant was promoted to the newly revived rank of lieutenant general and given supreme command of the Union armies. Halleck became chief of staff, while Meade continued in charge of the Army of the Potomac, although Grant went with him in the field. Grant now proposed a methodical hammering away at Lee's army until it was defeated.

Grant planned a multifaceted and simultaneous offensive. In the western theater, Sherman would move across Georgia to Savannah, while at the same time Major General Banks would try to take Mobile. The Army of the Potomac, now more than 100,000 men, would drive south from Culpepper on Richmond, while Major General Benjamin Butler's 36,000-man Army of the James would march up the south bank of the James and cut Lee off from the lower South. Other Union forces would move against the Shenandoah Valley from the west and north to seize the railheads of Staunton and Lynchburg. To oppose Meade and Grant, Lee had 60,000 men, supported by Beauregard and 30,000 men in the Richmond-Petersburg area.

The Union Overland Campaign began on May 4 when the Army of the Potomac crossed the Rapidan River and entered the so-called Wilderness. Attacking the Union left flank, Lee used the heavily wooded terrain to offset the Union numerical advantage. In the ensuing Battle of the Wilderness (May 5–6), Lee inflicted some

18,000 casualties while sustaining 10,000, but for the first time after a fight with Lee, the Army of the Potomac continued south.

Grant repeatedly tried to outflank Lee, who anticipated Grant's moves and proved too quick for him. Bloody fighting occurred at Spotsylvania Court House (May 8–12), followed by a battle at Cold Harbor on the Chickahominy (June 1–3). Grant again assaulted a well-entrenched Confederate line, and on June 3 he sent three corps in a frontal assault against Lee; in seven minutes 7,000 Union troops were shot down. In one month of fighting Grant had suffered nearly 60,000 casualties, a figure equal to Lee's total strength, against Confederate casualties of 25,000–30,000. But the Army of Northern Virginia never really recovered from the heavy punishment inflicted.

Grant now sought to steal a march on Lee and move his army south of the James River to Petersburg, 20 miles below Richmond, in order to approach the Confederate capital from the rear and cut its transportation connections to the south and west. Butler's inept generalship prevented Grant from taking Petersburg, which withstood four days of battering on June 15–18, costing Grant another 8,000 casualties.

Both sides now dug in. A nine-month siege followed. On July 30, Union forces exploded a huge mine under the Confederate lines in a costly but unsuccessful attempt to break the siege.

Meanwhile, Union forces were endeavoring to secure the Shenandoah Valley. Major General Franz Siegel's men met defeat at the hands of Major General John C. Breckinridge in the Battle of New Market (May 15). Major General David Hunter then replaced Siegel and resumed the offensive, taking Staunton and reaching as far as Lynchburg before he was turned back by Confederate forces under General Early. When Hunter withdrew into West Virginia, Early embarked on an raid north into Maryland (June 28–July 21) that carried to five miles from Washington. After testing and finding the Washington defenses too strong, Early withdrew back into the valley.

During March 10–May 22, 1864, the Union mounted its largest combined operation of the war. The Red River Campaign was an attempt to capture Shreveport, Louisiana, and gain access to Texas from the east. Mansfield was the decisive battle of the campaign. There on April 8, Major General Richard Taylor and some 8,800 Confederates attacked and defeated Major General Nathaniel Banks's far larger but drawn-out Union march column, of which only about 12,000 Union troops were able to join the fray. Despite numerical superiority Banks then withdraw, necessarily followed by Rear Admiral Porter's Union naval force on the Red River. The expedition was a fiasco.

In the eastern theater, Grant gave Major General Philip J. Sheridan command of the Union Army of the Shenandoah in August and ordered him to clear the valley. Sheridan laid waste to it and defeated Early in a series of battles, including the Third Battle of Winchester (Opequon, September 19, 1864), the Battle of Cedar Creek (October 19), and finally the Battle of Waynesboro (March 2, 1865), after which Sheridan rejoined Grant.

In early May 1864, Sherman had set out from Chattanooga with 100,000 men to begin his invasion of Georgia. Johnston, who had replaced Bragg, was continually forced to retreat. For two and a half months Johnston slowed the advance of Sherman's superior forces to an average of only a mile a day, but his continued retreats led to Johnston's relief on July 19 and replacement with Lieutenant General John Bell Hood. In two pitched battles, Peachtree Creek (July 20) and Atlanta (July 22), he attacked Sherman but, after suffering heavy losses, withdrew into Atlanta's entrenchments.

Hood finally abandoned Atlanta, and Sherman entered the city on September 2. This Union victory severed Confederate communications westward and helped secure Lincoln's reelection, dashing the last Southern hopes for a negotiated settlement.

Sherman then destroyed such supplies as might be useful to the Confederates and set out with 60,000 men on a march to the sea (November 14–December 22, 1864), cutting a swath across Georgia some 300 miles in length and 60 miles in width. Union troops systematically destroyed factories, public buildings, warehouses, bridges, and railroads. Sherman encouraged foraging, and there was widespread looting. Sherman's advance was virtually unopposed, and on December 10 he reached Savannah, which fell on December 22.

Sherman's troops then moved northward through South Carolina, inflicting even greater destruction than in Georgia. Union forces burned more than a dozen towns in whole or in part, including much of the state capital of Columbia on February 17, 1865, although at least some of the fires resulted from deliberate Confederate destruction of cotton stores.

Meanwhile, Hood had set out after Union forces under Thomas and made contact with part of them under Major General John M. Schofield at Franklin, Tennessee. In a battle there on November 30, Hood with 22,000 men sustained 6,300 casualties in repeated frontal attacks against 28,000 Union troops in prepared defenses; Union losses were only about 3,100. Schofield then joined Thomas at Nashville, again defeating Hood in a two-day battle (December 15–16), with 55,000 Union troops inflicting 6,000 casualties on Hood's 30,000 men for half that number themselves.

Both sides and especially the Confederates suffered a difficult winter in the trenches at Petersburg. Grant now had an advantage of 115,000 men to Lee's 54,000. With Grant systematically hammering away at the Confederate lines, on April 1 Lee made his last assault of the war, against Grant's left flank at Five Forks near Petersburg, only to be repulsed by Sheridan coming up from the Shenandoah Valley. The next day, April 2, Lee evacuated Petersburg and Richmond and headed west, hoping to reach Lynchburg and then move by rail to North Carolina and join forces with General Johnston.

With Grant in pursuit, Lee's movement south and west was blocked by Sheridan's cavalry. Following a series of engagements and with few rations left, Lee surrendered his remaining force of fewer than 30,000 men on April 9 at Appomattox Court House. Grant paroled Lee's men and allowed them to return to their homes. On April 18 General Joseph Johnston surrendered his 37,000 men to Sherman. Some Confederate forces remained in the field into late May, and the Confederate commerce raider *Shenandoah* continued its depredations of American whalers in the Pacific until August.

Lincoln did not live to see the end of the war. After visiting Richmond on April 5, he returned to Washington to work on his plans for the peace and for reconciliation, not a popular policy in the North. On April 14 he was shot by a Southern sympathizer while attending a play at Ford's Theatre and died the next day. Vice President

Andrew Johnson succeeded him and tried to carry out Lincoln's reconstruction policies but was impeached in 1868, although acquitted. The war ended by declaration on May 9, although the last Confederate command surrender occurred on June 2, 1865.

Significance

The Civil War was by far the costliest U.S. war in terms of casualties. It claimed between 33 and 40 percent of the combined Union and Confederate forces. Union dead amounted to 360,000 (110,000 killed in battle or died of wounds) and 275,000 wounded. Confederate dead came to 258,000 (94,000 in battle or from wounds) and at least 100,000 wounded. In the South, one-quarter of all white males of military age lay dead. A study by J. David Hacker based on census statistics persuasively argues that the above long-accepted death toll should be increased by more than 20 percent, to some 750,000.

The United States had some 1 million men under arms at the end of the war, 183,000 by November 1865, and only 25,000 by the end of 1866. The number of Union Army generals went from 600 to 11.

The Civil War ended slavery in the United States, although it would be a century before African Americans achieved full civil rights. The war brought the modern staff system to the U.S. Army, the Medal of Honor, national cemeteries, and ultimately battlefield parks. Also, the war impoverished the South and brought more than a decade of Northern-imposed Reconstruction. At the same time, the war greatly stimulated economic activity in the North especially in the industrial sector, which placed the United States at the forefront of the Industrial Revolution. Preservation of the Union also meant that the United States would be able to fill the role of a major player in the family of nations. The war also probably hastened the British government's decision to create the Dominion of Canada in 1867.

Further Reading

Beringer, Richard E., et al. *Why the South Lost the Civil War.* Athens: University of Georgia Press, 1986.

Canney, Donald L. *Lincoln's Navy: The Ships, Men and Organization, 1861–65.* Annapolis, MD: Naval Institute Press, 1998.

Catton, Bruce. *The Civil War.* New York: Houghton Mifflin, 1987.

Davis, William C. *Look Away! A History of the Confederate States of America.* New York: Free Press, 2003.

Davis, William C. *Stand in the Day of Battle: The Imperiled Union, 1861–1865.* Garden City, NY: Doubleday, 1983.

Donald, David, Jean H. Baker, and Michael F. Holt. *The Civil War and Reconstruction.* New York: Norton, 2001.

Eicher, David J. *The Longest Night: A Military History of the Civil War.* New York: Simon and Schuster, 2001.

Foner, Eric. *The Fiery Trial: Abraham Lincoln and American Slavery.* New York: Norton, 2010.

Foote, Shelby. *The Civil War: A Narrative.* 3 vols. New York: Random House, 1968–1974.

Gallagher, Gary W. *The Confederate War.* Cambridge, MA: Harvard University Press, 1999.

Guelzo, Allen C. *Fateful Lightning: A New History of the Civil War and Reconstruction.* Oxford: Oxford University Press, 2012.

Hacker, J. David. "A Census-Based Count of the Civil War Dead." *Civil War History* 57 (2011): 307–348.

Hattaway, Herman, and Archer Jones. *How the North Won: A Military History of the Civil War.* Urbana: University of Illinois Press, 1981.

Jones, Howard. *Abraham Lincoln and a New Birth of Freedom: The Union and Slavery in the Diplomacy of the Civil War.* Lincoln: University of Nebraska Press, 1999.

McPherson, James M. *Battle Cry of Freedom: The Civil War Era.* Oxford: Oxford University Press, 1988.

McPherson, James M. *This Mighty Scourge: Perspectives on the Civil War.* Oxford: Oxford University Press, 2007.

Nevins, Allan. *The War for the Union.* 8 vols. New York: Scribner, 1947–1971.

Thornton, Mark, and Robert Burton Ekelund. *Tariffs, Blockades, and Inflation: The Economics of the Civil War.* Lanham, MD: Rowman and Littlefield, 2004.

Tucker, Spencer C., ed. *American Civil War: The Definitive Encyclopedia and Document Collection.* 6 vols. Santa Barbara, CA: ABC-CLIO, 2013.

Tucker, Spencer C. *Blue and Gray Navies: The Civil War Afloat.* Annapolis, MD: Naval Institute Press, 2006.

Tucker, Spencer C., ed. *The Civil War Naval Encyclopedia.* 2 vols. Santa Barbara, CA: ABC-CLIO, 2010.

Weigley, Frank R. *A Great Civil War: A Military and Political History, 1861–1865.* Bloomington: Indiana University Press, 2004.

Wars of German Unification (1864–1871)

Dates	1864–1871
Location	Germany, Denmark, Austria, France
Combatants	German states vs. Denmark; Prussia and Italy vs. Austria; Prussia and other German states vs. France
Principal Commanders	Prussia: Otto von Bismarck, Albrecht von Roon, Helmuth von Moltke Austria: Franz Joseph I, Ritter Ludwig August von Benedek, Archduke Albrecht, Wilhelm von Tegetthoff Italy: Émile Olivier, Alfonso Ferrero di La Marmora, Carlo Pellion di Persano France: Napoleon III, Émile Ollivier, Patrice de MacMahon, Achille Bazaine, Léon Gambetta, Louis Jules Trochu
Principal Battles	Dybbøl; Königgrätz (Sadowa), Fröschwiller (Wörth), St. Privat–Gravolette, Sedan, Metz, Orléans, Paris
Outcome	Germany is unified and the German Empire is proclaimed, with Germany acknowledged as the most powerful state of Europe.

Causes

For centuries Germany was little more than a geographical term. The division of Germany into many small states was very much in the interest of its neighbors, especially France. Efforts by successive Holy Roman emperors to unify Germany under their leadership ran afoul of religious turmoil and opposition from the princes and free cities. Germany became a battleground involving outside powers, including France, Denmark, Sweden, and Russia. The 16th-century wars of religion were destructive, but the Thirty Years' War of 1618–1648 may have claimed half the German population.

As a consequence of the Treaty of Westphalia of 1648, Germany was essentially atomized into some 350 different political entities, each able to conduct its own foreign policy and make alliances. This was a recipe for repeated outside intervention. Two states, Austria and Prussia, predominated, with the Habsburg rulers of Austria most often the Holy Roman emperors, the largely figurehead rulers of Germany.

The French Revolution and Napoleonic periods changed German attitudes, for Napoleon Bonaparte greatly stimulated German nationalism. France provided the example of what a unified, well-administered state might accomplish. Napoleon also had formed the Confederation of the Rhine and reduced the number of German political entities down from some 350 to only 38. Then in 1813 the German people were swept up in a war to expel the French, with many Germans believing that the overthrow of Napoleon would bring the desired unification of Germany.

It was not to be, for the Congress of Vienna of 1814–1815 basically reestablished the old system. There was a new confederation of German states, and with some reshuffling of territorial boundaries Napoleon's consolidation was allowed to stand, but the new political arrangement had Austria as its permanent president.

In 1848 revolutions swept much of Europe, and Germany was not immune. Indeed, revolutions occurred in both Prussia and Austria, but both were soon reversed. During that revolutionary year, however, German nationalists had elected the Frankfurt Assembly, which they hoped would yield a unitary state. The assembly sharply divided on the form of government and whether the new state should only include Germans. In the end it decided on a constitutional monarchy and a *kleindeutsch* (little German) approach, offering the crown to King Frederick William IV of Prussia. He, however, rejected what he called a crown "offered from the gutter," and the work of the Frankfurt Assembly came to

naught. The Prussian king's own plan for a smaller German state under Prussian leadership within a large entity that would include Austria was blocked by Austria and Russia in the 1850 Punctuation of Olmütz (known to many Germans as the "Humiliation of Olmütz"). The old German Confederation was restored. It was clear that if Germany was to be unified, it would come only in defiance of Austria, and Prussia was the only German state capable of that.

Significant change was taking place, however. For one thing, Germany was rapidly overcoming the economic deficiencies that had plagued it for 300 years. During 1850–1870 Germany's iron and coal production would increase sixfold, and by the latter date it was producing more iron than France. German cities were now linked by railroad and telegraph.

Much of this heightened economic activity was the result of the Zollverein, the customs union established by Prussia in 1819. Its purpose was to standardize tariffs in the various Prussian territories, but it proved to be a powerful incentive for unification. A great success, the Zollverein was expanded to other states. By 1848 it included all Germany except Hanover, Oldenburg, Mecklenburg, the three Hanse cities, and Austria. Prussian leaders did not want to see Austria in the union. The smaller German states were now bound to Prussia by strong economic ties.

Prussia hardly played a major role in European affairs in the 1850s, remaining neutral in the Crimean War of 1854–1856. In 1859 during the war with France and the Kingdom of Sardinia (Piedmont-Sardinia) against Austria, many German nationalists urged Prussian military intervention against France. Prince William, now directing Prussian affairs for his brother Frederick William IV, who was experiencing a mental breakdown, mobilized the Prussian Army, but Austria rejected Prussian demands for joint control over the forces of the German Confederation, and Prussia did not join the war. Austria was then obliged to conclude an armistice with France.

The Prussian mobilization revealed serious problems in its military, and William, who became king on his brother's death in 1861 and ruled until 1888, was determined to address them. William was convinced that Prussia could assert its proper role in German affairs only with a highly effective military force. Like Prussian king Frederick II (the Great), William believed that "diplomacy without arms is music without instruments."

William appointed Albrecht von Roon as minister of war with orders to expand and modernize the army. General Helmuth von Moltke became chief of the general staff. William sought a much larger army, but the Prussian Landtag (legislature) balked. The Landtag was dominated by men of wealth, and increasingly these were men associated with industry and not members of the landed aristocracy or Junkers, from which the officers of the army were drawn. The business classes could see little use for a large army in time of peace and balked at spending tax revenues on it. They believed that Prussia could best win the support of the smaller German states through the example of democratic reform.

An army bill introduced by the government in 1860 would have greatly increased the size of the standing army and brought compulsory military service. The Landtag was willing to go along but wanted the Landwehr or reserve army to be retained in the standing army and the period of military service reduced from three to two years. The government took the position that only the king could determine the size and composition of the army and that the sole function of the Landtag was to vote the funds required. Deadlock ensued, with liberal strength in the Landtag increased following new elections in December 1861 and larger numbers in yet another election in May 1862.

William believed army reform so important that he considered abdication. Roon urged that he govern in defiance of the Landtag, merely collecting existing taxes and spending them as he pleased. A forceful minister-president (chief minister) was needed, and Roon secured the appointment of his friend Otto von Bismarck, then Prussian ambassador to France. Bismarck, an archconservative and staunch Prussian patriot, assumed the post in September 1862 and announced at his first budget committee meeting that "The great questions of the day will not be decided by speeches and the will of majorities—that was the blunder of 1848 and 1849—but by iron and blood."

Bismarck, who was to be one of the great heroes of German history and one of the most important modern statesmen of the modern world, now controlled German affairs. He was the classic practitioner of realpolitik (politics of reality)—a complete opportunist for whom anything was acceptable to achieve the desired end. He now pursued war as an instrument of state policy.

As Bismarck anticipated, Prussian citizens continued to pay their taxes, regardless of the Landtag, and army expansion and modernization went forward. In 1863–1864 Bismarck, who had earlier served as ambassador to Russia, won the lasting gratitude of Czar Alexander II (r. 1855–1881) for sending Prussian troops to seal off the Prussian border with Poland during

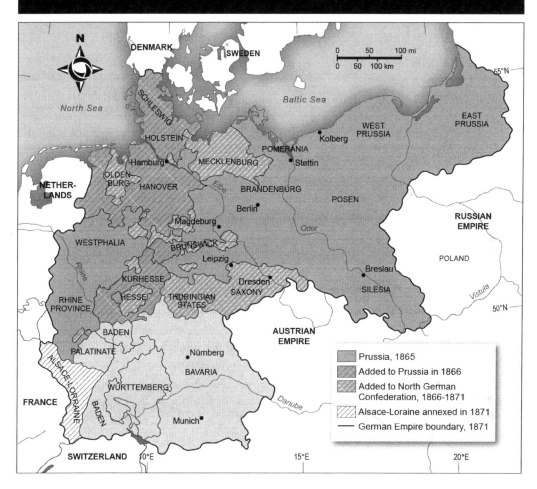

UNIFICATION OF GERMANY, 1864 – 1871

Legend:
- Prussia, 1865
- Added to Prussia in 1866
- Added to North German Confederation, 1866–1871
- Alsace-Loraine annexed in 1871
- German Empire boundary, 1871

a revolt there against Russian rule, greatly aiding the Russian Army in crushing it.

The first test of the Prussian Army reforms came in 1864 in a war with Denmark. The issue was complex, but the two duchies of Schleswig and Holstein in northern Germany contained a mixed population of Danes and Germans (Holstein was almost entirely German) and were the personal possession of the king of Denmark. In the revolutionary year of 1848, new Danish king Frederick VII had agreed to the incorporation of the two duchies into Denmark in lieu of losing his

throne, and many in the German population had protested and appealed to the Frankfurt Assembly, which called on military action. German troops, including those of Prussia, had invaded the duchies and Denmark. The Armistice of Malmö in December set up a joint commission of Danes and Germans to rule the two duchies, a situation unacceptable to either side. In February 1849 Denmark renounced the armistice, and fighting resumed. German troops again invaded Denmark, and a new armistice was concluded that July. In May 1852 Prussia, Austria, France, Russia,

Sweden, and Great Britain (though not the two duchies or the German Confederation) concluded the London Protocol, which settled the succession to the two duchies not on Frederik August, Duke of Augustenburg, who was supported by the German Confederation, but on Christian, Prince of Glücksburg. The southernmost duchy, Holstein, was to remain a member of the German Confederation.

Neither side was satisfied with the London Protocol, and on March 30, 1863, with the major powers occupied with the Polish Revolution, in a clear violation of the London Protocol, Frederick VII announced the annexation of Schleswig to Denmark. The Diet of the German Confederation demanded both duchies to be taken from Denmark and given to the rule of the Duke of Augustenburg. On October 1, the Diet voted for military action and called on Hanover and Saxony to furnish troops.

Frederick VII died on November 15, the day the Danish parliament voted a new constitution for Denmark and Schleswig. The Danish throne went to his designated successor, Christian, Prince of Glücksburg. The new king agreed to the new constitution, probably in lieu of losing his throne. Bismarck could now separate Prussia from the actions of the Diet of the German Confederation and claim that Prussia was merely upholding the London Protocol. He persuaded a reluctant Austria to join in alliance against Denmark, with the two powers to settle the future of Holstein and Schleswig "by mutual agreement" while secretly planning to annex both to Prussia. In mid-January 1864 Prussia and Austria demanded that Denmark abrogate the incorporation of Schleswig, threatening war if this was not done. The Danes refused, and what is sometimes called the Second Schleswig War began on February 1.

Course of the Second Schleswig War (1864)

When the Danes refused to withdraw their troops from Schleswig, on February 1 Austrian and Prussian forces crossed the Eider Canal, and the war began. The Second Schleswig War (February 1–October 30, 1864) was the first test of the reworked Prussian Army. Prussian field marshal Friedrich Graf von Wrangel commanded the allied force. The Prussians initially committed 38,400 men and 110 guns; later 23,000 additional men and 64 guns were sent. The Austrians committed 23,000 men and 48 guns.

The Danes were overconfident, and their strategic plan was flawed as a result of political interference. The Danish army numbered about 38,000 men, but for political reasons the defense was far to the south along the so-called Dannevirke Line 13.5 miles in length near the city of Schleswig, which required more men to be secure and was vulnerable to flanking attack.

The allies were able to turn the Danish flanks, and with the Dannevirke Line now a trap, on the night of February 5 Danish commander Lieutenant General Christian Julius De Meza withdrew his army northward, forced to leave behind some 150 heavy guns, to a secondary defensive position at Dybbøl, which the Danish political leadership demanded be defended to the last. The Siege of Dybbøl opened on March 17, with the Danes repelling a number of attacks. On April 2, Prussian siege guns commenced shelling the Danish positions. Fort Dybbøl fell on April 18 after a valiant defense to an assault by 10,000 Prussian infantry following a six-hour bombardment. The Prussians sustained some 1,200 casualties, the Danes 5,000 (including prisoners).

A conference in London beginning on May 12 came to naught largely owing to the efforts of Bismarck to torpedo it and the stubbornness of the Danes regarding territorial boundaries. Combat resumed, and the Danish troops were forced off the mainland and onto the islands. The last fighting occurred in early July. A preliminary peace treaty was concluded on August 1, 1864, with Christian IX renouncing all rights in the duchies in favor of Austria and Prussia. Casualties in the war were more than 1,700 Prussians and Austrians killed or wounded, while the Danes lost an estimated 1,570 killed, 700 wounded, and 3,500 taken prisoner.

In the definitive Treaty of Vienna of October 30, Denmark definitively ceded not only Schleswig and Holstein but also the Duchy of Lauenburg and enclaves in western Schleswig that were legally part of Denmark proper. The peace settlement decreased Danish land area by 40 percent and the population by almost the same, from 2.6 million to 1.6 million people.

Causes of the Austro-Prussian War (1866)

The Convention of Gastein of August 14, 1865, provided for joint Prussian and Austrian sovereignty over Schleswig and Holstein. Austria would administer Holstein, and Prussia would have charge of Schleswig. Lauenburg was awarded to Prussia outright in return for a payment of 2.5 million thalers. Austrian Schleswig was thus an enclave within Prussian territory.

Bismarck now skillfully worked to create tension between Prussia and Austria to bring about war. He was confident that Prussia could defeat Austria militarily, but he needed to secure the neutrality of the other major powers. Russia was still grateful to Bismarck for his actions in helping to put down the Polish revolt of 1863 and also wanted to see Austria humbled for having blocked its aspirations against the Ottoman Empire.

France was another matter, however. For centuries French interests had been served by a divided Germany. In October 1865, Bismarck met with French emperor Napoleon III at Biarritz and secured French neutrality by allowing Napoleon to believe that, following a Prussia victory, France would be allowed to annex Belgium and Luxembourg or receive other territorial compensation along the Rhine. On his part, Napoleon expected Austria to win the war or for it to be lengthy, as the last war between Prussia and Austria had lasted from 1756 to 1763. If protracted, France could enter the conflict late and dictate a settlement advantageous to itself.

Napoleon actually encouraged the war, urging Bismarck to take the Kingdom of Italy as an ally to tie down Austrian forces in the south and receive Venetia from Austria in compensation. Napoleon could thus gain credit with Italy as furthering Italian unification.

In November 1865 the Prussian government offered to buy Holstein outright from Austria in a cash settlement, as with Lauenburg. Vienna refused. This may have been Austrian emperor Franz Joseph I's worst mistake, for had Vienna done so, this would have made it far more difficult for Bismarck to create war.

Italy was at first reluctant to ally with Prussia in fear that Prussia might lose. So anxious for war was Napoleon, however, that he guaranteed Italy Venetia no matter the outcome. On April 8, 1866, Prussia and Italy concluded an offensive alliance against Austria in which Italy insisted that the war had to occur within three months.

On June 12 with war between Prussia and Austria apparently inevitable, Austria concluded a secret treaty with France. In return for a pledge by Napoleon III to work to ensure Italian neutrality, Austria agreed to cede Venetia to France, which would then cede it to Italy, no matter the war's outcome. In the event of an Austrian victory, Vienna would consult with Napoleon III on any major changes in Germany. Austria also made a verbal promise not to oppose the creation of a new French-dominated state along the Rhine.

Bismarck now worked to create the war. Casting himself as a good liberal, he ordered the Prussian representative to the Diet of the German Confederation at Frankfurt to demand that the body be abolished and a new German political entity based on universal manhood suffrage be created without the participation of Austria. The thrust of this, of course, was to bring on war.

Both sides commenced military mobilization, and Austria foolishly allowed its governor of Holstein on June 6 to call its Diet into session to discuss the future of the duchy. Bismarck denounced this as contrary to the Convention of Gastein and ordered Prussian troops into the duchy. On June 14 on the motion of Austria, the Diet of the German Confederation at Frankfurt voted for war against Prussia for the latter's invasion of Holstein. The vast majority of the German states, including Bavaria, Hanover, and Saxony, sided with Austria. Prussia declared this a violation of the federal constitution and also declared the German Confederation to be at an end.

Course of the Austro-Prussian War (1866)

Although the war also involved Italy, it is generally referred to as the Austro-Prussian War or, for its duration, the Seven Weeks' War. Bismarck intended it to be short. Fighting occurred in three theaters: Germany, Bohemia, and Italy.

Chief of the Prussian General Staff General von Moltke sought to make maximum use of the railroad and telegraph to strike quickly and catch his opponents by surprise. Austria, meanwhile, had done little to prepare for a two-front war that would involve Italy, which declared war on June 20.

With the south German states slow to mobilize, Moltke sent General Vogel von Falkenstein's 40,000-man West Army against Hanover's 19,000-man army under King George and General Alexander von Arentschildt before it could link up with the Bavarian Army. The West Army entered Hanover and converged on the Hanoverians at Langensalza (Bad Langensalza) from the south, west, and north.

Eager for glory, General Eduard Flies, commanding the southern Prussian force, disregarded Moltke's orders and attacked prematurely on June 27 before the other Prussian forces could arrive. Flies's men were badly mauled by the Hanoverians and were forced to withdraw in disorder. This victory went for naught, however, as the next day the other Prussian corps arrived, and on June 29 Hanoverian king George was forced to surrender at Nordhausen. The Prussians disarmed the Hanoverians and sent them home.

Meanwhile, the bulk of the German forces were moving southward against the Austrians, placed by intelligence reports concentrating northwest of Olmütz (present-day Olomouc in the Czech Republic). Moltke utilized the railroad to move and the telegraph to coordinate three separate Prussian armies. Prussian king Wilhelm I had nominal commands. The Army of the Elbe, under General Karl Herwarth von

Bittenfeld, occupied Dresden in Saxony on June 19, then moved to join the First Army under Prince Friedrich Karl to enter Bohemia via passes in the Erzgebirge and Riesengebirge during June 22–23. Meanwhile, the Second Army under Crown Prince Friedrich moved south through Silesia.

At Münchengrätz on June 28, the Army of the Elbe and the First Army joined to defeat retreating Saxon troops under Prince Albert and the Austrian I Corps under General Count Eduard Clam-Gallas. The Prussians suffered 341 casualties and inflicted some 2,000 (1,400 of them prisoners). There was also fighting at Burkersdorf, Rudersdorf, and Skalice (Skalitz).

Austrian general Ritter Ludwig August von Benedek commanded the Austria North Army and allied Saxon forces in Silesia. An incompetent strategist whose military experience was confined to Italy, he had never before commanded large numbers of troops. Meanwhile, the far more capable field marshal Archduke Friedrich Rudolf Albrecht was assigned command of Austrian forces in Italy, where the House of Habsburg was most likely to be victorious.

On July 2, Moltke learned that Benedek's North Army was concentrating along the upper Elbe, north of Königgrätz (today Hradec Králové). The Austrians were within striking distance of two of Moltke's armies, Bittenfeld's Army of the Elbe and Prince Friedrich Karl's First Army. In numbers of men, the two sides were about equal. Moltke commanded about 221,000 men and 702 guns, while Benedek commanded some 206,000 men (184,000 Austrians and 22,000 Saxons) and 650 guns. The Prussians had a distinct advantage in small arms, however. Their Dreyse breech-loading needle gun could fire six times as fast as the Austrian Lorenz muzzle-loader.

Moltke, who was in contact with all three of his advancing armies by telegraph, attempted a double envelopment. That night, however, the telegraph link with Crown Prince Friedrich's Second Army broke down. Moltke nonetheless decided to proceed with the other two armies and sent a courier to ride the 20 miles to the crown prince to tell him to bring up his army as soon as possible.

The ensuing Battle of Königgrätz (Hradec Králové), also known as the Battle of Sadowa (Sadová), was the largest European land battle until World War I. The Army of the Elbe and the First Army attacked in a pouring rain at dawn on July 3. Crowded onto too narrow a front, they thus were ideal targets for the Austrian artillery but were saved only by foolish Austrian bayonet counterattacks, which forestalled the artillery and brought little result. Nonetheless, by 11:00 a.m. the Austrians had blunted the Prussian attacks. Benedek might have won the day had he committed his cavalry, but he refused. At about 1:30 p.m., the Prussian Second Army at last arrived and fell on the Austrian northern line, quickly reversing the situation. Benedek ordered a retreat, covered by his artillery. Moltke did not pursue.

Austrian and Saxon losses were nearly five times those of Prussia. The Prussians sustained some 9,000 casualties (1,900 killed, 6,800 wounded, and 275 missing). Austrian and Saxon losses were roughly 44,000 (5,735 killed, 8,440 wounded, some 22,000 prisoners, and 7,925 missing). Austria also lost 116 guns. The battle was decisive. With its heavy losses, on July 22 Vienna had no choice but to agree to an armistice on Prussian terms.

To the south, the Italian strategic plan called for an invasion of Austrian Venetia along the Mincio and Po Rivers by 200,000 men and 370 guns, defended by Archduke Albrecht's Austrian South Army, with only 75,000 men and 168 guns. The critical battle of the campaign occurred at the old battlefield of Custoza, southwest of Verona. In a major tactical blunder, Italian commander General Alfonso Ferrero di La Marmora, who was unaware of the South Army's strength and dispositions, managed to get only 65,000 troops and 122 guns across the Mincio before they were confronted by virtually the entire Austrian South Army.

In the daylong Battle of Custoza on June 24, the Austrians defeated the Italians piecemeal, with the Austrian Light Cavalry Brigade playing the major role and the Italians driven back across the Mincio into Lombardy. Albrecht did not pursue. The Italians suffered 3,800 killed or wounded and 4,300 taken prisoner. Austrian casualties were 4,600 killed or wounded and 1,000 missing. Despite the outcome of the battle, on July 3 Napoleon III arranged the transfer of Venetia to France, then ceded it to Italy.

Given command of 10,000 men and a flotilla on Lake Garda, Italian general Giuseppe Garibaldi fought a series of small, indecisive engagements with the Austrians during July 3–21. He was about to attack Trent when he was ordered to withdraw. Bismarck made it clear to the Italian government that it would not be allowed to secure part of the Trentine Tyrol.

The only sea battle of the war was at Lissa in the Adriatic on July 20, between virtually the entire Italian and Austrian Navies. Commanders proved important. The incompetent Admiral Count Carlo Pellion di Persano commanded the Italians; capable young rear admiral Wilhelm von Tegetthoff had charge of the Austrian side. Persano sortied on July 15. He proceeded

not to Pola, where the Austrian fleet was located, but against the Austrian island of Lissa. For two days the Italians bombarded Lissa with little effect. Persano was landing men there when informed of the Austrian approach. Tegetthoff had 21 ships, Persano 31. Each side had a half dozen ironclads. Tegetthoff immediately attacked and won the battle, with the Italians withdrawing. The Italians lost 2 ships; 4 others were badly damaged (1 of which subsequently sank). They also suffered 619 dead and 39 wounded. The Austrians had only several ships damaged and 38 men killed and 138 wounded. The Battle of Lissa was the first between oceangoing ironclad fleets at sea and the only major fleet encounter between ironclads in which the principal tactic was to ram the opposing vessel.

On July 5 a badly shaken Napoleon III had offered his good offices to end the war. Bismarck accepted on condition that the terms of peace were agreed to before any armistice was concluded. Napoleon, ill and his army unready to intervene, agreed to the Prussian terms imposed in the Preliminary Peace of Nikolsburg in southern Moravia on July 26. Prussia annexed the states of Hanover, Hesse-Kassel, and Nassau as well as the free city of Frankfurt. The German Confederation was abolished, and Austria was excluded from German affairs. Prussia then reorganized Germany north of the Main River into the North German Confederation under its leadership. The south German states of Bavaria, Baden, and Württemberg remained independent. King William I wanted an indemnity, a parade in Vienna, and additional territory from Austria, but Bismarck set himself against this and won his point. Austria retained all its territory, and there was no indemnity. The August 23 Peace of Prague merely confirmed these terms.

The long struggle between Prussia and Austria for mastery in the Germanies, which began with the War of the Austrian Succession in 1740, was over. Prussia now dominated Germany.

Causes of the Franco-Prussian War (1870–1871)

With the end of the Austro-Prussian War, on August 5, 1866, Napoleon III put forth his claims for compensation. Bismarck rejected these out of hand. Indeed, Bismarck used the French demands as proof of that country's aggressiveness to secure defensive military alliances with the three south German states of Bavaria, Baden, and Württemberg.

When Napoleon continued to press the issue, Bismarck requested that French ambassador to Prussia Count Vincent Benedetti put the French demands in a draft treaty. In it Napoleon III proposed that France be awarded Luxemburg and Belgium, while also agreeing to the union of north and south Germany under Prussian leadership. Bismarck used personal illness as an excuse not to respond and, in December, rejected the treaty outright. In 1870 he released the draft treaty to the press, helping to win support for Prussia abroad, particularly in Britain.

Bismarck knew that he could not realize his dream of fully unifying Germany under Prussian leadership without first defeating France. Napoleon III had been humiliated by events, outwitted by Bismarck at every turn. French leaders were bent on revenge. They did little to prepare their country for war, however. Austrian leaders, made aware of France's duplicity, were now hostile to that country, while Russian leaders remembered France's leading role in the Crimean War of 1854–1856. Britain, meanwhile, held itself aloof.

Convinced that his own forces were ready for war with France, in 1870 Bismarck attempted to isolate that country further and perhaps create circumstances for armed conflict by presenting Paris with a diplomatic fait accompli. In 1868 a revolution had occurred in Spain, and Bismarck intrigued to place Prussian Catholic prince Leopold of Hohenzollern Sigmaringen on its throne. The French government learned of the plan, and Foreign Minister Duc Antoine de Gramont demanded through ambassador to Prussia Benedetti that the candidacy be withdrawn. Prussian king Wilhelm I, at Ems and away from Bismarck in Berlin, agreed.

France thus achieved a limited diplomatic victory, but Gramont wanted to inflict a personal defeat on Bismarck and ordered Benedetti to secure a pledge that no Prussian prince would ever be a candidate for the throne of Spain. Wilhelm politely but firmly rejected the request and communicated this to Bismarck, who then edited the communication and released it to the press. This famous Ems Dispatch was so cleverly worked and presented that it inflamed opinion in both France and Prussia and ultimately led to war. Bismarck's hand in events was not clear to most Europeans at the time, who blamed France for the conflict. That was certainly the prevailing attitude in Britain.

In the meantime, French government ministers had whipped up public opinion to the point that it was next to impossible to back down. Premier Émile Ollivier encouraged the national illusions by announcing that he "accepted war with a light heart." But despite Minister of War Edmund Leboeuf's assertions that the army was ready "down to the last gaiter button," this was far from the case. Among French leaders, only Napoleon III expressed doubts.

On July 15, 1870, the French Corps Législatif (lower house of parliament) voted war credits. Prussia mobilized immediately. From this point there was no wavering on either side, and on July 19 the French government declared war.

Course of the Franco-Prussian War (1870–1871)

The Franco-Prussian War of 1870–1871 deserves to be known as the Franco-German War as Prussia's defensive treaties with the south German states came into operation; in effect, France had blundered into war with all Germany. By the end of July, Moltke had positioned three armies of some 386,000 men in the Rhineland along the French frontier: General Karl F. Von Steinmetz's First Army of 66,000 men, Prince Friedrich Karl's Second Army of 175,000 men, and Crown Prince Friedrich Wilhelm's Third Army of 145,000 men. Moltke held 95,000 troops in reserve until it was certain that Austria would not intervene. King Wilhelm I had nominal command, but Moltke exercised actual command authority. The Prussians were fully prepared for the war, and their military intelligence and maps of France were both excellent.

All was confusion on the French side, however. France's military mobilization was not even complete by the time the war began. The French had 224,000 men in eight army corps. The army had élan, but its recent military experience was in North Africa. French weaponry was equal or superior to that of the Prussians in all except heavy artillery, Leboeuf having rejected an opportunity to acquire new breech-loading Krupp artillery before the war. Logistical arrangements were sadly lacking, and ammunition was in short supply. There was no general staff in the Prussian sense of the term, and the senior French military leadership was inept and unimaginative. Intelligence regarding Prussian dispositions was nonexistent. French units were not even issued maps of France; the army presumed that the fighting would be entirely on German soil. French numbers were sufficient to fight a delaying action until additional manpower could be brought up, but the French were thinking only of an invasion of Germany. The strategic plan was that espoused by the French public: "À Berlin!"

At the end of July, Napoleon III ordered a general advance into Germany. The emperor was not well but nonetheless chose to personally accompany the army in the field. Napoleon III grouped his eight separate corps into two armies: the Army of Lorraine of five corps under Marshal François Achille Bazaine and the Army of Alsace of three corps under Marshal Patrice MacMahon, Duc de Magenta. On August 2, Bazaine's advancing forces encountered the Prussians in the Saar at Saarbrücken. With six divisions to only one Prussian infantry regiment supported by limited artillery and cavalry, the French won the engagement.

On August 4, however, Prussian crown prince Friedrich Wilhelm's Third Army invaded eastern Alsace and at Wissenbourg, along the Lauter River, completely surprised General Abel Douay's leading division of MacMahon's army. In a battle pitting 50,000 advancing Prussians and Bavarians against only 6,000 French, the outcome was hardly in doubt. The French suffered some 1,600 killed or wounded, with 700 prisoners, against German casualties of 700 killed and 850 wounded.

On August 6, 1870, also in Alsace, Crown Prince Friedrich Wilhelm's Third Army met MacMahon's Army of Alsace near the village of Fröschwiller (Wörth), on the Sauer River. MacMahon counted on having 78,000 men available, but the failure of one of his corps commanders to obey orders gave him only 48,000 men and 119 guns. Deploying 125,000 men and 312 guns, Friedrich Wilhelm attempted a double envelopment. The sheer weight of German numbers and their superior artillery decided the battle.

MacMahon sacrificed his cavalry and escaped, withdrawing without German pursuit to Châlons-sur-Marne during August 7–14. German losses were 10,500 killed or wounded and 1,373 missing. French casualties were about the same in killed or wounded (10,760), but they also lost 9,200 men captured. The battle opened the way for a German advance on Paris.

That same day, August 6, Steinmetz's First Army and Prince Frederick Karl's Second Army were advancing on Saarbrücken when they discovered General Charles Auguste Frossard's II Corps of the Army of Lorraine. Bazaine had separated his forces into three major bodies, none within supporting distance of the other. The ensuing battle had the German First Army and a corps of the Second Army attacking the French II Corps on the Spicheren heights to the southeast of Saarbrücken. Bazaine was slow to reinforce Frossard, who held off the Germans for an entire day. Threatened with envelopment, the French withdrew at nightfall. Of nearly 30,000 men engaged, the French lost 1,982 killed or wounded and more than 2,000 missing, with the majority of these taken prisoner. Of their 45,000 troops committed to the battle, the Germans lost 4,491 killed or wounded and 371 missing.

Ill and shaken by the French defeats, Napoleon III ordered Metz abandoned.

His defeatism rapidly spread through the army. On August 12 Napoleon yielded field command to Bazaine, who now commanded a reorganized Army of the Rhine. Napoleon departed for Châlons-sur-Marne to join MacMahon's efforts to reconstitute his army.

Determined to give the French no respite, Moltke pushed his First and Second Armies against Bazaine on a wide front, attempting to place his own forces between the two French armies and threaten Bazaine's line of communications westward. Steinmetz's First Army forced Bazaine to withdraw the Army of the Rhine across the Moselle in the hopes of reaching Verdun and linking up with MacMahon, but Prince Friedrich Karl's Second Army cut him off. In the ensuing battle between Borny and Colombey on August 14, Prussian general Karl von der Goltz attacked with his VII Corps, and instead of continuing his withdrawal as Napoleon III ordered, Bazaine decided to stand and fight.

Although the French lost some 3,500 men killed or wounded (Bazaine slightly by a shell fragment) against Prussian losses of nearly 5,000 men, the Prussians had delayed by a day Bazaine's effort to escape from Metz. Not until late in the morning of August 15 did Bazaine order a continuation of the retreat.

On August 16, Prince Friedrich Karl's Second Army again engaged Bazaine's Army of the Rhine, on the Verdun-Metz road. Beginning as a piecemeal engagement, this became a large-scale battle, with the German infantry pushing into Rezonville. The French suffered 13,761 casualties to 15,780 for the Germans. The battle was a strategic victory for the Prussians, however, as Bazaine now abandoned his withdrawal and retired back on the fortress of Metz.

The bulk of the German armies, some 200,000 men, now moved into the area between Metz and Paris, and Motlke assumed personal command of the Second and First Armies facing Bazaine. Moltke attacked, hoping to destroy the Army of the Rhine. The battle was fought between the villages of St. Privat la Montaigne and Gravolette, with the major point of combat the walled village of St. Privat. This battle differed from previous engagements in its great size, for it pitted more than 188,000 Prussians with 732 guns against 112,000 French with 520 guns.

At St. Privat, Second Army commander Prince Friedrich Karl sent in the elite Prussian Guard against Marshal François Certain Canrobert's VI Corps. Bazaine ignored Canrobert's pleas for reinforcement, but the latter's 23,000 men held against some 100,000 attacking Prussians, who lost 8,000 men. Not until the arrival of a Saxon corps to the north that threatened to cut him off did Canrobert withdraw toward Metz.

On the French right, meanwhile, two Prussian corps battled their way east of Gravolette only to become trapped in a ravine, leading to a panicked withdrawal. The French counterattack was checked only by effective Prussian artillery fire and Moltke's personal intervention with reinforcements.

Although the French withdrew, the Germans had lost some 20,163 men, the French only 12,273. The tragedy of St. Privat–Gravolette for the French was that had Bazaine made a concerted effort there he would most likely have won a victory and broken free. As it was, on August 19 the French were back at Metz, where the Prussians sealed them in. The separation of their two field armies proved disastrous for France.

Responding to urgent appeals by the French government, on August 21 MacMahon set out from Châlons-sur-Marne with 120,000 men and perhaps 450 guns to try to relieve Bazaine at Metz. MacMahon's only chance at success rested on speed, which was beyond the capability of his large, poorly trained, and badly equipped army. Napoleon III accompanied MacMahon in an operation that was in any case widely reported in the French press and known to the Prussians.

Foolishly, MacMahon selected a northerly approach, allowing Moltke to execute a turning movement against him. Leaving his First Army and a part of the Second Army to continue the investment of Metz, Moltke ordered the remainder of the Second Army, now designated the Army of the Meuse and commanded by Crown Prince Albrecht of Saxony, to join him and Prussian crown prince Friedrich Wilhelm's Third Army against MacMahon.

MacMahon crossed the Meuse River at Douzy with part of his army as Moltke was bringing up his forces. Prince Albrecht's Army of the Meuse was to serve as the anvil for the hammer of Prince Friedrich Wilhelm's far larger Third Army. Albrecht's advancing forces encountered the French at Nouart on August 29, with the two sides together sustaining some 600 casualties.

Major fighting occurred the next day, August 30, at Beaumont when two Bavarian Army corps came on the camp of French general Pierre Louis de Failly's V Corps unawares, with no sentries posted. The immediate Bavarian attack drove the French eastward to the Meuse. The French lost some 7,500 men, the Germans 3,500. The Germans also captured considerable French equipment, stores, guns, and horses. That night MacMahon ordered his army to fall back on the fortress of Sedan on the Meuse River some 120 miles northeast of Paris and close to the Belgian border.

Moltke now assembled against MacMahon 250,000 Prussian and Bavarian troops, along with some 500 artillery pieces. Although the French established their positions on high ground, the Germans held still higher ground dominating the city and its environs. The Battle of Sedan opened at dawn on September 1 with a German artillery bombardment against 85,000 French troops packed into an area of less than two square miles. The more modern breech-loading rifled Prussian guns outranged the French artillery.

Napoleon III, who was with the army but ill from kidney stones, seemed resigned to his fate. Heedless of danger, he rode about to encourage the men, perhaps hoping for martyrdom that might help secure the throne for his son. French marines mounted a fine defensive stand in the outlying village of Bazeilles, but it was nonetheless lost.

MacMahon was wounded early in the battle and thus escaped onus for the result. His successor, General Auguste Ducrot, immediately ordered an attempt to break out. Before this could be accomplished, however, General Emmanuel de Wimpffen arrived, having been appointed to command by the Ministry of War. Wimpffen countermanded Ducrot's order and insisted that Bazeilles be retaken.

That afternoon the Germans repelled desperate French cavalry charges by the Chasseurs d'Afrique at Floing, a mile north of Sedan. With French casualties steadily mounting in what was clearly a lost cause, Napoleon III took the initiative and, despite Wimpffen's objections, opened surrender talks. A truce was arranged that evening. Talks continued into the night, and the next

morning, September 2, Napoleon insisted that Wimpffen sign a surrender document. The emperor was among the 83,000 French soldiers taken prisoner. He was escorted to Bismarck and King William I, who were with Moltke observing the battle.

The Germans secured substantial French supplies, more than 1,000 wagons, 6,000 horses, and 419 guns. Prior to the surrender, the Germans had captured another 21,000 Frenchmen. French dead numbered 3,000; another 17,000 were wounded and among the prisoners. Prussian and Bavarian losses totaled about 9,000.

The way to Paris was now completely open, and news of the French defeat at Sedan brought political upheaval in the capital. Crowds converged on the Corps Législatif and established the Third French Republic. General Louis Jules Trochu, commander of the Paris garrison, was the new president.

Full of the myth of the Battle of Valmy in 1792, many Frenchmen believed that a great national effort might yet bring victory. Dynamic young Léon Gambetta, the chief figure in the new government, became both minister of war and minister of the interior and set about organizing the national defense. On September 6, Foreign Minister Jules Favre announced that France would not yield an inch of its soil.

On September 19, troops of the Prussian Third Army and the Army of the Meuse reached the outskirts of Paris and commenced siege operations. Although several forts guarded the city and it was also ringed by a bastioned enceinte, very little had been done to prepare for a prolonged siege, including laying in supplies. Trochu manned the defenses with 120,000 soldiers (including veterans, reservists, and 20,000 marine infantry), 80,000 Gardes mobiles (untrained recruits under the age of 30), and 300,000 Gardes nationales (untrained recruits between the ages of 30 and 50). By September 23, Paris was completely surrounded. Eventually the only way out was by balloon.

The Prussians set up their headquarters at the château of Versailles outside the city. Moltke had no intention of trying to take Paris by storm but ringed it with two belts of German troops, cut off food supplies, and waited for hunger to do its work.

On October 7 in order to organize other forces for the relief of Paris, Gambetta made the hazardous trip out by balloon and then traveled on foot to southeastern France. Gambetta had reason to hope, for Bazaine and his 173,000-man Army of the Rhine, although besieged at Metz, were nonetheless tying down there 135,000 Germans. The Siege of Paris required another 250,000 German troops, while other forces were necessary to maintain the lines of communication to the German frontier, now under harassment from irregular French forces (franc-tireurs), who were shot out of hand when captured by the Germans. Gambetta's hopes were dashed, however, when the defeatist Bazaine surrendered Metz on October 27.

Bazaine had rejected a Prussian offer of the honors of war and inexplicably refused to order the destruction of his arms. The Prussians thus gained 600 French guns in working order. More important, Bazaine's action released the Prussian First and Second Armies for operations elsewhere. Although surrender of Metz was inevitable, by careful planning Bazaine might have held out at least until mid-November.

Gambetta, meanwhile, organized new forces in the south as the Army of the Loire. Mistakenly believing that Paris could not hold out long, Gambetta sent his inadequately trained and equipped forces into combat prematurely in November 1870. This led to large-scale combat in the Loire and Sarthe Valleys against Prussian veterans drawn from the Siege of Paris.

On November 9, 1870, the 70,000-man Army of the Loire commanded by General D'Aurelle de Paladines attacked the I Bavarian Corps of 20,000 men and 110 guns under General Ludwig Freiherr von und zu der Tann-Rathsamhause at Coulmiers about 12 miles northwest of Orléans. For the first time employing percussion fuses in their shells, the French artillerymen wreaked havoc on the Bavarians, who withdrew that afternoon. The Germans then withdrew from Orléans.

The Army of the Loire offensive was soon halted by the arrival of German reinforcements released by the surrender of Metz, however. On November 28, German forces defeated an attack by the Army of the Loire at Beaune-la-Rolande, an attack undertaken under objection by de Paladines and with the Germans having intercepted letters from Gambetta and army orders that enabled them to anticipate the French moves. In the fighting the French sustained 1,300 men killed or wounded and 1,800 captured. German losses were fewer than 900.

Fighting also continued on the perimeter around Paris, despite increasingly difficult conditions inside the city. Paris was now alone in its hunger, cold, and disease. A black market flourished, with all manner of animals sold for gold. Plague also arrived and reached alarming proportions.

Three times Trochu attempted to break the siege: in November, December, and January. All were unsuccessful, although the strongest attempt, on November 29–30 by 140,000 men and 400 guns, almost broke free and destroyed a Bavarian corps before it was turned back.

On December 2–4 the French Army of the Loire attempted to break through the German lines and raise the siege. Fighting was heavy, with the German troops being those of Prince Friedrich Karl's Second Army, released from the siege of Metz. In the fighting on December 2 at Poupry and Loigny, sometimes referred to as the Battle of Orléans, 35,000 German defenders defeated 45,000 French attackers. The French suffered 6,000–7,000 killed or wounded and 2,500 prisoners, while German killed or wounded were only 139. Gambetta ordered Paladines to withdraw southwesterly to Bordeaux.

Taking the offensive, the Germans cut the largely untrained Army of the Loire in two. Reoccupying Orléans on the night of December 4–5, the Germans held this important crossing point on the Loire for the remainder of the war. In additional fighting, the French lost 2,000 killed or wounded and 18,000 prisoners.

Fighting continued in northern France, where in early December General Louis Léon Faidherbe took command and engaged the Germans at the Hallue River (December 23) and Bapaume (January 2–3, 1871). In the Battle of Saint-Quentin of January 19, however, Faidherbe suffered a major defeat by reinforced German forces under General August Karl von Goeben, losing 3,000 killed or wounded and 11,000 missing, or a third of his army of 43,000. Faidherbe then distributed the remainder of his men among the northern French fortresses, bringing an end to fighting in the north.

On January 5, 1871, on Bismarck's insistence, the Germans commenced shelling Paris on the assumption that this would hasten its capitulation. During January 5–26 an estimated 12,000 shells fell on the city, inflicting some 400 civilian deaths

but if anything hardening the French will to resist.

Moltke also ordered Prince Friedrich Karl to finish off the French Army of the Loire, now commanded by General Antoine Eugène Chanzy. Fighting centered on the city of Le Mans, defended by the French, where the Germans defeated the French during January 10–12, inflicting French losses of more than 25,000 killed, wounded, and captured. Another 50,000 French soldiers deserted. German losses were perhaps 3,400. The battle ended French resistance in the south. Chanzy withdrew with the remainder of his forces, first to Alençon and then toward Laval.

In eastern France only one major French fortress still held out, that of Belfort in Franche-Comté. In December 1870 General Charles Denis Sauter Bourbaki had assumed command of the virtually untrained and ill-equipped 110,000-man French Army of the East, and he now advanced on Belfort to raise the siege of that place by 40,000 German troops under General Karl Wilhelm Werder.

During January 15–17, Bourbaki attacked Werder's positions along the Lisaine River line. The battle was hard-fought, but confusion in orders, Bourbaki's lack of drive, the ineptitude of Italian Giuseppe Garibaldi (fighting as a volunteer general on the French side), terrible weather, and the inexperience of the French soldiers, coupled with the competence of the well-trained Germans, gave the Germans victory. The French sustained more than 6,000 casualties, the Germans nearly 1,900. Bourbaki attempted suicide but only wounded himself. General Justin Clinchant succeeded to the command.

With the arrival of another German army under Edwin von Manteuffel, Clinchant's men were in danger of being crushed between the two German forces. Abandoning much equipment, he crossed into western Switzerland with some 80,000 men on February 1. The Swiss disarmed his men, interning them until the end of the war, when they were repatriated.

With the end of the war fast approaching, on January 18, 1871, in the great Hall of Mirrors at Versailles, the seat of French power and hegemony over Europe during the reign of King Louis XIV, Bismarck announced the establishment of the German Empire. The Crown was to rest with the House of Hohenzollern, with Prussian king Wilhelm I as emperor. The constitution of the North German Confederation was then modified to include the south German states of Baden, Bavaria, and Württemberg. Although the states retained considerable power in the new empire, the constitution was structured so as to assure the domination of Prussia and the emperor.

On January 19 the French mounted a sortie from Paris by 90,000 men, about half of them members of the Garde Nationale. It failed utterly, although the French successfully resisted the German counterattacks. In this Battle of Buzenval, the French sustained some 4,000 killed or wounded against German losses of only 700. The battle sealed the fate of Paris and gave finis to the myth that untrained mass levies could defeat a well-trained professional army.

Cold, lack of food and fuel, and the spread of disease brought the Siege of Paris to an end on January 28. On that date, with only about a week of food remaining and despite strong objections by Gambetta, Favre accepted Bismarck's armistice terms. The Paris garrison and the Gardes Mobiles became prisoners of war. Some 12,000 of the Paris garrison were allowed to retain their arms as a police force for the city. All French perimeter forts around the city were surrendered, and Paris had to pay a tribute of 200 million francs. The Germans were also permitted a triumphal march into the city (March 1).

The Germans agreed to a rapid reprovisioning of Paris. There was to be an armistice of three weeks throughout France, except in the departments of the Jura, Côte d'Or, and Doubs. This exclusion was at French insistence, as Gambetta hoped that the Army of the East could achieve victory at Belfort.

On February 8, French voters went to the polls in perhaps the strangest election in French history. Indeed, the chief purpose of the armistice was to allow the French people to decide whether to continue the war. Except in Paris and northeastern France, they voted overwhelmingly in favor of peace. Of 650 members of the new National Assembly, more than 400 were avowed monarchists elected on the program of an immediate peace. On February 17 the National Assembly, meeting at Bordeaux, elected Adolphe Thiers, who had strongly opposed the war, as chief of the executive power and entrusted him with negotiating a peace settlement.

On February 15 under orders from the National Assembly, Colonel Pierre Philippe Denfert-Rochereau surrendered Metz. Its garrison of 17,600 men, most of them Gardes Mobiles and Gardes Nationales, had held out for 105 days. The Germans permitted the garrison the full honors of war, and it marched out with all its weapons, arms, baggage, and equipment, with flags flying. The siege had claimed some 4,800 French military casualties. Another 336 civilians died in the German bombardment. German losses were about

2,000. In 1880, sculptor Frédéric Bartholdi completed his mammoth *Lion of Belfort,* which soon became a symbol of French courage and resistance.

During February 21–26 at Versailles, Thiers negotiated with Bismarck an end to the war. Bismarck would later blame the harsh terms on German Army insistence as a consequence of continued French resistance, but he had earlier talked of annexing all of northeastern France up to Paris. Any mitigation of his conditions was at least in part the result of British and Russian pressure. The terms were nonetheless harsh. Under the Versailles Diktat, France was forced to surrender all Alsace (except Belfort, which Thiers secured as a consequence of its heroic defense in the war) and the city of Strasbourg as well as much of Lorraine, including Metz. France also had to pay what at the time seemed an astronomical indemnity of 5 billion francs (2.5 times the cost of the war to Prussia). One billion francs was to be paid by the end of 1871 and the remainder within three years, with Prussian troops to occupy northeastern France until this was done.

Significance

The effects of the war and the peace treaty that ended it were momentous. France lost 1.6 million people, and the French nation of 36 million people now faced a united Germany of 41 million. France also gave up major natural resources, including the bulk of its iron ore deposits. The indemnity also fueled a subsequent major German industrial expansion.

Although Germany was now at last united, the harsh treaty may have been a great mistake. Bismarck's foreign policy after the war had to be directed toward the isolation of France, while French foreign policy has been described in a single word, *revanche* (revenge). Bismarck would boast that he had personally caused three wars. This is undoubtedly correct, but the peace settlement following the Franco-Prussian War sowed the seeds for both World War I and World War II.

Further Reading

Baldick, Robert. *The Siege of Paris.* New York: Macmillan, 1964.

Béringer, Jean. *A History of the Habsburg Empire, 1700–1918.* Translated by C. Simpson. New York: Longman, 1997.

Bucholz, Arden. *Moltke and the German Wars, 1864–1871.* New York: Palgrave MacMillan, 2001.

Crankshaw, Edward. *Bismarck.* New York: Viking, 1981.

Horne, Alistair. *The Fall of Paris: The Siege and the Commune, 1870–1871.* New York: Doubleday, 1965.

Howard, Michael. *The Franco-Prussian War: The German Invasion of France, 1870–1871.* New York: Routledge, 2001.

Kann, Robert A. *History of the Habsburg Empire, 1526–1918.* Berkeley: University of California Press, 1974.

Mann, Golo. *The History of Germany since 1789.* Translated by Marion Jackson. New York: Praeger, 1968.

Quintin, Barry. *The Franco-Prussian War, 1870–1871,* Vol. 1, *Helmuth von Moltke and the Overthrow of the Second Empire.* Solihull, UK: Helion, 2010.

Quintin, Barry. *The Franco-Prussian War, 1870–1871,* Vol. 2, *After Sedan: Helmuth von Moltke and the Defeat of the Government of National Defence.* Solihull, UK: Helion, 2010.

Showalter, Dennis E. *Railroads and Rifles: Soldiers, Technology, and the Unification of Germany.* Hamden, CT: Hailer Publishing, 1975.

Wawro, Geoffrey. *The Austro-Prussian War: Austria's War with Prussia and Italy in 1866.* New York: Cambridge University Press, 1996.

Wawro, Geoffrey. *The Franco-Prussian War: The German Conquest of France in 1870–1871.* New York: Cambridge University Press, 2005.

Wetzel, David. *Duel of Giants: Bismarck, Napoleon III, and the Origins of the Franco-Prussian War.* Madison: University of Wisconsin Press, 2003.

Sino-Japanese War (1894–1895)

Dates	August 1, 1894–April 17, 1895
Location	Korean Peninsula, China, Manchuria
Combatants	China vs. Japan
Principal Commanders	China: Yuan Shikai, Ding Ruchang Japan: Ōshima Yoshimasa, Ito Yuko, Yamagata Aritomo
Principal Battles	Pingdo, Pyongyang, Yalu River, Weihaiwei
Outcome	China's military backwardness is made evident, with Japan recognized as the dominant military power in Asia and with Chinese influence in Korea ended.

Causes

Unlike the leaders of China, the men ruling Japan recognized the need for their nation to Westernize, at least to the point of acquiring advanced Western military technology. Initially this was undertaken to prevent the country from falling under the control of a Western power, but by the last decade of the 19th century Japanese leaders were ready to embark upon their own program of imperial expansion. Largely bereft of national resources, they were especially desirous of securing Korea, the Chinese tributary kingdom across the Korea Strait. Japanese interference in Korean affairs eventually brought war between Japan and China.

In March 1894, the antiforeign Tonghak Society rebelled against the Korean government. With Tonghak forces advancing on Seoul, on June 1, 1894, King Yi Myeong-bok of Korea requested Chinese military assistance. The Qing government duly informed Japan under the provisions of the 1885 Convention of Tianjin (Tientsin) and dispatched General Yuan Shikai (Yuan Shih-kai) and 2,800 troops. Ignoring Qing suzerainty over Korea, however, the Japanese claimed that the Chinese action was a violation of the Convention of Tianjin. They then sent to Korea their own expeditionary force of some 8,000 men, rushing them through Seoul's port of Incheon (Chemulpo, Inchon).

Efforts at mediation between China and Japan in July failed, and on July 23, although the Chinese troops were already leaving Korea with the Tonghak rebellion crushed, Japanese troops entered the capital city, seized the Korean king, and established a new pro-Japanese government that terminated all Sino-Korean treaties and granted the Imperial Japanese Army the right to expel Chinese troops from Korea by force. China refused to recognize the legitimacy of the new government, and the war was on.

Course

Although both sides did not officially declare war until August 1, 1894, fighting

BATTLE OF THE YALU (YELLOW SEA)
SEPTEMBER 17, 1894

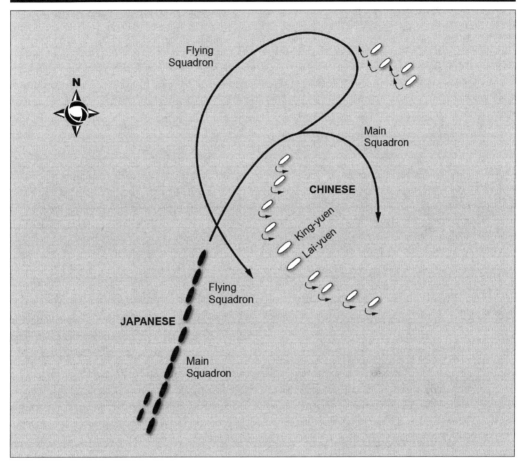

actually began in late July. On July 25 in the Battle of Pingdo, three Japanese cruisers under Admiral Kozo Tsuboi attacked a Chinese troop convoy under Fang Boqian consisting of a cruiser, two gunboats, and the transport *Kowshing*. The Japanese sank the *Kowshing* and severely damaged its escorts, resulting in 1,100 Chinese killed or wounded for no losses of their own. At the same time, fighting began on land when Major General Ōshima Yoshimasa, commander of Japanese forces in Seoul, led his forces against the Chinese at Songhwan, about 10 miles northeast of Asan.

The Japanese mounted a diversionary attack accompanied by a successful flanking maneuver, defeating the Chinese on the night of July 28–29. The Chinese then withdraw to Asan.

Both sides dispatched troop reinforcements by sea. The Chinese sent their men by means of the Yalu River and ports in North Korea, while Japanese forces arrived through Incheon and Busan (Pusan) in far southern Korea and the port most easily accessible to Japan. Neither side made any effort to interfere with the other's troop convoys.

Japanese troops under Lieutenant General Nozu Michitsura marched north toward Pyongyang, joined en route by reinforcements landed at Busan and Wonsan. Some 20,000 Japanese then converged on the walled city of Pyongyang in northern Korea, defended by 14,000 Chinese. On the morning of September 15, 1894, the Japanese attacked. An unexpected Japanese flanking attack produced heavy Chinese casualties, and late in the afternoon the garrison surrendered.

Heavy rain and nightfall, however, enabled many Chinese to escape to the coast and the border town of Uiju (Wiju) on the lower Yalu River. Chinese admiral Ding Ruchang (Ting Ju-ch-ang) had just arrived there with the main Chinese fleet and troop reinforcements. Chinese casualties in the Battle of Pyongyang were estimated at 2,000 killed and some 4,000 wounded. The Japanese lost 102 killed, 433 wounded, and 33 missing. The Japanese occupied Pyongyang early on September 16.

A significant naval battle occurred on September 17. Known as the Battle of the Yalu River, the Battle of Haiyang Island, and the Battle of the Yellow Sea, it conclusively demonstrated that old unarmored wooden ships were no match for newer steel warships. Chinese admiral Ding Ruchang's Beiyang Fleet included two newer ironclad battleships, the *Dingyuen* (*Ting Yuen*) and *Zhenyuan* (*Chen Yuen*). Historians disagree on the number of ships on each side, but Ding may also have had eight light cruisers and several smaller vessels. The Chinese warships were escorting six transports carrying 4,500 troops and 80 guns to the Yalu.

At the same time, Japanese admiral Ito Yuko was disembarking troop reinforcements some 100 miles farther down the Korean coast, after which he sailed north to locate Ding's squadron. Ito probably had four heavy cruisers, five light cruisers, one corvette, and one gunboat.

At about 10:00 a.m. on September 17, Ito came upon Ding's ships between the mouth of the Yalu River and Haiyang Island. On paper the two sides appeared somewhat evenly matched. Despite Ding's advantage in having the heaviest, longest-range guns in the battle (four 12-inch guns on each of his two battleships), Ito had newer and faster ships and enjoyed a considerable advantage in his many 4.5-inch and 6-inch quick-firing guns—the most effective naval guns of the period. Japanese gunnery and ship handling were also far superior to those of the Chinese, and Japanese shells soon riddled the unprotected Chinese ships, setting their exposed wooden areas ablaze.

The Chinese lost three of their cruisers and two smaller vessels. A number of Ito's ships were hit, but only one was seriously damaged, and no ships were sunk. Fearing the power of the two larger Chinese battleships, however, Ito failed to press his attack. Unknown to him, the Chinese had used up most of their ammunition, and during the night the remaining Chinese ships escaped to Lüshunkou (Lüshun Port and Port Arthur).

After taking Pyongyang, Japanese lieutenant general Nozu Michitsura moved north to the Yalu. Reinforced to 20,000 men, his forces were reorganized into the First Army under Field Marshal Yamagata Aritomo. The Japanese crossed the Yalu during October 24–25 and proceeded into Manchuria with no initial Chinese opposition. As the Japanese proceeded, however, they found themselves in hard-fought engagements with Chinese forces under General Song Jing (Sung Ching). Cold weather and supply problems also hindered the Japanese advance, and they were hard-pressed to retain their base at Haicheng in Liaoning Province.

Meanwhile moving by sea, Japanese field marshal Oyama Iwao's Second Army of some 26,000 men and 13,000 auxiliaries landed on October 14 at Pitzuwu north of Lüshunkou, the base for China's Beiyang Fleet. There was little Chinese opposition as the Japanese closed on Lüshunkou. Surprisingly, the Japanese allowed Chinese admiral Ding to escape with his ships across the Strait of Bohai to Weihaiwei.

Major General Yamaji Motoharu's 1st Division of the Japanese Second Army arrived at Lüshunkou and there began an artillery bombardment on the night of November 20. The next morning, the Japanese assaulted and captured the city and port with but little Chinese resistance. Many city residents had already fled westward by land or sea. Infuriated by the discovery of several mutilated Japanese bodies displayed at the entrance to the city, upon taking Lüshunkou the Japanese reportedly massacred a number of the Chinese who remained. The scale of this massacre is still a matter of scholarly dispute.

To eliminate any threat from the Chinese Beiyang Fleet, the Japanese decided to take the Chinese naval base at Weihaiwei, located across the Gulf of Pohai from Lüshunkou. During January 20–24, 1895, Oyama's Second Army, less one brigade left in garrison at Lüshunkou, landed without Chinese resistance at Jiurongcheng (Jungcheng), on the eastern tip of the Shandong (Shantung) Peninsula.

Upon consolidation, Japanese forces advanced west on Weihaiwei along two routes, facing vigorous resistance from the Chinese Beiyang Army. In assaulting the Chinese forces defending the port, the Japanese had the advantage of naval gunfire support from their ships offshore. Most of the forts and the town of Weihaiwei fell following a nine-hour battle on February 1, and the Japanese occupied the port the next day.

The Japanese capture of Weihaiwei trapped the Chinese Beiyang Fleet in the harbor between Oyama's troops at Weihaiwei and Ito's fleet offshore. Chinese admiral Ding's Beiyang Fleet consisted of the 2 ironclad battleships *Dingyuan* and *Zhenyuan,* 4 cruisers, 6 gunboats, and 15 torpedo boats. Ito, however, commanded 25 warships and 16 torpedo boats and could call on artillery fire from the Japanese in the port, who now had at their disposal the captured Chinese forts and coast-defense artillery. Ito send a note to Ding, a personal friend, calling on him to surrender in order to prevent a needless bloodletting. Despite the hopelessness of the situation, Ding was determined to fight and rejected the appeal.

Beginning on February 7, the Japanese carried out a series of night torpedo boat attacks, while the captured shore batteries shelled the Chinese ships during the day. The Japanese torpedo boats sank the *Dingyuan* and several other ships. Ding sent out his torpedo boats in the hope they could escape to Yantai, but the Japanese sank six and captured another seven.

On February 12, Ding surrendered what remained of the Beiyang Fleet ships in the harbor and the Chinese-held forts and stores to the Japanese on condition that the Chinese military and civilians be permitted to depart Weihaiwei unmolested. Ito agreed, despite Japanese Army demands that the Chinese be made prisoners of war. Ding rejected Ito's personal offer of political asylum in Japan, however, and committed suicide. The Japanese Navy then took control of the surrendered battleship *Zhenyuan,* three cruisers, and six gunboats. The Japanese had completely eliminated the Northern Chinese Fleet and secured absolute control of the Gulf of Pohai.

Japanese military operations in Manchuria continued. The Japanese First Army, now commanded by Lieutenant General Nozu Michitsura, linked up with the Second Army while at the same time beating back repeated Chinese attacks against their base at Haicheng. In the Battle of Tapingshan on February 21–23, Nozu defeated Chinese forces under General Sung Ching. Then in a battle near Yingkou (also known as the Battle of Newchwang) on March 9, the Japanese eliminated the last major Chinese military resistance in Manchuria.

With the Japanese Army now in position to advance on Beijing, the Qing court entered into peace negotiations. In the Japanese-dictated Treaty of Shimonoseki of April 17, 1895, the Qing were forced to cede to Japan the island of Taiwan (Formosa), the Pescadores, and the Liaodong (Liaotung) Peninsula in southern Manchuria. China was also forced to pay an indemnity of 300 million taels ($150 million) and to recognize Korea as an independent kingdom, a step toward its absorption by Japan.

Significance

The Sino-Japanese War conclusively demonstrated Japanese success in its modernization and industrialization program. The Westernized Japanese military was clearly superior to that of China. The war greatly enhanced Japanese prestige and established Japan as the dominant military power in Asia. The Japanese also promptly ended Korean independence and integrated Korea's economy into that of Japan. Japanese efforts to "modernize"

the economic and social spheres, however, had a profound effect on Korea, disrupting traditional structures. Japan's seizure of a third of the country's arable land without compensation also caused widespread suffering and resentment.

For China, the war had been a disaster. It revealed for all to see the corruption and inefficiency of the Qing dynasty and its backward military. The Chinese had traditionally viewed Japan as a subordinate part of the Chinese sphere of influence. That now changed. The Japanese victory came on the heels of defeats by the Western powers in the mid-19th century, but this defeat had been administered by an "inferior" Asian state. Antiforeign sentiment and agitation grew in China, helping to bring on the Boxer Rebellion five years later.

For Japan, however, the victory turned out to be bittersweet. Although Japan had achieved what it had set out to accomplish, mainly to end Chinese influence over Korea, its acquisition of a foothold on the Asian mainland was particularly distasteful to Russian leaders, who then secured the support of France and Germany. In the Triple Intervention of April 23, 1895, these three powers "advised" Japan to refrain from annexing any part of the Chinese mainland. Japan was in no position to fight three Western powers at once and therefore gave up claim to territory on the Asian mainland and in return received from China an additional indemnity. Russia then secured in 1898 a 25-year lease from China of the Liaodong Peninsula in Manchuria, including Lüshunkou, now renamed Port Arthur, that had originally been assigned to Japan. This greatly infuriated the Japanese and was a major factor in bringing on the Russo-Japanese War a decade later.

Further Reading

Chamberlin, William Henry. *Japan over Asia.* Boston: Little, Brown, 1937.

Duus, Peter. *The Abacus and the Sword: The Japanese Penetration of Korea.* Berkeley: University of California Press, 1998.

Evans, David C., and Mark R. Peattie. *Kaigun: Strategy, Tactics, and Technology in the Imperial Japanese Navy, 1887–1941.* Annapolis, MD: Naval Institute Press, 1997.

Jansen, Marius B. *The Emergence of Meiji Japan.* Cambridge: Cambridge University Press, 1995.

Jansen, Marius B. *The Making of Modern Japan.* Cambridge, MA: Harvard University Press, 2002.

Kim, Jinwung. *A History of Korea: From "Land of the Morning Calm" to States in Conflict.* Bloomington: Indiana University Press, 2013.

Lone, Stewart. *Japan's First Modern War: Army and Society in the Conflict with China, 1894–1895,* New York: St. Martin's, 1994.

Paine, S. C. M. *The Sino-Japanese War of 1894–1895: Perceptions, Power, and Primacy.* Cambridge: Cambridge University Press, 2002.

Schencking, J. Charles. *Making Waves: Politics, Propaganda, and the Emergence of the Imperial Japanese Navy, 1868–1922.* Stanford, CA: Stanford University Press, 2005.

Sondhaus, Lawrence. *Naval Warfare, 1815–1914.* London: Routledge, 2001.

Spanish-American War (1898)

Dates	April 25–August 12, 1898
Location	Cuba, Puerto Rico, Caribbean Sea, Philippine Islands
Combatants	United States vs. Spain
Principal Commanders	United States: William McKinley, George Dewey, William R. Shafter, William T. Sampson, Nelson A. Miles Spain: Práxedes Mariano Mateo Sagasta y Escolar, Patricio Montojo y Pasarón, Arsenio Linares Pomba, Pascual Cervera y Topete
Principal Battles	Manila Bay, Las Guásimas, El Caney, San Juan Heights (Hill), Santiago de Cuba, Manila
Outcome	The United States secures Cuban independence but begins a long period of interventionism in the Caribbean and Latin America. U.S. acquisition of the Philippines (which triggers the Philippine-American War of 1899–1902), establishes that country as a Pacific power, leading to the future confrontation with Japan.

Causes

Fighting in Cuba lay behind the U.S. decision to go to war against Spain in 1898. Located only 110 miles off the southern coast of Florida, the island of Cuba had necessarily been forced into a close relationship with the United States. There had been several revolts on the island against inept but not overly oppressive Spanish rule, including the Ten Years' War (1868–1878) and the Small War (1879–1880). The failure of the Spanish government to implement promised reforms following these conflicts and a high tariff on sugar into the United States imposed by the Dingley Tariff of 1897 led to a new widespread Cuban insurrection. Spanish captain general Valeriano

Weyler attempted to put down the rebellion in compartmentalization of the island through *trochas,* or fortified lines, and the establishment of concentration camps to isolate the insurgents from support by the civilian population.

The so-called yellow press in the United States reported widely on events in Cuba. Reporters for William Randolph Hearst's and Joseph Pulitzer's newspapers vied with one another in sensationalist accounts of Spanish atrocities, both real and imagined, while largely ignoring those committed by the insurgents. American sympathy was particularly stirred by the plight of those in the concentration camps, and Cuban exiles in the United States adroitly fanned the flames of anti-Spanish sentiment.

The struggle in Cuba threatened to go on indefinitely, as 150,000 Spanish troops were unable to subdue an estimated 40,000 rebels. U.S. presidents Grover Cleveland and William McKinley had both refused to get involved. Then in October 1897 a new Spanish premier, Práxedes Mariano Mateo Sagasta y Escolar, proposed abandonment of the concentration policy, recalled General Weyler, and promised Cuba a measure of home rule. The crisis apparently had passed.

The continuing Cuban insurgency, the Dupuy de Lôme Letter, and the sinking of USS *Maine* all brought rapid deterioration in U.S.-Spanish relations. Spanish ambassador to the United States Enrique Dupuy de Lôme wrote to an acquaintance in Cuba covering events there for a Spanish newspaper. In the letter Dupuy de Lôme was sharply critical of President McKinley, characterizing him as "weak" and a "low" politician who pandered to the "rabble." Cuban revolutionaries intercepted this and turned it over to the Hearst publishing empire. The letter appeared in the *New York Journal* on February 9, 1898, and played a significant role in increasing popular support in the United States for war against Spain. Dupuy de Lôme meanwhile promptly resigned his post and returned to Spain.

In a provocative step, the U.S. government had dispatched the second-class battleship *Maine* to Havana, ostensibly to protect U.S. interests in Cuba but really designed to intimidate Spain into granting concessions to the Cuban insurgents. On the night of February 15, 1898, the *Maine* was riding at anchor in Havana Harbor when its forward magazines with nearly 5 tons of powder charges exploded, sinking the ship and resulting in the deaths of 266 members of its crew. A naval court of inquiry blamed the blast on an external mine. More recent scientific research has concluded that the explosion resulted from excessive heat caused by spontaneous combustion in a coal locker touching off the magazines.

Encouraged by the yellow press, most Americans held the Spaniards responsible, although it is impossible to see how sinking a U.S. warship would have been in their interest. If it was a mine, it could well have been the work of the Cuban insurgents. In any case, Americans took up the cry "Remember the *Maine*—to hell with Spain!"

McKinley, a veteran of the American Civil War, did not want war with Spain. But Congress, the press, and the so-called congressional Young Republicans did. Imperialism was in the air, and American expansionists were eager to join the race for overseas territory. Influential figures such as U.S. Navy captain Alfred Thayer Mahan saw this as an opportunity for the United States to secure overseas bases and assert itself as a world power.

On March 8, the U.S. Congress passed a $50 million national defense appropriation bill, to be spent at the discretion of the president, and on March 17, moderate Republican senator Redfield Proctor, just returned from an inspection trip to Cuba, delivered a major speech before the U.S. Senate denouncing the methods employed by the Spanish authorities in Cuba. This speech helped convince many that the United States had a humanitarian duty to intervene in Cuba.

McKinley finally gave way to the argument that failure to act regarding Cuba would split the Republican Party. On March 22, the day after the report of the board of inquiry concerning the loss of the *Maine,* the president sent Madrid an ultimatum demanding an immediate armistice, release of prisoners, and American mediation between Spain and Cuba. Spain's formal reply to this unwelcome demand was unsatisfactory, but the Sagasta government did not want war with the United States and took steps to avert it. On April 9 the governor-general of Cuba offered an armistice to the insurgents, and on April 10 U.S. ambassador to Madrid Stewart L. Woodford cabled Washington that if nothing was done to humiliate Spain, the Cuban situation could be settled on the basis of autonomy, independence, or even cession of the island to the United States.

On April 11, McKinley sent Congress a long review of the situation with only a passing, deceptive reference to Woodford's dispatch, concluding that he had "exhausted every effort to relieve the intolerable condition of affairs which is at our doors" and asking for authority to intervene. On April 19 Congress passed a joint resolution (311 to 6 in the House of Representatives and 42 to 35 in the Senate) that recognized the independence of Cuba, demanded the withdrawal of Spanish armed forces from the island, called on the president to use the U.S. armed forces to carry out these demands, and disclaimed any U.S. intention to exercise sovereignty over the island (the Teller Amendment). President William McKinley signed the resolution on April 20 and that same day sent it to Spain. The Spanish government held the ultimatum to be a declaration of war and declared war itself on April 23. The United States responded in kind on April 25. However, because of McKinley's order of a naval blockade of Cuba on April 22, the U.S. declaration was made retroactive to that date.

Course

Americans were united behind the war, with scant consideration of its probable consequences. On paper, Spain appeared formidable. Its regular army was far larger, and its navy had more cruisers and torpedo craft than did the United States. Yet many of Spain's ships were obsolete and inadequately armed. The larger U.S. Navy ships were of recent construction and mounted a heavier armament than those of the Spaniards, and their crews were better trained.

On the other hand, the small U.S. Army of only 28,000 men was unready. Given this, it would have been a far better strategy to impose a naval blockade on Cuba, which would have prevented Spain from reinforcing. Army commanding general Major General Nelson Miles wanted a period of training and then an invasion, but public opinion demanded an immediate descent on Cuba. The result was near chaos. The regular army was immediately authorized a increase in size to 60,000 men, with a volunteer force created for the duration of the conflict. By May 1898, regular and

CARIBBEAN THEATER NAVAL MOVEMENTS

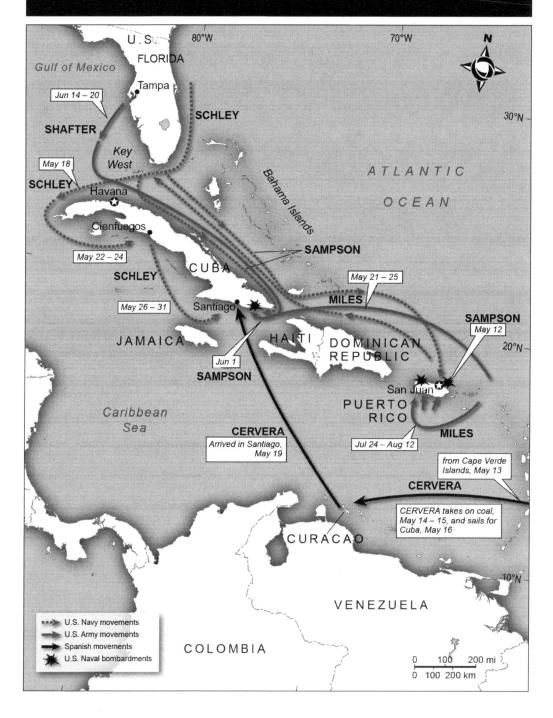

volunteer strength totaled 168,929 men; this rose to 274,717 by August.

Spanish forces in Cuba were equipped with the superior smokeless powder Mauser rifle, and while there were enough modern Krag Jorgenson rifles for the regular army, the volunteers had to be armed with the old .45-caliber black powder trapdoor Springfield. Shortages abounded and assembly areas were all chaos, with everything in short supply, spoiled food, and the volunteer forces neglecting even elementary sanitation. It took months for the logistical problems to be worked out.

This was not to be a war of hopes deferred, however. While the army was assembling for a descent on Cuba, the navy was winning an overseas empire. The U.S. Asiatic Squadron was at Hong Kong when its commander, Commodore George Dewey, learned that war had begun. Pursuant to orders, Dewey proceeded to the Philippines with his squadron of four protected cruisers (the *Olympia,* flagship), two gunboats, and a revenue cutter, along with two colliers. On May 1 in the Battle of Manila Bay, the American ships engaged and destroyed Spanish rear admiral Patricio Montojo y Pasarón's squadron of two large cruisers and four small cruisers, which were inferior in both armament and crew training to those of the Americans. Dewey also secured the surrender of the naval station at Cavite. The battle claimed Spanish casualties of 167 dead and 214 wounded—all but 10 aboard the ships. The Americans sustained but 8 wounded.

Rarely had such an important victory been more cheaply obtained. Dewey occupied Cavite and, awaiting U.S. troops to take Manila, blockaded the city. At this point, Washington conceived of the Philippines merely as a bargaining chip, an inducement for Spain to conclude peace, but that would soon change. On June 20 also, U.S. warships escorting troopships en route to the Philippines stopped at Agana, Guam, and took possession of that strategically situated island.

On May 19, meanwhile, Spanish rear admiral Pascual Cervera y Topete had eluded U.S. rear admiral William T. Sampson's North Atlantic Squadron and arrived at Santiago, Cuba, from the Cape Verde Islands with four cruisers and two torpedo boat destroyers. Sampson's squadron appeared off Santiago on June 1 and imposed a blockade, adding the ships of Commodore Winfield Scott Schley's Flying Squadron to his own squadron to form the North Atlantic Fleet. The U.S. blockaders numbered five battleships, two armored cruisers, and a number of smaller cruisers and auxiliaries.

On June 3 the navy attempted to prevent the departure of Cervera's squadron by blocking the Santiago Channel, but this failed when the collier *Merrimac,* sunk with explosive charges, failed to go down in the proper location.

Meanwhile, U.S. troops were being hastily assembled in Florida for a descent on Cuba. These consisted of three divisions of 16,888 men in V Corps commanded by Major General William Shafter, including 15 regiments of regulars and 3 of volunteers (including the 1st Volunteer Cavalry, later known as "Roosevelt's Rough Riders" but first commanded by Colonel Leonard Wood, with Roosevelt as lieutenant colonel and then by Roosevelt when Wood assumed command of a brigade). Few horses were available for the 6 cavalry regiments sent to Cuba, and they were forced to fight on foot.

In a chaotic operation on June 22 supported by ships of the U.S. Navy, Shafter's men began coming ashore at Daiquiri on the southeast coast of Cuba about 16 miles east of Santiago. That day some 6,000 men landed. Spanish Army lieutenant general Arsenio Linares y Pomba commanded the Santiago area, and although he had some 12,000 men, he chose not to contest the landings, despite the considerable casualties that even a small Spanish force might have inflicted. On June 23 Shafter sent one of his divisions to secure Siboney, 7 miles closer to Santiago, which proved as deserted of Spanish forces as Daiquiri. Siboney became Shafter's headquarters for the assault on Santiago.

Lieutenant General Linares, Spanish commander in Cuba, had almost 200,000 men and ample warning of a U.S. invasion, but fewer than 35,000 of his men were in the Santiago area, and the city's actual garrison was only 13,000. Linares was able to concentrate just 1,700 men for the first big battle with the Americans, on July 1.

Shafter and Sampson were unable to agree on a plan to attack the city of Santiago and destroy Cervera's squadron. After U.S. forces defeated the Spanish at Las Guásimas on June 24, 1898, Shafter moved to take the high ground east of Santiago known as San Juan Heights (Ridge), including the prominent points of San Juan Hill and Kettle Hill. If U.S. forces could capture this terrain, they would control access to Santiago.

Shafter's plan called for Brigadier General Jacob Ford Kent's division to attack San Juan Hill while Brigadier General Samuel Sumner's dismounted cavalry assaulted nearby Kettle Hill. At the same time, Brigadier General Henry Lawton's division would take nearby El Caney. Shafter expected the latter operation to take about two hours, which would allow Lawton's division to take part in the attack on the San Juan Heights. As it turned out, Lawton was caught up in a daylong fight, and his men were unable to participate in the San Juan Heights attack.

Following a morning artillery duel on July 1, 1898, in which the more modern Spanish guns soon silenced those of the Americans, the ground assault opened at 1:00 p.m. American élan, leadership, and superior numbers overcame Spanish superior firepower. Roosevelt won renown for leading the dismounted Rough Riders up Kettle Hill. In the fighting for San Juan Heights and El Caney, the Americans lost 1,572 killed or wounded for Spanish losses of 850.

With the American land forces closing on Santiago from the east, Madrid ordered Cervera to sortie with his squadron of four cruisers and two destroyers. On the morning of July 3, the Spanish ships began exiting the channel. Awaiting the Spaniards was the far more powerful U.S. squadron of four battleships, one armored cruiser, and three armed yachts. Sampson had just departed in another battleship (the *New York*) for a conference with Shafter, and Schley exercised command in his absence.

The Spanish ships were soon in flames, overwhelmed by superior U.S. firepower. They tried to make the shore, and the Americans turned to rescuing their crews. In this four-hour Battle of Santiago de Cuba, the Spanish lost all six ships either sunk or scuttled; 323 men were killed and 151 wounded, and 1,720 were taken prisoner, including Cervera. Later a bitter public controversy erupted when Schley and Sampson feuded over deserved credit for the victory.

On the night of July 4, the Spaniards attempted to block water access to Santiago by scuttling in the channel to Santiago Harbor the cruiser *Reina Mercedes,* which had been serving as a guard ship. Two U.S. battleships opened fire and hit the cruiser five times. The Spanish crew managed to set off the scuttling charges, but the ship took too long to sink and drifted out of the channel before grounding.

On July 1 General of Brigade José Toral y Vázquez succeeded Linares, who had been wounded in the Battle of San Juan Heights, as commander of the Santiago area. Toral was unaware that Shafter's men were rapidly falling prey to disease, and on July 3 following the Battle of Santiago de Cuba, Shafter demanded that Toral surrender. Following a land and sea bombardment of the city during July 10–11 and with freshwater cut off and supplies running low, Toral surrendered on July 17. In the negotiations, Shafter had offered to return all prisoners taken to Spain at U.S. expense.

The siege of Santiago claimed 1,614 U.S. casualties; the Spaniards suffered some 2,000 dead and wounded and 11,500 prisoners. Eight Spanish vessels were also captured in the harbor. The surrender of Santiago largely ended fighting in Cuba.

On July 25, U.S. forces under commanding general of the army Major General Nelson A. Miles landed in Puerto Rico. The original invasion force numbered 3,500 men, but by early August Miles had 17,000 men and their artillery on the island. In sharp contrast to the chaotic Cuban campaign, that in Puerto Rico proceeded smoothly. By the time a general armistice in the war took effect on August 13, U.S. forces had fought a half dozen engagements, suffering only 3 dead and 40 wounded, and captured half of the island. Spanish casualties were at least 10 times that number.

In the Philippines, meanwhile, the first 2,500 men of Major General Wesley Merritt's VIII Corps arrived from San Francisco on June 30. All of Merritt's 10,800 men were in place by the end of July. Spanish honor demanded a battle before the surrender of Manila, and Merritt's troops, supported by Cuban insurgents led by Emilio Aguinaldo and naval gunfire, attacked. Following a short nominal defense, Manila surrendered on August 13.

With the armistice of August 13, 1898, Spanish and U.S. negotiators met in Paris to bring the war to a formal close. The only sticking point was the future of the Philippines, which McKinley now decided to retain, partly as a result of clear German interest in acquiring the islands. (After the Battle of Manila Bay, Kaiser William II had sent out a powerful naval squadron and some 1,400 troops.) As McKinley explained it to a visiting Mexican delegation to Washington, it was the duty of Americans "to take them all and to educate the Filipinos, and uplift and civilize and Christianize them." A majority of the Filipinos, of course, had been Roman Catholic for centuries.

Significance

In the Treaty of Paris of December 10, 1898, Spain relinquished sovereignty over Cuba, ceded to the United States the islands of Puerto Rico and Guam, and sold it the Philippine Archipelago for $20 million. Also, during the war on July 7, 1898, in a joint resolution of Congress, the United States had annexed the Hawaiian Islands, perceived as a naval coaling station and base to the Philippines.

The U.S. military did much to improve public services in Cuba, and a team of doctors headed by Walter Reed definitively established the link between the mosquito and yellow fever, helping to bring an end to a scourge that had ravaged the tropics. Cuba was duly granted its independence, but the new government was endued to grant the United States the Guantánamo naval base and to recognize the right of the United States to intervene to preserve Cuban independence or restore order there. The treaty provisions for intervention (the Platt Amendment) were only revoked in 1934.

Won at surprisingly little human cost (the war claimed 289 men killed or mortally wounded in battle, although 13 times that number died of disease), the Spanish-American War had immense repercussions for the United States. The great success of the U.S. Navy and its new overseas responsibilities led to support for naval expansion, and by 1917 the United States had the third-largest navy in the world. The war was certainly a major turning point in U.S. history, marking the arrival of the United States as a world power. Unanticipated at the time, the acquisition of the Philippines set up future confrontation with Japan.

The U.S. annexation of the Philippines also immediately brought a far more costly and longer struggle than the Spanish-American War. In January 1899 Filipino nationalist Aguinaldo proclaimed Philippine independence, and fighting began the next month. Eventually the United States committed 126,000 troops to the Philippine-American War (known at the time as the Philippine Insurrection). Although President Theodore Roosevelt officially pronounced the war at an end in 1902, fighting in the Moro Rebellion in the southern Philippines continued until 1913. Some 80,000–100,000 Filipinos fought the United States, suffering an estimated 16,000 military deaths. Another 250,000–1 million Filipinos died as a consequence. Perhaps 100,000 Filipino civilians died in the Moro Rebellion. The United States suffered 6,165 dead and another 3,000 wounded.

Further Reading

Balfour, Sebastian. *The End of the Spanish Empire, 1898–1923.* New York: Oxford University Press, 1997.

Blow, Michael. *A Ship to Remember: The Maine and the Spanish-American War.* New York: Morrow, 1992.

Bradford, James C., ed. *Crucible of Empire: The Spanish-American War and Its Aftermath.* Annapolis, MD: Naval Institute Press, 1993.

Conroy, Robert. *The Battle of Manila Bay: The Spanish-American War in the Philippines.* New York: MacMillan, 1968.

Cosmas, Graham A. *An Army for Empire: The United States Army in the Spanish-American War.* Columbia: University of Missouri Press, 1971.

Hendrickson, Kenneth E., Jr. *The Spanish-American War.* Westport, CT: Greenwood, 2003.

Linn, Brian McAllister. *The Philippine War, 1899–1902.* Lawrence: University Press of Kansas, 2000.

Nofi, Albert A. *The Spanish-American War, 1898.* Conshohocken, PA: Combined Books, 1996.

O'Toole, G. J. A. *The Spanish War: An American Epic, 1898.* New York: Norton, 1984.

Silbey, David J. *A War of Frontier and Empire: The Philippine-American War, 1899–1902.* New York: Hill and Wang, 2006.

Trask, David F. *The War with Spain in 1898.* Lincoln: University of Nebraska Press, 1996.

Tucker, Spencer C. *The Encyclopedia of the Spanish-American and Philippine-American Wars: A Political, Social, and Military History.* Santa Barbara, CA: ABC-CLIO, 2009.

Russo-Japanese War (1904–1905)

Dates	February 8, 1904–September 5, 1905
Location	Manchuria, Korea, Yellow Sea
Combatants	Russia vs. Japan
Principal Commanders	Russia: Nicholas II, Stepan Ossipovitch Makarov, Aleksei Kuropatkin, Zinovi Petrovitch Rozhdestvenski Japan: Tōgō Heihachirō, Kuroki Tamemoto, Oku Yasukata, Oyama Iwao
Principal Battles	Chemulpo, Port Arthur, Yellow Sea, Ulsan, Shao-Ho, Sandepu, Mukden, Tsushima Straits
Outcome	Japan secures effective control of Korea as well as the Russian holdings in Manchuria. The war also reveals Russian military weakness and confirms Japan as the dominant military power in Asia.

Causes

The Russo-Japanese War was the direct result of a clash of imperial interests between Russia and Japan. In the 1890s Russia's leaders temporarily set aside their ambitions in the Balkans to seek influence over, or outright control of, Manchuria and Korea in the Far East. These areas would provide warm-water ports to supplement Vladivostok, which was closed by ice part of each year. Control of Manchuria would also allow Russia to establish a more direct rail line to Vladivostok. Resource-starved Japan, however, was determined to acquire Manchuria's rich natural resources for itself.

One of the provisions of the peace settlement imposed by Japan following its victory over China in the Sino-Japanese War of 1894–1895 provided that China would surrender the Liaotung (Liaodong) Peninsula in southern Manchuria. Russian leaders desired that territory for themselves and therefore opposed the Japanese acquisition. For reasons of their own, France and Germany agreed to support Russia in its position. The governments of all three pressed the Japanese leaders to surrender the territory. Japan could not contemplate war against a coalition of major European powers and eventually ceded its claim to territory on the Asian mainland in return for an additional indemnity from China.

Russia then advanced its own position in China under the pretense of defending Chinese territorial integrity. In 1896 the two states concluded a treaty in which Russia agreed to aid China if it was attacked by a third power. Russia also secured economic concessions, including the right to build the Chinese Eastern Railway across Manchuria to Vladivostok. This railway, protected by Russian troops, would connect Russia's port in the Far East with inland Siberia and European Russia by a much shorter and more direct route than the Trans-Siberian Railway. In 1898 Russia also secured a lease of about 500 square miles of territory—including part of the land surrendered by Japan in 1895—at the end of the Liaotung Peninsula and the right to construct a branch line to connect this territory with the Chinese Eastern Railway at Harbin. Subsequently the Russians improved the harbor of Darien and constructed a powerful fortress and naval base at Port Arthur. Russia now had a warm-water port/outlet for the Trans-Siberian Railway, and it appeared that Manchuria would pass under Russian control. Indeed, during the 1900 Boxer Rebellion, Russia sent troops into Manchuria apparently with a view to detaching it from China and then failed to withdraw them, despite Japanese anger and diplomatic protests by that nation.

In 1902 Japan concluded an alliance with Britain, which was also worried about Russian expansion in the Far East. The terms assured Japan that Great Britain would remain neutral in the event of war between Japan and Russia and that if any power assisted Russia in such a war Great Britain would fight on the side of Japan.

In 1903 Japanese leaders offered the Russians a compromise. Japan would recognize Russian ascendancy in the greater part of Manchuria if Russia withdrew its troops from Manchuria, recognized Japan's right to intervene in Korea, and gave Japan the right to build a railroad from Korea into Manchuria that would connect with the Chinese Eastern Railway. When Russian leaders hesitated, Japan broke off diplomatic relations. Japanese statesmen believed that Russia was merely trying to postpone war until it had completed its strategic rail net in the region. Czar Nicholas II (r. 1894–1917) and his advisers anticipated a war with Japan, but they believed that it would occur in circumstances favorable to Russia and that Japan certainly would never begin it. The sole voice of reason in the cabinet against this was Minister of Finance Sergei Witte. His opposition to the czar's Manchurian policy

led in 1903 to his being removed from his post. (In 1905 Witte would be called upon to pick up the pieces of the czar's disastrous Far Eastern policies.) The Japanese, however, decided not to wait for Russia's convenience and prepared a preemptive strike to secure control of the seas, an essential precondition for the transportation of troops to Manchuria and Korea.

To the casual observer, war between Russia and Japan in 1904 would appear to be a mismatch. Although Russia was vastly superior in resources and manpower (its army numbered on paper some 4.5 million men), it was seriously handicapped at the outset of the war because it was unable to bring its full strength to bear. The conflict was far distant from the heart of Russia, and troops and supplies would have to be shipped 5,500 miles over the single-track Trans-Siberian Railway. A gap in the line at Lake Baikal complicated logistical problems.

The Russian Navy was divided into three main squadrons, again widely separated—the Baltic, the Black Sea, and the Pacific—and it was difficult to concentrate them. Russian troops lacked enthusiasm for the war, the purpose of which they either did not understand or did not approve. Indeed, the war never did receive the wholehearted support of the Russian people. Inefficiency and corruption, which had so often undermined Russian armies in the past, again appeared in this conflict. Finally, it was Russia's misfortune to have a supreme command lacking in both initiative and strategic ability.

Japan, on the other hand, had a highly disciplined, efficient, and enthusiastic army and navy. It was well trained and ably led and was loyally supported by the populace at home. Also, many of the more powerful ships of the Japanese Navy were new.

RUSSO-JAPANESE WAR, 1904 – 1905

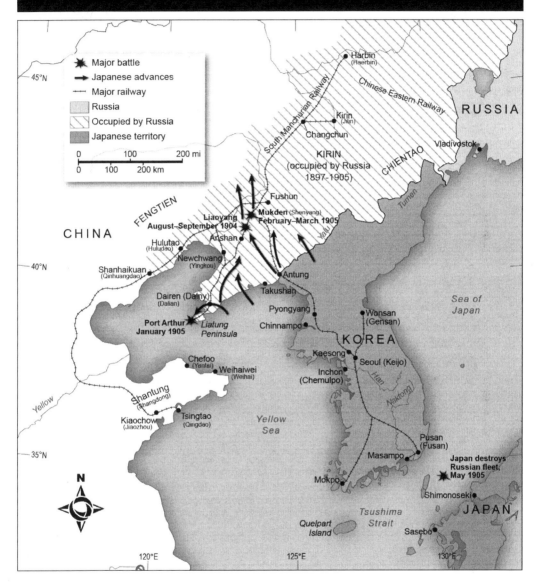

Furthermore, Japan was in close proximity to the seat of hostilities and, assuming control of the sea, could place its forces in the field with a minimum of difficulty.

Course

On February 6, 1904, Japanese vice admiral Tōgō Heihachirō's Combined Fleet sailed from Japan for Port Arthur (present-day Lüshunkou). At the same time, Vice Admiral Uryu Sotokichi sailed with a squadron of four heavy cruisers for Chemulpo Bay in western Korea, there to ensure the safe landing of transports bearing troops of the Japanese Army's 12th Division.

Outside the harbor of Chemulpo (present-day Inchon) in the early afternoon of February 8, Uryu joined a flotilla of torpedo boats and three transports carrying 3,000 men as well as horses and equipment of the 12th Division. At Chemulpo another Japanese cruiser had been keeping close watch on three Russian ships in the harbor: a cruiser, a gunboat, and a transport. The gunboat, the *Koreetz,* had already put to sea with dispatches and mail for Port Arthur when it encountered the Japanese ships.

Realizing that the Japanese presence meant war, the captain of the *Koreetz* attempted to return to port. The opening shots of the war occurred about 2:15 p.m. The Japanese claimed that the *Koreetz* fired its one gun first, which seems highly unlikely. Uryu's torpedo boats attacked the *Koreetz,* but their torpedoes missed. That evening Japanese troops, protected by their warships, began coming ashore. The landing continued until the next morning, when some of the soldiers set off to capture the Korean capital of Seoul. Uryu then sent an ultimatum to the Russians demanding that their ships take to the sea or be attacked in the harbor, a violation of international law.

The Russians decided that honor dictated that they fight, although the cruiser *Varyag* was their only ship capable of battle. In the late morning of February 9, the two Russian warships exited the harbor. In an hour-long battle both ships were badly damaged, but both regained the harbor, where the Russians scuttled all three of their ships. The Japanese claimed that in the battle they suffered no casualties and no damage to their ships.

Aside from the warships at Chemulpo, the Russians had at Vladivostok 4 heavy cruisers and 17 torpedo boats, but their most powerful naval force, consisting of 7 battleships and 4 cruisers, was at Port Arthur. Because early on February 7 the

Japanese had cut the cable between Port Arthur and Korea, the Russians were unaware of the Japanese attack at Chemulpo and the start of the war.

During the night of February 8–9, 1904, Tōgō launched a surprise torpedo attack against the Russian squadron just outside the harbor at Port Arthur. The attack badly damaged two Russian battleships and a cruiser. The next day, February 9, Tōgō brought up his heavy ships to shell the shore batteries, town, and Russian ships from long range. Although four Russian ships were damaged, in the exchange of fire most Japanese vessels were also struck, and Tōgō reluctantly ordered the Combined Fleet to withdraw.

There were no pangs of conscience in Tokyo regarding the surprise Japanese attacks of February 8, and not until February 10 did Japan formally declare war.

On February 17, Japanese general Kuroki Tamemoto's First Army began coming ashore at Chemulpo. Once the men were assembled and organized, the Japanese began moving north toward the Yalu River. In mid-March, other Japanese troops of Kuroki's army landed at Chinnampo midway between Chemulpo and the Yalu River and advanced north to Pyongyang and then to the Yalu.

Tōgō, meanwhile, was frustrated at his inability to destroy the Russian naval forces at Port Arthur in the initial attack, and he was now obliged to keep up the pressure and adopt attrition tactics. A new Russian commander, Vice Admiral Stepan Ossipovitch Makarov, took command at Port Arthur and initiated a series of sorties to harass the Japanese cruisers, while avoiding contact with Tōgō's battleships. Both sides also laid minefields, but Makarov was killed and his battleship lost when it ran over a known Japanese minefield in

April. The Japanese also lost two battleships to mines off Port Arthur. But Japan now rushed troops into southern Manchuria. General Nogi Maresuke and his Third Army cut off Port Arthur and drove back to the north Russian forces attempting to relieve the fortress.

Following the first Japanese land assault on Port Arthur, Czar Nicholas II ordered Admiral Vilgelm Vitgeft, Makarov's successor, to break free and steam to Vladivostok. Vitgeft was determined to take the whole squadron, and on August 10 he sortied with 18 ships. That afternoon Tōgō closed on the Russians with 34 ships and 29 torpedo boats. In the Battle of the Yellow Sea, Tōgō's omnipresent good luck held. Although themselves struck hard, the Japanese ships scored two hits late in the day that killed Vitgeft and put the flagship out of control and the Russian battle line into complete confusion. The Russian squadron then scattered. No Russian ship had been destroyed or taken in the battle, however. Five battleships, 1 cruiser, and 3 destroyers regained Port Arthur. Most others were interned in Chinese ports and Saigon.

News of the Battle of the Yellow Sea reached Vladivostok on August 11, but not until August 13 did three cruisers under Rear Admiral Nikolai von Essen steam to the assistance of the Port Arthur Squadron. On August 14 they ran into Admiral Kammimura Hikonojo's four armored cruisers. In the resulting Battle of Ulsan, the Japanese sank one of the Russian cruisers. The others were able to regain Vladivostok, but Japan now had complete control of the sea.

That autumn in Manchuria, Japanese land forces under General Oyama Iwao engaged the main Russian forces under General Alexsei Kuropatkin. In the great Battle of Liaoyang (August 25–September 3, 1904), the Japanese lost 23,000 men against only 19,000 Russians. Kuropatkin repulsed three days of Japanese assaults but, believing he had been defeated, began a well-managed, systematic withdrawal toward Mukden. During October 5–17 the two sides fought another battle at the Shao-Ho (Shaho, Sha River). In this battle the Russians lost some 40,000 men, the Japanese 20,000.

On January 2, 1905, Port Arthur, now blockaded by land and sea, surrendered. This released the bulk of Nogi's Third Army for deployment north. During January 26–27 another land battle occurred in Manchuria at Sandepu (Heikoutai). The Russians, now reinforced to 300,000 men, took the offensive against Oyama's 220,000 Japanese. Kuropatkin was close to victory but failed to press his advantage, and the battle ended in stalemate.

By the third week in February, Russian forces were drawn up along a 47-mile line south of the city of Mukden (present-day Shenyang), an important rail center in southeastern Manchuria. The Russians deployed three armies, the Japanese four. Estimates of strength vary widely, but the two sides appear to have been evenly matched in numbers, with each side fielding as many as 310,000 men. The battle, during February 21–March 10, 1905, saw the Japanese attacking the entrenched Russians.

Oyama's initial attacks came at the strongest point of the Russian line, against the First Army on the eastern flank. Kuropatkin sent in reserves, halting the attack. Oyama then dispatched Nogi's Third Army in a wide flanking maneuver across the Hun River, attempting to turn the Russian right flank, held by the Russian Third Army under Baron General A. V. Kaulbars.

By the end of the first day's fighting, the Japanese had driven the Russian right back so that it faced west, defending the rail line to the north instead of to the south. Russian reserves again blunted the Japanese attack, however. Attacks and counterattacks continued. Oyama then reinforced Nogi, and the Japanese again tried to outflank Kaulbars on the Russian right. During heavy fighting on March 6–8, the Russians were driven back to the point that Kuropatkin feared that his lines of communication north might be cut. On March 10 Kuropatkin withdrew his forces northward in orderly fashion, on the cities of Teih-ling (Tieling) and Harbin. Casualty figures vary widely, but the Russians lost something on the order of 100,000 men and much equipment, while Japanese casualties may have totaled 70,000 men. Kuropatkin's forces were still largely intact. Nonetheless, the heavy losses sustained at Mukden and in prior battles, coupled with increasing domestic unrest in Russia, culminated in the start on January 22 of the Russian Revolution of 1905, giving the czar and his advisers pause. Russia's leaders, however, were determined on one more toss of the dice, committing their Baltic Fleet, renamed the 2nd Pacific Squadron, that had been sent around the world to the Far East. If the Russians could gain control of the sea, they could cut off Japanese forces in Manchuria and bombard Japanese coastal cities, forcing Japan from the war.

On October 15 Rear Admiral Zinovi Petrovitch Rozhdestvenski's 36 warships had set out on what would be a seven-month odyssey. The most powerful units were the 4 new 13,500-ton Borodino-class battleships: the *Borodino, Alexander III, Orel,* and *Kniaz Suvarov.* The voyage went badly from the start. On October 21 off the Dogger Bank in the North Sea, jittery Russian crews opened fire on their own cruiser, the *Aurora,* and the British Hull fishing fleet, mistaking them for Japanese torpedo boats and sinking several trawlers. This incident almost brought war with Britain.

After the fleet rounded Portugal, some ships proceeded eastward through the Mediterranean and the Suez Canal, while the main detachment continued south around Africa. With the British (a Japanese ally) refusing to supply coal, the Russians were forced to secure it from German colliers. The lack of coaling stations led Rozhdestvenski to order the ships to take on whatever they could, placing it in every possible space and precluding training and gunnery practice.

Reunited at Madagascar, on March 16 the fleet started across the Indian Ocean, refueling five times at sea—an unprecedented feat. Rozhdestvenski hoped to get to Vladivostok without battle, but the fleet made one last stop to take on supplies and coal at Cam Ranh Bay, in French Indochina. The Russian ships then slowly made their way north through the South China Sea and up the Chinese coast.

Rozhdestvenski sent most of his auxiliary vessels to anchor at the mouth of the Yangtse River, and he timed his advance through the Tsushima Straits to be at night. He also sent two cruisers toward the east coast of Japan in a vain attempt to persuade the Japanese that the entire fleet would follow.

At sea for eight months and halfway around the world from their Baltic bases, the Russians prepared to meet Fleet Admiral Tōgō's modern, efficient, battle-tested Japanese fleet in its home waters. Tōgō gambled that Rozhdestvenski would choose the most direct route to Vladivostok, by means of the Tsushima Straits, and planned a trap there. The Japanese also had cut off Vladivostok by sowing 715 mines at the entrance to Peter the Great Bay.

On the night of May 26–27 Japanese picket ships sighted the Russian fleet in the straits; Tōgō's ships immediately left their bases, dumping coal as they went to increase their speed. Tōgō relied on radio messages to keep informed of the location of the Russian ships (Tsushima was the first naval battle in which the radio was used in action). The total Russian fleet consisted of eight battleships, eight cruisers, nine destroyers, and several smaller vessels. The firepower of the two fleets was slightly to the Russian advantage, but this was offset by the fact that the Japanese crews were far superior to the Russians in gunnery.

Tōgō had 4 battleships, 8 cruisers, 21 destroyers, and 60 torpedo boats. Many factors favored Tōgō. His ships had been recently overhauled and repaired. They also possessed the important advantage of superior speed; the ships were, on the average, about 50 percent faster than the Russian vessels, even the newest of which were fouled from the long voyage. Tōgō's men were fresh and eager, battle-tested, sailing in their own waters, and led by highly skilled officers.

On the afternoon of May 27 the 2nd Pacific Squadron, trailed by Japanese cruisers, sailed past Tsushima Island. When the Russian ships came out of some fog at 1:19 p.m., Tōgō in the battleship *Mikasa* to the northeast at last sighted his prey. The Russian ships were steaming in two columns. Rozhdestvenski had his flag in the *Suvarov*, the lead ship in the starboard column.

The Russians assumed that Tōgō would turn south and bridge the gap, allowing his battleships to fire on the weaker Russian divisions, but this would have left the Russian ships headed toward Vladivostok, with the Japanese moving in the opposite direction. Instead Tōgō made a daring move, ordering his cruisers to make a

270-degree turn to the northeast in order to cut the Russians off from Vladivostok. This brought the Japanese ships onto a course parallel to that of the Russians; with their superior speed they would turn east and cross the Russian "T" at leisure.

This maneuver carried grave risks, because during the long turn Tōgō exposed in succession his entire line of ships to the full broadsides fire of the Russian fleet. Seconds after the *Mikasa* began its turn, the *Suvarov* opened fire at a range of about 6,400 yards. Other Russian ships followed suit. As the fleets formed into two converging lines, each blasted away at the other. Rozhdestvenski altered course slightly to port, reducing the range, but the Russian fire rapidly deteriorated as the range closed. The Russians scored few direct hits.

Russian fire damaged three Japanese ships, hit many others, and forced a cruiser out of the battle line. But soon the *Suvarov* was on fire, and another battleship, the *Oslyabya*, was holed in its side. The Japanese concentrated their fire on these two crippled battleships, and their superior gunnery gradually told.

By nightfall the Japanese victory was nearly complete. Wounded in the battle, Rozhdestvenski yielded command to Rear Admiral Nicholas Nebogatov. That night Tōgō sent his destroyers and torpedo boats to finish off those Russian vessels not already sunk or escaped. Isolated fighting continued throughout the night, but by the next day the Japanese had sunk, captured, or disabled eight Russian battleships.

Of 12 Russian ships in the battle line, 8 were sunk, including 3 of the new battleships, and the other 4 had been captured. Of the cruisers, 4 were sunk and 1 was scuttled; 3 limped into Manila and were interned; another made it to Vladivostok. Of the destroyers, 4 were sunk, 1 was captured, 1 was interned at Shanghai, and 2 reached Vladivostok. Three special service ships were sunk, 1 was interned at Shanghai, and 1 escaped to Madagascar.

Tōgō lost only three torpedo boats. Although other ships suffered damage, all remained serviceable. The Russians had 4,830 men killed or drowned and just under 7,000 taken prisoner. Japanese personnel losses were 110 killed and 590 wounded.

In just one day Russia ceased to be a major Pacific power. Fifty years would pass before it regained status at sea. The battle also led the Japanese to believe that wars could be turned by one big battle. Ironically, Tsushima was also the only major decisive fleet action in the history of the steel battleship. Only the gun had counted. In the future, underwater or aerial weapons would often exercise the dominant influence at sea.

Both Kaiser Wilhelm II and U.S. president Theodore Roosevelt had urged peace upon the belligerents. Although Russia, with its vast resources and manpower, might possibly have sent new armies to continue the war, popular discontent and political unrest at home alarmed the czar's ministers, and they were therefore willing to consider peace proposals. On the other hand, its military efforts had nearly bankrupted Japan (a fact that Japanese leaders had carefully concealed from the Japanese people), so its leaders were also ready to halt military operations.

On Roosevelt's invitation a peace conference opened in the unlikely venue of Portsmouth, New Hampshire. Sergei Witte ably represented Russia at the conference and succeeded in saving his country from the worst consequences of the defeat. The September 5, 1905, Treaty of Portsmouth transferred Russia's cessions in southern Manchuria to Japan, converting that area into a Japanese sphere of influence. Russia also recognized Japan's preponderant interest in Korea and its right to control and "protect" the Korean government. In addition, Russia surrendered to Japan the southern half of Sakhalin Island, which Japan had occupied during the war. The treaty, favorable as it was to Japan, was not popular there, for Japanese leaders had not obtained the indemnity they wanted, and the Japanese people were unaware how close the country was to bankruptcy.

Significance

The Russo-Japanese War showcased the high stakes involved in Great Power rivalry in East Asia. The 1890s had witnessed a significant imperial push in the Far East, perhaps best exemplified by the Sino-Japanese War of 1894–1895, the Spanish-American War of 1898, and the Philippine-American War of 1898–1902. Coming on the heels of turn-of-the-century expansionism and the Boxer Rebellion, the Russo-Japanese War capped off a feverish scramble for hegemony in the Far East driven by a search for markets, imperial aspirations, and military and geostrategic concerns. The war saw the emergence of the machine gun as an important weapon, but the European powers, with the exception of the Germans, seemed not to take much notice.

Japanese had not only halted Russian expansion in the Far East but had shown the world that a new Great Power had arisen in Asia. Indeed, the war confirmed Japan as the premier military power of the Far East. The Japanese victory also rocked all Asia in the sense that the myth of European military supremacy had been forever shattered and helped set the stage for the showdown between Japan and the United States in 1941.

Further Reading

Busch, Noel F. *The Emperor's Sword.* New York: Funk and Wagnalls, 1969.

Corbett, Julian S. *Maritime Operations in the Russo-Japanese War, 1904–1905.* 2 vols. Rockville, MD: Sidney Kramer, 1994.

Evans, David C., and Mark R. Peattie. *Kaigun: Strategy, Tactics, and Technology in the Imperial Japanese Navy, 1887–1941.* Annapolis, MD: Naval Institute Press, 1997.

Grove, Eric. *Big Fleet Actions: Tsushima, Jutland, Philippine Sea.* London: Arms and Armour, 1995.

Hough, Richard. *The Fleet That Had to Die.* New York: Viking, 1958.

Warner, Denis, and Peggy Warner. *The Tide at Sunrise: A History of the Russo-Japanese War, 1904–1905.* New York: Charterhouse, 1974.

World War I (1914–1918)

Dates	July 28, 1914–November 11, 1918
Location	Europe, Africa, Middle East, Atlantic Ocean, Pacific Ocean
Combatants	Central Powers of Austria-Hungary, Germany, Ottoman Empire, Bulgaria vs. Allied Powers of Serbia, Belgium, Russia, Britain, France, Japan, Italy, Romania, the United States
Principal Commanders	Austria-Hungary: Franz Joseph I, Karl I, Franz Conrad von Hötzendorf Germany: Kaiser Wilhelm I, Helmuth von Moltke, Erich von Falkenhayn, Paul von Hindenburg, Erich Ludendorff Ottoman Empire: Enver Pasha, Liman von Sanders Bulgaria: Czar Ferdinand I, Nikola Zhekov Russia: Czar Nicholas II, Pavel Rennenkampf, Aleksandr Samsonov, Grand Duke Nicholas, Aleksei Brusilov, Aleksandr Kerensky France: Georges Clemenceau, Joseph Jacques Césaire Joffre, Robert Nivelle, Philippe Henri Pétain, Ferdinand Foch Great Britain: Herbert Henry Asquith, David Lloyd George, Winston Churchill, Sir John French, Sir Douglas Haig Japan: Emperor Taishō Italy: King Victor Emmanuel III, Luigi Cadorna, Armando Diaz Romania: King Ferdinand I United States: Woodrow Wilson, John J. Pershing Belgium: King Albert I
Principal Battles	Frontiers, Mons, Tannenberg, Masurian Lakes (first), Marne (first), Ypres (first), Falkland Islands, Champagne (first), Aisne (first), Dardanelles, Gallipoli, Verdun, Somme, Brusilov Offensive, Jutland, Nivelle Offensive, Ypres (third), Caporetto, Kerensky Offensive, Marne (second), Somme Offensive (Second Battle of the Somme), Saint-Mihiel, Meuse-Argonne
Outcome	The Allies are victorious, bringing the demise of all the continental empires. The United States becomes the world's leading financial and industrial power. Dissatisfaction with the peace settlement and the unwillingness of the victors to enforce it bring a renewal of the fighting a generation later in World War II.

Causes

Impetus for a general European war had been building for decades, and all the major European powers bore some measure of responsibility for the war that began in 1914. Historians usually identify five underlying causes: nationalism (the triumph of statism over internationalism but also the desire of subject minorities to have their own nation states), two hostile alliance systems, imperialist and trade rivalries, an arms race, and economic and social tensions.

Nationalism was the major impetus, and nowhere was this more obvious than in Austria-Hungary, a mélange of at least a dozen minorities. Germans (23 percent) and Magyars (19 percent) dominated, but early in the 20th century Slavic nationalism, championed by neighboring Serbia, threatened the Dual Monarchy. Enjoying the support of Russia, Serbia had long sought to be the nucleus of a large state embracing all the southern Slavs. In 1908 in an effort to diminish Serb influence and cut it off from access to the sea, the Dual Monarchy annexed Bosnia-Herzegovina. This almost brought war with Russia. Austria-Hungary also insisted on the creation of an independent Albania.

Germany—Europe's preeminent military power—was Austria-Hungary's closest ally and supported its action in Bosnia-Herzegovina. The German Empire had come into being as a consequence of the Franco-Prussian War of 1870–1871. Having imposed a draconian peace settlement on France, German chancellor Otto von Bismarck sought to isolate that country, which was bent on revenge. An arrangement with both Austria-Hungary and Russia (the Dreikaiserbund, or Three Emperors' League) shattered on their competition in the Balkans. Forced to choose, Bismarck in 1879 selected Austria-Hungary as Germany's principal ally. This Dual Alliance was the bedrock of German foreign policy into World War I. Not prepared to cast Russia adrift, however, in 1887 Bismarck concluded the so-called Reinsurance Treaty with it, which he kept secret from Austria.

As long as Bismarck was chancellor France remained isolated, but in 1888 Wilhelm II became emperor. Young, rash, and headstrong, he soon clashed with Bismarck and in 1890 dropped him as chancellor and dramatically changed Germany's foreign policy. Relations with Russia were already frayed, but the situation was made worse when in 1890 Wilhelm ordered that the Reinsurance Treaty not be renewed. Russia was rapidly industrializing and seeking foreign capital, and France stepped into the breach. By 1894 the two had forged a military alliance against Germany.

Thus, by 1914 there were two mutually antagonistic alliance systems in Europe. The first consisted of Germany and Austria-Hungary. Separate from it was the Triple Alliance of 1882 of Germany-Austria-Hungary and Italy, made possible because of Italian anger over France's seizure of Tunis, but Italy was an increasingly reluctant ally.

France and Russia formed the second alliance, to which Britain was informally linked. During World War I the latter three (with Japan and then Italy after 1915) became known as the Entente Powers, the Entente, the Allied Powers, or simply the Allies. Germany and Austria-Hungary (later the Ottoman Empire and Bulgaria) were, for their geographical location, the Central Powers.

Wilhelm II was not content with Germany being the preeminent European

WESTERN FRONT, 1914

power; he wanted it to be the preeminent world power. He reversed Bismarck's wise policy of not building a strong navy so as not to antagonize Britain, and the result was a naval-building contest between the two powers beginning in the mid-1890s. Wilhelm II and Grand Admiral Alfred von Tirpitz saw Germany challenging Britain on the seas for world mastery. Wilhelm II's bellicose actions alienated would-be allies and created a climate of uncertainty. Many Germans, however, saw themselves encircled and denied their rightful place in the sun.

The economic transformation experienced by Germany after 1871 brought social change and worker unrest, the rise of socialism, and the antagonism of most political parties toward the government, which despite a democratic veneer was controlled by the kaiser and the military. Some German leaders saw a general European war as a means to unite the country.

France also looked forward to war. In addition to an indemnity of more than twice the cost of the war to Prussia, the Treaty of Frankfurt of 1871 had stripped it of Alsace and Lorraine. French foreign policy after 1871 is said to have been dominated by one word: revenge. France had found immediate gratification in empire building, but this almost brought war with Britain. In 1904, however, the two ended decades of rivalry in an agreement on colonial issues. Britain and Russia concluded a similar arrangement in 1907.

Russia was beginning to enter the modern age, although Czar Nicholas II would make no concessions to political change. Russia sought ascendancy in the Balkans and control of the straits to ensure free access from the Black Sea into the Mediterranean. Humiliated in the Russo-Japanese War (1904–1905), Russia had expended considerable resources in rebuilding its military. Russian industrial and military growth, which included the construction of new strategic railroads, raised alarm bells in Berlin. Chief of the German General Staff Colonel General Helmuth von Moltke said in May 1914 that in several years Russia would be rearmed and the Entente Powers would then be so powerful that it would be difficult for Germany to defeat them. Germany therefore had no alternative but to seek a preventive war while there was a chance of victory.

Britain followed its traditional pattern of involving itself in continental affairs only to preserve vital national interests or the European balance of power, but Germany's decision to build a powerful navy drove it to the side of France. The British also viewed growing German industrial might and trade as a threat. Although aligned with France and Russia, Britain's sole military responsibility in 1914 was a 1912 pledge to protect France's coasts from German naval attack.

Several crises almost brought general European war in the decade before 1914. Two, in 1904–1905 and in 1911, involved Morocco when Germany, with no vital interests at stake, threatened war to block a French takeover. In 1908 war almost erupted over Austria's annexation of Bosnia-Herzegovina, but Russia backed down. In 1911 Italy went to war with the Ottoman Empire to secure present-day Libya and the Dodecanese islands. Then in 1912 and 1913 two regional wars raged in the Balkans, both of which had threatened to draw in the big powers and bring world war.

In 1914 a Serb nationalist organization linked to the Serbian military undertook the assassination of Archduke Franz Ferdinand, heir to the Austrian throne and believed to favor greater rights for Slavs within the Dual Monarchy. This was a threat to Serbian aspirations. On June 28, 1914, in Sarajevo, Bosnia, young Bosnian Serb nationalist Gavrilo Princip shot to death Franz Ferdinand and his wife as they rode in an open car. This event touched off World War I, also known as the Great War.

Austrian leaders sought to use the assassination to advantage, envisioning a localized Balkan conflict in which the Serbian question would be settled "once and for all." But Austria required German support, as this might bring on a general European war. Russia had backed down in 1908, but this made a second retreat less likely. German leaders were well aware that Austria-Hungary intended to attack Serbia, but because the Dual Monarchy was its only reliable ally, on July 6, 1914, Berlin again pledged its support in the famous blank check.

On July 7 Vienna proposed a surprise attack on Serbia, but the Hungarians insisted on diplomacy first. To cloak the intention to crush Serbia, the Austro-Hungarian council of ministers approved an ultimatum couched so that Serbia must reject it. On July 22 Germany approved the terms, and a day later it was sent to Belgrade with the demand for a reply within 48 hours.

To the world's surprise, Serbia responded within the time limit, accepting all the Austrian demands except those directly impinging on its sovereignty but offering to accept arbitration by the Hague Court or a decision of the big powers regarding these. Vienna declared the response unsatisfactory, severed diplomatic relations with Serbia, and ordered partial military mobilization; Serbia had already mobilized.

In St. Petersburg the Russian government hoped to bluff Vienna into backing down by ordering "preparatory measures" for a partial military mobilization. This step on July 26 had the support of the Russian General Staff, which believed that war was inevitable.

On July 28 the Third Balkan War began when Austria-Hungary formally declared war on Serbia; later that day it commenced shelling Belgrade. On July 29 Russia ordered actual mobilization in four Russian military districts. Czar Nicholas II made the decision only with great difficulty and after an exchange of telegrams with Kaiser Wilhelm. On July 30 Russia ordered a general mobilization. This ensured that the Balkan war would become a general European conflict, for military timetables came into play.

In planning for the possibility of a two-front war against France and Russia, General of Cavalry Alfred von Schlieffen, chief of the German General Staff during 1891–1906, envisioned sending most German military strength against France with a holding action against a slowly mobilizing Russia. Following the rapid defeat of France, Germany would then deal with Russia. Implicit in this was that Germany could not allow the Russians to mobilize and still win the war. The German government therefore demanded that Russia halt its mobilization. With no answer forthcoming, on August 1 Germany ordered general mobilization.

The French cabinet had refused to mobilize the army but did order troops to take up position on the frontier, although far enough from it so as to convince British public opinion that France was not initiating hostilities. The Schlieffen Plan, however, mandated that there be no delay in opening an attack against France. Thus, on August 1 the Germans demanded to know how France would respond to war between Germany and Russia. Berlin insisted that even if France pledged neutrality, it would have to surrender certain eastern fortresses as proof of sincerity. No French government could agree to this, and Premier René Viviani replied that France would act in accordance with its interests. That same day France ordered military mobilization. On August 3, Germany declared war on France.

Course

Four of the five great European powers were now at war. Britain held back. As early as July 31, London had demanded assurances from both Paris and Berlin to respect Belgian neutrality, guaranteed by the major powers since 1839. France replied affirmatively, but German declined. Again, the Schlieffen Plan drove German policy. Schlieffen had regarded the heavily fortified frontier of eastern France, where the French Army would undoubtedly mass, as a formidable obstacle. The quickest way to defeat France was to invade from the northeast through Belgium.

On August 2, German troops occupied Luxembourg. The same day Berlin demanded the right of transit through Belgium. Brussels rejected this on August 3, and early the next morning German troops invaded. This brought Britain into the war, and on August 5 it announced a state of war with Germany. Italy declared that the Triple Alliance did not obligate it to fight an aggressive war and remained neutral. Within a few weeks, however, the

Ottoman Empire joined the Central Powers, and Japan sided with the Allies.

For the Allies, the most potent weapon was Britain's Royal Navy. Britain also had the world's largest merchant marine, vital for securing and transporting war materials. With 19 million tons of shipping, it was half the world's total.

On land, the advantage lay with the Central Powers. Germany had the world's largest and most efficient army and the largest reserve of male citizens, second to Russia. France had the next largest army but was weak in reserves because its population was some 25 million less than that of Germany. France could, however, draw on its colonial population for manpower.

Considering everything, the Allies were much stronger than the Central Powers. One calculation for August 1914 has the Allies with 199 infantry divisions and 50 cavalry divisions to 137 and 22, respectively, for the Central Powers. The combined Allied population was also much larger—279 million to 120 million—and the Allies were much better placed economically. Industrial output and agricultural strength were keys to the outcome. If the war could be prolonged and all other factors remained equal, economics and demography would give the Allies victory. The German General Staff had no intention of fighting a prolonged war and had made careful preparations to defeat France in one quick blow.

The advance into Belgium went as planned, with Liège and other Belgian fortresses pounded into submission by August 16. The actual delay to the Germans was only several days. In Schlieffen's plan everything depended on a preponderance of strength on the invading right wing. The vast wheeling movement through Belgium would roll up the French Army to the east

of Paris and smash it against the German frontier. Schlieffen had 68 divisions marching west and only 10 with supporting local troops facing the Russians. Of the force sent against France, the right wing north of Metz would have 59 divisions, the left only 9—a ratio of 7:1.

Schlieffen's successor Moltke made key modifications to the plan, weakening the ratio of right-wing to left-wing forces by adding 8 of 9 new divisions to the left wing and only 1 to the right, with 55 divisions on the right wing and 23 on the left. Schlieffen was prepared to accept temporary defeat in Lorraine and even draw French forces into Germany to secure overall victory. Then, with the campaign in progress and because the Russians moved faster than anticipated, Moltke detached some 80,000 men from the right wing and sent them east. Given the excellent French rail net that allowed quick troop movements, the Schlieffen Plan might not have worked in any case, but Moltke gave it no chance.

Meanwhile, French Army chief of staff General of Division General Joseph Jacques Césaire Joffre, a staunch advocate of offensive action, planned a massive easterly drive to retake Alsace and Lorraine. Despite knowledge that the Germans were likely to attempt a strong thrust through Belgium, Joffre's Plan XVII of 1913 placed three of the five French armies on the borders of Alsace and Lorraine. Only one army, the Fifth Army, was in the critical area of the Belgian frontier. Plan XVII met quick defeat, but thanks to the French railroads, Joffre was able to shift forces northward.

Meanwhile, the British transported all available troops to the continent. The British Expeditionary Force (BEF) of 160,000 men commanded by Field Marshal Sir

John French was small in size but highly trained. It assumed position on the left wing of the French Fifth Army. At Mons (August 23) the BEF encountered the full weight of Colonel General Alexander von Kluck's First Army. Although heavily outnumbered, the British inflicted some 5,000 casualties for 1,638 of their own. With the Germans outnumbering the Allied forces facing them and moving in a wider arc than supposed, the Fifth Army and the BEF were in danger of being cut off. The Allies then staged a general withdrawal to within 25 miles of Paris. With the city's fall seeming certain, the French government departed for Bordeaux.

By September 4, five German armies pressed along a line that sagged below the Marne River east and northeast of Paris. These forces had been thinned, however, by the two corps sent to the Eastern Front and troops in occupation duties. Indeed, the Allies now had a slight numerical advantage. The time had come for the French to stand; as Joffre put it, they were to "die in their tracks rather than retreat." French reconnaissance aircraft and cavalry patrols revealed that Kluck was swinging east of the capital, exposing his army's flank to the French Sixth Army and the Paris garrison. Military governor of Paris General of Division Joseph Gallieni secured approval from Joffre for a flanking attack.

The ensuing Battle of the Marne (September 5–12) involved more than 2 million men. With the Allies able to exploit a gap between the German First and Second Armies, the Germans began a withdrawal on September 9. What the French called the "Miracle of the Marne" denied Germany the quick victory it needed to win the war. Losses in the battle are largely guesswork, but the Allies probably sustained some 263,000 casualties (81,700

dead), with German losses about the same. On September 14, General of Infantry Erich von Falkenhayn replaced Moltke as chief of the General Staff.

A race to the sea now ensued, with each side endeavoring to turn the other's flank. Falkenhayn attempted to capture the English Channel ports, but heavy fighting occurred all the way south to Verdun. The holdout Belgian port of Antwerp surrendered to the Germans on October 10, and King Albert I brought out what remained of the Belgian army to behind the Yser River. In the Battle of the Yser (October 18–November 30), Belgian and French forces held off the Germans. The Belgians opened sluice gates and flooded the countryside, forcing the Germans to shift their efforts southward. Belgian and British troops held a small sector of northwestern Belgium for the remainder of the war.

In the sanguinary First Battle of Ypres (October 22–November 22), Falkenhayn again sought unsuccessfully to outflank the British. The battle was particularly costly to the Germans, who called it the Kindermord von Ypren (Massacre of the Innocents at Ypres) for the 134,000 men, most of them young draftees, lost there. The BEF suffered 58,000 casualties, while French losses were some 50,000 and Belgian losses were about 19,000. But the channel ports, vital for British resupply, had been saved. The battle ended the war of movement and began that of trenches and stalemate.

The front now extended some 350 miles from the English Channel to the Swiss frontier. Both sides constructed dugouts and laid barbed wire. Trenches were necessary for protection against the machine-gun and quick-firing artillery. Multiple trench lines soon appeared. The area between the two opposing frontline trenches

EASTERN FRONT, 1914 – 1918

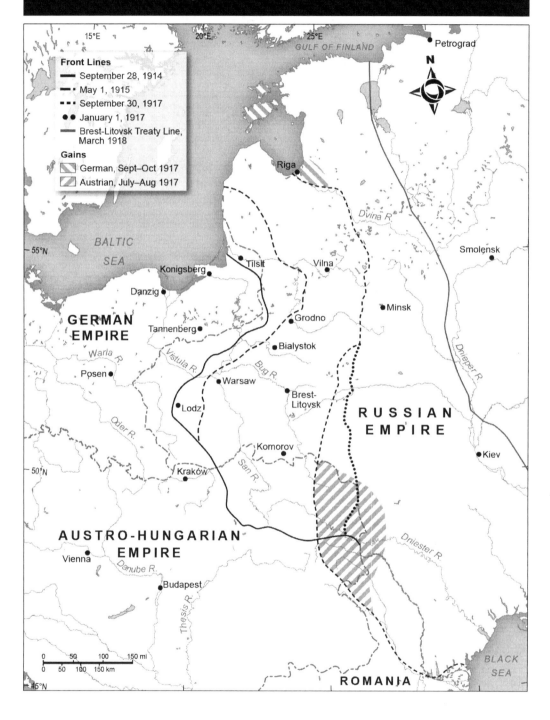

Front Lines
— September 28, 1914
–·– May 1, 1915
---- September 30, 1917
•• January 1, 1917
— Brest-Litovsk Treaty Line, March 1918

Gains
▨ German, Sept–Oct 1917
▨ Austrian, July–Aug 1917

GULF OF FINLAND
Petrograd

15°E 20°E 25°E

N

Riga

Dvina R.

Smolensk

BALTIC SEA

55°N

Tilsit
Konigsberg
Vilna
Danzig
Minsk
GERMAN EMPIRE
Grodno
Tannenberg
Bialystok
Warla R.
Vistula R.
Posen
Warsaw
Bug R.
Brest-Litovsk
Lodz
Dnieper R.
Oder R.
RUSSIAN EMPIRE
Komorov
Kiev
50°N
San R.
Kraków
AUSTRO-HUNGARIAN EMPIRE
Dniester R.
Vienna
Danube R.
Budapest

0   50   100   150 mi
0 50 100 150 km

Thesis R.

BLACK SEA

45°N

ROMANIA

was no-man's-land. From the end of 1914 until early 1918, there was no change of more than 10 miles in the front lines on the Western Front, with the sole exception being a 1917 voluntary German withdrawal from the Noyon salient.

Convinced that his armies could break through the German lines, Joffre pressed the offensive, targeting the Noyon salient between Arras and Reims that pointed toward Paris. Joffre planned to strike both its sides: from the Artois plateau against its western side and northward from Champagne. These met failure in the First Battle of Artois (December 17–January 4) and the First Battle of Champagne (December 20–March 17). Five months of war on the Western Front in 1914 had cost some 1.7 million casualties.

Simultaneous with the German invasion of Belgium and France, fighting began on the Eastern Front. Owing in large part to the length of the front, combat here was much more fluid.

In prewar planning, Russia had agreed to strike early to divert German strength east. Commander of the Northwest Front Group General Yakov Zhilinsky had some 300,000 men each in General Pavel K. Rennenkampf's First Army and General Aleksandr V. Samsonov's Second Army. Although Russian forces outnumbered those of the Germans in East Prussia by almost three to one, they were seriously deficient in weapons and logistical support.

Colonel General Maximilian von Prittwitz und Gaffron's Eighth Army consisted largely of garrison troops and reserves. If unable to defend East Prussia, Prittwitz was to withdraw to the Vistula and hold there until help could arrive from the Western Front.

On August 17 the First Army, the northernmost of the two Russian pincers,

began crossing the frontier. Two days later the Second Army also advanced. Once past the physical obstacle of the Masurian Lakes between them, the two armies were to link up and drive on Berlin, but cooperation seemed remote because the two commanders were bitter enemies. The Germans also were aware of Russian plans and dispositions thanks to Russian radio messages sent without code.

Two German attacks on the Russians heightened Rennenkampf's innate sense of caution, but Prittwitz panicked on learning of Samsonov's advance and ordered a withdrawal. His deputy, Colonel Max Hoffmann, convinced Prittwitz to change his mind and order a concentration against Samsonov. Unaware of Prittwitz's change of heart, Moltke sacked him. The Eighth Army's new commander was Colonel General Paul von Beckendorff und Hindenburg, with Major General Erich Ludendorff as his chief of staff. They drew up a plan nearly identical to that by Hoffmann. Three corps would move south by train to join the one already there, leaving only a single cavalry division to oppose Rennenkampf who, had he moved, could have taken the Eighth Army in the rear. Zhilinsky repeatedly urged this, to no avail.

In the resultant Battle of Tannenberg (August 26–31) the Germans had some 165,000 men, the Russians 205,000, but the Second Army was widely spread. The Germans slowly closed the ring on Samsonov, who committed suicide. The Russians sustained 122,000 casualties (90,000 prisoners) and lost 500 guns; German losses were only 10,000–15,000 men.

The Germans then returned north, reinforced by Moltke's Western Front addition, to reengage Rennenkampf. The Russians still held a numerical advantage, but in the First Battle of the Masurian

Lakes (September 7–13) Rennenkampf was defeated. The Russians lost 100,000 killed or wounded, 45,000 prisoners, and 150 guns. German casualties were around 70,000. Rennenkampf did manage to withdraw what was left of his army.

Concurrently, the Russians met success against the Austrians in Galicia. Here the Austrians had about 1 million men, the Russians 1.2 million. Russian Southwestern Front commander General Nikolai I. Ivanov expected the Austrians to attack due east from the fortress of Lviv (Lemberg, in present-day Ukraine). He positioned two armies to defend there while sending two other armies south from Russian Poland to cut the Austrians off from Kraków (Cracow) and capture their fortresses of Lviv and Przemyśl. Ivanov then planned to clear the Carpathian passes and advance on Budapest and Vienna.

Meanwhile, chief of the Austro-Hungarian General Staff General of Infantry Conrad von Hötzendorf ordered most of his forces to advance to Lublin against Russian positions east of Warsaw. This attack of August 23 immediately collided with Ivanov's two southward-advancing armies near Lviv, the major city of eastern Galicia. The Austrians were soon in retreat, and Conrad abandoned Lviv. The Russians advanced more than 100 miles to the Carpathians and in late September laid siege to some 100,000 Austrians at Przemyśl. Altogether the Austrians sustained some 300,000 casualties, including 100,000 prisoners, and lost 300 guns. The Russians lost some 255,000 men (45,000 prisoners) and 182 guns, but they now held most of Galicia and were in position to outflank Germany's major industrial center of Silesia.

On September 29 the Germans opened an offensive in Poland with their new Ninth Army. It reached almost to Warsaw before Hindenburg withdrew on October 17. Faced with the prospect of an invasion of Silesia but privy to Russian plans through radio intercepts, Hindenburg moved the Ninth Army 250 miles north to Toruń at the northern tip of the Polish salient. The Austrian Second Army took over the Ninth Army's former positions.

Oblivious to the German presence, in mid-November the Russians began their Silesia offensive. The Ninth Army caught Rennenkampf's First Army on its right flank, taking 12,000 prisoners in two days and resulting in Rennenkampf's dismissal. The Germans then smashed into the flank of the Second Army. Defeated in the Battles of Łódź and Łowicz (November 16–25), the Russians withdrew back on Łódź. On December 6 they retired to before Warsaw. German losses totaled approximately 35,000; Russian casualties approached 95,000, including 25,000 prisoners.

Fierce fighting also occurred in Serbia. Austrian commander General Oskar Potiorek's forces greatly outnumbered Field Marshal Radomír Putnik's 200,000-man Serbian Army. The Austrians finally captured Belgrade on December 2, but the Serbs counterattacked and by the end of the year had cleared Serbia of the invaders. Austria-Hungary had lost 227,000 men, Serbia around 70,000.

At sea, the Royal Navy chased down German merchant ships or drove them into neutral ports and also hunted down isolated German warships. Then on August 28, the British attacked German naval units at Heligoland Bight, suffering one light cruiser and two destroyers badly damaged but sinking three German light cruisers and one destroyer and damaging three other cruisers. The Germans retaliated with battle cruiser raids against

Yarmouth in November and Hartlepool, Whitby, and Scarborough in December.

Two naval battles also occurred off South America. At the start of hostilities, Vice Admiral Maximilian Graf von Spee moved his East Asia Squadron of two heavy cruisers and three light cruisers from China to Easter Island. He there learned that British vice admiral Sir Christopher Cradock's North American and West Indies Station Squadron was nearby. Cradock had two old heavy cruisers, a light cruiser, and a converted auxiliary cruiser. The two sides clashed off Chile on November 1 in the Battle of Coronel. Both heavy British cruisers were sunk, one with 895 of its 900 men, including Cradock; none of the other ship's 675-man complement survived. The two light British ships managed to escape.

This first defeat for the Royal Navy at sea in a century shocked the British. London sent out to Port Stanley in the Falklands Vice Admiral Sir Frederick Sturdee with two modern battle cruisers, five cruisers, and an auxiliary cruiser. On December 8 Spee, unaware of Sturdee's presence, moved to attack Port Stanley. Discovering the British, Spee endeavored to escape, but Sturdee pursued. The circumstances of Coronel were now reversed. In the Battle of the Falklands it was the British who engaged in a long-range battle that the Germans could not win. Both German heavy cruisers were sunk, as were two of the cruisers. Some 2,000 Germans perished. Sturdee's ships sustained only light damage and just 21 casualties.

The submarine became Germany's most effective weapon at sea. On September 22, one submarine sank three old British cruisers off the Dutch coast. This event signaled a new era in naval warfare.

The Ottoman Empire's entry into the war brought fighting in the Middle East and

Caucasia. The claim of Sultan Mohammed V as leader of Islam and his proclamation of a jihad (holy war) had implications for millions of Muslims in the British and French Empires and southern Russia. The Ottoman Empire also controlled the vital water passageway from the Mediterranean to the Black Sea, through which passed Western military aid to Russia and Russian goods to pay for this. Without this passageway, goods would have to move through the Arctic or to Vladivostok and then overland 5,000 miles on the Trans-Siberian Railway.

On July 28, 1914, the British had sequestered two Ottoman dreadnoughts paid for by popular subscription. This action angered the Turks and greatly aided the pro-German faction in Istanbul. Then with the start of the war, German vice admiral William Souchon escaped Allied warships in the Mediterranean and reached Istanbul with the powerful battle cruiser *Goeben* and the light cruiser *Breslau*. Souchon transferred both to Ottoman control. The ships retained their German crews, and Souchon became commander of the Ottoman Navy. With the secret support of Minister of War Enver Pasha, on October 29 Souchon bombarded Russian bases on the Black Sea under the guise of a training exercise, then falsely reported that the Russians had attacked him first. Russia declared war.

The Ottoman entry into the war led the British to send mostly Indian Army forces to Basra to protect oil facilities in Mesopotamia and to Egypt to guard the vital Suez Canal waterway. There was also heavy fighting between Russian and Ottoman forces in Caucasia, where Russian major general Nicholay Yudenich with 80,000 men defeated an offensive by the Ottoman Third Army of 120,000 men in the Battle of Sarikamish (December 22, 1914–January 17, 1915). The Ottomans sustained 50,000 casualties, the Russians 22,000.

In Asia, Japan capitalized on the preoccupation of the Western powers with Europe to further its imperial ambitions, laying siege to and capturing Qingdao (Tsingtao) and acquiring the German concession of the Shandong (Shantung) Peninsula in China and ultimately the German Pacific islands north of the equator. The Japanese also sought, unsuccessfully, to establish a protectorate over China.

Fighting also occurred in Africa, where French, British, and imperial (South African) forces moved against the German colonies. Although the Allies enjoyed considerable initial success, German colonel Paul von Lettow-Vorbeck, with never more than about 14,000 men (3,000 Germans and 11,000 Africans), tied down some 300,000 British, South African, Belgian, and Portuguese troops in German East Africa, Mozambique, and Rhodesia until the end of the war.

At the end of 1914 the rough parity of forces on the Western Front led Wilhelm II to order Falkenhayn to give priority in 1915 to the war against Russia. Joffre, however, continued to champion an Allied breakthrough on the Western Front. While a renewal of the offensive in Champagne in February gained some ground, it could not be exploited because of poor weather and was halted in mid-March. The British attacked at Neuve Chapelle during March 10–12 as General Douglas Haig sought to capture Aubers Ridge and threaten Lille. Although the British took Neuve Chapelle, their offensive soon collapsed. The Allies concluded that they needed longer and larger preparatory artillery fire and broader attack frontages. The Germans believed that well-entrenched troops, supported by

reserves, could repulse numerically superior attackers. This was well demonstrated in the Battle of the Woëvre (April 5–30), when they halted an attack by the French First Army against both sides of the Saint-Mihiel salient.

Joffre was not deterred. The capture of Vimy Ridge would give command of the Douai plain and put the Allies in position to sever key German rail lines in the Lille area, forcing a German withdrawal. Preparations were disrupted by the Second Battle of Ypres (April 22–May 25), which saw the first successful use of poison gas in the war.

Falkenhayn sought to reduce the Ypres salient and mask transfer of reinforcements eastward. On April 22 after a brief preliminary bombardment, the Germans released 268 tons of chlorine gas; it wiped out two French divisions manning four miles of front. By the end of the day the Allies had sustained 15,000 casualties (5,000 dead and 2,000 prisoners) but had sealed the breach, the Germans having failed to position sufficient reserves. Thereafter the Allies developed their own poison gas, and both sides introduced gas masks.

With the Ypres front stabilized, the French began the Second Battle of Artois (May 9–June 18) following a five-day preliminary bombardment. One French corps reached the crest of Vimy Ridge, only to be thrown back because reserves were too distant. Haig's BEF diversionary attack against Aubers Ridge was ended after only one day.

Joffre still hoped to drive the Germans from the Noyon salient, and he planned simultaneous offensives in Champagne and Artois. The British were to attack near Loos. The offensives began on September 25 following a four-day preliminary bombardment. The Second Battle of Champagne

(September 25–November 6) began well enough. The French outnumbered the Germans almost two to one, but the attackers came up against the second German defensive line well ahead of schedule, and the French artillery opened fire there just as they arrived, forcing the attackers back. The French made several other attempts and briefly penetrated the second German line before German reinforcements halted them. The offensive gained little ground at a cost of 144,000 French casualties to 85,000 for the Germans.

In the Third Battle of Artois (September 25–October 16) Joffre again attempted to take Vimy Ridge. Again he chose firepower and élan over surprise. A four-day preliminary bombardment opened on September 21. Although the French registered some gains, nowhere did they pierce the German second defensive line. On September 25 Haig's British First Army launched a diversionary attack at Loos. It ended in failure, leading London to replace Field Marshal French with Haig. In 1915 on the Western Front, the French suffered 1.292 million casualties and the British 279,000. The Germans lost only 612,000.

A new front opened in 1915, in Italy. Both sides had courted Italy, but the Allies offered territorial gains at the expense of Austria-Hungary, promising the Trentino and southern Tirol (the subsequent Alto Adige) up to the Brenner Pass, Trieste and the Istrian Peninsula, North Dalmatia and islands facing it, and the Dodecanese Islands. On May 23, Italy declared war on the Dual Monarchy.

Italian Army commander General Luigi Cadorna had 875,000 men but was short of heavy guns, ammunition, and motor transport. The border between Austria-Hungary and Italy in the Alps also limited any offensive to the narrow and extremely rugged Isonzo River front. Cardona planned to stand on the defensive on the Trentino front and make the major attack along the Isonzo. Archduke Eugene, the Austrian commander, had heavily fortified the frontier, and the Austrians beat back the Italians in the First (June 23–July 7, 1915), Second (July 18–August 3), Third (October 18–November 4), and Fourth (November 10–December 2) Battles of the Isonzo.

The major German efforts in 1915 came on the Eastern Front. Hindenburg wanted concentration in the north, but Falkenhayn insisted it be in the south to keep Austria-Hungary in the war. The Russians planned to renew their drive into East Prussia but were preempted by the Germans in two offensives: a drive to the north by the Eighth and Tenth Armies from the Masurian Lakes and a southern attack by the new Südarmee (South Army) northwest through the Carpathians toward Lviv but also to relieve the siege of Przemyśl. In order to distract the Russians, at the end of January the German Ninth Army feinted an attack toward Warsaw.

The northern offensive is known as the Second Battle of the Masurian Lakes (February 7–22, 1915). The new German Eighth Army struck the left flank of the Russian Tenth Army, and the German Tenth Army then struck the Russian right. The battle ended after a German advance of some 70 miles. The Russians sustained some 200,000 casualties, including 90,000 prisoners.

The southern offensive was not as successful. The Austrians were unable to relieve Przemyśl, and on March 22 that fortress and its 110,000-man garrison surrendered. The Russians then resumed their Carpathian advance, but the new German-Austrian Südarmee halted it by the end of April.

Falkenhayn planned a major effort in Galicia, with the Austro-Hungarian Fourth and Second Armies supporting the new German Eleventh Army of men from the Western Front. Four Russian armies opposed them. The attack began on May 2, and in two weeks the Central Powers advanced 80 miles. On June 3 they retook Przemyśl, and on June 22 they occupied Lviv, the Russians withdrawing all the way to the Bug River. The Central Powers had retaken all territory lost in 1914.

The southern offensive resumed on July 13, with the German Twelfth Army attacking the northeastern edge of the Polish salient. By the end of July the Germans had taken Lublin. The Russians abandoned Warsaw (August 4–7). Brest-Litovsk fell (August 25), and the Russians withdrew across the Niemen River. By early September the Polish salient ceased to exist, and the Germans stood on Russian soil. The culmination of the drive was the capture of Vilnius (Vilna) on September 19.

In mid-August Falkenhayn unleashed Hindenburg, but bad weather halted him at the end of September, and the front then stabilized. The Russians had given up a swath of territory 300 miles deep. Despite shortages of every kind, Grand Duke Nicholas had managed to preserve the bulk of his forces, only to be relieved of command of the army on August 21 and assigned to the Caucasus front. Czar Nicholas II then assumed personal command, with General Mikhail V. Alekseyev as his chief of staff. For the year Russian losses totaled some 2 million men, half of them prisoners. Germany and Austria-Hungary together lost more than 1 million.

Yet another front opened in 1915 with the Dardanelles Campaign. Stalemate on the Western Front led British leaders to consider utilizing their sea power

advantage in what was one of the war's most controversial campaigns and great missed opportunities. The British hoped to get Greece to enter the war and secure the Gallipoli Peninsula at the northern entrance of the Dardanelles, then send naval forces to Istanbul and drive the Ottoman Empire from the war. Although promised Cyprus in reward, the Greeks refused.

British first lord of the admiralty Winston Churchill believed that warships could do it alone, and the War Council approved the enterprise on this basis. British admiral Sackville Carden assembled a powerful force of 1 dreadnought, 1 battle cruiser, 16 old battleships (4 French), and 20 destroyers (6 French) as well as minesweeping trawlers and auxiliaries.

The Ottomans had about 100 guns in a dozen forts and some two dozen German-supplied mobile howitzers. Only two Ottoman infantry divisions were available to oppose a landing, one on each side of the straits. The British Naval Division was available, and had troops been sent at the onset, they might easily have secured the Gallipoli Peninsula.

The British silenced the outer forts in a bombardment beginning on February 19. The fleet then steamed into the straits and began bombarding the inner forts. The Ottoman howitzers, firing from behind the crests of the hills, were not accessible to the flat-trajectory naval guns and scored a growing number of hits on the minesweepers. Carden meanwhile suffered a collapse and was replaced by Admiral John de Robeck.

Disaster struck an attempt to force the Narrows on March 18. A French battleship suffered a hit to a magazine and blew up, the British battle cruiser struck a mine and had to be withdrawn, and another mine disabled a battleship. A second battleship was sent to its rescue, but it too struck a mine. That night both battleships succumbed to a small minefield. Churchill urged de Robeck to press on, but he decided against it. Unknown to the British, the shore batteries were down to their last armor-piercing shells, and the Ottomans had expended all their mines.

The campaign continued but too late became a land operation by the two-division Australian and New Zealand Corps (ANZAC) then in Egypt, a British Army division, the Royal Naval Division, and a French division. General Sir Ian Hamilton commanded the 70,000 troops.

German general Liman von Sanders, ably assisted by Ottoman colonel Mustapha Kemal, had six widely dispersed divisions, but the Gallipoli Peninsula was ideal defensive terrain. On April 25, Allied troops landed at Cape Helles on the end of the peninsula and a nearby beach still called Anzac Cove. French troops came ashore on the Asiatic side, but advance there proving impossible, they were taken off and moved to Cape Helles.

The fighting soon resembled the trench warfare of the Western Front. Although the Allies sent out seven additional divisions, shore bombardment monitors, and more aircraft, the defenders also increased their strength. Both sides also dispatched submarines. A surprise British landing at Suvla Bay on August 6–7, designed to draw off defenders from Anzac Cove and trigger a breakout there, failed to have the desired result.

Allied plans to send additional troops to Gallipoli were postponed when Bulgaria joined the Central Powers, and Hamilton had to send two of his divisions to Salonika in northern Greece. The British War Cabinet then decided on evacuation. Predicted heavy losses did not occur, with

the evacuation (December 8, 1915–January 9, 1916) the only well-executed part of the entire campaign. Allied losses in the entire campaign totaled some 265,000 (46,000 dead); the Ottomans may have lost 300,000.

In 1915 also, the Austrians opened a new offensive against Serbia. Defeating Serbia was necessary to send military supplies to the Ottoman Empire by the Berlin-to-Istanbul railroad through Serbia. Typhus broke out in Serbia and ravaged the country and the army. By May 1915 it had killed 100,000 people.

Bulgaria also joined the war. The Allies had pressed Bulgaria to join their side, but its price was Macedonia. The Allies thought this reasonable on ethnic grounds, but Serbia refused to yield that territory. The Central Powers, however, were prepared to promise this.

Also influenced by Central Powers successes on the Eastern Front and in the Gallipoli Campaign, Bulgaria on September 6, 1915, concluded an alliance with Germany and Austria-Hungary providing for a joint attack on Serbia. When Bulgaria mobilized, Serbia appealed to Britain and France but also to Greece under a 1913 treaty between the two states. Greek premier Eleftherios Venizelos wanted his nation to join the Allies but insisted that the Entente provide the 150,000 men that Greece was bound to send to the Bulgarian frontier according to the treaty. The Allies agreed, and Venizelos acceded to their request to land troops at Salonika. But the Allies were unable to send the men immediately. And despite the promise of Cyprus, London and Paris were unable to persuade Greek king Constantine, and Venizelos resigned.

On October 6 the Austrians invaded. Five days later the Serbs were caught by surprise when the Bulgarians joined in. Belgrade fell on October 10, and by early November half of Serbia was in enemy hands. The British and French made only a belated, halfhearted advance into Serbia before withdrawing to Salonika.

The Serbs then carried out at great cost a retreat across the mountains into Albania. The Allies evacuated the 75,000 survivors to the Greek island of Corfu, which the French had occupied in early January without Greek consent. The Central Powers now occupied Serbia, Montenegro, and Albania.

In Middle East fighting, the British authorized a largely Indian army advance on Baghdad. At first successful, Major General Charles Townshend's force was rebuffed in November and was withdrawing when it was besieged by Ottoman forces at Kut-al-Amara (December 7–April 29, 1916). Its surrender was a powerful blow to British prestige in the Middle East.

In the war at sea, the Royal Navy tightened its blockade of Germany. In March 1915 it became total with the inclusion of foodstuffs. On January 24, 1915, the first fleet action of the war occurred off the Dogger Bank in the North Sea. German Navy commander Admiral von Ingenohl dispatched Vice Admiral Franz Ritter von Hipper there with 3 battle cruisers, an armored cruiser, 4 light cruisers, and 19 destroyers. Intercepting and decoding the orders, the British ordered the Grand Fleet out. On the morning of January 24, Vice Admiral Sir David Beatty with 5 battle cruisers, 7 light cruisers, and 35 destroyers made contact.

Outgunned, Hipper reversed course, but Beatty caught up with the Germans and in the ensuing engagement sank the armored cruiser *Blücher* (792 men lost) and damaged two other German ships. The British suffered two ships damaged.

The German naval staff, meanwhile, won the kaiser over to unrestricted submarine warfare. On February 4, 1915, Berlin declared that from February 14 the waters around Great Britain and Ireland were a war zone, with every ship, including neutral vessels, subject to attack. The Germans justified this as a countermeasure to the British blockade. Berlin said that if London lifted the prohibition on imports into Germany of food and raw materials, it would abandon the practice. While willing to lift the ban on foodstuffs in return for an end to submarine attacks, the British were not willing do so for raw materials.

Germany began its U-boat campaign with only 29 boats, and the campaign carried great risks regarding the United States. On May 7 a German submarine torpedoed the Cunard passenger liner *Lusitania* en route from New York to Liverpool off southwestern Ireland, drowning 1,201 of 1,965 on board. At least 124 of the dead were Americans. Although many Americans sought war with Germany, President Woodrow Wilson strongly opposed it.

On June 5, Berlin ordered U-boat captains not to sink large passenger ships on sight. Nevertheless, on August 19, 1915, the *U-24* sank the British passenger liner *Arabic,* killing 40 people, including 3 Americans. American pressure brought a temporary halt to unrestricted submarine warfare, but proponents of the campaign finally won the kaiser's approval, and unrestricted submarine warfare resumed on February 23, 1916, but with the proviso that only armed freighters were to be sunk without warning. On March 14, however, a submarine sank the French passenger ship *Sussex* off Boulogne. Although no Americans were lost, a sharp note from Washington brought a pledge that no merchant ships would be sunk without warning and provision for the safety of those aboard. This ended unrestricted submarine warfare until early 1917.

Airplanes came into their own in 1915. The most important early World War I types were two-seaters for reconnaissance and artillery observation. Both sides developed antiaircraft guns to shoot down enemy planes, but the best way to accomplish this was by one's own planes. Pilots and observers began carrying up small arms, but a machine gun mounted on the upper wing became the key weapon. It was, however, difficult to operate because of location. Dutch aircraft designer Anthony Fokker then developed a cam-operated synchronizer that allowed bullets to fire through the arc of the propeller and miss the blades. Beginning in August 1915, the Germans dominated the skies over the Western Front for eight months until the Allies developed their own effective synchronizer system.

Specialized aircraft appeared in single-seater fighters (first known as "scouts" and "fighting scouts") to shoot down enemy aircraft and carry out ground attacks. Five generations of fighter aircraft appeared during the war. The last were single-wing all-metal craft.

By 1917, aircraft were an integral part of ground operations. Fortunately for the Allies, they outproduced Germany. One estimate puts total aircraft production by all powers during the war at 150,000 planes.

The British Royal Naval Air Service probably conducted the first effective strategic bombing raids of the war in September and October 1914 in attacking sheds housing zeppelins at Düsseldorf. The Germans employed these lighter-than-air craft in aerial reconnaissance and bombing. Indeed, the zeppelin was the first strategic bomber. Fifty-one zeppelin attacks (208 sorties) against the British Isles dropped 196 tons of bombs, killing 557 people and wounding 1,358. By mid-1916, defenders had gained the upper hand. Countermeasures included searchlight batteries, antiaircraft guns, and incendiary bullets, to which the hydrogen-filled zeppelins were vulnerable. Zeppelin raids declined steadily to only four in 1918. The German Navy also employed zeppelins in reconnaissance.

Aircraft were not as vulnerable to antiaircraft fire. The Germans developed the twin-engine Gotha, some of which could carry a 2,200-pound bomb. Most Gotha raids were against London. In all the Germans mounted 435 bomber sorties over Britain, killing some 1,300 people, injuring 3,000, and inflicting a fair amount of material damage. The British had their twin-engine Handley-Page bomber with a bomb load of nearly 1,800 pounds.

Aircraft were also employed at sea to hunt submarines, locate enemy battle fleets, and adjust naval gunfire. The British also experimented, using them to launch torpedoes in the Dardanelles. Aircraft carriers also appeared, although none had full-length flight decks. Planes taking off from them were expected to land on shore or, in extremis, in the water to float on air bags until they could be hoisted aboard. Only the Royal Navy used aircraft carriers in combat. Its *Ark Royal* was the first ship that might be called an aircraft carrier.

The year 1916 saw the war's two biggest land battles and its largest sea battle. On December 6–8, 1915, the Allies agreed on a coordinated military strategy with simultaneous attacks on the Western Front and the Italian and Eastern fronts. On the Western Front there was to be a late summer British-French offensive north and south of the Somme River, but the Germans struck first.

Falkenhayn was well aware that time was working against Germany, with the British blockade creating major food and raw materials shortages. Falkenhayn therefore planned his own decisive blow for 1916. France had already sustained 2 million casualties, half of them killed, and Falkenhayn reasoned that one big push might drive it from the war. His objective was the fortress city of Verdun, which lay in a narrow salient into German-controlled territory with its southern face the Saint-Mihiel countersalient. The Verdun sector was only lightly garrisoned, and many of its heavy guns had been removed elsewhere. Not until the last week of January did Joffre begin to improve its defenses.

The Verdun salient lent itself to a converging German attack and allowed concentrated artillery fire from three sides. Its woods and hills screened troops and artillery, easily brought up via railway and Metz. The French would also find it difficult to resupply and reinforce Verdun. Only one road and railroad line connected it to the rest of France.

Taking Verdun would provide security for German rail lines only 15 miles to the east. The Germans also hoped to boost German civilian morale, shaken by the beginning of rationing. At the very least Falkenhayn expected to capture the east bank of the Meuse, thereby securing a shortened front with fewer men. The attack would be on a narrow front supported by massive artillery fire. Believing that the French would commit all available manpower to defend Verdun, Falkenhayn planned to bleed France white in a battle of attrition.

Falkenhayn entrusted the offensive to the Fifth Army, commanded by Crown Prince Wilhelm. By February 11, the Germans had assembled seven divisions and

more than 850 guns. The French had only 270 guns and 34 infantry battalions in half-completed positions. Bad weather delayed the attack, however, enabling detection of the German buildup and also French reinforcement, although Joffre discounted a major German attack. Joffre also failed to give proper attention to the Verdun sector because of his own planned Somme offensive.

The preliminary German bombardment opened early on February 21. Late that afternoon the ground attack began on a six-mile front. The French fought doggedly but by February 24 had lost half their 20,000 men, and the Germans had taken the French reserve trench. Through a command error, Fort Douaumont, linchpin of the French defensive system, was only lightly held. It was captured by the Germans in an almost fatal blow.

General of Division Henri Philippe Pétain took command at Verdun. He immediately rushed in reinforcements, then developed an elastic defensive scheme to canalize German advances. He also questioned the strategic value of Verdun and the decision to hold there, but the government would not permit withdrawal. As Falkenhayn anticipated, Verdun became a matter of national honor for the French. But the same reason kept the Germans from breaking off their attack.

Falkenhayn now extended the front, but Pétain had anticipated this and reinforced. Pétain also rotated men in and out of the battle, frustrating German plans to wear them down. The French also organized an effective supply system along what became known as the Sacred Way from Bar-le-Duc to Verdun. Despite German artillery fire, up to 6,000 trucks a day in each direction around the clock brought in supplies and carried out the wounded.

Sixty-six divisions—three-quarters of the entire French Army in the war—fought at Verdun. "Ils ne passeront pas" ("They shall not pass") became the French rallying cry.

On May 1 Pétain assumed command of an army group, and General of Division Robert Nivelle took over at Verdun. On June 7 the Germans succeeded in taking Fort Vaux. Their last major assault came on July 11. It got to less than 2.5 miles from Verdun, but French counterattacks drove them back.

The British Somme offensive and the Russian Brusilov offensive helped relieve pressure on Verdun. In the fall the French took the offensive and retook Douaumont (October 24) and Vaux (November 2). Not until August 1917 did they recover their positions of February 1916, however.

The Germans had not bled France to death or even taken Verdun. The butcher's bill was nonetheless high. The French suffered 377,231 casualties in the battle. The Germans lost roughly 337,000. The French estimate for both sides at Verdun in the war is 420,000 dead and 800,000 gassed or wounded. Germany was unable to mount another such attack on the Western Front until the spring of 1918 after the collapse of Russia. Verdun also discredited Falkenhayn.

The Battle of the Somme, the second great 1916 land battle on the Western Front, was closely tied to Verdun. That battle shifted the burden on the Somme to the British, with the goal now to relieve German pressure on Verdun. The offensive occurred on a 20-mile front north of the Somme River, with General Sir Henry Rawlinson's Fourth Army making the main effort. South of the Somme the French Sixth Army mounted a supporting attack, while in the north the British Third Army staged a diversion.

Haig hoped to pierce the German lines, widen the gap, and employ reserves to exploit the breakthrough. Rawlinson had a more realistic bite-and-hold plan involving a lengthy bombardment, a limited infantry advance, consolidation, and then destruction of German counterattacks to inflict maximum casualties. In Haig's defense, appeals from Joffre caused the offensive to be launched six weeks before planned, and the French troop number commitment to the battle was less than envisioned.

Falkenhayn expected an effort to relieve pressure on Verdun but assumed that it would come in Alsace. Second Army commander General of Infantry Fritz von Below believed that it would occur in his sector and had his men build deep underground bunkers and a defensive belt of up to five miles in depth.

Haig committed 18 divisions, 11 of which were from the half-trained so-called New Army. The British planned a massive artillery preparation, enabling the infantry to shoulder their 70-pound packs and simply walk across no-man's-land. The preliminary barrage began on June 24, but the British lacked sufficient heavy guns to destroy the new German defenses. The shelling also merely rearranged the barbed wire.

The British attack on July 1 was preceded by the denotation of mines under the German positions. But doing so 10 minutes before the assault alerted the Germans, and their artillery immediately fired on every British forward trench. As soon as the British shelling shifted rearward, the Germans left their bunkers, set up machine guns, and began slaughtering the attackers. By the end of the day Rawlinson had committed 143 battalions, and almost half of his men were casualties, with the rate for officers 75 percent. That day the British suffered 57,470 casualties, 19,240 of them killed or mortally wounded. German losses were about 8,000.

Virtually none of the first day's objectives were met, but Haig continued the offensive, confident of eventual success. On September 15 he employed tanks for the first time in the war. Their debut was plagued by mechanical problems, inadequate tactical plans, and poor training. The offensive continued until a blizzard hit on November 19.

Losses on the Somme were even higher than those at Verdun. The British sustained some 420,000 casualties, the French 195,000, and the Germans 650,000. The Somme battles did help relieve pressure on Verdun, and their heavy losses here contributed to the German decision to withdraw to a shorter position that could be held with fewer men. As with Verdun for the French, the Battle of the Somme also carried a heavy psychological cost for the British and helped fuel postwar pacifism.

Both sides had anticipated a major naval battle in the North Sea that might decide the war and world mastery. This almost occurred on May 31 when the British Grand Fleet and the German High Seas Fleet met off the coast of the Jutland Peninsula near the Skagerrak Strait (the German name for the battle).

New High Seas Fleet commander Admiral Reinhard Scheer favored a series of attacks to reduce the strength of the Grand Fleet piecemeal followed by an all-out encounter. Jutland was an attempt to reduce the odds, but it was also prompted by political pressure that the navy not remain idle while the army was fighting at Verdun.

On May 30 Scheer took the High Seas Fleet into the North Sea in hopes of engaging a portion of the British Grand Fleet. Hipper's scouting force of 40 fast vessels, including 5 battle cruisers, preceded the main German force. Hipper's task was to lure part of the Grand Fleet back into the main body of the High Seas Fleet.

Alerted by heavy German signal traffic and unknown to the Germans, the entire Grand Fleet was at sea. Admiral Sir John Jellicoe had 151 ships (28 dreadnoughts, 9 battle cruisers, 34 cruisers, and 80 destroyers) against Scheer's 101 (16 dreadnoughts, 6 predreadnoughts, 5 battle cruisers, 11 cruisers, and 63 destroyers). As the German ships steamed north, a British scouting force of 52 ships rushed to meet them. It included Beatty's 6 battle cruisers and Rear Admiral Hugh Evan-Thomas's 4 new fast dreadnoughts.

At about 2:30 p.m. on May 31 and 100 miles off Jutland, the two opposing scouting forces made contact. Hipper then turned south to draw the British ships into Scheer's trap. The aggressive Beatty did as Hipper hoped, signaling Evan-Thomas to follow. The dreadnoughts, however, missed Beatty's signal and were slow to close. The result was a disaster for Beatty's battle cruisers, their inadequacy in turret armor and magazine protection soon apparent. Beatty's flagship, the *Lion,* took a direct hit on one of its turrets and was saved only by quick flooding of the magazine. Two other British battle cruisers were also hit and blew up. To this point the Germans had suffered no losses.

Beatty now played the decoy, reversing course to join Jellicoe and drawing Scheer after him. This so-called Chase to the North continued for more than an hour. At about 6:00 p.m. a third British battle cruiser was hit and blew up.

At about 6:30 p.m. the Germans were proceeding north in line-ahead formation, expecting soon to finish off the rest of Beatty's ships, when Jellicoe's main body suddenly appeared out of the mist in one long line on the horizon. British shells immediately struck three of the leading German ships. Jellicoe had crossed the "T" of the German line, allowing all his ships to fire, whereas only a limited number of German guns could do so.

Although the Germans enjoyed advantages in long-range gunnery and fire control, their ships were outclassed by the more numerous British dreadnoughts. Sensing disaster, Scheer ordered a difficult high-speed 180-degree turn, and the German warships disappeared back into the mist. Jellicoe tried to cut the Germans off and it appeared that the Germans might not escape this time, but Scheer again reversed course, ordering his destroyers to lay down smoke and launch torpedoes. Jellicoe had his ships turn about to outrun the torpedoes. This tactic, approved by the sea lords, may have cost the British opportunity for a decisive victory, but pressing the attack could also have brought disaster.

On June 1 the High Seas Fleet was back in its bases. The British had suffered higher casualties and lost 14 ships (3 battle cruisers, 3 cruisers, and 8 destroyers) to only 11 German ships (1 battle cruiser, 1 predreadnought, 4 cruisers, and 5 destroyers). But Scheer's claim of victory rang hollow. Within 24 hours Jellicoe had 24 dreadnoughts available for action, whereas Scheer had only 10. The upshot was that the blockade remained in place, and the Germans abandoned risking their capital ships in a showdown fight. Increasingly the big ships rode at anchor as the Germans concentrated on the submarine war.

The Italian front remained inconclusive in 1916. Cadorna launched the Fifth Battle of the Isonzo (March 11–29), and Conrad responded with the Trentino or Asiago Offensive (May 15–June 17, 1916), an effort to seize the northern Italian plain and trap the two Italian armies on the Isonzo front. Cadorna did not believe that Conrad would risk a major operation in the Trentino, and thus any attack there would be a feint.

The attack began on May 15 and overran the Italian First Army but failed to break out onto the Asiago plateau. By June 2 the threat was over, for the Russian Brusilov Offensive forced Austria-Hungary to shift men there. Cadorna then retook some lost territory.

Noting that the Austrians had weakened the Isonzo front for the drive in the Trentino, Cadorna again attacked it in the Sixth Battle of the Isonzo (August 6–17) but failed to achieve a breakthrough. The year ended with three more Isonzo battles: the Seventh (September 14–20), Eighth (October 10–12), and Ninth (November 1–14).

Fighting on the Eastern Front, calm from November 1915 to March 1916, resumed in response to Verdun. While Czar Nicholas II nominally commanded the Russian Army, he left actual management to Stavka, the Russian high command. Nicholas's presence at headquarters had a most unfortunate effect in Petrograd, where the reactionary Czarina Alexandra and the monk Gregorii Rasputin dominated affairs of state and near chaos reigned.

Still, chief of staff General Mikhail V. Alekseev accomplished much, and by the beginning of 1916 he had largely rebuilt the army. On March 18 the Russians responded to the French appeal for action to draw off German forces from Verdun by launching a two-pronged attack in the Vilna–Lake Naroch area against the German Tenth Army. Russian gains in the Battle of Lake Naroch (March 18–April 14) were, however, soon halted.

The Austrian Trentino Offensive brought an appeal from Italy, and Russian Army leaders debated a new offensive.

Most believed that the army was too weak, but General Aleksei Brusilov, new commander of the Southwestern Front and arguably the most able senior Russian general of the war, thought otherwise. The others finally agreed, and Stavka adopted a plan whereby Brusilov would attack in the direction of Kovel (Kowel, in present-day northern Ukraine), with supporting attacks aimed at Lviv in Galicia and Chernivtsi (Czernowitz, in present-day western Ukraine). When the Central Powers moved resources to block these, General Aleksei Evert's powerful northern army group would launch the main Russian drive toward Vilnius.

Brusilov's 55 divisions faced 50 entrenched Austro-Hungarian divisions along a 300-mile front. Brusilov had his men sap their frontline trenches close to the Austrian lines and dig tunnels under the Austrian wire. The Russians also stockpiled shells and constructed dugouts for reserves. Brusilov used aerial photography to locate enemy guns and positioned his own artillery close to the front. He held a manpower advantage of 600,000 to 500,000 and a weapons advantage of 1,938 guns to 1,846, although the Austrians had more heavy pieces.

On June 4 the Russians began a massive and accurate barrage that silenced many Austrian guns. The next day the infantry attacked and broke through, with some units advancing 10 miles. By June 23 Brusilov had taken 204,000 prisoners and 219 guns. Austria-Hungary seemed near collapse, but Brusilov was forced to pause. His own losses had been heavy, he had outrun his supply lines, and he lacked reserves.

Now it was up to Evert with 1 million troops and two-thirds of the Russian artillery—a three to one superiority in men

and guns—to attack the Germans in the north. His offensive was to commence on June 14, but Evert repeatedly claimed shortages and put the attack off until July 3, dooming any chance for Russian military success in 1916.

The Germans insisted that the Austrians transfer forces from the Italian front to the Eastern Front, and they sent troops south. On June 16 the Germans launched a counteroffensive near Kovel, temporarily checking Brusilov.

On July 28 Brusilov resumed the offensive. During August 7–September 2 the Russians reached the Carpathian foothills. During the next month, however, the advance bogged down, handicapped by supply problems. The Germans stabilized the front and eventually forced Brusilov to abandon Bukovina and Galicia.

The Brusilov Offensive was the greatest feat of Russian arms of the war. During June 4–August 12 he had taken nearly 379,000 prisoners and 496 guns. Brusilov contended that had Evert attacked on schedule, Austria-Hungary would have been driven from the war. Even so, the offensive probably marked the end of the Dual Monarchy as a military power, helped bring Conrad's removal from command in February 1917, and may have saved the Italian Army with the transfer of Austrian units to the Russian front. It also weakened the German attack at Verdun and helped bring the fall of Falkenhayn. The Brusilov Offensive also brought some 1.4 million Russian casualties, and the Russian people saw it as just another military failure. As such, it contributed to revolution the next year.

The Brusilov Offensive also helped bring Romania into the war. The Allies exploited Romanian territorial claims against Austria-Hungary. Germany's failure at

Verdun and that of Austria in the Asiago Offensive were also factors in Romania's decision, but the most important influence was the Brusilov Offensive. Romanian premier Ian Brătianu and King Ferdinand I had long coveted Hungarian Transylvania. Fearing that it might now fall to the Russians, they signed a secret treaty with the Allies promising them Transylvania, the Bánát of Temesvár, and Bukovina. The Allies also pledged a simultaneous Russian advance and offensive from Salonika.

On August 27, 1916, Romania declared war on the Dual Monarchy. Romanian forces then invaded Hungary. Their 620,000-man army was, however, poorly trained and badly led, and it suffered from severe shortages and outdated equipment. Russian pledges to make up shortages did not materialize. Romania's entry into the war did bring the dismissal of Falkenhayn, as he had declared that it would not happen. The kaiser replaced him with Hindenburg, who shifted the major German effort to the Eastern Front.

In a month the Romanians took about a quarter of Transylvania; indeed, most of their difficulties resulted from logistical incompetence. Russian support was, however, limited because of heavy casualties in the Brusilov Offensive, although many Russians believed that the Romanians had waited until the Brusilov advance was spent before entering the war. The Russians sent only two divisions to the Dobrudja to reinforce the Romanians there, while Brusilov reluctantly sent an army into Bukovina. The promised Salonika offensive fizzled out, halted by Bulgarian troops.

The Central Powers moved decisively. Falkenhayn assumed command of the German Ninth Army and the reduction of Romania. His brilliant three-pronged counteroffensive soon drove the Romanians back to their own frontier. At the same time, Colonel General August von Mackensen led a mixed German, Bulgarian, and Ottoman force against the Romanian Dobrudja. By mid-November the Germans had entered the central Wallachian Plain. Bucharest fell on December 6. What remained of the Romanian Army withdrew into Moldavia, shielded there by the Russians. The Central Powers acquired Romania's rich agricultural lands and could now hold their eastern lines with fewer troops than before.

Greece meanwhile struggled to remain neutral. King Constantine preferred neutrality, while ex-premier Venizelos favored the Allies, who now embarked on a policy of coercion. In June 1916 Britain and France blockaded Greek ports and demanded demobilization of the Greek Army and a new government. On September 29 Venizelos set up a pro-Allied provisional government at Salonika, and on November 23 it declared war on Bulgaria and Germany.

The Allies demanded surrender of the Greek Navy, to which the Athens government agreed, but it rejected the next Allied demand, that Athens surrender war material. On December 8 the Allies declared Greece under blockade, and on December 19 they recognized the Venizelos government.

In the Caucasus, meanwhile, Yudenich built up Russian strength, and on February 16, 1916, he attacked and defeated the Ottomans at Erzurum, inflicting 25,000 casualties and taking 327 guns. The Ottoman Third Army barely escaped annihilation. In September Yudenich turned back an offensive by the Ottoman Third Army, inflicting another 30,000 casualties.

In the Middle East the Ottomans, urged on by the Germans, attempted to capture the Suez Canal from the Sinai (January 13–February 3) but were defeated. The British then built up their forces in Egypt to take the offensive, constructing both a water line and a railroad into the Sinai to support offensive operations. They repulsed an Ottoman attack on the railroad at Rumani (August 3) and also supported the so-called Arab Revolt against the Ottomans in the Hejaz (Hijaz), while also suppressing a Senussi revolt in Libya.

In December 1916 David Lloyd George replaced Herbert Asquith as British prime minister. Lloyd George blamed Haig for the great British manpower losses of the Western Front and tried to reduce Haig's freedom of action while supporting less costly peripheral operations in the Middle East.

At the end of 1916 Allied leaders agreed to continue the Western Front as the critical sector of war, with the French Army to mount a major offensive in 1917. Blamed for previous failures and for being surprised at Verdun, Joffre was replaced in December 1916 by Nivelle.

Although Nivelle was supremely confident of success, his plan for massive frontal assaults against well-fortified defensive positions was essentially the same failed tactic of the preceding two years. Fluent in English, Nivelle convinced Lloyd George to send Haig six additional divisions to take control of 20 miles of French trenches. Lloyd George also insisted that Haig place his forces under Nivelle's operational command. Haig reluctantly agreed, but only for this offensive.

In September 1916 Hindenburg had ordered construction of a new heavily fortified defensive line, the Siegfried Stelling, known to the Allies as the Hindenburg Line. Located 20 miles behind the existing German positions, this new line would eliminate the Noyon salient, shorten the

German front by 25 miles, and free up 14 divisions. It also incorporated innovations such as better-sited front lines and an elastic defense or defense in depth. It featured reinforced concrete bunkers as well as tunnels, underground electric lighting, and concrete machine-gun positions.

Hindenburg and Ludendorff believed that Russia was on the verge of collapse and that withdrawing to the Siegfried Line would enable Germany to maintain its defensive posture on the Western Front while delivering a knockout blow on the Eastern Front. The withdrawal, Operation ALBERICH, occurred during March 16–April 5. The Germans also evacuated 125,000 French civilians and left behind a booby-trapped wasteland. The Allies realized too late what had happened. ALBERICH should have given the Allies pause, but Nivelle persisted with his plan. The Germans were well aware of his intentions from his public posturing, aerial reconnaissance, spies, and a trench raid that captured a set of plans.

In the Battle of Arras (April 9–15) the British attempted to draw off German reserves. The key objective was Vimy Ridge. It fell to the Canadian Corps on April 10 in one of the notable feats of arms of the war. This was, however, the only major Allied success of the battle, and no German reserves were drawn from the Aisne sector.

The Nivelle Offensive, also known as the Second Battle of the Aisne and the Third Battle of Champagne, involved some 1.2 million French soldiers along a 40-mile front between Soissons and Reims. Their objective was the Chemin des Dames ridges paralleling the front. A 14-day bombardment by 5,544 guns preceded the April 16 attack, although much of this was wasted against lightly held German forward positions. The attackers also had 128 tanks, the first French use of them in the war.

The offensive produced only minimal gains. Although the French took most of the German first-line trenches, their artillery failed to silence the German guns or hardened machine-gun positions. Nivelle had promised to call off the offensive immediately if it was unsuccessful, but he did not do so. The attacks continued until May 9.

The results compared favorably to Joffre's earlier attacks, but Nivelle had promised breakthrough and victory. Widespread French Army mutinies occurred, seriously affecting 46 of 112 divisions. (The Germans did not learn of the mutinies until too late.) On May 15 Pétain replaced Nivelle as commander of the army. Pétain visited the disaffected units and talked to the men. He promised to address their complaints of poor food, inadequate medical services, and insufficient leave. He reminded the troops that the Germans were still in France but promised no future attacks without real hope of success.

Pétain's appeals were successful. Of some 35,000 mutineers, 2,873 were court-martialed and received sentences, many of which were suspended. Although 629 death sentences were handed down, only 43 were actually carried out.

The French Army mutinies and events in Russia played into the hands of defeatists in France, and by the fall of 1917 there were serious doubts as to whether France could continue the struggle. In November the government fell, and staunch nationalist Georges Clemenceau became premier. France would fight on.

Meanwhile, in April the United States had entered the war. In 1914 President Wilson had proclaimed strict American neutrality and had insisted on the right to trade with all the belligerents. But because the Entente controlled the seas, the United States traded only with it.

In early 1917 in what was probably the most fateful decision of the war, Berlin decided to resume unrestricted submarine warfare. Without this Russia would still have collapsed, and Germany would have had to deal with only France and Britain on the Western Front in 1918, conceivably giving it victory. By the end of 1916 despite having to provide for the safety of merchant ship crews, U-boats had been sinking some 300,000 tons of Allied shipping monthly. This was well ahead of 1915 totals and formed the rationale for the resurrection of unrestricted submarine warfare, when submarines would no longer have to attack on the surface and be vulnerable to Allied armed merchant ships and decoy-armed British Q-ships.

Britain imported more than half its food and raw materials, and the German high command believed that an all-out submarine offensive would soon bring Britain to its knees. If this occurred, France would have to surrender. Resumption of unrestricted submarine warfare would probably bring the United States into the war, but by the time this could have a major impact the war would be over. On January 31 the German Foreign Ministry announced that unrestricted submarine warfare would resume the next day.

Americans were also angered by the infamous Zimmermann Telegram, the public release of an intercepted January 1917 communication from German state secretary for foreign affairs Arthur Zimmermann endeavoring to bring Mexico in on Germany's side should the United States enter the war and pledging German assistance in the Mexican recovery of territory lost to the United States in 1848.

Another factor was the involvement of German diplomats in sabotage activities in the United States.

German torpedoes soon claimed American lives, and on April 6 the United States declared war. In addition to being a great morale boost for the Entente, this meant immediate financial assistance in the form of loans. The United States also provided food and significant industrial assistance (U.S. annual steel production was 93.4 million tons, three times that of Germany and Austria-Hungary combined.)

The United States quickly seized German ships interned in its ports and began an ambitious shipbuilding program to "build a bridge to France." The U.S. Navy was the world's fifth-largest navy, and U.S. destroyers were soon involved in escort and antisubmarine duties. A battleship division also went to Scapa Flow, although it did not see action during the war.

The army was not ready. It counted just 133,000 regulars and 67,000 national guardsmen. President Wilson appointed General John J. Pershing to command the American Expeditionary Forces, but only four U.S. divisions had reached France by December 1917.

In February 1917 German submarines sank about 540,000 tons of Allied shipping, and from April to June 1917 they sank another 2 million tons. In April alone the tally was 350 ships of 849,000 tons. The U-boats were sinking ships faster than they could be built. If this rate continued, Britain would indeed be driven from the war.

Allied technology played an important role in the antisubmarine campaign. This included more lethal depth charges and hydrophone technology but also a new technique of sending a beam of sound through the water to strike an object and reflect back as an echo. This was known as asdic and later sonar. The convoy system was the key, however. Senior British commanders had rejected this course, because focused on fleet actions, they preferred to build battleships and cruisers rather than destroyers and subchasers. Convoys were instituted in May 1917 on the insistence of Prime Minister Lloyd George and U.S. vice admiral William S. Sims, then in London.

In the convoy system, large numbers of merchant vessels traveled together. Although German submarines still registered kills, the proportion of ships sunk to those sailing was only a small fraction of merchant ships traveling singly. Merchant ship losses now dramatically declined, while losses of submarines rose.

Fighting on the Western Front resumed in the summer. Given the French Army mutinies and Pétain's penchant for the defense, the initiative passed to the British. Haig hoped to achieve a breakthrough in the Ypres salient and outflank the German defenses from the north. He knew time was limited before Lloyd George diverted some of his assets to other theaters.

Haig's first objective was Messines Ridge; it dominated the southern part of the salient. He assigned the task to General Herbert Plumer and his Second Army. Plumer made careful preparations that included tunneling and more than 1 million pounds of explosives.

On May 21, 1917, the British began a 17-day artillery bombardment. Royal Flying Corps aircraft also won air superiority over the point of attack. On June 7 the British exploded mines beneath Messines Ridge. A massive barrage and assault by nine divisions with tanks followed. That day the attackers secured the eastern sides of Messines Ridge and straightened the Ypres salient.

Seven weeks then passed before Haig followed up this success. He gave General Hubert Gough responsibility for the offensive, and Gough's Fifth Army had to be relocated to the area held by Plumer. But Haig was buoyed by intelligence reports claiming that the Germans were near collapse. Haig's choice for the attack area was unfortunate. The Germans held the high ground and were able to observe British preparations, and they brought up reinforcements.

The series of battles that followed are collectively known as the Third Battle of Ypres and also the Passchendaele Campaign (July 31–November 10, 1917). On July 17 the British began a 14-day preliminary bombardment of 4,283,550 shells, their heaviest of the war. Then on July 31, 12 divisions attacked on an 11-mile front. The heaviest rains in years and all the shelling destroyed systems protecting the otherwise swampy terrain, however, making transport nearly impossible. Tanks were useless.

On August 2 Haig suspended the attack. A second British push on August 16 was less successful. At the end of August, Haig gave the main effort to Plumer.

The weather turned dry, and on September 20 Plumer launched a series of limited narrow-front attacks. Special assault groups outflanked German strongpoints. Shallow rushes kept within artillery support, and divisions had shorter frontages with sufficient reserves to meet counterattacks.

In October the rains returned, however. The Germans also employed mustard gas for the first time and, in the first massive air support for ground troops, employed planes to strafe the British infantry. Plumer's tactics, however, forced the Germans to revert to defending forward areas, and

this produced heavy German casualties from artillery fire. With possession of both Passchendaele Ridge and the village, Haig ended the campaign on November 10.

Deepening the Ypres salient by some five miles had cost the British 245,000 casualties. More than 90,000 of these were missing in action, many having simply disappeared into the mud. These heavy losses were greatly felt in 1918.

Within a few weeks Haig had initiated a new battle, that of Cambrai (November 20–December 5). The British committed 19 divisions and three tank brigades of General Julian Byng's Third Army. The Germans initially had 6 divisions, later 20. The objective was Cambrai, 35 miles south of Lille.

For the first time in the war, tanks were employed en masse as the key element. There was firm, dry ground with sufficient cover to assemble attackers in secrecy. Haig and Byng expanded the attack from a mere raid into an offensive to smash a six-mile-wide gap in the German lines, through which five cavalry divisions would be launched into the German rear.

Success depended on surprise and securing Bourlon Ridge before the Germans could deploy reserves. The British used low-flying aircraft to mask the noise of the tanks' arrival and brought up additional artillery to provide supporting fire. The assault by nine tank battalions (374 tanks) followed by five infantry divisions began early on November 20. There was only a short but intense shelling of the German front line before the artillery shifted rearward to disrupt the movement of reserves and to blind direct-fire artillery with smoke.

On the first day the attack went largely according to plan. By nightfall the British had penetrated the Hindenburg Line up to five miles. But the Germans held

Bourlon Ridge and rushed up reinforcements. Thanks to Passchendaele, the British did not have the reserves to counter them. Also, too many tanks had suffered mechanical breakdowns or were put out of action by German field guns. The Germans mounted a counterattack on November 29, and by the end of the battle on December 5 they had retaken most of the territory lost as well as some original British positions. Despite its failure, the Battle of Cambrai demonstrated that tank and infiltration tactics could restore battlefield fluidity.

Meanwhile, there was near disaster on the Italian front. Despite his pledge to attack simultaneously with his Western Front allies, Cadorna did not begin his own offensive until May 12. This Tenth Battle of the Isonzo (May 12–June 8) produced only slight gains. The Eleventh Battle of the Isonzo (August 18–September 15) was more successful, and new Austro-Hungarian chief of staff General Arz von Straussenburg requested German assistance. This led to the Twelfth (and final) Battle of the Isonzo, better known as the Battle of Caporetto (October 24–November 12, 1917).

Ludendorff created the new Fourteenth Army, commanded by German general of infantry Otto von Below. Seven of its 15 divisions were German. In all, the Central Powers massed 35 divisions (28 Austrian and 7 German) against 41 Italian, planning to employ surprise and new tactics to offset their numerical disadvantage. These came to be called "Hutier tactics," for German general of infantry Oscar von Hutier. These were centered on highly trained assault forces, massed at the last moment by night. A short, intense barrage firing a mix of high-explosive, gas, and smoke shells to mask enemy strongpoints, cause confusion, and disrupt the enemy replaced the

old long-preliminary bombardment. The artillery preparation was immediately followed by an infantry assault led by specially trained elite forces. Armed with rapid-fire small arms and supported by light artillery, they bypassed enemy strongpoints and created corridors rather than trying to advance along an entire front.

Deserters warned of an imminent major assault, but Cadorna discounted a large-scale offensive on the Isonzo. He expected the attack to occur in the Trentino sector, seemingly confirmed by an October 27 diversionary thrust there. Cadorna did order a defense in depth along the entire line with only light forces in forward positions, but Second Army commander General Luigi Capello failed to implement it. Capello also had his worst troops in the area of greatest danger.

The Germans opened their barrage at 2:00 a.m. on October 24 from 4,126 guns on a 25-mile front. Six hours later the infantry attacked, and by the end of the first day they had advanced up to 12 miles. Cadorna ordered a retreat to the Tagliamento River, and by the evening of October 31 the Italians were over it, but on November 4 Cadorna ordered a withdrawal behind the wide Piave, the bridges of which were blown up on November 9. That same day General Armando Diaz replaced Cadorna.

The Italians now had only 33 divisions, 3,986 guns, and six airfields behind the Piave, but the attackers had outrun their supply lines and artillery support, and Diaz now had a shorter front. The attackers were also worn down from the advance. Efforts by German and Austro-Hungarian forces in mid-December to force the Piave line and flank failed, and the offensive ended on December 25.

Five British and six French divisions also arrived to bolster Italian resolve.

Nonetheless, Italy had sustained in the battle 320,000 casualties (265,000 of them prisoners) and lost 3,152 guns and more than 300,000 rifles. Austro-German losses were only about 20,000 men.

Surprisingly, the Italian Army quickly recovered. By the summer of 1918 Diaz had 7,000 guns along the Piave, including 1,100 from France and Britain. He also had 50 Italian and 4 Allied divisions. An important result of Caporetto was an Allied conference at Rapallo on November 5, leading to the creation of the Supreme War Council, the first real Allied effort to bring about unity of command.

Although Italy continued in the war, Russia did not. What happened in Russia was attributable more than anything else to the failed leadership of Czar Nicholas II. Political ineptitude, economic disarray, and general war weariness brought revolution and Nicholas's forced abdication. On March 16, 1917, a provisional government was established of moderate to conservative Duma (parliament) leaders. The exception was socialist Aleksandr F. Kerensky, minister of justice.

The Allied governments assumed that the March Revolution would stimulate the Russian people to greater sacrifice, and the country's new leaders were determined to continue the war. This decision, more than anything else, brought the Bolsheviks to power.

The new government initiated sweeping reforms, but lawlessness took hold. Army discipline collapsed, and increasing numbers of soldiers deserted. The provisional government meanwhile secured a pledge from the political parties for a political truce. Initially the leaders of the small militant Bolshevik Party agreed. But on his return to Russia, Bolshevik Vladimir I. Lenin called for a break with the provisional government and an end to the "predatory" war. The Germans had aided Lenin's return to Russia, and they now spent vast sums to destabilize the new government and help the Bolsheviks, the only Russian party openly opposing the war.

In April, Kerensky became minister of war and staked all on a great summer offensive. Local attacks were to hold the Germans in the north, with the major blow against Austro-Hungarian forces in Galicia. In May, Kerensky appointed Brusilov to command the army. Brusilov called for a drive by three armies (45 divisions), with Lviv as the objective.

Relations between Germany and Austria-Hungary were now tense. Emperor Franz Josef had died in November 1916, and Berlin was well aware that his successor, Karl I, wanted to extract the Dual Monarchy from the war. Although nothing came of this, in early 1917 Karl initiated secret negotiations with the Allies.

Russia's last great military effort, known as the Kerensky or Second Brusilov Offensive, opened on July 1. Initially the Russian forces made significant gains. Many Austrian troops simply fled, and the Russians took thousands of prisoners and great quantities of war supplies. But Brusilov lacked reserves. The Russians also outran their supply lines, and the drive came to a halt as German reinforcements stiffened Austro-Hungarian resistance.

Deserters betrayed Russia's plans, and de facto German commander Paul Hoffmann was ready with a counterstrike. Augmented by reinforcements from the Western Front, he launched his own offensive toward Tarnopol on July 19. It gained nine miles the first day. Tarnopol's fall on July 25 triggered widespread Russian withdrawals, and by early August the Russians had evacuated Galicia and Bukovina.

The entire Southwestern Front collapsed. Many Russian soldiers refused to fight, and some shot their officers. The gains of 1916 were wiped out, and there was no Russian army south of the Pripet Marshes. The German offensive then halted on the border of Galicia.

News of the military collapse coincided with the July Days in Petrograd, when the Bolsheviks and other radicals attempted to seize power. The provisional government responded by jailing a number of Bolsheviks, although Lenin escaped and went into hiding in Finland. As unrest and demoralization spread, Kerensky became head of the provisional government.

In August, Kerensky named General Lavr Kornilov to replace a spent Brusilov. Many hoped that Kornilov, who had come up through the ranks and was widely respected, could restore the situation. Demanding a free hand, he soon clashed with the strong-willed Kerensky. Kornilov then attempted a coup d'état, supported by most of the army's officers, the middle class, and the Allied governments.

The coup attempt was made possible by the fall of Riga. In early August, Ludendorff ordered Hoffmann to cross the Dvina River and seize Riga to open the way to Petrograd. Ludendorff believed that this might cause the Russians to seek an armistice. Hutier's Eighth Army took Riga on September 3. The Russian Twelfth Army was already withdrawing when the Germans attacked, but Hutier introduced here the new assault techniques employed at Caporetto. The Germans also carried out amphibious landings on islands in the Gulf of Finland as well as on the mainland.

The Baltic coast was now completely exposed, and Petrograd was undefended. In these circumstances Kornilov demanded that Kerensky transfer authority to

him, but Kerensky refused and dismissed Kornilov, who then ordered his troops to march on the capital. This led Kerensky to release stocks of arms in Petrograd to leftist groups, including the Bolsheviks. This was unnecessary, as leftist agitators halted the troop trains before they could reach Petrograd and persuaded the soldiers to go home. Kornilov was arrested on September 12, but Kerensky was now at the mercy of the radical Left.

Conditions in Russia continued to deteriorate, especially in the cities, where there were major food shortages because of transportation bottlenecks. In late September the Bolsheviks, buoyed by an infusion of German funds, advanced the slogan of "peace, bread, and land." More than any other Russian leader, Lenin understood the extent of Russian war weariness and desire for peace at almost any price.

On October 6 Kerensky formed a new government with a majority of socialists. On September 27 he declared Russia a republic and initiated arrangements for a constitutional assembly. Lenin, meanwhile, secured party approval for a coup attempt. It occurred on the night of November 6–7 with revolutionary soldiers, sailors, and Red Guards occupying strategic points in Petrograd and arresting members of the provisional government, although Kerensky escaped abroad. The communist era in Russia had begun.

On June 11, 1917, meanwhile, the French demanded that King Constantine of Greece abdicate as Allied troops moved into Thessaly and the Isthmus of Corinth. Constantine complied, succeeded by his second son Alexander, who on June 26 appointed Venizelos premier. A day later Greece declared war on the Central Powers.

In Mesopotamia, the British reinforced and again took the offensive. On the Sinai front, General Archibald Murray met rebuff in two efforts to take Gaza (March 26 and April 17–19). Lloyd George replaced Murray with able Lieutenant General Edmund Allenby, who after careful preparation captured Gaza and Beersheba on October 31. Allenby's forces entered Jerusalem on December 9.

At the beginning of 1918, both sides were reeling. The Allied blockade was, however, strangling Germany. If Germany was to win the war it would have to be in 1918, with its forces bearing the brunt of the effort. This, however, hinged on peace on the Eastern Front and transferring forces west before American manpower could count.

The day after coming to power, Lenin suggested an immediate armistice on all fronts followed by peace talks. The Western Allies rejected this, but Berlin responded positively, and talks opened at Brest-Litovsk on December 3. Two weeks later an armistice went into effect on the Eastern Front. Peace talks followed on December 22. Leon Trotsky headed the Russian delegation and sought delay for an anticipated communist revolution in Germany to drive that country from the war. The Russians also naively expected the Germans to negotiate on the basis of no annexations or indemnities. Hoffmann soon disabused the Russians of this when he presented Germany's crushing demands.

During a brief Christmas recess Trotsky returned to Petrograd and urged a policy of "no war, no peace." He then announced that the Russians simply considered the war at an end. Hoffmann responded by signing a separate peace with Ukraine and resuming offensive operations. On February 18, German troops crossed the Dvina River and captured Pskov.

Although most of the Bolshevik leaders wanted to fight, they had destroyed the

army in coming to power and were in no position to do so. Lenin convinced them to agree to peace, telling them that Germany was on the brink of revolution and that any treaty would not last. The most important thing, he said, was to consolidate Bolshevik power in Russia. Lost territory could be recovered later. Meanwhile, German forces reached Narva within 100 miles of Petrograd, precipitating transfer of the Russian government to Moscow.

On March 3, 1918, the Bolsheviks signed the Treaty of Brest-Litovsk. In it Russia lost Poland, Courland (western Latvia), and Lithuania. Russia also had to evacuate Livonia, Estonia, Finland, and the Åland Islands; quit Ukraine and recognize the treaty between the Ukrainian People's Republic and the Central Powers; and surrender Ardahan, Kars, and Batum to the Ottomans. Finally, Russia agreed to pay Germany an indemnity estimated at from 4 billion to 5 billion gold rubles. In all, the treaty stripped Russia of nearly 1.3 million square miles of territory and 62 million people, a third of its population. This included a third of its arable land, three-quarters of its coal and iron, and a third of its factories. German troops landed in Finland, and German and Austro-Hungarian troops occupied Ukraine and established a military dictatorship there under General Pavlo Skoropadski. In view of subsequent German protestations regarding the 1919 Treaty of Versailles, it is worth remembering that the Treaty of Brest-Litovsk was far harsher. It was also approved by the German Reichstag, which in 1917 had passed a resolution calling for peace with no territorial annexations.

On May 7 the Central Powers forced Romania to sign the equally punitive Treaty of Bucharest. Romania was forced to cede the Dobrudja to Bulgaria and the

Carpathian mountain passes to Hungary. Germany secured a 90-year lease on Romania's oil wells and mineral rights.

Germany would have to act quickly on the Western Front. Yet Ludendorff erred in retaining 1 million soldiers on the Eastern Front. Ultimately another half million men were ordered west. Had they been available at the onset of the offensive, they probably would have given Germany victory.

The spring 1918 German drive is known as the Ludendorff Offensive. It envisioned a series of attacks to push British forces back on the English Channel, isolating them from the French and then mounting a decisive blow to defeat the British, whereupon the French would have to give up.

The first German drive, code-named MICHAEL, was directed at the hinge where the British and French armies met. By its start, Ludendorff had 207 divisions against only 173 Allied (including 4.5 U.S. divisions, which at 27,000 men each are here calculated at 9 divisions). The attack itself involved 74 German divisions supported by 6,473 guns and 730 aircraft. The British had only 27 divisions (3 cavalry) at the point of attack and at some points were outnumbered four to one. The defenders had 2,804 guns, 579 aircraft, and 217 tanks.

The Allies knew that an attack was imminent. The Supreme War Council sought the creation of a 30-division reserve that could be committed after the German attack began. Pétain and Haig both objected, and in the end each went his own way, with only limited arrangements to reinforce the other.

The Germans utilized their already-proven infiltration tactics. They also instituted an elaborate deception plan, convincing Pétain that the main German attack would come in the Verdun sector and that the attack to the north was merely

a feint. Early in 1918 the British had extended their front southward, with Gough's Fifth Army assuming control of 28 miles of French trenches, which as it turned out were largely devoid of defenses. This was where the brunt of the attack fell. Haig also underestimated the threat here and kept the bulk of his reserves in Flanders. Also, in Gough's sector the forward defensive zone was too densely held.

The Germans opened MICHAEL, now dubbed the Kaiserschlacht (Emperor's Battle) and also known as the Second Battle of the Somme, early on March 21. Their preliminary bombardment lasted only five hours but fired 1.2 million shells. Heavy fog and the plentiful use of gas and smoke shells greatly inhibited Allied visibility. The Germans then attacked along a 50-mile front held in the north by the Third Army and in the south by the Fifth Army.

The Germans easily forced back the heavily outnumbered Fifth Army. On the second day the British lost contact with French forces to their right, and Gough ordered a retirement beyond the Somme. To the north, however, the Germans encountered the better-prepared defenses of Byng's Third Army.

Although they withdrew, the British did not break, and the Germans soon outran their supply lines. They also had sustained heavy casualties and lacked reserves to exploit breakthroughs. Their troops in the open also fell prey to British air attacks.

Nonetheless a great tactical success, MICHAEL saw the Germans recapture much of the ground abandoned in 1916 and create a 10-mile-wide gap in the Allied lines. But the Germans lacked the resources to exploit the opportunity. MICHAEL also sufficiently scared the Allied leaders that they finally instituted a uniform command structure. They knew that the Germans had greatly benefited from the lack of cooperation between British and French commanders. On March 26 the Allies entrusted overall command on the Western Front to French general of division Ferdinand Foch, and on April 3 he became commander in chief of all Allied armies on the Western Front, including the Americans. Foch proved to be a capable commander, and his positive attitude had immediate effect.

Ludendorff now prepared another assault. Shifting emphasis to the center and right and code-named MARS, it began on March 28 with Arras as its objective. The stronger British positions there held, and at the end of the month Ludendorff again shifted emphasis to take Amiens, but by now the Germans were exhausted. Clear weather also allowed Allied aircraft to savage the German forces, and on April 5 Ludendorff suspended the offensive.

By that date the British had been pushed back up to 40 miles. Unfairly singled out, Gough was removed from command. Rawlinson replaced him, and the Fifth Army was renamed the Fourth Army. Thus far the British had suffered 178,000 casualties (72,000 prisoners) and lost more than 1,100 guns, 200 tanks, and about 400 aircraft. The French sustained some 77,000 casualties (15,000 prisoners). But the Germans had suffered 239,000 casualties and now needed more men to hold a longer line.

In this perilous situation, the British dispatched to the continent its reserve of 355,000 men. By March also some 325,000 American troops were in France; then during May through July more than 675,000 arrived. By the end of the war the U.S. Army had grown to 4 million men, 2.1 million of whom were in France. Ultimately 1.3 million reached the firing line.

Ludendorff now launched his second blow to the north in Flanders. A smaller version of the original GEORGE, it was code-named GEORGETTE. The German Fourth and Sixth Armies attacked just south of Ypres on both sides of the east-west–running Lys River, which gave its name to the battle during April 9–21.

Ludendorff hoped to break the BEF or at least cripple it sufficiently to allow him to shift back to the south and finish the job. His sole aim here was destruction of British forces. The two German armies had 2,208 artillery pieces; the British First Army opposing them had only 511.

The Sixth Army's attack on April 9 fell in a sector near Neuve Chapelle held by the 2nd Portuguese Division, one of two in France under British control since 1916. Of poor quality and in the line longer than was normal, it immediately broke, leaving a six-mile-wide gap. The next day the Germans attacked to the north and drove the British from Messines Ridge and Armentières. On April 11 Haig issued a desperate order calling on positions to be held to the last man, with no retirement.

Although the British were forced back 15 to 20 miles in places, their lines did not break. By April 19 also, the French had taken over 9 miles of front previously held by the British, but Plumer reluctantly ordered the Second Army to withdraw from Passchendaele Ridge to just east of Ypres.

On April 24 the Germans again struck toward Amiens, but Ludendorff had to regroup, and on April 29 he called off the offensive. In the Lys River battle the Allies lost more than 146,000 men (two-thirds of them British) and at least 573 guns. German losses were some 109,000 men.

By early May, Ludendorff had replaced approximately 70 percent of his losses. He still had a numerical advantage on the Western Front—206 divisions against 160—but these were not the fine troops of the start of MICHAEL, and there were many reports of lapses in discipline.

Ludendorff's next drive again aimed at the juncture between the British and French armies. He saw it as the final decisive blow to drive the British back against the channel and from the war. Before that offensive was launched, however, he planned a diversionary attack against the French Army on the Chemin des Dames front. He believed that French reinforcements had twice saved the British (certainly not how the British saw it), and this attack was to hold the French in place.

This third major drive, code-named Operation BLÜCHER and also known as the Third Battle of the Aisne, began on May 27 and lasted until June 3. The Germans secretly positioned 30 divisions of the Seventh Army in the Chemin des Dames sector, giving Crown Prince Wilhelm's army group there 41 divisions. The Germans had 5,263 guns against only 1,422 British and French, the highest ratio for them on the Western Front in the war.

The Germans were aided by the fact that Sixth Army commander General of Division Denis Auguste Duchêne, commanding the Aisne sector, ignored Pétain's call for an elastic defense. In order to retain the high ground of the Chemin des Dames, won at such high cost, he placed most of his 16 divisions, including 5 British, forward along the crest of the 25-mile front. An elastic defense would have had only outposts there and the bulk of his forces behind the Aisne.

The May 27 massive 160-minute preliminary bombardment shattered the French defenders in their forward positions. The German Seventh Army easily broke through and secured the bridges over the Aisne and undefended terrain behind it. Within two days the Seventh Army

had taken Soissons, and by the end of the month it was in the Marne River Valley, the natural route to Paris just 50 miles distant.

Lulled by the 40-mile advance, Ludendorff continued the attack too long. The French withdrew in good order and brought up supplies and reinforcements, including fresh U.S. Army divisions, by rail. On May 28 the U.S. 1st Division recaptured Cantigny. American forces also helped blunt the subsequent German advance at Château Thierry and Belleau Wood.

The Germans had again made a tremendous advance but were unable to exploit it. They were now in a deep salient that was difficult to supply and hold. And in three offensives, they had sustained more than 600,000 casualties.

Ludendorff's next goal was to link the salient north along the Somme with the other to the south on the Marne and shorten his lines. His fourth drive, known as GNEISENAU and mounted by Hutier's Eighteenth Army, began on June 9 on a 22-mile front between Noyon and Montdidier. Foch anticipated this, and German deserters gave away the timing, enabling the French to open counterbattery fire against the German assault positions just before the German barrage commenced. Again the Germans made a spectacular advance on the first day of 6 miles, but the Americans halted it. On June 11 the French counterattacked, and Hutier's drive ended. Losses in the June 9–14 fighting came to 35,000 French (15,000 prisoners) and 30,000 Germans.

Austro-Hungarian forces were also making a final drive against the Italians along the Piave. Diaz learned the exact timing of the attack on June 15 and ordered artillery to fire on the Austrian staging areas, inflicting heavy losses. Nonetheless the attackers enjoyed some success, getting 100,000 men across the Piave. A flood on June 17, however, swept away the majority of the bridges essential for logistical support. On June 18 Diaz counterattacked, and within a week the Italians recovered all the territory south of the river. Instead of knocking Italy out of the war, the battle cost Austria-Hungary 150,000 casualties (25,000 captured). The Italians lost 85,000 (30,000 prisoners) and the British and French 2,500. It was the Dual Monarchy's last great effort of the war.

On the Western Front, Ludendorff did what he could to reequip and reinforce his troops. A monthlong delay, however, enabled the Allies to bring more U.S. troops into the line. At dawn on July 15 Ludendorff launched his fifth offensive, known as the Champagne-Marne Offensive or the Second Battle of the Marne (July 15–18). Ludendorff committed 50 divisions east and west of Reims with the goal of capturing that city and the vital Paris-to-Nancy rail line. He expected to then return to Flanders and finish off the British. There was, however, no guarantee that the Germans would not continue up the Marne Valley to Paris, and fear gripped the French capital. Many on both sides believed that if the Germans took Reims they would win the war.

Increasing numbers of German deserters betrayed most of Ludendorff's plan, including its timing, enabling Foch to order counterbattery fire against German assembly areas during the night of July 14–15. Although some troops of the German Seventh Army crossed the Marne near Château Thierry, they got little farther. East of Reims the French Fourth Army stopped the German First and Third Armies. The farthest German advance was barely six miles.

The strategic initiative now passed to the Allies. Even as the battle for Reims

had raged, Foch assembled a 20-division reserve and 350 tanks, and on July 18 he launched his counteroffensive. The U.S. 1st Infantry and 2nd Infantry Divisions spearheaded the French Tenth Army's attack, which fell on the right side of the Reims salient five miles south of German-held Soissons. Although Allied casualties were heavy, the attack succeeded brilliantly. The threat to Paris was ended. On July 20 Ludendorff called off his planned Flanders drive to concentrate on holding the area to the south, rejecting sound advice that the army withdraw to the Siegfried Line.

A week later Allied commanders met in Paris, where Foch, now marshal of France, informed them of his plans for a series of continuing attacks from Flanders to the Marne that would allow the Germans no respite. The first of these, entrusted to Haig, was the Amiens Offensive (August 8–September 4) to reduce the German salient south of the Somme.

Haig's Allied army group consisted of 24 divisions in the Fourth Army and the French First Army. Fourteen German divisions opposed them. The main blow came south of the Somme, delivered by the Canadians and Australians. By the end of the first day at little cost to themselves, the British had advanced up to 6 miles on a 12-mile front. Ludendorff called August 8 "the black day of the German Army in the history of this war." This was not for the ground lost but rather for the large number of Germans who surrendered after at best token resistance. The three-day total was some 75,000 German casualties (30,000 prisoners) and 500 guns, with Allied casualties of some 45,000. By September 9 the Allies had retaken all the territory lost in the spring offensives. The Amiens Offensive revealed the collapse of German fighting ability, paralleling war weariness at home.

With the German threat to Paris ended and following acrimonious debate with Foch, Pershing received permission for an independent U.S. Army action to reduce the Saint-Mihiel salient south of Verdun. The Germans, who recognized the need for a shorter line, were already withdrawing when on September 12 the U.S. First Army and four French divisions attacked. The attackers reduced the salient in just two days, capturing 15,000 Germans and 250 guns for 7,000 casualties of their own. Pursuant to orders, they then halted.

Pershing had wanted to drive on Metz. But with the Amiens Offensive going well, Foch ordered him to limit his assault to reaching the base of the salient, then shift his forces west to attack north of the Marne. This was probably a mistake, for Pershing's plan offered the promise of greater gains than Haig's attack toward Cambrai, the basis of Foch's subsequent plan.

Foch's strategy was essentially one great continuous pushing action all the way from Ypres to Verdun. On September 26 the French and Americans launched what became known as the Meuse-Argonne Offensive, continuing until the end of the war. The U.S. First Army and the French Fourth Army steadily drove the Germans back. By November 11 the Germans had suffered more than 100,000 casualties (26,000 prisoners) and lost 846 guns.

The Italians, who had remained largely quiescent after their June victory on the Piave, also resumed the offensive. It was clear that Austria-Hungary was breaking apart, and Italian leaders were anxious to be in a strong negotiating position at any peace conference. Diaz had available 57 infantry and 4 cavalry divisions, 7,720 guns, and 600 aircraft against 60.5

Austro-Hungarian divisions supported by 6,145 guns and 564 aircraft.

The Battle of Vittorio-Veneto (October 24–November 4) began with stiff resistance but ended in a rout, with many Austro-Hungarian units deserting en masse. Some 30,000 troops were killed or wounded, but an incredible 427,000 were captured, along with 5,000 guns. Allied losses were approximately 41,000 (38,000 Italian). Vienna asked for an armistice on October 30. It was signed on November 3, and fighting on the Italian front ceased the next day.

Bulgaria was, however, the first Central Power to break. In July, General of Division Louis Félix François Franchet d'Esperey had assumed command of Allied troops at Salonika. He had 700,000 men in 29 divisions, although those available for duty probably numbered half that figure. On September 15 the Allies began an offensive and drove back the 400,000 Bulgarians. In the Battle of the Vardar (September 15–24), the Serbs and French advanced 40 miles. On September 29, French cavalry took Skopje. The Bulgarian government appealed for an armistice, which was concluded on September 30. On October 4 Czar Ferdinand abdicated, succeeded by his son Boris.

Franchet d'Esperey also sent a force into Thrace to open the straits into the Black Sea. Belgrade fell on November 1, and on November 10 the Allies crossed the Danube. Franchet d'Esperey had liberated the Balkans and was preparing to move on Budapest and Dresden when the war ended. Allied troops also crossed into Romania, and on November 10 it reentered the war.

In Mesopotamia, British forces launched an offensive that secured Mosul, although not until November 14, after the armistice. Allenby meanwhile broke the Ottomans in Palestine following his spectacular attack at Megiddo (September 19). Operating with Arab forces, Allenby captured Damascus (October 1) and Aleppo (October 25). In Africa, Lettow-Vorebeck surrendered on November 25.

In Caucasia, the disintegration of Russian forces in late 1917 produced a virtual vacuum. Although the Ottoman Army was now hardly capable of major offensive operations, the situation favored the Ottomans and Armenians. In February 1918 the Ottoman Third Army took the offensive, and by early April it had retaken all the territory lost to Russia earlier. The Ottomans went on to take Kars, then moved into Persia and Azerbaijan, taking Baku in September 1918. All this was rendered meaningless with the Ottoman surrender.

Hindenburg and Ludendorff knew that the war was lost. Indeed, on September 29 they called for a new German government and immediate negotiations for an armistice. The duo, who had been in complete control of German policy for the past two years, blamed the defeat on others and refused to take ownership of it.

On October 3, Prince Max of Baden became chancellor of a new liberal German government. On October 26, both Hindenburg and Ludendorff offered to resign; the kaiser accepted only that of Ludendorff. On October 28, a mutiny broke out in the High Seas Fleet at Kiel on word that the admirals planned a last-ditch naval foray. By early November the mutiny had spread to other German seaports, where councils on the Russian model sprung up. With revolution threatening and the kaiser refusing to act on his own, Prince Max simply announced in Berlin on November 9 that the kaiser had abdicated. Wilhelm then went into exile in the Netherlands.

In these circumstances, Allied leaders at Paris discussed the options of an armistice or continuing the war until Germany surrendered. An armistice would merely halt the fighting, with peace negotiations to follow. Foch believed that two additional weeks of fighting would have forced a German surrender, but general war weariness and French and British fears of growing American influence worked in favor of an armistice. On November 8, Foch received a German armistice delegation in his command railroad car at Compiègne. To spare the German Army the onus of defeat, Hindenburg insisted that it be headed by a civilian.

The Germans were given 72 hours to accept the terms. After several days of negotiation, the parties reached agreement. The Germans signed the armistice at 5:00 a.m. on November 11, and it went into effect six hours later.

The agreement provided that within two weeks the Germans would evacuate all captured territory as well as Alsace and Lorraine. Within four weeks German troops were to quit the left (west) bank of the Rhine River and its right bank to a depth of 18 miles (30 kilometers). Allied troops would occupy that territory and control crossing points over the Rhine at Köln (Cologne), Koblenz (Coblenz), and Mainz. Germany was also forced to turn over sufficient equipment to ensure that it would be unable to resume the war. This included the bulk of its surface navy and all submarines as well as substantial quantities of artillery pieces, machine guns, and aircraft, along with large numbers of locomotives, railway cars, and trucks. Germany would have to make reparation for war damages, and all Allied prisoners of war were to be returned immediately without reciprocity. The most controversial provision was the continuation of the naval blockade, which had exacted a high price on German civilians, until a peace agreement was signed, although London did promise to allow such provisioning of the German people as it deemed necessary.

The Allied failure to insist on German surrender undoubtedly saved lives but had momentous consequences. Because Germany was spared invasion and the German armies marched home in good order with battle flags flying, many Germans believed in the "stab in the back" legend of the German political Right that the German armies had not been defeated in the field but had been betrayed by corrupt politicians, Jews, war profiteers, and disaffection on the home front. Later this provided considerable grist for Adolf Hitler's hate mill, especially when leading German generals testified that it was fact.

The war was over. Now it was up to the politicians to resolve the peace. On January 18, 1919, the conference opened in Paris. Russia did not take part. Civil War was raging there, and efforts to cobble together a united delegation proved fruitless. Although five delegations (those of Britain, France, the United States, Italy, and Japan) played important roles, the conference was dominated by the Big Three of Britain, France, and the United States. Wilson and Lloyd George stood together on most issues, meaning that Clemenceau of France was the odd man out.

On April 28, the conferees approved creation of the League of Nations. Wilson's cherished project, the league emerged not as a binding international organization with its own military force, as the French and many smaller powers desired; instead, it was based on voluntary membership with emphasis on moral suasion.

Sanctions were its strongest enforcement weapon. Unfortunately, many people saw the league as a cure-all for the world's security problems when other guarantees were what really mattered.

The peace treaties, all named for Paris suburbs, were as follows: the Treaty of Versailles with Germany (June 28, 1919), the Treaty of Saint-Germain with Austria (July 20, 1919), the Treaty of Neuilly with Bulgaria (November 27, 1919), the Treaty of Trianon with Hungary (March 21, 1920), and the Treaty of Sèvres with the Ottoman Empire (August 10, 1920), superseded by the Treaty of Lausanne (July 24, 1923).

The most important of these treaties was the one with Germany. France sought to detach the entire Rhineland from Germany and make it independent with a permanent Allied occupation force. Britain and the United States were strongly opposed and wanted all troops to depart on the signing of the treaty. To break this impasse, Britain and the United States offered France a guarantee that they would come to its support should it ever be attacked by Germany. Clemenceau was forced to yield. But the U.S. Senate never approved this Anglo-American Treaty of Guarantee, and the British government claimed that its agreement was contingent on American acceptance. The French thus lost the security guarantee they had so desperately sought.

The Treaty of Versailles restored Alsace and Lorraine to France and gave Belgium the small border enclaves of Moresnet, Eupen, and Malmédy. In recompense for the deliberate destruction of French coal mines by the withdrawing Germans, France was to receive the coal production of the Saar region of Germany for 15 years. The Saar itself would be under League of

Nations administration, with Saarlanders to vote at the end of the period whether to continue that status or to join Germany or France.

Plebiscites were to decide the future of northern and southern Schleswig. Germany was also to cede most of Posen and West Prussia to the new state of Poland, with a plebiscite to be held in districts of Upper Silesia. Gdansk (Danzig) would be a free city under the League of Nations but within the Polish customs union to provide that new state with a major seaport. Germany ceded Klaipėda (Memel, now part of Lithuania) to the Allies, and all the German colonies were to be organized as mandates under League of Nations supervision.

The Rhineland and a belt east of the Rhine 30 kilometers (18 miles) deep were to be permanently demilitarized. The Allies were allowed to occupy the Rhineland for up to 15 years, with Germany to bear the costs. The Kiel Canal was to be open to the warships and merchant ships of all nations, and Germany's rivers were internationalized. The German Army was restricted to 100,000 officers and men, and it was denied all military aircraft, heavy artillery, and tanks. The German Navy was limited to six predreadnought battleships in capital ships and was not permitted submarines.

In highly controversial Article 231, Germany accepted responsibility for having caused the war, establishing the legal basis for reparations. Germany was to pay for all civilian damages in the war. (The bill, presented in May 1921, was $33 billion.) In the meantime, Germany was to pay $5 billion. Germany was also to hand over all merchant ships of more than 1,600 tons, half of those of 800–1,600 tons, and a quarter of its fishing fleet. It was also to build 200,000 tons of shipping for the Allies annually for a period of five years. While the other major signatories approved the Treaty of Versailles, the United States Senate never ratified it.

The treaties with the other defeated powers imposed restrictions on their military establishments and demanded reparations. That with Austria confirmed the breakup of the former Dual Monarchy. Hungary, Czechoslovakia, Yugoslavia, and Poland were all independent. Austria was forced to cede from its own territory Eastern Galicia to Poland as well as the Trentino, Trieste, and Istria to Italy. Italy also secured the South Tirol (Tyrol), even though this violated Wilson's "self-determination of peoples" because of its German-speaking population of some 240,000 people. Shorn of its raw materials and food-producing areas, Austria was hard-hit economically, and many Austrians favored union with Germany (Anschluss), which was, however, forbidden.

Hungary lost almost three-quarters of its pre–World War I territory and two-thirds of its people. Czechoslovakia gained Slovakia, Austria secured western Hungary, and Yugoslavia took Croatia and Slovenia and part of the Banat of Temesvar. Romania received the remainder of the Banat and Transylvania, with its large Magyar population, along with part of the Hungarian plain.

Bulgaria was forced to yield territory to the new Yugoslavia and to cede Western Thrace to Greece and thus port facilities on the Aegean Sea. Bulgaria gained minor territory at the expense of the Ottoman Empire.

The Ottoman Empire renounced all claim to non-Turkish territory. The Kingdom of the Hejaz in southwestern Asia became independent. France secured a mandate over a new state of Syria (to include Lebanon), while Britain gained a mandate over Mesopotamia (the future Iraq, to include Mosul) and Palestine. Smyrna (present-day Izmir) in eastern Anatolia and the hinterland was to be administered by Greece for five years after which a plebiscite would decide its future, while Italy gained the Dodecanese Islands and Rhodes, and Greece received the remaining Turkish islands in the Aegean as well as Thrace. Armenia was made independent. The treaty also established an autonomous Kurdistan under the League of Nations. The straits were internationalized, and territory adjacent to them was demilitarized.

Turkish nationalists such as General Mustafa Kemal were outraged by this treaty, and they set out to drive the Greeks from Anatolia. As a result of their military successes, the dictated Treaty of Sèvres was superseded by the negotiated settlement of the Treaty of Lausanne in 1923. Although the new Republic of Turkey still gave up all claim to the non-Turkish areas, it recovered much of Eastern Thrace as well as Imbros and Tenedos. The remainder of the Aegean Islands went to Greece. Italy retained the Dodecanese Islands, and Turkey recognized British control of Cyprus. The Kurds and the Armenians lost out. There was no mention of autonomy for Kurdestan and no independent Armenia. The straits were to be demilitarized and open in times of peace to ships of all nations and in times of war if the Republic of Turkey was neutral. If Turkey was at war, enemy ships but not those of neutral nations might be excluded.

There was much debate about the Paris settlement in subsequent years. Critics on the Right claimed that World War II would

not have occurred had the French been allowed to write the settlement, while those on the Left maintained that the Treaty of Versailles was too harsh to conciliate the Germans. However, the peace settlement was a compromise, and the reality is that it did not significantly diminish German power. In any case, Britain, France, and the United States failed to cooperate on enforcement of the treaty in the postwar period, and there is no reason to suppose they would have done any better with a different treaty. The United States almost immediately withdrew into isolation, while the British had little interest in postwar collective security arrangements binding them to France and Europe. This left enforcement of the peace settlement to France, a burden it proved incapable of bearing alone.

Significance

Almost all of the predictions of 1914 had been proven wrong. The belief in a short war over by Christmas gave way to a four-year-long slaughterhouse and the largest conflict in world history to that point. Victory was almost indistinguishable from defeat. The human costs alone were staggering. More than 68 million men had been mobilized, and at least 10 million had died (8 million from combat and the remainder from disease and malnutrition). Another 21 million men were wounded, and nearly 8 million had been taken prisoner or declared missing. In the French and Russian Armies three-quarters of the men were casualties. At least 6.6 million civilians also perished, some 1 million of these starving to death as a consequence of the British blockade. These heavy casualties fueled pacifist sentiment, especially in Britain, and helped prevent timely rearmament in the 1930s against Hitler's Germany.

World War I introduced or saw increased use of new weapons including the tank, airplane, machine gun, and submarine. The war also introduced penicillin and focused attention on shell shock, now known as post traumatic stress disorder (PTSD). The war led vast numbers of women to enter the workforce, which would have profound social, economic, and political ramifications. World War I also greatly influenced literature and the arts.

The war was much more than a vast military holocaust. It toppled all of continental Europe's dynastic empires: the German, Austro-Hungarian, Ottoman, and Russian Empires. It used up the capital and treasure accumulated over centuries. The war established the United States as the leading creditor nation and world financial capital. World War I was followed by a crippling economic downturn that lasted into the mid-1920s in some countries, producing economic chaos in Italy, which Benito Mussolini used to advantage to seize power in 1922.

World War I greatly stimulated unrest in the colonial areas of the world, paradoxically advancing both Zionism and Arab nationalism, leading to today's problems in that region. Wilson's statements about "self-determination of peoples" found ready acceptance overseas in Africa and Asia that is still playing out. It is also hard to imagine the Bolsheviks coming to power in Russia without the war. World War I also occupied a central place in the rise to power of Adolf Hitler in Germany. His effort to reverse the outcome of the Great War brought World War II. In this sense, World War II was simply a continuation of World War I. Given all this, World War I was quite simply the most important single event of the 20th century.

Further Reading

Chickering, Rodger. *Imperial Germany and the Great War, 1914–1918.* Cambridge: Cambridge University Press, 2004.

Doughty, Robert A. *Pyrrhic Victory: French Strategy and Operations in the Great War.* Cambridge, MA: Belknap, 2005.

Falls, Cyril Bentham. *The First World War.* London: Longmans, 1960.

Farwell, Byron. *The Great War in Africa, 1914–1918.* New York: Norton, 1989.

Gilbert, Martin. *The First World War: A Complete History.* New York: H. Holt, 1994.

Halpern, Paul G. *A Naval History of World War I.* New York: Routledge, 1995.

Herwig, Holger H. *The First World War: Germany and Austria-Hungary, 1914–1918.* New York: Arnold, 1997.

Herwig, Holger H., and Richard F. Hamilton. *The Origins of World War I.* New York: Cambridge University Press, 2003.

Kennett, Lee. *The First Air War, 1914–1918.* New York: Free Press, 1991.

Lyons, Michael J. *World War I: A Short History.* 2nd ed. New York: Prentice Hall, 1999.

Meyer, Gerald J. *A World Undone: The Story of the Great War, 1914 to 1918.* New York: Random House, 2006.

Neiberg, Michael S. *Fighting the Great War: A Global History.* Cambridge, MA: Harvard University Press, 2005.

Sachar, Howard Morley. *The Emergence of the Middle East, 1914–1924.* New York: Knopf, 1969.

Strachan, Hew. *World War I: A History.* New York: Oxford University Press, 1998.

Tucker, Spencer C. *The Great War, 1914–18.* Bloomington: Indiana University Press, 1998.

Tucker, Spencer C., ed. *World War I: The Definitive Encyclopedia and Document Collection.* 5 vols. Santa Barbara, CA: ABC-CLIO, 2014.

Chinese Civil War and Communist Revolution (1927–1949)

Dates	1927–1949
Location	China
Combatants	Guomindong (Nationalists) vs. Communists
Principal Commanders	Guomindong: Jiang Jieshi (Chiang Kai-shek), Zang Fakuei, Feng Yuxiang Communists: Mao Zedong (Mao Tse-tung), Zhou Enlai, Zhu De, Li Lisan, Lin Biao
Principal Battles	Nanchang Uprising, August Harvest Uprising, Changsha, Shanghai (first), Long March, Xiang River, Liaoxi Corridor Offensive, Jinan, Huai-Hai, Shanghai (second), Ghangzhou, Chongqing
Outcome	Mainland China is unified under the communists, who have been in power ever since.

Causes

The Chinese Civil War and Communist Revolution, which is generally divided into two phases during 1927–1936 and 1946–1949, was an internecine conflict between the Republic of China government led by the Guomindang (GMD; also known as the Kuomintang, or Nationalist) and supporters of the Chinese Communist Party (CCP). The conflict ended with the defeat of the GMD and the establishment of the People's Republic of China (PRC).

The CCP was founded in 1921 by Chen Duxiu and Li Dazhao in the city of Shanghai. While there had been informal communist groups in China and among Chinese overseas in 1920, the first CCP Congress was held in Shanghai and attended by 53 men in July 1921. Soviet representatives of the Communist International (Comintern) advised the CCP early on to collaborate with other political groups supporting the Chinese revolution, especially the GMD, which had been founded by Sun Yixian (Sun Yat-sen), the revered revolutionary leader who was elected provisional president of the new Republic of China (ROC) in 1911.

Unfortunately for China, Sun died in March 1925. He was succeeded by Jiang Jieshi (Chiang Kai-shek), who had undergone military training in Japan and headed the Whampoa Military Academy. Jiang, who was based in Guangzhou (Canton), immediately moved to eliminate all potential rivals. In July 1926 he led northward substantial GMD forces, many of them trained by German advisers, in an effort to defeat the northern warlords and unify China.

Jiang's first objective was territory held by warlord Wu Peifu (Wu Pei-fu). GMD forces captured Hankou (Hankow) on September 6. Following a siege, they took Wuchang (Wuch'ang) on October 10. Jiang then transferred the capital from Guangzhou to Hankou. Jiang next moved east against warlord Sun Chuanfang (Sun Ch'uan-fang) in the lower Changjian (Yangxi, Yangtze) River Valley, centered on the city of Nanjing (Nanking), which GMD forces captured on March 24, 1927.

Although his campaign against the northern warlords had gone well, Jiang became alarmed about the rising power of his allies, the communists. The CCP had staged bloody although unsuccessful uprisings in several industrial cities, most notably the great commercial center of Shanghai. Jiang now purged CCP members from GMD institutions. Fearful of an alliance between the communists and leftist elements within the GMD, on April 12, 1927, he also ordered his troops to seize control of the Chinese portion of Shanghai and break the back of the CCP there. An estimated 3,000–4,000 communists in Shanghai and neighboring areas were killed. Another 30,000 suspected communists, peasant association members, and leftists died in purges from April through August 1927. Understandably, this action brought a split in the GMD. Denounced by the Hankou government for his actions in Shanghai, Jiang established his own government at Nanjing.

During April–June 1927, the two rival ROC governments each mounted campaigns against the northern warlords, now supported by Marshal Zhang Zuolin (Chang Tso-lin), warlord of Manchuria and northeastern China. Hankou government forces, however, enjoyed only mixed success in northern Hubei (Hupeh) and southern Henan (Honan) Provinces, while the Nanjing forces under Jiang advanced through Anhui (Anhwei) Province against Sun Chuanfang in Xuzhou (Hsuchow). In June warlord Feng Yuxiang (Feng Yuhsiang), known as the Christian General, moved southwest from Shaanxi (Shanhsi) against Jiang, who then withdrew into northern Henan. On June 21, however, Feng met with Jiang and agreed to support him.

Course

In July 1927 the Nationalist government in Hankou, having discovered a communist plot to seize control, forced all known communists from government posts and expelled Soviet political and military advisers. Following this action, on August 1 communist elements in the Hankou Army stationed in the city of Nanchang in Jiangxi (Kiangsi) Province mutinied, hoping that this would be the trigger for a communist revolution throughout China. Proposed by communist leader Li Lisan (Li Li-san), the mutiny was led by Generals Ye Ting (Yeh T'ing), He Long (Ho Lung), and Zhu De (Chu Te).

Nationalist troops loyal to the Hankou government crushed the rebellion. Although most of the rebel troops were caught or dispersed, Zhu De escaped with a small force into the mountains of western Jiangxi. The Nanchang Uprising is usually recognized as the beginning date for the Chinese Workers and Peasants Red Army (the future People's Liberation Army [PLA]) as well as the long civil war between the Nationalists and communists in China.

Jiang refused to try to reach an agreement with the more radical GMD leaders at Hankou and, in order to restore unity within the GMD, resigned on August 8. He then traveled to Japan, while the two GMD factions reunited at Nanjing.

On September 7, communist leader Mao Zedong (Mao Tse-tung) led a peasant insurrection in Hunan and Jiangxi Provinces and established the short-lived Hunan Soviet in what becomes known as the Autumn Harvest Uprising. GMD forces soon defeated Mao's small forces centered on peasants and miners, but in a significant ideological shift, Mao and Red Army founder Zhu De established a rural strategy that concentrated on the peasantry as the center of revolutionary activity. Traditional communist theory heretofore had

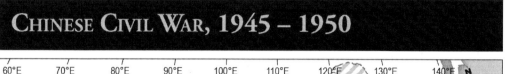

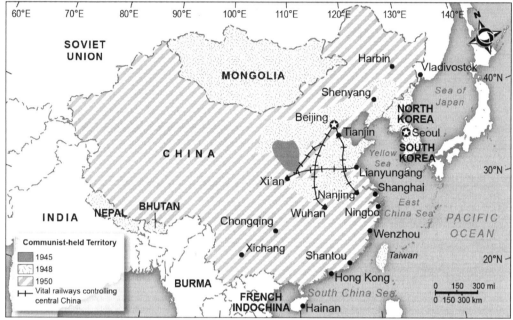

called for revolution to be based on industrial workers.

Seeking to take advantage of the split in GMD ranks and the communist uprisings in central China, in September 1927 warlords of northern China launched a counteroffensive in the Changjiang Valley. Sun Chuanfang led 70,000 men across the Changjiang but was met and defeated by Nationalist General Li Zongren (Li Tsung-jen) in the five-day Battle of Longtan (Lung-tan) in September 1927. Li lost some 5,000 dead, while Sun suffered as many as 20,000 dead and perhaps 30,000 taken prisoner. Sun then withdrew back into northern China. During December 11–15 also, some 50,000 GMD troops put down a communist uprising in Guangzhou, resulting in the deaths of some 15,000 soldiers and civilians.

Jiang returned to China on January 6, 1928, and was reappointed commander of

the GMD Army and head of the reunited Nationalist government as chairman of the GMD Central Executive Committee. He then prepared for a renewal of the offensive into northern China to defeat the warlords there and reunify China, while at the same time continuing the struggle against the communists.

On April 1, Jiang launched some 700,000 troops against the northern warlords, with some 500,000 men. The offensive was led by Generals Li Zongren, Feng Yuxiang, and He Yingqin (Ho Ying-ch'in) as well as Yan Xishan (Yen Hsi-shan), the allied warlord of Shanxi (Shansi). GMD forces crossed the Huang He (Yellow River) and advanced on Beijing (Peking), taking the former imperial capital on June 8. Jiang then changed the city's name to Beiping (Peiping, meaning "Northern Peace"). Prominent warlord in northeastern China and Manchuria Marshal Zhang Zuolin (Chang Tso-lin) tried to withdraw into Manchuria but, having rejected cooperation with the Japanese, was assassinated by them when his train blew up near Shenyang (Mukden) on June 4. He was succeeded by his son Zhang Xueliang (Chang Hsueh-liang), known as the "Young Marshal," who acknowledged Nationalist authority over Manchuria.

The Japanese presence rendered Jiang's efforts to control all China far more difficult. The Japanese had secured the German concession in China as a consequence of World War I, and the GMD northern advance led them to rush troops from Tianjin (Tientsin) to Jinan (Tsinan), the capital of Shandong (Shantung), in order to establish their control over that entire province. A skirmish occurred on April 30, followed by a more serious confrontation on May 3. Following a truce on May 5, the Japanese demanded that the Chinese withdraw from Jinan within 12 hours. When the Chinese did not do so fighting resumed, with the Chinese forced to withdraw on May 11. China then appealed to the League of Nations, which took no action. On March 28, 1929, however, the Japanese and Chinese reached agreement, and Japanese troops were withdrawn from Jinan, ending the immediate crisis over Shandong.

The Soviet Union was also active in China, and in 1929 a dispute occurred between the GMD and the Soviets as to ownership of the Chinese Eastern Railroad, whereupon in October Moscow sent troops into Manchuria. This action forced the Chinese, and most especially Manchurian warlord Zhang Xueliang, to acknowledge that the Soviets had indeed inherited the assets belonging to former imperial Russia, whereupon the Russian troops withdrew in January 1930.

In 1930, CCP chairman Li Lisan, one of the leaders of the 1927 Nanchang Uprising, judged the time right for a communist uprising among the urban proletariat. Mao opposed Li but was overruled. Li then ordered communist guerrillas to take control of the principal cities of central China.

The only communist success came at Changsha (Ch'ang-sha) in Hunan Province, which was briefly secured by forces under Peng Dehuai (P'eng Teh-huai) on July 28. Li ordered a new effort to retake Changsha, but this met bloody failure from GMD reinforcements, and Li was soon called for consultations in Moscow. The communist failure at Changsha substantially increased Mao's influence in the CCP.

The CCP, now largely led by Mao, established a rural base in Jiangxi in southern China that became the Jiangxi Soviet Republic. By 1933 it boasted a military force of some 200,000 men. Jiang now regarded the communists as an even greater threat to his regime than the Japanese. Between December 1930 and September 1934, Jiang waged five campaigns against the communist Ruijin (Juichin) base in Jiangxi. Jiang referred to these as bandit suppression (or extermination) campaigns. The first two campaigns (December 1930–January 1931 and April–May 1931) were easily turned back by the communists. Jiang commanded in person the third campaign (July–September 1931). His forces were converging on Ruijin when word was received of the Mukden Incident. This caused Jiang to break off the offensive and withdraw.

The Mukden Incident of September 18, 1931, saw Japanese staff officers of the elite Kwantung (Guandong) Army in southern Manchuria set off an explosion near the main line of the South Manchuria Railway near Mukden (present-day

Shenyang), then blame the act on nearby Chinese soldiers. The event is known in Japan as the Manchurian Incident. Claiming that the Chinese intended to blow up the rail line from Port Arthur to Shenyang, the Japanese military quickly seized control of Shenyang, forcing the Chinese to withdraw. The Japanese then began the conquest of all Manchuria. Presented with a fait accompli by its military, the Japanese government in Tokyo supported the action, and on February 18, 1932, Japan proclaimed the independence of Manchuria in the form of the new state of Manchukuo (Manzhouguo), headed by former Qing boy emperor Henry Puyi (Pu-i), who had been deposed in 1912. A protocol in September 1932 established a Japanese protectorate over Manchukuo.

The Chinese responded to the Mukden Incident with a boycott of Japanese goods, and to break this the Japanese sent 70,000 troops into Shanghai on January 28, 1932. In what is known as the First Battle of Shanghai (January 28–March 4, 1932), the Chinese Nineteenth Route Army put up a surprisingly effective resistance before it was driven out after a month of fighting. The Chinese government then agreed to end its boycott of Japanese goods.

Following this agreement, Jiang resumed action against the communists. Jiang's summer 1932 offensive against the Eryuwan (Oyuwan) soviet in the Anhui-Henan-Hubei border area was largely successful. A fourth offensive during April–June 1933 was again disrupted, however, by increased Japanese activity in northern China. Claiming that this Inner Mongolian province was actually part of Manchuria, the Japanese sent troops into Rehe (Jehol) and added it to their Manchurian holdings. In early April they also moved against Chinese forces south of the

Great Wall to within a few miles of Beijing and Tianjin. In May, Chinese forces evacuated Beijing, then under the control of pro-Japanese Chinese.

On May 31, 1933, the Beijing leaders concluded the Tanggu Truce (T'ang-ku Truce) with Japan. It required that all Chinese troops be withdrawn south and west of a line running roughly from Tianjin to Beijing, while Japanese troops would be withdrawn north of the Great Wall. This created a zone administered by the Demilitarized Peace Preservation Corps controlled by Chinese friendly to Japan. The GMD government was now forced to recognize that for the present at least, Manchuria was lost.

Jiang's carefully prepared Fifth Bandit Extermination Campaign during December 1933–September 1934 benefited from German military assistance in the form of advisers headed by General Hans von Seeckt, retired head of the German General Staff. This well-planned and methodical offensive by some 300,000 GMD troops included the use of blockhouses and was slowly closing on Ruijin when the communist leadership, consisting of Bo Gu (Po Ku), Zhou Enlai (Chou En-lai), and Comintern agent Otto Braun, decided on a breakout. Jiang's anticommunist campaigns, while ultimately enjoying success, were extraordinarily costly in terms of lives and resources, and they prevented the Chinese from concentrating on the encroaching Japanese in the north.

The communist breakout leading to the Long March of October 1934–October 1935 began with a diversionary attack by some 130,000 communist troops, allowing 86,000 other troops, 11,000 political cadres, and many thousands of civilian porters to break free of the GMD encirclement. The remaining communist forces sought to fight a delaying action, then disperse as best they could.

The escaping communists easily broke through the first Nationalist strongpoints but then encountered reinforced GMD troops at the Xiang (Hsiang) River in Hunan Province. Here during November 30–December 1, 1934, the communists lost 40,000 men and virtually all of their porters. Those communists who remained now had to fight their way across some of the most difficult terrain of western China before proceeding north. The trek extended over 370 days, and during it the communists came under near-constant Nationalist attacks from the ground and air. Many died, others were left behind as underground cadres, and there were desertions. But adding others who joined en route, about 100,000 people reached the remote northwestern Chinese province of Shaanxi. Although the communists later embellished the story of the Long March to near-legendary proportion, claiming a distance traveled of up to 8,000 miles (recent scholarship posits 3,700 miles), it was nonetheless an extraordinary feat. As a consequence, Mao and his supporters became the leaders of the CCP.

During 1935–1936 Jiang ordered troops commanded by his ally, Manchurian warlord Zhang Xueliang, to attack and eliminate the remaining communists. The soldiers refused, insisting that Chinese should be fighting the Japanese and not each other. In the December 1936 Xi'an Incident, Zhang met with Jiang and forced him to agree to a united front with the communists against the Japanese. The GMD-CCP relationship remained strained, however.

Japan continued its effort to control all China. Tokyo demanded an end to Western loans and military advisers to China,

threatening force if this continued. Increasing numbers of young Chinese and the military demanded an end to Jiang's appeasement of the Japanese. Then on the night of July 7, 1937, a clash occurred west of Beijing at the Lugouqiao (Lukouch'iao), or Marco Polo Bridge, between Japanese and Chinese troops. Known as the China Incident, it marked the beginning of the Second Sino-Japanese War (1937–1945), which would merge into World War II.

Later that month after the Chinese government at Nanjing rejected a Japanese ultimatum, the Japanese invaded the coveted northern provinces. In short order they occupied both Beijing (July 28) and Tianjin (July 29). By the end of December, Japan had control of the five Chinese provinces north of the Huang He. In mid-December Japan installed a new government in Beijing. Japan never declared war on China, however. This enabled it to avoid U.S. neutrality legislation and purchase raw materials and oil. But it also allowed the United States to send aid to China. Japanese expansionary policies in China and Southeast Asia brought increasing U.S. resistance, culminating in American economic sanctions and the Japanese attack on Pearl Harbor (December 7, 1941).

In the Second Sino-Japanese War, some 300,000 well-trained and highly motivated Japanese soldiers (backed by 2 million trained reserves in Japan), equipped with the most modern weapons and assisted by 150,000 less well-trained and well-equipped allied Manchurian and Mongolian troops, faced 2 million poorly equipped, indifferently trained Chinese GMD troops and some 150,000 communist guerrillas in northern China. Japan also possessed the third-largest and in many respects most modern navy in the world. Its air force was also large and well trained. China was deficient in both.

During the next 18 months, Jiang gradually abandoned northern and eastern China to the Japanese, withdrawing his government and GMD forces to Chongqing (Chungking) in the far southwestern China province of Sichuan. Meanwhile, the communist Eighth Route Army and the New Fourth Army controlled northwestern China. Despite the assertion by Mao that the war against the Japanese would be protracted, the buildup in their military strength resulted in a communist decision to try to drive the Japanese from northern China. Led by Peng Dehuai, the communist offensive began on August 20, 1940. Some 115 regiments ultimately took part in what came to be known as the Hundred Regiments Offensive, a series of strikes against key Japanese rail and road communications as well as Japanese-held cities. The communist forces destroyed some 600 miles of track, but their biggest success was to put the Jingjing (Chingching) coal mine out of operation for six months, which severely impacted Japanese industrial production. Nonetheless, Japanese lieutenant general Tada Hayao's better-equipped North China Army responded in force beginning in November, defeating CCP forces in pitched battles and convincing Mao and the CCP leadership to change strategy to guerrilla operations behind Japanese lines in northern and central China. This policy provoked ferocious Japanese reprisals against both the communists and the civilian population in the so-called Three Alls Campaign ("burn all, loot all, kill all"), but it helped disrupt Japanese control and served to enhance both the reputation of the communists as dedicated opponents of Japanese rule and their postwar political position.

In December 1940 Jiang ordered the communist New Fourth Army, operating south of the Changjiang in Anhui and Jiangsu (Kiangsu) Provinces, to withdraw north of the river. New Fourth Army commander General Ye Ting refused to obey the order, evidently because it conflicted with that of Mao. Jiang repeated the order and then dispatched GMD troops. Ye finally obeyed the order, and at the end of December his troops began to cross the river. When most of the troops were across, a far larger GMD force under General Shangguan Yunxiang attacked the remainder, killing or capturing some 7,000 men. Ye was among those taken prisoner. Communist bitterness over this incident was perhaps the final blow to CCP-GMD collaboration against the Japanese, although an uneasy alliance continued until 1944.

Throughout the Second Sino-Japanese War, both Jiang and Mao focused on a postwar military confrontation. Jiang drove his U.S. advisers to distraction with his reluctance to commit his troops and the substantial military equipment provided by the Americans against the Japanese.

Jiang's refusal to focus on the Japanese and his failure to deal with the vast corruption that characterized many top officials of his regime eroded his hold on popular loyalties. However, morale remained high in the areas controlled by the communists. The idealistic communist rhetoric, the Spartan living conditions of their leaders at Yan'an in Shaanxi, their willingness to use troops to help the peasants, and their small-scale partisan operations against the Japanese all caught the popular imagination and impressed many visiting Western journalists and officials.

World War II ended in August 1945 with Japan's surrender, but some 1.45 million Japanese troops remained in central

China, and 900,000 more remained in Manchuria. The communists now controlled a wide swath of northwestern China, with some 90 million people and military forces numbering some 1 million.

Jiang insisted that the Japanese surrender only to GMD forces, then numbering about 2.7 million men. During the war the Japanese had stockpiled substantial stocks of arms in Manchuria in order to hold that resource-rich area. Despite objections from Jiang, Soviet forces that had invaded Manchuria in early August turned over much of this equipment to the poorly equipped communist troops. To forestall a communist takeover of all of northern China, beginning in August 1945 Jiang's chief of staff U.S. general Albert C. Wedemeyer provided U.S. aircraft and ships to move GMD troops to Manchuria. By mid-October half a million GMD soldiers had been relocated there.

At the same time, U.S. leaders, especially Ambassador Patrick J. Hurley, urged Jiang to strengthen his position with the Chinese people by carrying out meaningful reforms. Jiang stubbornly resisted this, claiming that reform had to await the defeat of the communists. Jiang simply did not understand the powerful appeal of such policies with the Chinese people. Increasingly, many Chinese saw the CCP rather than the GMD as the only source of long-overdue reform.

Hurley also worked to encourage GMD-CCP reconciliation and the formation of a coalition government in which the communists would have some influence, albeit as junior partners. After several attempts to bring this about, on August 28, 1945, Hurley personally escorted CCP leaders, including Mao and chief lieutenant Zhou Enlai, to Chongqing for a peace conference. Prolonged talks collapsed, however,

and a frustrated Hurley resigned his post on November 26.

Communist forces under Lin Biao now moved into southwestern Manchuria. The Soviet Union rejected a request from Jiang to allow GMD troops to proceed there through the Soviet-occupied Liaodong (Liaotung) Peninsula, and the troops were transported by sea. Beginning on November 15, GMD troops attacked communist forces in areas not controlled by the Soviet army. The much better armed GMD forces made steady progress. Between November 1945 and July 1946 the GMD VI and LII Corps drove the communists from the Shenyang area toward the Yalu River, winning control of much of Manchuria.

The last and most sustained American effort to bring about a reconciliation between the two sides came in the 13-month mission to China of former U.S. Army chief of staff General George C. Marshall. Arriving in China in December 1945, the next month he secured a temporary cease-fire. It was broken later that spring when, as Soviet units withdrew, GMD forces attacked Chinese communist troops moving into areas occupied by the Soviets in Manchuria. In January 1946 also the communists rechristened their military forces the PLA.

Full-scale fighting resumed on July 20, 1946, when Jiang launched a full-scale offensive by more than 100 brigades against communist-held areas in Hubei and Henan Provinces. The United States continued to provide massive loans and large amounts of military equipment to the GMD but refused to commit American troops.

In early November Jiang ordered a unilateral cease-fire and informed Marshall that he was willing to resume negotiations with the communists. The communists rejected this, and the fighting continued. A frustrated Marshall departed China on

January 8, 1947, blaming both sides for the failure to secure an agreement. Some 12,000 U.S. marines remaining in northern China were then ordered to withdraw.

By 1947 with inflation and corruption both rampant in GMD-controlled areas, large numbers of Chinese businessmen and members of the middle class began to desert the GMD, many quitting China altogether. The CCP's introduction of land reform was a powerful incentive for peasant support. By 1947 also, the communists were strong enough to commence offensive operations, and during January–March PLA commander in Manchuria general Lin Biao launched three separate offensives with his Fourth Field Army across the Songhua (Sungari) River. GMD forces, which had assumed a defensive posture with the end of U.S. military assistance in July 1946, repulsed all three. During May and June 1947 some 270,000 PLA troops converged on the Manchurian population centers of Changchun (Ch'angch'un), Jilin (Kirin), and Siping (Szeping). With these cities cut off, GMD forces had to be resupplied by air, and the GMD abandoned its bridgehead across the Songhua. Jiang rushed two additional GMD armies northward. In the Third Battle of Siping during June–July, the GMD repulsed PLA efforts to take the city. A lull in the fighting then occurred as both sides reinforced and prepared for the showdown battles in Manchuria.

Meanwhile, a successful GMD offensive in Shaanxi Province in northwestern China brought the capture of the communist capital of Yan'an on March 19, 1947. The PLA continued its offensives elsewhere, however, for Mao refused to pull back troops to defend the communist capital.

In Manchuria in September 1947 the PLA began its Liaoxi Corridor Offensive, attempting to cut off the city of Shenyang (Mukden) from land communication with northern China. GMD forces managed to secure the corridor from the PLA in early October, however. In January and February 1948, PLA forces mounted a second offensive to secure the vital Liaoxi Corridor. Jiang flew to Manchuria and assumed personal command of the GMD forces, which in February 1948 again secured the corridor, whereupon Jiang returned to Nanjing. PLA forces recaptured the communist capital of Yan'an on April 19, however.

PLA forces continued to pressure the GMD in Manchuria. This brought a GMD withdrawal from Jilin in order to strengthen the large city of Changchun. The GMD's continued defensive posture and its withdrawals adversely affected morale.

In May PLA forces under Generals Chen Yi and Liu Bocheng opened an offensive in the Huang He Valley of north-central China, taking GMD positions north of the river. The offensive culminated in the Battle of Jinan during September 14–24 in which 80,000 GMD troops were captured or defected to the PLA side.

On September 12, meanwhile, the PLA renewed its campaign against the Liaoxi Corridor, seizing control of it on September 12. Despite repeated efforts, GMD forces failed to reopen it. Jiang then flew to Beijing to assume military command. With the military situation in Manchuria now hopeless, he ordered his forces there to fight their way south. A substantial portion of the GMD forces at Changchun defected to the communists, however, and many remaining units surrendered. In the Battle of Shenyang of October 17–30, the PLA attacked three withdrawing GMD columns. Most Nationalist soldiers involved were killed, captured, or simply fled.

GMD commander General Liao Yuexiang (Liao Yueh-hsiang) was among the dead. Shenyang itself fell to the PLA on November 1. By the end of the year, the PLA controlled all Manchuria. The effort to reclaim Manchuria had resulted in 380,000 GMD casualties from combat and disease as well as simple desertion.

In east-central China, remaining GMD forces controlled a cross-shaped area with two major rail lines running east-west from the Yellow Sea through the city of Xuzhou in Jiangsu Province to Kaifeng in Henan and north-south from Jinan in Shandong through Xuzhou to Nanjing in Jiangsu. At Kaifeng and Xuzhou on November 7, 1948, the communist PLA opened its largest major offensive of 1948, the Battle of Huai-Hai for the Huai River and the Longhai (Lung-hai) Railroad that roughly paralleled the river. It is also sometimes called the Battle of Xuzhou.

Each side ultimately committed some 600,000 men to the battle. The GMD enjoyed complete air superiority, but poor communications with ground forces largely nullified this advantage. General Chen Yi, commander of the New Fourth Army, had overall command of the PLA forces. General Bai Chongxi (Pai Ch'ung-hsi) commanded the Nationalist Central China Bandit Suppression Headquarters, but Du Yuming was the GMD general in command of ground in Xuzhou. GMD forces consisted of four army groups: the 2nd, 7th, 13th, and 16th. The 13th was situated at Xuzhou, the 7th was to the east at the juncture of the Longhai Railroad and the Grand Canal, the 2nd was to the west along the railroad to Kaifeng, and the 16th was to the south along the rail line to Bengbu (Peng-pu) on the Huai River.

The battle opened on November 7, 1948, with Chen's New Fourth Army attacking from the east against the GMD 7th Army Group, while General Liu Bocheng's Central Plains Army drove eastward against the GMD 2nd Army Group. Liu's troops forced the GMD troops back into Xuzhou, then swung south to link up with Chen's army and cut off a GMD retreat to the Huai. Liu's rapid advance and further Nationalist defections led to the encirclement of the 7th Army Group about 30 miles east of Xuzhou. Generalissimo Jiang, who took personal charge during the battle, ordered 15 divisions of his 2nd and 16th Army Groups to relieve the surrounded 7th Army Group, but they were slow to respond, and the GMD 7th Army Group surrendered on November 22. Only about 3,000 of its original strength of 90,000 men escaped. Meanwhile on November 16, PLA forces surrounded the GMD 13th Army Group at Xuzhou.

Jiang ordered relief columns of the 12th Army Group and the Eighth Army to advance from the south to assist the escape of the 13th Army Group. Poor leadership again plagued the Nationalist side, however, with the two relief columns unable to join before they came under PLA attack. Liu's PLA forces attacked from the east against the 12th Army Group, while Chen's troops fell on the GMD Eighth Army.

Jiang now decided to abandon Xuzhou altogether. The 13th Army Group departed Xuzhou on December 1, but inept leadership led to it and remnants of other Nationalist forces, altogether about 200,000 men, being surrounded at Yongcheng (Yung-ch'eng) five days later. Jiang's last effort was to commit his Sixth Army from Bengbu, but its advance ground to a halt under fierce PLA guerrilla attacks. With morale in the trapped GMD 12th Army Group at a nadir, many men simply defected. The last GMD units surrendered on

January 10, 1949, bringing the campaign and the battle to an end. Nationalist casualties, including prisoners and defected, totaled about 327,000 men, or more than half of the GMD force engaged. This defeat broke the back of the GMD forces and removed the principal Nationalist defensive line north of the Changjiang, opening the way to the GMD capital of Nanjing.

On January 21, 1949, Jiang resigned. Vice President Li Zongren (Li Tsung-jen) became acting president. On January 31, PLA forces entered the city of Beiping, soon to return to its earlier name of Beijing. On March 25 Mao proclaimed Beijing as again the capital of China.

On April 1, acting GMD president Li Zongren offered a peace settlement with the CCP, suggesting a division of the country at the Changjiang. The communists rejected this and called for the GMD to surrender. The relentless communist military advance continued. On April 20 PLA troops began crossing the Changjiang, and two days later they took the GMD capital of Nanjing. What remained of the GMD government withdrew to Guangzhou. The great city of Shanghai fell on May 25. During the next month, many GMD troops and their commanders simply defected. The GMD capital, meanwhile, was relocated to Chongqing.

On October 1, 1949, in Beijing, Mao announced the establishment of the PRC. Initial recognition came from the Soviet Union, India, Burma, and Ceylon (present-day Sri Lanka). Britain followed suit in January 1950. The PLA took Ghangzhou on October 15 and Chongqing on November 30. The last GMD capital was at Chengdu (Ch'eng-tu).

On December 7, 1949, GMD forces completed their evacuation of the Chinese mainland to the island of Taiwan (Formosa), where the ROC government had relocated. The Nationalists also retained control of the islands of Jinmen (Quemoy) and Mazu (Matsu) and several dozen smaller islands off the Chinese coast. Jiang then carried out a program of reforms in Taiwan that, had they been enacted on the mainland earlier, might have won the support of the Chinese population during the civil war.

Significance

In addition to having led to the establishment of the PRC, the Chinese Civil War and continuing U.S. military and economic assistance to the GMD government on Taiwan created a prolonged legacy of distrust and suspicion that prevented dialogue between the United States and mainland China for several decades. Americans came to see the establishment in China of a communist government sympathetic to the Soviet Union as a major Cold War defeat for the West, abetted by the PRC's participation in the Korean War (1950–1953).

For at least two decades PRC leaders regarded the United States as their country's major international adversary, especially with ongoing U.S. support for the ROC government on Taiwan. This perspective only began to change after U.S. president Richard Nixon moved to reopen relations with China in the early 1970s, but considerable mistrust continues today.

Further Reading

Dreyer, Edward L. *China at War, 1901–1949.* New York: Longman, 1995.

Eastman, Lloyd E., ed. *The Nationalist Era in China, 1927–1949.* Cambridge, MA: Harvard University Press, 1991.

Fairbank, John K., and Albert Feuerwerker, eds. *The Cambridge History of China,* Vol. 13, *Republican China, 1912–1949,* Part 2.

Cambridge: Cambridge University Press, 1986.

Fairbank, John King. *China: A New History.* Cambridge, MA: Harvard University Press, 1994.

Liu, F. F. *The Military History of Modern China, 1924–1949.* Princeton, NJ: Princeton University Press, 1956.

Lynch, Michael. *The Chinese Civil War, 1945–49.* London: Osprey, 2010.

Westad, Odd Arne. *Cold War and Revolution: Soviet-American Rivalry and the Origins of the Chinese Civil War, 1944–1946.* New York: Columbia University Press, 1993.

Westad, Odd Arne. *Decisive Encounters: The Chinese Civil War, 1946–1950.* Stanford, CA: Stanford University Press, 2003.

Zarrow, Peter Gue. *China in War and Revolution, 1895–1949.* London: Routledge, 2005.

World War II (1939–1945)

Dates	September 1, 1939–September 2, 1945
Location	Europe, Asia, Africa, Middle East, Pacific and Atlantic Oceans
Combatants	Allied Powers of China, Poland, Great Britain, France, Soviet Union, and the United States vs. the Axis Powers of Germany, Italy, and Japan
Principal Commanders	China: Jiang Jieshi, Mao Zhedong Poland: Edward Rydz-Śmigły Great Britain: Winston Churchill, Dudley Pound, Bernhard Montgomery, Hugh Dowding France: Charles de Gaulle, Jean de Lattre de Tassigny Soviet Union: Joseph Stalin, Semyon Timoshenko, Georgy Zhukov United States: Franklin D. Roosevelt, George C. Marshall, Dwight D. Eisenhower, Douglas MacArthur, Chester W. Nimitz, Ernest J. King, Henry H. Arnold Germany: Adolf Hitler, Hermann Göring, Eric Raeder, Karl Dönitz, Gerd von Rundstedt, Heinz Guderian, Erich von Manstein, Erwin Rommel Italy: Benito Mussolini, Pietro Badoglio Japan: Emperor Hirohito, Tōjō Hideki, Yamamoto Isoroku, Yamashita Tomoyuki
Principal Battles	Polish Campaign, Norwegian Campaign, France Campaign, Britain, Operation BARBAROSSA, Pearl Harbor, Singapore, Coral Sea, Midway, Guadalcanal, El Alamein (second), Stalingrad, Kursk, Normandy, Bulge, Iwo Jima, Okinawa, Berlin
Outcome	Germany, Italy, and Japan are all defeated. The United Nations is established. The United States and the Soviet Union emerge as the two world superpowers, and the Cold War begins.

Causes

World War II was the most wide-ranging, destructive, and costly conflict in human history, ultimately involving virtually every major country and region. The war pitted the totalitarian Axis states of Germany, Italy, and Japan against the Allied nations, with the principal powers here being Britain, France, the United States, and the Soviet Union. Some historians date the war as beginning with the Japanese invasion of China in 1937. Japanese official histories, however, start with 1931, when their forces overran Manchuria. Most histories of the war, however, start with September 1939 and the German invasion of Poland.

World War II was in many respects a continuation of World War I (1914–1918). The centerpiece of the Paris Peace Conference of 1919 was the Versailles Treaty with Germany. Often unfairly depicted as a piece of French villainy too harsh on Germany, it was in fact too harsh to conciliate and too weak to destroy. It was also not enforced. This, rather than its severity or lack thereof, is what made possible the renewal of World War I by Germany 20 years later.

Under the peace settlement, Alsace and Lorraine were returned to France, while Belgium received several border enclaves. France received the coal production of the Saar for 15 years, with the Saar itself placed under the new League of Nations and with its inhabitants to decide their future at the end of the 15 years.

The chief bone of contention was the German territory west of the Rhine. French hopes of detaching this from Germany and forming it into one or more independent states maintaining a permanent Allied military presence encountered British and American opposition. The French yielded in return for a treaty pledging Britain and the United States to aid France should Germany ever again strike westward. The Rhineland would also be permanently demilitarized, along with a belt of German territory east of the Rhine 30 miles deep. Allied garrisons would remain in the Rhineland for up to 15 years.

Unfortunately for France, the treaty for which it had traded away its security never came into effect. The U.S. Senate refused to ratify it, and the British government claimed that its acceptance was contingent on American approval.

Germany lost northern Schleswig to Denmark and a portion of Silesia and the Polish Corridor to the new state of Poland. A corridor of German territory allowed Poland access to the sea but also separated East Prussia from the remainder of Germany. Germans keenly felt these territorial losses, although they were modest and did not materially alter German power. Germany was still the most powerful state of Europe.

The Treaty of Versailles limited the German Army to 100,000 men. It was also denied heavy artillery, tanks, and military aviation, and the General Staff was to be abolished. The German Navy was sharply limited in size and could not have submarines. Germany violated these provisions and worked out arrangements with other states, notably the Soviet Union, for the development of new weapons and the training of military personnel. Article 231, the so-called war guilt clause, fixed blame for the war on Germany and its allies and was the justification for reparations, which were set at $33 billion in 1920.

The new German democratic government, the Weimar Republic, had to bear the shame of Versailles. Many Germans believed the lie known as the "stab in the back." It held that their army had not been defeated in the field but had been forced to surrender because of a collapse of the home front.

The breakup of the Austro-Hungarian Empire as a consequence of the war led to creation of new states in Poland, Czechoslovakia, and Yugoslavia. They allied and, known as the Little Entente, were linked to France through a 1925 treaty of mutual assistance between that country and Czechoslovakia. The Soviet Union refused to recognize Poland's new eastern border, the Curzon Line. But Poland won the ensuing Soviet-Polish War (1919–1921) fought over this.

Allied unity disappeared almost immediately with the end of the war. The United States withdrew into isolation, and Britain disengaged from the European continent. This left France to enforce the settlement. Yet France was weaker in both population and economic strength than Germany, despite the latter's 1919 losses. In effect it was left up to the Germans themselves to decide whether they would abide by the treaty provisions.

The German government adopted obstructionist policies to break the treaty and by 1923 halted major reparations payments. French premier Raymond Poincaré responded in January 1923 by sending troops into the Ruhr, the industrial heart of Germany. Chancellor Wilhelm Cuno's government then adopted a policy of "passive resistance," urging workers not to work and promising to pay their salaries in order to buy time for the United States and Britain to pressure France into withdrawal. Although such pressure was forthcoming, Poincaré stood firm, and the result was catastrophic German inflation. By November 1923 the mark had fallen to 4.2 trillion to the dollar. This wiped out the savings of the German middle class and caused many Germans to lose all faith in democracy.

Seemingly Poincaré had won. Germany agreed to pay reparations under a scaled-down schedule, and French troops were withdrawn from the Ruhr in 1924. Although the French people approved of Poincaré's action, they noted its high financial cost and the opposition of Britain and the United States. These factors helped bring the Left to power in 1924, and it reversed Poincaré's go-it-alone approach.

The new German government of Chancellor Gustav Stresemann also announced a policy of living up to its treaty obligations. "Fulfillment" and "conciliation" replaced "obstruction" and brought the Locarno Pacts of 1925, in which Germany voluntarily guaranteed its western borders as final and promised not to resort to war with its neighbors and to resolve disputes through arbitration. Britain, while it promised at Locarno in 1925 to defend France and Belgium in the event of German attack, refused to make any such pledge regarding the states of Central and Eastern Europe.

By the 1930s the leaders of Germany, Italy, and Japan were not satisfied with the 1919 settlement, and the Western powers seemed powerless to resist their demands. This was partly the result of the heavy human cost of World War I. For example, the French Army had suffered a casualty rate of 73 percent. France adopted a defensive military strategy, beginning construction in 1929 of a belt of forts known as the Maginot Line running from Switzerland to Belgium. This helped condition the French military to a defensive mind-set.

In Britain the costs of World War I had also been heavy. Some influential figures also were sympathetic toward fascism and dictators seen as opposing communism. British governments avoided commitments to continental Europe and embraced "appeasement," the notion that meeting the more legitimate demands of the dictators would obviate the need for war. Prime Minister Neville Chamberlain (1937–1940) was its principal architect. There was also great concern in Britain, as elsewhere, about air attacks on cities in any future war.

The United States had greatly benefited from World War I. At modest human cost (its military battle deaths totaled 50,585), it had become the world's leading financial power. Yet Americans believed that they had been misled by wartime propaganda and drawn into the war by the arms merchants. The U.S. Congress enacted legislation preventing the loan of money or the sale of arms to combatants in a war. Such legislation benefited the aggressor states, which were already well armed, and handicapped their victims, who were not. But most Americans eschewed involvement in world affairs.

The Soviet Union was largely absorbed in its internal affairs. It had suffered immense losses in World War I, and during 1918–1922 it underwent a fierce civil war between the communist "Reds" who had seized power and the opposition "Whites" supported by the Western Allies. The Reds won, and by 1929 Joseph Stalin was in control. He insisted on the collectivization of agriculture that brought the deaths of millions of people but also pushed industrialization. Stalin did not accept the new frontiers in Eastern Europe as final. Poland was a particular concern; it had been partially carved from former Russian territory, and more land had been lost to Poland in the 1921 Treaty of Riga ending the Soviet-Polish War.

Stalin was quite concerned about Germany after Adolf Hitler came to power in 1933, for the German leader had openly expressed his opposition to communism and his intention to secure "Lebensraum" (living space) for Germany in Eastern Europe. With Stalin's full support, Soviet Union commissar for foreign affairs Maksim Litvinov pursued an internationalist course.

This occurred even as Stalin was carrying out unprecedented actions against his own people that may have brought the deaths of 20 million people, including the vast majority of the military leadership.

The chain of events that culminated in world war began in Asia in 1931, when Japan seized Manchuria. In World War I, Japan had secured at scant cost to itself the German colonial possessions of the Shandong (Shantung) Peninsula in China and islands north of the equator. Japanese nationalists sought to take advantage of the world economic depression and continuing upheaval in China to rectify their nation's lack of natural resources. They sought not only to secure Manchuria but also to control Mongolia, China, and South Asia.

Although Japan had many of the trappings of a democracy, it was not such. The army and navy departments were independent of the civilian authorities, and from 1936 the ministers of war and the navy had to be serving officers. This gave them a veto over public policy, as no government could be formed without their concurrence. Army leaders had little sympathy for civilian rule, and in the 1930s they dominated the government and even resorted to political assassinations.

On September 18, 1931, officers of the elite Japanese Kwantung Army in southern Manchuria set off an explosion near the South Manchuria Railway near Mukden. Blaming this on Chinese soldiers, the Japanese took control of Mukden and soon began the conquest of all Manchuria. Presented with this fait accompli by its military, Tokyo supported the action.

China appealed to the League of Nations. The League Council was reluctant to embark on tough action without the collaboration of the United States (not a League of Nations member), which was not forthcoming. The British also opposed drastic action. Without these, the league could do little. Japan ignored league calls for both sides to withdraw their troops and continued its military operations. Then in February 1932 Japan proclaimed Manchuria independent as Manchukuo, although a protocol established it as a Japanese protectorate.

The League of Nations Lytton Commission submitted a report in October 1932 that largely exonerated China and condemned the Japanese. The report concluded that Manchukuo was possible only because of Japanese troops and recommended an autonomous government under Chinese sovereignty that would recognize Japan's special economic interests. The commission also urged nonrecognition of Manchukuo. On February 24, 1933, of 42 members of the League Assembly, only Japan voted against the report. The Japanese delegation then walked out, and in March Tokyo gave notice that it would withdraw from the League of Nations.

Manchukuo was larger than France and Germany combined, but in March 1933 Japanese troops added the Chinese province of Jehol. Early in April they moved to within a few miles of Beijing and Tianjin (Tientsin). In May Chinese forces evacuated Beijing, controlled by pro-Japanese Chinese leaders who then concluded a truce with Japan, creating a demilitarized zone administered by Chinese friendly to Japan.

The economic depression and general Western indifference to the plight of Asians precluded Western military action, but a worldwide financial and commercial boycott in accordance with Article 16 of the League Covenant might have brought Japanese withdrawal, but even this was beyond Western will. The failure to enforce collective security here encouraged other states with similar goals.

Germany was next to take advantage. Hitler, who came to power in January 1933 by entirely legal means, soon precipitated a series of crises. In October 1933 he withdrew Germany from the League of Nations and the Geneva disarmament conference. In response, in June 1934 the Soviet Union, Poland, and Romania mutually guaranteed their existing frontiers. That September the Soviet Union joined the League of Nations.

On July 25, 1934, Austrian Nazis attempted to seize power in Vienna in order to achieve Anschluss, or union with Germany, which was forbidden by the 1919 peace settlement. Although Chancellor Engelbert Dollfuss was assassinated, Austrian authorities put down the coup attempt. Italian dictator Benito Mussolini rushed troops to the Brenner Pass. Germany, still largely unarmed, was in no position to oppose Italy, and Hitler, who had initially expressed his support, now disavowed the coup attempt.

To prevent Germany from annexing Austria, in January 1935 France secured a pact with Italy. The pact called for close cooperation between the two powers regarding Central Europe and reaffirmed the independence and territorial integrity of Austria. In secret provisions, Italy promised to support France with its air force in the event of a German move to remilitarize the Rhineland, and France agreed to provide troops to aid Italy should the Germans threaten Austria. France also transferred some of its African territory to the Italian colonies of Libya and Eritrea, and French foreign minister Pierre Laval apparently pledged that France would not oppose Italy's colonial ambitions.

In January 1935 the Saar voted overwhelming to rejoin Germany. On March

16, Hitler announced that the Reich would reintroduce compulsory military service and increase its army to more than 500,000 men, justifying this step by the failure of the Allies to disarm. Paris, London, and Rome protested but took no action to compel Berlin to observe its treaty obligations. In April 1935 leaders of these three states met at Stresa and agreed to oppose "unilateral repudiation of treaties that may endanger the peace of Europe."

On May 2, 1935, France and the Soviet Union signed a five-year mutual assistance pact, but the French never did agree to a military convention to coordinate an actual response to German aggression. On May 16 the Soviet Union and Czechoslovakia signed a similar pact, but the Soviet Union was not obligated to provide armed assistance unless France first fulfilled its commitments, already extended to Czechoslovakia.

Britain took the first step in the appeasement of Germany, shattering the so-called Stresa Front. On June 18, 1935, it signed a naval agreement with Germany that violated the Versailles Treaty. In spite of having promised the French in February that it would take no unilateral action toward Germany, London agreed to Germany building a surface navy of up to 35 percent the tonnage of the Royal Navy. In effect this permitted Germany a navy larger than those of either France or Italy. It also allowed Germany 45 percent of the Royal Navy in submarines, which had specifically been prohibited. The Anglo-German Naval Agreement was the first occasion when any power sanctioned Germany's misdeeds.

On October 1935 Mussolini invaded Ethiopia (Abyssinia). The outcome was a foregone conclusion, and in May 1936 Italian forces captured Addis Ababa, and Mussolini proclaimed the annexation of Ethiopia. The League of Nations voted to condemn Italy, the first time it had branded a European state an aggressor, but British foreign secretary Sir Samuel Hoare and French foreign minister Laval worked behind the scenes in their infamous Hoare-Laval Proposals to broker away Ethiopia to Italy in return for Italian support against Germany. Public anger when this became known forced both men to resign.

Ultimately the League of Nations voted to impose sanctions but not on oil, which would have severely crippled Italy. The argument against this was that Italy could always turn to the United States, which was not bound by league decisions. In the end, even the ineffectual sanctions were lifted. Another blow had been dealt to collective security.

Probably the seminal event on the road to World War II was Hitler's remilitarization of the Rhineland. On March 7, 1936, he sent 22,000 German troops, armed with little more than rifles and machine guns, into the Rhineland. This violated the Treaty of Versailles but also the Locarno Pacts voluntarily entered into by Germany. The operation occurred while France was in the midst of a bitterly contested election campaign that brought the leftist Popular Front to power.

Incredibly, France had no contingency plan, and its intelligence services grossly overestimated the size of the German forces involved and believed Hitler's false claims that the Luftwaffe (German Air Force) had achieved parity with the French Armée de l'Air. Paris appealed to London, which made it clear that Britain would not fight for the Rhineland. Had the French acted alone, their forces would have rolled over the Germans, and this probably would have been the end of Hitler, who admitted as much.

Remilitarization of the Rhineland provided protection for the industry of the Ruhr and a springboard for invading France and Belgium. It also had another important effect, for Belgium now renounced its treaty of mutual assistance with France and again sought security in neutrality. Germany promptly guaranteed that state's inviolability and integrity.

Almost immediately another international crisis erupted in Spain, where civil war began on July 18, 1936. The republican Popular Front of leftist parties won a narrow victory in the elections of 1936, and Spanish traditionalists, known as the nationalists, took up arms. Germany and Italy aided the nationalists, with the German aviation contingent known as the Kondor Legion a key factor in the ultimate nationalist victory.

Surprisingly, the Western democracies cut the Spanish republic adrift. France wanted to help, but Britain threatened that if this led to a general European war it would not honor its pledge of military support; France then reversed course. British leaders came up with a noninterventionist policy, but although all the Great Powers promised to abide by it, only the Western democracies did so.

Among major powers, only the Soviet Union assisted the republic. Stalin apparently hoped for a protracted struggle entangling the Western democracies and Germany at the other end of the continent. Aid from the Soviet Union, paid for in gold by the republicans, eventually brought a communist takeover of that government. In March 1939 nationalist forces took Madrid, and by April hostilities ended. Some 600,000 Spaniards had died in the fighting; the nationalists executed another 200,000 after the war, and it is likely that a similar number died of starvation and disease.

The Spanish Civil War brought together Germany and Italy. On October 25, 1936, they formed what became known as the Rome-Berlin Axis. On November 25 Germany and Japan signed the Anti-Comintern Pact to oppose activities of the Comintern (Third International), created by Moscow to spread communism. Germany and Japan also signed a secret agreement providing that if either state was the object of an unprovoked attack by the Soviet Union, then the other would do nothing to assist the Soviet Union. On November 6, 1937, Italy joined the Anti-Comintern Pact.

Shortly afterward Mussolini announced that Italy would not act to prevent Anschluss. Italy also withdrew from the League of Nations and recognized Manchukuo as an independent state in November 1937. (Germany followed suit in May 1938.) By 1938 the Great Powers were again divided into two antagonistic groups.

Japan, meanwhile, asserted its right to control China. Tokyo demanded an end to Western assistance to that state and threatened force if it continued. In 1935 Japan also began encroaching upon several of China's northern provinces. The Chinese government at Nanjing headed by Generalissimo Jiang Jieshi (Chiang Kai-shek) was more concerned with the Chinese communists and initially favored appeasement, but students and the Chinese military demanded action. The Chinese communists expressed a willingness to cooperate against the Japanese.

On July 7, 1937, a clash occurred near Beijing between Japanese and Chinese troops. Later that month after the nationalist government rejected their ultimatum, the Japanese invaded the coveted northern provinces. In a few days they had occupied both Tianjin and Beijing, and by the end of the year Japan controlled all five

Chinese provinces north of the Yellow River. In mid-December Japan installed a pro-Japanese government in Beijing. Japan never declared war against China, enabling it to avoid U.S. neutrality legislation and purchase raw materials and oil. But this also allowed Washington to aid China.

The fighting was not confined to northern China, for in August 1937 the Japanese attacked the great commercial city of Shanghai. It fell in November. Japanese forces then advanced up the Yangtse and in December took Nanjing, where they committed wide-scale atrocities.

China again appealed to the League of Nations, which again condemned Japan. But the Western powers failed to withhold critical supplies and financial credits from Japan. By the end of 1938 Japanese troops controlled the great commercial cities of Tianjin, Beijing, Shanghai, Nanjing, Hankow, and Guangzhou (Canton), and the nationalist government had relocated to the interior city of Chongqing (Chungking).

Japanese troops also clashed with the Soviet Union. Fighting began in 1938 in the poorly defined triborder area of Siberia, Manchukuo, and Korea. Although no state of war was declared, significant battles occurred, no doubt giving Tokyo a new appreciation of Soviet fighting ability and helping to influence the 1941 decision not to strike north into Siberia but instead proceed against the European colonial possessions of Southeast Asia.

In Western Europe, by 1938 the situation was such as to encourage Hitler to embark upon his own territorial expansion. Mussolini was now an ally, France was experiencing governmental instability, and in Britain appeasement was in full force.

Austria was first. On February 12, 1938, Hitler demanded that Austrian chancellor Kurt von Schuschnigg appoint Austrian

Nazis to key cabinet positions. On March 9 Schuschnigg attempted an end run by announcing a plebiscite on Anschluss only four days hence. Hitler was determined that there be no plebiscite and demanded Schuschnigg's resignation and postponement of the vote under threat of German invasion. Schuschnigg gave way and resigned. Austrian Nazi leader Seyss-Inquart then took power and invited in German troops "to preserve order," although they had already crossed the border.

On March 13 Berlin declared Austria to be part of the Reich, and the next day perhaps 1 million Austrians welcomed Hitler to Vienna. France and Britain lodged formal protests, but that was the extent of their action. After the war Austrian leaders denied culpability by successfully positing that their country was the first victim of Nazi aggression.

Anschluss greatly strengthened Germany's strategic position, as Germany was now in direct contact with Italy, Yugoslavia, and Hungary. Czechoslovakia was almost isolated, with its trade largely at German mercy, and Germany outflanked the powerful western Czech defenses. Thus, despite his pledges to respect its territorial integrity, Hitler next moved against Czechoslovakia.

Some 3.5 million Germans lived in Czechoslovakia. They had long complained about discrimination in a state in which Czechs were only the largest minority. Czechoslovakia was the keystone of Europe. It had a military alliance with France, a well-trained 400,000-man army, the important Skoda munitions complex at Pilsen, and strong western fortifications. Unfortunately for the Czechs, the latter were in the Erzegeberge (Ore Mountains), where the population was almost entirely German. Also Bohemia-Moravia, almost one-third German in population, now protruded into the Reich. Hitler pushed the demands of the Sudetendeutsch (Sudeten German) Party to address legitimate complaints into outright union of the German regions with Germany.

In May 1938 during key Czechoslovakian elections, German troops massed on the border and threatened invasion. Confident in French support, Czechoslovakia mobilized. Both France and the Soviet Union stated their willingness to go to war to defend Czechoslovakia, and in the end nothing happened. Hitler then ordered construction of fortifications along the German western frontier. Called by the Germans the West Wall, it was clearly intended to prevent France from supporting its eastern allies.

Western leaders now pondered whether Czechoslovakia, formed only in 1919, was really worth a general European war. British prime minister Chamberlain sent a mediator to Prague, and on his suggestions Prague offered their German minority practically everything they demanded short of independence.

By mid-September Hitler was insisting on "self-determination" for the Sudeten Germans and threatening war if this was not granted. If Germany intervened militarily, France would have to decide whether to honor its pledge to defend Czechoslovakia. If it did so, this would bring on a general European war.

In this critical situation Chamberlain flew to Germany to meet with Hitler. Hitler informed him that the Sudeten Germans must be able to unite with Germany and that he was willing to risk war to accomplish this. London and Paris then decided to force self-determination on Prague.

The British and French decision to desert Czechoslovakia resulted from many factors. Both countries dreaded a new general war with the threat of air attacks against London and Paris. Britain had begun to rebuild the Royal Air Force (RAF) only the year before, and the Germans succeeded in duping the French as to actual Luftwaffe strength. The Western Allies also believed that they could not count on the Soviet Union, the military of which was still recovering from Stalin's purges. In France and especially in Britain there were also those who viewed Nazism as a bulwark against communism and who hoped to encourage Hitler to move against Russia so that communism and fascism might destroy one another.

Chamberlain desperately hoped to prevent a general European war. A businessman before entering politics, he believed in the sanctity of contracts and, despite evidence to the contrary, could not accept that the leader of the most powerful state in Europe was a blackmailer and a liar. But the West had in 1919 championed "self-determination of peoples," and by this Germany had a right to all it had hitherto demanded. The transfer of the Sudetenland to the Reich did not seem too high a price for a satisfied Germany and a peaceful Europe. Finally, there were Hitler's statements that once his demands upon Czechoslovakia had been satisfied he would have no further territorial ambitions in Europe.

Under heavy British and French pressure, on September 21 Czechoslovakia accepted the Anglo-French proposals. Chamberlain again traveled to Germany and so informed Hitler. To his surprise Hitler upped the ante, demanding that all Czechoslovak government officials be withdrawn from the Sudeten area within 10 days and that all military and economic establishments be left in place.

Hitler's demands led to the most serious international crisis in Europe since 1918. On September 24 Prague informed London that Hitler's demands were unacceptable, as they would not allow Prague time to organize its military defense. London and Paris agreed with the Czech position and decided not to pressure Prague to secure its acceptance. A general European war appeared inevitable.

U.S. president Franklin Roosevelt now urged an international conference, and Mussolini secured Hitler's reluctant agreement. Chamberlain, French premier Edouard Daladier, and Mussolini traveled to Munich and met with Hitler on September 29. The Soviets were not invited, and Czechoslovakia itself was not officially represented. The object was simply to give Hitler what he wanted and avoid war.

The Munich agreement of September 30 gave Hitler everything he demanded, and on October 1 German troops marched across the frontier. Poland and Hungary now demanded and also received Czechoslovakian territory that contained their national minorities.

Even though France and Britain were far from ready for war, it would have been better to have fought Germany in September 1938. Even if the Soviet Union and Poland had not joined in, the German Army would have been forced to fight against France, Britain, and Czechoslovakia. Germany was not then ready for war. The Luftwaffe would have had to fight on two fronts and was short of bombs. Also, only 12 German divisions were available to hold against eight times that number of French divisions. And there would be 35 well-trained and well-equipped Czechoslovak divisions, backed by substantial numbers of artillery, tanks, and aircraft. Later those responsible for the Munich

agreement claimed that it bought a year for the Western democracies to rearm, but in fact a year later Britain and France were in a much worse position than they had been at the time of the Munich crisis.

The Munich agreement had far-reaching international effects. It effectively ended the French security system. Poland, Romania, and Yugoslavia now questioned the worth of French commitments. Stalin saw the Western surrender to Hitler as an effort by the Western powers to encourage Germany's *Drang nach Osten* (Drive to the East) and precipitate a war between Germany and the Soviet Union.

Despite Hitler's assurance that the Sudetenland was his last territorial demand, events soon proved the contrary. The day after Munich, Hitler told his aides that he would annex the remainder of the country at the first opportunity. Seizing upon internal dissension in Czechoslovakia, in March 1939 Hitler announced support for the complete independence for Slovakia, and on March 14 Slovakia and Ruthenia declared their independence. Hitler then summoned Czechoslovak president Emil Hácha to Berlin, where Luftwaffe commander Hermann Göring threatened the immediate destruction of Prague from the air unless Bohemia and Moravia became German protectorates. Hácha signed, and on March 15 Nazi troops occupied what remained of Czechoslovakia, which became the Protectorate of Bohemia and Moravia. Slovakia became a vassal state of the Reich. Hungary soon seized Ruthenia. On March 21 Germany demanded that Lithuania return Memel, with its mostly German population, secured after World War I to provide access to the sea. The Lithuanian government complied.

In the former Czechoslovakia the Wehrmacht secured 1,582 aircraft, 2,000 artillery pieces, and sufficient equipment for 20 divisions. Hitler had more than offset any increase in armaments that Britain and France had achieved. Between August 1938 and September 1939 Skoda produced nearly as many arms as all British arms factories combined.

Hitler's actions, however, proved that his demands were not limited to Germans. His repudiation of the formal pledges given Chamberlain at Munich also finally convinced the British that they could no longer trust Hitler. Indeed, Britain and France responded by a series of guarantees to the smaller states now threatened by Germany.

With the German press now attacking Poland for its treatment of its German minority, on March 31, 1939, Great Britain and France extended a formal guarantee to support that country in the event of a German attack. At the 11th hour and under the worst possible circumstances, with Czechoslovakia lost and the Soviet Union alienated, Britain had reversed its East European policy and agreed to do what the French had sought in the 1920s.

Mussolini took advantage of the situation and strengthened Italy's position in the Balkans by seizing Albania in April 1939. Britain and France then extended guarantees to defend Greece and Romania. On April 28 Hitler reiterated earlier demands for the Baltic port city of Gdansk (Danzig) and insisted that Germany receive extraterritorial rights in the Polish Corridor. Poland refused. On May 23 Hitler met with his leading generals and stated his intention to attack Poland at the first suitable opportunity.

In April, Britain and France initiated negotiations with the Soviet Union for a mutual assistance pact. But their guarantee to Poland gave the Soviet Union protection on its western frontier. Although negotiations continued until August, these failed to produce agreement. Poland, Latvia, Lithuania, and Estonia all feared the Russians as much as or more than the Germans, and all were unwilling to allow Soviet armies within their borders to defend against German attack. Polish leaders also refused to believe that Hitler would risk war with Britain and France. In the end, the British and French negotiators refused to give Poland and the Baltic States to Stalin the way they had handed Czechoslovakia to Hitler.

While the Kremlin negotiated more or less openly with Britain and France, it also sought an understanding with Germany. Stalin held equal suspicion for all foreign governments; his preoccupations were remaining in power and what was in the best interest of the Soviet Union. Signals from Stalin, including the dismissal of Foreign Minister Maksim Litvinov, a Jew, convinced Hitler that Stalin truly wanted an agreement.

Stalin personally negotiated with German foreign minister Joachim von Ribbentrop in Moscow on August 23, and a Soviet-Nazi agreement was signed that night. It consisted of an open 10-year nonaggression pact, but there were two secret protocols, not publicly acknowledged by Moscow until 1990. The first secret provision partitioned Eastern Europe between Germany and the Soviet Union. The Soviet sphere included eastern Poland, Romanian Bessarabia, Estonia, Latvia, and Finland. Lithuania and western Poland went to Germany. A month later Hitler traded Lithuania to Stalin in exchange for further territorial concessions in Poland. The second secret provision was a trade convention whereby the Soviet Union would supply vast quantities of raw materials to Germany in exchange for military technology and finished goods. This was of immense assist to the German war machine early in World War II.

Although Hitler's and Stalin's interests coincided over Poland, Stalin failed to understand the danger of the alliance. He expected that the Germans would face a protracted war in the West, which would allow the Soviet Union time to rebuild its military. Also, Stalin assumed that an eventual clash would occur with Germany but not before 1943, and by then the Red Army would be ready to meet it.

The Nazi-Soviet Non-Aggression Pact shocked the West. Communism and Nazism, supposed to be ideological opposites on the worst possible terms, had come together. The German invasion of Poland was originally set for August 26 but was delayed owing to Italy's decision to remain neutral. Uncertain of German victory, Mussolini insisted on armaments and raw materials that he knew Germany could not supply. He did agree to keep secret the decision to remain neutral and continue military preparations so as to fool the English and French. The weight of Italy in the German calculus was so slight that it took only a few days for Germany to reset its military plans and go it alone.

Course

On September 1, 1939, following false charges that Polish forces had crossed into Germany and killed German border guards, German forces invaded Poland. On September 3 in fulfillment of its guarantee to Poland, Britain and then France declared war on Germany. World War II had begun.

The German Army was far from being ready for war in 1939. Including reserves, France and Poland together had the equivalent of 150 divisions, although some

French forces had to remain overseas. Germany had 98 divisions, but 36 of these were still undergoing formation. But Hitler had supported the creation of 14 new types of divisions—6 armored, 4 mechanized (light), and 4 motorized infantry—and ultimately these were worth more than the rest of the army combined.

The Germans had incorporated ideas developed by British and French military theorists. The new German armor divisions were charged with achieving sudden breakthroughs at weak points in the enemy lines, followed by motorized infantry and mobile antitank guns, all supported by flying artillery in the Junkers Ju-87 Stuka dive-bomber. The Polish campaign was the first example of the blitzkrieg (lightning war).

The French had all the elements of an up-to-date army, but it was still organized along World War I lines. The French actually had more tanks than the Germans, and many were larger and more heavily armored than any of the German tanks. But the French high command still saw tanks as best used in packets in an infantry support role. The French, and even more so the Poles, lacked air support for their ground forces.

In invading Poland, the Germans also had the advantage of being able to attack from three directions simultaneously. They committed 1.25 million men, along with 2,900 tanks and more than 1,500 aircraft. Polish leader Marshal Edward Śmigly-Rydz did not want to meet the Germans as far east as Warsaw, and the bulk of his forces were therefore dispersed forward along the 800-mile western frontier, where they could be cut off and surrounded.

Luftwaffe control of the air inhibited the Polish mobilization and prevented any Polish military concentration. German aircraft also spread panic by attacking cities, including Warsaw. Polish pilots fought bravely, but their aircraft were no match for the far larger Luftwaffe. On September 19 the campaign was all but over when remnants of 19 Polish divisions and three cavalry brigades, 100,000 men in all, surrendered.

On September 17, the Red Army had invaded Poland from the east in accordance with the secret provisions of the Nazi-Soviet Non-Aggression Pact. The Russians also proceeded into the Baltic States of Estonia, Latvia, and Lithuania.

Following a stout defense, Warsaw surrendered on September 27. Nearly 150,000 troops were taken prisoner. The last organized Polish resistance occurred on October 5.

The Poles had expected to be able to hold out until the French and British launched a massive offensive in the West. The British and French air forces were to strike Germany immediately, and the French were to launch a ground offensive on the 15th day. The French had 72 divisions, 1,600 guns, and 3,200 tanks. The French and British air forces counted 1,700 aircraft. Opposing these, the Germans had in the West 40 divisions, but only 4 of these were fully manned and equipped. The Germans had only 300 guns and had no tanks and almost no aircraft.

The mobilization of their trained reserves and the need to bring artillery out of storage imposed delay, and the best the French could do was a token offensive toward Germany's West Wall with nine divisions that advanced a maximum of 5 miles on a 16-mile front. Casualties were light, but the French then halted; when Warsaw surrendered, the French began a withdrawal. Had the French undertaken a major offensive early, it would have reached the Rhine and had a great impact on the course of the war.

Britain did even less. The British Expeditionary Force (BEF) had not even completed its assembly by early October. Polish pleas for previously promised RAF bombing raids against Germany met no response.

The Polish campaign cost the Germans 16,000 dead and 32,000 wounded. They also lost up to a third of their tanks and aircraft. For fewer than 1,000 dead, the Soviet Union had gained a third of Poland. The Poles suffered 66,300 killed, 133,700 wounded, and 587,000 taken prisoner (200,000 of these by the Soviets). Some 90,000 Polish troops escaped and continued the fight on land, at sea, and in the air, winning renown in the 1940 Battle of Britain.

Hitler now offered Britain and France peace on a forgive-and-forget basis. The Allies rejected this, and the war continued. Poland, meanwhile, disappeared from the map. Germany annexed outright about half of the territory it had taken, and Poles were forced from it. The remainder under German jurisdiction, called the General Government, was to be exploited for cheap labor. Einsatzgruppen—special extermination units—moved into Poland to imprison or kill the Polish intelligentsia and potential leaders as well as Jews.

Hitler's hatred of Jews was pathological and long-standing. Already expressed in *Mein Kampf,* its horror was fully revealed in November 1938 in Kristallnacht (Night of Broken Glass), an orgy of government-condoned anti-Semitic violence. The Einsatzgruppen had begun killing Jews during the Polish Campaign, and Poland then became one vast network of work camps and extermination centers, with Jews shipped there from all over Europe. During the war some 6 million Jews were systematically slaughtered in what was called the Final Solution of the Jewish Question but is better known as the Holocaust. The extermination of much of the Jewish population of Europe, along with gays and Gypsies, is the greatest of Nazi crimes against mankind, and many Germans and other nationalities were complicit in it.

The Russians also imposed a brutal regime in their part of Poland. They deported some 1.2 million Poles to the Soviet Union, and in April 1940 they executed up to 15,000 Polish officers and intellectuals in the Katyn Forest near Smolensk (a deed they steadfastly refused to admit until 1990).

The Poles did provide an important contribution to the ultimate Allied victory. The Germans had adopted for transmission of highly classified messages an encrypting device invented by Dr. Arthur Scherbius and christened Enigma. Japan also bought the machine and used it. Enigma resembled a typewriter and enabled the operator to encode a plain text in any of 150 million possible combinations, with settings regularly changed. The Germans believed that messages so encoded were unbreakable.

In the 1930s the Poles formed a special cryptology group at the University of Poznan and were largely successful in figuring out how to decipher the messages. Before their defeat, the Poles got some of their machines to France and England. The British then assembled a team of experts at Bletchley Park outside London and there developed additional devices that, given time, could sort their way through the possible variations of an encoded text. Ultimately the delay was only a matter of hours. Enigma intelligence (code-named Top Secret Ultra) was of immense benefit

to the Allies and undoubtedly shortened the war.

Stalin now attacked Finland. Believing that there would be an eventual military confrontation with Germany (although he thought not before 1943) and seeking to obtain security for the second-largest Russian city of Leningrad only 20 miles from the Finnish border, Stalin demanded that Finland yield territory in its south. With only 3.7 million people, Finland hardly seemed cable of resistance. While the Finns were open to compromise on the issue of Leningrad, they rejected Stalin's demand for a naval base on the Hango peninsula to the west, which Stalin wanted in order to deny a potential enemy (Germany) access to the Gulf of Finland. True, Stalin offered considerably more Russian territory in exchange for these concessions, but this was far to the north. When the Finns refused to yield Hango after nearly two months of negotiations, Stalin alleged border incidents and ordered an invasion.

The Soviet-Finnish War (November 30, 1939–March 13, 1940), also known as the Winter War, was a foregone conclusion but an embarrassment for Stalin. Despite its fortyfold advantage in manpower, it took the Red Army four months to defeat Finland. Finnish morale, equipment, and tactical leadership were all superior to those of the Russians. By the end of the war Stalin had been forced to commit 1 million men, and the Red Army had suffered at least 200,000 dead—many from the cold in addition to inadequate medical services. The Russians also lost 1,800 tanks and 634 aircraft. On their side, the Finns suffered 25,000 killed and 44,000 wounded. The Finns had to yield about a 10th of their territory (16,173 square miles, including the Karelian Isthmus, with the original demand having been 1,066 square miles, with the Soviet Union giving 2,134 in return). A half million Finns also left the ceded territory. The war brought the Soviet Union's expulsion from the League of Nations.

On November 23, 1939, Hitler again met with his military chiefs and informed them of his intention to secure for Germany "a larger lebensraum" on a "secure basis." Toward this end he intended to attack Russia, but its army was then of "little worth" and would remain so for the next year or two. Germany could oppose Russia only when it was free in the West. Time was on the side of the Allies, and he was determined to attack France and England at the earliest favorable opportunity.

All was then quiet on the Western Front. The French occupied the Maginot Line. British had sent only a dozen divisions to France, and the Germans remained behind their West Wall. Hardly any air action took place, with dire predictions that once unleashed, the bombing of cities would shatter civilian morale and decide the war.

Hitler worried about an Allied offensive through Belgium and the Netherlands against the Ruhr. He need not have worried. The Allies had pressed Belgium to permit their armies to advance into that country to meet an expected German invasion, but they had no plans for an offensive against Germany. Indeed, the Allies seemed content to wage a war of attrition in the form of economic strangulation by naval blockade, which had proven so successful in World War I. But 1939 was not the same as 1914. Germany could now rely on resources shipped to it through Italy and the Soviet Union, both of which were benevolent neutrals.

First Lord of the Admiralty Winston Churchill did convince the British War Cabinet to mount an operation to mine Norwegian territorial waters. High-grade Swedish iron ore accounted for some 40 percent of German prewar imports. In winter the Baltic was frozen, and the ore was shipped through Narvik in northern Norway and then almost entirely within Norwegian territorial waters to Germany. The mining operation, a blatant violation of Norway's neutral rights, would force the German ships out to sea, where they could be legally intercepted. No doubt Germany would react militarily, but this would be the justification for the British to land troops in Norway.

British and French leaders discussed this as well as the possibility of sending an expeditionary force to aid the Finns against the Soviet Union that would also seize the iron mines in Sweden. Fortunately the other operations were dropped, but on March 28 the Supreme War Council approved the Norway operation and set the date for April 5. It also approved Operation ROYAL MARINE, Churchill's plan for aerial mining of Germany's inland waterways, especially the Rhine. French reluctance regarding ROYAL MARINE, which could bring retaliatory German bombing of France, led to a postponement of the Norwegian operation until April 8.

The Germans had a good idea of what the British intended, and Hitler was determined to beat them to the punch. He set April 9 as the date for a German invasion of Norway. The British knew from signals traffic that German warships were active in the Baltic, but they failed to guess the German intention or its scale.

Hitler committed virtually the entire German Navy to Operation WESERÜBUNG. On April 7, German ships sailed for Norway. A number of German ore and merchant ships, secretly loaded with troops, were already in harbors there.

The Germans quickly secured Oslo, Bergen, and Trondheim along with vital airfields, from which German aircraft were soon operating. They sank lighter British warships and drove the rest out to sea as their troops consolidated control of southern Norway.

The British and French landed forces, but this effort was seriously handicapped by logistical failures, and the first troops did not come ashore until April 18. Ultimately, 25,000 were landed. Two Royal Navy carriers flew off RAF Hurricane fighters to be based on land. In their first major land victory of the war, on May 28 the Allies captured Narvik, but mounting aircraft losses, the unsatisfactory situation elsewhere in Norway, and the German invasion of France and the Low Countries in May all brought evacuation on June 7–8. On June 10, Norway surrendered.

On June 8 the German battleships *Scharnhorst* and *Gneisenau* caught the British aircraft carrier *Glorious* and two escorting destroyers, sinking all three. One of the destroyers damaged the *Scharnhorst* with a torpedo, however, and a few days later the *Gneisenau* was also damaged by a British submarine. Indeed, the Norwegian campaign ruined the German surface navy. The Germans lost 3 cruisers and 10 destroyers, half their total. This was, however, scant price to pay for Norway's agricultural production and the protection it brought for the Reich's Baltic flank. Most important, the Kriegsmarine now had new bases from which to strike the North Atlantic convoys and later the Arctic convoys bound for the Soviet Union.

The Germans set up a puppet state in Norway headed by Norwegian Nazi Vidkun Quisling, while King Haakon VII established a government-in-exile in London. Most of Norway's 4.7 million tons of merchant shipping passed into Allied hands, an invaluable addition. The German occupation of Norway also stretched the Reich's manpower resources; by 1944 Germany had 365,000 of its best troops there, providing security and protecting against invasion. Denmark was easily overrun in one day, also on April 9, for only 20 German casualties.

Allied operations at sea were largely defensive, despite the considerable German inferiority in surface warships. The Royal Navy had given little attention to naval aviation, the threat posed by aircraft against warships, or antisubmarine warfare, although it did immediately implement the convoy system.

Hitler had told German Navy commander Grand Admiral Erich Raeder not to expect war before 1944, and Raeder had thus concentrated on building a balanced fleet. Consequently, at the beginning of the war Germany had only 55 operational submarines. The submarine force did have an able commander in Commodore Karl Dönitz, but Hitler ordered that the submarines concentrate on enemy warships rather than merchantmen, probably so as to not draw the United States into the war as had occurred in 1917. Hitler also virtually halted U-boat construction in the first year of the war in anticipation of a quick victory on the continent and Britain then suing for peace.

The resultant Battle of the Atlantic was one of the most important struggles of the war. The convoy system saw large numbers of merchant ships sailing together, protected by destroyers and destroyer escorts. The U-boats still registered kills but a much smaller percentage than with ships sailing singly, and the subs were also subject to attack from the escorting warships.

Dönitz developed new tactics. In the Rudeltaktik (Wolfpack) a single submarine would locate a convoy, then shadow it and radio for reinforcements for a massed night surface attack and then a submerged secondary attack. Submarine "milk cows" were also utilized to enable the submarines to remain on station for longer periods. The Germans also had success in breaking the British convoy codes.

German surface ships carried out commerce raiding, and occasionally there were spectacular engagements such as when the British cruisers *Exeter, Achilles,* and *Ajax* outmaneuvered and outfought the pocket battleship *Graf Spee* in the Battle of the River Plate (December 13, 1939), leading to its scuttling off Montevideo. Then in May 1941, the German battleship *Bismarck,* at the time the world's largest and most powerful warship, sank the British battle cruiser *Hood* (all but 3 of its 1,500-man crew were lost) and severely damaged the battleship *Prince of Wales* before itself falling prey to pursuing British warships, including the carrier *Ark Royal* and the battleships *Rodney* and *King George V* (May 27, 1941).

After his conquest of Norway and Denmark, Hitler's next move was against France and the Low Countries of the Netherlands, Belgium, and Luxembourg. He believed that defeating France would force the British to sue for peace. Planned for November, the invasion was repeatedly postponed owing to one of the worst winters in years. Then on January 10, 1940, a German military aircraft landed by mistake in Belgium. Its German officer passenger was carrying the full invasion plans. Compromise of these forced Hitler to order a new plan, which imposed further delay.

The old plan had called for a movement through Belgium and the Netherlands against France, similar to the 1914 Schlieffen Plan. Its implementation would have had the Germans encountering the best British and French forces. The new plan, drawn up by Lieutenant General Erich von Manstein, was known as SICHELSCHNITT (CUT OF THE SICKLE). It envisioned the Allied forces advancing into Belgium to meet the German offensive there, only to have the bulk of the German panzer divisions massed to southward push through the hilly and wooded Ardennes region, which the Allied high command considered impassable for tanks. The panzers would then cross the Meuse River at Sedan and drive for the English Channel, cutting off the Allied forces in Belgium. As a result, Army Group B, charged with the invasion of Belgium and the Netherlands, was downgraded from 37 to 28 divisions, including 3 rather than 8 armor divisions. Army Group A, which was to drive into the Ardennes, was increased from 17 to 44 divisions, including 7 armored divisions rather than 1. At the point of their planned breakthrough the Germans would have 44 divisions, the French 9.

On paper at least, the two sides seemed about even. The Allies had 136 divisions, although some French divisions were in the Maginot Line. The Allies had 3,254 tanks to only 2,574 for the Germans. But despite the Polish example, the French were slow to understand the new armor warfare tactics. The first two French tank divisions had only assembled for training in January 1940, and their conversion was not yet complete by May. The vast majority of the French tanks were divided into small groups of up to 10 tanks apiece in support of infantry.

Allied weakness was even more glaring in the air. The Luftwaffe deployed 3,226 combat aircraft against only 1,563 for the

Armée de l'Air and the RAF. The Luftwaffe also fielded 9,300 antiaircraft guns; the French had only some 1,500. French military leadership was also ineffective or worse. French Army commander General Maurice Gamelin's headquarters was well to the rear, with messaging by carrier pigeon and motorcycle dispatch rider, imposing delay. There was also no reserve to contain a German breakthrough. Finally, French military intelligence was grossly incompetent. Although French pilots reported what was the largest concentration of armor yet seen in war and poised to strike into the Ardennes, the reports were disbelieved, and no action was taken until it was too late.

The German offensive opened on May 10, 1940. Operating according to prearranged plan, the best British and French units left their prepared defensive positions and advanced to the relief of Belgium. Then on the night of May 12–13, the Germans launched their drive in the Ardennes. Greatly aided by Stuka dive-bombers, they quickly captured Sedan. They were across the Meuse River by May 14 and then swung northward in order to trap the major Allied armies in Belgium.

Hitler now intervened. On May 24 he halted his tanks for three critical days. This stop order originated with Army Group A commander Colonel General Gerd von Rundstedt, who believed that a brief pause was necessary, but Hitler made this a firm order. The campaign had thus far been far more successful than Hitler had hoped. He did not understand the true situation on the ground; a delay would allow the infantry to catch up and thus minimize tank losses in the drive to the sea. Göring also convinced Hitler that the Luftwaffe could destroy the BEF from the air, preserving the German tanks for the final effort to defeat the French.

Then on May 28 despite a pledge not to act unilaterally, King Leopold III surrendered Belgian forces. This opened a 30-mile gap in Belgium between BEF positions and the sea and placed the Allies who had come to the rescue of Belgium in great jeopardy. General Maxime Weygand, commanding the French Army since May 20, urged BEF commander Field Marshal John Vereker, sixth Viscount Gort, to attack southward against the German thrust while the French moved from the south. Gort believed that the battle was now lost, and in one of the critical decisions of the war he refused and withdrew northerly to the coast.

During May 28–June 4 the British carried out Operation DYNAMO, the evacuation of their forces from France. Originally the British hoped to bring off 40,000 men. They ended up evacuating some 338,226, of whom 225,000 were British. Civilian as well as military vessels participated, and not just from Britain. Of 861 vessels in the operation, 243 were sunk, including 6 British destroyers (19 other destroyers were put out of action). The evacuation was carried out under very limited air cover because head of Fighter Command Air Chief Marshal Hugh Dowding was unwilling to lose valuable aircraft in a battle already lost and wanted to hold back resources for the defense of Britain.

The British lost 30,000 men, including prisoners, and were forced to abandon virtually all their equipment, but the vast bulk of the BEF had escaped to fight another day. In exalting the so-called Miracle of Dunkerque (Dunkirk), the British public tended to ignore the fact that they had left the French to deal with the Germans alone and that it was a holding action by the 50,000-man French First Army (which suffered 30,000–40,000 casualties) that had made possible the escape.

Much of the French Army now simply disintegrated, and Weygand quickly concluded that the situation was hopeless. Some in the cabinet urged an immediate armistice, but Premier Paul Reynaud was determined to fight on. On June 10, however, the French government left Paris for Bordeaux and, to spare Paris the fate of Warsaw and Rotterdam, declared it an open city.

That same day Mussolini, concluding that Germany had won the battle for France and indeed the war, cast his lot with Hitler and declared war on France and Britain. Some 32 Italian divisions attacked 5 French divisions in southeastern France but made little progress before conclusion of the armistice.

German troops made a peaceful entry into Paris on June 14. Reynaud hoped to continue the fight in North Africa if necessary, but on June 16 after the Germans had captured Verdun and had begun to cut off the Maginot Line from the rear and penetrate it in frontal assaults, a majority of the cabinet voted to ask Hitler for terms, and Reynaud was forced to resign. Eighty-four-year-old Marshal Philippe Pétain became the premier and sent an armistice team to treat with Hitler. To rub salt in the French wounds, Hitler received it on June 22 in the same railroad coach at Compiègne in which Marshal Ferdinand Foch had handed the Germans the armistice terms of 1918. Two days later an armistice was signed, and fighting ceased on June 25, 1940.

Since May 10, the western offensive had cost the Germans 27,000 killed, 18,000 missing, and 111,000 wounded. Britain had sustained 68,000 dead or wounded, Belgium 23,000, and the Netherlands 10,000. France had lost 90,000 men dead and 200,000 wounded. Another 2 million

were prisoners, not to be released until a peace treaty was signed.

The Germans occupied northern and western France, constituting some two-thirds of the country including Paris. The French Army was restricted to 100,000 officers and men. In what Hitler later admitted was a serious mistake, the French Navy remained under French control, to be disarmed in French ports. France also had to pay for the German occupation; this came to some 60 percent of the national income.

Many Frenchmen blamed the defeat on the communists, poor equipment, or defeatism. But morale had plummeted only after the German breakthrough. The collapse of the French Army was rather a matter of failed military policy and poor leadership. No prominent French leader escaped abroad to continue resistance, but young Brigadier General Charles de Gaulle made it to London. There he established the Free French, a resistance movement and ultimately a government-in-exile.

Despite pledges by the French not to surrender the fleet to the Germans, the British took unilateral action. In Operation CATAPULT they offered French naval commanders the choice of joining the British in continuing the fight, sailing to neutral ports to disarm, or be sunk. The British secured their ends peacefully at Portsmouth, Gibraltar, and Alexandria but not at Mers-el-Kebir in Algeria, where on July 3 they sank the battleship *Bretagne,* the new battle cruiser *Dunkerque,* and several destroyers. The battle cruiser *Strasbourg,* though damaged, got away. Some 1,300 French seamen died, and 350 were wounded. In part the action was designed to demonstrate, particularly to American leaders, that Britain was committed to continuing the fight, but it produced great French bitterness. In Operation CATAPULT the British did acquire some 130 French ships, including 2 battleships, 2 light cruisers, 8 destroyers, and 5 submarines.

The French parliament, meeting at Vichy in the unoccupied southern third of the country, voted to hand over power to Pétain, who then set up an authoritarian state. Pétain believed that Germany would soon defeat Britain and would then have won the war and that for the indefinite future France would be a German satellite. Given this, he embarked on policies intended to curry favor and lesson the harsh armistice terms. Some in Pétain's circle were also openly pro-Nazi.

Paying back Hitler for not having informed him ahead of time of German plans to invade France, Mussolini on October 28, 1940, sent Italian forces into Greece from Albania without informing the Germans ahead of time. Italy also attacked the British in Africa. Since both the Germans and the Italians were on good terms with Franco in Spain and since the Soviet Union was benevolently neutral, they now dominated the entire continent. The Germans created Festung Europa (Fortress Europe) and organized their conquests for their economic benefit.

Only Great Britain remained at war, and the British people now awaited invasion. Hitler regarded the British as a rational people who would see reason and treat with him, but Winston Churchill, who had become prime minister on May 10, 1940, and had promised his countrymen nothing but "blood, toil, tears and sweat," vowed to fight on. He appealed to the United States for material assistance to continue the battle.

The United States had been anything but neutral. Roosevelt believed strongly in the Allied cause and was convinced that American security was at stake. With American opinion still strongly isolationist, however, he sought ways to assist Britain short of outright participation. Roosevelt also ordered sharp increases in weapons production, particularly aircraft. In 1940 the United States adopted conscription and planned the construction of a two-ocean navy that would be the world's largest. In November 1939 American neutrality legislation was amended with repeal of the ban on arms sales. Then by executive order on September 2, 1940, Roosevelt answered a plea from Churchill and provided 50 old U.S. Navy destroyers in return for the right to maintain American bases in Newfoundland, Bermuda, and the British Caribbean Islands.

Then on March 8, 1941, in one of the most important legislative actions of the war, the U.S. Congress passed Lend-Lease. This legislation empowered the president to provide arms, raw materials, and food to countries at war with the Axis. Lend-Lease worked in reverse as well, for the British shared radar technology, then the world's most advanced.

The United States also became involved in the Battle of the Atlantic. Roosevelt secured bases in Greenland and Iceland (then belonging to Denmark) and ordered that American shipping be convoyed as far east as Iceland. In September 1941 a German submarine fired a torpedo against the U.S. destroyer *Greer*, and Roosevelt responded with a "shoot on sight" order. Then on October 31, German submarines sank the U.S. destroyer *Reuben James*, and 100 men were lost. No doubt war with Germany would have eventually come from the sinking of U.S. ships.

Britain, meanwhile, was in a perilous state. Abandoned in France were some 85,000 vehicles, virtually all the 445 tanks sent to France, and more than 1,500 artillery and antiaircraft guns, virtually all the army's machine guns, and half a million tons of stores and ammunition. In June 1940 there was only one properly equipped division in all Britain, and the navy ordered its ships to the far north to escape the Luftwaffe. Hitler, however, had been caught off guard by the rapid defeat of France, and no plans were in place for the logical next step of an invasion of Britain.

Several of his key advisers sensed what Hitler did not: that Germany's only chance for a successful invasion of Britain was in the immediate aftermath of the Dunkerque Evacuation. On June 3 RAF Fighter Command had only 413 serviceable aircraft, while Luftwaffe strength was some 1,500 fighters and about 3,000 bombers. Major General Kurt Student, commander of German Airborne Forces, urged that all available men be sent by air and by such ships as could be gotten across the English Channel to secure a toehold in Britain. Hitler refused, believing that Britain would see reason and soon sue for peace.

Hitler let a month pass. Even then, plans for an invasion of Britain, Operation SEA LION, were halfhearted. Part of this was the hazardous nature of the English Channel, with storms and rough waters the rule. The essential prerequisite for any sea invasion, however, was command of the air. Destruction of the RAF was left to the Luftwaffe.

The ensuing Battle of Britain began on July 10, 1940, and continued until October 31, going through a succession of targeting phases. The Germans lost the battle for a number of reasons. For one thing, Göring proved to be an inept leader, intervening in fits and starts with disastrous result. Believing exaggerated pilot claims, he shifted the targeting from vectoring stations and radar

masts just as it was having major impact. Radar—an acronym for "radio detection and ranging"—and the Ultra code-breaking operation were also important; they enabled the RAF to know in advance the size and direction of the German bomber streams. A crippling disadvantage for the Germans was the range limitation of their fighter aircraft. The fighter pilots could count on only about 20 minutes of flying time over Britain and often ran out of fuel and crashed short of their bases. Another factor in the battle was the sheer strain on the German aircrews flying as many as five sorties a day. Also, if they were forced to bail out over Britain they would be captured, whereas British pilots doing the same would be recovered. Many of the German aircraft were also either ill-suited (the Stuka) or, because of the crash German building program, obsolescent. The Luftwaffe was a tactical force, designed for close air support at which it excelled, not for long-range strategic bombing. On the British side, the Hawker Hurricane bore the brunt of the battle, but the RAF Supermarine Spitfire, with its self-sealing gas tanks, was superior to any German fighter.

British deceptions and camouflage were also successful, with decoys drawing perhaps half the German attacks on airfields. British aircraft production and the ability to rapidly return damaged aircraft to service also played important roles. As a result, the number of aircraft available to Fighter Command continued to increase throughout the battle. Indeed, 1940 saw the British outproduce German in aircraft by 50 percent.

Finally, there was the German concentration on London. On August 24, some German bombers missed their intended target and struck London by mistake. Churchill immediately ordered a retaliatory strike on Berlin. Hitler responded by an order to concentrate on London rather than against the vastly more important RAF airfields and production facilities. Dowding heralded the shift to bombing London on September 7 as a "supernatural intervention," for it ended any chance of the Luftwaffe obtaining air superiority over southern England.

The Germans hoped that their concentration on London would bring up the remaining British fighters so they might destroy them. But Dowding refused to be drawn into a fight for the city or other forward areas. Instead, he concentrated on defending vital sectors, particularly airfields. Unpopular at the time, Dowding's decision was decisive. Although the bombing killed some 14,000 people in London alone, the city was able to absorb the punishment. Contrary to the predictions of airpower theorists, the bombings did not break civilian morale but instead served to strengthen it. The power of the bomber was overestimated, and the Battle of Britain was the first proof of this.

Finally, with the Luftwaffe taking aircraft losses of two and three to one on November 1, the Germans shifted to night bombing, what Londoners called the Blitz. During its height the Germans sent an average of 200 planes over London 57 days in a row. This continued into May 1941. On May 10 London had its worst night, with 1,500 killed and another 1,800 seriously injured.

German Army and Navy leaders, who dreaded an invasion of Britain, were glad of the excuse provided by the failure of the battle for the suspension of SEA LION (October 12, 1940). Had Hitler concentrated on defeating Britain through combined air and submarine pressure to starve it of resources, he could have brought about its defeat, but his focus now became the Soviet Union. Hitler claimed that the only reason Britain continued in the war was the hope that Germany and the Soviet Union might come to blows: defeat the Soviet Union, and Britain would have to give up.

Raeder and Göring both tried to convince Hitler to pursue a Mediterranean option. In this, Spain would be brought into the war and Gibraltar taken to prevent an Anglo-American invasion of North Africa. Malta would also be secured, and German forces would join the Italians in seizing Egypt and the Suez Canal and then the Persian Gulf oil. Such a plan offered a far better chance of success than the invasion of the Soviet Union. In the summer of 1942, even two additional panzer divisions in North Africa might have given the Axis victory there. Hitler ordered an invasion of the Soviet Union not from sound strategic reasons but to secure Lebensraum.

Hitler grossly underestimated Soviet resources and ability and was confident of success. "We have only to kick in the door," he said, "and the whole rotten structure will come crashing down." Planning now began for the invasion, code-named Operation BARBAROSSA, and in the winter of 1940–1941 the Germans shifted the bulk of their resources eastward.

Both Hitler and Stalin, foreseeing eventual war with the other, had entered into their partnership to secure time. Germany gained much more from the pact than did the Soviet Union, securing immense quantities of raw materials and other goods that the Russians obtained from third parties. All this would be lost to Germany in an invasion, although Hitler believed that he would then be able to take the resources by force. Wishing to give his partner no excuse, Stalin fulfilled his obligations to the letter right up to the German invasion.

OPERATION BARBAROSSA, 1941 – 1942

Shocked by the rapid defeat of France, Stalin had immediately cashed in his outstanding chips. In June 1940 Soviet troops occupied Lithuania, followed by Latvia and Estonia. In early August all three were incorporated into the Soviet Union as separate union republics. Later that month, Stalin also annexed the Romanian province of Bessarabia (assigned to the Soviets under the Nazi-Soviet Pact) and Northern Bukovina (it, however, had not been assigned to the Soviet Union and had never been part of the territory of Imperial Russia).

To counter these moves and secure his flank, Hitler sought to bring the Balkans under German control. By early 1941 he pressured Romania, Bulgaria, and Hungary to join the Axis. They were quickly occupied by German troops. Yugoslavia, which had also agreed, underwent a coup d'état and withdrew from the alliance, only to be invaded on April 6, 1941, with the Luftwaffe flattening Belgrade.

The Germans also invaded Greece to rescue the Italians who had been driven out by the Greek Army, which then moved into Albania. Upon the German invasion of Greece, Churchill mistakenly halted a successful British offensive in North Africa and sent troops to Greece, where they were soon defeated and evacuated to Crete.

After securing Greece, Hitler decided on an airborne invasion of Crete (May 20–21, 1941). He took this step largely to prevent the British using Crete for air strikes on the vital Ploesti oil fields. Thanks to Ultra intelligence, the British knew the exact timing and location of the German drop zones, which is how they were able to kill 4,000 Germans in the first assault wave. Unfortunately, Ultra also indicated a German naval invasion, which turned out to be inconsequential and was easily turned back at sea. The threat, however,

led to a misapplication of British resources and eventual German victory. The high casualties of the operation caused Hitler to scrap his airborne forces when in fact he should have utilized them for an assault on Malta. Ironically, the Crete operation led the Allies to embrace airborne forces.

Final preparations for BARBAROSSA now went forward. So confident was Hitler of success in a single campaign of three months' duration that he did not believe it necessary to put Germany on a full wartime mobilization; some German troops were also actually being demobilized to return to industry. Nor did Hitler consider it necessary to coordinate plans with his Japanese ally.

The German Balkan campaign, the need to relocate men and equipment and effect repairs, and heavy rains had all imposed delay, however. Originally planned for May 15, the campaign did not occur until June 22. The delay may have been the final blow preventing German victory in the Soviet Union.

Britain and the United States provided ample warning to Stalin of German intentions, but he brushed these aside, seeing only an attempt to drive a wedge between the Soviet Union and Germany. Reportedly Moscow received more than 100 reports of the impending invasion.

Early on June 22, 1941, the German Army, with Finnish, Romanian, Hungarian, and Italian contingents totaling some 3 million men, moved into Russia along a 2,000-mile front. The appallingly bad generalship of Stalin saw the bulk of the Red Army in forward positions, where these units were quickly cut off and surrounded. In the first day alone some 1,200 Soviet aircraft were destroyed, most of them on the ground. Within two days the total was 2,000 aircraft lost. Stalin had rejected appeals to place his border troops on alert, not wishing to provoke the Germans. Even when informed that German troops were invading, Stalin initially refused to allow the troops to return fire. He even claimed that Hitler had to be ignorant of events. Only after four hours did Stalin authorize return fire. For more than a week he was virtually incommunicado. Finally brought to his senses, he proclaimed the Great Patriotic War, appealing to Russian patriotism and downplaying communism.

General Dimitry Pavlov, who commanded the sector of the front that bore the brunt of the German attack, had pleaded with Stalin a week before the invasion to set up rearward defensive positions. Stalin had refused and now made Pavlov the scapegoat. Accused of collaboration with the Germans, Pavlov was tried and shot along with others.

In the early fighting Stalin repeatedly ignored sound military advice, with disastrous result. Thus, instead of letting his armies escape a pincer on Kiev, Stalin insisted that they hold in place, and some 665,000 soldiers were taken prisoner along with vast quantities of weapons. At Smolensk the Germans took another 475,000 Russians prisoner.

No wonder Hitler was confident. Within a week of the start of the invasion the Germans had advanced 350 miles. By autumn they had conquered Belarus (White Russia) and most of Ukraine. The Red Army had lost 1 million dead or wounded and 2 million prisoners. German forces were in three principal columns. In the north they placed Leningrad under siege, in the center they were driving on Moscow, and in the south they entered the Crimean peninsula and laid siege to Sebastopol.

The blitzkrieg had worked well in short distances but broke down in the vast expanses of the Soviet Union. Most roads in the Soviet Union were unpaved, and the autumnal rains turned these into quagmires of mud, impassable for tanks. The winter was also severe, with temperatures plummeting to 60 degrees below zero while many of the German soldiers were still in summer uniforms. The German logistics system simply broke down. The Russians were more accustomed to such conditions.

Hitler also greatly miscalculated Soviet resources. The Germans expected to meet 200 divisions, and by mid-August they had defeated these. They now had to contend with another 160. Germany had 3,600 tanks, the Soviets 24,000 (12,000 in Europe); Germany had 2,000 planes, the Soviets 8,000 (6,000 of them in Europe). Even with these disadvantages, Moscow might have been taken if the panzers had been permitted to drive on Moscow in the summer, without waiting for the infantry. Stalin was aware from Viktor Sorge's spy network in Tokyo that the Japanese were not planning to attack the Soviet Union but would instead move south. By the end of November he had moved west from Soviet Asia 22 Siberian divisions, along with 1,500 planes and 1,700 tanks. In December General Georgy Zhukov led a counteroffensive that pushed the Germans back from the Moscow suburbs.

Hitler, disgusted by what he claimed was ineptitude on the part of his generals, assumed command of military operations himself, and in the spring of 1942 he shifted the main attack to the south toward the oil fields of the Caucasus. Sebastopol soon fell. But Hitler also sent forces against Stalingrad on the Volga River. Increasingly his forces experienced the consequences of strategic overstretch, made all the worse because of fighting in the Mediterranean theater.

Fighting in North Africa had begun in September 1940 when Mussolini ordered Italian forces to invade Egypt from Libya. Determined to keep control of the Suez Canal and the vital supply route to India, Churchill had diverted vitally needed supplies and men to the Middle East during the Battle of Britain. A British counteroffensive by Major General Richard N. O'Connor's Western Desert Force attacked the Italians beginning on December 9. Although only numbering 31,000 men—one-quarter the size of the Italian forces—the British soon ejected the Italians from Egypt and invaded Libya. In just two months O'Connor had advanced 500 miles, destroyed 9 Italian divisions, and taken more than 130,000 prisoners, 380 tanks, and 845 guns. British losses were 500 killed, 1,373 wounded, and 55 missing. British forces also overran Ethiopia, ending Mussolini's short-lived empire there. Britain's mechanized force could have driven on to Tripoli and cleared Africa of the Axis completely, but it had been halted on Churchill's decision to send an expeditionary force to Greece.

The Italian breakdown had led Hitler to send German reinforcements to North Africa under Lieutenant General Erwin Rommel. His Afrika Korps launched an offensive in Libya in the spring of 1941. But Hitler never did make a major effort to seize control of North Africa or the Mediterranean choke points of Gibraltar, Malta, and Suez. Indeed, he merely opened a fresh drain on German resources. The fighting in North Africa shifted back and forth, but by mid-1942 Rommel, although badly outnumbered, succeeded in repulsing the British and penetrating Egypt. In the First Battle of El Alamein (July 1–27), however, Rommel was halted only 70 miles from the Suez Canal.

In December 1941 the war widened when the Japanese attacked the United States. As in World War I, the Japanese saw in World War II an opportunity to expand their territory. With their home islands 70 percent mountains and largely bereft of natural resources, Japanese leaders saw in the war an opportunity to secure the rich natural resources and agricultural production of South Asia, including the much-needed oil of the Dutch East Indies (present-day Indonesia).

In July 1940 an army-dominated government had taken power in Tokyo, determined to exploit circumstances to build a "New Order" in Asia, one in which Japan would supplant British, French, Dutch, and American interests. The United States was the major obstacle to its realization.

On September 27, 1940, Japan entered into an alliance with Germany and Italy. This Tripartite Pact recognized Japanese leadership in "Greater East Asia" and German-Italian leadership in "a new order" in Europe. All three agreed to assist any of the others should they be attacked "by a power presently not involved in the European war or the Sino-Japanese conflict." Their military bogged down in fighting in China, Japanese leaders saw the defeat of France and the Netherlands in addition to British weakness as the ideal opportunity to strike.

Following the defeat of France, in September 1940 the Japanese sent 35,000 troops into northern French Indochina, ostensibly to close the supply routes to nationalist forces in China. Then in July 1941 following Hitler's invasion of the Soviet Union, Japanese forces moved into southern Indochina. This put Siam (present-day Thailand), Malaya (Malaysia), the Dutch East Indies, and the Philippines all within range of Japanese bombers and brought joint retaliation by the United States, Britain, and the Netherlands. Roosevelt froze Japanese assets in the United States and prohibited exports to it of oil, rubber, and scrap iron. Japan had no oil of its own and only a two-year reserve. Without fuel its forces would have to evacuate China, a loss of face unacceptable to the Japanese military. Tokyo branded this an "unfriendly act."

The United States was the first obstacle to Japanese expansion. The second was the Soviet Union. Red Army forces had more than held their own against the Japanese in 1938. Although surprised by the German invasion of the Soviet Union in June 1941, the Japanese were delighted by the initial German victories, for this removed any immediate Soviet threat to their East Asian holdings and allowed them to contemplate a thrust southward.

Negotiations occurred between the United States and Japan, but in fact it was a case of an irresistible force and an immovable object. The United States insisted that Japan remove its troops from China and Indochina, and the Japanese refused. The basic reason the United States was negotiating was its own unreadiness for war. With only 190,000 men in September 1939, the U.S. Army ranked 19th in the world in size. American factories were only beginning to produce substantial quantities of war materials, but much of this was going to Britain. The longer Roosevelt could delay participation in the fighting, the better prepared U.S. forces would be.

With negotiations between the United States and Japan at an impasse, on December 7, 1941, Japan attacked without warning the U.S. Pacific Fleet as it lay at anchor at Pearl Harbor, Hawaii. Japan had the world's largest and most effective naval air arm, and its leading advocate, commander of the Combined Fleet Admiral Yamamoto Isoroku, developed the attack plan of a preemptive strike to purchase time for Japan to conquer Southeast Asia and establish a defensive ring. Then when the Americans had rebuilt their naval strength and attempted to cross the Pacific, Japanese naval aviation, submarines, and warships utilizing the deadly Long Lance torpedo would savage the U.S. fleet and force the Americans to recognize Japanese control of Asia.

The Pearl Harbor attack caught American forces there by surprise, despite a "war warning" resulting from code breaking. (Japanese plans to present a declaration of war just in advance of the attack ran afoul of decoding the long declaration at the Washington embassy.) The Japanese strike force, centered on six aircraft carriers, inflicted terrific damage, sinking four of eight U.S. battleships and severely damaging four others. They also sank three destroyers and four smaller vessels and badly damaged three light cruisers and a seaplane tender; 188 American aircraft were destroyed and 63 badly damaged. The Japanese lost only 29 planes destroyed and 70 damaged, apart from five midget submarines lost. In human casualties, the Americans lost 3,535 killed or wounded; Japanese killed were under 100.

The Pearl Harbor attack brought great advantages to Japan. The U.S. Pacific Fleet was virtually hors de combat, and operations in the Southwest Pacific could now proceed without major interference. The Japanese had won time to secure their defensive ring. The main military drawback for Japan was that they had missed the U.S. carriers, their prime target. They were then at sea on maneuvers. For some inexplicable reason the Japanese also did not strike the oil tanks and other important installations, the destruction of which would have greatly slowed the American recovery. Most important, the Japanese had now united Americans behind the war effort.

On December 11 Germany (and Italy) declared war on the United States. The Tripartite Pact did not cover acts of aggression, so Hitler need not have done this. If he had not, Roosevelt might have been obliged to fight Japan only.

The Japanese now had nearly a free hand. They secured Guam and Wake Island, and they attacked the Philippines by air. Soon General Homma Masaharu's Fourteenth Army invaded Luzon. U.S. commander General Douglas MacArthur mismanaged its defense, believing that he could prevent a Japanese lodgement. When this failed and his troops were forced to fall back on the original plan to withdraw into the Bataan Peninsula, insufficient supplies were in place there for a sustained defense.

Roosevelt ordered MacArthur to Australia on March 11, and command fell to Lieutenant General Jonathan Wainwright. On April 9, 1942, remaining U.S. and Filipino forces withdrew to the island of Corregidor. But Wainwright was forced to surrender the Philippines on May 6. Meanwhile, 76,000 prisoners taken in the Battle for Bataan—some 64,000 Filipino soldiers and 12,000 Americans—were forced to endure what came to be known as the Bataan Death March.

The Japanese also moved against the British possessions of Hong Kong and Malaya. General Yamashita Tomoyuki commanded the invasion of northern Malaya. His forces proceeded southward, and although British forces outnumbered those of Japan two to one, on February 15, 1942, Lieutenant General Arthur Percival

surrendered the great British naval base of Singapore, long held to be impregnable. The Japanese took 70,000 prisoners and destroyed British prestige in Asia in what was one of the most humiliating defeats in British military history. The Japanese also sunk by air at sea while they were under way the new British battleship *Prince of Wales* and the battle cruiser *Repulse,* a feat pronounced impossible by naval experts.

Japanese forces also invaded and took the Dutch East Indies (January–March 1942). They then overran Burma (present-day Myanmar, January–May), completing their control of the western gateways to China and the Pacific. British forces in Burma had to carry out a 1,000-mile retreat. The Japanese also invaded New Guinea and threatened Australia, and they sent their fleet into the Indian Ocean and seemed ready to invade India.

With so many of their troops also fighting in China, the Japanese were in fact stretched far beyond their capacity to hold their gains. U.S. industrial capacity also dwarfed that of Japan. Japanese steel production in 1941 was only 7 million tons versus 92 million for the United States. Japan was not to have the time to exploit the resources of the conquered territory.

Barring some sort of miracle weapon, if the Soviet Union survived and America's strength developed, defeat of the Axis Powers was nearly certain. This did not seem apparent at the end of 1941 and early 1942, however, as German forces were at the Caucasus and close to the Nile. They were also sinking Allied shipping at an unprecedented and disastrous rate, and they were wreaking havoc in the Mediterranean.

The United States and Britain formed the Combined Chiefs of Staff to develop a unified strategy. Germany was deemed the major threat, and its defeat became the primary goal. Sufficient resources were available to permit American operations against Japan, with Australia the chief base of operations. In mid-1942 American, British, and Australian forces brought Japanese expansion southward to a halt and frustrated Japanese efforts to cut the supply line to Australia.

At the beginning of April 1942 the United States assumed responsibility for the whole Pacific area, except Sumatra; the British retained responsibility for it and the Indian Ocean area. China was a separate theater of war under American tutelage. There was, however, no unified U.S. command with the Pacific divided between MacArthur and Admiral Chester Nimitz. The Southwest Pacific area was placed under MacArthur, the Pacific Ocean area under Nimitz.

In 1942 the United States won two Pacific naval victories. The Battle of the Coral Sea (May 4–8) was the first major naval action fought by aircraft without the fleets of the two sides actually coming in sight of one another. Although it was a tactical draw, the United States won a strategic victory in turning back the Japanese invasion of Port Moresby.

The Battle of Midway (June 4–6) is often regarded as the turning point in the Pacific War. In it, Japanese Combined Fleet commander Yamamoto flung a vast armada against American Midway Island with a diversionary/secondary thrust against the Aleutians. Almost the entire Japanese Navy participated. Yamamoto planned to secure Midway as a base for future operations against Pearl Harbor and draw out and destroy the U.S. Pacific Fleet.

Aware of the broad outlines of the Japanese plan thanks to code breaking, Nimitz in Hawaii scrambled to meet the Japanese. Yamamoto had some 200 ships, including

8 carriers (more than 600 aircraft), 11 battleships, 22 cruisers, 65 destroyers, and 21 submarines. Transports carried some 7,400 ground troops. Nimitz could count on only 76 ships, and a third of these, belonging to the North Pacific force, never came into the battle.

Rear Admiral Raymond A. Spruance fought the battle with great skill, but luck played a major role, as 37 U.S. dive-bombers from the U.S. carrier *Enterprise* swept down to attack the Japanese carriers, while the Japanese fighters that had been dealing with the torpedo bombers were close to sea level. Soon the *Akagi* and *Kaga* were flaming wrecks, with the torpedoes and fuel on their decks feeding the fires. The *Sōryū* took three hits from the U.S. carrier *Yorktown*'s dive-bombers that also arrived on the scene, and soon it too was abandoned.

The *Hiryū*, the only Japanese fleet carrier still intact, then sent its planes against the *Yorktown,* forcing the Americans to abandon it. Then 24 U.S. dive-bombers, including 10 from the *Yorktown,* caught the *Hiryū*. It sank the next day. Yamamoto now suspended the attack on Midway, hoping to trap the Americans by drawing them westward. Spruance, however, refused to take the bait. The Battle of Midway was a crushing defeat for Japan, with the loss of four fleet carriers and 350 aircraft with their highly trained aircrews. The United States lost only the *Yorktown* and 150 aircraft.

In August 1942 American forces landed at Guadalcanal in the Solomon Islands to contest Japanese construction of an airstrip. A fierce struggle ensued ashore and in the surrounding waters until the Japanese withdrew their remaining ground forces in February 1943. U.S. forces then embarked on a long series of island-hopping operations. The U.S. Marine Corps took the lead, assisted by the U.S. Army and made possible by the great buildup in naval forces and development of the fleet train concept of supply and repair vessels accompanying the battle fleet. Strong Japanese installations were on occasion simply bypassed and cut off.

At the same time also, the U.S. Navy embarked on a campaign that would see it become the most effective practitioner of submarine warfare in history. The U.S. Navy entered the war with 114 submarines, Japan with about 50. The United States built another 206, Japan only 112. At the beginning of the war Japan had a marginal capability of 6 million tons of merchant shipping. It built another 2 million tons during the war, but 4.8 million of the 8 million tons were sunk by submarines. Particularly grievous for the Japanese was the shortage of aviation fuel occasioned by the sinking of tankers. U.S. submarines also sank some 200 Japanese Navy ships.

Meanwhile, plans by the Western Allies to invade continental Europe had to be delayed as U.S. ground forces underwent training and acquired equipment. This greatly displeased the Soviets, who understandably sought relief from the 300 Axis divisions on their territory and accused the British and Americans of "wanting to fight to the last Russian." In the meantime, the Western Allies concentrated on the air bombardment of Germany.

British and American air commanders believed strongly that strategic bombing could win the war. The Americans were confident that the well-armed, supposedly self-defending four-engine Boeing B-17 Flying Fortress and the newly developed Norden bombsight would allow precise bombing of German targets in broad daylight. The British, who had tried and failed at daylight bombing, had gone over to area bombing of cities at night. Pinpoint bombing simply could not work in World War II. Although the fiction of it was maintained, the United States in effect accepted the argument that the way to win the war was to shatter civilian morale by area bombing of cities. Such arguments were specious, particularly in a totalitarian state. Again and again, bombing of civilians has been shown to stiffen rather than weaken civilian resolve. The first Allied 1,000-bomber raid, against Köln (Cologne), Germany's fifth-largest city, on May 30–31, 1942, did, however, bring home to many Germans which side was winning the war.

An alternative strategy directed against vital choke points in the German war economy, especially oil refineries and ball-bearing plants, brought high losses and disappointing results. U.S. strategic bombing was much more effective in the Pacific theater, however.

Hopes that the Western Allies might soon open a true second front with a cross-channel invasion suffered a severe blow in a disastrous raid on German-held Dieppe (August 19, 1942) that cost the Allies, especially the Canadians, more than 1,000 dead. Moreover, a major increase in U-boat strength made large troop movements across the Atlantic in 1942 risky. By May 1943, half of the 5,600 merchant ships of the world in 1939 had been sunk by U-boats. A shortage of shipping (along with that of landing craft) was one of the key problems facing the Allies throughout the war. By the first part of 1943 the submarine menace was reduced to tolerable proportions, but the land invasion of Europe was postponed until 1944.

The U-boats were tamed thanks to convoys, better depth charges, escort carriers,

PACIFIC THEATER, 1941 – 1945

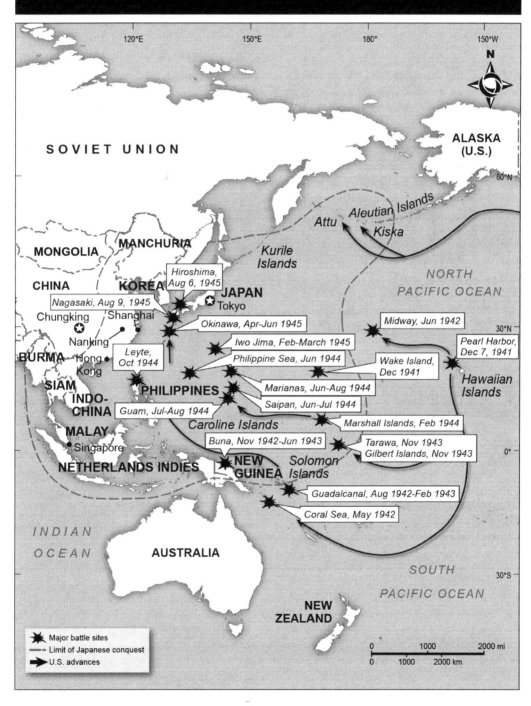

SOVIET UNION

ALASKA (U.S.)

60°N

Aleutian Islands

Attu

Kiska

Kurile Islands

NORTH PACIFIC OCEAN

MONGOLIA

MANCHURIA

CHINA

KOREA

Hiroshima, Aug 6, 1945

JAPAN

Tokyo

Nagasaki, Aug 9, 1945

Chungking

Shanghai

Okinawa, Apr-Jun 1945

Midway, Jun 1942

30°N

Nanking

Iwo Jima, Feb-March 1945

Pearl Harbor, Dec 7, 1941

BURMA

Hong Kong

Leyte, Oct 1944

Philippine Sea, Jun 1944

Wake Island, Dec 1941

Hawaiian Islands

SIAM

INDO-CHINA

PHILIPPINES

Marianas, Jun-Aug 1944

Guam, Jul-Aug 1944

Saipan, Jun-Jul 1944

MALAY

Singapore

Caroline Islands

Marshall Islands, Feb 1944

0°

Buna, Nov 1942-Jun 1943

Tarawa, Nov 1943
Gilbert Islands, Nov 1943

NETHERLANDS INDIES

NEW GUINEA

Solomon Islands

Guadalcanal, Aug 1942-Feb 1943

INDIAN OCEAN

AUSTRALIA

Coral Sea, May 1942

SOUTH PACIFIC OCEAN

30°S

NEW ZEALAND

Major battle sites
Limit of Japanese conquest
U.S. advances

0   1000   2000 mi
0   1000   2000 km

hunter-killer groups operating independent of convoys, and new 10cm radar sets carried in long-range aircraft. Ultra helped guide aircraft to the submarines. By the autumn of 1943 the Battle of the Atlantic had been won.

Indeed, at the end of 1942 the tide in Europe began to turn. On November 8, 1942, in Operation TORCH, Anglo-American forces carried out a surprise amphibious operation of hitherto unparalleled proportion at Casablanca in Morocco and at Oran and Algiers in Algeria. French forces loyal to Vichy contested the landings, which were successful and provided training for the subsequent invasion of Europe. Lieutenant General Dwight D. Eisenhower had overall command.

These forces consolidated and then pushed eastward to meet British general Bernard Montgomery's Eighth Army, which had broken out in the Second Battle of El Alamein (October 23–November 4). Montgomery was slow to pursue the Afrika Korps, and Axis forces were able to withdraw in good order into Tunisia. Two American divisions also suffered a serious rebuff at the hands of Rommel in the Battle of Kasserine Pass (February 14–21, 1943).

In November 1942 the Germans took over the rest of unoccupied France, but they were frustrated in an effort to gain possession of the French fleet. True to their word, the French managed to scuttle 77 of the 80 ships of their navy at Toulon. Meanwhile, on November 7 the Red Army closed a ring around the Germans at Stalingrad.

Too late, Hitler now reinforced in North Africa, only to see the Germans and Italians defeated in the Battle of Tunis (May 3–13, 1943), with 275,000 taken prisoner. Unfortunately for the Allies, the best German units were evacuated. But Africa was at last cleared of the Axis forces, the Mediterranean was open, and the threat to Egypt and Suez was ended. The Germans also suffered a major defeat in the Battle of Stalingrad (August 24, 1942–January 31 1943).

In 1942 Hitler still had a good chance of victory in the Soviet Union, but he had greatly reduced his chances by splitting German resources between two objectives 500 miles apart: the lower Volga River transportation hub of Stalingrad and the Caucasus oil fields. The campaign in the Caucasus stalled owing to lack of fuel and Hitler's decision to drain off resources from Field Marshal Paul von Kleist's First Panzer Army to support the growing battle at Stalingrad. Stalingrad might have been taken in July had troops not been diverted then to the Caucasus, only to be stripped away in September and, too late, sent to Stalingrad.

By September the Germans had entered Stalingrad itself, but Stalin ordered his namesake city held at all costs. Hitler became obsessed with taking the city and wore down the Sixth Army in the process. It was not necessary for Stalingrad to be taken to control the transportation on the Volga, but Hitler insisted that it be secured in the traditional sense. From September 15 for a month, the Sixth Army and the Fourth Panzer Army attempted to take the city by storm. Heavy Luftwaffe bombing had created piles of rubble and turned the city into a fortress. Fighting was house by house and room by room.

The German Army's greatest strength of mobility counted for nothing, while the Soviets' greatest strength of tenacious defense was all. General Vasily Chuikov's Sixty-Second Army managed to hold the west bank of the Volga. The German front in Russia was now more than 2,000 miles long and well beyond overstretched. His generals were concerned, but Hitler claimed that the Russians lacked the resources to exploit the situation and ordered Sixth Army commander General of Armored Troops Friedrich Paulus to continue.

The Germans had taken most of Stalingrad when Soviet forces under Zhukov launched an encirclement and cut off the Sixth Army. Hitler forbade any withdrawal, convinced that the Sixth Army could be supplied from the air (Göring was later blamed). But bad weather made flying difficult, and in any case the Luftwaffe was stretched thin supplying Axis forces in North Africa and lacked the airlift capacity.

Paulus should have acted on his own and attempted a breakout, but he had been appointed precisely because he would follow orders. Hitler would permit only a linkup, not a breakout that would surrender territory already taken. A hastily assembled German relief force got to within 30 miles of the Sixth Army, but Paulus rejected appeals that he act to save his army. This doomed the Sixth Army. Twenty-two German divisions and 330,000 German troops were lost in the battle. When Paulus surrendered on January 31, only 90,000 of his men were still alive, and only 5,000 of these would ever return to Germany.

The situation was not irredeemable. In the spring the Germans again held the initiative, and the Russians were suffering defeats. The war on the Eastern Front might still have been fought to a draw. But a withdrawal and a shortened front was the only realistic course. Hitler's generals urged this, but he obstinately refused, insisting that there be no retreat. This only ensured that each inevitable withdrawal would be more costly.

By the summer of 1943 Germany and its allies and the Soviet Union each had some 250 divisions, but the advantage in matériel had passed to the Russians. Soviet industrial output had increased and more U.S. Lend-Lease aid was reaching the Soviet Union via the Arctic and Iran. Ultimately the Soviets received 22,000 planes, 12,000 tanks, 375,000 trucks, 51,000 jeeps, and 15 million pairs of American boots. American food aid alone amounted to some half a pound per soldier per day.

Still, the Soviets bore the brunt of the ground combat in the war. The United States eventually committed 60 divisions to the battle for Europe, but the Russians lost more men in the Battle of Stalingrad alone than the United States did in battle during the entire war in all theaters combined. From June 1941 the Russians had to contend most of the time with four-fifths of the German Army and never less than three-fourths of it.

Both sides now focused on the German buildup for a major offensive that became the Battle of Kursk (July 5–16, 1943). Manstein had wanted only a spoiling attack, but Hitler broadened his plan into an all-out offensive. The Soviets knew the German plans thanks to the "Red Orchestra," their spy apparatus in Berlin. Code-named Operation CITADEL, the offensive came against well-prepared, deep Soviet defenses, and on July 12 the Soviets launched a counteroffensive.

Kursk was actually the largest battle of World War II, involving some 4 million Russian and German troops, as many as 70,000 artillery pieces, and 12,000 planes. With 13,000 tanks, it also saw the heaviest armor battles in history. In the battle the Germans suffered 198,000 casualties, the Russians 254,000, but the strategic initiative was now with the Soviets. Kursk was the true turning point on the Eastern Front.

Meanwhile, having secured North Africa the Western Allies moved against

Southern Europe. In Operation HUSKY (July 9–August 17, 1943), U.S., British, and Canadian forces invaded and conquered Sicily. The victory was marred by the rivalry between Lieutenant General George C. Patton's U.S. Seventh Army and Montgomery's Eighth Army in a race to Messina and by the success of the Germans in evacuating the bulk of their forces to Italy. The Germans removed 100,000 men and considerable vehicles and equipment across the narrow straits. The invasion did bring the end of Mussolini's regime on July 24 (the Germans subsequently rescued him and set him up as head of a rump Italian state in the north), and the new Italian government led by Marshal Patrice Badoglio promptly opened secret peace talks with the Allies.

On September 3 the Allies invaded Italy from the south, but the Germans promptly took over the Italian positions. In October 1943 the Badoglio government declared war on Germany, and the Allies recognized Italy as a cobelligerent. But German forces blocked the advance on Rome, and the Italian campaign became a bloody stalemate as the Western Allies concentrated on building up their forces in Britain for the invasion of France. Rome was only liberated on June 4, 1944, and the German surrender in Italy did not occur until May 2, 1945.

Meanwhile, the Allies continued their strategic bombing of Germany. In the summer of 1943 British and American bombers launched devastating raids against German cities. The raid on Hamburg in July killed some 45,000 Germans in great firestorms. But raids on August 17, 1943, on a ball-bearing plant at Schweinfurt and the Messerschmitt aircraft factory at Regensburg proved costly. In the subsequent October 14 return U.S. raid at Schweinfurt,

the Germans destroyed or damaged 198 attacking aircraft out of 291.

Losses were reversed in late 1943 with the arrival of the long-range North American P-51 Mustang and Republic P-47 Thunderbolt. Equipped with drop tanks, these superb fighters protected the bombers to and from their targets. The Germans could replace aircraft but not the trained pilots lost. By the summer of 1944 the chief threat to Allied bombers was antiaircraft fire.

In February 1945 the bombers struck Dresden, crowded with a million refugees from the East. The death tally approached 45,000, although some historians claim that many more perished. Such terror bombing could not topple the Hitler regime, however. In September 1944 the Allies made the destruction of the petroleum industry a priority, and then in 1945 the bombing was largely directed against industrial targets and lines of communication. But strategic bombing, while important, was not decisive in the war. Germany actually attained its highest levels of military production at the end of the war. The bombing also cost the United States 9,949 bombers and the RAF 10,045. Personnel losses were 79,281 for the RAF and 79,265 for the U.S. Army Air Forces.

Meanwhile, the Western Allies were preparing for the invasion of Europe. The Atlantic coastline bristled with thousands of fortifications, and French ports became fortresses, but the Allies brought their own artificial harbors (Mulberries) with them and, in Operation PLUTO, even an oil pipeline across the English Channel. Elaborate deceptions in Operations FORTITUDE NORTH and FORTITUDE SOUTH convinced Hitler that the Allies were intending to invade Norway and that the Normandy operation was a feint, with the main landing

NORMANDY INVASION, 1944

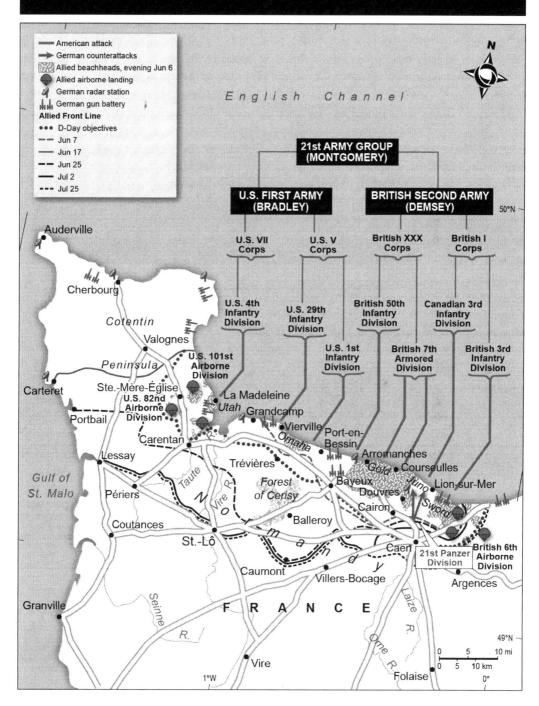

Legend:
- American attack
- German counterattacks
- Allied beachheads, evening Jun 6
- Allied airborne landing
- German radar station
- German gun battery

Allied Front Line
- ••• D-Day objectives
- --- Jun 7
- — Jun 17
- --- Jun 25
- — Jul 2
- ---- Jul 25

English Channel

21st ARMY GROUP (MONTGOMERY)

U.S. FIRST ARMY (BRADLEY)

BRITISH SECOND ARMY (DEMSEY)

50°N

U.S. VII Corps

U.S. V Corps

British XXX Corps

British I Corps

U.S. 4th Infantry Division

U.S. 29th Infantry Division

British 50th Infantry Division

Canadian 3rd Infantry Division

U.S. 1st Infantry Division

British 7th Armored Division

British 3rd Infantry Division

Auderville

Cherbourg

Cotentin

Valognes

Peninsula

U.S. 101st Airborne Division

Carteret

Ste.-Mère-Église

U.S. 82nd Airborne Division

Portbail

La Madeleine

Utah Grandcamp

Vierville

Port-en-Bessin

Carentan

Omaha

Lessay

Trévières

Gulf of St. Malo

Périers

Taute

Vire R.

Forest of Cerisy

Bayeux

Douvres

Gold Courseulles

Arromanches

Juno

Lion-sur-Mer

Cairon

Sword

Coutances

N o r m a n d y

Balleroy

St.-Lô

Caen

21st Panzer Division

British 6th Airborne Division

Caumont

Villers-Bocage

Argences

Granville

Seinne R.

F R A N C E

Laize R.

49°N

Orne R.

Vire

Folaise

1°W

0°

| 0 | 5 | 10 mi |
| 0 | 5 | 10 km |

to occur in the Pas de Calais area. The invasion itself saw 10,000 aircraft provide protection, and there were also 138 bombarding warships, 221 destroyers and other convoy escorts, 287 minesweepers, 495 light craft, 441 auxiliaries, and some 4,000 landing ships and other craft of various sizes.

D-day (decision day) began before dawn on June 6, 1944, with airborne forces landing behind German lines to prevent reinforcements from reaching the beaches. Because the Allied forces were fully mechanized and the bulk of the German defenders were not, the Germans had to prevent the Allies from establishing a beachhead and building up their strength. Hitler did not grasp this, and FORTITUDE SOUTH caused him to hold his armor formations back until it was too late.

Some 130,000 men came ashore the first day, and a million came ashore within a month. Nonetheless, the going was slower than expected. Not until the end of July were the Allies able to break free, in Operation COBRA (July 25–31, 1944). Lieutenant General Omar Bradley's U.S. First Army forced the German line west of Saint-Lô.

Patton's Third Army now took up the right of the Allied line, and Bradley assumed command of the 12th Army Group, with Lieutenant General Courtney Hodges taking over First Army. In the British zone of operations Montgomery's 21st Army Group also expanded, comprising the Canadian First Army and the British Second Army. The Third Army achieved the greatest success, and Patton was certainly the outstanding general of the campaign for France. In a single month his army liberated most of France north of the Loire River.

On August 15 meanwhile in Operation DRAGOON, Lieutenant General Alexander Patch's Seventh Army invaded southern France near Cannes. Originally planned to coincide with D-day, the operation had to be postponed because of a shortage of landing craft from OVERLORD and British reluctance to divert assets from Italy. In one day 86,000 men and 12,000 vehicles came ashore, and aircraft dropped a provisional airborne division. The Seventh Army then drove northeast.

Paris was liberated at the end of August by General Philippe Leclerc de Hauteclocque's French 2nd Armored Division. The city was spared the fate of Rotterdam and Warsaw because German general of infantry Dietrich von Choltiz refused to employ heavy weaponry to defend the city or to destroy it as Hitler ordered.

The Allies now wasted a golden opportunity. While Montgomery made little progress, Patton's Third Army carried out a wide enveloping movement that prevented the Germans from making a stand along the Seine and trapped large numbers of two German field armies, including seven Panzer divisions, in the so-called Falaise Pocket. The Allies might well have had victory in Europe in 1944 if they had closed the 15-mile-wide gap between Argentan and Falaise. Argentan had been assigned to the British, but they had not arrived there when Patton on August 12 urged Bradley to permit him to drive farther north and close the ring. Bradley refused. The pocket was not closed until August 18. Although 60,000 Germans were killed or captured along with substantial amounts of arms and equipment, some 100,000 Germans escaped.

By August 31 Patton's Third Army had reached the Meuse at Verdun, and the following day it was at the Moselle. To the north Montgomery drove into Belgium. Arguing that there was insufficient logistical support for more than one major drive, Montgomery proposed that Bradley's forces halt and that all logistical support go to his 21st Army Group for a last decisive blow against the Wehrmacht. Although Montgomery received 80 percent of the support he requested, he missed an opportunity to shorten the war. British tanks captured Brussels on September 3 and then Antwerp on September 4 so quickly that the Germans could not destroy its port facilities. Opening the Scheldt estuary would relieve the growing Allied supply difficulties. Montgomery was also in position to trap the German Fifteenth Army withdrawing up the coast. An advance of less than 10 miles beyond Antwerp would have accomplished this, but in one of the great mistakes of the war, Montgomery halted at Antwerp, and the Fifteenth Army got across the Scheldt to Walcheren Island and then into Holland.

By the end of August the German Army had sustained 500,000 casualties and lost 1,600 tanks. Few troops and only 100 tanks and 570 aircraft were in position to block an Allied drive eastward. One major thrust might have been decisive, but the advance stalled. Allied forces were still being supplied over the Normandy beaches, and supply lines were lengthening and tenuous, while those of the Germans were eased. Supplies were certainly insufficient for General Eisenhower's broad-front strategy, and the Allied advance now ground to a halt. There were also natural obstacles to be overcome in the Vosges Mountains, the Ardennes, and the Hürtgen Forest. The front stabilized.

By 1944 most German leaders knew that the war was lost. It was also clear that Hitler was determined to fight to the last, even at the cost of the complete destruction of Germany. A number of individuals set out to assassinate Hitler, which would free German officers from their oath of allegiance and make possible a coup d'état. After several abortive attempts, on July 20, 1944, Colonel Klaus von Stauffenberg placed a bomb in Hitler's conference room in East Prussia. Although it exploded, Hitler survived, and some 5,000 opponents of the regime were executed during the next several months.

Surprisingly given his hitherto cautious approach, Eisenhower gave Montgomery permission to try a narrow-front attack. His Operation MARKET GARDEN (September 17–26, 1944) was an effort to seize a crossing over the Rhine River at Arnheim and allow an offensive into the Ruhr. It involved three airborne divisions—two U.S. and one British—and the British Second Army. The U.S. airborne forces were to secure bridges over the Maas (Meuse), Waal (Rhine), and Lek (Lower Rhine) Rivers and hold them until the Second Army could move up a narrow 60-mile corridor from Belgium and across the succession of rivers to secure Arnhem on the far side of the lower Rhine. The inexperienced British 1st Airborne was assigned the most difficult task, that of taking and holding the farthest bridge at Arnhem.

The operation was fraught with risk, yet Allied planners, believing that Germany was on the verge of defeat, were overconfident. Warnings by the Dutch underground, Ultra intercepts, and late photographic evidence revealed two German panzer divisions recuperating and reequipping around Arnhem. The major tactical error, however, was dropping the 1st Airborne some 7–8 miles from the highway bridge at Arnhem, allowing the German panzers to isolate it.

Beginning on September 17 in the largest airborne attack of the war, 1,400 aircraft transported 34,000 paratroopers (20,000 in the first day) to their drop zones, and the Second Army began its drive north. Although the U.S. airborne divisions secured their objectives, the ground advance slowed. Despite orders to the contrary, an American officer had a complete set of plans aboard one of the gliders. He was killed, and the plans were soon in German hands. The operation ended on September 26, a complete failure.

Meanwhile, the Soviets had begun Operation BAGRATION (June 22–August 19, 1944). Involving some 1.67 million troops, it inflicted 300,000–600,000 German casualties and destroyed German Army Group Center. The Soviets then halted before Warsaw. They encouraged the Poles to rise up against the Germans in the city, but they sat idly by for two months. This resulted in the deaths of some 10,000 Germans and 300,000 Poles and a far easier subsequent Soviet subjugation of Poland. In December 1944, however, the Red Army crossed the German frontier, driving millions of German refugees ahead of them.

Hitler placed his faith in new weapons such as the Messerschmitt Me-262 jet aircraft, the V-1 buzz bomb cruise missile, and the V-2 rocket. These came too late, however. The Eastern Front had remained static for several months while the Allied offensive on the Western Front was gaining ground, and in September 1944 Hitler decided to put together a large offensive to take the Western Allies by surprise and recapture Antwerp. This was the Ardennes Offensive, known to the Allies as the Battle of the Bulge (December 16, 1944–January 16, 1945). Western Front commander Field Marshal von Rundstedt protested, as did other high-ranking officers, but Hitler was not to be dissuaded, and substantial reinforcements were now transferred from the Eastern Front for what would be the biggest battle fought on the Western Front in the war and the largest engagement ever fought by the U.S. Army.

In a major Western intelligence failure, the German attack caught the Western Allies entirely by surprise. Bad weather also grounded Allied aircraft and enabled the Germans to advance quickly. Eisenhower immediately ordered up the 82nd and 101st Airborne Divisions, and late on December 18 the 101st took up position near the key road hub of Bastogne, Belgium, which held. Patton's relief effort—one of the more memorable mass military maneuvers of the war—and clearing skies that enabled Allied aircraft to attack the German tanks blunted the offensive, which nonetheless created a bulge in the American line some 50 miles deep and 70 miles wide.

Unfortunately, Montgomery decided to remain on the defensive, overruling an American plan to cut off the bulge by striking from each shoulder. Finally, the Allies attacked midway up the salient, passing up the chance to surround the Germans. Of the 600,000 U.S. troops involved, 19,000 were killed, 50,000 were wounded, and 20,000 were taken prisoner. Nearly 800 tanks were destroyed. The Germans sustained nearly 100,000 killed, wounded, or captured.

Before the Germans could switch resources eastward, the Soviets launched their great Vistula-Oder Offensive (January 12–February 2, 1945) with 2.2 million men against only some 450,000 Germans. In effect the Ardennes Offensive hastened the end of the war. Hitler, meanwhile, rejected all appeals to end the slaughter and the suffering of the German people. He forbade retreat. If unavoidable, then everything was to be destroyed. The fate of the German people was irrelevant.

Soviet forces now swept through the Baltic States, White Russia, Ukraine, and Poland and forced the capitulation of Romania, Finland, and Bulgaria. Early in 1945 the Red Army entered East Prussia, Czechoslovakia, and Hungary and began its drive into Germany. On April 16 the Red Army launched the Berlin Strategic Offensive Operation to take the German capital.

In April, meanwhile, Eisenhower sent 18 divisions to clear out the Ruhr. A more daring thrust might have hastened the final German defeat. U.S. forces might have taken both Berlin and Prague, but Bradley estimated that capturing Berlin would have cost 100,000 casualties, and Berlin, deep inside the designated Russian zone of occupation, would in any case have passed to them. Eisenhower was focused on a phantom Alpine German redoubt and turned much of his strength south to reduce it. As it worked out, Bradley was prescient, as more than 100,000 Russians died in the campaign to take Berlin.

The Allies offered no terms to Hitler or to any Germans. Mussolini was captured in northern Italy by the antifascist resistance and shot. Hitler committed suicide in the ruins of Berlin, and the Germans surrendered unconditionally on May 8, 1945. By that time forces driving from the west had met the Red Army on the Elbe and in Bohemia and Austria. The war in Europe was over.

In the Pacific, American forces had moved in a northwesterly direction from the Solomon Islands, the easternmost fringe on the Indonesian archipelago, toward the Japanese home islands. The Americans had to assault and take the Japanese-held islands and atolls in the mid-Pacific. These were the Gilbert Islands (Tarawa and Makin, November 20–24, 1943), the Marshalls (Kwajalein

and Eniwetok, January 29–February 21, 1944), and the Carolines (Saipan, Guam, and Tinian, June 15–August 2, 1944). For the most part these were desperate struggles, with the Japanese choosing to fight to the death rather than surrender.

U.S. naval forces inflicted major losses on the Japanese in the Battle of the Philippine Sea (June 19–21, 1944), the first fleet encounter in two years. Particularly grievous to Japan was the loss of 460 trained aircrews.

On October 20, U.S. forces began landing on Leyte in the Philippines. This triggered the largest naval battle in terms of men and ships engaged in history. The polycentric Battle of Leyte Gulf (October 23–26) involved 282 ships: 218 U.S. and 64 Japanese. It also ended the Japanese fleet as an organized fighting force. In the disparate fight Japan lost 4 carriers, 3 battleships, 6 heavy and 4 light cruisers, 11 destroyers, and 1 submarine; nearly every other ship was damaged. About 500 planes were lost. American losses were 1 light carrier, 2 escort carriers, 2 destroyers, 1 destroyer escort, and more than 200 aircraft.

During February 19–March 24, 1945, U.S. marines took the island of Iwo Jima. In fighting to secure the island, the marines suffered 6,891 killed and 18,070 wounded. More than 21,000 Japanese were counted dead, and only 212 surrendered. Iwo Jima then became a base for fighter aircraft and an emergency landing point for damaged B-29 bombers striking Japan.

Finally, in one of the war's greatest and final battles the U.S. Army and Marine Corps secured Okinawa, 300 miles from Japan itself. This battle during April 1– June 22 saw Japanese suicide kamikaze aircraft kill 5,000 navy personnel and wound more than 4,600. The navy suffered more casualties here than in all previous

American wars combined. The fighting on land claimed more than 130,000 Japanese killed and only 7,400 prisoners. U.S. Tenth Army casualties were 7,374 killed and 32,056 wounded.

Meanwhile, heavy Boeing B-29 Superfortress bombers flying first from China, then from the Carolines, pounded Japan. The first firebomb raid was carried out against Tokyo on March 9–10, 1945, with 334 B-29s dropping 1,667 tons of incendiary bombs in the single most destructive air raid in history. Widespread firestorms destroyed 15 square miles of Tokyo, killing more than 83,000 people and injuring 100,000. Other Japanese cities were also burned out. Carrier aviation joined in. The combined effort, which included U.S. submarines as well as ships of the Royal Navy, shattered Japanese industry, all but destroyed intraisland shipping, and obliterated what was left of the Japanese Navy.

With the capture of Okinawa, the stage was set for a full-scale invasion of Japan itself, with anticipated heavy U.S. casualties. On August 6, 1945, however, an atomic bomb, developed in great secrecy, was dropped on the city of Hiroshima. In a single instant the city of 200,000 people was destroyed, with 70,000 dead. Two days later the Soviet Union, which had pledged to enter the conflict in the Far East within three months of the surrender of Germany, declared war on Japan and invaded Manchuria. On August 9 a more powerful bomb struck Nagasaki, and the Japanese cabinet decided in favor of surrender the next day. A number of Japanese military leaders wanted to fight on, but on August 15 Emperor Hirohito addressed the Japanese people in a recorded message and announced the surrender. On September 2, 1945, final terms of surrender were signed. World War II was over at last.

Significance

World War II was immensely destructive. The butcher's bill exceeded 60 million dead. Most of continental Europe's cities were masses of rubble, and the transportation infrastructure was all but gone. The firebombing of Japanese cities, which were largely of wood, had been especially destructive.

Among the major powers, the Soviet Union was the hardest hit. It had suffered as many as 27 million dead. Aside from the catastrophic human cost, the Germans had occupied Russia's most productive regions, and the scorched-earth policy practiced by both sides resulted in the total or partial destruction of 1,700 towns, 70,000 villages, and 6 million buildings. Perhaps a quarter of the property value of the Soviet Union was lost in the war, and tens of millions of Soviet citizens were homeless. Simply feeding the Soviet population was a staggering task. All of this goes a long way toward explaining the subsequent policies, both internal and external, of the Soviet Union.

The Soviet Union gained considerable territory. It retained control of the Baltic States of Estonia, Latvia, and Lithuania and kept territory taken from Finland in 1940 and 1944 (after Finland had reentered the war on the German side in an effort to regain the territory lost in the Winter War), which gave it the port of Petsamo and the province of Karelia. The Soviets also received land from Romania and from Poland (with the restoration of the Curzon Line). Poland received compensation in eastern Germany. Peace treaties later confirmed most of these changes. In addition, Italy gave up some territory to France, Yugoslavia, and Greece. Italian colonies in Africa (Eritrea, Libya, and Italian

Somaliland) were placed under a trustee-ship by the United Nations. Hungary lost territory to Bulgaria and Czechoslovakia. Transylvania was restored to Romania, and Romania ceded land to Bulgaria. Japan lost its territories outside the home islands, including Korea and parts of China.

The Soviets received from Japan South Sakhalin Island and the Kuriles as well as concessions in Dalien, China, including the return of Port Arthur as a naval base. Outer Mongolia would continue to be independent of China, but China regained sovereignty over Manchuria. In effect these concessions sanctioned the replacement of Japanese imperialism with Soviet imperialism, but the Western leaders had thought these necessary to secure the timing of the Soviet entry into the Pacific War.

Far from destroying the Soviet Union and communism as he had sought, Hitler had strengthened it. Indeed, the Soviet Union emerged from the war regarded with the United States as one of the two so-called superpowers. The Soviet armies that had liberated Eastern Europe remained in place. Obsessed as always by security concerns and with much of his western territories devastated by the fighting, Stalin was determined to establish a tier of buffer states to protect the Soviet Union from the West and its influences. The only way to have prevented this was for the United States to have gone to war with the Soviet Union, which the American public was not prepared to sanction in 1945. Indeed, American military strategy had been predicated on defeating the Germans and Japanese at the least cost in American lives rather than securing long-range strategic goals. Churchill's pleas for the Western powers to "shake hands with the Russians as far east as possible" was largely ignored.

In China, the physical destruction and loss of life had also been great, but the end of the war and a struggle over Manchuria brought a renewal of the Chinese Civil War and an eventual communist victory.

The vast destruction in Western Europe did help to promote the movement for European integration, strongly aided by the United States in the 1947 Marshall Plan. This led to the European Common Market. The war also helped boost internationalism with the 1945 establishment of the United Nations, which had somewhat more power than its ineffectual predecessor, the League of Nations.

The war also greatly stimulated colonial unrest around the world. Where the colonial powers sought to hold on to their empires after August 1945, there was often fighting. France, seeking to retain its status as a Great Power, insisted on retaining its empire. This prompted the long Indochina War (1946–1954). Fighting also erupted in many other places, including Malaya and the Netherlands Indies, Africa, and the Middle East. Even where the European powers chose to withdraw voluntarily, as in the case of Britain in Palestine and the Indian subcontinent, there was fighting as competing forces sought to fill the vacuums. Wartime decisions about postwar occupation zones led to major confrontations regarding Germany that brought the Berlin Blockade (1948–1949) and the Korean War (1950–1953). The Soviet Union and the United States and their respective allies soon clashed in what became known as the Cold War (1946–1991), a direct result of World War II and in many ways a continuation of it.

Further Reading

Black, Jeremy. *World War Two: A Military History.* London: Routledge, 2003.

Dear, I. C. B., and M. R. D. Foot, eds. *The Oxford Companion to World War II.* New York: Oxford University Press, 1995.

Frank, Richard B. *Guadalcanal: The Definitive Account of the Landmark Battle.* New York: Penguin, 1992.

Hastings, Max. *Inferno: The World at War, 1939–1945.* New York: Knopf, 2011.

Keegan, John. *The Second World War.* New York: Viking, 1989.

Liddell Hart, B. H. *History of the Second World War.* New York: Putnam, 1970.

Morison, Samuel Eliot. *History of United States Naval Operations in World War II.* 15 vols. Boston: Little, Brown, 1947–1962.

Murray, Williamson, and Allan R. Millett. *A War to Be Won: Fighting the Second World War.* Cambridge, MA: Belknap, 2000.

Neillands, Robin. *The Bomber War: The Allied Air Offensive against Nazi Germany.* Woodstock, NY: Overlook, 2001.

Prange, Gordon W., Donald M. Goldstein, and Katherine V. Dillon. *At Dawn We Slept: The Untold Story of Pearl Harbor.* New York: McGraw-Hill, 1981.

Shirer, William L. *The Rise and Fall of the Third Reich: A History of Nazi Germany.* New York: Simon and Schuster, 1960.

Sledge, Eugene B. *With the Old Breed: At Peleliu and Okinawa.* New York: Presidio, 2007.

Spector, Ronald. *Eagle against the Sun: The American War with Japan.* New York: Free Press, 1985.

Tucker, Spencer C. *The Second World War.* New York: Palgrave Macmillan, 2004.

Tucker, Spencer C., ed. *The Encyclopedia of World War II: A Political, Social, and Military History.* 5 vols. Santa Barbara, CA: ABC-CLIO, 2004.

Weinberg, Gerhard L. *A World at Arms: A Global History of World War II.* New York: Cambridge University Press, 1994.

Willmott, H. P. *The Great Crusade: A New Complete History of the Second World War.* Revised ed. Washington, DC: Potomac Books, 2008.

Indochina War (1946–1954)

Dates	December 19, 1946–July 21, 1954
Location	Indochina
Combatants	France and French Indochina (State of Vietnam, Cambodia, and Laos) vs. Viet Minh
Principal Commanders	France: Philippe Leclerc, Jean de Lattre de Tassigny, Henri Navarre Viet Minh: Ho Chi Minh, Vo Nguyen Giap
Principal Battles	Haiphong, Hanoi, Cao Bang, Vinh Yen, Mao Khe, Hoa Binh, Dien Bien Phu
Outcome	The 1954 Geneva Conference establishes the states of Indochina as independent, but in the case of Vietnam there is a temporary division at the 17th Parallel, with national elections to reunify the country set for 1956.

Causes

Although there were other explosions of nationalist sentiment in the French Empire after World War II (most notably in Algeria in 1945 and in Madagascar in 1947), that in Indochina was by far the most damaging. Fought during 1946–1954 between the French and Vietnamese nationalists, the Indochina War was the first phase of what might be called the Second Thirty Years' War (the second phase being the Vietnam War of 1958–1975), the longest war of the 20th century.

The French had established themselves in Indochina in the 1840s, and by 1887 they had formed French Indochina, made up of the three divisions of Vietnam (Tonkin, Annam, and Cochin China) and the kingdoms of Cambodia and Laos. The cause of the war was the French refusal to recognize that the days of colonialism were over. In the aftermath of World War II, a weakened France was determined to hold on to its richest colony.

In 1941 veteran Vietnamese communist leader Ho Chi Minh had formed the Viet Minh to fight the Japanese, then in military occupation of Vietnam, and the French. A fusion of communists and nationalists, the Viet Minh had by 1944 liberated most of the northern provinces of Vietnam. The defeat of Japan in August 1945 created a power vacuum (all French troops in Indochina were in Japanese prison camps) into which Ho moved. At the end of August 1945, he established in Hanoi the provisional government of the Democratic Republic of Vietnam (DRV, North Vietnam), and on September 2, 1945, he proclaimed Vietnamese independence.

With no support from either the Soviet Union or the United States, Ho was forced to deal with France. He and French diplomat Jean Sainteny concluded an agreement in March 1946 to allow 15,000 French troops into North Vietnam, with the understanding that 3,000 would leave each year and all would be gone by the end of 1951. In return, France recognized North Vietnam as a free state within the French Union. France also promised to abide by the results of a referendum in Cochin China (southernmost Vietnam) to determine if it would be reunited with Annam (central Vietnam) and Tonkin (northern Vietnam).

The Ho-Sainteny Agreement fell apart with the failure of talks in France, the Fontainebleau Conference in the summer of 1946, to resolve outstanding substantive issues and with the decision of new French governor-general of Indochina Admiral Georges Thierry d'Argenlieu to proclaim on his own initiative the independence of a republic of Cochin China. Paris officials were not worried. They believed that the Vietnamese nationalists would not go to war against France and that if they did they would be easily crushed. Violence broke out in Hanoi in November 1946, whereupon d'Argenlieu ordered military action to bring the nationalists to heel. On November 23, 1946, the French cruiser *Suffren* shelled the port of Haiphong. Following a cease-fire, fighting began in Hanoi on December 19. The failure of the French government to realize that the days of colonialism were over had collided with Vietnamese nationalism.

Course

The French fought the Indochina War not so much for economic reasons (by 1950 French military expenditures surpassed the total value of all French investments there) but rather for political and psychological reasons. Perhaps only with its empire could France be counted a Great Power. Colonial advocates also argued that if France were to let go of Indochina, the rest of their overseas possessions, including those in North Africa, would soon follow. This idea bore some similarity to the domino theory held by many in the United States during the Vietnam War.

Course

Ho Chi Minh predicted how the war would be fought. It would be, he said, the war of the tiger and the elephant. The tiger could not meet the elephant in an equal contest, so he would lie in wait for it, drop on its back from the jungle, and rip huge hunks of flesh with his claws. Eventually, the elephant would bleed to death. The war played out very much along those lines.

Initially, it did not appear that way. With the defeat of Japan in World War II, French general Jacques-Philippe Leclerc arrived in Indochina with reinforcements. He used his small yet mobile force of about 40,000 men to dash through the country and secure southern Vietnam and Cambodia. The nationalist Viet Minh were quickly forced out into the countryside, and life returned to normal, or almost so. There were those who dreaded the Viet Minh's retreat into the jungle. Leclerc was one; he was convinced that the Viet Minh was a nationalist movement that France could not subdue militarily. Unlike most of his compatriots, he was aware of the great difficulties of jungle warfare and favored negotiations. In a secret report to Paris, Leclerc said that there would be no solution through force in Indochina.

Although the French Socialist Party showed interest in ending the war through peace talks, the steady drift of the French coalition government to the right and increasing bloodshed prevented this. Admiral d'Argenlieu and other French colonial administrators opposed meaningful concessions to the nationalists, and in the summer of 1946 Leclerc departed Indochina in frustration.

Leclerc was but the first in a succession of French military commanders. He was followed by Generals Jean-Etienne Valluy, Roger Blaizot, Marcel Carpentier, Jean de Lattre de Tassigny, Raoul Salan, Henri Navarre, and Paul Henri Romuald Ely. This frequent change in command undoubtedly affected the overall efficiency and morale of the French Far East Expeditionary Corps.

Most French leaders assumed that the conflict would be little more than a classic colonial reconquest, securing the population centers and then expanding outward in the classic oil slick (*tache d'huile*) method they had practiced so effectively in Morocco and Algeria. Meanwhile, the Viet Minh, led by former history teacher General Vo Nguyen Giap, steadily grew in strength and controlled more and more territory.

In May 1947 the French did make a stab at settling the war peacefully when Paul Mus traveled from Hanoi to meet with Ho Chi Minh in the latter's jungle headquarters. Mus was an Asian scholar sympathetic to the Vietnamese nationalist point of view and a personal adviser to Emile Bollaert, who had replaced d'Argenlieu as high commissioner. Mus told Ho that France would agree to a cease-fire on condition that the Viet Minh lay down some of their arms, permit French troops freedom of movement in their zones, and turn over some deserters from the French Foreign Legion. Ho rejected this offer, which was tantamount to surrender. In May, Bollaert declared that "France will remain in Indochina."

Despite its stated determination to hold on to Indochina, the French government never made the commitment in manpower necessary for it to have a chance to win. The war was essentially fought by the professional soldiers: officers and noncommissioned officers who led the French Expeditionary Corps. The French government never allowed draftees to be sent to

BATTLE OF DIEN BIEN PHU, MARCH 13, 1954

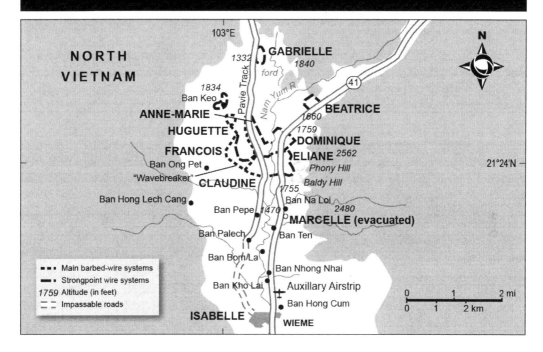

Indochina. The small number of effectives available to French commanders left them very few options as far as strategy was concerned. Shortages of noncommissioned officers, a lack of trained intelligence officers and interpreters, and little interest in or knowledge of the mechanics of pacification all hampered the French military effort.

The French held much of Cochin China in large part because the powerful religious sects and Buddhists there opposed the Viet Minh. The French also controlled the Red River Delta in the north, along with the capital of Hanoi. But the Viet Minh controlled much of the countryside, and the area they dominated grew as time went on. Initially, the Viet Minh largely withdrew into the jungle to indoctrinate and train their troops. The French invested little attention and resources to

pacification efforts, and their heavy-handedness alienated many Vietnamese. The French scenario had the Viet Minh eventually tiring of their cause and giving up. It never played out that way.

To increase available manpower, attract Vietnamese nationalist support, and quiet critics at home and in the United States, Paris sought to provide at least the facade of an indigenous Vietnamese regime as a competitor to the Viet Minh. After several years of negotiations, in March 1949 the French government concluded the Elysée Agreements with former emperor Bao Dai. These created the State of Vietnam, with Paris making the key concession that Vietnam was in fact one country.

The State of Vietnam allowed the French government to portray the war as a conflict between a free Vietnam and the communists—and thus not a colonial war at all. The U.S. government, which supported France in Indochina because with the arrival of the Cold War it desperately needed French military support in Europe, claimed to be convinced.

The problem for Vietnamese nationalists was that the State of Vietnam never truly became established. The French continued to control all of its institutions, and its promised army never really materialized. France simply took the recruited soldiers and added them to the French Expeditionary Corps, in which they were commanded by French officers. In effect, there were only two choices for the Vietnamese: either the Viet Minh or the French. The French therefore pushed Vietnamese nationalists into the Viet Minh camp.

In October 1947 the French mounted Operation LEA. Involving some 15,000 men and conducted over a span of three weeks, it was devoted almost exclusively to the capture of Ho Chi Minh and the Viet Minh leadership and the destruction of their main battle units. Operation LEA involved 17 French battalions, and while it succeeded in taking Thai Nguyen and some other Viet Minh–controlled cities, it failed both to capture the Viet Minh leadership and to destroy the main communist units. It also showed the paucity of French resources in Indochina. The troops in LEA were badly needed elsewhere, and their employment in the operation opened up much of the countryside to Viet Minh penetration. As time went on the military situation continued to deteriorate for the French, despite the fact that by the end of 1949 Paris had expended $1.5 billion on the war.

The Indochina War changed dramatically in the fall of 1949 when the communists came to power in China. That event and the recognition of the DRV by the People's Republic of China, while helping to change Washington's attitude toward the war, in effect lost the war for the French then and there. The long Chinese-Vietnamese border allowed the Chinese to supply arms and equipment to the Viet Minh across their common border and provided sanctuaries in China in which the Viet Minh could train and replenish their troops. And there were plenty of arms available from the substantial stocks of weapons, including artillery that the United States had previously supplied to the Chinese Nationalists.

With arms from China, the People's Army of Vietnam (PAVN, North Vietnamese Army) shifted rapidly to conventional forces. In April 1949 Giap commanded 32 regular battalions and 137 regional battalions. Two years later the PAVN included 117 regular battalions—progressively formed into regiments—and 37 regional battalions. Giap then brought the regiments together into brigades and then into divisions of some 10,000 men each. By mid-1952 the PAVN fielded five infantry divisions. They were soon joined by a heavy division of 12 infantry and 8 engineer regiments. The division provided heavy weapons support to the other divisions as needed. Giap now had a real army. PAVN forces were both well equipped and well trained. The troops were also highly motivated in consequence of intense political indoctrination.

The Korean War, which began in June 1950, profoundly affected the U.S. attitude toward the war in Indochina. Korea and Vietnam came to be viewed as mutually dependent theaters in a common Western struggle against communism. Washington now recognized the State of Vietnam and changed its policy of providing only indirect aid to the French effort in Indochina. In June 1950 President Harry S.

Truman announced that the United States would provide direct military assistance to French forces in Indochina and establish a military assistance and advisory group there. By the end of the Indochina War in 1954, the United States had provided a total of $2.5 billion in military aid to the French and was paying three-quarters of the cost of the war.

The French insisted that all U.S. military assistance be given directly to them rather than channeled through the State of Vietnam. Although a Vietnamese National Army was established in 1951, it remained effectively under French control, and France continued to dominate the State of Vietnam down to the 1954 Geneva Conference. Regardless, the Truman and Dwight D. Eisenhower administrations assured the American people that real authority in Vietnam had been handed over to the Vietnamese. With Paris refusing to concede real authority to the State of Vietnam, however, Vietnamese nationalists had no other recourse but the Viet Minh. In the end, Vietnamese nationalism was completely usurped by communism.

The Indochina War became an endless quagmire. By 1950, it was costing France between 40 and 45 percent of its entire military budget and more than 10 percent of the national budget. That same year, Giap and the Viet Minh won control of Colonial Highway (Route Coloniale) 4 (RC4), taking its French outposts. Located in the far north, it paralleled the Chinese frontier and ran from the Gulf of Tonkin to Cao Bang. The RC4 debacle cost the French 4,800 killed or missing. To make matters worse, the Viet Minh captured 13 artillery pieces, 112 mortars, 160 machine guns, and nearly 10,000 pistols, submachine guns, and rifles—enough weapons to arm an entire PAVN division.

With the loss of this critical China frontier section, for all practical purposes the war was over for France. The Viet Minh now had ready access to China. That the war was allowed to drag on past this point is proof of the dearth of political leadership in Paris.

In 1951 Giap, who believed that the circumstances were ripe for conventional large-unit warfare, went on the offensive in a effort to take Hanoi in Operations HOANG HOA THAM (March) and HA NAM NINH (May–June). His divisions were stopped cold by French forces led by General Jean de Lattre de Tassigny, probably the most capable of French commanders in the war. After these rebuffs, Giap simply shifted back to his phase two strategy of engaging the French in circumstances of his own choosing.

In late 1951 de Lattre initiated a battle outside the important Red River Delta area. What became the Battle of Hoa Binh (November 14, 1951–February 24, 1952) was a meat-grinder battle, as de Lattre envisioned, but for both sides. By the end of the battle the Viet Minh had suffered some 9,000 casualties, while the French had lost 894 killed or missing. But all the Viet Minh divisions had participated, and the troops had learned how to deal with French tactics and weapons. The Viet Minh had also penetrated the French defensive ring around Hanoi as never before.

Giap now undertook the conquest of the Thai Highlands in northwestern Vietnam. By the end of November 1952, Viet Minh units had penetrated to the Lao border. De Lattre had departed at the end of December, consumed by cancer. New French commander General Raoul Salan tried to halt this offensive by striking at Viet Minh supply lines. But Giap refused to take the bait, and Operation LORRAINE, which involved 30,000 French troops in special airborne, commando, and support formations, was soon in reverse. By December, Viet Minh units were still at the Lao border, and the French were back within their heavily fortified "de Lattre" defensive line of the Red River Delta.

The Viet Minh also made significant gains in central Vietnam. French control in the plateau area of the Central Highlands was narrowed to a few beachheads around Hue, Da Nang, and Nha Trang. The only areas where the French enjoyed real success were in Cochin China, thanks to the antipathy of religious sects and the Buddhists toward the Viet Minh, and in neighboring Cambodia.

In the spring of 1953, Giap assembled a powerful force to invade Laos. That country had an army of only 10,000 men supported by 3,000 French regulars. Giap employed four divisions totaling 40,000 men, and he had the assistance of 4,000 communist Pathet Lao troops. Once more, the French were compelled to disperse their slender resources. They were, however, successful in preventing the communists from overrunning the Plaine des Jarres, and in late April the French halted the Viet Minh and inflicted heavy casualties on them. The onset of the rainy season forced the Viet Minh to fall back on their bases, and Laos was saved for another summer.

In July 1953, new French commander General Henri Navarre arrived in Indochina. Buoyed by promises of increased U.S. military aid, Navarre attempted a "general counteroffensive." The press in both France and the United States gave much attention to the so-called Navarre Plan. Unknown to the public, however, was Navarre's own secret pessimistic assessment to his government that the war

could not be won militarily and the best that could be hoped for was a draw.

Using his increased resources (French forces, including troops of the French Union, and the Vietnam National Army, now numbered about 517,000 men, while the Viet Minh had perhaps 120,000), Navarre vowed to go over to the offensive. He ordered the evacuation of a series of small posts, and this was accomplished successfully. At the same time, the Vietnam National Army was given more responsibility, although this was a case of too little, too late.

To keep Giap off balance and on the defensive, Navarre launched a series of small attacks. The first of these, Operation HIRONDELLE (SWALLOW) on July 17, was a three-battalion (2,000-man) paratroop operation against the important Viet Minh base of Lang Son. The paratroopers then made their way overland to the coast and were evacuated by the French Navy. Although the operation secured quantities of Viet Minh weapons and supplies, it was more of a psychological lift than anything else.

Concurrently, Giap was gathering additional resources for a larger invasion of Laos. With five divisions he hoped to overrun all of Laos and perhaps Cambodia, then join up with Viet Minh units in the south for an assault on Saigon itself. In the meantime, some 60,000 guerrillas and five regular regiments would tie down the French in the north. In December 1953 and January 1954, the Viet Minh overran much of southern and central Laos.

Navarre's response was Operation CASTOR, the establishment of an airhead in far northwestern Vietnam astride the main Viet Minh invasion route into Laos. Navarre envisioned this either as a blocking position or as bait to draw some Viet Minh forces into a set-piece conventional battle, in which they would be destroyed by French artillery and airpower. The location Navarre selected, the village of Dien Bien Phu, was in a large valley, and the French conceded the high ground around it to the Viet Minh. When he was asked later how he got into this position, in an astonishing statement Navarre said that at the time the French arrived there the Viet Minh did not have artillery, so there was no danger from the heights. Dien Bien Phu was also a considerable distance, some 200 miles, by air from Hanoi, and the French had only a very limited transport airlift capability (approximately 100 aircraft).

Giap took the bait, but he sent four divisions rather than the one that Navarre had envisioned, to engage the French at Dien Bien Phu. The cumulative total of the French garrison was 16,544 men, while Giap committed some 50,000 troops, not counting logistical personnel. The siege of the French fortress lasted from March 13 to May 7, 1954. The battle's outcome was largely decided by two key factors: the Viet Minh's ability to bring Chinese-supplied artillery to the heights by means of an extensive supply network of coolies (the "People's Porters," Giap called them) and the inadequacy of French air support. Although there was some debate in Washington over possible U.S. military intervention (Operation VULTURE), President Dwight D. Eisenhower rejected it because the British refused to go along. On May 7, Brigadier General Christian Marie Ferdinand de la Croix de Castries surrendered the French garrison. During the siege the French suffered 1,600 killed, 4,800 wounded, and 1,600 missing. The Viet Minh immediately sent their 8,000 prisoners off on foot on a 500-mile march to prison camps. Less than half returned. Of Vietnamese taken, only 10 percent were seen again. The Viet Minh had

also shot down 48 French planes and destroyed 16 others on the ground. Viet Minh casualties amounted to some 7,900 killed and 15,000 wounded.

The French defeat at Dien Bien Phu allowed political leaders in Paris to shift the blame to the generals and at last bring the war to an end. Attention now turned to a conference previously scheduled in Geneva to deal with a variety of Asian problems. New French premier Pierre Mendès-France imposed a 60-day timetable for an agreement, threatening to resign if one was not reached. The Geneva Accords were announced on July 21.

At Geneva, the People's Republic of China and the Soviet Union pressured the Vietnamese into an agreement that gave them less than they had won on the battlefield. Cambodia and Laos were declared independent, but the key provision was recognition of the unity of Vietnam. Pending unification, however, there were to be an armistice and a *temporary* dividing line at the 17th Parallel. The agreements also provided for the compulsory regroupment of troops and, if they desired, civilians. Nationwide elections were to be held in two years.

In the Indochina War, the French and their allies sustained 172,708 casualties: 94,581 dead or missing and 78,127 wounded. These are broken down as 140,992 French Union casualties (75,867 dead or missing and 65,125 wounded), with allied Indochina states losing 31,716 (18,714 dead or missing and 13,002 wounded). Viet Minh losses were perhaps three times those of the French and their allies. Some 25,000 Vietnamese civilians also died.

Significance

Ultimately, a new government in South Vietnam headed by Ngo Dinh Diem refused to permit the elections, and the United States supported Diem in his stand. This led to a renewal of the war in an American phase.

For France, the struggle had been a distant one. Paris had not dared send draftees to Indochina, and the conflict had been fought largely by the professionals. The French government almost immediately transferred these men to Algeria, where an insurrection against French rule had begun. The soldiers pledged that this time there would be no political betrayal. In 1958 when this appeared imminent, the French Army brought down the Fourth Republic.

Further Reading

Duiker, William J. *The Communist Road to Power in Vietnam.* Boulder, CO: Westview, 1981.

Dunn, Peter M. *The First Vietnam War.* New York: St. Martin's, 1985.

Fall, Bernard, B. *Hell in a Very Small Place: The Siege of Dienbienphu.* Philadelphia: J. B. Lippincott, 1966.

Fall, Bernard B. *Street without Joy.* Harrisburg, PA: Stackpole, 1961.

Fall, Bernard B. *The Two Vietnams.* New York: Praeger, 1964.

Gras, General Yves. *Histoire de La Guerre d'Indochine.* Paris: Éditions Denoël, 1992.

Hammer, Ellen J. *The Struggle for Indochina.* Stanford, CA: Stanford University Press, 1954.

Kelly, George A. *Lost Soldiers: The French Army and Empire in Crisis, 1947–1962.* Cambridge, MA: MIT Press, 1965.

Maneli, Mieczyslaw. *The War of the Vanquished.* New York: Harper and Row, 1969.

Porch, Douglas. *The French Foreign Legion: A Complete History of the Legendary Fighting Force.* New York: HarperCollins, 1991.

Israeli War of Independence (1948–1949)

Dates	May 14, 1948–January 7, 1949
Location	Palestine
Combatants	Israel vs. Arab states of Egypt, Iraq, Lebanon, Syria, and Transjordan
Principal Commanders	Israel: David Ben Gurion, Yigel Allon, David Marcus Arab states: Ahmed Ali el-Mawawi
Principal Battles	Jerusalem, Malkya, Degania, Lod, Ramle, Gaza
Outcome	Israel secures its independence, but much of the Palestinian Arab population is displaced, and the Arab states refuse to recognize the existence of Israel.

Causes

The causes of the Israeli War of Independence, also known as the First Arab-Israeli War, are deep-rooted. Nineteenth-century nationalism in Europe also impacted Jews. Persecutions of Jewish populations in Europe late in that century, especially in Russia and Poland but also to a lesser extent in Central and Western Europe (for example, the Dreyfus Affair in France), led to the establishment of the Zionist movement, or desire among many Jews for a national state. Palestine, the historic homeland of the Jews before the Diaspora, was the favored and most likely location for such a state, and Jews throughout Europe contributed to the purchase of land there. Mostly

East European Jews emigrated and settled in Palestine.

In order to secure the support of world Jewry for the Allied cause in World War I, in 1917 the British government issued the Balfour Declaration, which expressed support for the formation of a Jewish national homeland in Palestine. Increased Jewish immigration and continued loss of Arab lands through purchase by Jews, however, inflamed the Arab population of Palestine, which as a consequence of World War I became a British mandate. Violence flared in Palestine in what became a triangular struggle among the British authorities, the Arabs, and the Jews.

There was thus already considerable violence in Palestine by World War II, when the Holocaust, the Nazi effort to eradicate the Jewish people, which resulted in the deaths of about 6 million Jews, heightened sympathy worldwide for the survivors. The Holocaust also greatly increased the determination of Jews to establish a nation-state as the only effective means to guarantee their future security. Sympathy for this was especially strong in the United States, which had the largest population of Jews in the world and where Jews were an important political pressure group.

After World War II and with Britain determined to quit an increasingly divided and violent Palestine, efforts were made to partition Palestine into Jewish and Arab states. These plans failed—largely on Arab intransigence—and the neighboring Arab states mobilized their forces for the anticipated military showdown.

Violence between Arabs and Jews was already under way when, with the expiration of the British mandate on May 14, 1948, Jewish Palestinian leader David Ben-Gurion announced the independence of the State of Israel. The United States,

closely followed by the Soviet Union, recognized the new Jewish state. The Jewish declaration, however, touched off the first Arab-Israeli war of May 15, 1948–January 7, 1949.

Course

Arab forces ranged against Israeli included regulars from Egypt, Iraq, Lebanon, Syria, and Transjordan, supplemented by volunteers from Libya, Saudi Arabia, and Yemen. Officially, the Arab forces operated under the auspices of the Arab League, formed in 1945. King Abdullah of Transjordan was named commander in chief of the Arab armies, although cooperation among the Arab forces was almost nonexistent, which was a chief cause of their military failure throughout the course of the war.

The Arab states anticipated an easy military victory, and on paper the odds certainly favored them. The Arab armies not only heavily outnumbered Jewish forces but also retained a wide edge in heavy weaponry.

On May 14, the Arab League announced its intention to create a unified Palestinian state to include the Jewish and Arab regions of the United Nations (UN) partition plan. On May 26, the Israeli government created the Israel Defense Forces (IDF), incorporating the irregular Jewish militias that had existed under the British mandate, to include the Haganah, led by Israel Galili, and the Palmuch, commanded by Yigel Allon. The IDF initially numbered fewer than 30,000 troops, but by mid-July it had more than doubled in size. The IDF continued to grow exponentially, and by the end of 1948 it numbered more than 100,000 troops. At least initially, these forces had virtually no heavy weapons in the form of artillery, armored vehicles, or aircraft.

ARAB-ISRAELI WAR, 1948

Principal Arab attacks from outside Palestine

Territory allocated to the state of Israel by the United Nations, but overrun by Arabs between May 15 and Jun 1, 1948

Territory remaining under Israeli control on Jun 1, 1948

● Jewish settlements overrun by the Arabs between May 15 and Jun 1

● Jewish settlements surrounded by Arab forces, but resisting repeated attempts to overrun them between May 15 and Jun 1

LEBANON

SYRIA

33°N

Malkiya
Kadesh
Nahariya
Acre
Mishmar Hayarden
Haifa
Ein Gev
Naharayim
Afula
Degania
Gesher
IRAQI TROOPS

Mediterranean
Sea

Hadera

Nablus

Herzliya
Tel Aviv
Jaffa

TRANSJORDAN 32°N

Ben Shemen
Atarot
Neve Yaakov
Kfar Menachem
Mt Scopus
Hartuv
Kallia
Bet Haarava
Nitzanim
Kedma
Massuot Yizhak
Revadim
Ein Tzurim
The Jewish Quarter: Old City of Jerusalem
Gat
Galon
Gush Etzion
Yad Mordechai
Dead Sea

Kfar Darom

Beersheba
Nirim
Nevatim

Sodom

31°N

EGYPT

ISRAEL

SINAI

NEGEV

Jordan R.

0   10   20 mi
0   10   20 km

34°E   35°E   36°E

N

The combined Arab armies, which began the conflict with some 30,000 troops, increased in size to only 40,000 men in July 1948 and 55,000 by October. Most independent observers expected the Arabs to score a quick military victory largely because they enjoyed a crushing superiority in heavy weapons at the beginning of the conflict.

As the fighting continued, the Israeli government was able to secure some arms from abroad, beginning with a shipment of 25 aircraft from Czechoslovakia in late May. That nation continued to provide weapons to the IDF for the remainder of the war, even during UN-mandated cease-fires that prohibited arms sales to any belligerent.

During the first phase of the war of May 14–June 1, in the central part of the front Arab armies from Transjordan and Iraq advanced on Jerusalem with the aim of driving all Jews from the city. The best Arab fighting force in the war, the Transjordan Arab Legion, secured the eastern and southern portions of the new part of the city. It also occupied most of Old Jerusalem and laid siege to the remainder. Although Jewish forces, ably led by American volunteer Colonel David Marcus, failed to break through the Arab roadblock on the Tel Aviv–Jerusalem road, they managed to construct a new access road to Jerusalem through the mountains just before a UN-sponsored truce went into effect on June 11.

Meanwhile, Lebanese and Syrian forces invaded Palestine from the north. The Lebanese were stopped at Malkya. The Syrian invasion, which was both larger and supported by tanks and artillery, was defeated by Jewish settlers at Degania, the oldest kibbutz in Palestine, although they possessed only light weapons. The Israelis

also blunted an ineffective Iraqi invasion that crossed the Jordan River south of the Sea of Galilee. Soon the Iraqi Army shifted to a defensive posture in the regions of Jenin and Nablus.

Only in the south did Arab forces register significant territorial gains. Here two Egyptian brigades commanded by Major General Ahmed Ali el-Mawawi advanced into Palestine. The principal Egyptian force moved up the coastal road to take Gaza and threaten Tel Aviv. A smaller force moved inland from Abu Ageila by way of Beersheba toward Jerusalem. Although the Egyptian coastal force secured Ashdod, only 25 miles from Tel Aviv, it bogged down shortly thereafter. The inland column succeeded in making contact with the Arab Legion at Bethlehem on May 22.

The first phase of the war ended with a UN-declared truce that went into effect on June 11. Although the truce included an arms embargo for all belligerents, both sides in the war saw this as an opportunity to rest, resupply, and reequip their forces, and the Israelis were able to smuggle in arms and ammunition from Czechoslovakia during the monthlong truce.

During the cease-fire, UN mediator Folke Bernadotte advanced a new partition plan, but both sides immediately rejected it. On July 9 the cease-fire collapsed, and the IDF assumed the offensive. The second phase of the war occurred during July 9–18.

In the renewed fighting, the primary IDF objective was to regain control of the vital Tel Aviv–Jerusalem corridor in the central sector. In heavy fighting, the IDF secured the corridor after a massive assault on Lod (Lydda) that included the first Israeli use of bomber aircraft. Defended by Transjordanian troops and supplemented by Palestinian irregulars and units of the Arab

Liberation Army, Lod surrendered on July 11. The next day the IDF captured Ramle, another key location in the vital corridor.

In the north the IDF launched Operation DEKEL, a major push against Syrian and Lebanese troops in the lower Galilee region. The IDF captured Nazareth on July 16. Only against Egyptian forces in the southern sector did the IDF fail to make any significant progress in the July fighting. Here the IDF goals were to sever Egyptian supply lines and reopen communications with the Negev. The second phase of the war (July 9–18) ended with another UN-brokered truce, which went into effect on July 18.

Bernadotte presented yet another partition plan, this time calling for Transjordan to annex the Arab regions. It also called for the creation of an independent Jewish state and the establishment of Jerusalem as an international city. All belligerents again rejected the plan, and on September 17, the day after Bernadotte had presented his latest solution to the conflict, he was assassinated by Israeli members of Lehi, a Zionist militia.

The truce remained in effect until October 15, when the third phase of the war (October 15–November 5, 1948) began. The IDF ended the cease-fire with a series of offensives designed to drive Arab armies completely from Israeli territory. The first strike was against Egyptian Army troops in the Negev. Operation YOAV, commanded by Yigal Allon, sought to cut off the Egyptian troops along the coast from those to the interior in the Negev. The success of this operation forced the Egyptian Army to abandon the northern Negev.

The IDF also enjoyed success in the northern sector. On October 24 Operation HIRAM commenced in the upper Galilee region, with the IDF destroying remnants of the Arab Liberation Army, driving Lebanese forces completely out of Palestine, and pushing several miles into Lebanon. Shaky cease-fires were arranged in the north between Israeli and Syrian and Lebanese forces on November 30.

The fourth and final phase of the war occurred between November 19, 1948, and January 7, 1949, beginning with an Egyptian Army offensive on November 19. Although they failed in their design of relieving the Faluja pocket, the Egyptians were able to expand their coastal holdings around Gaza.

With cease-fires holding elsewhere, beginning on December 20, 1948, the IDF launched a major offensive designed to drive Egypt from the war. The IDF isolated Rafah on December 22 and secured Asluj and Auja during December 25–27. Halted by Egyptian forces in their effort to take El Arish, the Israelis turned to the northeast. With the IDF about to launch a major attack on Rafah, Egypt requested an immediate armistice, which the UN Security Council granted. The cease-fire went into effect on January 7, 1949.

With the cease-fire, UN mediator Dr. Ralph Bunche began armistice discussions between Israel and the Arab belligerent states. Armistice agreements, but no peace treaties, were ultimately concluded between Israel and all the Arab belligerents except Iraq. The arrangement with Egypt went into effect on February 24. It left Egyptian troops in occupation of the Gaza Strip. In the March 23 agreement with Lebanon, Israel agreed to withdraw from territory it had captured in southern Lebanon. The Israeli-Transjordan armistice of April 3 allowed Transjordanian troops to remain in control of the West Bank and East Jerusalem. The Israeli-Syrian armistice of July 20 resulted in the creation of a demilitarized zone along the Israeli-Syrian border.

Significance

The Israeli War of Independence ended with the new Jewish state occupying about three-fourths of the former British mandate of Palestine, or about 50 percent more land than offered in Bernadotte's original partition proposal. The war claimed about 6,000 Israeli lives, one-third of them civilians. Arab losses were much higher, about 10,000 killed.

Although the figure is in dispute, as many as 1 million Arab Palestinians may have either voluntarily left or were driven from their homes and lands, forced to live in makeshift refugee camps in the adjacent Arab states, which insisted on keeping them in refugee camps until they were allowed to return. Refugee status has been passed on to their descendants, who have been denied citizenship in their host countries on the insistence of the Arab League in order to preserve their Palestinian identity "and protect their right of return to their homeland." More than 1.4 million Palestinians still live in 58 recognized refugee camps, while more than 5 million Palestinians live outside Israel and the Palestinian Territories.

Some 10,000 Jews were displaced by the war. After the war, many Jews either voluntarily left or were expelled by the Arab states, and a number of them and other Jews living elsewhere in the world moved to Israel to help build the new Jewish state. From May 1948 to the end of 1951 some 700,000 Jews settled in Israel, in effect doubling its Jewish population.

This relatively small and short war had immense consequences. The surprising Israeli victory humiliated the Arab states and fueled demand for revenge, which continues in 2015. Indeed, this dynamic resulted in two major wars—the 1967 Six-Day War and the 1973 Yom Kippur/Ramadan War—as well as many smaller conflicts, incursions, and terror attacks. Failure to reach a comprehensive peace settlement would see vast sums spent on armaments (in both Israel and Arab nations) rather than on infrastructure and social programs. The lack of a peace settlement also embroiled the major world powers in a series of crises, many of which revolved around the securing of the area's vast oil supplies, and would become a constant source of unrest in the Middle East. In the 21st century, this perennially unstable environment produced a major war in Iraq and significant rebellions in Yemen, Egypt, Libya, and Syria. It has also led to the rise of extremist, fundamentalist Islamic groups such as the Islamic State of Iraq and the Levant (ISIS), which now imperils Iraq as well as Syria.

Further Reading

Bowyer Bell, John. *Terror Out of Zion: The Fight for Israeli Independence.* New Brunswick, NJ: Transaction Publishers, 1996.

Bregman, Ahron. *Israel's Wars: A History since 1947.* London: Routledge, 2002.

Heller, Joseph. *The Birth of Israel, 1945–1949: Ben-Gurion and His Critics.* Gainesville: University Press of Florida, 2001.

Herzog, Chaim. *The Arab-Israeli Wars: War and Peace in the Middle East.* New York: Random House, 1982.

Joseph, Dov. *The Faithful City: The Siege of Jerusalem, 1948.* New York: Simon and Schuster, 1960.

Karsh, Efraim. *The Arab-Israeli Conflict: The Palestine War, 1948.* New York: Osprey, 2002.

Krämer, Gudrun. *A History of Palestine: From the Ottoman Conquest to the Founding of the State of Israel.* Princeton, NJ: Princeton University Press, 2011.

Kurzman, Dan. *Genesis 1948: The First Arab-Israeli War.* New York: World Publishing, 1970.

Lustick, Ian. *From War to War: Israel vs. the Arabs, 1948–1967.* New York: Garland, 1983.

Morris, Benny. *1948: The First Arab-Israeli War.* New Haven, CT: Yale University Press, 2008.

Pollack, Kenneth M. *Arabs at War: Military Effectiveness, 1948–1991.* Lincoln: University of Nebraska Press, 2002.

Rogan, Eugene L., and Avi Shlaim, eds. *The War for Palestine: Rewriting the History of 1948.* 2nd ed. Cambridge: Cambridge University Press, 2007.

Sachar, Howard M. *A History of Israel.* New York: Knopf, 1979.

Tucker, Spencer C., ed. 2 vols. *The Encyclopedia of the Arab-Israeli Conflict: A Political, Social, and Military History.* 2 vols. Santa Barbara, CA: ABC-CLIO, 2008.

Korean War (1950–1953)

Dates	June 25, 1950–July 27, 1953
Location	Korea
Combatants	Democratic People's Republic of Korea (North Korea) and People's Republic of China vs. Republic of Korea (South Korea), the United States, and 15 other nations formed into the United Nations Command
Principal Commanders	North Korea: Kim Il Sung, Pak Hun Yong, Choe Yong Gun China: Mao Zedong, Peng Dehuai South Korea: Syngman Rhee, Chae Pyong Dok, Chung Il Kwon United States: Harry S. Truman, Dwight D. Eisenhower, Douglas MacArthur, Walton Walker, Matthew B. Ridgway, Mark Wayne Clark, James Van Fleet
Principal Battles	Kaesong, Seoul (first), Osan Taejon, Busan (Pusan) Perimeter, Incheon (Inchon), Seoul (second), Wonsan, Pyongyang, Ch'ongch'on River, Changjin Reservoir Campaign
Outcome	Communist forces are driven from South Korea, but the Korean Peninsula remains divided and continues as one of the world's flashpoints.

Causes

The Korean War was a watershed event in the history of the 20th century. It was both the first shooting war of the Cold War and the first limited war of the nuclear age. The Korean War was also the first United Nations (UN) war and the only time since World War II that two major powers—the United States and China—had met on the battlefield.

Situated as it was between the major powers of China, Russia, and Japan, Korea was fated to have a stormy history. The country was long the nexus of big-power confrontation and war, first between China and Japan and then between Japan and Russia. After having defeated both China in 1894–1895 and Russia in 1904–1905, Japan controlled Korean affairs and integrated it into the Japanese economy. Korea has been a single entity during its modern history, however. The 38th Parallel dividing line between the present Democratic People's Republic of Korea (DPRK, North Korea) and the Republic of Korea (ROK, South Korea) is simply an arbitrary political line that divides a country forming a single geographic, ethnic, and economic unit.

The division of Korea (and that of Vietnam, another post–World War II hot spot) into two hostile states resulted from arbitrary decisions taken at the end of World War II concerning the surrender of Japanese forces. In these decisions, neither the Koreans nor the Vietnamese were consulted.

As World War II (1939–1945) drew to a close, U.S. president Franklin Roosevelt was determined to get the Soviet Union into the war against Japan in order to reduce anticipated heavy American casualties in an invasion of the Japanese home islands, even if the price for this might be temporary Soviet occupation of much of Northeast Asia. Roosevelt also staked his presidency on cooperation with the Soviet Union, which he saw as essential in preserving stability in the postwar world. In endeavoring to reach some arrangement with Soviet leader Joseph Stalin on the future of Northeast Asia, Roosevelt and his advisers proposed that a postwar international trusteeship be set up for Korea under the United States, Great Britain, China, and the Soviet Union. Although the Cairo Declaration stated that Korea was to become "independent in due course," there was no agreement on specifics.

U.S.-Soviet relations deteriorated following the war when it became clear that for the Soviet Union, the alliance had been a marriage of convenience only. This became evident with the end of the fighting in Europe, when Soviet territorial and

security demands became manifest. U.S. president Harry S. Truman, who took office following the death of Roosevelt in April 1945, then took a harder line toward Moscow.

After the United States dropped two atomic bombs on Japan and the Soviet Union had declared war on that country, on August 10, 1945, Japan requested an armistice. This spurred efforts to secure a Korean occupation agreement. With Soviet troops rapidly advancing in Manchuria and the nearest U.S. troops 600 miles from Korea on Okinawa, two American officers were instructed to secure the best possible territorial arrangement. They recommended the 38th Parallel, which divided the country roughly in half and placed the Korean capital of Seoul in the American zone. President Truman approved this arrangement on August 15, and it was sent to Moscow. Stalin did not object. On August 15 Tokyo agreed to allied surrender terms, and on September 8 U.S. occupation forces began arriving at the Korean port of Incheon (Inchon).

The Korean occupiers, north and south, found a land seething with pent-up political frustration and rampant nationalism, all fueled by returning exiles. Koreans of whatever political stripe, having suffered nearly a half century of Japanese occupation, wanted immediate independence and not a trusteeship or allied occupation. Certainly they did not want a divided nation. But few outside of Korea thought of these arrangements as anything other than temporary.

Both the Soviets and the Americans each now installed a group of Korean advisers in their two zones. These were hardly democratic and were certainly strongly conservative in the American zone and staunchly procommunist in the northern zone. In

Korean War, 1950 – 1953

Limit of North Korean advance, Jun-Sep 1950
Limit of United Nations advance, Nov 1950
Limit of Chinese advance, Jan 1951
Armistice Line, Jul 27, 1953
Battle site
Principal railroads
Principal Chinese railroad supply lines
Principal roads

December 1946 a legislative assembly opened in the American zone.

By September 1947, frustrated with the failure to settle the future of Korea by direct negotiation with the Soviet Union, the United States referred the problem to the UN. The UN General Assembly recognized Korea's right to independence and planned for the establishment of a unified government and withdrawal of the occupation forces. The General Assembly established the United Nations Temporary Commission on Korea (UNTCOK) with the goal of securing a free and independent Korea. In January 1948 UNTCOK representatives arrived in Seoul to supervise elections for a national constituent assembly.

UNTCOK was refused admission to the Soviet zone, and it then recommended elections in South Korea for a new national assembly. This duly met in May 1948; its invitation for representatives of North Korea to attend was ignored. In August 1948 the ROK was officially proclaimed in South Korea, with a strong presidential regime headed by the staunchly conservative former exile Syngman Rhee. He was also widely detested by more democratic elements in Korea, and many of the ROK's key figures, including military leaders, had served the Japanese. But Washington wanted stability, although its slavish support of Rhee brought the enmity of many Korean radicals. The U.S. military government was terminated, and the new Korean government entered into an agreement with the United States for the training of its forces.

In September 1948 the DPRK, which also claimed authority over the entire country, was inaugurated in North Korea under the presidency of veteran communist Kim Il Sung. Kim, leader of the so-called Gapsan faction of former anti-Japanese guerrilla fighters, became the paramount leader.

In December the UN General Assembly endorsed South Korea as having the country's only lawfully elected Korean government. That same month the Soviet Union announced that it had withdrawn all its forces from North Korea. The United States completed withdrawal of its occupation forces from South Korea in June 1949.

In September 1949, UNTCOK reported its failure to mediate between the two Korean states and warned of impending civil war. Beginning in April 1948, there had been sporadic fighting. Indeed, Allan Millett states unequivocally that the Korean War began on April 3, 1948, in the Chejudo Rebellion, in which communist guerrillas mounted attacks against the South Korean government. Estimates of the dead in this rebellion during 1948–1950 range from 30,000 to as many as 100,000 people. There were also clashes along the 38th Parallel involving battalion-size units on both sides that claimed hundreds of lives. Two of the largest were launched by North Korea south of the 38th Parallel in the Ongjin Peninsula in May and August 1949.

Both Rhee and Kim Il Sung were fervent nationalists determined to unify their country during their lifetimes. Indeed, Rhee's support for a possible military solution to the reunification question led the U.S. State Department to go out of its way to disassociate itself from these activities. In April 1948 President Truman approved a policy statement to the effect that the United States should not become so irrevocably involved that an action taken by any faction in Korea or by any other power there could be considered a cause for war for the United States. This U.S. government attempt to adopt a hands-off policy encouraged Kim in his belief that the United States would not fight for Korea. Then on January 12, 1950, U.S. secretary of state Dean Acheson further distanced the United States when, in the course of a speech to the National Press Club, he specifically excluded both Korea and Taiwan from the Asian "defensive perimeter" of vital strategic interests that the United States would fight to defend.

The U.S. Joint Chiefs of Staff (JCS) reached the same conclusion, and in 1949 in two separate interviews, U.S. commander in the Far East General Douglas MacArthur outlined a defense perimeter for the United States that excluded Taiwan as well as Korea. Republicans in Congress then demanded U.S. defense for Formosa, but no such move was made regarding Korea.

On June 25, 1950, the DPRK's armed forces mounted a massive conventional invasion of South Korea across the 38th Parallel. The communist bloc claimed steadfastly that the war had begun in a South Korean attack on North Korea and that Rhee had hoped thereby to bring about American involvement and a war in which the two Koreas would be reunited under his leadership. The communists maintained that North Korean, Soviet, and Chinese policy was merely reactive. This position found a supporter in U.S. scholar Bruce Cumings, but more recent scholarship holds that border clashes diminished in the period from October 1949 to the spring of 1950, because Stalin sought to prevent the possibility of a war developing before North Korea was completely ready. Soviet foreign minister Gromyko informed ambassador to the DPRK Colonel General Terenti Shtykov that Pyongyang must cease all military operations without prior approval from Moscow, and the border between north and south remained quiet until the June invasion.

The timing of the North Korean attack was conditioned by the need to plant rice in March and then harvest it in September. Until the breakup of the Soviet Union, the reasons behind the attack were shrouded in mystery. At the time many observers believed it to be a diversionary attack by the communist world to divert U.S. attention away from Europe, where the Russians had just suffered a rebuff in the Berlin Blockade (1948–1949). Others considered it to be soft-spot probing to test U.S. resolve or a demonstration to show the world that America was a paper tiger. Some even saw it to be part of an elaborate plot by Stalin to unseat Mao Zedong in China. Most Americans believed that Moscow had initiated events in Korea as part of some global chess move.

But the reasons behind the invasion were local, not global. Rhee's government had suffered a major reversal in what was a relatively free election. Kim Il Sung judged that Rhee might be about to fall from power, and given the announced American position and his own attitude, the moment seemed ripe for an invasion. As early as September 1949 he had sought Soviet support for a military operation to seize the Ongjin peninsula and perhaps territory south of the 38th Parallel all the way to Kaesong. The Soviets demurred, believing that it would result in a protracted civil war that would be disadvantageous to North Korea and to the Soviets, allowing the United States to increase aid to the Rhee government and agitation against the Soviet Union.

Kim Il Sung secretly met with Stalin in Moscow in April 1950 concerning an invasion. Kim provided Stalin what turned out to be wildly exaggerated promises of the prospects of a North Korean military success, communist revolution in South Korea, and American abstention from intervention. Certainly both Moscow and Beijing were actively involved in preparations for the invasion as early as the spring of 1949.

Course

When the war began in June 1950, North Korea had every military advantage. Its Korean People's Army (KPA) numbered some 130,000 men with heavy artillery, 151 T-34 tanks, and about 180 aircraft, including fighters and twin-engine bombers. In South Korea, the Republic of Korea Army (ROKA) was unprepared militarily because of U.S. unease about Rhee unleashing a war to reunify Korea but also because there were insufficient funds in a shrunken U.S. defense budget. In 1950 the U.S. military itself was stretched thin and was relatively small, poorly trained, and inadequately equipped. The army was just nine divisions. ROK armed forces numbered about 95,000 men. No ROKA unit had progressed beyond regimental-level training, and the ROKA lacked heavy artillery, tanks, and even antitank weapons, to include mines. Its sole aircraft were trainers and liaison types. Worse, ROKA ammunition stocks were sufficient for only six days of combat.

Kim Il Sung fully expected to overrun South Korea quickly; indeed, the invasion plan called for this to be completed within 22–27 days. He also promised Stalin a concurrent communist revolution in South Korea and insisted that Washington would not intervene. Stalin himself concluded that even if the United States did move to defend South Korea, it would come too late. Soviet military aid was substantial, and its personnel in North Korea took a key role in planning the invasion.

Stalin's approval had been contingent on the support of Chinese leader Mao Zedong, and indeed Stalin insisted that Kim meet with Mao. As a result, Kim's KPA included at least 16,000 members of the People's Liberation Army, consisting of Korean volunteers who had fought against the Japanese in World War II and in the Chinese Civil War thereafter and were released by Mao, along with their weapons and equipment. They played a key role in the subsequent KPA invasion.

The invasion caught MacArthur, who was in Tokyo, and Washington by surprise. Fighting along the border between North and South Korea had died down, and U.S. government officials did not think that the communist camp would risk a nuclear war. Although Truman called it "the most difficult decision" of his presidency, U.S. intervention was certain, given the Truman Doctrine, domestic political fallout from the communist victory in China in 1949, and the belief that a communist success in Korea would embolden the communists elsewhere.

Within hours of the June 25, 1950, invasion, the UN Security Council called for an immediate cease-fire and the withdrawal of the KPA. A Soviet boycott allowed action, and on June 27 the Security Council asked member states to furnish assistance to South Korea. President Truman extended U.S. air and naval operations to include North Korea, and he authorized U.S. forces to protect the vital port of Busan (Pusan).

Upon the recommendation of U.S. Far Eastern Command (FEC) commander General MacArthur, Truman committed FEC ground forces to the war on June 30. The United States then had four poorly trained and equipped divisions in Japan. By cannibalizing his 7th Infantry Division,

MacArthur was able to dispatch the 24th and 25th Infantry Divisions and the 1st Cavalry Division to Korea within two weeks.

Meanwhile, the war was going badly for the ROK. At the time of the invasion, four ROKA divisions were stretched out over more than 200 miles of linear front. (The remaining ROKA divisions were engaged in training and counterguerrilla operations.) This was some 9.5 miles a regiment, far more than was possible to defend. There were few natural obstacles to impede the KPA, and the ROKA was also forced to defend the cul-de-sac of the Ongjin peninsula. Only a valiant effort by the 6th Division on the Chunchon front allowed the remainder of the ROKA to regroup and erect the Han River defensive line, delaying the KPA offensive. Seoul fell on June 28.

In one of the key strategic blunders of the war, KPA troops halted to regroup for three days. They did not begin crossing the Han River until July 1. A mistaken decision by ROKA chief of staff Major General Chae Pyong Dok led to the four bridges over the Han being blownup hours before this was necessary, preventing thousands of troops and their heavy equipment from reaching South Korea.

On July 5 the first American ground unit—Task Force Smith of only 540 men—entered the war at Osan, 50 miles south of Seoul. The false sense of optimism that the mere presence of American troops would give the North Koreans pause was quickly dispelled when KPA tanks easily brushed the poorly equipped Americans aside.

At the request of the UN Security Council, the UN set up a military command in Korea. Washington insisted on a U.S. commander, and on July 10 Truman appointed MacArthur to head the United Nations Command (UNC). Sixteen nations contributed military assistance, and at peak strength UNC forces numbered about 400,000 ROK troops, 250,000 U.S. troops, and 35,000 troops from other nations. The largest of these was the 1st Commonwealth Division from Britain and Canada, while Turkey provided a brigade. Other nations provided smaller numbers of troops or noncombat assistance in the form of medical units.

The communist revolution, predicted by Kim Il Sung for South Korea, failed to materialize. Meanwhile, difficult terrain, primitive logistics, poor communication, and floods of refugees delayed the North Korean advance as much as did the defenders, but by mid-July UNC troops had been pushed back into the so-called Pusan Perimeter, an area of 30–50 miles in southeastern Korea around Pusan. In desperate fighting, ROK and U.S. forces held. This may be attributed to their artillery, U.S. Air Force control of the skies, and the brilliant improvised mobile defense led by Lieutenant General Walton Walker, commander of the Eighth U.S. Army in Korea (EUSAK). The KPA also had failed early to employ its manpower advantage and mount simultaneous attacks along the entire perimeter.

Even as the battle for the Pusan Perimeter raged, MacArthur was planning an amphibious assault behind enemy lines. Confident that it could hold, he deliberately weakened EUSAK to build up an invasion force. He selected Incheon as the invasion site. Only 15 miles from Seoul, it was nearly astride the KPA's main supply line south. The recapture of nearby Seoul would also deal North Korea a major political blow.

A landing at Incheon was risky, and almost everyone except MacArthur opposed it. Mines were stacked and waiting but, fortunately, had not been laid. Still, the problems were daunting. On September 15 Major General Edward Almond's X Corps of the 1st Marine Division and the 7th Infantry Division commenced the invasion. Supported by naval gunfire and air attacks, the marines soon secured Incheon, and UNC forces reentered Seoul on September 24. EUSAK also broke out of the Pusan Perimeter. Driving north, it linked up with X Corps on September 26. Only one-quarter to one-third of the KPA escaped into North Korea. During their retreat northward, the KPA took with them thousands of South Koreans and forced them to serve in their army.

By this time, there was enormous pressure in the United States on Truman to expand the war. Both Republicans and Democrats sought to defeat the communists, not merely to "contain" them, and MacArthur was himself perhaps the most outspoken proponent of changing the war aims to include total victory. Truman, Secretary of State Dean Acheson, and new secretary of defense George C. Marshall had decided to take the war into North Korea, which exceeded the UNC's mission. On October 7 the UN General Assembly passed a resolution calling for "a unified, independent, and democratic" Korea. Washington used this as justification to enter North Korea.

With Pyongyang having ignored MacArthur's call for surrender, on October 1 ROKA troops crossed into North Korea. On October 9, MacArthur ordered U.S. forces to follow. The advance was rapid, and Pyongyang fell on October 19.

MacArthur now committed a major strategic blunder, retaining X Corps as a separate command under Almond and dividing his forces for the drive to the Yalu River. MacArthur ordered X Corps sent by sea to the east coast port of Wonsan with the task of clearing northeastern Korea, while EUSAK remained on the west coast to drive into northwest Korea. The two commands were now separated by a gap of between 20 and 50 miles. MacArthur believed, falsely as it turned out, that the Nangnim mountain range would obviate large-scale communist operations there.

All went well at first. EUSAK crossed the Ch'ongch'on River at Sinanju, and by November 1 elements of the 24th Division were only 18 miles from the Yalu. Several days earlier a reconnaissance platoon of the ROK 6th Division reached the Yalu, the only UNC unit to get there.

China now entered the war, albeit unofficially through the guise of "volunteers." Alarmed by a U.S. military presence adjacent to Manchuria, Mao had issued repeated warnings about potential Chinese military intervention. Actually, he was planning to intervene even before UNC troops crossed the 38th Parallel, but on September 30 Kim requested intervention. Mao was confident. He believed that the United States would be unable to counter Chinese numbers and that American troops were soft and unused to night fighting.

On October 2, Mao informed Stalin that China would enter the war. Stalin agreed to shift Soviet MiG-15 fighters already in China to the Korean border to cover the Chinese buildup and prevent U.S. air attacks on Manchuria. Soviet pilots began flying combat missions on November 1. Stalin ordered other Soviet air units to deploy to China, train Chinese pilots, and then turn over aircraft to them. Ultimately there were some 26,000 Soviet military personnel involved. Soviet pilots bore the brunt of the air war. Although ordered to pretend they were Chinese, they soon dropped this pretense because it was impractical in combat.

Stalin had no intention of using Soviet airpower for anything other than defensive purposes, but the Chinese later angrily claimed that he had promised full air support for their ground forces. Still, Stalin had helped China establish the world's third-largest air force.

On October 25 Chinese troops entered the fighting in northwestern Korea, and Walker wisely brought the bulk of EUSAK south of the Ch'ongch'on. The Chinese offensive then slackened. The Chinese also attacked in northeastern Korea before halting operations and breaking contact there as well. The initial Chinese incursion ended on November 7.

In a meeting with President Truman at Wake Island on October 15, MacArthur had assured the president that the war was all but won but that if the Chinese intervened their forces would be slaughtered by UNC airpower. Yet from November 1, 1950, to October 1951, MiGs so dominated the Yalu River area that U.S. B-29 bombers had to cease daylight operations. It is hard to understand how MacArthur, who touted himself as an expert on Asia, could so misread Chinese intentions and capabilities.

The initial Chinese intervention numbered 18 "volunteer" divisions. In early November the Chinese moved an additional 12 into Korea, totaling some 300,000 men. MacArthur now ordered the destruction of the bridges over the Yalu. Washington revoked the order, but MacArthur complained of the threat to his command, and Washington gave in. The bombing on November 8 had little effect, however; most of the Chinese were already in North Korea, and the Yalu was soon frozen. Sheer manpower numbers would overcome Chinese logistical limitations.

Meanwhile, American leaders in Washington debated how to proceed. The political leadership and the JCS under chairman General Omar Bradley believed that Europe had to remain the top priority. Washington decided that while Manchuria would remain off limits, MacArthur could take other military steps he deemed advisable, including resuming the offensive. The Democrats were especially reluctant to show lack of resolve in Korea, for the Republicans who blamed them for the "loss" of China had gained seats in the November 1950 congressional elections.

While much was made in the United States about the prohibitions of strikes on Manchuria, it should be pointed out that the communist side also exercised restraint. With the exception of a few ancient biplanes that sporadically struck UNC positions at night, communist airpower was restricted to north of Pyongyang. No effort was made to strike Pusan, and UNC convoys traveled without fear of air attack, even at night with lights blazing. Nor did communist forces attempt to disrupt UNC sea communications.

MacArthur had made X Corps dependent logistically on EUSAK instead of Japan, and Walker insisted on delaying resumption of the offensive until he could build up sufficient supplies. Poor weather was also a problem, but Walker agreed to resume the offensive on November 24. To the east, X Corps was widely dispersed.

MacArthur was oblivious to any threat, confident that this would be an occupation rather than an offensive. The offensive went well on the first day, but on the night of November 25–26 the Chinese struck EUSAK in force. On November 26 the ROKA II Corps gave way under the massive Chinese assault, exposing EUSAK's right flank. The Chinese poured 18 divisions into the gap, threatening the whole of EUSAK. In a brilliant delaying action at Kunu-ri, the U.S. 2nd Division bought time for the other EUSAK divisions to get across the Ch'ongch'on. MacArthur now ordered a retirement just below the 38th Parallel to protect Seoul.

Washington directed MacArthur to pull X Corps out of northeastern Korea. Under heavy Chinese attack, X Corps withdrew to the coast for seaborne evacuation along with the ROK I Corps. The retreat of the 1st Marine Division and some army elements from the Changjin Reservoir ranks as one of the most masterly withdrawals in military history. X Corps was then redeployed to Pusan by sea. At Hungnam through December 24, 105,000 officers and men were taken off, along with some 91,000 Korean refugees who did not want to remain in North Korea.

The Korean War had entered a new phase; in effect, the UNC was now fighting China. MacArthur refused to accept a limited war and publicized his views to his supporters, making reference to "inhibitions" placed upon him. UNC morale plummeted, especially with General Walker's death in a jeep accident on December 22. Not until Lieutenant General Matthew Ridgway arrived to replace Walker did the situation improve. In the United States, meanwhile, Truman found himself under heavy pressure from Republicans to pursue the war vigorously. But fearing a wider war, possibly even a worldwide conflagration involving the Soviet Union, the administration reduced its goal to restoring the status quo ante bellum.

UNC troops were again forced to retreat when the Chinese launched a New Year's offensive, retaking Seoul on January 4, 1951. But the Chinese People's Volunteer Army soon outran its supply lines, and Ridgway began a methodical, limited advance designed to inflict maximum

punishment rather than secure territory. Ridgway rejected suggestions from several of his key subordinates for an amphibious landing that might have trapped large numbers of communist troops. Nonetheless, by the end of March UNC forces had recaptured Seoul, and by the end of April they were north of the 38th Parallel.

On April 11, 1951, President Truman relieved MacArthur of command, appointing Ridgway in his stead. Lieutenant General James Van Fleet took over EUSAK. Truman and MacArthur saw the war quite differently. MacArthur saw the conflict as a great anticommunist crusade that would reverse the Chinese Revolution. He made no secret of his desire to expand the war and had made his case for this publicly. MacArthur sought to bomb Manchuria, employ Chinese nationalist troops in Korea, and unleash nationalist forces on Taiwan against the Chinese mainland. This position elicited some support from among so-called Asia Firsters in the United States, notably members of the Republican Party, but it found little support in the UN or among West European leaders.

Although widely unpopular at the time, MacArthur's removal was fully supported by the JCS. The general returned home to a hero's welcome, but political support soon faded, as did MacArthur's hopes, however faint, of a run for president in 1952.

On April 22, the Chinese counterattacked. Rather than expend his troops in a defensive stand, Van Fleet ordered a methodical withdrawal, employing artillery firepower and air strikes against the communist forces. The Chinese pushed the UNC south of the 38th Parallel, but the offensive was halted by May 19. UNC forces then counterpunched, and by the end of May the front stabilized just above the 38th Parallel. The JCS now generally limited EUSAK to that line, allowing only small local advances to secure more favorable terrain.

The war now became one of position, essentially a stalemate. In these circumstance, a diplomatic settlement seemed expedient. On June 23, 1951, Soviet UN representative Jacob Malik proposed a cease-fire. With the Chinese expressing interest, Truman authorized Ridgway to open negotiations. Meetings began on July 10 at Kaesong, although hostilities continued.

UNC operations from this point were essentially designed to minimize friendly casualties. Both sides had now built deep defensive lines that would be costly to break through. In August armistice talks broke down, and later that month the Battle of Bloody Ridge began, developing into the Battle of Heartbreak Ridge, which lasted until mid-October. In late October negotiations resumed, this time at Panmunjom. The fighting continued, with half of the war's casualties occurring during the period of armistice negotiations.

On November 12, 1951, Ridgway ordered Van Fleet to cease offensive operations. Fighting now devolved into raids, local attacks, patrols, and artillery fire. In February 1953 Lieutenant General Maxwell D. Taylor took command of EUSAK. UNC air operations intensified to choke off communist supply lines and reduce the likelihood of offensive action. By now also, the burden was shifting to the ROKA, which was adding one new trained division each month and was inflicting more than half of the casualties on KPA and Chinese units. The Chinese especially targeted South Korean units. In July 1953, the last month of the war, the ROKA suffered 25,000 casualties.

In the United States, meanwhile, Truman's popularity had plummeted because of the war, and he refused to stand for reelection. In November 1952 General Dwight Eisenhower was elected president on a mandate to end the war. With U.S. casualties running 2,500 a month, the conflict had become a political liability. Eisenhower instructed the JCS to draw up plans to end the war militarily, including the possible use of nuclear weapons. Talk of this was allowed to circulate publicly. More important in ending the conflict, however, was Stalin's death on March 5, 1953.

As the armistice negotiations entered their final phase in May, the Chinese stepped up military action, initiating attacks in June and July to remove bulges in the line. UNC forces gave up some ground but inflicted heavy casualties.

Prisoner repatriation remained the chief obstacle to an agreement, and the use of prisoners as propaganda tools was the main reason the war continued. The North Koreans and Chinese had forced into their army many South Koreans, and thousands of them had subsequently been taken prisoner. If all KPA prisoners were repatriated, many South Koreans would be sent to North Korea. Also, many Chinese prisoners did not wish to return to China but sought refuge on Taiwan. Truman, who had seen the consequences of the forced repatriation of Russian citizens from Western Europe after World War II, was determined that none would be repatriated against their will. The communist side rejected the UNC position out of hand and sought to use the prisoners to tar the UNC with the patent lie of germ warfare and immoral air operations against North Korea.

Following intense UNC air strikes on North Korean hydroelectric facilities and the capital of Pyongyang, the communists accepted a face-saving formula whereby a neutral commission would handle prisoner repatriation. Syngman Rhee, who was adamantly opposed to any peace settlement that did not include the reunification of the two Koreas, almost sabotaged the peace agreement with the release of some 27,000 North Korean prisoners just weeks before the final agreement. Rhee was only placated by Washington's pledge of military and financial aid in the U.S.-ROK Mutual Defense Treaty of August 1953. (Had Rhee not agreed to honor the armistice, the Eisenhower administration might have been forced to implement Operation EVER-READY, its secret but risky plan to remove him from office.) Finally, on July 27 an armistice was signed at Panmunjom, and the guns fell silent.

Of 132,000 North Korean and Chinese military prisoners of war, fewer than 90,000 chose to return home. Twenty-two Americans held by the communists also elected not to return home, a shock to the American public. Of 10,218 Americans captured by the communists, only 3,746 returned; the remaining 6,472 perished. Perhaps four times that number of South Korean prisoners also died. ROK forces sustained some 257,000 military deaths, while U.S. war-related deaths numbered 36,574. Other UNC killed came to 3,960. North Korea has released no casualty figures, but its military deaths are estimated at 295,000. Chinese deaths from all causes might approach 1 million. Perhaps 900,000 South Korean civilians died during the war from all causes.

Significance

The Korean War absolutely devastated the country and hardened the divisions between North Korea and South Korea. Democracy was also a casualty, for the corrupt Rhee regime rode roughshod over its opposition. Certainly the war was a sobering experience for the United States,

used to total victory. But after the war the United States, which had disarmed after previous conflicts, kept its military establishment strong with substantial, sustained increases in the national defense budget. The United States also saw a considerable expansion in presidential powers.

The Korean War institutionalized the Cold War national security state. The war also effectively militarized U.S. foreign policy. Before the war, Marshall Plan aid had been almost entirely nonmilitary. Aid now shifted heavily toward military rearmament.

The Korean War also solidified the role of the United States as the world's policeman and strengthened the country's relationship with its West European allies and the North Atlantic Treaty Organization (NATO). The war greatly facilitated the rearmament of the Federal Republic of Germany (West Germany) and dramatically impacted in a favorable way the Japanese economy. At the same time, the war also led Washington to extend direct military American assistance to the French fighting in Indo-China, placing the United States on the slippery slope to the Vietnam War.

The Korean War had important consequences for America domestically. The war ended 20 years of control by the Democratic Party, and the racial integration of the U.S. armed forces implemented during the war greatly impacted the civil rights movement of the 1960s. The war also accelerated an economic and political reorientation from the global North and Northeast to the South, Southwest, and West.

China gained greatly from the war, which added immensely to its prestige. China now came to be regarded as the preponderant military power in Asia. In the following decades, concerns over Chinese military strength was woven into the fabric of American foreign policy. These concerns influenced subsequent U.S. policy in Vietnam.

No formal peace has been concluded in Korea. Technically the two Koreas remain at war. The demilitarized zone and the Northern Limitation Line in the Yellow Sea constitute one of the world's flashpoints.

Further Reading

Allen, Richard C. *Korea's Syngman Rhee: An Unauthorized Portrait.* Rutland, VT: Charles E. Tuttle, 1960.

Appleman, Roy E. *United States Army in the Korean War: South to the Naktong, North to the Yalu.* Washington, DC: Office of the Chief of Military History, 1961.

Bai, Bong. *Kim Il Sung: A Political Biography.* 3 vols. New York: Guardian Books, 1970.

Bailey, Sydney D. *The Korean Armistice.* New York: St. Martin's, 1992.

Blair, Clay. *The Forgotten War: America in Korea, 1950–1953.* New York: Times Books, 1987.

Cumings, Bruce. *The Korean War.* New York: Modern Library, 2010.

Cumings, Bruce. *The Origins of the Korean War.* 2 vols. Princeton, NJ: Princeton University Press, 1990.

Edwards, Paul G. *The Inchon Landing, Korea, 1950.* Westport, CT: Greenwood, 1994.

Ent, Uzal E. *Fighting on the Brink: Defense of the Pusan Perimeter.* Paducah, KY: Turner, 1996.

Foot, Rosemary. *A Substitute for Victory: The Politics of Peacemaking at the Korean Armistice Talks.* Ithaca, NY: Cornell University Press, 1990.

Goncharov, Sergei, John W. Lewis, and Xue Litai. *Uncertain Partners: Stalin, Mao and the Korean War.* Stanford, CA: Stanford University Press, 1993.

Hermes, Walter, Jr. *U.S. Army in the Korean War: Truce Tent and Fighting Front.* Washington, DC: Office of the Chief of Military History, 1966.

Kim, Chum-Kon. *The Korean War, 1950–1953.* Seoul: Kwangmyong, 1980.

Kim, Jinwung. *A History of Korea: From "Land of the Morning Calm" to States in Conflict.* Bloomington: Indiana University Press, 2012.

Korean Institute of Military History. *The Korean War.* 3 vols. Seoul: Republic of Korea Ministry of National Defense, 1997–1999.

Li, Xiaobing. *A History of the Modern Chinese Army.* Lexington: University Press of Kentucky, 2007.

Millett, Allan R. *The War for Korea, 1945–1950: A House Burning.* Lawrence: University Press of Kansas, 2005.

Millett, Allan R. *The War for Korea, 1950–1951: They Came from the North.* Lawrence: University Press of Kansas, 2010.

Montross, Lynn, and Nicholas A. Canzona. *U.S. Marine Operations in Korea,* Vol. 2, *The Inchon-Seoul Operation.* Washington, DC: U.S. Marine Corps Historical Branch, 1954–1957.

Mossman, Billy C. *United States Army in the Korean War: Ebb and Flow, November 1950–July 1951.* Washington, DC: U.S. Army, Center of Military History, 1990.

O'Neill, Mark A. "The Other Side of the Yalu: Soviet Pilots in Korea." Unpublished PhD dissertation, Florida State University, 1996.

Paige, Glenn D. *The Korean Decision, June 24–30.* New York: Free Press, 1968.

Pierpaoli, Paul G., Jr. *Truman and Korea: The Political Culture of the Early Cold War.* Columbia: University of Missouri Press, 1999.

Sawyer, Robert K. *Military Advisors in Korea: KMAG in Peace and War.* Washington, DC: Office of the Chief of Military History, U.S. Army, 1962.

Scalapino, Robert A., and Lee Chong-Sik. *Communism in Korea,* 2 vols. Berkeley: University of California Press, 1973.

Simmons, Robert R. *The Strained Alliance: Peking, Pyongyang, Moscow, and the Politics of the Korean War.* New York: Columbia University Press, 1975.

Spanier, John W. *The Truman-MacArthur Controversy and the Korean War.* Cambridge, MA: Belknap, 1959.

Stueck, William W., Jr. *Rethinking the Korean War: A New Diplomatic and Strategic His-*

tory. Princeton, NJ: Princeton University Press, 2004.

Suh, Dae-Sook. *Kim Il Sung: The North Korean Leader.* New York: Columbia University Press, 1988.

Truman, Harry S. *Memoirs.* 2 vols. Garden City, NY: Doubleday, 1955–1956.

Tucker, Spencer C., ed. *Encyclopedia of the Korean War.* 3 vols., revised ed. Santa Barbara, CA: ABC-CLIO, 2010.

Van Ree, Eric. *Socialism in One Zone: Stalin's Policy in Korea, 1945–1947.* Oxford: Oxford University Press, 1988.

Vietnam War (1958–1975)

Dates	1958–1975
Location	Indochina
Combatants	Democratic Republic of Vietnam (North Vietnam) and South Vietnamese communists (Viet Cong) vs. Republic of Vietnam (South Vietnam), the United States, and allied nations
Principal Commanders	North Vietnam: Ho Chi Minh, Pham Van Dong, Vo Nguyen Giap South Vietnam: Ngo Dinh Diem, Nguyen Van Thieu United States: Lyndon Baines Johnson, Richard M. Nixon, Paul Harkins, William C. Westmoreland, Creighton Abrams
Principal Battles	Ap Bac, Gulf of Tonkin Incident, Ia Drang Valley, Operation BARREL ROLL, Operation ROLLING THUNDER, Khe Sanh, Tet Offensive, Hue, Hamburger Hill, Cambodian Incursion, Easter Offensive, Operation LINEBACKER II, Quang Tri (first), Loch Ninh, An Loc, Quang Tri (second), Buon Me Thuot, Xuan Lac
Outcome	South Vietnam falls to the communist forces, and North and South Vietnam are reunited as the Socialist Republic of Vietnam.

Causes

The Vietnam War (also known as the Second Indochina War) grew out of the First Indochina War (1946–1954). The 1954 Geneva Conference, called to deal with Asian problems, ended the First Indochina War between France and the Vietnamese nationalists, dominated by the communists and known as the Viet Minh. Pressed by its chief backers, the People's Republic of China and the Soviet Union, the Viet Minh settled for less than they had won on the battlefield. The Geneva Accords provided for the independence of Cambodia, Laos, and Vietnam. In a victory for the Viet Minh, the agreement established Vietnam as one nation but also temporally divided it at the 17th Parallel, pending national elections to be held in 1956. Viet Minh political cadres were permitted to remain in southern Vietnam to prepare for the elections that would unify the country. In the meantime, Viet Minh military forces were to withdraw north of that line and French forces south of it. The war left two competing entities, the northern communist-led Democratic Republic of Vietnam (DRV) and the southern French-dominated State of Vietnam (SV), created during the war. Each claimed to be the legitimate government of a united Vietnam.

In June 1954, SV titular head Emperor Bao Dai appointed as premier Roman Catholic Ngo Dinh Diem, whom Bao Dai believed to have the backing of the United States. Diem's base of support was narrow, being limited largely to minority Catholics, rich and powerful Vietnamese, and foreign interests. But his base of support was greatly strengthened by the addition of some 800,000 northern Catholics who took advantage of the Geneva Accords that allowed relocation north and south and who had been moved from the Hanoi area to southern Vietnam in large measure by the U.S. Navy.

Diem solidified his hold on power by moving against and defeating the religious sects and the organized crime syndicate in Saigon, the Binh Xuyen. In a subsequent power struggle between Bao Dai and Diem, in October 1955 Diem established the Republic of Vietnam (RVN), with himself as president.

Eager to support this new "democracy" during this Cold War era of containing the spread of communism, U.S. president Dwight D. Eisenhower and Secretary of State John Foster Dulles began sending aid to the new regime. During Eisenhower's last six years as president, U.S. aid to the RVN totaled $1.8 billion. Most of this went to the RVN military budget. Only minor sums were set aside for education and social welfare programs. The aid thus little affected the lives of the preponderantly rural South Vietnamese populace and therefore provided communist organizers a powerful propaganda issue with which to generate opposition to the SV government among the neglected peasantry.

As Diem consolidated his power, U.S. military advisers reorganized the RVN armed forces. Known as the Army of the Republic of Vietnam (ARVN), it was equipped with American weaponry. The U.S. Military Advisory Group (MAAG) overrode Vietnamese arguments for a lightly armed, highly mobile force capable of combating guerrillas and insisted that the military be organized to fight a conventional invasion from northern Vietnam, as in the recently concluded Korean War (1950–1953) that still exerted a psychological hold on the U.S. military.

Fearing a loss, Diem refused to conduct the scheduled 1956 elections. This jolted veteran communist DRV leader Ho Chi Minh. Ho had not been displeased with Diem's crushing of his internal opposition but was now ready to reunite the country under his sway and believed that he would win the elections. Northern Vietnam was more populous than southern Vietnam, and the communists were well organized there. The Eisenhower administration backed Diem's defiance of the Geneva Agreements, fortified by the containment policy that sought to halt the spread of communism wherever it threatened; the domino theory, which held that if southern Vietnam were to fall to the communists, the other states of Southeast Asia would surely follow; and the belief that the communists, if they came to power, would never permit a democratic regime.

Course

Diem's decision led to a renewal of fighting, which became the Vietnam War. Various dates have been advanced for its start, from 1954 to as late as 1959. (The U.S. government has settled on 1958.) Fighting certainly occurred in earnest in 1957 when Diem moved against the 6,000–7,000 Viet Minh political cadres who had been allowed to remain in southern Vietnam to prepare for the 1956 elections. Although this is a matter of some controversy, the Viet Minh in southern Vietnam probably began the insurgency on their own initiative but were subsequently supported by the DRV government.

The insurgents came to be known as the Viet Cong (VC, for "Vietnamese Communists"). In December 1960 they established the National Liberation Front (NLF) of South Vietnam. Supposedly independent, it was certainly completely controlled by Hanoi. The NLF program called for the overthrow of the Saigon government, its replacement by a "broad national democratic coalition," and the "peaceful" reunification of Vietnam.

In September 1959 DRV defense minister Vo Nguyen Giap established Transportation Group 559 in order to send supplies and men south along what came to be known as the Ho Chi Minh Trail, much of which ran through supposedly neutral Laos. The first wave of infiltrators was native southerners and Viet Minh who had relocated in northern Vietnam in 1954. The trail grew increasing complex and sophisticated as time went on, and the resupply effort came to include a naval group that moved supplies south by sea.

VC sway meanwhile expanded, spreading out from safe bases to one village after another. The insurgency was fed by the weaknesses of the central government, by communist use of terror and assassination, and by Saigon's appalling ignorance of the movement and corruption within its government. By the end of 1958 the insurgency had reached the status of conventional warfare in several South Vietnamese provinces. In 1960 the communists carried out even more assassinations, and guerrilla units attacked ARVN regulars, overran district and provincial capitals, and ambushed convoys and reaction forces.

By mid-1961 the Saigon government had lost control over much of rural South Vietnam. Infiltration was as yet not significant, and most of the communist weapons were either captured from the ARVN or left over from the war with France. As had been the case with another American ally, Generalissimo Jiang Jieshi (Chiang Kai-shek) of China, Diem rejected American calls for meaningful reform until the defeat of the VC and establishment of full security. He did not understand that the war was primarily a political problem and could be solved only through political means. Diem used 80 percent of his aid funds for internal security. He also estranged himself from the peasants. Little was done to carry out land reform, and by 1961 75 percent of the land in South Vietnam was owned by 15 percent of the population.

Diem, who practiced the divide-and-rule concept of leadership, remained largely isolated in Saigon from his people, choosing to rely on family members and a few other trusted advisers for advice. He increasingly delegated authority to his brother Ngo Dinh Nhu and the latter's secret police. Diem resisted U.S. demands that he promote senior officials and military officers on the basis of ability rather than loyalty to him and that he pursue the war aggressively.

By now the John F. Kennedy administration, which took office in January 1961, was forced to reevaluate its position toward the war, but increased U.S. involvement was inevitable, given Washington's commitment to resist communist expansion and the domino theory. In May 1961 Kennedy sent several fact-finding missions to Vietnam. These led to the Strategic Hamlet program—concentrating the rural population in locations for better defense and isolating South Vietnamese peasants from NLF influence—as part of a general strategy emphasizing local militia defense,

VIETNAM WAR, 1964 – 1967

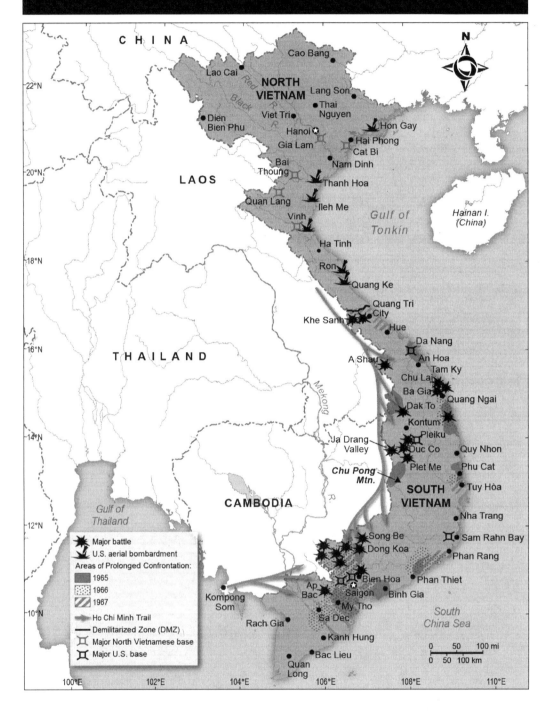

C H I N A

Cao Bang

Lao Cai

NORTH VIETNAM

Lang Son

Thai Nguyen

Viet Tri

Dien Bien Phu

Hon Gay

Hanoi

Gia Lam

Hai Phong

Cat Bi

Bai Thoung

Nam Dinh

LAOS

Thanh Hoa

Quan Lang

Ileh Me

Vinh

Gulf of Tonkin

Hainan I. (China)

Ha Tinh

Ron

Quang Ke

THAILAND

Quang Tri City

Khe Sanh

Hue

Da Nang

A Shau

An Hoa

Tam Ky

Chu Lai

Ba Gia

Quang Ngai

Dak To

Kontum

Pleiku

Ia Drang Valley

Duc Co

Quy Nhon

Chu Pong Mtn.

Plet Me

Phu Cat

Tuy Hòa

SOUTH VIETNAM

Nha Trang

Gulf of Thailand

Song Be

Dong Koa

Sam Rahn Bay

Phan Rang

Bien Hoa

Phan Thiet

Ap Bac

Saigon

Binh Gia

Kompong Som

My Tho

South China Sea

Rach Gia

Sa Dec

Kanh Hung

Quan Long

Bac Lieu

CAMBODIA

Mekong

Legend:

Major battle

U.S. aerial bombardment

Areas of Prolonged Confrontation:

1965

1966

1967

Ho Chi Minh Trail

Demilitarized Zone (DMZ)

Major North Vietnamese base

Major U.S. base

0   50   100 mi

0   50   100 km

and to the commitment of additional U.S. manpower. The United States also steadily increased its military presence in South Vietnam. By the end of 1961 U.S. strength there had grown to around 3,200 men, mostly in helicopter units and as advisers.

In February 1962 the United States established a military headquarters in Saigon, when the MAAG was replaced by the Military Assistance Command, Vietnam (MACV), under General Paul D. Harkins to direct the enlarged American commitment. Harkins, who rarely ventured outside of Saigon, agreed with Diem that reforms should await the defeat of the VC. The infusion of U.S. helicopters and additional support for the ARVN probably prevented a VC military victory in 1962. The VC soon developed tactics to effectively cope with the helicopters, however, and again the tide of battle turned in the communists' favor.

Meanwhile, Nhu's crackdown on the Buddhist opposition to government policies increased opposition to Diem's rule. A number of frustrated and ambitious South Vietnamese generals now planned a coup, and after Diem rejected repeated calls for reforms, Washington gave the plotters tacit support. On November 1, 1963, the generals overthrew Diem, murdering both him and Nhu. Kennedy, who was shocked at Diem's assassination, was also soon dead. Himself assassinated on November 22, he was succeeded by his vice president, Lyndon B. Johnson.

The United States seemed unable to win the war either with Diem or without him. A military junta now took power, but none of those who followed Diem had his prestige. Coups and countercoups occurred, and much of South Vietnam remained in turmoil. Not until General Nguyen Van Thieu became president in 1967 was there a degree of political stability.

Both sides steadily increased the stakes, apparently without foreseeing that the other might do the same. In 1964 Hanoi took three major decisions. The first was to send south units of its regular army, the People's Army of Vietnam (PAVN, known to the Americans as the North Vietnamese Army, or NVA). The second was to rearm its forces in South Vietnam with modern communist-bloc weapons, giving the PAVN a firepower advantage over the ARVN, still equipped largely with World War II–era U.S. infantry weapons. The third was to order direct attacks on American installations, provoking a U.S. response.

On August 2, 1964, the so-called Gulf of Tonkin Incident occurred when DRV torpedo boats attacked the U.S. destroyer *Maddox* gathering electronic intelligence in international waters in the Gulf of Tonkin. A second reported attack two days later on the *Maddox* and another U.S. destroyer, the *Turner Joy,* most certainly never occurred, but Washington believed this was the case, and this led the Johnson administration to order retaliatory carrier air strikes against DRV naval bases and fuel depots (Operation PIERCE ARROW) on August 5, the start of U.S. air operations over North Vietnam. The Johnson administration also went to Congress to secure what amounted to a blank check to wage war in Vietnam. Congress voted nearly unanimously on August 7 for the Gulf of Tonkin Resolution. Signed into law on August 10, it authorized the president to use whatever force he deemed necessary to protect U.S. interests in Southeast Asia.

Johnson would not break off U.S. involvement in Vietnam, stating privately that he feared possible impeachment if he did so. At the same time, he refused to make the tough decision of fully mobilizing the country for the war and committing the resources necessary to win it, concerned that this would destroy his cherished Great Society social programs.

The ARVN was not faring well against the VC. Communist forces had employed hit-and-run tactics, but in the Battle of Binh Gia (December 28, 1964–January 1, 1965) 40 miles southwest of Saigon, some 1,800 VC engaged a total of 4,300 supposedly elite ARVN troops in a conventional battle and soundly defeated them. The ARVN suffered 201 killed, 192 wounded, and 68 missing. Five U.S. advisers were also slain. VC killed were 34–200. Both sides saw the battle as a watershed in that well-trained VC forces supplied with modern weapons were capable of fighting and winning large battles. The battle also signaled the beginning of a mix of guerrilla and conventional warfare.

During June 9–12, 1965, two VC regiments totaling some 1,500 men attacked the newly established special forces camp at Dong Xoai in Phuoc Long Province held by 400 Montagnard Civilian Irregular Defense Group (CIDG) troops and 24 U.S. personnel staffing the camp. In their attack, the VC employed AK-47 assault rifles (the first time in the war by a VC unit). Saigon dispatched reinforcements, which were then ambushed. Some 2,000 ARVN troops were eventually involved fighting the VC. On the ARVN side, the battle claimed 416 killed, 174 wounded, and 233 missing. U.S. forces lost 29 killed or wounded and 13 missing. Some 200 civilians also died. MACV estimated VC casualties at 700, although dead left behind totaled only 134. (Throughout the war MACV and communist casualty claims were always widely different, with each side exaggerating enemy losses.)

The North Vietnamese leadership expected to win the war in 1965. Taking their cue from Johnson's own pronouncements

to the American people, they mistakenly believed that Washington would not commit ground troops to the fight. Yet Johnson did just that. Faced with Hanoi's escalation, however, in March 1965 U.S. marines arrived with the mission of protecting the large American air base at Da Nang, South Vietnam's second-largest city. The marines' mission soon expanded to seeking out nearby communist forces.

A direct attack on U.S. military advisers at Pleiku in February 1965 led to a U.S. and Republic of Vietnam Air Force (RVNAF) air campaign against North Vietnam (Operation FLAMING DART, February 7–14). The operation targeted PAVN military bases north of the demilitarized zone (DMZ) dividing North and South Vietnam near the 17th Parallel.

Johnson hoped to win the war on the cheap, relying heavily on airpower. Known as Operation ROLLING THUNDER (March 2, 1965–October 31, 1968) and paralleled by Operation BARREL ROLL (December 14, 1964–March 29, 1973), the secret bombing of Laos, which became the most heavily bombed country in the history of warfare, the air campaign would be pursued in varying degrees of intensity over the next three and a half years. Its goals were to force Hanoi to negotiate peace and to halt infiltration into South Vietnam.

The bombing resulted in the destruction of more than half the DRV's bridges, almost all of its large petroleum storage facilities, and nearly two-thirds of its power-generating plants. It also killed some 52,000 Vietnamese. DRV air defenses cost the United States nearly 1,000 aircraft, hundreds of prisoners of war, and hundreds of airmen killed or missing in action. Altogether the U.S. Air Force, U.S. Navy, and U.S. Marine Corps flew almost 1 million sorties (one plane, one mission) and dropped nearly three-quarters of a million tons of bombs. ROLLING THUNDER failed, however, to achieve its stated major political and military objectives.

In the air war, Johnson decided on "graduated response" rather than the massive strikes advocated by the military. He and his secretary of defense Robert McNamara believed that there was some point at which North Vietnamese leaders would halt their support for the southern insurgency, but what would have been unacceptable to the United States was perfectly acceptable to the DRV leadership. Gradualism became the grand strategy employed by the United States in Vietnam. Haunted by the Korean War, at no time would Johnson consider an invasion of North Vietnam, fearful of provoking a Chinese intervention.

By May and June 1965 with PAVN forces regularly destroying ARVN units, General William C. Westmoreland, who had replaced Harkins in June 1964 as MACV commander, appealed for U.S. ground units, which Johnson committed. As PAVN regiments appeared ready to launch an offensive in the rugged Central Highlands and then drive to the sea, splitting South Vietnam in two, Westmoreland mounted a spoiling attack with Major General Harry W. O. Kinnard's recently arrived 1st Cavalry Division (Airmobile) formed around some 450 helicopters.

In the Battle of the Ia Drang Valley (October 19–November 26), the 1st Cavalry Divison won one of the war's rare decisive encounters in what was also the first battle between American regulars and PAVN forces. Although there are conflicting opinions over PAVN commander Chu Huy Man's strategic objective, the outcome may have derailed Hanoi's hopes of winning a decisive victory before full American might could be deployed. During the

hard-fought battle, Boeing B-52 Stratofortress strategic bombers were called in to provide close ground support. MACV gave casualty figures of 305 killed, while PAVN dead were estimated at 3,561.

Heavy personnel losses on the battlefield, while regrettable, were entirely acceptable to the DRV leadership. Ho remarked at one point that the DRV could absorb an unfavorable loss ratio of 10:1 and still win the war. Washington never did understand this and continued to view the war through its own lens of what would be unacceptable in terms of casualties.

From 1966 on Vietnam was an "escalating military stalemate," as Westmoreland requested and received increasing numbers of men from Washington. By the end of 1966, 400,000 U.S. troops were in Vietnam. In 1968, U.S. strength was more than 500,000 men. Johnson also made a major effort to enlist support from other nations. In all, some 40 nations provided some assistance, while the flags of the United States, the Republic of Korea, Thailand, Australia, New Zealand, the Philippines, the Republic of China, and Spain flew alongside the colors of the Republic of Vietnam at MACV headquarters in Saigon. Of the 60,000 troops from other nations, the Republic of Korea provided the greatest number, some 50,000, receiving offset payments from a grateful Johnson administration. This number exceeded the 39,000-man international coalition of the Korean War.

Capturing terrain was not judged important. The goals were to protect the population and kill the enemy. MACV waged attrition warfare and measured success in terms of body count, which in turn led to abuses. During 1966 MACV mounted 18 major operations dubbed "search and destroy," each resulting in more than

500 supposedly verified VC/PAVN dead; 50,000 enemy combatants were supposedly killed in 1966. By the beginning of 1967, the PAVN and VC had 300,000 men versus 625,000 ARVN troops and 400,000 Americans.

Ultimately more than 2.5 million Americans served in Vietnam, and nearly 58,000 of them died there. At its height, Washington was spending $30 billion per year on the war. Although the conflict was the best-covered war in American history (it became known as the first television war), it was conversely the least understood by the American people.

Hanoi meanwhile had reached a point of decision, with casualties exceeding available replacements. Instead of scaling back, North Vietnamese leaders prepared a major offensive that would employ all available troops to secure a quick victory. Hanoi believed that a major military defeat for the United States would end its political will to continue.

Giap now prepared a series of peripheral attacks, including a modified siege of some 6,000 U.S. marines at Khe Sanh in far northwestern South Vietnam near the DMZ, beginning in January 1968. These were designed to draw U.S. and ARVN forces to the periphery. With U.S. attention riveted on Khe Sanh, Giap planned a massive offensive to occur during Tet, the Vietnamese lunar new year holiday. Hanoi mistakenly believed that this massive offensive, called the "General Offensive–General Uprising," would lead the South Vietnamese people to rise up and overthrow the RVN government, bringing an American withdrawal. The attacks were mounted against the cities. Although U.S. and South Vietnamese officials believed that an attack was imminent, in a major intelligence blunder they failed to anticipate both the timing and strength of the attack, finding it inconceivable that the attack would come during Tet, which would sacrifice public goodwill.

The Tet Offensive began on January 31 and ended on February 24, 1968. Poor communication and coordination plagued Hanoi's effort. Attacks in one province occurred a day early, alerting the authorities. Hue, the former imperial capital, was especially hard hit, but within a day 5 of 6 autonomous cities, 36 of 44 provincial capitals, and 64 of 245 district capitals were under attack.

Hanoi's plan failed. ARVN forces generally fought well, and the people of South Vietnam did not support the attackers. In Hue the communists executed 3,000 people, and this horror caused many South Vietnamese to rally to the RVN. Half of the 85,000 VC and NVA who took part in the offensive were killed or captured. It was the worst military setback for North Vietnam in the war.

Paradoxically, it was also the communist side's most resounding victory, in part because the Johnson administration and Westmoreland had before Tet trumpeted prior allied successes and encouraged the American people to believe that the war was being won. The intensity of the fighting and heavy casualties came as a profound shock to the American people. They were disillusioned and, despite the victory, turned against the war.

Washington was also shocked by Westmoreland's post-Tet request for an additional 200,000 troops, which Johnson turned down. In June Westmoreland returned to Washington, D.C., to serve as chief of staff of the army, succeeded in Vietnam by his capable deputy General Creighton Abrams. This decision, which had been made in later 1967, was announced shortly after the Tet

Offensive and was widely seen by the press and the media as a punishment for being caught off guard by the communist assault.

Abrams changed the conduct of the war in fundamental ways. He abandoned Westmoreland's attrition strategy of search-and-destroy tactics and emphasis on body counts. Abrams stressed population security and held that the keys to victory rested on combat operations, pacification, and upgrading South Vietnamese forces. In combat operations he cut back on the multibattalion sweep operations, replacing these with multiple small-unit patrols and ambushes.

At the end of March 1968, meanwhile, Johnson announced a partial cessation of the bombing and withdrew from the November presidential election in the stated hopes of securing a peace settlement. Hanoi persisted, however. In the first six months of 1968, communist forces sustained more than 100,000 casualties, and the VC was virtually wiped out; 20,000 ARVN, U.S., and other allied troops died in the same period. All sides now opted for talks in Paris in an effort to negotiate an end to the war.

American disillusionment with the war was a key factor in Republican Richard M. Nixon's razor-thin victory over Democrat Hubert H. Humphrey in the November 1968 presidential election. In his bid to become president, Nixon deliberately and secretly sabotaged the Paris peace talks and also gave the American electorate the false impression that he had a plan to win the war. In fact, with no plan of his own Nixon embraced Vietnamization, which had actually begun under Johnson and involved turning over more of the war to the ARVN.

U.S. troop withdrawals began. Peak U.S. strength of 550,000 men occurred in early 1969; there were 475,000 men by the end of the year, 335,000 by the end

of 1970, and 157,000 at the end of 1971. Massive amounts of equipment were also turned over to the ARVN, including 1 million M-16 rifles and sufficient aircraft to make the RVNAF the fourth largest in the world. Extensive retraining of the ARVN was begun, and training schools were established. The controversial counterinsurgency Phoenix Program also operated against the VC infrastructure, reducing the insurgency by 67,000 people between 1968 and 1971, but PAVN forces remained secure in sanctuaries in "neutral" Laos and Cambodia.

Nixon's policy was to limit outside assistance to Hanoi and pressure Hanoi to end the war. For years, American and RVN military leaders had sought approval to attack the sanctuaries. In March 1970 a coup in Cambodia ousted Prince Norodom Sihanouk. General Lon Nol replaced him, and secret operations against the PAVN Cambodian sanctuaries soon began. During a two-month span there were 12 cross-border operations in the so-called Cambodian Incursion. Despite widespread opposition in the United States to the widened war, the incursions resulted in the destruction of considerable communist arms and supplies, raised allied morale, allowed U.S. withdrawals to continue on schedule, and purchased additional time for Vietnamization. U.S. interference in Cambodia also created chaotic conditions that helped the communist Khmer Rouge seize power there in 1976, with dire consequences for the Cambodian people. PAVN forces now concentrated on bases in southern Laos and on enlarging the Ho Chi Minh Trail.

In the spring of 1971 ARVN forces mounted a major invasion into southern Laos, known as Operation LAM SON 719. This overly ambitious operation was designed to cut the Ho Chi Minh Trail and demonstrate the success of Vietnamization. There were no U.S. ground troops or advisers with the ARVN. The operation set back Hanoi's plans to invade South Vietnam but took a considerable toll on ARVN's younger officers and pointed up serious command weaknesses. In large part due to the bravery of U.S. Army helicopter pilots, about half of the original ARVN force of 15,000 men were able to reach safety. At least 5,000 ARVN troops were killed or wounded, and more than 2,500 were unaccounted for and listed as missing. Additionally, 253 Americans were killed and another 1,149 wounded, although no Americans fought on the ground inside Laos.

By 1972, PAVN forces had recovered and had been substantially strengthened with new weapons, including heavy artillery and tanks from the Soviet Union. The PAVN now mounted a major conventional invasion of South Vietnam. The DRV had 15 divisions. Confident that the United States would not interfere, Hanoi left only 1 division in the DRV and 2 divisions in Laos and committed the remaining 12 to the invasion.

The attack began on March 30, 1972. Known as the Spring or Easter Offensive, it began with a direct armor strike across the DMZ at the 17th Parallel and caught the best South Vietnamese troops facing Laos. Allied intelligence misread its scale and precise timing. Hanoi risked catastrophic losses but hoped for a quick victory before ARVN forces could recover. At first it appeared that the PAVN would be successful. Quang Tri fell, and rain limited the effectiveness of airpower.

But in May, Nixon authorized B-52 bomber strikes on Hanoi's principal port of Haiphong and the mining of its harbor. This new air campaign was dubbed Operation LINEBACKER and involved the use of new precision-guided munitions, so-called smart bombs. The bombing cut off much of the supplies for the invading PAVN forces. Allied aircraft also destroyed 400–500 PAVN tanks. In June and July the ARVN counterattacked and in September regained Quang Tri. The invasion cost Hanoi half its force—some 100,000 men died—while ARVN losses were only a quarter of that, at 25,000.

With both Soviet and People's Republic of China leaders anxious for better relations with the United States in order to obtain Western technology and pressing the DRV, Hanoi gave way and switched to negotiations. Nixon's landslide victory against the "peace candidate" George McGovern in the November 1972 presidential election was also likely a major factor in Hanoi's decision to negotiate. Finally, an agreement was hammered out in Paris that December. But President Thieu balked and refused to sign, whereupon Hanoi made the agreements public. A furious Nixon blamed Hanoi for the impasse and ordered a resumption of the bombing, officially known as LINEBACKER II (December 18–29) but also dubbed the December Bombings and the Christmas Bombings. Although 15 B-52s were lost, Hanoi had fired away virtually its entire stock of surface-to-air missiles and now agreed to resume talks.

After a few cosmetic changes, an agreement was signed on January 23, 1973, with Nixon forcing Thieu to agree or risk the end of all U.S. aid. The United States recovered its prisoners of war and departed Vietnam. The Soviet Union and China continued to supply arms to Hanoi, however, while Congress constricted U.S. supplies to Saigon. Tanks and planes were not replaced on the promised one-for-one basis as they were lost, and spare parts and fuel were both in short supply. All this had a devastating effect on ARVN training, operations, and morale. At the start of 1975, the ARVN had twice the number of combat troops, three times the amount of artillery, and twice the number of tanks as the PAVN. The ARVN also had 1,400 aircraft, but rising oil prices meant that much of this equipment could not be used.

In South Vietnam both sides violated the cease-fire, and fighting steadily increased in intensity. In January 1975 communist forces attacked and quickly seized Phuoc Long Province on the Cambodian border north of Saigon. Washington took no action. The communists next took Ban Me Thuot in the Central Highlands, then in mid-March President Thieu precipitously decided to abandon the northern part of his country. This brought confusion and then disorder and disaster. Six weeks later PAVN forces controlled virtually all South Vietnam. Saigon fell on April 30, 1975, to be renamed Ho Chi Minh City. The long war was over at last.

Significance

Vietnam was now reunited but under a communist government. In the war the ARVN had suffered between 220,000 and 313,000 military deaths, the communist side 400,000 to 1.1 million. Some 3 million Vietnamese, both military personnel and civilians, had died in the struggle. Much of the country was devastated by the fighting, and Vietnam suffered from the effects of the widespread use of chemical defoliants.

Communist governments also appeared in Laos and Cambodia. Kampuchea (the renamed communist Cambodia) especially suffered. Its 1970 population of some 7.1 million experienced a human catastrophe unparalleled in the 20th century. Cambodia lost nearly 4 million of its people to fighting, famine, and mass murder, perhaps 2.4 million of these murdered by the communist Khmer Rouge.

The effects were profound in the United States. It suffered 58,220 dead and 303,644 wounded (other allied dead totaled nearly 6,000). A significant percentage of the participants suffered from drug addiction and post-traumatic stress disorder. The American military was shattered by the war and had to be rebuilt. Under President Nixon, Congress had done away with the draft and substituted an all-volunteer force. The voting age was also reduced to 18. Congress also moved to curtail the "imperial presidency" with the War Powers Act, which restricted the ability of presidents to wage war without congressional consent.

Inflation was rampant from the failure to face up to the true costs of the war, and there were major social problems. The country also wrestled with an influx of several hundred thousand Vietnamese refugees. The war certainly contributed to a distrust of government and also fractured the Democratic Party, as many blue-collar Democrats saw the party as dominated by antiwar liberals and either joined the Republican Party or became independents. Certainly the war weakened the U.S. commitment to international peacekeeping and institutions. Many questioned U.S. willingness to embark on such a crusade again, at least to go it largely alone. In this sense, the war forced Washington into a more realistic appraisal of U.S. power.

Further Reading

Berman, Larry. *Lyndon Johnson's War: The Road to Stalemate in Vietnam.* New York: Norton, 1999.

Brocheux, Pierre. *Ho Chi Minh: A Biography.* Cambridge: Cambridge University Press, 2007.

Currey, Cecil B. *Victory at Any Cost: The Genius of Viet Nam's General Vo Nguyen Giap.* Washington, DC: Brassey's, 1997.

Dommen, Arthur J. *Conflict in Laos: The Politics of Neutralization.* Revised ed. New York: Praeger, 1971.

Dong Van Khuyen. *The Republic of Vietnam Armed Forces.* Washington, DC: U.S. Army Center of Military History, 1980.

Duiker, William J. *The Communist Road to Power in Vietnam.* 2nd ed. Boulder, CO: Westview, 1996.

Karnow, Stanley. *Vietnam: A History.* New York: Viking, 1983.

Maclear, Michael. *The Ten Thousand Day War, Vietnam: 1945–1975.* New York: St. Martin's, 1981.

McMaster, H. R. *Dereliction of Duty: Johnson, McNamara, the Joint Chiefs of Staff and the Lies That Led to Vietnam.* New York: Harper Perennial, 1998.

McNamara, Robert S., and Brian VanDemark. *In Retrospect: The Tragedy and Lessons of Vietnam.* New York: Vintage Books, 1996.

O'Ballance, Edgar. *The Wars in Vietnam, 1954–1960.* New York: Hippocrene Books, 1981.

Oberdorfer, Don. *Tet! The Turning Point in the Vietnam War.* Baltimore: Johns Hopkins University Press, 2001.

Palmer, Bruce, Jr. *The 25-Year War.* Lexington: University Press of Kentucky, 1984.

Prados, John. *Vietnam: The History of an Unwinnable War, 1945–1975.* Lawrence: University Press of Kansas, 2009.

Pribbenow, Merle L., and William J. Duiker. *Victory in Vietnam: The Official History of the People's Army of Vietnam.* Lawrence: University Press of Kansas, 2002.

Tucker, Spencer C. *Vietnam.* Lexington: University Press of Kentucky, 1999.

Tucker, Spencer C., ed. *The Encyclopedia of the Vietnam War: A Political, Social, and Military History.* 4 vols. Santa Barbara, CA: ABC-CLIO, 2011.

Willbanks, James H. *Abandoning Vietnam: How America Left and South Vietnam Lost Its War.* Lawrence: University Press of Kansas, 2004.

Six-Day War (1967)

Dates	June 5–10, 1967
Location	Middle East (Israel and bordering states)
Combatants	Israel vs. Egypt, Syria, Jordan, and Iraq
Principal Commanders	Israel: Levi Eshkol, Moshe Dayan, Yitzhak Rabin, Ariel Sharon Egypt: Gamal Abdel Nasser, Abdel Hakim Amer, Abdul Munim Riad Syria: Hafez al-Assad, Nur al-Atassi Jordan: King Hussein I, Mubarak Abdullah
Principal Battles	Gaza, Sinai Peninsula, Jerusalem, Jordan River West Bank, Golan Heights
Outcome	Israel is victorious and secures the territory on the West Bank of the Jordan River.

Causes

In the spring of 1967 the Middle East was poised on the brink of a new war. Israel's neighbors still refused to recognize Israel as an independent state, but their military defeats in the Israeli War of Independence of 1948–1949 and the 1956 Suez Campaign sparked by the Suez Crisis had made even the most belligerent Arab leaders reluctant to embark on a new conflict. Indeed, the fighting after 1956 had shifted to a low-intensity struggle marked by Palestinian raids against the Jewish state from Israeli neighbors Syria and Jordan. Yasir Arafat's al-Fatah movement was a leader in this effort.

Israel met this undeclared war on its territory by retaliatory strikes against guerrilla camps and villages in the Golan Heights of Syria and in Jordan. The year 1965 saw an Arab attempt to divert the flow of the Jordan River, and this brought a series of Israel Defense Forces (IDF) attacks against the diversion sites in Syria. This in turn led to a mutual defense pact between Egypt and Syria against Israel, signed on November 4, 1966.

On November 13, 1966, the IDF mounted a large-scale attack on Es Samu in Jordan, a Palestinian refugee camp held by the Israelis to be a base for Syrian terrorists. Then on April 7, 1967, two decades of sporadic raids across the Israel-Syria border exploded into an aerial battle over the Golan Heights, with IDF aircraft downing six Syrian Mikoyan-Gurevich MiG-21 jet aircraft, after which IDF warplanes flew over Damascus in a show of force.

With Israeli's chief supporter, the United States, heavily engaged in Vietnam, the leaders of the Soviet Union saw an opportunity to alter the balance of power in the Middle East that would favor their client states of Egypt and Syria. On May 13, the Soviets provided the Egyptian government with false information that Israel was mobilizing troops along the Syrian border. As a consequence, on May 16 Egyptian president Gamal Abdel Nasser declared a state of emergency (Israel's subsequent protestations that the Soviet report was untrue were ignored), and the next day the Egyptian and Syrian governments proclaimed a state of "combat readiness." Jordan also mobilized.

As a consequence of this belligerency, Nasser's popularity soared in the Arab world, and this impacted what followed. On May 16 also, Nasser requested that with Egyptian forces massing in the Sinai and the possibility of an Israeli attack on Egypt, the United Nations Emergency Force (UNEF), stationed in the Sinai, depart immediately. Since the 1956 War the UNEF had served as a buffer between Egyptian and Israeli forces. The UNEF complied on May 19. The day before Syria and Egypt placed their armed forces on maximum alert, while the Iraqi and Kuwaiti governments announced that their forces were also mobilizing.

In a meeting with the Arab press, Nasser also announced Egypt's intention to close the Straits of Tiran to Israeli shipping. The straits were the principal avenue for Israeli trade with Asia and the transit point for 90 percent of its oil imports. Closing the straits to Israel would severely disrupt the Israeli economy. Indeed, Israel had already let it be known that it would consider such a step to be justification for war. Nasser knew that Israel would probably react militarily, but he assumed that the United States would not support the anticipated Israeli military response, while Egypt and its allies would have the support of the Soviet Union. The Kremlin, however, reacted negatively to Nasser's announcement. Having stirred the pot, it now urged restraint. Responding to a hotline message to Soviet leaders from U.S. president Lyndon Johnson, the Soviets on May 27 insisted that the Egyptians not strike first.

Nasser's proposal regarding the Straits of Tiran was apparently in part bluff. He

BALANCE OF FORCES, MAY 14 – 24, 1967

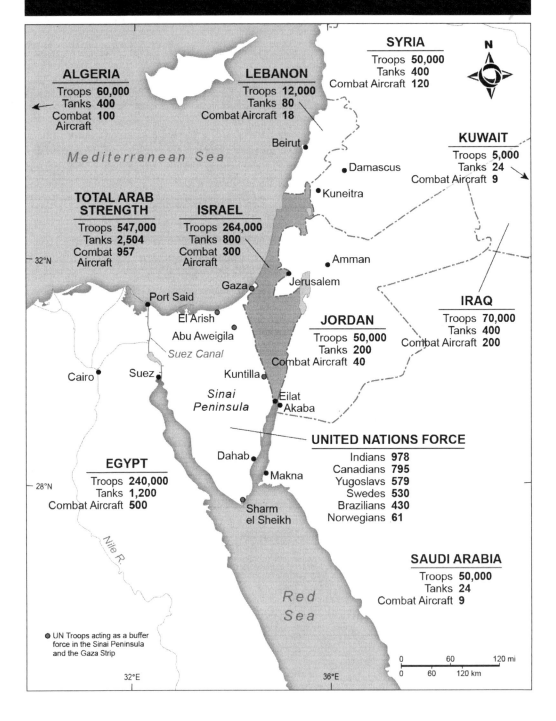

SYRIA
Troops **50,000**
Tanks **400**
Combat Aircraft **120**

N

ALGERIA
Troops **60,000**
Tanks **400**
Combat **100**
Aircraft

LEBANON
Troops **12,000**
Tanks **80**
Combat Aircraft **18**

Mediterranean Sea

Beirut

Damascus

Kuneitra

KUWAIT
Troops **5,000**
Tanks **24**
Combat Aircraft **9**

TOTAL ARAB STRENGTH
Troops **547,000**
Tanks **2,504**
Combat **957**
Aircraft

ISRAEL
Troops **264,000**
Tanks **800**
Combat **300**
Aircraft

Gaza

Jerusalem

Amman

32°N

Port Said

El Arish

Abu Aweigila

Suez Canal

JORDAN
Troops **50,000**
Tanks **200**
Combat Aircraft **40**

IRAQ
Troops **70,000**
Tanks **400**
Combat Aircraft **200**

Cairo

Suez

Kuntilla

Eilat
Akaba

Sinai Peninsula

UNITED NATIONS FORCE
Indians **978**
Canadians **795**
Yugoslavs **579**
Swedes **530**
Brazilians **430**
Norwegians **61**

Dahab

Makna

EGYPT
Troops **240,000**
Tanks **1,200**
Combat Aircraft **500**

28°N

Sharm
el Sheikh

Nile R.

SAUDI ARABIA
Troops **50,000**
Tanks **24**
Combat Aircraft **9**

Red Sea

● UN Troops acting as a buffer
force in the Sinai Peninsula
and the Gaza Strip

0   60   120 mi
0   60   120 km

32°E

36°E

assumed that the threat of closing the straits would at least force Israel to withdraw its supposed increased forces along the Syrian border, greatly enhancing his own standing in the Arab world. On May 22, however, Egyptian minister of defense Field Marshal Abdel Hakim Amer ordered Egyptian forces to close the Straits of Tiran the next day. A countermanding order from Nasser would have signaled weakness on his part, and the Egyptian leader issued orders to the Egyptian military to prepare for war.

On May 20, meanwhile, Israel completed a partial mobilization. The Arab states were also mobilizing, and Iraqi and Algerian forces began moving to Syria and Egypt. On May 26 Nasser announced that if Israel were to strike either Egypt or Syria, this would result in a general war, with the Arab goal "the destruction of Israel." On May 30 Jordanian king Hussein arrived in Cairo and Egypt, and Jordan concluded a mutual security pact.

On paper, the balance of forces heavily favored the Arab states. At the beginning of June 1967, Israel had mobilized 230,000 men, 1,100 tanks, 200 artillery pieces, 260 combat aircraft, and 22 naval vessels. Egypt and Syria together had 263,000 men, 1,950 tanks, 915 artillery pieces, 521 combat aircraft, and 75 naval vessels. Counting Iraqi and Jordanian forces, the Arab advantage swelled to 409,000 men, 2,437 tanks, 1,487 artillery pieces, 649 combat aircraft, and 90 naval vessels.

Now certain that there would be war and unwilling to allow the Arab forces time to fully mobilize their larger resources, on June 4, despite strong U.S. opposition, Israeli prime minister Levi Eshkol authorized a preemptive strike against Israel's strongest enemy, Egypt. Minister of defense General Moshe Dayan passed the word to Lieutenant General Yitzhak Rabin and the Israeli General Staff.

Course

The Arab-Israeli War of 1967, known to history as the Six-Day War, commenced on the morning of June 5. For all practical purposes, the war was over by noon. The Israeli Air Force offensive of that day remains one of the most stunning successes in modern warfare.

Egyptian Front

Destruction of the Egyptian Air Force was essential if the Israeli Army was to enjoy success on the ground, yet Israel was outnumbered by Egypt and Syria two to one in combat aircraft. Also, it would be difficult for Israel to defend against Egyptian and Syrian air attacks because the attackers would come from two different directions and also because Israel was too small in area for early warning systems to provide sufficient time for Israeli fighters to scramble. The Israeli capital of Tel Aviv was 25 minutes' flying time from Cairo but only 4.5 minutes from the nearest Egyptian air base at El Arish.

The initial Israeli air attack plan relied on accurate, timely, and precise intelligence information. The plan called for a first strike against Egypt, the most formidable of Israel's opponents. Israeli aircraft were to take off from airfields all around Israel and fly west, under radio silence and at low altitude to avoid radar, out over the Mediterranean, then turn south to strike Egyptian airfields as simultaneously as possible. Rather than attacking at dawn, the strikes were timed to coincide with the return of Egyptian aircraft to base from morning patrols, when most Egyptian pilots would be having breakfast.

The Israeli Air Force was certainly one of the best-trained air forces in the world and was well prepared for its mission. The aircrews had been thoroughly briefed as to objectives and procedures. Israeli Air Force ground crews were also highly trained and able to reduce turnaround time between missions to a minimum. Thus, Israeli aircraft could fly up to four sorties a day versus only half that number for their opponents. The operation was, however, extremely risky in that it employed almost all Israeli bomber and fighter aircraft, leaving only a dozen fighters behind to fly combat air patrol in defense of Israel itself.

The Israeli Air Force achieved complete tactical surprise, going into action at 7:45 a.m. (8:45 a.m. Cairo time). One unexpected development was that Egyptian field marshal Abdel Hakim Amer and his deputy, General Mamoud Sidky, were in the air, flying from Cairo to inspect units in the Sinai, when the attacks commenced. Unable to land in the Sinai, they returned to Cairo, and during 90 minutes two key Egyptian commanders were out of touch with their units and unable to give orders.

The first Israeli Air Force attack wave struck 10 Egyptian airfields, hitting all of them within 15 minutes of the scheduled time. On their final approach to their targets, the Israeli pilots climbed to make their aircraft suddenly visible on radar in order to induce Egyptian pilots to attempt to scramble in the hopes of catching them in their aircraft on the ground. Only four Egyptian aircraft, all trainers, were in the air at the time of the first strikes, and all were shot down. Subsequent waves of Israeli attacking aircraft, about 40 per flight, arrived at 10-minute intervals. These met increased Egyptian opposition, mostly in the form of antiaircraft fire. Only eight Egyptian MiGs managed to take off during the strikes, and all were shot down.

In all, the Israeli Air Force attacked 17 major Egyptian airfields with some 500 sorties (a sortie being one mission by one individual aircraft) in just under three hours, wiping out half of Egyptian Air Force strength of 431 combat aircraft. Most of the Egyptian aircraft were destroyed by accurate Israeli cannon fire, but the Israelis also dropped 250-, 500-, and 1,000-pound bombs. Special bombs with 365-pound warheads, developed to crack the hard-surface concrete runways, were dropped on Egyptian airfields west of the Suez Canal, but none of these were employed against the Sinai airfields, which the Israelis planned for subsequent use by their own aircraft.

Later that same day, June 5, Israeli aircraft struck Syria and Jordan. Following an Iraqi air strike on Israel, Israeli Air Force aircraft also attacked Iraqi air units based in the Mosul area. With opposing air forces largely neutralized, the Israeli Air Force could then turn to close air support and other missions in support of Israeli mechanized ground forces, which had begun operations in the Sinai simultaneous with the initial air attacks. In all during the war, the Arab side would lose 390 aircraft of their prewar strength of 969 aircraft of all types (Egypt, 286 of 580; Jordan, 28 of 56; Syria, 54 of 172; Iraq, 21 of 149; and Lebanon, 1 of 12). Total Israeli Air Force losses were 32 aircraft shot down of 354 of all types at the beginning of the war, only 2 to aerial combat.

Israeli ground forces were also on the move against Egypt. The Egyptians, it should be noted, were handicapped by the fact that 50,000 of their best troops were tied down in the ongoing civil war in Yemen. Israeli ground forces sent against

Egypt consisted of a mechanized brigade under Colonel Yehuda Resheff, a mechanized division commanded by Major General Israel Tal, an armored division under Major General Avraham Yoffe, and a mechanized division under Major General Ariel Sharon. Tal's division drove into the Rafah–El Arish area, Resheff advanced into the Gaza Strip, and Sharon moved toward fortifications in the area of Abu Ageila and Kusseima. Yoffe headed southward toward the central Sinai to cut off an Egyptian retreat.

On June 6, Egyptian troops in Gaza surrendered to Resheff's forces. Meanwhile, Tal's mechanized division and Yoffe's armored division linked up. Sharon sent part of his mechanized division to Rafah and El Arish and the remainder toward Nakhle and the Mitla Pass, while Yoffe attacked the main Egyptian force at Jabal Libni in central Sinai. Egyptian Army commander Field Marshal Amer ordered all Egyptian units in the Sinai to withdraw.

On June 7 the major elements of Tal's mechanized division arrived at Bir Gifgafa, while his northern task force passed Romani. The leading brigade of Yoffe's armored division arrived at the eastern end of the Mitla Pass out of fuel and short of ammunition. Egyptian forces quickly surrounded it, but shortly thereafter Yoffe's other brigade arrived and relieved the first. Sharon's mechanized division advanced closer to Nakhle, while other units captured northeastern Sinai and Israeli air and amphibious forces secured Sharm al-Shaykh.

On June 8, Egyptian armored units attempted to provide cover for other forces withdrawing from the Sinai. Tal's mechanized division drove them back, however, advancing toward the Suez Canal between Qantara and Ismailiyya. Meanwhile, Yoffe's armored division transited Mitla Pass and reached the canal opposite Port Suez, while Sharon's mechanized division captured Nakhle and moved through Mitla Pass. By the end of the day, the Sinai was firmly under Israeli Army control. Egypt had lost 80 percent of its military equipment and had some 11,500 troops killed, 20,000 wounded, and 5,500 taken prisoner. IDF losses were 338 killed.

On June 9, the United Nations Security Council called for a cease-fire. This left Israel in control of the Sinai east of the Suez Canal. While Israel accepted it immediately, Egypt did not agree to the cease-fire until the next day, June 10. On June 9, meanwhile, Nasser had offered his resignation as president, but it was rejected, the consequence of large Egyptian public demonstrations.

Jordanian Front

Israeli leaders had urged King Hussein of Jordan to stay out of the war, informing him at the onset of fighting that the dispute was with Egypt. Hussein wanted to avoid participation but came under heavy pressure to act. He was also deceived by early broadcasts from Cairo claiming major Egyptian military successes. Hussein hoped to satisfy his allies with minimum military action short of all-out war. Jordanian 155mm "Long Tom" guns went into action against Tel Aviv, and Jordanian aircraft attempted to strafe a small airfield near Kfar Sirkin. These steps, however, led the Israeli government to declare war on Jordan.

The Jordanians commenced firing on Israeli territory from their part of Jerusalem. Israeli brigadier general Uzi Narkiss then commenced an offensive against Jerusalem with three brigades under Colonel Mordechai Gur. The Israelis surrounded the Old

City, defended by Jordanian forces under Brigadier General Ata Ali. That same day in the Battle of Jenin-Nablus, Major General David Elazar, who headed the Israeli Northern Command, received orders to seize Jenin and Nablus and advance to the Jordan River. Elazar dispatched one division and an armored brigade toward Jenin.

On June 6, the Israelis continued their attacks on the Old City but encountered fierce Jordanian opposition. They were able, however, to prevent Jordanian efforts to relieve the Old City. An Israeli tank brigade seized Ramallah, and another captured Latrun. The road between Tel Aviv and Jerusalem was open to Jewish traffic for the first time since 1947. To the north, Jenin fell after midnight to the Israelis after fierce combat.

On June 7 Gur's forces stormed the Old City, forcing the Jordanians to withdraw. That same day, the Israelis captured Bethlehem, Hebron, and Etzion. At the same time despite Jordanian counterattacks, the Israelis advanced on and seized Nablus. Jordanian forces then withdrew across the Jordan River, and both Israel and Jordan agreed to a cease-fire, to take effect at 8:00 p.m.

Syrian Front

At the onset of fighting, Syria had positioned on the Golan Heights six brigades on line, with six others in reserve east of Quneitra (Kuneitra). For four days Israeli commander of the Northern Front Major General David Elazar engaged in artillery duels against the Syrians, who showed no signs of wishing to initiate offensive action. On June 8, however, a United Nations–brokered cease-fire collapsed, the consequence of artillery fire from both sides.

On June 9 with resources released from other fronts, Elazar initiated major offensive action in an advance toward the Dan-Banyas area along the foothills of Mount Hermon. The Israelis broke through the first line of Syrian defenses in the northern Golan, with three brigades poised to follow. Other units forced their way north of the Sea of Galilee, while Elazar ordered units recently engaged in the Jenin-Nablus area to attack the Golan south of the Sea of Galilee.

Syrian defenses rapidly deteriorated on June 10 as Israeli forces drove into the northern Golan. The Israelis resisted calls from the United States not to occupy the Golan Heights or to agree to a cease-fire and advanced on Quneitra from the north, west, and southwest. Troops from the Jordanian front pushed northeastward toward the Yarmouk (Yarmuk) Valley and occupied the southern Golan. The Israelis then surrounded Quneitra and captured it. Only when the Golan Heights were firmly in their hands did the Israelis agree to a cease-fire. It went into effect on the Syrian front at 6:30 p.m. on June 10.

Fighting at Sea

In the last few days just before the beginning of the war, during June 3–4 the Israelis trucked landing craft by day from the Mediterranean to Eilat, then returned them at night. This deception led the Egyptians to believe that the Israelis were massing resources at Eilat for operations in the Gulf of Aqaba and caused the Egyptians to shift naval assets into the Red Sea, redressing the imbalance of naval forces in the Mediterranean.

With the start of the war on June 5, Israeli and Egyptian naval units clashed off Port Said. An Israeli destroyer and several motor torpedo boats reached Port Said and were there met by two Egyptian Osa-class missile boats. After an inconclusive battle, the Egyptian missile boats withdrew into the harbor. Israeli frogmen entered the harbors of both Port Said and Alexandria and inflicted some damage on Egyptian ships at Alexandria before they were taken prisoner. On June 6 as a consequence of the Israeli air attacks and the advance on land, Egyptian naval units withdrew from Port Said to Alexandria.

On the night of June 6–7, three Egyptian submarines shelled the Israeli coast near Ashdod and north and south of Haifa, but Israeli air and naval forces returned fire and drove them off. On June 7 with the Israeli capture of Sharm al-Shaykh, Israeli warships were able to transit the Strait of Tiran to the Red Sea unobstructed.

On June 8 the *Liberty,* a U.S. electronic intelligence-gathering ship, was steaming in international waters some 13 miles off El Arish on the Sinai Peninsula when it came under attack by Israeli air and naval units. Thirty-four American personnel died in the attack; another 172 were wounded, many seriously. Although their ship was badly damaged, the *Liberty*'s crewmen managed to keep it afloat, and it was able to make Malta under its own power, escorted by ships of the U.S. Sixth Fleet. The Israeli government later apologized for the attack and paid nearly $13 million in compensation. The reasons for the attack and charges of a cover-up have been the topics of conspiracy theories, but inquiries in both the United States and Israel have concluded that it was a matter of mistaken identity.

In all the Six-Day War claimed on the Israeli side some 800 dead, 2,440 wounded, and 16 missing or taken prisoner. Arab losses, chiefly Egyptian, were estimated at 14,300 dead, 23,800 wounded, and 10,500 missing or taken prisoner. Israel lost 100 tanks and 40 aircraft, while the Arab side lost 950 tanks and 368 aircraft.

Significance

The Six-Day War vastly increased the amount of territory controlled by Israel. From Egypt, Israel gained all of the Sinai east of the Suez Canal, including the Gaza Strip; from Jordan, it secured the entire east bank of the Jordan River and the Old City of Jerusalem; and from Syria, it added the Golan Heights. Despite calls by the United Nations and the passage of Security Council Resolution 242 of November 17, 1967, which called for the Israelis to return the captured territories and the Arab states to negotiate peace treaties with Israel, it would be 12 long years and more fighting before the first formal peace treaty between Israel and an Arab nation, Egypt, with the return of the Sinai.

Indeed, warfare between the two sides simply entered a new stage in what would become known as the War of Attrition, with Egypt and Syria supporting enhanced terrorist attacks against Israel. By 1969 also, Arafat's al-Fatah had gained complete control of the Palestine Liberation Organization, which supported terrorist activities against Israeli citizens around the world.

The territorial acquisitions by Israel as a consequence of the war made securing a Middle East peace settlement much more difficult. Although Israel returned the Sinai to Egypt in 1978 and withdrew from the Gaza Strip in 2005, it has showed a marked reluctance to yield up the Golan Heights, the West Bank, and Old Jerusalem. Politically conservative Israelis and ultraorthodox Jews consider the West Bank part of the ancient Jewish state, not to be given up on any basis. Yet some 1.7 million Arabs constitute 21 percent of the Israeli population, raising issues of Israeli's survival both as a Jewish state and a democracy. Increasing construction of Jewish settlements and Israel's determination to retain significant parts of the West Bank and all of Jerusalem certainly constitute major barriers to a comprehensive peace settlement. All of these can be traced to the 1967 War.

Further Reading

Bowen, Jeremy. *Six Days: How the 1967 War Shaped the Middle East.* London: Simon and Schuster, 2003.

Bregman, Ahron. *Israel's Wars: A History since 1947.* London: Routledge, 2002.

Finkelstein, Norman G. *The Rise and Fall of Palestine: A Personal Account of the Intifada Years.* Minneapolis: University of Minnesota Press, 1996.

Friedman, Thomas L. *From Beirut to Jerusalem.* New York: Anchor, 1990.

Gawrych, George W. *The Albatross of Decisive Victory: War and Policy between Egypt and Israel in the 1967 and 1973 Arab-Israeli Wars.* Westport, CT: Greenwood, 2000.

Goldschmidt, Arthur. *Modern Egypt: The Formation of a Nation State.* Boulder, CO: Westview, 2004.

Hammel, Eric. *Six Days in June: How Israel Won the 1967 Arab-Israeli War.* New York: Simon and Schuster, 1992.

Herzog, Chaim. *The Arab Israeli Wars.* New York: Random House, 1982.

Morris, Benny. *Righteous Victims: A History of The Zionist-Arab Conflict, 1881–2001.* New York: Vintage, 2001.

Mutawi, Samir A. *Jordan in the 1967 War.* Cambridge: Cambridge University Press, 2002.

Ochsenwald, William, and Sydney Nettleson Fisher. *The Middle East: A History.* Boston: McGraw-Hill, 2004.

Oren, Michael B. *Six Days of War: June 1967 and the Making of the Modern Middle East.* New York: Presidio, 2003.

Parker, Richard B. *The Six-Day War: A Retrospective.* Gainesville: University Press of Florida, 1996.

Pollack, Kenneth. "Air Power in the Six-Day War." *Journal of Strategic Studies* 28(3) (2005): 471–503.

Pollack, Kenneth. *Arabs at War: Military Effectiveness, 1948–1991.* Lincoln: University of Nebraska Press, 2002.

Sachar, Howard M. *A History of Israel from the Rise of Zionism to Our Time.* New York: Knopf, 1967.

Yom Kippur War (1973)

Dates	October 6–25, 1973
Location	Middle East (Israel and bordering states)
Combatants	Israel vs. Egypt and Syria
Principal Commanders	Israel: Golda Meir, Moshe Dayan, David Elazar, Ariel Sharon Egypt: Muhammad Anwar el-Sadat, Ahmed Ismail Ali Syria: Hafez al-Assad, Mustafa Tlass, Yousef Chakour
Principal Battles	Suez Canal, Latakia, Mount Hermon, Golan Heights, Rafid, Quneitra, Chinese Farm
Outcome	A costly Israeli victory, the war restores Arab military prestige, resulting in successful peace talks between Egypt and Israel.

Causes

The Yom Kippur War of October 6–25, 1973, also known as the Ramadan War, the October War, and the 1973 Arab-Israeli War, was a major conflict between Israel and its Arab neighbors that had a profound effect on the Middle East. Egyptian president Gamal Abdel Nasser died in

September 1970. His successor, Muhammad Anwar el-Sadat, was determined to change the status quo regarding Israel. He called for a gradual peace settlement that would lead to Israeli withdrawal from the Sinai but without formal general peace agreement. Sadat expelled the Soviet advisers brought in by Nasser and resumed negotiations with the United States that Nasser had ended in 1955.

The failure of his diplomatic efforts in 1971, however, led Sadat to begin planning a military operation that would break the political stalemate along the Israeli-Egyptian front. Sadat believed that even a minor Egyptian military success would change the military equilibrium and force a political settlement. Israel's strength was in its air force and armored divisions, which were well trained in maneuver warfare. Egyptian strengths lay in the ability to build a strong defense line and in new Soviet-supplied surface-to-air missiles (SAMs) deployed in batteries along the canal and deep within Egypt. Sadat hoped to paralyze the Israeli Air Force by the SAMs and counter the Israelis' advantage in maneuver warfare by forcing them to attack well-fortified and well-defended Egyptian strongholds.

In an attempt to dilute the Israeli military forces on the Sinai front, Sadat brought in Syria. A coordinated surprise attack by both states would place maximum stress on the Israel Defense Forces (IDF). Above anything else, the key to the plan's success was secrecy. Were Israel to suspect that an attack was imminent, it would undoubtedly launch a preventive attack, as in 1967. That part of Sadat's plan, at least, was successful.

A combination of effective Egyptian deceptive measures and Israeli arrogance contributed to Israel's failure to comprehend what was happening. One deception consisted of repeated Egyptian drills along the Suez Canal, simulating a possible crossing. The Israelis thus became accustomed to large Egyptian troop concentrations at the canal and interpreted Egyptian preparations for the actual crossings as just another drill. Even the Egyptian soldiers were told that it was simply a drill. Only when the actual crossing was under way were they informed of its true nature. Even with the actual attack, however, the real intent of Egyptian and Syrian forces remained unclear to the Israelis, and they initially refrained from offensive action.

On the Israeli-Egyptian front, Egypt amassed nearly 800,000 soldiers, 2,200 tanks, 2,300 artillery pieces, 150 SAM batteries, and 550 aircraft. Along the canal Egypt deployed five infantry divisions with accompanying armored elements, supported by additional infantry and armored independent brigades. This force was backed by three mechanized divisions and two armored divisions. Opposing this impressive Egyptian force on the eastern bank of the Suez Canal, Israel had only a single division, supported by 280 tanks.

On October 4–5, 1973, Sadat expelled some 15,000 Soviet advisers and all their dependents. Not until the early morning hours of October 6 did Israeli military intelligence conclude that an Egyptian attack was imminent. Brigadier General Eilhau Zeira, Israeli director of intelligence, warned Lieutenant General David Elazar, IDF chief of staff, of this, but Prime Minister Golda Meir decided against a preemptive strike.

Course of Operations on the Sinai Front

At 2:00 p.m. on October 6, Egypt launched a massive air strike against Israeli artillery and command positions. At the same time, Egyptian artillery shelled the Israeli Bar Lev Line fortifications along the Suez

OCTOBER WAR, 1973

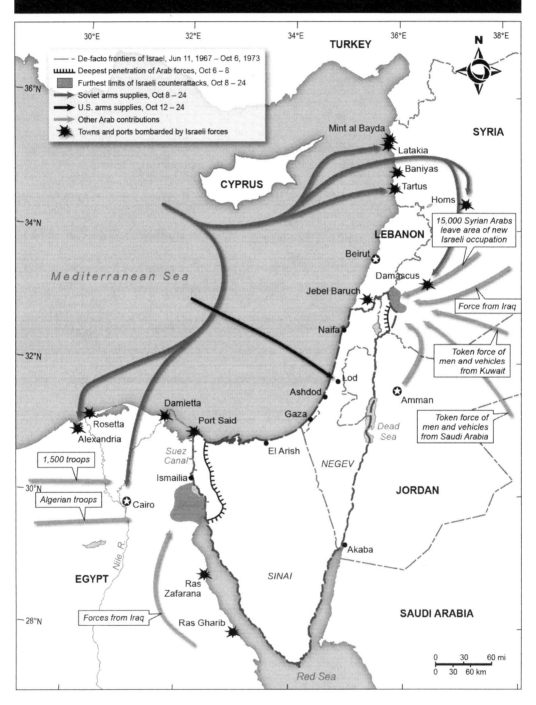

Legend:
- De-facto frontiers of Israel, Jun 11, 1967 – Oct 6, 1973
- Deepest penetration of Arab forces, Oct 6 – 8
- Furthest limits of Israeli counterattacks, Oct 8 – 24
- Soviet arms supplies, Oct 8 – 24
- U.S. arms supplies, Oct 12 – 24
- Other Arab contributions
- Towns and ports bombarded by Israeli forces

TURKEY

SYRIA

CYPRUS

Mint al Bayda
Latakia
Baniyas
Tartus
Homs

15,000 Syrian Arabs leave area of new Israeli occupation

Mediterranean Sea

LEBANON

Beirut

Damascus

Jebel Baruch

Force from Iraq

Naifa

Token force of men and vehicles from Kuwait

Lod

Ashdod
Gaza

Amman

Dead Sea

Token force of men and vehicles from Saudi Arabia

Damietta
Rosetta
Alexandria

Port Said

El Arish

NEGEV

JORDAN

1,500 troops

Suez Canal

Ismailia

Algerian troops

Cairo

Akaba

EGYPT

Nile R.

Ras Zafarana

SINAI

SAUDI ARABIA

Forces from Iraq

Ras Gharib

Red Sea

0   30   60 mi
0   30   60 km

Canal. Egyptian commandos crossed the canal followed by engineers who quickly constructed bridges, allowing the Egyptians to get sizable numbers of infantry and armor across. By October 8, the Egyptians had established a three- to five-mile-deep penetration on the east bank of the canal with some 500 tanks. They then fortified this zone with more troops. Two Egyptian divisions held the seized area, which was also defended by SAM batteries.

The Israelis, meanwhile, mobilized two armored divisions under Major Generals Ariel Sharon and Abraham (Bren) Adan and on October 8 launched a quick counteroffensive in an attempt to repel the Egyptian troops. The undermanned and underequipped Israeli troops, however, came up against the far larger, well-organized, and well-equipped Egyptian force protected by highly effective handheld antitank missiles. The Egyptians crushed the Israeli counteroffensive. In the fighting, Israeli ground support aircraft also suffered heavy losses against Egyptian antiaircraft defenses, especially from the SAMs. Following this setback, the Israeli General Staff decided to halt offensive actions on the Suez Front and give priority to the fighting in the north against Syria.

Sadat now overruled his ground commander, Field Marshal Ahmed Ismail Ali, and, following Syrian pleas for assistance, ordered a resumption of the offensive in the Sinai on October 11. This, however, took Egyptian forces out of their prepared defensive positions and removed them from the effective SAM cover on the other side of the canal, which was to Israeli advantage. On October 14 the Israelis threw back the Egyptians and inflicted heavy losses on them, especially in tanks.

On October 15–16 the Israelis located a gap between the two Egyptian divisions defending the occupied area that had gone unnoticed by the Egyptian command. Sharon's division then drove through that gap, and part of the division crossed the canal. An Israeli paratroop brigade established a bridgehead on the west bank. The Israeli high command now had two goals: establishing a SAM-free zone over which Israeli aircraft could maneuver free from the threat of missile attack and cutting off Egyptian troops east of the canal from their bases west of it.

The Egyptian Second Army then closed behind Sharon, isolating his division on both sides of the canal. Adan's division, however, broke through, bringing a bridge forward to the crossing point. The Egyptian Second Army, assisted by units of the Third Army, was unable to close the Israeli supply corner and cut off the Israelis at the canal.

Fighting during October 16–18 was known as the Battle of the Chinese Farm. It took its name from a former Japanese experimental agricultural station there, which the Israelis assumed to have been Chinese. The Egyptians suffered heavy losses, especially in tanks, and on the night of October 17–18 Adan's division crossed the canal.

Adan's division then pushed westward, rolling up Egyptian base camps and capturing antiaircraft positions and SAM sites, which greatly facilitated Israeli aircraft support. On October 19, however, Sharon was unsuccessful in seizing Ismailia. During October 20–22 Sharon continued his attacks on Ismailia but encountered heavy resistance from the Egyptian Second and Third armies. Adan enjoyed more success, cutting the Suez-Cairo road northeast of Suez.

On October 22 Egypt and Israel agreed to a cease-fire, to take effect that evening, but this was soon broken. The Israeli high command then dispatched strong reinforcements across the canal, while Adan was ordered to continue his drive southward to the Gulf of Suez. Another Israeli division, commanded by Major General Kalman Magen, followed after Adan, reaching Adabiya on the Gulf of Suez.

The Egyptians turned back an Israeli effort to take Suez during October 23–24. A second cease-fire was concluded on October 24 and went into effect the next day. Despite some military activity thereafter, it eventually took hold.

Course of Operations on the Syrian Front

Syrian president Hafez al-Assad's chief motivation in joining Egyptian president Sadat in the war was to regain the Golan Heights along the 45-mile Syria-Israeli border. This volcanic lava plateau of about 480 square miles is bordered by Mount Hermon on the north, the upper Jordan River Valley of the Sea of Galilee to the west, the Yarmouk Valley on the south, and the Ruqqad stream to the east. Israeli forces had captured the Golan Heights from Syria in the 1967 Six-Day War, thereby gaining security for Israel's northern settlements from sporadic Syrian bombardment. Unlike Sadat, Assad had no diplomatic goals and no intention of using the war as leverage for a settlement with Israel.

At 2:00 p.m. on October 6 simultaneous with the Egyptian air strikes to the south, Syria launched a massive air strike accompanied by a heavy artillery bombardment against Israeli positions on the Golan Heights. Syrian ground forces then advanced in an effort to recapture this area and drive on Jerusalem from the north. Syrian Army major general Yousef Chakour commanded the attacking force

of some 60,000 men in two armored divisions (600 tanks) and two infantry divisions (another 300 tanks). The Syrians also had some 140 artillery batteries, including long-range 130mm and 154mm guns. Opposing them, Israeli major general Yitzhak Hofi's Northern Command numbered some 12,000 troops, 177 tanks, and 11 artillery batteries.

With the exception of one important outpost, however, Israeli forces were not taken by surprise. Israeli intelligence had accurately detected the massive Syrian buildup, and Israeli forces on this front were on full alert. The tanks were in hull-down positions behind earthen barricades, with the infantry in their fighting positions.

The one exception was Mount Hermon. At the very start of the war on the northern front, four helicopters carried Syrian commandos to the back of the fortified Israeli observation post on Mount Hermon that provided an excellent view of the Golan Heights and the Damascus Plateau. The two-platoon Israeli garrison there was taken completely by surprise, with most of the soldiers at prayer. Within a few minutes most of the defenders were dead, and some of those who surrendered were subsequently butchered by their captors.

The main Syrian attack by the four divisions occurred in three axes against two Israeli brigades in defensive positions. Israel mobilization was excellent, and reservists were soon on the scene, but it took time to ready their equipment and tanks for action and bring them forward. Nonetheless, within a day the Israeli 7th Armored Brigade halted the northernmost thrust by the Syrian 7th Infantry Division, destroying most of the Syrian tanks. The Israelis also repulsed an attack by the Syrian 3rd Tank Division, which was to pass through the 7th Infantry Division.

The two Syrian thrusts in the south nearly entered the Jordan River Valley, however. At Rafid during October 6–7, the Syrian 5th Mechanized Division broke through and virtually destroyed the Israeli 188th Armored Brigade. Reinforced by the Syrian 1st Tank Division, the 5th Mechanized Division pushed to the western escarpment of the Golan Heights, where it halted as much for logistical reasons as from the actions of Israeli reserve units, which were now entering the fighting. If the Syrians could push beyond the escarpment, they could cross the Jordan River and Galilee, cutting Israel in two. The Israeli troops realized what was at stake; if they failed here, the Syrians would spill into the valleys that contained the defenders' family homes.

Israeli McDonnell-Douglas F-4 Phantoms and Douglas A-6 Skyhawk aircraft went into action immediately following the first Syrian attacks. They attacked the clusters of many Syrian tanks, armored personnel carriers, and artillery pieces. Some 1,500 tanks of the two sides were now crammed into a relatively small space, and the Golan Heights quickly became one vast graveyard of armored vehicles (especially for the Syrian T-55 tanks) and abandoned guns, but many of the Israeli jets also fell prey to Syrian SAMs and mobile antiaircraft guns. And many of the Israeli M-48 Patton and A41 Centurion tanks were also knocked out. Only the Israeli close air support, rapid arrival of Israeli reserves, and unimaginative Syrian attacks prevented the Syrians from overrunning the Israeli positions and retaking the southern Golan Heights on the second day of fighting.

During October 8–9 the Israelis counterattacked in the south, assisted by the 7th Armored Brigade brought down from the northern Golan Heights. On October 9 the Israeli 7th Brigade halted a Syrian thrust north of Quneitra (Kuneitra), and the next day the Israelis mounted a major counteroffensive north of the Quneitra-Damascus road. Three divisions pushed the Syrian 5th Mechanized and 1st Tank Divisions back to and beyond the prewar Israeli-Syrian border.

Beginning on October 12, the Israelis began to withdraw some units south to fight on the Sinai front. Nonetheless, by October 14 the Israelis had opened up a salient inside Syria some 10 miles deep, 30 miles wide, and only 25 miles from Damascus. The Israelis held here during October 15–19 against fierce Syrian and Iraqi counterattacks, Iraq and Jordan having now entered the war. On October 15 the Israelis repulsed the Iraqi 3rd Armored Division, and on October 19 they halted another Arab counterattack against the salient, this one spearheaded by Jordanian units. The Israelis maintained these positions until the cease-fire of October 24.

On October 22 following two failed assaults on October 8 and 21 and just before a cease-fire went into effect, Israeli helicopter-borne paratroopers captured the Syrian observation post on Mount Hermon, above the original Israeli position. At the same time, Israeli infantry retook the original Israeli observation post. The cease-fire on the Golan front went into effect at 6:52 p.m.

The constrained area of the Golan Heights and the large forces involved ensured both fierce fighting and heavy losses on both sides. In the fighting for the Golan Heights, Israel lost nearly 800 dead and 250 tanks put out of action, along with a number of ground support aircraft shot down. Certainly a key factor in Israeli success was their ability to quickly return disabled tanks to battle. Syrian losses were significantly greater: perhaps 8,000 men killed, 1,150 tanks destroyed, and 118 aircraft lost.

Course of the Air War

Israeli ground support aircraft first arrived over the Sinai and Golan fronts on October 6 some 40 minutes after the commencement of the Arab attack but immediately encountered heavy Arab antiaircraft fire and SAMs. The Israelis lost more than 30 aircraft, and for the first few days of the war Israeli air support was ineffective. Beginning on October 8 with the employment of electronic countermeasures and chaff, Israeli aircraft were able to provide far greater assistance to the troops on the ground. They also destroyed some Egyptian bridges over the Suez Canal and attacked Arab airfields.

Beginning on October 9, using the excuse of Syrian surface-to-surface missile attacks against the Hula Valley, Israel launched a major aerial campaign against Syria. Israeli aircraft struck deep within that country, hitting the Syrian Ministry of Defense in Damascus as well as seaports, industrial sites, and fuel storage areas. These attacks profoundly affected the Syrian economy and continued until October 21.

Meanwhile, the Israelis won control of the air over the Suez front. The success of Adan's armor division in capturing Egyptian antiaircraft units and SAM sites on the western bank of the Suez Canal greatly aided the Israeli Air Force in its highly effective support of the Battle of the Chinese Farm and the Israeli army breakout to the south.

Course of the War at Sea

On the start of the war, the Egyptians imposed a naval blockade of Israel's coasts to disrupt its Mediterranean trade, while Egyptian destroyers and submarines at the Strait of Bab al-Mandab halted seaborne traffic to Eilat.

On the first night of the war, however, Israeli Saar- and Reshef-class missile boats attacked the chief Syrian Mediterranean port of Latakia (Ladhaqiyya). Syrian missile boats engaged the attackers, and in the first naval battle in history between missile-firing ships, the Israelis defeated the incoming Syrian fire-and-forget Styx missiles while using their own radar-guided Gabriel ship-to-ship missiles to destroy one Osa- and two Komar-class missile boats and a minesweeper. No Israeli vessels were lost. The Syrian Navy then remained in port for the rest of the war. The Battle of Latakia brought new prestige for the Israeli Navy, previously regarded as only a poor relation of its highly regarded army and air force. Israeli electronic countermeasure techniques employed in the battle set a new standard for subsequent naval engagements employing missiles.

A second Israeli strike at Latakia on the night of October 7–8 was inconclusive, as were engagements that same night between Israeli and Egyptian naval units in the Mediterranean and Red Seas. In all instances, however, the Syrian and Egyptian ships withdrew. On October 8–9 in a naval action off the Egyptian port of Damietta, Egyptian missile boats sortied to engage an Israeli missile boat task force, which sank four of them. There were no Israeli losses. In an action the next night off Egyptian Port Said, another Egyptian missile boat was sunk. The remaining Egyptian missile boats were then withdrawn to Damietta and Alexandria.

During the nights of October 9–10 and 12–13, Israeli missile boats struck Syrian ports. In the first attack they bombarded

Latakia, Tartus, and Banias. No Syrian missile boats challenged them. In the second raid, the Israelis again struck Latakia and Tartus. This time Syrian missile boats sought to engage the Israelis, though without success.

During October 15–16 Israeli missile boats attacked the Nile Delta and sank a number of Egyptian landing craft. Finally on October 21–22, the Israelis attacked Abu Kir (Aboukir) Bay and Alexandria and there sank two Egyptian patrol boats.

Both the United States, supporting Israel, and the Soviet Union, supporting the Arab states, were caught off guard by the war, although the Soviets probably learned of the Egyptian and Syrian plans several days in advance of the actual attacks. Both sides in the war were soon in need of resupply. On October 8 Israel sent El Al aircraft to the United States to procure supplies, and the next day the Soviet Union commenced an airlift of supplies to Syria and Egypt through Hungary and Yugoslavia. On October 13 the United States augmented the Israeli airlifts by sending American C5A transport planes to Israel by way of the Azores. Between October 14 and 21 the United States airlifted some 20,000 tons of supplies to Israel, as opposed to some 15,000 tons supplied by the Soviet Union to the Arab states.

On October 24 the Soviet Union had threatened intervention in announcing that it was placing seven airborne divisions on alert, presumably to be sent to Egypt if necessary to break the Israeli stranglehold on the Egyptian Third Army east of the Suez Canal. The next day, U.S. secretary of state Henry Kissinger announced that the United States had placed its armed forces—including its nuclear assets—on "Precautionary Alert," based on the possibility of Soviet intervention.

Any possibility of a Soviet-U.S. armed clash over the Middle East ended with a United Nations (UN) Security Council resolution—with both the Soviet and U.S. representatives voting in the affirmative—to establish a 7,000-man UN emergency force to be sent to the Middle East to enforce the cease-fires in the Sinai Peninsula and the Golan Heights.

Casualty figures for the war vary depending on the source and especially for Egypt and Syria, which did not release any official figures. Israel suffered 2,521–2,800 killed in action and 7,250–8,800 wounded; 293 were captured. Some 400 Israeli tanks were destroyed; another 600 were disabled but returned to service. The Israeli Air Force lost 102 airplanes and 2 helicopters. There were no navy losses.

Arab casualties were much higher. Most estimates fall in the range of 5,000–15,000 Egyptians and 3,000–3,500 Syrians killed; the number of wounded is unknown. Iraq lost 278 killed and 898 wounded, while Jordan suffered 23 killed and 77 wounded. A total of 8,372 Egyptians, 392 Syrians, 13 Iraqis, and 6 Moroccans were taken prisoner. The Arab states lost 2,250–2,300 tanks, 400 of which were taken by the Israelis in good working order and added to their inventory. Arab aircraft losses are estimated at 450–512. Nineteen Arab naval vessels, including 10 missile boats, were sunk.

Significance

The war revealed the vulnerability of tanks, aircraft, and ships to the new missile weapons. In the end, however, the outcome of the war secured Israel's borders. Nonetheless, the war shocked Israel. Following the rapid overwhelming victory in the 1967 Six-Day War, the Israeli public and military had become complacent. The early losses and hard fighting of the 1973 Yom Kippur War brought new respect for the Egyptian and Syrian armed forces. Yet there was anger over the surprise of the Arab attack. An investigatory agency, the Agranat Commission, fixed blame on several military officers and recommended they be dismissed, including IDF chief of staff General Elazar. The commission did not assess the responsibility of the civilian leadership, but Meir resigned in April 1974, and Dayan resigned at the same time. Yitzhak Rabin became prime minister.

Although the Arab states lost the war, the conflict certainly erased the trauma of their rapid defeat in the Six-Day War of 1967 and allowed them to negotiate as equals with Israel. Yet the Yom Kippur War had seen Israel secure additional Arab territory, and this may have helped convince many in the Arab world that Israel could not be defeated militarily. The war brought the removal of a number of Arab military commanders.

Talks between Egyptian and Israeli military representatives on the west bank of the canal on October 28, 1973, led to an agreement that Egypt might send noncombatant supplies to its Third Army trapped east of the Suez Canal. Nonmilitary supplies were also allowed to pass, and prisoners of war were to be exchanged.

In December 1973 a summit conference, recognized by UN Security Council Resolution 344 calling for a "just and durable peace," opened in Geneva. All parties to the war were invited, but the talks adjourned on January 9, 1974, after Syria refused to participate. Kissinger commenced shuttle diplomacy ending in the initial military disengagement agreement, signed by Israel and Egypt on January 18, 1974, known as Sinai I. Israel agreed to pull back

its forces from west of the Suez Canal and also from the length of the front to create security zones for Egypt, UN observers, and Israel, although Israel still held nearly all of Sinai. Another agreement of September 4, 1975, known as Sinai II saw Israel withdrawing another 20–40 kilometers, with UN observer forces taking over that area. Still, Israel held more than two-thirds of Sinai.

A peace agreement between Israel and Egypt known as the Camp David Accords was finally reached on September 17, 1978, following negotiations hosted by President Jimmy Carter. In accordance with the treaty, Israeli forces withdrew gradually from Sinai, with the last troops exiting on April 26, 1982. There is still no formal peace agreement between Israel and Syria. Sadat was assassinated on October 6, 1981, while attending a military review commemorating the ninth anniversary of the start of the war by Islamist Egyptian Army members outraged at his negotiations with Israel.

On the Syrian front, from February to May 1974 Syria engaged Israel in a war of attrition along the Golan Heights, consisting of artillery fire along the cease-fire line between Quneitra and Damascus. The Syrians hoped thereby to force Israel to agree to withdraw its troops from the Golan Heights. On May 31 following 32 days of shuttle diplomacy by U.S. secretary of state Kissinger, the two sides agreed to disengage. An exchange of prisoners occurred, and Israel relinquished all territory taken from Syria in the October 1973 war, two small strips taken in 1967, and the town of Quneitra. A cease-fire line was established between the two states, to be patrolled by troops of the United Nations Disengagement Observer Force.

Finally, the Yom Kippur War brought a major world economic shock. On October 17, 1973, in response to U.S. support of Israel, the Arab members of the Organization of Oil Exporting Countries, led by Saudi Arabia, decided to reduce oil production by 5 percent per month. When on October 19 U.S. president Richard Nixon authorized a major allocation of arms supplies and $2.2 billion in appropriations for Israel, Saudi Arabia declared an embargo against the United States, later joined by other oil exporters and extended against other states as well. Unlike the ineffective embargo of the 1967 Six-Day War, this resulted in a full-blown energy crisis in much of the West and great havoc for the Western economies. The embargo lasted five months, until March 18, 1974.

Further Reading

Adan, Avraham. *On the Banks of the Suez: An Israeli General's Personal Account of the Yom Kippur War.* Novato, CA: Presidio, 1980.

Dunstan, Simon. *The Yom Kippur War 1973.* 2 vols. Oxford, UK: Osprey, 2003.

El-Gamasy, Mohamed Abdul Ghani. *The October War: Memoirs of Field Marshal El-Gamasy of Egypt.* Translated by Gillian Potter, Nadra Morcos, and Rosette Frances. Cairo: American University in Cairo Press, 1993.

Gawrych, George W. *The 1973 Arab-Israeli War: The Albatross of Decisive Victory.* Leavenworth Papers No. 21. Fort Leavenworth, KS: Combat Studies Institute, 1996.

Heikal, Mohammed Hasanyn. *The Road to Ramadan.* New York: Quadrangle/New York Times Book Company, 1975.

Kahalani, Avigdor. "Israeli Defense of the Golan." *Military Review* 59(10) (October 1979): 2–13.

Kahana, Ephraim. "Early Warning versus Concept: The Case of the Yom Kippur War, 1973." *Intelligence and National Security* 17 (Summer 2002): 81–104.

Pollack, Kenneth M. *Arabs at War: Military Effectiveness, 1948–1991.* Lincoln: University of Nebraska Press, 2002.

Rabinovich, Abraham. *The Yom Kippur War: An Epic Encounter That Transformed the Middle East.* New York: Schocken Books, 2004.

Shazli, Saad al. *The Crossing of the Suez.* San Francisco: Mideast Research, 1980.

Soviet-Afghan War (1979–1989)

Dates	December 24, 1979–February 15, 1989
Location	Afghanistan
Combatants	Soviet Union and Democratic Republic of Afghanistan vs. Mujahideen rebels
Principal Commanders	Soviet Union: Leonid Brezhnev, Mikhail Gorbachev, Dimitry Ustinov Afghanistan government: Babrak Karmal, Mohammad Najibullah, Abdul Rashid Dostum Mujahideen: Ahmad Shah Massoud, Abdul Haq, Abdullah Azzam
Principal Battles	Kabul
Outcome	A major military defeat for the Soviet Union, the war helps bring the collapse of the Soviet Union and also leads to the creation of an Afghan Islamic state.

Causes

The Soviet-Afghan War of December 24, 1979–February 15, 1989, a major military conflict during the Cold War (1947–1991), was caused by the Soviet desire to control Afghanistan. In August 1975 the Soviets had signed a 30-year economic assistance agreement with the Afghans, but in early 1978, alarmed over growing Soviet influence in his country, Afghan president Mohammed Daoud Khan reduced the number of Soviet advisers in the country from 1,000 to 200. Daoud also moved, albeit too late and ineffectively, against the Afghan communists.

On April 19, 1978, on the occasion of a funeral for prominent leftist political leader Mir Akbar Khyber, up to 30,000 Afghans gathered to hear speeches by Afghan communist leaders Nur Muhammad Taraki, Hafizullah Amin, and Babrak Karmal. Daoud ordered the arrest of the communist leaders. Taraki was caught after a week, but Karmal escaped to the Soviet Union, and Amin was merely placed under house arrest. Operating from his home and employing his family as couriers, Amin directed planning for a coup d'état against Daoud, who was unpopular with many Afghans for his authoritarian rule.

On April 26 Daoud placed the Afghan Army on alert, but on April 27 anti-Daoud military units at Kabul International Airport were nonetheless able to launch the coup attempt. During April 27–28, army units both opposing and loyal to the government battled in and around Kabul. Daoud and most of his family were caught and executed in the presidential palace on April 28, the coup leaders announcing that Daoud had "resigned for reasons of health." Soviet involvement in the coup, known as the Saur Revolution, is unclear, but Moscow certainly welcomed the change of government.

On May 1, Nur Mohammad Taraki assumed the Afghan presidency. He was also the prime minister and the secretary-general of the communist People's Democratic Party of Afghanistan (PDPA). The country was renamed the Democratic Republic of Afghanistan (DRA); it lasted until April 1992. Hafizullah Amin, who was foreign minister in the new government, was its driving force as the Taraki regime rooted out its opponents and embarked on an extensive modernization program that included women's rights and freedom of religion. It also implemented an extensive land reform program. The majority of Afghan city dwellers either welcomed the reforms or were ambivalent about them. The secular nature of the reforms were, however, highly unpopular with the very religiously conservative Afghan countryside, where there was strong sentiment for traditionalist Islamic restrictions regarding women.

On February 14, 1979, U.S. ambassador to Afghanistan Adolph Dubs was taken hostage by Muslim extremists and killed that same day in the exchange of gunfire when Afghan security forces and their Soviet advisers stormed the hotel in Kabul where he was being held. The U.S. government protested the Soviet role.

Opposition was building against the regime, and Afghan Muslim leaders soon declared a jihad against "godless communism." By August 1978 the Taraki regime faced an armed revolt that included the defection of a portion of the army. On March 27, 1979, Taraki was forced to appoint Amin premier. In these circumstances, U.S. president Jimmy Carter's administration extended covert assistance to the conservative Islamic antigovernment

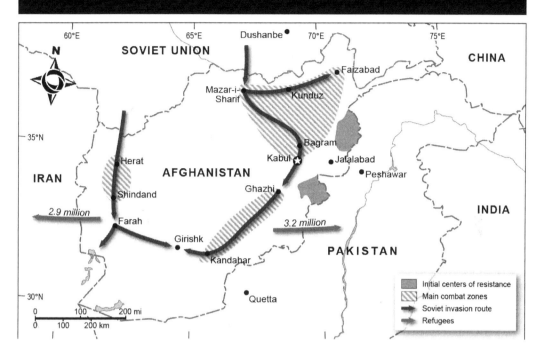

SOVIET INVASION OF AFGHANISTAN, 1979

mujahideen (freedom fighters, holy warriors) now fighting the Afghan communist government. This program, spearheaded by U.S. national security adviser Zbigniew Brzezinski, aided and trained the mujahideen through the Pakistani Inter-Services Intelligence (ISI). The mujahideen continued to make steady gains in the rural areas of the country.

On September 14, 1979, Amin ousted President Taraki, who was slain in the coup. This change of power was apparently accomplished without Soviet approval, and friction between the Soviets and Amin increased.

As the mujahideen registered steady gains in the countryside against the communist government, Moscow grew increasingly concerned. The Soviet leadership was then committed to the so-called Brezhnev Doctrine, elucidated by Soviet

leader Leonid Brezhnev. First employed in Czechoslovakia in 1968, it held that the Soviet Union had the right to interfere militarily to prevent the overthrow of a communist government. Moscow was also fearful of the possible impact of an Islamic fundamentalist regime on the large Muslim population of Soviet Central Asia, specifically in the republics bordering on Afghanistan. As a consequence, the Soviet leadership moved toward military intervention.

During the last months of 1979, the Brezhnev government dispatched some 4,500 Soviet advisers to assist the DRA while also allowing Soviet aircraft to conduct bombing raids against mujahideen positions. Soviet deputy defense minster Ivan G. Pavlovskii, who had played an important role in the Soviet invasion of Czechoslovakia, opposed a full-scale intervention, but his superior, Defense Minister

Dmitrii Ustinov, convinced Brezhnev to undertake it, arguing that this was the only sure means to preserve the Afghan communist regime. Ustinov also postulated a short and victorious intervention. The deciding factor for Brezhnev was apparently Amin's coup and the death of staunch Soviet ally Taraki in September 1979. Beginning in November, the Soviets increased the size of their garrisons at the two air bases in Kabul and began quietly prepositioning forces just north of Afghanistan, most notably the Fortieth Army composed largely of Central Asian troops.

Course

On December 24, 1979, Soviet troops invaded Afghanistan. Moscow cited as justification the 1978 Treaty of Friendship, Cooperation and Good Neighborliness between the two countries and claimed that the Afghan government had invited them in. The invasion began with Soviet special forces seizing control of the Kabul airport. Deputy minister of internal affairs Lieutenant General Viktor S. Paputin commanded the operation.

Having secured the Kabul airport, on December 25 the Soviets began a massive airlift, flying three airborne divisions—the 103rd, 104th, and 105th—into Kabul, while four motorized rifle divisions invaded overland from the north. During December 25–28 the 105th Division occupied Kabul against considerable resistance from elements of the Afghan Army and the local population.

Afghan president Amin and his ministers were cut off in the presidential palace. The Soviets attacked the palace, and Amin was killed either in the fighting or by execution. Soviet commander Paputin was also killed during the battle. On December 28 the Soviets installed Babrak Karmal,

former Afghan vice president and then Afghan ambassador to Czechoslovakia, as president.

The more moderate Kemal attempted without great success to win popular support by portraying himself as a devoted Muslim and Afghan nationalist. Meanwhile, Soviet forces occupied the major Afghan cities and secured control of the roads.

Unable to meet the Soviets in conventional battle, the mujahideen resorted to protracted guerrilla warfare, ambushing Soviet road-bound convoys and laying siege to several Soviet-occupied towns. During February 21–23, 1980, a popular Afghan uprising occurred in Kabul, but Soviet troops crushed it. Some 500 Afghans were killed and 1,200 were imprisoned.

The invasion of Afghanistan had immediate adverse international consequences for the Soviet Union. For one thing, it effectively ended détente. Having expended considerable effort to improving relations with the Soviet Union, U.S. president Jimmy Carter felt betrayed by Moscow and reacted swiftly and strongly to the invasion. On December 28 he publicly denounced the Soviet action as a "blatant violation of accepted international rules of behavior." On December 31 he accused Moscow of having lied about the reasons behind its intervention, and on January 3, 1980, he asked the U.S. Senate to delay consideration of the SALT II treaty. On January 23, 1980, in his State of the Union address, Carter warned that the Soviet action in Afghanistan constituted a serious threat to world peace, because should the Soviets be able to control Afghanistan, it would be able to dominate the Persian Gulf and thus be in position to interdict at will the flow of Middle East oil.

Carter then enunciated what became known as the Carter Doctrine, declaring that any effort to dominate the Persian Gulf would be interpreted as an attack on American interests, to be countered by force if necessary. Carter also moved to limit the transfer of technology and the sale of agricultural products, including grain, to the Soviet Union. He imposed restrictions on Soviet fishing privileges in U.S. waters, and he canceled U.S. participation in the 1980 Moscow Summer Games and called on America's allies to do the same.

Carter also called for increased defense spending and registration for the draft, pushed for creation of a rapid-deployment force capable of intervening in the Persian Gulf or other areas threatened by the Soviets, offered increased military aid to Pakistan, moved to enhance ties with the People's Republic of China, and approved expanded covert assistance to the mujahideen. These steps, except for the last, all had but limited impact. Key U.S. allies rejected both economic sanctions and the Olympic boycott. Also, other states, notably Argentina, offset the grain embargo by increasing their own grain sales to the Soviet Union. There was also little interest among the American public for involvement in Afghanistan.

Republican Ronald Reagan, who defeated Carter in the November 1980 presidential election, took an even harder stand toward the Soviet Union, which he characterized as an "evil empire." The Reagan administration poured vast sums of money into a massive military buildup to include development of a missile defense system, the Strategic Defense Initiative, known as "Star Wars" by its critics. This led Moscow to increase its defense spending, a major factor in the subsequent financial collapse of the Soviet Union.

In the spring of 1980 the Soviets mounted offensive operations. The Soviet strategy called for, in order, relieving besieged towns; driving the mujahideen from the towns, roads, and fertile agricultural regions back into the mountains; securing the frontier near the Khyber Pass to prevent the mujahideen from receiving weapons and other military supplies from Pakistan; and attacking and eliminating the mujahideen mountain camps.

The first two phases enjoyed considerable success. The Soviets employed jet aircraft to bomb rebel positions, followed by Mil Mi-24 armored helicopter gunships firing rockets and machine guns. Mil Mi-26 helicopters then ferried assault troops to attack the mujahideen in place.

Although the mujahideen inflicted significant casualties on the Soviets, they themselves suffered heavily and were driven from the towns and into the hills and mountains. The Soviets gradually increased the number of troops in Afghanistan to some 105,000 men, but this number was insufficient to defeat the insurgents. The Soviets never were able to control the mountainous areas where the guerrillas established their bases, nor did the Soviets always enjoy complete control of the fertile valleys, where the mujahideen continued to carry out hit-and-run attacks and secure much-needed Soviet weapons and equipment. The Soviets also were unable to seal the porous frontier with Pakistan, which remained a source of arms and equipment supplied by both Pakistan and the U.S. Central Intelligence Agency (CIA).

Frustrated, the Soviets responded with wanton attacks on villages. They also employed numerous small land mines that killed or maimed numerous innocent civilian victims and, according to some sources, employed biological and chemical weapons in violation of the 1925 and 1972 Geneva protocols. The Soviets also expanded their air bases and brought in additional aircraft and equipment.

The mujahideen, meanwhile, remained short of equipment and supplies and were bitterly divided among themselves, thanks to tribal and clan loyalties that prevented them from establishing a unified leadership. In May 1985, however, representatives of seven major mujahideen groups met in Peshawar, Pakistan, to try to establish a united front against the Soviets.

On May 4, 1986, in a bloodless coup engineered by the Soviet Union, Mohammed Najibullah, former head of the Afghan secret police, replaced Karmal as secretary-general of the communist PDPA. In November 1987, Najibullah was elected president of Afghanistan for a seven-year term.

After meeting with Soviet leader Mikhail Gorbachev, in October 1986 Najibullah offered the mujahideen a unilateral cease-fire agreement and limited power-sharing arrangement, but they rejected it and the war continued. As with the United States in the Vietnam War, the Soviet leadership found itself committed to waging a war that seemed to offer no acceptable ending.

As the Soviet military increased its offensives, the United States increased its aid to the mujahideen. This included food, vehicles, and weapons. Assistance provided by the CIA ran into the billions of dollars and became one of its most expensive and protracted operations. The most important CIA-supplied weapon was the shoulder-launched ground-to-air Stinger missile. It and the British-supplied Blowpipe proved to be key in defeating Soviet air-to-ground support and especially the Mil Mi-8 and Mil Mi-24 armored helicopter gunships. The seemingly unending war exacted a continued heavy toll as the Afghan fighters defeated several Soviet offensives. As casualties mounted, Moscow came under increased domestic criticism, including that by prominent dissidents such as Andrei Sakharov.

By 1986 the Soviet leadership, now headed by the reformist Mikhail Gorbachev, began consideration of how it might extricate itself from what many observers characterized as the "Soviet Union's Vietnam." In April 1988, Gorbachev agreed to a United Nations–mediation proposal worked out in Geneva between the warring parties that provided for the withdrawal of Soviet forces to occur during a 10-month period.

The Soviet withdrawal occurred in two phases: the first from May 15 to August 16, 1988, and the second from November 15, 1988, to February 15, 1989. The withdrawal was generally peaceful, with the Soviet military working out cease-fire agreements with local mujahideen insurgent commanders. The agreement allowed Soviet military advisers to remain in Afghanistan and provide aid assistance to the more than 300,000-man DRA Army. Moscow also continued to support the DRA with weapons and equipment totaling some $500 million a month.

The Soviet-Afghan War cost Soviet forces some 15,000 dead, 54,000 wounded, and 417 missing. Afghan losses can only be approximated, but the best estimates are more than 1 million Afghan mujahideen combatants and civilians killed and more than 5.5 million displaced, a large number of these relocating in northwestern Pakistan.

Significance

Afghanistan itself was devastated by the fighting. Already one of the world's poorest countries, after the war Afghanistan ranked, according to the United Nations, 170 of 174 nations.

The Soviet-Afghan War was a major military defeat for the Soviet Union. The war seriously damaged the Soviet Union's military reputation and further undermined the legitimacy of the Soviet system. Certainly the war's high financial cost was a major factor in the collapse of the Soviet Union in 1991. The Islamists held this to be the case, with the leader of the Al Qaeda Islamist terrorist organization Osama bin Ladin attributing the dissolution of the Soviet Union to God "and the mujahideen in Afghanistan."

The United States lost interest in Afghanistan after the Soviet military withdrawal and extended scant aid to try to influence events in that war-torn nation. The new administration of President William Clinton handed this over to Pakistan and Saudi Arabia. Pakistan quickly took advantage, developing close relations first with warlords and then with the Taliban, a group of radical young Islamists, to secure trade interests and routes. This brought much ecological and agricultural destruction, including the destruction of Afghan forests and the widespread cultivation of opium.

The Soviet Union continued to support Afghan president Najibullah, who declared martial law, increased the role of the PDPA, and adopted policies favored by the hard-liners. Many if not most observers concluded that Najibullah would soon be driven from power by the mujahideen. Yet the army of the Republic of Afghanistan, which appeared to be on the brink of collapse on the Soviet departure, proved more effective than it had ever been under the Soviets. In July 1989 it inflicted a surprising defeat on the rebel forces at Jalalabad. In October 1990, however, the mujahideen

opened a major offensive, taking the provincial capitals of Tarin Kowt and Qalat.

Although they controlled much of the countryside, the mujahideen lacked the heavy weaponry required to secure the cities. Handicapped by the lack of unified command, they were also often at odds with one another. The war appeared to be a stalemate.

Najibullah's government, though it failed to win popular support, territory, or international recognition, remained in power until 1992. A major reason for its collapse was the refusal in 1992 of new Russian president Boris Yeltsin to sell oil products to Afghanistan because it did not want to support communists. The defection from the government side of General Abdul Rashid Dostam and his Uzbek militia in March 1992 further undermined Najibullah's power. In April, Najibullah and his communist government fell to the mujahideen, who set up a new governing council.

In September 1996 the more Islamic fundamentalist Taliban came to power in Afghanistan and ruled the country as the Islamic Emirate of Afghanistan until December 2001, with Kandahar as the capital. It secured diplomatic recognition from only three states: Pakistan, Saudi Arabia, and the United Arab Emirates. The Taliban enforced sharia law and sharply curtailed women's rights. Their harsh policies included the deliberate destruction of farmlands, tens of thousands of homes, and Afghan archaeological treasures. Hundreds of thousands of Afghans fled their homeland, most to Pakistan and Iran.

Widely believed to have been supported by the Pakistani ISI and military, the Taliban also granted safe haven to Saudi Osama bin Laden and the Al Qaeda terrorist organization. After Al Qaeda's attack on the United States on September 11, 2001, the Taliban was overthrown by a U.S.-led invasion of Afghanistan working with the United Front Afghan opposition. Later the Taliban reemerged as an insurgency movement to fight the American-backed administration of Hamid Karzai and the North Atlantic Treaty Organization International Security Assistance Force. The Afghanistan War that began in 2001, and that is in many ways a legacy of the Soviet-Afghan War, continues.

Further Reading

Braithwaite, Rodric. *Afgantsy: The Russians in Afghanistan, 1979–89.* New York: Oxford University Press, 2011.

Crile, George. *Charlie Wilson's War: The Extraordinary Story of the Largest Covert Operation in History.* New York: Atlantic Monthly Press, 2003.

Feifer, Gregory. *The Great Gamble: The Soviet War in Afghanistan.* New York: Harper, 2009.

Galeotti, Mark. *Afghanistan: The Soviet Union's Last War.* London: Frank Cass, 1995.

Hauner, Milan. *The Soviet War in Afghanistan: Patterns of Russian Imperialism.* Lanham, MD: University Press of America, 1991.

Judge, Edward, and John W. Langdon, eds. *The Cold War: A History through Documents.* Upper Saddle River, NJ: Prentice Hall, 1999.

MacKenzie, David. *From Messianism to Collapse: Soviet Foreign Policy, 1917–1991.* Fort Worth, TX: Harcourt Brace, 1994.

Prados, John. *Presidents' Secret Wars: CIA and Pentagon Covert Operations from World War II through the Persian Gulf.* Chicago: I. R. Dee, 1996.

Russian General Staff. *The Soviet-Afghan War: How a Superpower Fought and Lost.* Lawrence: University of Kansas Press, 2002.

Iran-Iraq War (1980–1988)

Dates	September 22, 1980–August 20, 1988
Location	Iran, Iraq, Persian Gulf
Combatants	Iran vs. Iraq
Principal Commanders	Iran: Ayatollah Khomeini, Abal Hassan Bani Sadr Iraq: Saddam Hussein
Principal Battles	Khorramshahr (first), Qasr-a Shirn, Susangerd, Khorramshahr (second), Dezful, "War of the Cities," Basra, Majnoon Islands, Faw, al-Anfal Campaign
Outcome	The war ends with Iraqi troops withdrawing from land taken from Iran. Although Iraq still has the region's second most powerful military, with only Israel's being more powerful, it accumulated a vast debt, a key factor behind Saddam Hussein's subsequent invasion of Kuwait.

Causes

The war between Iran and Iraq during September 22, 1980–August 20, 1988, marked a continuation of the ancient Persian-Arab rivalry fueled by 20th-century border disputes and competition for hegemony in the Persian Gulf and Middle East regions. In the late 1970s the long-standing rivalry between these two nations was abetted by a collision between the Pan-Islamism and revolutionary Shia Islamism of Iran and the Pan-Arab nationalism of Iraq.

The border between the two states had been contested for some time, and in 1969 Iran had abrogated its treaty with Iraq on the navigation of the Shatt al-Arab waterway, Iraq's only outlet to the Persian Gulf. In 1971 Iran had seized islands in the Persian Gulf, and there had been border clashes between the two states in mid-decade. The rivalry between the two states was also complicated by minorities issues. Both states, especially Iraq, have large Kurdish populations in their northern regions, while an Arab minority inhabits the oil-rich Iranian province of Khuzestan.

Given their long-standing rivalry and ambitions, it was natural that the leaders of both states would seek to exploit any perceived weakness in the other. Thus, Iraqi president Saddam Hussein sought to take advantage of the upheaval following the fall of Mohammad Reza Shah Pahlavi and the establishment of Ayatollah Ruhollah Khomeini's Islamic Republic after the Iranian Revolution (Islamic Revolution) of 1978–1979. This event had been precipitated by the disbandment of the shah's military establishment and an end to U.S. military assistance to Iran, which meant a shortage of spare parts. Hussein saw in this situation an opportunity to punish Iran for its support of Kurdish and Shia opposition to Sunni Muslim domination in Iraq. More important, it was a chance for Iraq to reclaim both banks of the Shatt al-Arab as well as Khuzestan; acquire the islands of Abu Musa, Greater Tunb, and Lesser Tunb on behalf of the United Arab Emirates; and overthrow the militant Islamic regime in Iran.

On the eve of the war, Iraq enjoyed an advantage in ground forces, while Iran had the edge in the air. Iraq had a regular army of some 300,000 men, 1,000 artillery pieces, 2,700 tanks, 332 fighter aircraft, and 40 helicopters. Iran had a regular army

of 200,000 men, somewhat more than 1,000 artillery pieces, 1,740 tanks, 445 fighter aircraft, and 500 helicopters.

Course

The war began on September 22, 1980, when Iraqi forces invaded western Iran along their common border. The Iraqi attack came as a complete surprise to Iran. Hussein justified it as a response to an alleged assassination attempt sponsored by Iran on Iraqi deputy prime minister Tariq Aziz. Striking on a 300-mile front, Iraqi troops were initially successful against the disorganized Iranian defenders. The Iraqis drove into southwestern Iran, securing the far side of the Shatt al-Arab. In November they captured Khorramshahr in Khuzestan Province. In places, the Iraqis penetrated as much as 30 miles into Iran. But Iran is a large country, and the Iraqi forces moved too cautiously, throwing away the opportunity for a quick and decisive victory. Another factor in their stalled offensive was certainly the rapid Iranian mobilization of resources, especially the largely untrained but fanatical Pasdaran (Revolutionary Guard Corps) militia.

Recovering from the initial shock of the Iraqi invasion, the Iranians soon established strong defensive positions. Iran's navy also carried out an effective blockade of Iraq. On the first day of the war, Iraqi air strikes destroyed much of the Iranian Air Force infrastructure, but most of the Iranian aircraft survived, and Iraq lacked the long-range bomber aircraft to be truly effective strategically against a country as large as Iran. Indeed, Iranian pilots flying U.S.-manufactured aircraft soon secured air superiority over the Iraqi Air Force's Soviet-built airplanes. The Iranians were then able to carry out ground-support missions utilizing both airplanes and helicopters that played an important role in checking the Iraqi advance.

Far from breaking Iranian morale as Hussein had hoped, the Iraqi attack served to rally public opinion around the Islamic regime. Ideologically committed Iranians flocked to join the Pasdaran and the army. By March 1981, the war had settled into a protracted stalemate. With both sides having constructed extensive defensive positions, much of the combat came to resemble the trench warfare of World War I.

In January 1982, Jordanian volunteers began arriving to assist the Iraqis, but this addition had little impact on the fighting. Then on March 22, the Iranians launched a major counteroffensive. Their forces included large numbers of ill-trained but fanatical Pasdaran fighters. Lasting until March 30, the offensive enjoyed considerable success, driving the Iraqis back as far as 24 miles in places.

During April 30–May 20 the Iranians renewed their attacks, again pushing the Iraqis back. Then on the night of May 22–23, the Iranians encircled the city of Khorramshahr, which the Iraqis had captured at the beginning of the war, forcing its surrender on May 24. There the Iranians captured large quantities of Soviet-manufactured weapons. Flush with victory, the Iranians now proclaimed as their war aim the overthrow of Saddam Hussein.

With the war now going badly for his country, Hussein proposed a truce and the withdrawal of all Iraqi troops from Iranian soil within two weeks of a truce agreement. Iraq also declared a unilateral cease-fire. Sensing victory, Iran rejected the proposal and reiterated its demand for the ouster of Hussein.

Given the Iranian rebuff and realizing that he had no legitimate hope of retaining his forces in Iran, Hussein now withdrew

them back into well-prepared static defenses in Iraq, reasoning that Iraqis would rally to his regime in a fight to defend their homeland. For political reasons, Hussein announced that the purpose of the withdrawal was to allow Iraqi forces to assist Lebanon, which had been invaded by Israeli forces on June 6, 1982.

Meanwhile, Iranian leaders rejected a Saudi Arabian–brokered deal that would have witnessed the payment of $70 billion in war reparations by the Arab states to Iran and complete Iraqi withdrawal from Iranian territory in return for a peace agreement. Iranian leaders insisted that Hussein be removed from power, that some 100,000 Shiites expelled from Iraq before the war be permitted to return home, and that the reparations figure be set at $150 billion. There is some suggestion that Iran did not expect these terms to be accepted and hoped to use the failure of negotiations as justification to continue the war with an invasion of Iraq. Indeed, Iranian leader Ayatollah Khomeini announced his intention to install an Islamic republic in Iraq.

The Iranians now sought to utilize their numerical advantage in a new offensive, which was launched on July 20, 1982. It was directed against Shiite-dominated southern Iraq, with the objective being the capture of Iraq's second-largest city, Basra. Iranian human-wave assaults, occasioned by a shortage of ammunition, encountered well-prepared Iraqi static defenses, supported by artillery. Hussein had also managed to increase substantially the number of Iraqis under arms.

Although the Iranians did manage to register some modest gains, these came at heavy human cost. In the five human-wave assaults of their Basra offensive (Operation RAMADAN), the Iranians sustained tens of thousands of casualties. Particularly hard-hit were the untrained and poorly armed

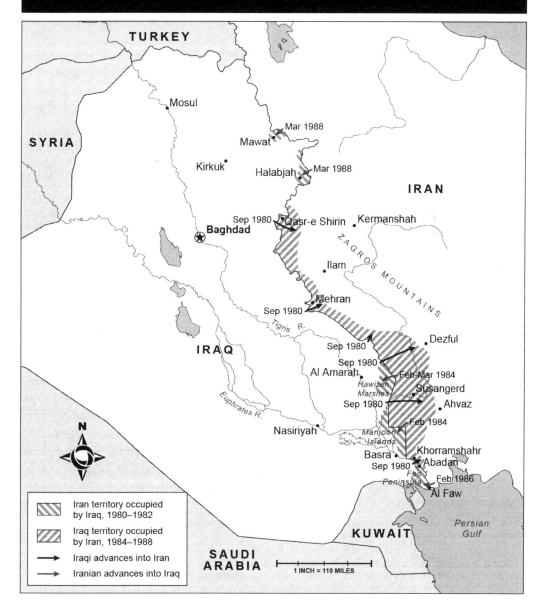

IRAN–IRAQ WAR, 1980 – 1988

units of boy-soldiers who volunteered to march into Iraqi minefields to clear them with their bodies for the trained Iranian soldiers who would follow. The Iraqis also employed poison gas against the Iranians, inflicting many casualties. On July 21, Iranian aircraft struck Baghdad. Iraq retaliated in August with attacks on the vital

Iranian oil-shipping facilities at Kharg Island, which also sank several ships.

During September–November, the Iranians launched new offensives in the northern part of the front, securing some territory near the border town of Samar, which Iraq had taken at the beginning of the war. The Iranians also struck west of

Dezful and, in early November, drove several miles into Iraq near Mandali. Iraqi counterattacks forced the Iranians back into their own territory. In the southern part of the front on November 17, the Iranians advanced to within artillery range of the vital Baghdad-Basra Highway.

Iran was now receiving supplies from such nations as the People's Republic of China, the Democratic People's Republic of Korea (North Korea), and Albania. Iraq was securing supplies from the Soviet Union and other Warsaw Pact states as well as from France, Great Britain, Spain, Egypt, Saudi Arabia, and the United States. Iraq's chief financial backers were Saudi Arabia, Kuwait, and the United Arab Emirates.

In the course of 1983, Iran launched five major offensives against Iraq. Before the first of these, however, during February 2–March 9 the Iraqi Air Force carried out large-scale air attacks against Iranian coastal oil-production facilities, producing the largest oil spill in the history of the Persian Gulf region. Again seeking to utilize their advantage in troop strength, during February 7–16 Iranian leaders launched a ground attack hoping to isolate Basra by cutting the Baghdad-Basra Highway at Kut. They drove to within 30 miles of their objective but were then halted and thrown back. In the fighting, the Iraqis claimed to have destroyed upward of 1,000 Iranian tanks.

During April 11–14, the Iranians attacked west of Dezful but failed to make meaningful gains. On July 20, Iraqi aircraft again struck Iranian oil-production facilities. Three days later, the Iranians attacked in northern Iraq but again registered few gains. The Iranians mounted a major offensive west of Dezful on July 30 but failed to break through. In the second week in August, however, the Iranians

blunted an Iraqi counterattack. Both sides suffered heavy casualties.

In late October the Iranians launched yet another attack in the north to close a salient there opened by Iranian Kurdish rebels. Iraqi leader Hussein was disappointed in his hope that the failed Iranian ground offensives and ensuing heavy casualties would make that regime more amenable to peace talks. Indeed, Iranian leader Ayatollah Khomeini restated his determination to overthrow the Iraqi regime.

Determined to prevent the spread of militant Islamism in the Middle East, the Ronald Reagan administration in the United States made a firm commitment to support Iraq. Washington supplied Baghdad with intelligence information in the form of satellite photography and also furnished economic aid and weapons. In a National Security decision directive of June 1982, Reagan determined that the United States must do whatever necessary to prevent Iraq from losing the war.

Believing that more aggressive tactics were necessary to induce Iran to talk peace, Hussein announced that unless Iran agreed to halt offensive action against Iraq by February 7, 1984, he would order major attacks against 11 Iranian cities. Iran then mounted a ground attack in the northern part of the front, and Hussein ordered air and missile attacks against the cities to proceed. These lasted until February 22. Iran retaliated in what became known as the "War of the Cities." There were five such air campaigns in the course of the war.

On February 15, 1984, the Iranians launched the first in a series of ground offensives. It fell in the central part of the front and pitted 250,000 Iranian troops against an equal number of Iraqi defenders. During February 15–22 in Operation DAWN 5 and during February 22–24 in Operation DAWN 6, the Iranians attempted to take the city of Kut to cut the vital Bagh-dad-Basra Highway there. The Iranians came within 15 miles of the city but were then halted.

The Iranians enjoyed more success in Operation KHEIBAR during February 24–March 19. This renewed drive against Basra came close to breaking through the stretched Iraqi defenders. The Iranians did capture part of the Majnoon Islands, with their undeveloped oil fields, then held them against an Iraqi counterattack supported by poison gas. The Iranians occupied these islands until near the end of the war.

With his forces having benefited from substantial arms purchases financed by the oil-rich Persian Gulf states, on January 28, 1985, Hussein launched the first Iraqi ground offensive since late 1980. It failed to register significant gains, and the Iranians responded with their own offensive, Operation BADR, beginning on March 11. Now better trained, the Iranian Army eschewed the costly human-wave tactics of the past, and its more effective tactics brought the capture of a portion of the Baghdad-Basra Highway. Hussein responded to this considerable strategic emergency with chemical weapons attacks and renewed air and missile strikes against 20 Iranian cities, including Tehran.

In February 17, 1986, in a surprise offensive employing commandos, Iranian forces captured the strategically important Iraqi port of Faw, southeast of Basra at the southeast end of the Faw peninsula on the Shatt al-Arab waterway. In January 1987, Iran launched Operation KARBALA 5, a renewed effort to capture Basra. When the operation ground to a halt in mid-February, the Iranians launched NASR 4 in northern Iraq, which threatened the Iraqi city of Kirkuk during May–June.

On March 7, 1987, the United States initiated Operation EARNEST WILL to protect

oil tankers and shipping lanes in the Persian Gulf. The so-called Tanker War had begun in March 1984 with the Iraqi air attack on strategic Kharg Island and nearby oil installations. Iran had then retaliated with attacks, including the use of mines, against tankers carrying Iraqi oil from Kuwait and on any tankers of the Persian Gulf states supporting Iraq. On November 1, 1986, the Kuwaiti government petitioned the international community to protect its tankers. The Soviet Union agreed to charter tankers, and on March 7, 1987, the United States announced that it would provide protection for any U.S.-flagged tankers. This would protect neutral tankers proceeding to or from Iraqi ports, ensuring that Iraq would have the economic means to continue the war.

On the night of May 17, 1987, an Iraqi French-manufactured Mirage F-1 fighter aircraft on antiship patrol fired two AM-39 Exocet antiship cruise missiles at a radar contact, apparently not knowing that it was the U.S. Navy frigate *Stark* (FFG-31). Although only one of the missiles detonated, both struck home and crippled the frigate, killing 37 crewmen and injuring another 50. The crew managed to save their ship, which then made port under its own power.

On July 20, 1987, the United Nations (UN) Security Council passed unanimously U.S.-sponsored Resolution 598. The resolution deplored attacks on neutral shipping and called for an immediate cease-fire and withdrawal of armed forces to internationally recognized boundaries.

Acting in retaliation for Iranian ground offensives, during February 1988 the Iraqis launched a renewed wave of attacks against Iranian population centers, and the Iranians reciprocated. These attacks included not only aircraft but also surface-to-surface missiles, principally the Soviet-built Scud type. Iraq fired many more missiles than did Iran (reportedly some 520 as opposed to 177). Also during February and extending into September, the Iraqi Army carried out a massacre of Kurds in northern Iraq, known as the al-Anfal (Spoils of War) Campaign. It claimed as many as 300,000 civilian lives and the destruction of some 4,000 villages.

Meanwhile on April 14, 1988, the U.S. Navy frigate *Samuel B. Roberts,* involved in Operation EARNEST WILL, was badly damaged when it struck an Iranian mine in the Persian Gulf. No one was killed, but the ship nearly sank. Four days later, the navy responded with Operation PRAYING MANTIS, the navy's largest battle involving surface warships since World War II. This one-sided battle also saw the first surface-to-surface missile engagement in U.S. naval history. U.S. forces damaged two Iranian offshore oil platforms, sank one Iranian frigate and a gunboat, damaged another frigate, and sank three Iranian speedboats. The United States lost one helicopter.

By the spring of 1988, Iraqi forces had been sufficiently reorganized to enable them to launch major operations. By contrast, Iran was now desperately short of spare parts, especially for its largely U.S.-built aircraft. The Iranians had also lost a large number of aircraft in combat operations. As a result, by late 1987 Iran was less able to mount an effective defense against the resupplied Iraqi Air Force, let alone carry out aerial counterattacks against a ground attack.

The Iraqis mounted four separate offensives in the spring of 1988. In the process they were able to recapture the strategically important Faw peninsula, which had been lost in 1986; drive the Iranians away from Basra; and make progress in the northern part of the front. The Iraqi victories came

at little cost to themselves, while the Iranians suffered heavy personnel and equipment losses. These Iranian setbacks were the chief factor behind Khomeini's decision to agree to a cease-fire as called for in UN Security Council Resolution 598.

On July 3, 1988, the crew of the U.S. Navy cruiser *Vincennes,* patrolling in the Persian Gulf and believing that they were under attack by an Iranian jet fighter, shot down Iran Air Flight 655, a civilian airliner carrying 290 passengers and crew. There were no survivors. The U.S. government subsequently agreed to pay $131.8 million in compensation for the incident. It expressed regret only for the loss of innocent life and did not apologize to the Iranian government. The incident may have served to convince Iranian leader Ayatollah Khomeini of the dangers of the United States actively entering the conflict against Iran and thus made him more amenable to ending the war.

War weariness and pressure from other governments induced both sides to accept a cease-fire agreement on August 20, 1988, bringing the eight-year war to a close. Total Iraqi casualties, including 60,000 men taken prisoner by Iran, numbered about 375,000 (perhaps 200,000 of these killed). This figure does not include those killed in the Iraqi government campaign against its own Kurdish population. Iran announced a death toll of nearly 300,000 people, but some estimates place the figure as high as 1 million or more. The war ended with a status quo ante bellum, with none of the outstanding issues resolved. The UN-arranged cease-fire merely ended the fighting, leaving these two isolated states to pursue an arms race with each other and with the other states in the region.

Negotiations between Iraq and Iran remained deadlocked for two years after the cease-fire. In 1990 Iraq, concerned with securing its forcible annexation of Kuwait, reestablished diplomatic relations with Iran and agreed to the withdrawal of Iraqi troops from occupied Iranian territory, the division of sovereignty over the Shatt al-Arab, and a prisoner-of-war exchange.

Significance

Iraqi leader Saddam Hussein, despite having led his nation into a disastrous war, emerged from it with the strongest military in the Middle East, second only to Israel. His power unchallenged in Iraq, he trumpeted a great national victory. The war, however, put Iraq deeply in debt to its Persian Gulf Arab neighbors, and this played a strong role in the coming of the Persian Gulf War. Indeed, the $14 billion debt owed to Kuwait was a key factor in Iraq's decision to invade that nation in 1990. In Iran, the war helped consolidate popular support behind the Islamic Revolution.

Further Reading

Cooper, Tom. *Iran-Iraq War in the Air: 1980–1988*. Atglen, PA: Schiffer Publishing, 2004.

Farrokh, Kaveh. *Iran at War: 1500–1988*. Oxford, UK: Osprey, 2011.

Hiro, Dilip. *The Longest War: The Iran-Iraq Military Conflict*. London: Routledge, 1990.

Johnson, Rob. *The Iran-Iraq War*. Houndmills, Basingstoke, Hampshire, UK: Palgrave Macmillan, 2010.

Karsh, Efraim. *The Iran-Iraq War: 1980–1988*. Oxford, UK: Osprey, 2002.

Murray, Williamson, and Kevin Murray. *The Iran-Iraq War: A Military and Strategic History*. New York: Cambridge University Press, 2014.

Pollack, Kenneth M. *Arabs at War: Military Effectiveness, 1948–1991*. Lincoln: University of Nebraska Press, 2004.

Rajaee, Farhang. *The Iran-Iraq War: The Politics of Aggression*. Gainesville: University Press of Florida, 1993.

Willet, Edward C. *The Iran-Iraq War*. New York: Rosen, 2004.

Iraq War (2003–2011)

Dates	March 20, 2003–December 15, 2011
Location	Iraq
Combatants	United States, Britain, and coalition partners vs. Iraq
Principal Commanders	United States: George W. Bush, Donald Rumsfeld, Paul Bremer, Barack Obama, Tommy Franks, Ricardo Sanchez, George W. Casey Jr., David Petraeus, Raymond T. Odierno Great Britain: Tony Blair, Brian Burridge Iraq: Saddam Hussein, Izzat Ibrahim ad-Douri
Principal Battles	Nasiriyah, Najaf, Karbala, Baghdad, Basra, Fallujah (first), Najaf (second), Fallujah (second), Habbaniyah
Outcome	Coalition forces overthrow Saddam Hussein and occupy Iraq, but the country is destabilized, with the majority Shiites taking power and ruling to the exclusion of the Sunnis and Kurds. The country then descends into chaos with an ensuing Sunni insurgency.

Causes

The Iraq War, also known as Operation
IRAQI FREEDOM, occurred in two phases:
the first was the invasion and rapid conquest of Iraq by coalition forces led by
the United States, and the second saw a
lengthy insurgency against the occupying
coalition forces and the new Iraqi government. Dates for the war are usually given
as March 20, 2003, to December 15, 2011,
when the last U.S. troops departed, but this
end date is misleading, as sectarian violence continued after the U.S. departure,
and it and outright warfare in Iraq are ongoing as of early 2015.

The historic roots of the violence in Iraq
go back at least as far as the peace settlement following World War I, which broke
up the old Ottoman Empire and created
new states in the Middle East in Palestine,
Lebanon, Syria, and Iraq and placed them
under European control in a mandate system. The arbitrary borders of these states
ignored religious rivalries, such as that between Shia and Sunni Muslims, and ethnic
divisions. Thus, the Kurds were denied a
state and found themselves a minority in
Iraq, Syria, Turkey, and Persia (Iran). By
1990, Iraq had a Shia majority (60 percent of the population) concentrated in
the south of the country and a Kurdish
minority (17 percent and Sunnis) in the
north but was ruled with an iron fist by
Saddam Hussein, a Sunni. The Sunnis (20
percent) were concentrated in western Iraq
and dominated the government and the
military.

Following a long, sanguinary, and financially costly war with Iran (1980–1988),
which he had initiated, Iraqi dictator Hussein sent his forces into oil-rich Kuwait
on August 2, 1990. He then proclaimed
Kuwait an Iraqi province. International

diplomatic efforts to remove the Iraqis
from Kuwait proving futile, a coalition of
34 states led by the United States attacked
Iraq and liberated Kuwait in the Persian
Gulf War (Operation DESERT STORM, January 17–February 28, 1991). With Kuwait
free of Iraqi army troops, U.S. president
George H. W. Bush, who had assembled
the impressive international coalition, ordered a halt to the fighting, allowing the
elite Republican Guard divisions, the Iraqi
Army's most effective units, to largely
escape intact, ensuring Hussein's continued hold on power. Coalition forces
commander U.S. general H. Norman
Schwarzkopf also erred in a cease-fire
agreement of March 3, 1991, that permitted the Iraqis to fly helicopters.

Hussein now quickly reestablished
his authority, employing the Republican
Guard units and helicopters to put down
rebellions by both the Shiites in the south
and the Kurds in the north. The United
States had encouraged both groups to rebel
against the central government during the
war but took no action while as many as
50,000 Shiites perished in the subsequent
repression. Hussein also began a program
of draining the swamps populated by the
southern so-called Marsh Arabs to better
control that restive group.

Hussein further defied United Nations
(UN) inspection teams by failing to account for and destroy all his biological and
chemical weapons, the so-called weapons
of mass destruction (WMDs). Stymied,
the UN withdrew its inspectors. In order
to help protect the Kurds and the Shiites,
the United States and Britain continued to
enforce the no-fly zone set by the cease-
fire north of the 36th Parallel and then a
southern zone set in 1992 at the 32nd Parallel and in 1993 extended to the 33rd Parallel, from which Iraqi fixed-wing aircraft

were prohibited. U.S. and British aircraft struck Iraqi ground radars and antiaircraft positions that on occasion fired on their aircraft, and larger strikes also took place.

Increasingly, though, the administration of U.S. president George W. Bush, elected in November 2000, adopted a tough attitude toward Iraq. This followed and was closely tied to the worst terrorist attack in U.S. history, carried out by the Islamist Al Qaeda terrorist organization on September 11, 2001, against the World Trade Center in New York and the Pentagon in Washington, D.C., resulting in the deaths of some 3,000 people. After the Taliban government of Afghanistan refused Washington's demands to hand over members of Al Qaeda and especially its leader, Osama bin Laden, U.S. forces invaded Afghanistan. They and opposition Northern Alliance (Afghan) forces easily overthrew the Taliban. However, they failed to secure bin Laden or, more important, to completely eliminate Taliban and Al Qaeda fighters, who subsequently mounted a years-long insurgency that continues today.

Encouraged by what appeared to be a quick victory in Afghanistan with a relatively modest commitment of U.S. ground troops, the Bush administration then shifted its attention to Iraq. In a speech to the U.S. Congress, Bush asserted his intention to root out international terrorism and to confront those states that supported it. He singled out an "Axis of Evil" of Iraq, Iran, and the Democratic People's Republic of Korea (North Korea). Under U.S. and British pressure, the UN Security Council unanimously passed Resolution 1141 calling on Iraq to reveal information regarding WMDs and on UN inspectors to report progress to the Security Council. It also threatened force unless Iraq fully complied.

Iraq claimed that it had nothing to hide and no WMDs, but the UN inspections went slowly and met many Iraqi-imposed obstacles. A frustrated President Bush and the so-called neocons (neoconservatives) in his administration now demanded military action against Iraq. The neocons saw such a war as a chance to not only overthrow Hussein but also produce a democratic, pro-U.S. Iraq and reshape the entire Middle East. Some held that given Iraq's oil, the war could be won at little cost in treasure to the United States.

A coalition of countries that had vested financial interests in the status quo in Iraq—France, Germany, and Russia— blocked U.S. and British efforts to secure a UN Security Council resolution supporting an invasion. President Bush and British prime minister Tony Blair then decided to proceed against Iraq without a UN resolution. Bush sought and won on October 11, 2002, a congressional mandate authorizing the use of force against Iraq if he deemed it necessary. Public opinion was very much divided, although a slight majority of the U.S. population supported such action, while Blair's government took its decision in the face of British popular opposition.

Despite the fact that since 1990 U.S. and British air and naval power had kept Hussein contained, Bush defended a ground invasion as necessary to locate and destroy Iraqi WMDs, to end Hussein's alleged effort to acquire nuclear weapons, and to terminate a claimed link between the Iraqi government and Al Qaeda. Misgivings voiced by lower-level experts at the State Department and the Central Intelligence Agency (CIA), who had a far better understanding of Iraqi realities, never reached the president or were brushed aside. Certainly there was a rush to war from his influential advisers, especially

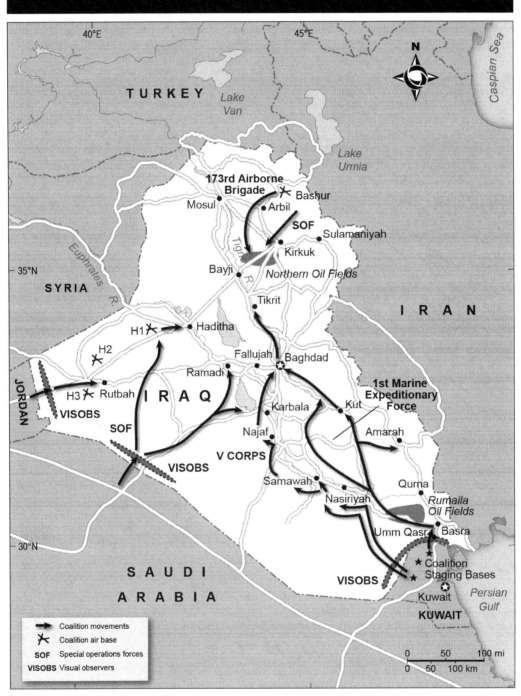

40°E · 45°E

Caspian Sea

N

TURKEY · Lake Van

Lake Urmia

173rd Airborne Brigade ✈ Bashur
Mosul ● Arbil
SOF
● Sulamaniyah
● Kirkuk
Bayji ● ● Tikrit *Northern Oil Fields*

35°N

SYRIA
Euphrates R.
Tigris R.

IRAN

H1 ✈ ● Haditha
✈ H2
Fallujah ● ● Baghdad
Ramadi ●
JORDAN
H3 ✈ ● Rutbah
VISOBS
IRAQ
Karbala ● ● Kut
1st Marine Expeditionary Force
● Amarah
SOF
Najaf ●
V CORPS
VISOBS
Samawah ● Qurna ●
Rumaila Oil Fields
Nasiriyah ●
Umm Qasr ● ● Basra

30°N

SAUDI
ARABIA
VISOBS
★ Coalition Staging Bases
★
☆ Kuwait
KUWAIT
Persian Gulf

Legend:
➤ Coalition movements
✈ Coalition air base
SOF Special operations forces
VISOBS Visual observers

0   50   100 mi
0   50   100 km

Vice President Dick Cheney, Secretary of Defense Donald Rumsfeld, and Deputy Secretary of Defense Paul Wolfowitz. No serious consideration was given to the risks involved, particularly the bitter rivalries among the religious/ethnic factions within Iraq. Both Cheney and Rumsfeld asserted that U.S. forces would be welcomed as liberators. Moreover, the seemingly quick and cheap victory in Afghanistan led Rumsfeld and others to publicly belittle and ignore assessments by military advisers, notably U.S. Army chief of staff General Eric Shinseki, that occupying and effectively controlling Iraq would require many hundreds of thousands of American ground troops.

Meanwhile, a military buildup had been under way for some time in Kuwait. More than 300,000 American military men and women were deployed under coalition commander U.S. Army general Tommy Franks, head of Central Command. Unlike DESERT STORM, however, there was no broad grouping of powers arrayed with the United States, and Saudi Arabia refused use of its bases for air strikes against Iraq. Although some Persian Gulf states, notably Kuwait and Qatar, did cooperate, members of this "Coalition of the Willing" ultimately included some 75 nations, but the military forces were drawn chiefly from the United States, Britain, and Australia. Notably absent were key U.S. European allies France and Germany.

Washington experienced a major setback when the Turkish parliament, despite promises of up to $30 billion in financial assistance, refused to allow U.S. forces to use Turkish territory to open up a northern front, a key component of the U.S. strategic plan. Three dozen ships laden with equipment for the 30,000-man U.S. 4th Infantry Division lay off Turkish ports but never were permitted to unload. Only after the war began were they redirected through the Suez Canal to Kuwait. In consequence, the 4th Infantry Division became part of the follow-on force. A disinformation campaign to the effect that the Turkish military would pressure Ankara to allow the forces of its NATO ally the United States to operate from Turkey apparently proved successful, as Hussein retained two regular Iraqi divisions north of Baghdad, and these troops took no part in combating the coalition offensive.

Course

The Iraq War—dubbed Operation IRAQI FREEDOM—began at 5:34 a.m. Baghdad time on March 20, 2003 (9:34 p.m., March 19, Washington time), just hours after the expiration of President Bush's ultimatum to Hussein, with a cruise missile strike against a purported meeting of the Iraqi leadership in Baghdad. This strike failed to decapitate the Iraqi government as intended, however. On succeeding nights, Baghdad was repeatedly hit from the air with cruise missile attacks and air strikes by Rockwell B-1 Lancer, Northrop Grumman B-2 Spirit, and Boeing B-52 Stratofortress bombers against key headquarters and command and control targets. This "Shock and Awe" air campaign employed 70 percent precision-guided (smart) aerial weapons and 30 percent unguided (dumb) munitions, as opposed to only 10 percent smart weapons during the 1991 Persian Gulf War. Also in contrast to 1991, a good many of the air strikes occurred away from the capital. As in the Persian Gulf War, coalition forces early on established complete air superiority.

Even before the start of hostilities, U.S., British, and Australian special forces had deployed into Iraq for both reconnaissance and strike roles. One of their missions was to destroy Iraqi watch posts on the southern border. Special forces also secured key bridge and crossing points across the Tigris and Euphrates Rivers.

On March 20, the 100,000-man coalition invasion ground force moved into southern Iraq from Kuwait. The few Iraqi missiles launched at allied staging areas in particular and Kuwait City in general were almost all downed by improved Patriot antimissile missiles. The coalition ground forces moved north on three axes: the U.S. Army V Corps to the west, the U.S. Marine Corps 1st Expeditionary Force in the center, and British forces to the east. The Iraqi capital of Baghdad, a city of 5 million people, lay 300 miles to the northwest.

In the west the offensive was led by Sikorsky UH-60 Black Hawk and Boeing AH-64 Apache helicopters, with the 7th Armored Cavalry Regiment the leading ground element, followed by the 3rd Infantry Division and follow-on units of V Corps. The western offensive made the most rapid progress, largely because it swung westward and moved through sparsely populated areas. In the center part of the front, the 1st Marine Expeditionary Force skirted to the west of the Euphrates River through the cities of Nasiriyah and on to Najaf and Karbala. On the eastern part of the front, the British had the task of securing the port of Umm Qasr and Iraq's second-largest city of Basra, with its largely Shia population of 500,000. It was not clear how the Shiites would react, following their abandonment by the United States in 1991. After clearing the channel for mines, a British ship docked at Umm Qasr with relief supplies.

Airpower played a key role in the allied advance. In northern Iraq, aircraft ferried men and supplies into the Kurdish-controlled zone, opening a front there against the Iraqi army but also against Ansar al-Islam, a militant Islamic group with a base camp and training facilities at Kalak on the Iranian border. Coalition airpower dominated the skies, with Iraqi aircraft and helicopters rarely even getting off the ground. Helicopter gunships and the Republic Fairchild A-10 Thunderbolt II (Warthog) tank buster proved highly effective. Another important factor was the technical and tactical ability of coalition troops to fight at night, whereas the Iraqis lacked the equipment and training to do so effectively.

U.S. marines were successful in seizing the oil fields north of Basra—some 60 percent of the nation's total production—and the key refineries. A few wellheads were set afire and some equipment was damaged, but overall damage was slight.

Meanwhile, the British were at Basra. Wishing to spare the civilian population and hoping for an internal uprising, they did not move into the city proper until the night of April 2. In the meantime the British imposed a loose blockade and, to demoralize the defenders, carried out a series of raids into the city to destroy symbols of the regime, such as Baath Party headquarters and images of Hussein. At the same time, they distributed relief supplies to win over the civilian population.

As U.S. special forces secured airfields in western Iraq, on the night of March 26 1,000 members of the 173d Airborne Brigade dropped into Kurdish-held territory in northern Iraq to operate in conjunction with lightly armed Kurdish forces, open a northern front, and threaten the key oil-production center of Mosul. Hussein loyalist Baath Party terror cells carried out attacks on civilians, including in Basra, while the so-called Saddam Fedayeen, or "technicals," irregulars often wearing civilian clothes, carried out attacks employing civilian vehicles mounting machine guns and rocket-propelled grenades against coalition supply convoys plying the lines of communication north from Kuwait. Near Najaf, Iraqi missiles destroyed two M1 Abrams tanks, the first time this had been accomplished, but the 7th Cavalry Regiment secured bridges south of the town, completing its encirclement.

A week into the war the coalition advance north stalled in an operational pause because of a *shamal* (strong sandstorm) on March 26; fierce U.S. Army and Marine Corps firefights for Nasiriyah, Najaf, and other places; and the need to protect lengthy logistical lines now under increasing Iraqi attack. Friendly-fire incidents remained a nagging problem. There were more casualties from these (including two aircraft—one British and one U.S.—shot down by Patriot missiles and a Patriot battery engaged by a U.S. aircraft) than during the 1991 Persian Gulf War.

The Iraqi leadership now repositioned the six elite Republican Guard divisions around the city of Baghdad to defend the capital. Reportedly Hussein had drawn a "Red Line," beyond which the allies would not be allowed to cross and within which he would employ WMDs. This seemed increasingly possible with coalition discoveries of caches of gas masks and the nerve gas antidote atropine and when some Iraqi Republican Guard troops with gas masks were taken prisoner. As the Baghdad and Medina Republican Guard divisions moved to take up new positions south of Baghdad, they came under heavy coalition air attack, seriously degrading their fighting ability.

The coalition advance quickened again during April 1–2. U.S. troops were within 50 miles of Baghdad, and U.S. secretary of state Colin Powell (who had been chairman of the Joint Chiefs of Staff during the Persian Gulf War) traveled to Ankara and secured Turkish government approval for coalition equipment to be moved through Turkey to troops on the Northern Front. U.S. forces reached the outskirts of Baghdad on April 3 and during the next two days secured Saddam International Airport, some 12 miles from the city center. Because of the speed of the advance, the airport was taken with minimal damage to its facilities. When the surrounding territory was secured, the airport became a major coalition staging area. The general Iraqi population seemed to sense the shift of momentum and an imminent coalition victory. Advancing troops reported receiving friendly receptions from civilians and increasing surrenders of Iraqi troops.

By April 5 the 3rd Infantry Division was closing on Baghdad from the southwest, the marines were closing from the southeast, and the 101st Airborne Division was repositioning to move in from the north. Baghdad in effect came under a loose blockade in which civilians were allowed to depart, and sanctuaries were created for civilians and surrendering Iraqi forces. On that day also, the 2nd Brigade of the 3rd Infantry Division pushed through downtown Baghdad in a three-hour operation named THUNDER RUN, inflicting an estimated 1,000 Iraqi casualties. This was a powerful psychological blow to Hussein's regime, which had claimed that U.S. forces were nowhere near the city and that the regime still controlled the international airport. The operation showed that allied forces could move at will and led to an exodus of Baath Party officials and Iraqi Army personnel, who now joined ordinary citizens trying to escape.

The U.S. raid into Baghdad was repeated on April 6 and 7. In a fierce firefight on April 6, U.S. forces killed an estimated 2,000–3,000 Iraqi soldiers for 1 killed of their own. U.S. forces also toppled a large statue of Hussein and occupied one of his presidential palaces. Also on April 6, the first C-130 aircraft landed at the renamed Baghdad International Airport, and the coalition announced that it was providing 24-hour air cover over Baghdad to protect U.S. forces there.

On April 7 three 3rd Infantry Division battalions remained in the city, while the next day U.S. Marine Corps elements moved into southeastern Baghdad, securing a military airfield. With the 101st Airborne coming in from the west and then fanning out to the north and with the 3rd Infantry Division moving in from the southeast, the ring around the capital was closed. By that day there was at least a brigade in the city.

On April 9, resistance in Baghdad collapsed as civilians, assisted by U.S. marines, toppled another large statute of Hussein. Sporadic fighting continued in parts of the city, however, as diehard Baath loyalists sniped at U.S. troops, but Iraqi government central command and control had ended.

The next day, April 10, a small number of Kurdish fighters, U.S. special forces, and 173rd Airborne Brigade troops liberated Kirkuk. They quickly took control of the northern oil fields from the Kurds to prevent any possibility of Turkish intervention. The next day Iraq's third-largest city, Mosul, fell when Iraq's V Corps commander surrendered some 30,000 men. Apart from some sporadic shooting in Baghdad and massive looting there and in other cities, the one remaining center of resistance was Hussein's ancestral home of Tikrit.

On April 12 the 101st Airborne relieved the marines and the 3rd Infantry Division in Baghdad, allowing them to deploy northwest to Tikrit. The battle for Tikrit, however, failed to materialize. Hussein's stronghold collapsed, and on April 14 allied forces entered the city. That same day the Pentagon announced that major military operations in Iraq were at an end; all that remained was mopping up. President Bush officially proclaimed victory on May 1 aboard the aircraft carrier *Abraham Lincoln* against a large banner with the words "Mission Accomplished."

With no WMDs discovered and no link with Al Qaeda proven, the Bush administration now modified its justifications for war. Although presidential candidate Bush had steadfastly denounced the Democrats for military interventions around the world and "nation building," he now claimed that the war was necessary to remove Hussein and his family from power and to democratize Iraq. Hussein, who was not taken prisoner until December 13, 2003, was tried by the interim Iraqi government and executed on December 30, 2006.

As of May 1, 2003, the United States had suffered 138 deaths: 114 from combat and 24 from other causes. The British sustained 42 dead, 19 of them from accidents. Estimates of Iraqi casualties vary widely, from 7,600 to 10,800 dead. Civilian dead may have topped 10,000.

Victory would have been even swifter had U.S. forces been able to operate from Turkey. It was also clear that had the additional American ground forces of up to 500,000—sought initially by U.S. military planners but rejected by Rumsfeld—been made available, this would have prevented some of the extensive looting in the wake of the coalition victories that did much to embolden the opposition. Additional forces would also have been able to secure Hussein's massive munitions and weapons stockpiles, which for months thereafter supplied resistance fighters with the stockpiles with which they could make the improvised explosive devices (IEDs) that would plague the occupation forces for years to come and produce the vast majority of U.S. and coalition casualties during the ensuing counterinsurgency operations.

Among major errors by the United States in Iraq following the overthrow of Hussein's regime were two disastrous decisions by Paul Bremer, administrator of the Coalition Provisional Authority. Bremer ordered the Iraqi Army disbanded and also ordered a purge of members of Hussein's Baath Party, who constituted the majority of experienced Iraqi governmental employees as well as a number of teachers. On Bremer's order, these skilled and mostly apolitical individuals were banned from holding any positions in Iraq's new government and public services. This decision created a formidable opposition to the new Shia-dominated government, which sought to impose Shia hegemony over the entire country. De-Baathification certainly fueled the insurgency that now swept Iraq. Disbanding the Iraqi Army destroyed security and let that burden fall solely on the occupying forces, most of whom could not speak Arabic and understood little of Iraq and its customs.

The insurgency appeared in the form of kidnappings, political assassinations, suicide bombings, car and truck bombs, IEDs, and other terrorist activities. The violence was carried out primarily by, but not limited to, Sunni Arabs—many of them former members of the armed forces—who now found themselves bereft of power and influence and under the thumb of the majority Shiites. Their attacks were directed against both the foreign troops now occupying Iraq, seen as propping up the new Shia-dominated government, and the Shiites themselves. The insurgents came to include foreign fighters—jihadists who came to Iraq to establish an Islamic state and to wage war against the West. Also present was Al Qaeda in Iraq, a branch of the international terrorist organization determined to strike at the United States.

Soon a virtual civil war had engulfed Iraq, waged by a large number of disparate groups against coalition military forces and the Iraqi government. Foreign governments, chiefly Syria and Iran, were not above supporting the insurgency, despite being coreligionists of the Iraqi Shia, because it served to weaken their longtime rival of Iraq and lengthened the odds against establishment of a strong pro-Western government there. Some former Baathists, including the acknowledged leader of the resistance, Ibrahim al-Duri, were in Syria. They also strongly opposed the establishment of U.S. bases and a permanent American presence in Iraq.

It would take considerable time to establish intelligence networks to deal with the insurgents, and initial U.S. and Iraqi government tactics were haphazard and ineffective. These consisted chiefly of indiscriminate and sometimes culturally insensitive night searches, interrogations, and blanket incarcerations. Such actions angered many formerly friendly or neutral Iraqis. Moreover, the revelations in late 2003 of widespread and systematic abuse of detainees perpetrated by U.S. military personnel and civilian contractor interrogators at Abu Ghraib Prison generated a massive international outcry and condemnation of the American-led occupation.

As the insurgency spread, full-scale military operations against insurgent-controlled areas ensued. They included Operations DESERT THRUST, carried out by the 1st Brigade of the 1st Infantry Division; PHANTOM FURY (also known as the Second Battle of Fallujah), carried out in the Sunni city by U.S., British, and Iraqi troops during November 7–December 23, 2004; and TOGETHER FORWARD, an unsuccessful effort by U.S. and Iraqi Army forces during June 14–October 24, 2006, to improve security in the capital of Baghdad. These large-scale operations had only a temporary and limited effect, however. As soon as security was reestablished and troops were withdrawn, the insurgents returned.

The most notable counterinsurgency effort was mounted during 2007. The so-called troop surge saw an additional 21,500 U.S. military personnel sent to Iraq. Critics, however, pointed out that violence had receded in some areas only because of ethnic cleansing in neighborhoods, whereby Shiites were driven out of predominantly Sunni areas and vice versa. In the spring of 2009, moreover, there was an upsurge in bombings in both Shia and Sunni areas of Baghdad. Most insurgent activity involved only Sunni-Shia confrontations, but there was also armed resistance against the Iraqi government by members of Muqtada al-Sadr's Mahdi Army.

Perhaps the key reason for the decrease in violence was the bargain struck beginning in 2005 by the U.S. military with Sunni tribal sheikhs that led to the creation of the National Council for the Salvation of Iraq, also known as the Sunni Salvation movement, the National Council for the Awakening of Iraq, the Sunni Awakening movement, and Sons of Iraq. It was a series of agreements between tribal Sunni sheikhs, especially in heavily Sunni Anbar Province, whereby local defense forces would be paid to maintain security in their communities.

The violence again increased when Shiite prime minister Nuri al-Maliki refused to integrate the Sons of Iraq into the Iraqi security services. By 2013 they had virtually ceased to exist. Many former members of the Sons of Iraq joined the radical Islamic State of Iraq and Syria (ISIS).

The steady withdrawal of coalition partners put pressure on the United States to do the same. U.S. president Barack Obama had planned to leave a residual U.S. force in Iraq that would have as its chief mission training the Iraqi Army, but the refusal of Iraqi prime minister Maliki, who took office in May 2006, to agree to a status of forces agreement that would provide immunity from Iraqi prosecution for U.S. armed forces led Obama to withdraw all remaining U.S. forces according to the timetable previously set by the Bush administration. The U.S. military withdrawal was completed on December 15, 2011.

The second phase of the Iraq War had claimed 4,487 U.S. military personnel killed. The United Kingdom lost 179, and other coalition forces lost 139. Wounded amounted to 32,226 from the United States, 315 from the United Kingdom, and more than 212 from other coalition partners. Even larger numbers of personnel had received medical treatment for noncombat injuries, illnesses, or diseases. The Iraqi Awakening Councils lost more than 1,000 killed and 500 wounded. By that date also, Iraqi insurgent dead numbered some 26,500, while the number of documented Iraqi civilians killed in the violence easily topped 100,000.

Significance

Since the U.S. withdrawal from the country, Iraq has experienced steadily increasing sectarian violence and actual armed conflict, leading to mounting civilian casualties.

In April 2014 alone, some 750 Iraqis died in bombings and other insurgency-related unrest. The players in the current violence are similar to those of the earlier insurgency and include Sunni extremists, Shiite militia groups, and a number of radical Islamist groups, including those with ties to Al Qaeda. A new threat emerged, however, in the form of the extremist Islamic State of Iraq and Syria (ISIS). By mid-2014, it had seized control of virtually all of Anbar Province and was actually threatening Baghdad. As it came to control the entire border with Syria, ISIS was able to link its new Iraqi holdings with territory previously won from the Syrian government in the civil war in that country that began in March 2011. It has now proclaimed a caliphate and introduced sharia (Islamic) law. At the same time, the Kurds moved toward establishing what amounted to at least autonomy in their areas of northern Iraq.

The Iraq War clearly resulted in increased Sunni-Shia tensions throughout the Middle East. The war also significantly advanced Iranian influence in the region. Iran has increased its military assistance to its coreligionists in Lebanon, to Hamas against Israel, to the regime of President Bashar al-Assad in Syria, and now to Iraq.

This is certainly not what the Bush administration had sought or anticipated when it plunged the United States into a war to topple Saddam Hussein from power. Hussein was indeed a cruel dictator and mass murderer who ruled by terror, but he also had held Iraq together. A more inclusive post-Hussein Iraqi government might have carried off this difficult task as well, but Maliki and his Shiite colleagues rejected this course. As of this writing, the long-term consequences of the Iraq War remain quite unclear, but certainly it has brought greater instability to the region. The long war may well result in the redrawing of state borders in the Middle East, to include Syria and Iraq, this time not by peacemakers in Paris but by fighting on the ground between rival religious sects.

Further Reading

Atkinson, Rick. *In the Company of Soldiers: A Chronicle of Combat.* New York: Little, Brown, 2004.

Cavaleri, David. *Easier Said Than Done: Making the Transition between Combat Operations and Stability Operations.* Ft. Leavenworth, KS: Combat Studies Institute Press, 2005.

Cordesman, Anthony H. *The Iraq War: Strategy, Tactics, and Military Lessons.* Washington, DC: Center for Strategic and International Studies, 2003.

DiMarco, Louis A. *Traditions, Changes and Challenges: Military Operations and the Middle Eastern City.* Ft. Leavenworth, KS: Combat Studies Institute Press, 2004.

Franks, Tommy R. *American Soldier.* New York: HarperCollins, 2004.

Gaddis, John Lewis. *Surprise, Security and the American Experience.* Cambridge, MA: Harvard University Press, 2005.

Gordon, Michael R., and Bernard E. Trainor. *Cobra II: The Inside Story of the Invasion and Occupation of Iraq.* New York: Pantheon, 2006.

Murray, Williamson, and Robert H. Scales Jr. *The Iraq War: A Military History.* Cambridge, MA: Belknap, 2005.

North, Richard. *Ministry of Defeat: The British War in Iraq, 2003–2009.* New York: Continuum Publishing, 2009.

Pirnie, Bruce R., and Edward O'Connell. *Counterinsurgency in Iraq (2003–2006).* Santa Monica, CA: Rand Corporation, 2008.

Ricks, Thomas E. *Fiasco: The American Military Adventure in Iraq.* New York: Penguin, 2006.

Sanchez, Ricardo S., and Donald T. Phillips. *Wiser in Battle: A Soldier's Story.* New York: Harper, 2008.

Trainor, Bernard E., and Michael R. Gordon. *Cobra II: The Inside Story of the Invasion and Occupation of Iraq.* New York: Pantheon, 2006.

Woodward, Bob. *Bush at War.* New York: Simon and Schuster, 2002.

Woodward, Bob. *Plan of Attack.* New York: Simon and Schuster, 2004.

Woodward, Bob. *State of Denial: Bush at War,* Vol. 3. New York, Simon and Schuster, 2007.

Zinmeister, Karl. *Boots on the Ground: A Month with the 82d Airborne Division in the Battle for Iraq.* New York: St. Martin's, 2004.

Zinmeister, Karl. *Dawn over Baghdad: How the U. S. Military Is Using Bullets and Ballots to Remake Iraq.* New York: Encounter Books, 2004.

Index

About the Author

SPENCER C. TUCKER, PhD, held the John Biggs Chair of Military History at his alma mater, the Virginia Military Institute in Lexington, for 6 years until his retirement from teaching in 2003. Before that, he was professor of history for 30 years at Texas Christian University, Fort Worth. He has also been a Fulbright Scholar and, as a U.S. Army captain, an intelligence analyst in the Pentagon. Currently the senior fellow of military history at ABC-CLIO, he has written or edited 53 books, including the award-winning *American Civil War: The Definitive Encyclopedia and Document Collection; Battles That Changed History: An Encyclopedia of World Conflict;* and *World War I: The Definitive Encyclopedia and Document Collection,* all published by ABC-CLIO.